Availability

This text is available in both digital and print formats. Pearson offers its titles in eText format through **MyLabs, CourseSmart®, Kindle®, Nook®,** and more. And going digital saves students money — up to 60%.

To learn more about our programs, pricing options, and customization, visit

www.pearsonhighered.com

Public Speaking

Strategies for Success

SEVENTH EDITION

David Zarefsky
Northwestern University

PEARSON

Boston Columbus Indianapolis New York San Francisco Upper Saddle River
Amsterdam Cape Town Dubai London Madrid Milan Munich Paris Montreal Toronto
Delhi Mexico City São Paulo Sydney Hong Kong Seoul Singapore Taipei Tokyo

For My Students

Publisher, Communication: Karon Bowers
Editorial Assistant: Kelly Clark
Development Editor: Brenda Hadenfeldt
Senior Marketing Manager: Blair Zoe Tuckman
Senior Managing Editor: Linda Mihatov Behrens
Project Manager: Richard DeLorenzo
Senior Operations Supervisor: Mary Fischer
Operations Specialist: Mary Ann Gloriande
Cover Art Director: Jayne Conte
Cover Images: Top left, Bottom right: Fotolia; Top right, Bottom left: Alamy
Senior Digital Editor: Paul DeLuca
Digital Media Editor: Lisa Dotson
Text Permissions Specialist: Craig A. Jones
Text Permissions Project Manager: Jillian Santos/PreMediaGlobal
Photo Researcher: Joanne Casulli/Bill Smith Group
Full-Service Project Management, Composition, and Design: PreMediaGlobal
Printer/Binder: Courier/Kendalville
Cover Printer: Lehigh-Phoenix Color/Hagerstown

Credits and acknowledgments borrowed from other sources and reproduced, with permission, in this textbook appear on appropriate page within text (or on page 447).

This work is protected by United States copyright laws and is provided solely for the use of instructors in teaching their courses and assessing student learning. Dissemination or sale of any part of this work (including on the World Wide Web) will destroy the integrity of the work and is not permitted. The work and materials from it should never be made available to students except by instructors using the accompanying text in their classes.

All recipients of this work are expected to abide by these restrictions and to honor the intended pedagogical purposes and the needs of other instructors who rely on these materials.

Copyright © 2014, 2009, 2005 by Pearson Education, Inc. All rights reserved. Printed in the United States of America. This publication is protected by Copyright and permission should be obtained from the publisher prior to any prohibited reproduction, storage in a retrieval system, or transmission in any form or by any means, electronic, mechanical, photocopying, recording, or likewise. To obtain permission(s) to use material from this work, please submit a written request to Pearson Education, Inc., Permissions Department, One Lake Street, Upper Saddle River, New Jersey 07458 or you may fax your request to 201-236-3290.

Many of the designations by manufacturers and seller to distinguish their products are claimed as trademarks. Where those designations appear in this book, and the publisher was aware of a trademark claim, the designations have been printed in initial caps or all caps.

Library of Congress Cataloging-in-Publication Data is available on request from the Library of Congress.

10 9 8 7 6 5 4 3 2

PEARSON

www.pearsonhighered.com

Student Edition:
ISBN-13: 978-0-205-85726-5
ISBN-10: 0-205-85726-4

Instructor's Review Copy:
ISBN-13: 978-0-205-93138-5
ISBN-10: 0-205-93138-3

À la Carte:
ISBN-13: 978-0-205-93137-8
ISBN-10: 0-205-93137-5

Brief Contents

Contents

Special Features

CHOOSE A STRATEGY

A Question of Ethics

Rhetorical Workout

Strategies for Speaking to Diverse Audiences

To the Student

I was fortunate to have an excellent education in both high school and college. I had many stimulating and useful courses, interesting and challenging teachers, and rewarding and enjoyable experiences. But if I had to single out the *most* important course I had, without a doubt it would be public speaking. I think my experience was not unique and I hope yours will be similar.

You may be taking this course because you want to improve your voice or physical delivery, or to overcome speech anxiety, or to organize your thoughts better, or to learn how to do good research. You may have picked this class because a friend is in it, or because it meets at a convenient time, or even because it is required. I'm willing to predict that if you take the course seriously and work at it, you not only will achieve your goals but will go far beyond them. I know I did.

I wanted to become more comfortable in speaking before a group and to learn how to use my voice effectively and how to control distracting mannerisms. I accomplished those goals but also learned how to think analytically, how to organize ideas, how to do research, how to assess an audience, how to inform and persuade. It was not long before I realized that these skills and habits were valuable not just in public speaking, but in every other course and, indeed, in almost every aspect of life. When my daughter and my son each took a public speaking course, they experienced very similar results and, of course, I greatly enjoyed observing the positive effect the course had on each of them.

For over 2,500 years, men and women have studied the art of public speaking, both because it is valuable in its own right and because, in the best sense of the term, it is a liberal art—one that frees and empowers people. It does so by providing the knowledge, cultivating the skills, and modeling the habits of effective thought and expression that can be applied to any area of life. You are the latest link in this chain and I hope that this book, and the course of which it is a part, will help you to have a similar experience.

The title of this book is *Public Speaking: Strategies for Success*. That title has a double meaning. First, this book is about strategies for success in public speaking. Second, the premise of the book is that public speaking will provide you with strategies for success in life. Certainly it does not promise fame or fortune, but it does offer a blend of reflective judgment and carefully chosen action that should enable you, whatever your experience, to enjoy a life well lived.

I have used the term strategy to emphasize that public speaking is about choices. It is an art and not a science. When you speak, you will be faced with situations that offer both opportunities and constraints. You will want to decide how to work within this situation to achieve your goals, and your plan for doing so is a strategy. And even as you make choices in response to a situation, the pattern of your choices actually helps to define what the situation is. It affects you, but you also affect it.

Thinking strategically about public speaking means abandoning the belief that there is an all-purpose magic formula that will always produce a good speech. You will have to make judgments each time you speak about what your goals should be and the best way to achieve them. With experience and practice, you should find choices easier to make. Although, as you will see, there are some general norms and expectations, a speech is good not because it follows some formula, but because it deals effectively with a specific situation. A speech that is good in one context may be weak in another. It is always necessary to get down to cases.

For that reason, you will find many examples and case studies in this book. Some come from student speakers and some from speakers in the "real world." Some are actual situations and some are hypothetical ones that I have designed to illustrate important principles. Some describe what speakers actually did, and some ask you what you might do. Just as lawyers learn the law, in part, through the case method, so you will cultivate and sharpen the skills of public speaking by trying them out on specific cases.

Case material will be provided not only by this book, but also by your class. You will have the opportunity not only to present speeches, but to listen to many as well. Listening to speeches is important, not just a necessary evil to be endured while you wait your turn to speak. You develop habits of analysis and memory, you see a large array of choices other students make in specific situations, and you gain skill in assessing whether strategies succeed or fail and in deciding whether or not they are strategies that you might wish to use.

At the same time, *Public Speaking* does not study cases in a vacuum. It draws on underlying theory to explain these situations. Theory does not refer to that which is impractical; nor does it refer to a lot of fancy terms or ideas that seem isolated from reality. Although sometimes the theory and practice of public speaking are studied in isolation, the premise of *Public Speaking* is that they need to be integrated at every step. Theory informs our understanding of practice by enabling us to explain what is happening in particular situations. And practice applies and modifies our understanding of theory. What you learn about theories of arrangement, for instance, will help you to organize a speech, but your experience in organizing speeches will also contribute to your thinking about theories of arrangement.

More than 50 years have passed since I first enrolled in a course in public speaking. Now you are starting the same journey. This book, your own experience, and the interaction with other students and your instructor are all vital parts of the course. Participate fully and try to get as much from the course as you can. I hope that, like me, you will find that you not only achieve your original goals, but actually transcend them and I hope that a course in public speaking contributes as much to your life as it has to mine.

David Zarefsky

To the Instructor

If you are using this textbook for the first time, welcome. If you are a previous user, I am grateful for your support and enthusiasm and I hope you will like the approach of this seventh edition.

Public Speaking: Strategies for Success is based on the premise that successful public speaking is *strategic*. It involves understanding the circumstances in which one speaks, making deliberate choices about how to deal with these circumstances, and planning in order to achieve one's speaking goals. The key elements in a strategic approach to public speaking are *critical thinking* and *strategic planning*, skills emphasized throughout this book. Equipped with the necessary knowledge and skills, students can learn to make skillful and intelligent choices in public speaking situations throughout their lives.

A consequence of a strategic perspective is the recognition that public speaking is not a science with universally applicable principles or a set of formulas that can be applied mechanically or by rote. It is more complicated than that, involving subjective judgment and human choice. We do our students a disservice if we pretend otherwise. Instead, by equipping them with necessary knowledge and skills, we should help to prepare them to make these choices skillfully and intelligently. That is a goal of this book.

To say that the subject matter is complex, though, is certainly not to say that the textbook must be dull, tedious, or unreadable. I have tried to make the text readily accessible to students without compromising the integrity of the subject matter.

The title of the book, *Public Speaking: Strategies for Success,* has a double meaning. The book offers a strategic perspective that should lead students to become more successful public speakers. And the art of public speaking provides many of the strategies for students to succeed in many different walks of life. I hope that this book will help you to empower your students to achieve those goals.

New to This Edition

In this new edition, *Public Speaking: Strategies for Success* maintains its solid foundations of strategy, practical skills, rhetorical theory, diversity, ethics, and civic participation, while revising and updating key areas to reflect the needs of today's beginning speakers. Some key areas revised in this edition include:

1. ***Further integration of Learning Objectives:*** Learning Objectives have been refined and visually emphasized in the chapter-opening sections; numbered identifiers for each objective appear in the chapter margins near related discussions; and the objectives now provide the framework for the end-of-chapter summary sections, "What Have You Learned?"
2. ***Expanded oral citation coverage:*** More discussion of how to create and use oral citations, including examples, gives students additional guidance on this often-challenging aspect of preparing a speech.
3. ***Updated coverage of technology:*** Updated discussions of technology-related issues in public speaking include such areas as social media and the public forum, speaking for the camera, mediated audiences, search engines,

LEARNING OBJECTIVES

After studying this chapter, you should be able to:

Objective 4.1	Distinguish between hearing and listening and explain why listening skills are important to speakers.
Objective 4.2	Identify obstacles to effective listening.
Objective 4.3	Listen carefully by mapping the central ideas of a speech and by taking notes.
Objective 4.4	Describe how critical thinking is applied in the speaking situation.
Objective 4.5	Evaluate speeches as a result of critical listening.

databases and catalogs, and audiovisual media and multimedia presentations, including additional advice for creating slides.

4. ***Expanded material on creating speeches for diverse audiences:*** More examples and practical tips are given for how students can respect diversity in their speeches, including areas such as the use of volume and gestures, strategies for building good will, language choices, and respectful uses of reasoning.
5. ***The rhetorical situation:*** Discussion of the rhetorical situation appears earlier in Chapter 1, linking it more closely to the process of communication, and includes discussion of interference.
6. ***The public forum:*** Expanded discussions include effects of social media on the public forum; when the public forum is present; and how informative speeches fit within the public forum.
7. ***Examples:*** Along with a variety of updated and revised examples in the text, new examples of complete preparation and presentation outlines from a student speech are included and extensively annotated, and a new student speech is in the appendix. Additionally, examples have been visually distinguished throughout the text to better highlight them for student learning.
8. ***Revised appendix of sample speeches:*** Featuring a more focused collection of student and public speeches, the appendix includes the full text of a new student speech—"The Internet and Intellectual Property," utilizing a mix of informative and persuasive strategies—and a new "For Further Study" section recommending additional speeches for analysis and discussion, annotated with notes on what students should look for when reading or listening to the speeches.
9. ***New and updated research:*** Every chapter includes new or updated research to keep the text current on topics from technology issues and speech anxiety to gestures and language choice.

Public Speaking Teaches Strategic Planning

Far too often, students leave a public speaking class with nothing more than a recipe for how to prepare and deliver a seven-minute speech in class. Certainly, being able to prepare and deliver that classroom speech well is a start. The goal of this book, however, is to help students also learn how to apply the skills required for that seven-minute classroom speech to the range of public speaking situations they will encounter throughout their lives. Students should recognize how often they will find themselves participating in speaking situations, whether as a public speaker or as an audience member. They need to think through and about the public speaking process and to develop strategies to achieve their goals.

OBJECTIVE 13.1

Planning Your Strategy

Broadly speaking, speech goals are achieved through the strategies of informing, persuading, and entertaining. These are sometimes mistaken as resulting in three fundamentally different kinds of speeches. In fact, though, because successful sharing of information also affects people's attitudes, informing and persuading occur together. Likewise, a successful persuasive speech is also entertaining and enjoyable to listen to, and an entertaining speech usually also conveys new information.

The broad strategies overlap, then, and they do not exclude each other. So if your assignment is to present "an informative speech," this does not mean that you should avoid saying anything entertaining or persuasive. Rather, you should achieve your purpose primarily through strategies of informing.

CHOOSE A STRATEGY: Organizing Your Speech

The Situation

You and a number of other students are dismayed by your university's decision to limit Internet access to certain sites on campus. You've been attending rallies against the policy and have been invited to speak at the next student government meeting about your objections.

Making Choices

1. How should you decide what main points you want to relay to your audience, and in what order should you present them?
2. What do you know about the school board's position that would affect your organizational choices?
3. What kind of supporting material would be important to include—and where in the speech should you include it?

What If...

How would your organizational decisions change if the following were true?

1. There was evidence of illegal Internet activity among the student population.
2. The university had asked for student feedback before making the decision to limit Internet access.

Choose a Strategy.

The *Choose a Strategy* boxes in each chapter present students with a case study allowing them to decide how the skills and concepts discussed can be adapted to a concrete rhetorical situation. Although these open-ended situations usually have no "correct" solutions, they train students to size up a situation, understand its opportunities and constraints, assess ideas, and reason with an audience in mind.

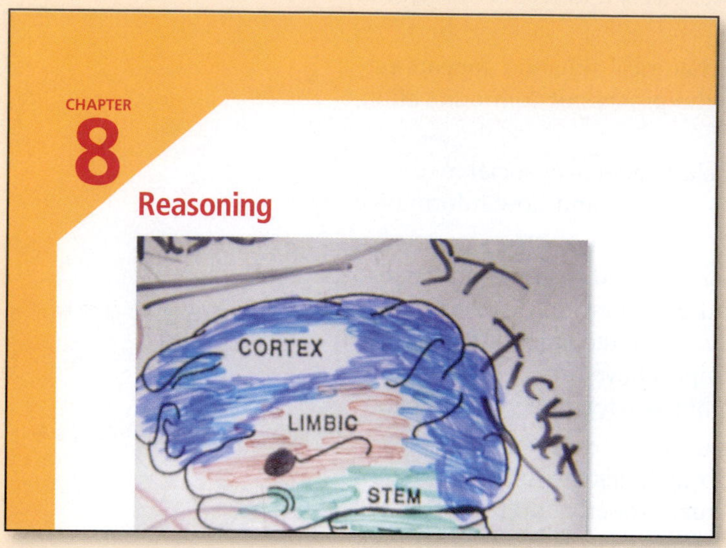

Public Speaking Teaches Rhetorical Theory and Critical Thinking Skills

Grounded in the tradition of the art of rhetoric, this text provides students with a beginning knowledge of rhetorical theory as they learn how to speak in public. Theory and practice are integrated as a seamless fabric, explaining clearly what students should do and why.

A full chapter focuses on reasoning in the context of the entire speaking situation (not limited to persuasive speeches).

Rhetorical Workout. The *Rhetorical Workout* feature in each chapter offers students a focused, step-by-step application of public speaking concepts. Each workout strengthens the student's public speaking skills just as a physical workout strengthens the muscles.

Rhetorical Workout

Learn About Your Listeners

You have been asked by the head of the non-profit organization where you volunteer once a week to give a presentation to several people who want to start their own non-profit organization on how to use the Internet for publicity. Before you prepare your speech, you want to understand more about your audience in order to decide what to cover.

1. What clues about your listeners have you been given so far, in the above description?
2. The head of your non-profit will be hosting the presentation. What are some questions you could ask her ahead of time that would help you prepare?
3. Which of the following audience demographics, if known, might affect how you approach your speech topic: audience size, diversity of views, age, gender, religion, ethnicity, native language, educational level, socioeconomic

5. You learn that all those who will be present receive a monthly newsletter via e-mail, and you are able to find the back issues online. How might this information help you analyze your listeners?
6. You do some research to learn more about people interested in starting a non-profit. How useful would each of the following be for you: (1) a national statistic that 75 percent of people who wish to start a non-profit have no experience with Internet publicity; (2) an article profiling people wishing to start non-profits in another state who have limited budgets for promotional activities; (3) the history of your own non-profit; (4) a list of people interested in starting non-profits and the businesses in which they previously have worked? Explain why.
7. If you prepared for an audience of 10 people and 30

ustify a tax cut may not square hat there are significant needs ation and health care that the

are intended to help you de- what a speaker is asking you do. They will help you to form ent about whether to agree critically does not mean that an inquisition before accept- ther, it is a way to "trust, but he speaker but not to depend

CHECKLIST 4.2

Critical Thinking About a Speech

- ❒ Are the main ideas identifiable?
- ❒ Are the links among the ideas reasonable?
- ❒ Are the ideas supported where necessary?
- ❒ How does accepting or rejecting the thesis affect my other beliefs?

Critical Thinking Skills. Practical applications of critical thinking skills are emphasized throughout, such as active listening skills, topic analysis, and reasoning. These and many other applied concepts are recapped through the Checklists.

Public Speaking Stresses Analysis, Research, and Evaluating Sources

The investigation and research process is covered in detail, with specific advice and guidance for analyzing a thesis to discover new subtopics and approaches. Emphasizing critical evaluation of sources, the research chapter helps students learn how to choose effective supporting material, how to judge if a source is credible, and how to cite sources. Evaluation of Internet sources receives special attention.

In addition, Chapters 7 and 15 incorporate the information technology that students know and use today, both for research and for presentation aids. With the distinction between electronic and printed materials becoming more blurred, each chapter offers a unified perspective, treating research sources and visual aids without regard to their medium.

The Quality of Internet Evidence

There are additional concerns that relate to evidence obtained from the Internet. The Internet has been described as the most democratic means of publishing there is. Virtually anyone can post virtually anything on the Web. As a consequence, there is almost no editorial or quality control except whatever is exercised by the producer of the site. An online version of a printed publication—an electronic copy of a print journal article, for example—can be assumed to reflect the same editorial judgment as the printed publication itself. At the other extreme, an individual's personal website may not have been checked at all. And some organizations whose mission is to promote a particular viewpoint can be deceptive, presenting propaganda as if it were scholarship.

Search engines attempt to distinguish between reliable and unreliable websites, but they cannot do so perfectly. And whether the site looks "professional" is not a reliable indicator either, because it is easier to design a sophisticated-looking site than it is to produce a book. In fact, sophisticated websites that look like those of easily recognized organizations have been created for the purpose of coaxing individuals to reveal their Social Security and credit card numbers in order to facilitate identity theft. This, of course, is fraud.[4] Extra vigilance is needed to be sure that you take only reliable evidence from the Web. For these reasons, the responsibility to evaluate Internet evidence rests with you. We need, therefore, to note some special precautions about supporting materials from electronic sources. The following questions are especially pertinent:[5]

- **Does the site meet the basic standards of credibility?** At a minimum, a credible website should contain the name of the sponsor, identification of

CHECKLIST 7.3

Testing the Credibility of Supporting Material[6]

- ❒ Is the evidence available for inspection?
- ❒ Is the evidence accurate?
- ❒ Is the source credible?
- ❒ Is the source making statements within his or her expertise?
- ❒ Is the evidence internally consistent?
- ❒ Is the evidence contradicted by the best evidence from other sources?
- ❒ Is the evidence recent enough?
- ❒ Is the evidence relevant to the point that it supports?

Table 7.3 Bibliographic Formats

American Psychological Association (APA)—References	
Type of Source	**Sample Format**
Book	White, R. C., Jr. (2009). *A. Lincoln: A biography.* New York, NY: Random House.
Chapter from an edited book	Hauser, G. A. (2008). Rethinking deliberative democracy: Rhetoric, power, and civil society. In T. F. McDorman and D. M. Timmerman (Eds.), *Rhetoric and democracy: Pedagogical and political practices* (pp. 225–264). East Lansing, MI: Michigan State University Press.
Magazine or newspaper article (online)	Stolberg, S. G., & Zeleny, J. (2009, September 10). Obama, armed with details, challenges Congress. *The New York* Times. Retrieved from http://www.nytimes.com
Magazine or newspaper article (print)	Stolberg, S. G., & Zeleny, J. (2009, September 10). Obama, armed with details, challenges Congress. *New York Times,* p. A1.
Journal article (online)	Howell, B. W. (2008). Reagan and Reykjavik: Arms control, SDI, and the argument from human rights. *Rhetoric & Public Affairs, 11,* 389–415. doi: 10.1353/rap.0.0045
Journal article (print)	Bostdorff, D. M. (2009). Judgment, experience, and leadership: Candidate debates on the Iraq war in the 2008 presidential primaries. *Rhetoric & Public Affairs, 12,* 223–277.
Web page	Mehltretter, S. A. (2009). John F. Kennedy, "Inaugural Address," 1961. *Voices of Democracy.* Retrieved from http://www.voicesofdemocracy.umd.edu/documents/Mehltretter-Kennedy.pdf

Table 7.3 Bibliographic formats

American Psychological Association (APA)—References	
Type of Source	**Sample Format**
Book	White, R. C., Jr. (2009). *A. Lincoln: A biography.* New York, NY: Random House.
Chapter from an edited book	Hauser, G. A. (2008). Rethinking deliberative democracy: Rhetoric, power, and civil society. In T. F. McDorman & D. M. Timmerman (Eds.), *Rhetoric and democracy: Pedagogical and political practices* (pp. 225–264). East Lansing, MI: Michigan State University Press.
Magazine or newspaper article (online)	Stolberg, S. G., & Zeleny, J. (2009, September 10). Obama, armed with details, challenges Congress. *The New York Times.* Retrieved from http://www.nytimes.com
Magazine or newspaper article (print)	Stolberg, S. G., & Zeleny, J. (2009, September 10). Obama, armed with details, challenges Congress. *The New York Times,* p. A1.
Journal article (online)	Howell, B. W. (2008). Reagan and Reykjavik: Arms control, SDI, and the argument from human rights. *Rhetoric & Public Affairs, 11,* 389–415. doi: 10.1353/rap.0.0045
Journal article (print)	Bostdorff, D. M. (2009). Judgment, experience, and leadership: Candidate debates on the Iraq war in the 2008 presidential primaries. *Rhetoric & Public Affairs, 12,* 223–277.

Public Speaking Integrates Theory and Practice

An approach that views public speaking as a set of formulas or rules to be followed is of limited value. Few actual speaking situations will match exactly those for which the "rules" were written; students need instead to be able to adapt to the particular situations in which they find themselves. In order to do that, they must understand the theory behind the rules. Recognizing this fact, some books try to "import" theory, including all the latest specialized terms and jargon. This book instead integrates theory into the underlying discussions of practice, not by highlighting obscure writers or technical terms, but by explaining clearly what students should do and why. The book is solidly grounded in rhetorical theory, but no prior knowledge of that field is either required or assumed. Theory and practice are treated as a seamless fabric.

Public Speaking Features a Variety of Challenging Examples and Applications

Because public speaking is situation-specific, this book includes a large number of cases and examples encompassing a wide range of topics and issues. Some examples come from actual speaking situations, and others are hypothetical examples to illustrate points in the text. Also, some examples compare speeches in the classroom with speeches in the field, and there are both brief examples and some extended examples that can be followed throughout an entire chapter. The examples emphasize a need to analyze and respond to audiences as an integral part of the strategic thinking process. Both historical and contemporary examples are featured. In keeping with the book's emphasis on civic engagement, many of the examples come from the realm of public affairs.

CHOOSE A STRATEGY: Presenting Yo

The Situation

You are a teacher at a grade school and your principal has asked you to present the new curriculum plan to the parents in your community and also to answer any questions they may have regarding these changes. There have been several major additions to the curriculum, and you want to make sure that each change is explained clearly to t... be presenting in the school gymnasium w... and podium will be set up the evening of ... is two weeks from today.

3. How will ... pare to ...

What If...

How would y... lowing were ... Would your p...

An Example of Rhetorical Proof

After introducing a speech about the effect of tax increases on a family's budget, student Catherine Archer claimed

> Taxes have taken a bigger bite out of the average paycheck each year. Just look at the record. Our state sales taxes have gone up faster than our income. Local property taxes have gone through the roof. And now the federal government is proposing to raise gasoline taxes again. Where does it all stop?

After the speech, she invited questions from the floor. "What about Social Security?" one woman asked. Catherine replied

> Thank you. That's still one more example of a tax that has gone up faster than income. In fact, many people today pay more in Social Security tax than in their income tax.

Then a man in the audience said, "Since you mentioned income taxes, I want to ...

Public Speaking Emphasizes Ethics and Respect for Diverse Audiences

Every aspect of public speaking is affected by the need to be ethical and to understand and respect diversity in audiences.

Some textbooks have a single chapter on ethics, as if it could be studied in isolation. In contrast, this book reflects the view that ethical issues are involved in virtually every aspect of public speaking.

A Question of Ethics. Each chapter includes the feature *A Question of Ethics* to highlight ethical issues students should consider as they prepare their own speeches or listen to the speeches of others. While some ethical standards—such as avoidance of plagiarism or racial stereotyping—are clear-cut, many involve subjective and case-specific judgments. For this reason, many of the ethical issues are presented as problems about which students should think and deliberate.

A Question of Ethics

Ethnocentric Assumptions

It is important for speakers to avoid making ethnocentric assumptions about the audience. However, sometimes you will know quite a bit about your audience that could help you to target a message to your listeners. For instance, your audience may be people of the same age group, from the same community, or with the same religious beliefs. If you tailor your message to take advantage of this knowledge, is that ethnocentric? Is it pandering to the audience? Is it acceptable to be ethnocentric if your audience is in fact homogeneous? How do you maintain a balance between appealing to your audience and being careful not to pander to their prejudices?

Strategies for Speaking to Diverse Audiences. Far from being a "buzzword" or an emblem of "political correctness," diversity of audiences on virtually every dimension is a fact with which speakers must be prepared to deal. It is a condition that affects every aspect of public speaking. Accordingly, throughout the book diversity is reflected in precepts and examples, and every chapter includes a feature entitled *Strategies for Speaking to Diverse Audiences* that includes tips on how that chapter can be applied in an increasingly diverse environment.

Strategies for Speaking to Diverse Audiences

Respecting Diversity Through Persuading

Successful persuasion meets listeners where they are and adapts to the opportunities and constraints of a situation. These factors are all more complex when an audience is diverse. Here are strategies for success in persuading diverse audiences:

1. With diverse audiences, identification is both more important (since it cannot be taken for granted) and more difficult (since you must acknowledge the variety of your audience members' beliefs and commitments). Identify with your listeners before moving them to a new commitment.
2. Consider the diversity of values and commitments. For instance, "family values" in Mexico include the expectation that children live with their parents until they are married, whereas this is much less common in the United States.
3. Consider how different cultures may present you with different constraints or opportunities. If your emotional appeal relies on a culturally specific value, then you may need to plan ahead and think about other possible strategies you might use.
4. Suggest actions that are appropriate and "do-able" for your specific audience. Calling on an audience to solve the Israel-Palestine conflict not only is asking for too much but may alienate certain audience members who think you are trivializing the issue.
5. Establish a positive *ethos* that invites trust from members of a diverse audience.

Public Speaking Emphasizes the Public Forum

This book grounds public speaking in the concept of the public forum and illustrates these speaking situations with both historical and contemporary examples. Beginning speakers will learn what makes a healthy public forum and how to apply strategies to situations outside of the classroom—on campuses, in communities, and in other realms of public affairs.

Rhetorical Workout

Find the Public Forum in Your Neighborhood

You and several of your neighbors would like to plan a neighborhood rummage sale. You set up a meeting to talk about when to have the sale and how to work together to promote it. Let's look at what makes this meeting a public forum.

1. What are the issues or problems affecting the group collectively? What kinds of issues might affect you and each of your neighbors individually? Outside of your group, who might be affected by what you decide?
2. Why is cooperative action needed in your meeting? Is it important for every person to participate in the decision? Why or why not?
3. In the public forum, a decision requires subjective judgment, which means there is no one obvious solution and the participants may all have different opinions. How might this factor play out in your neighborhood meeting?
4. Why is a decision needed in your meeting?
5. Suppose you have recently moved in and don't know your neighbors very well yet. How can your speaking and communication skills help you contribute to the meeting and the group's decision?

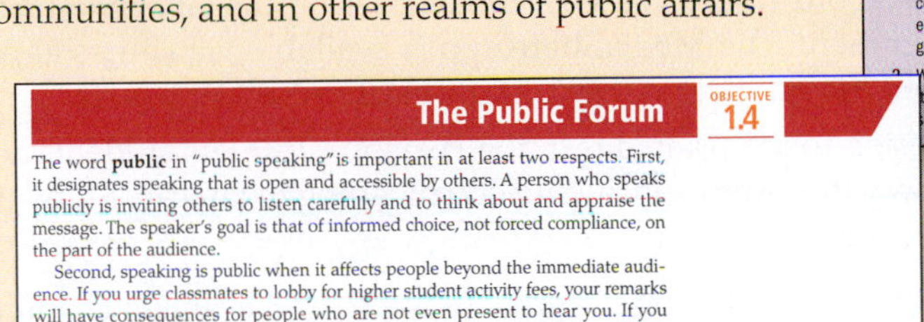

The Public Forum OBJECTIVE 1.4

The word **public** in "public speaking" is important in at least two respects. First, it designates speaking that is open and accessible by others. A person who speaks publicly is inviting others to listen carefully and to think about and appraise the message. The speaker's goal is that of informed choice, not forced compliance, on the part of the audience.

Second, speaking is public when it affects people beyond the immediate audience. If you urge classmates to lobby for higher student activity fees, your remarks will have consequences for people who are not even present to hear you. If you explain how to examine the terms of a lease before signing it, listeners can follow your directions in ways that will affect others as well.

I believe that public speaking is the single most important course in the curriculum because of the immense contribution it can make to students' lives. Good luck as you work to make that happen. I hope that this book will help you.

David Zarefsky

Instructional Resources

A wide array of additional instructor and student resources are available with this book, including

- Instructor's Resource Manual
- Test Bank
- MyTest Computerized Test Bank
- PowerPoint Presentation Package
- Pearson Public Speaking Video Library

For a current, complete list of accompanying student and instructor supplements, visit www.pearsonhighered.com/communication. Select instructor supplements are available at www.pearsonhighered.com/irc (instructor login required).

MyCommunicationLab®

MyCommunicationLab is an online homework, tutorial, and assessment program that truly engages students in learning. It helps students better prepare for class, quizzes, and exams—resulting in better performance in the course—and provides educators a dynamic set of tools for gauging individual and class progress. And, MyCommunicationLab comes from Pearson, your partner in providing the best digital learning experiences.

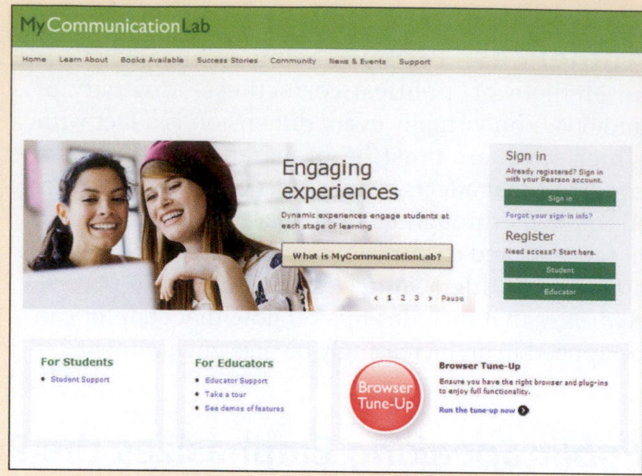

www.mycommunicationlab.com

MyCommunicationLab Highlights:

- **MediaShare:** This comprehensive file upload tool allows students to post speeches, outlines, visual aids, video assignments, role plays, group projects, and more in a variety of file formats. Uploaded files are available for viewing, commenting, and grading by instructors and class members in face-to-face and online course settings. Integrated video capture functionality allows students to record video directly from a webcam and allows instructors to record videos via webcam, in class or in a lab, and attach them directly to a specific student and/or assignment. The MediaShare app is available via iTunes at no additional charge for those who have purchased MediaShare or MyCommunicationLab access.
- **The Pearson eText:** Identical in content and design to the printed text, the Pearson eText lets students access their textbook anytime, anywhere, and any way they want—including downloading to an iPad. Students can take notes and highlight, just like a traditional text.
- **Videos and Video Quizzes:** Videos provide students with the opportunity to watch and evaluate chapter-related multimedia. Many videos include automatically graded quiz questions.
- **PersonalityProfile:** PersonalityProfile is Pearson's online library for self-assessment and analysis. Online resources provide students with opportunities to evaluate their own and others' communication styles. Instructors can use these tools to show learning and growth over the duration of the course.
- **Study Tools:** A personalized study plan, chapter assessment, key term flashcards, an audio version of the text, and more provide a robust range of study tools to focus students on what they need to know, helping them succeed in the course and beyond.
- **Class Preparation Tool:** Finding, organizing, and presenting your instructor resources is fast and easy with Pearson's class preparation tool. This fully searchable database contains hundreds of resources such as lecture launchers, discussion topics, activities, assignments, and video clips. Instructors can search or browse by topic and sort the results by type. Personalized folders can be created to organize and store content or download resources, as well as upload your own content.

Acknowledgments

Reviewers for the Seventh Edition

Articulating this perspective on public speaking in a textbook that is accessible to students has been a stimulating challenge. All or part of the manuscript was read by Marty Birkholt, Creighton University; Jodi Gaete, SUNY Suffolk County Community College; Laura Keimig, Creighton University; James L. Leighter, Creighton University; Daryle Nagano, El Camino College; Lynette Sharp Penya, Abilene Christian University; Samuel Rindell, Three Rivers Community College; Brent Sleasman, Gannon University.

Reviewers of Previous Editions

Elizabeth R. Alcock, Bristol Community College; Ellen Arden-Ogle, Consumnes River College; Susan Baack, Montana State University; Ernest Bartow, Bucks County Community College; John Bee, Ohio State University; Sandra Berkowitz, Wayne State University; Vincent Bloom, California State University–Fresno; Barbara Blackstone, Slippery Rock University; Robert Bookwalter, Marshall University; Kristine S. Bruss, University of Kansas; Ferald J. Bryan, Northern Illinois University; C. Leilani Carver, University of Kansas; Leah Ceccarelli, University of Washington; Faye Clark, DeKalb College; Lisa Inzer Coleman, Southwest Tennesee Community College; Melanie Conrad, Berry College; Marion Couvillon, Mississippi State University; Marilyn Cristiano, Paradise Valley Community College; Jim Dittus, Highland Community College; Michael Howard Eaves, Valdosta State University; Susan Redding Emel, Baker University; Patricia Faverty, Thomas More College; Mindy Fenske, University of South Carolina; William Fusfeld, University of Pittsburgh; Kathleen Galvin, Northwestern University; John Giertz, Bakersfield State University; Joseph Giordana, University of Wisconsin–Eau Claire; William Goodbar, Old Dominion University; Andrea Gregg, Penn State University; Mark A. Gring, Texas Tech University; Rose Gruber, Gloucester County College; Richard Halley, Weber State University; Kelby K. Halone, Clemson University; Katherine L. Hatfield, Creighton University; Diane Hill, Providence College; Heather Hundley, California State University—San Bernardino; Stephen K. Hunt, Illinois State University; Carol Jablonski, University of South Florida; Karla Kay Jensen, Texas Tech University; Richard Jensen, University of Nevada–Las Vegas; Jack Johnson, University of Wisconsin–Milwaukee; Nicole Johnson, Berry College; William Jordan, North Carolina State University; Douglas Kresse, Fullerton College; Elizabeth Lamoureux, Buena Vista University; Amy London, Oxnard College; Thomas A. Marshall II, Robert Morris College; Al Montanaro, SUNY Plattsburgh; Craig Monroe, California State University, San Bernardino; John M. Murphy, University of Georgia; Daryle Nagano-Krier, El Camino College; Stephen Neilson, University of Nevada–Las Vegas; Patrick O'Sullivan, Illinois State University; Cate Palczewski, University of Northern Iowa; Jay Pence, University of North Carolina–Chapel Hill; Bonnie Peterson, University of Wisconsin-Parkside; Lee Polk, Baylor University; Benjamin Ponder, Ponder Media; Kenna J. Reeves, Emporia State University; Kurt Ritter, Texas A&M University; Kellie Roberts, University of Florida; Rebecca L. Roberts, University of Wyoming; Paul Sabelka, Iowa Wesleyan College; Noreen Schaefer-Faix, Kutztown University; David Schneider. Saginaw Valley State University; Deanna Sellnow, North Dakota State University; Ryan Shepard, University of Kansas; Kenneth G. Sherwood, Los Angeles City College; Calvin Smith, Eastern Illinois University; Cynthia Duquette Smith, Indiana University, Bloomington; Jessica Stowell, Tulsa Junior College; Robert Terrill, Indiana University; Denise Vrchota, Iowa State University; Beth Waggenspack, Virginia Polytechnic Institute and State University; Rita Kirk Whillock, Southern Methodist University; Roy Wood, University of Denver; Quentin Wright, Mountain View College.

The comments and suggestions of the reviewers listed above were quite helpful and often pointed the way for substantial improvement in the manuscript. The responsibility for what I have written, of course, remains with me.

Additional Thanks

My debt to Leah Ceccarelli, now on the faculty at the University of Washington, continues from the first edition. She helped in the development and selection of examples and end-of-chapter features and helped significantly to shape the tone of the book. I also appreciate the work of those who prepared supplementary materials for previous editions: Victoria Gallagher, North Carolina State University; Glen Williams, University of Akron; Melissa Beall, University of Northern Iowa; Robert Brookey, Northern Illinois University; Robert Bookwalter, Marshall University; Calvin Troup, Duquesne University; Terry Doyle, Northern Virginia Community College; Sherilyn Marrow, University of Northern Colorado; Renee Brokaw, The University of North Carolina, Charlotte; and Kristine Greenwood, Marshall University.

I am grateful to those who assisted in the preparation of this seventh edition. Elliot Heilman, currently a Ph.D. candidate at Northwestern University, helped me with the revision and updating of examples, the reorganization of key chapters, the enhanced coverage of technology, and additions to the end-of-chapter discussion questions and activities. Additionally, I am grateful to Thomas Lessl of the University of Georgia, who prepared the *Instructor's Resource Manual*; Kristine Greenwood of Marshall University, who prepared the *Test Bank*; and Bjorn Stillion Southard of the University of Georgia, who prepared the *PowerPoint*™ presentation package for this edition.

At Pearson, Steve Hull and Joe Opiela first persuaded me to undertake this project and Bill Barke placed his faith in my ability to complete the book in a reasonable period of time. For this edition I again worked closely with Brenda Hadenfeldt, whose keen insights and editorial suggestions strengthened the book considerably. I have benefited from the editing of Karon Bowers, Carol Alper, Shannon Morrow, Brian Wheel, and Cate Dodson. I also am grateful for the diligent efforts of all the production staff at Pearson, often working against short deadlines.

CHAPTER 1

Welcome to Public Speaking

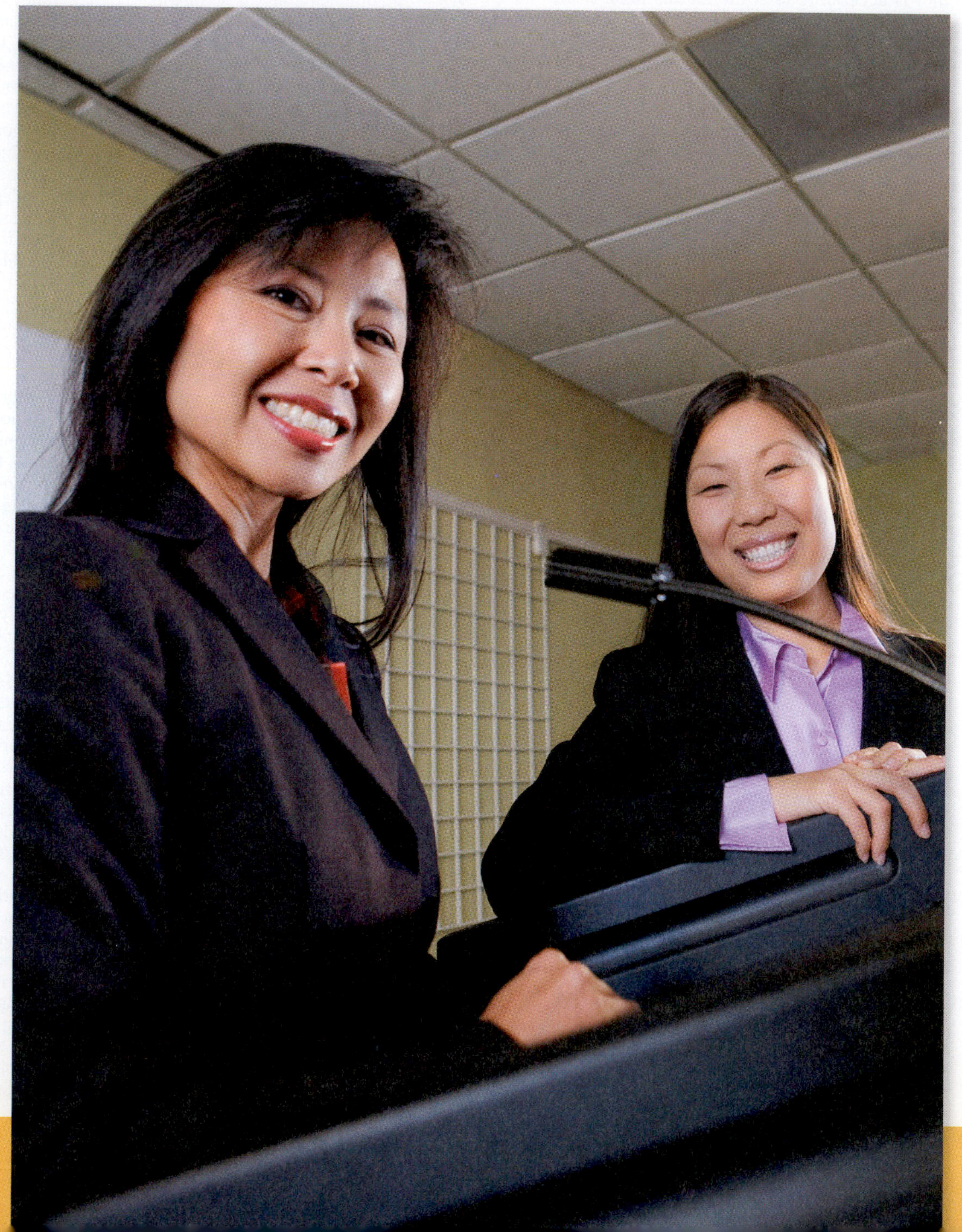

LEARNING OBJECTIVES

After studying this chapter, you should be able to:

Objective 1.1	Identify the principal things you will learn in this course and how they will benefit you outside the classroom.
Objective 1.2	Describe public speaking as a communication process in which the speaker and listeners jointly create meaning and understanding.
Objective 1.3	Name the elements of a rhetorical situation and explain the steps by which a speech affects the situation.
Objective 1.4	Define the public forum and describe how studying public speaking will prepare you to participate effectively in it.
Objective 1.5	Identify the principal ethical obligations of listeners and speakers.

Listen to the **Audio Chapter** at **MyCommunicationLab**

OUTLINE

Welcome to Public Speaking, one of the most important courses you will ever take. If that sounds like too strong a claim, consider what these students had to say after taking a public speaking course:

> I used to be terrified of speaking in public. I've learned that solid preparation is the key to overcoming my fears. I still get nervous, but now I know how to control my nervousness and focus on communicating with my audience.
>
> This class has taught me to be a better listener. I'm more aware of weak arguments, fuzzy logic, and unsupported claims. I think critically about what I am being persuaded to do and why.
>
> Before taking this class, I used to be the most boring speaker! My speeches were well researched, but my delivery was poor. Now I make eye contact with my audience members and use my voice and pauses to set a tone and emphasize key points.
>
> I've learned more about the structure of speeches, especially the importance of an attention-grabber at the beginning of my speech and a preview of my main points to give the audience a "road map" of what I'm going to say.

These students noticed right away that a public speaking course helped them to develop or to refine their communication skills. You will notice a difference by the end of your course, too—and as you move beyond the classroom, you will find that the knowledge and experience you gain from the course also help you to be a more successful worker and a more effective citizen.

Why Study Public Speaking?

You may have enrolled in this course because you expect to be making public presentations and you want to learn how to do that better and more easily. Maybe your goal is to speak more forcefully or to be less nervous. Perhaps you want to become better organized, to learn more about how to prepare a speech, or to think more clearly and more critically. You may even have chosen the course because it meets at a convenient time, is a requirement for graduation, or has a good instructor.

Develop Specific Communication Skills

Explore the Exercise "Personal Report of Communication Apprehension" at **MyCommunicationLab**

Whatever your reasons for studying public speaking, this class will enable you to develop or improve a variety of communication skills, such as how to:

- Listen carefully and critically in order to understand and evaluate what others say.
- Decide what you want to speak about.
- Select what to say.
- Find the material for a speech by examining your own experience, consulting with others, using the Internet, and visiting a library.
- Think critically about what you read and observe so that you will reason soundly when addressing an audience.
- Organize a speech to make it clear, coherent, sensible, and effective.
- Use language skillfully to convey both meaning and mood.

- Use your voice and your body to present yourself and your message in an effective, compelling way.
- Overcome speech anxiety and use any nervousness to your advantage.
- Use visual aids to enhance your message.
- Adapt general principles to your speaking situation, with emphasis on the dimensions of informing, persuading, and entertaining.
- Understand and benefit from reactions to your speeches so that the audience's response helps you improve your skills.

As one in a group of speakers, this advocate must make his message distinctive and adapt it to the audience. These tasks require good strategic planning.

This set of skills has been studied and taught for about 2,500 years (in different ways over the years, of course), so you are taking part in a very old and valuable academic tradition.

Focus on Critical Thinking and Strategic Planning

Besides improving these specific skills as a communicator, you also will be applying and refining two invaluable general skills that are emphasized throughout this book: critical thinking and strategic planning.

Critical Thinking.

Public speaking is in large measure an exercise in **critical thinking**, the ability to form and defend your own judgments rather than blindly accepting or instantly rejecting what you hear or read. Critical thinkers can analyze and understand various points of view, and they can quickly recognize the difference between fact and opinion.

Facts, as we will see in detail later, are statements that—at least in theory—can be *verified* by someone else. If a speaker says that the world's population has doubled every 25 years, that statement can be tested by checking population statistics. In contrast, **opinions** are *subjective* statements that presumably are based on experience or expertise. If a speaker asserts that the world's population is growing too fast, that opinion cannot be verified externally; it stands or falls depending on the insight and judgment of the person who offers it.

As a listener, critical thinking will help you to recognize a speaker's unstated assumptions. As a speaker, it will help you to form precise statements that embody your thoughts. Overall, critical thinking will place ideas into a broader context, showing how they relate to other things that you already know or believe.

Strategic Planning.

A speaker operates in a world of choices, including whether to speak, when to speak, what to say, how to phrase a point and how to explain or defend it, how to organize the message, what tone to give it, and exactly how to relate a message to the audience. Some speakers make these choices unconsciously, without real thought (and relying on luck). But effective speakers make their choices *strategically*; through **strategic planning** they identify their goals and then determine how best to achieve them.

critical thinking
The ability to form and defend your own judgments rather than blindly accepting or instantly rejecting what you hear or read.

facts
Statements that can be verified by someone other than the speaker.

opinions
Subjective judgments based on experience or expertise, not capable of being verified by someone else.

strategic planning
The process of identifying your goals and then determining how best to achieve them.

Apply What You Learn

Public speaking combines theory and practice that you can apply to your daily life. As you study creative and critical thinking, sensitivity to audiences, and effective speech presentation, the skills you learn will:

- Help you critically evaluate messages and appeals of all kinds.
- Make you more sensitive to people and situations.
- Enable you to recognize and adapt to diverse audiences and complex occasions.
- Increase your self-confidence and your willingness to engage in serious dialogue with others.[1]

Explore the **Exercise** "Principles of Communication" at **MyCommunicationLab**

Outside the classroom, these attributes will enhance your personal, professional, and civic life. Sensitivity to others and to their perspectives will help you in personal relationships as well as when, for instance, you speak to neighborhood groups, Scout troops, parent-teacher associations, or religious organizations. Employers and career counselors often put "good communication skills" at the top of the list of qualities they seek in people.[2] The reason is simple: Each year our economy becomes more dependent on information and the ability to communicate it.

Your study of public speaking also will help make you a more competent, more active citizen. You will be better able to understand public issues and controversies, to decide what you think about them, and to participate effectively in addressing them—whether on your campus, in your neighborhood, or in the larger public forum.

OBJECTIVE 1.2

Public Speaking and Communication

In one sense, we all know what public speaking is: a speaker transmits a message orally to an audience. But this simple view does not explain just how the speaker and listeners participate in **communication**, interacting in order to build connections whereby they can understand each other and recognize common interests.

Early theories of communication viewed public speaking as a series of one-way messages sent from speaker to audience. In fact, however, the audience participates along with the speaker in creating shared meaning and understanding. The speaker's ideas and values are tested and refined through interaction with the audience, and listeners' knowledge and understanding are modified through interaction with the speaker. Thus, public speaking is a *continuous* communication process in which messages and signals circulate back and forth between speaker and listeners.

The Audience's View

From the audience's point of view, each listener comes to the speech with a framework of prior knowledge, beliefs, and values, and each listener "decodes," or interprets, the speaker's message within this personal framework. In a large or culturally diverse audience, the frameworks used by listeners may vary greatly.

communication
Interaction that builds connections between people that helps them to understand each other and to recognize common interests.

To a particular listener, some ideas will be more important, or *salient*, than other ideas. In a speech about carrying weapons on campus, for example, some listeners will be focused on personal liberty, others on campus safety, and still others on the dangers of gun violence. The speech may support, challenge, or modify any of these frameworks, but each listener's framework will shape how he or she interprets and understands the speech. Audience members work actively to assess what the speaker says against what they already know or believe, and they constantly make judgments about the message and convey them back to the speaker through facial responses and other nonverbal clues.

The Speaker's View

From the speaker's point of view, knowing about the audience is crucial in preparing and delivering a speech. A speech about campus social life, for example, would be different for an audience of prospective students than for an audience of alumni, or even for an audience of current students. Even if the basic points of the speech were the same, the nature of the audience would affect how they are developed and explained and what tone or attitude the speaker projects. In preparing the speech, the speaker would analyze the audience and try to match listeners' expectations appropriately. Moreover, as listeners respond during the speech (by frowning, nodding approval, looking puzzled, etc.), the speaker would constantly modify how key points are organized and phrased and would try to acknowledge or respond to the audience's concerns.

The Interplay

Figure 1.1 depicts this interplay between speaker and audience. Suppose that you plan to speak about the benefits of a vegetarian diet. In preparing the speech, you'll remember that some listeners think vegetarianism is healthful; others think it is a passing fad; others come from cultures in which eating meat is prohibited, so that vegetarianism is not a matter of choice; and still others associate vegetarianism with eccentrics who don't really understand nutrition. As you speak, you'll be watching for **feedback**, responses from the audience that signal how they are reacting to what you say. Most responses will be nonverbal, such as frowns or

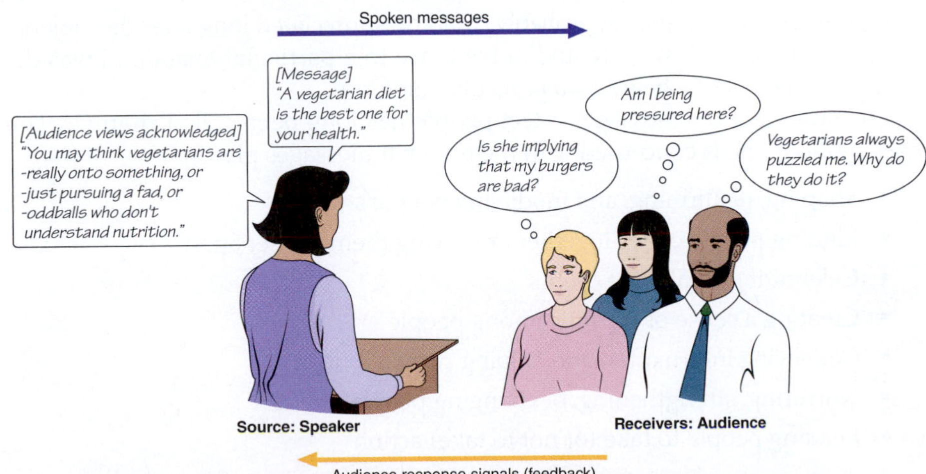

Figure 1.1 Public speaking as a communication process.

feedback
Responses from the audience to the speaker, often in the form of nonverbal cues.

nods of agreement. Feedback might prompt you to acknowledge that some people doubt the merits of vegetarian diets; you might even admit that you had doubts yourself but now are a committed vegetarian. Throughout the speech—from its preparation through its presentation—you will be sensitive to how well your ideas match your audience, and you'll use feedback to improve the fit as you speak.

You may convince some audience members to change their beliefs; others may interpret your message in ways consistent with their beliefs; and if the discrepancy between their beliefs and your message is too great, some listeners will reject your message. In any case, the audience will be actively involved as you speak, interpreting and testing what you say against their own beliefs and values, and letting you know their reactions. In short, the speaker and listeners simultaneously participate in creating the message.

Watch the Video
"Persuasive Speech: Starbucks" at
MyCommunicationLab

The Rhetorical Situation

Public speaking occurs *in a specific situation*. Unlike great dramatic or literary works, which "speak to the ages," the principal test of a good speech is whether it responds most effectively to the needs of the situation in which it is presented.[5]

The **situation** is the specific context in which a speech is given. Compared with poems and stories, which are read long after they were written, most speeches have a short life span. For example, student Jeremy Johnson's first speech to his classmates concerned an important and timely issue:

> Almost every week, there are new reports of genocidal violence in the Darfur region of Sudan. Innocent civilians, women and children among them, are killed or raped every day by marauding bands of Janjaweed militia whose goal is ethnic cleansing of the non-Arab peoples in their region. The crisis of Darfur is one of the greatest human catastrophes of our time—worse than Bosnia, Kosovo, Rwanda, or even Iraq. But our government and our attention have been so preoccupied with other wars and conflicts around the world that we have forgotten the people of Darfur and have abandoned our international human rights ideals.

Although Jeremy's speech probably could be appreciated long after the violence in Sudan subsides, it was created in response to a particular event and was designed primarily to be heard by a particular audience.

The study of how messages affect people has long been called **rhetoric**. This ancient discipline is concerned with the role that messages play in:

- Shaping, reaffirming, and modifying people's values
- Binding people closer together or moving them farther apart
- Celebrating significant events
- Creating a sense of identity among people
- Conveying information and helping people to learn
- Nurturing, strengthening, or changing people's beliefs
- Leading people to take (or not to take) action

A **rhetorical situation**, then, is a situation in which people's understanding can be changed through messages.[6] The following example shows how student Katie

situation
The particular context in which a speech takes place.

rhetoric
The study of how messages affect people.

rhetorical situation
A situation in which people's understanding can be changed through messages.

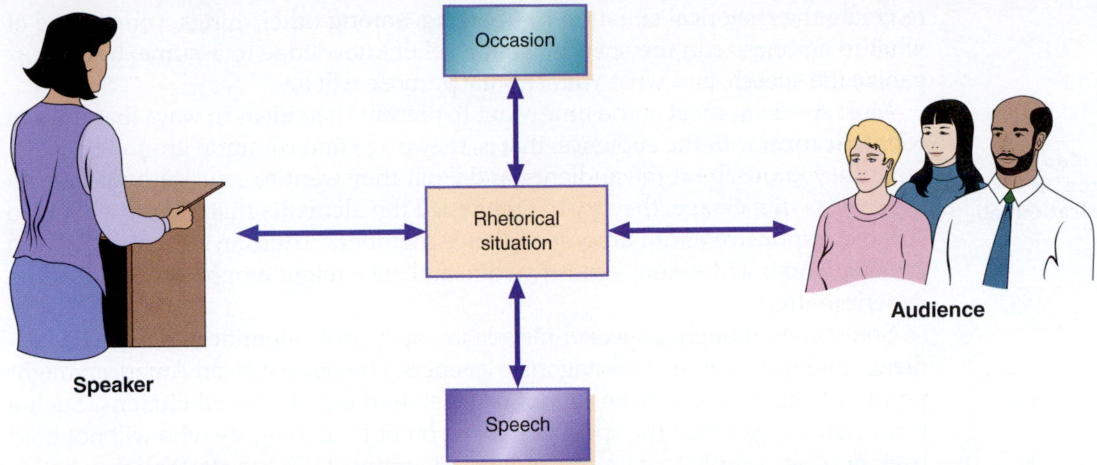

Figure 1.2 Determinants of the rhetorical situation.

Jacobson responded to a rhetorical situation posed by recent armed robberies on her university campus:

> It's easy to feel safe on our familiar campus, but crime is on the rise, and the university is partly to blame. Poor lighting both on and off campus provides many shadows for crimes to take place unseen. University police seem more interested in patrolling weekend parties than making weeknight walks between dorms and the library. And campus shuttle services are unreliable late at night, forcing students to walk through dangerous, unlit areas. We need to contact the university administration and let them know that they should take our safety seriously.
>
> But it's not just up to the administration. We also need to take our personal safety seriously. Take self-defense classes. Lock your bikes. Familiarize yourself with the emergency telephone boxes on campus. Don't leave valuables in plain sight. Be careful where you publish your personal identification information. Show the university officials that you are doing what you can to be safe; then ask them to do what they can.

Katie's message addressed a particular audience and asked its members to consider a specific problem and solution. The speech was timely—Katie knew that the recent robberies would be on her audience members' minds. The message also affected how students thought about the problem and how they understood possible solutions, both those that university administrators could effect and those that students could implement.

Figure 1.2 shows the four basic factors that determine the success of any rhetorical situation: the audience, the occasion, the speaker, and the speech itself. Each of the arrows goes in two directions. That is because each of the factors affects our understanding of the rhetorical situation, but our understanding of the situation also affects how we view each of the factors. As we will see, rhetorical situations both impose constraints and create opportunities.

The Audience

Unlike a poem or a novel, a speech is presented for a specific audience, and its success in achieving its goals depends on the reactions of those listeners. This is why audience analysis, discussed in Chapter 5, is so important. The audience helps to create the rhetorical situation by affecting, among other things, your choice of what to emphasize in the speech, what level of knowledge to assume, how to organize the speech, and what your specific purpose will be.

Watch the Video "Hmong Culture" at **MyCommunicationLab**

Most speakers, most of the time, want to present their ideas in ways that achieve **identification** with the audience; that is, they try to find common ground between what they know about the audience and what they want to say.[7] Without distorting their own message, they try to emphasize the elements that are most likely to strike a responsive chord among audience members. Thus, an African American speaker who is addressing a mostly white audience might emphasize their shared American dream.

Sometimes, though, a speaker may deliberately *avoid* identification with the audience and may even try to antagonize listeners. The same African American might point out that the American dream is *not* shared equally by all citizens. Such a tactic may suggest that the speaker is a person of high integrity who will not hold back punches simply to gain the audience's approval. Or the strategy may be intended to influence some other audience that is overhearing the speech.[8] Whether the goal is to identify or to criticize, however, knowledge of the audience is critical in assessing the rhetorical situation.

Sometimes, audience members are prepared to incorporate what the speaker says into their systems of beliefs. At other times they may be skeptical or downright hostile. The degree of interference they offer to the speaker's purpose is an important factor when assessing how the audience contributes to the nature of the rhetorical situation.

Audiences also provide important feedback. If listeners frown or stare blankly when you make an important point, they may not understand you. To respond to the rhetorical situation, you will want to explain that point further. If listeners appear lost, you may want to summarize your main points before moving on. If you've said something that you think is funny but no one laughs or smiles, you might either rephrase the comment or decide to let it pass. And when listeners nod supportively, you should feel more confident and reassured. Audience feedback will let you know whether you have assessed the rhetorical situation accurately and responded to it appropriately.

You can also get valuable feedback by placing yourself in the role of an audience member. If possible, review a video of your speech. At first, you may feel uncomfortable watching a recording of yourself; you may be oversensitive to details that no one else would notice. But do not worry about these details. Instead, try to view yourself as the audience saw and heard you. Watching a video after the fact allows you a critical distance that helps you to assess aspects you can improve before giving your next speech.

identification
Formation of common bonds between the speaker and the audience.

ceremonial
Speaking that focuses on the present and is usually concerned with praise.

deliberative
Speaking that focuses on the future and is usually concerned with what should be done.

The Occasion

The occasion is the place and event where the speech is given. It may be a community meeting, a classroom speech assignment, a business presentation, a local fundraising reception, an informal group gathering, or any other time and place where people assemble and relate to one another.

Some speech occasions are **ceremonial** (this is also known as *epideictic*, and is discussed in Chapter 16), such as presenting or accepting an award, introducing someone, delivering a eulogy, or commemorating an event. Others are primarily **deliberative**, such as making an oral report, delivering a sales presentation, advocating a policy, or refuting another person's argument. Ceremonial speaking focuses on the present and is usually concerned with what is praiseworthy in the subject. Deliberative speaking focuses on the future and is usually concerned with what should be done.

Many occasions combine ceremonial and deliberative elements. For example, a chief executive officer (CEO) who has been newly appointed in the wake of a fiscal scandal in the company will likely have to speak to the company's employees and stockholders. The occasion is deliberative in that the CEO speaks about the state and the direction of the company in light of the financial circumstances. The occasion is also ceremonial, though, because the CEO's presence demonstrates both a new chapter in the company's history and a personal interest in the well-being of the workers and stockholders, and also because the speech seeks to reassure and reaffirm the company's dedication to employees and investors.

Similarly, the president's State of the Union address is a ceremonial ritual prescribed by the U.S. Constitution. But, especially in recent years, it's the occasion when the president is expected to persuade the public to support, and the Congress to enact, the administration's legislative proposals. This expectation makes the State of the Union a deliberative occasion as well.

A third category of speech occasion, traditionally known as **forensic**, is concerned with rendering judgments about events in the past. Although this is the dominant form of speaking in courts of law, it plays only a small role in public speaking elsewhere.[9]

Whatever the occasion, the audience arrives with ideas about what is and what is not *appropriate behavior*. Such expectations have developed over time, and they limit what a speaker can do in responding to the rhetorical situation. For example, listeners expect a eulogy to offer a favorable view of the deceased, and they normally would think it inappropriate for a speaker to dwell on the person's failings. On the other hand, an after-dinner speech is usually expected to be lighthearted; a speaker who instead presents a highly technical lecture would not be responding appropriately to the occasion.

Simultaneous events further define the occasion. For example, the fact that a presidential campaign is under way helps to define the occasion for a speech about health care reform. The retirement of a popular athlete helps to set the stage for a speech about retirement trends in industry. And if listeners only last week were urged to give up tobacco, that may affect their judgments about a speech that now asks them to give up red meat.

Another way to think about the occasion is to note that it presents the speaker with an **exigence**—a problem that cannot be avoided but that can be solved, or at least managed, through the development of an appropriate message. Of course, the exigence is not always clear-cut. In designing the speech, often the speaker will play a major role in describing what the exigence is. In any event, satisfactorily addressing the exigence is the goal of the speech.

"A commencement speech about school reform, delivered at Western State University in June 2013" is an example of an occasion; "growing unease about the quality of public education" is the rhetorical situation to which this speech was a response. The speech responds to the rhetorical situation of growing unease among people about the quality of public education, but the expectation that a commencement speech will inspire the graduates also helps to define the rhetorical situation.

Each type of occasion raises certain expectations about what is appropriate behavior, and these expectations help to define the rhetorical situation. For example,

forensic
Speaking that focuses on the past and is usually concerned with justice.

exigence
A problem that cannot be avoided but that can be solved, or at least managed, through the development of an appropriate message.

if an engineer is presenting the features of a new product to the marketing group, everyone will be focused on the product's best features and how to make them more salable. The occasion will be deliberative. Unlike a ceremonial occasion, it will not emphasize good wishes or feelings about the product or the staff. And unlike a forensic occasion, it will not concentrate on the company's past sales performance with other products. Rather, the focus will be on how best to design the new product to achieve a strong sales record in the future.

The Speaker

The same speech delivered by different speakers can produce quite different reactions and effects. Your interest in the subject—as made evident through voice, delivery, and the vividness of your imagery—helps to determine how the audience will react to the speech. Your *ethos* affects whether listeners will pay attention and will regard you as believable. Fortunately, many of the skills that enable speakers to contribute positively to a rhetorical situation can be learned. Previous public speaking experience will also affect your comfort level, and the ability to respond to audience feedback will make you more flexible in any rhetorical situation.

Speakers have a purpose in mind. The three most general purposes of speeches are to inform, to persuade, and to entertain.

- **Informing** provides listeners with new information or ideas.
- **Persuading** influences listeners' attitudes and behavior (either to strengthen existing beliefs or to support new ones).
- **Entertaining** stimulates a sense of community by celebrating common bonds among speaker and listeners.

Although these general purposes may seem to be completely separate, they often coexist in a single speech—as when a speaker aims *both* to share new information and also to use that information to influence attitudes and behavior (or to stimulate a sense of community). For this reason, in Chapter 6 we will classify purposes in a more detailed way. For now, though, focus on the general purposes and realize that you must have (1) something about which to inform the audience, (2) some position you want to persuade them to take, or (3) some subject with which to entertain them. Therefore any speaker also has one or more specific purposes. Here are some examples:

GENERAL PURPOSE: Informing
SPECIFIC PURPOSE: Explaining the main steps in the construction of the college library.

GENERAL PURPOSE: Persuading
SPECIFIC PURPOSE: Urging listeners to endorse the president's economic proposals and to send supportive e-mails to the president and our elected officials.

GENERAL PURPOSE: Entertaining
SPECIFIC PURPOSE: "Roasting" the boss on the eve of her retirement.

In each case, the specific purpose is the standard to use in deciding whether the speaker achieved the goal and responded adequately to the rhetorical situation.

By this standard, good speeches are ones in which the speaker achieved the purpose; bad speeches are those in which the speaker did not. Yet clearly this standard is not enough. We do not want to regard as good a speech that misleads

informing
Providing listeners with new information or ideas.

persuading
Influencing listeners' attitudes and behavior.

entertaining
Stimulating a sense of community through the celebration of common bonds among speaker and listeners.

or manipulates the audience, even if it achieves the speaker's purpose. And if the speaker's purpose itself is unworthy—such as reinforcing negative cultural or racial stereotypes, for instance—we would evaluate the speech harshly even if it does achieve the speaker's purpose.

The Speech

Although we tend to think of the situation as something to which the speech responds, the message itself also works to *shape the situation.* Before Katie Jacobson spoke about crime on campus, her audience thought it was a problem for the campus police to solve, but during the speech, they began to see campus crime as a problem that called for individuals to take responsibility for the solution. The message had redefined the situation.

In most cases, an audience's understanding of a situation can be improved by a speech that is organized effectively, that includes interesting examples and memorable phrases, and that is presented enthusiastically. Although many factors determine whether a speech responds successfully to a rhetorical situation, by understanding the basic factors involved you can better shape your message as a speaker and can participate more fully as a listener.

Constraints and Opportunities

Your speech not only responds to the situation but also modifies it. In doing that, you face opportunities as well as constraints. Your goal is to devise a **strategy**—a plan of action—that will respond to the constraints and take advantage of the opportunities.

strategy
A plan of action to achieve stated goals.

CHOOSE A STRATEGY: Understanding the Rhetorical Situation

The Situation

You are a member of a seven-person campus committee that wants to propose a new intramural activity for your school. First, your committee must agree on one activity to support. Each member will have five minutes to present an idea to the committee at your next meeting. You would like to propose lacrosse, which you have always been interested in since you learned the game as a child, but you know it is not a popular sport.

Making Choices

1. For your presentation, would you plan to try to identify with your audience or would you avoid identification with them? What are the potential benefits or drawbacks of each strategy?
2. What type of behavior is most appropriate for this situation: Will listeners expect a lighthearted tone, a serious demeanor, or something in between? A broad overview or a detailed one?
3. In this situation, is the purpose of your presentation to inform, to persuade, to entertain, or a combination of some or all of these? Explain why.

What If...

The committee decides to support your idea for a new intramural activity and asks you to present it to the student government. You will have 5 to 10 minutes to make your pitch. How would your answers above be affected by the following conditions?

1. In addition to presenting your idea, you need to include estimates for how much it will cost to fund the program for a year, and you know that student government officials will balk at what seems to be a very high cost.
2. A campus-wide poll taken by your committee shows that most students in the governing group aren't interested in your activity but that large numbers of students overall are excited about your proposal.

President George W. Bush addresses a joint session of Congress and the nation after the terrorist attack on the World Trade Center on September 11, 2001. How would you describe this specific rhetorical situation? What needs were posed by the audience, occasion, speaker, and speech?

The following example illustrates the double-sided nature of the rhetorical situation. On September 11, 2001, the nation watched in horror as two commercial airplanes crashed into the World Trade Center in New York City. A third plane crashed into the Pentagon in Washington, D.C. A fourth plane, thought to be headed for another national landmark, crashed in a field in Pennsylvania, following heroic efforts by the passengers to thwart the hijackers' plans. Thousands of lives were lost in the crashes and the destruction of the twin towers of the World Trade Center, from office personnel to rescue workers. This was the single deadliest act of terrorism on U.S. soil in history. Americans needed to know what their government was doing to protect them.

This context defined a rhetorical situation. The audience was the American people, who needed to be consoled and protected. The occasion was one of collective grief, uncertainty, and fear. In times of national crisis, people look to the president for leadership. President George W. Bush was still in his first year of office after the contested vote count of the 2000 election. He needed to prove that he could handle the crisis and lead the nation.

On the evening of September 20, 2001, in what is widely recognized as the finest hour in an otherwise controversial presidency, President Bush spoke to a joint session of Congress and to the nation. His speech consisted of both the prepared text and its oral presentation by the president. His text, prepared by lead speechwriter Michael Gerson and other staff members, began responding to the situation by honoring those who had died in the terrorist attack. He said that the courage of those who died spoke for the strong "state of the union." At the same time, the speech set forth plans to calm fears and prevent further attacks. President Bush set out his new foreign policy to combat terrorism around the world and also announced a new administrative position of coordinator of homeland security to strengthen domestic defenses.

The speech responded to the immediate situation of the terrorist attack and created a new situation of a war on terrorism, refocusing Americans' attention from fear, grief, and mourning to indignation, resolve, and unity. In short, although President Bush was *constrained* by the needs to provide meaning, reassurance, and focus, he made the choice to characterize the situation as a war on terrorism, and by doing so he took advantage of an *opportunity.* Every rhetorical situation consists of a mix of constraints and opportunities.

Similarly, when you give a speech in class, your rhetorical situation is influenced by the audience and by the values its members hold. These are your situation's constraints. At the same time, you have the opportunity to modify listeners' beliefs and values by what you say.

Since ancient times, a speaker's opportunities—the speech elements about which the speaker can make choices—have been grouped under five major headings:

invention
The generation of materials for a speech.

- **Invention** is the generation of materials for the speech. You produce (or "invent," to use the rhetorical term) these materials through a combination of analysis, research, and judgment. You begin by identifying what *could* go into the speech, then you conduct research to determine what ideas are supportable, and then you select the most effective materials for your purpose and audience.

- **Arrangement** is the structuring of ideas and materials in the speech. This includes the organization of materials for each main idea, the ordering and connecting of main ideas within the body of the speech, and the overall structure of the introduction, the body, and the conclusion.
- **Style** is the distinctive character that may make a speech recognizable or memorable. Style is achieved primarily through language, and it reflects the speaker's awareness of how language can be used both to "show" and to "tell"—both to evoke emotions and to convey descriptive meaning.
- **Delivery** is the presentation of the speech. Whereas the preceding activities are performed by the speaker alone, delivery involves actually sharing the message with the audience. Skillful delivery involves the effective use of voice, gesture, facial expression, physical movement, and visual aids.
- **Memory** was an extremely important category of skills at a time when most speeches were memorized. Today, however, most speakers use either **extemporaneous presentation** (referring to an outline) or **manuscript presentation** (reading a written script). Even so, some dimensions of memory are still very important—for example, keeping track of main ideas, phrasing ideas so that listeners will remember them, and precisely wording an effective introduction and conclusion. Memory skills also are critical in rehearsing your speech mentally and in practicing it aloud before presentation.

arrangement
The structuring of materials within the main ideas, the organization of main ideas within the body of the speech, and the overall structure of introduction, body, and conclusion.

style
The distinctive character that may make a speech recognizable or memorable.

delivery
The presentation of the speech to an audience.

memory
Mental recall of the key ideas and the basic structure of the speech.

extemporaneous presentation
A mode of delivery in which the speech is planned and structured carefully but a specific text is not written in advance nor memorized.

manuscript presentation
A mode of delivery in which the speaker reads aloud the prepared text of the speech.

The Public Forum

OBJECTIVE 1.4

The word **public** in "public speaking" is important in at least two respects. First, it designates speaking that is open and accessible by others. A person who speaks publicly is inviting others to listen carefully and to think about and appraise the message. The speaker's goal is that of informed choice, not forced compliance, on the part of the audience.

Second, speaking is public when it affects people beyond the immediate audience. If you urge classmates to lobby for higher student activity fees, your remarks will have consequences for people who are not even present to hear you. If you explain how to examine the terms of a lease before signing it, listeners can follow your directions in ways that will affect others as well.

From the speaker's point of view, giving a speech means entering into the **public forum**. Centuries ago, the forum was a physical place where citizens gathered to discuss issues affecting them. Today, the public forum is not an actual place to which we go; instead, it is an imagined "space" that exists wherever people have the freedom to exchange ideas about matters that affect themselves and others. For example, in the United States religion usually is thought to be a private matter, but religious freedom is an important public value. So when, in early 2012, the federal government proposed rules requiring religious institutions to offer health insurance coverage for contraception, the resulting controversy prompted vigorous debates among citizens who wrote letters and made telephone calls to express their opinions.

public
Open to or accessible by others; affects others.

public forum
A space (imagined, rather than physical) in which citizens gather to discuss issues affecting them; discussion characterized by certain assumptions about the need for cooperative action and subjective judgment to resolve a problem.

We sometimes think of the public forum only when large questions of national or international affairs are involved, but *anytime* you deliberate about matters that affect you and others, you are participating in the public forum. Holding a classroom discussion, determining the rules for a residence hall, making policy in your local community, urging students to volunteer their time for a worthy cause, campaigning on behalf of a candidate for mayor, and trying to raise funds for a new city park are all examples of participation in the public forum. In principle, everyone has the chance not only to listen but to be heard as well.

The public forum used to develop only slowly and gradually, as individuals came to see that they shared a problem or concern about which something needed to be done. Now, however, electronic communication can make the emergence of the public forum almost instantaneous. Examples include the speed with which social media brought people together around the "Arab spring" protests of 2011, the Occupy movement in the United States in the fall of 2011, and in early 2012 a reversal of a prominent cancer research foundation's decision to discontinue support for Planned Parenthood.

Characteristics of the Public Forum

The public forum is created whenever the following conditions are met:

1. *Some problem affects people collectively* as well as individually.
2. *Cooperative action is needed* to address the problem. Speakers and listeners participate in deciding what to do.
3. *The decision requires subjective judgment.* What should be done is not obvious; there is more than one possible solution, and there is no way for anyone to gather all the information that conceivably might bear on the decision.
4. Nevertheless, *a decision is required.* People stand at a fork in the road, and a choice cannot be avoided.

Of course, the public forum does not come into being only at the moment of decision. When people seek information in order to understand the background of important issues, to recognize competing viewpoints, or to have a clear frame of reference, the public forum is present. Whether your main purpose is to inform or to persuade, or even to entertain, you will be addressing a public forum if these four conditions are present.

Strategies for Speaking to Diverse Audiences

Recognizing Diversity

The first step in recognizing diversity is to become aware of your own frameworks and assumptions, so that you might avoid unconsciously assuming that everyone "naturally" shares them. To help you do that, consider:

- What beliefs on your topic do you "take for granted"? How can you best anticipate these before addressing your audience? Can you account for all the assumptions on which your ideas depend?
- How might your assumptions and "taken for granted" beliefs be challenged by someone who did not share them? Does the way in which a challenge is made make a big difference in how you would respond to it? What types of challenges might be most productive?
- Assuming you receive constructive challenges, how might you reshape your message? Do you need to account for everything your respondent said? How much change do you need to make? What risks do you run by following the advice of one audience member over others?

Just as the public forum exists in many places, many subjects call for communication in the public forum. For example, consider how the topic of immigration policy reform reflects each of the four conditions for a public forum:

1. For many years, immigration was at the heart of American economic expansion. Early on, however, several ethnic and national groups were discriminated against, as with the Chinese Exclusion Act of 1882. In the following decades, strict quotas were placed on who could immigrate legally. Slowly, many realized that immigration policy was *not just an individual matter*, because all were harmed by acts of discrimination against individual ethnicities or nationalities.
2. When people came to see immigration as more than a private matter, *speakers and listeners together began to discuss* how and why to best reform immigration policy. Audiences heard descriptions of how various plans would work. They identified and evaluated speakers' claims, arguments, and evidence. They considered a variety of proposals, accepting some ideas and rejecting others. Speakers analyzed their audiences' beliefs and values and tried to adapt their ideas to what listeners regarded as most important.
3. *No one person can just impose a solution.* No one can be certain which proposal is best, and no one can ever get all the information that might help in making that decision. So there is a give-and-take process as speakers and listeners consider alternative ideas and proposals, trying their best to decide which are the most sensible or compelling.
4. *And yet a decision has to be made,* because doing nothing will make the problems of immigration worse—for individuals as well as for society as a whole.

Over time, the participants in the public forum come to an understanding about which approach should be tried. The understanding that they reach is always tentative and always subject to revision if better ideas emerge into the forum. Because no final answer has been found on the subject of immigration reform, for example, it returns to the public forum every few years. It has been in the public forum ever since the Alien and Sedition Acts of 1798 but was vigorously debated beginning early in the twentieth century. After World War II, immigration reform allowed many refugees from Eastern Europe to settle in the United States. A 1986 Act provided amnesty for many illegal aliens but imposed sanctions against employers hiring illegal aliens. The DREAM Act proposed in 2011 would allow illegal immigrants who have been in the United States since they were children and who have been educated in U.S. schools to become citizens.

The topic of immigration reform is typical of many subjects in the public forum. The specifics of the discussion change over time, decisions are subject to change as a result of new information or perspective, and the issue is not settled with finality. Also, although immigration reform is discussed in legislative halls, it is a topic for human rights activists, family organizations, workers and employers concerned about job security, legal immigrants, and those interested in the future demographic composition of the United States. In discussing the topic of immigration reform, all these people, wherever they are physically located, are participating in the public forum.

When you speak, you are joining an ongoing discussion in the public forum. The status of that discussion will tell you what people are thinking about and, therefore, what topics will be of interest and what positions are being considered. You may learn, for example, that just as terrorism eclipsed health care as a topic of public interest after September 11, 2001, so the financial crisis that began in 2008 eclipsed considerations of foreign policy. Closer to home, shortfalls in the college

Rhetorical Workout

Find the Public Forum in Your Neighborhood

You and several of your neighbors would like to plan a neighborhood rummage sale. You set up a meeting to talk about when to have the sale and how to work together to promote it. Let's look at what makes this meeting a public forum.

1. What are the issues or problems affecting the group collectively? What kinds of issues might affect you and each of your neighbors individually? Outside of your group, who might be affected by what you decide?
2. Why is cooperative action needed in your meeting? Is it important for every person to participate in the decision? Why or why not?
3. In the public forum, a decision requires subjective judgment, which means there is no one obvious solution and the participants may all have different opinions. How might this factor play out in your neighborhood meeting?
4. Why is a decision needed in your meeting?
5. Suppose you have recently moved in and don't know your neighbors very well yet. How can your speaking and communication skills help you contribute to the meeting and the group's decision?

budget may eclipse discussion of new academic programs in the public forum. This knowledge will help you to decide what to speak about and determine the specific questions you may want to address.

The Health of the Public Forum

As you become skilled in public speaking, you become a more effective participant in the public forum. You are able to analyze important issues of public concern, to articulate your ideas and to relate them to others, to listen carefully and critically to other points of view, to weigh and evaluate arguments and evidence, and to bring your best judgment to issues that have no easy or automatic answer. As you exercise these skills, you strengthen the ties that unite participants in the public forum into a community or society. This is a benefit above and beyond the gains in personal self-esteem and performance on the job that come with competence in communication.

"Citizen comment" periods at city council meetings permit representatives of local groups to speak on their behalf. You might find yourself in this role.

Traditionally, the public forum has been associated with political questions. But the boundary between public and private is always shifting, and any subject might easily find its way into the public forum. Styles in popular music, for example, become more than just private or individual choices in response to claims that the noise level is harmful to health or that the content leads children to violence. Personal choices of deodorants or clothing are no longer just private matters when they are alleged to cause destruction of the ozone layer or exploitation of Third-World labor markets. And speculating in the stock market becomes a public matter when one's investment choices affect so many others. Whatever subject you discuss—whether or not it is usually regarded as political—you are entering into the public forum.

Discussion of public issues is best advanced when the public forum is active and vibrant. Maintaining a healthy public forum, like maintaining our personal health, takes work. In the 2008 presidential election campaign, for example, after years of decline and apathy, many people, especially college students, developed an interest in public affairs. In formal discourse and informal conversation, public issues were discussed with vigor. But we should not assume that an engaged public is always the norm. More often, private citizens are put off by the difficulty of understanding important but complex issues. In the early months of the 2012 presidential campaign, for example, people were less inclined to participate, although more were aroused as Election Day approached. Even in informal conversation, according to recent research, many people are reluctant to talk about public issues.[3] Others are satisfied with sources of information that oversimplify issues and turn them into slogans. Or they may seek out and pay attention only to information that agrees with their point of view.

When large numbers of people become convinced that they have the power to effect change, the public forum becomes the centerpiece of democracy. But when citizens disengage from issues of public concern, a free society should sound the alarm.

Public Speaking and the Public Forum

If the public forum is allowed to weaken, critical public decisions will be made unilaterally, whether by experts or by rulers, so those who are affected by the decisions really won't have any part in making them. Without a well-cultivated public forum, the two alternatives are autocratic rule and anarchy.

Remember that the public forum extends beyond the realm of traditional politics. Many who disdain traditional politics are involved actively in their own communities on issues that affect the general good. For these citizens, the public forum, rather than weakening, is becoming more localized and many new forums are emerging. What it means to be a citizen is changing but not necessarily eroding.[4] This is an encouraging development but one that requires that many more people be able to participate actively.

Nationwide, colleges and universities are stressing "civic engagement" in order to help students to become more competent citizens who will become involved with public affairs. Fortunately, studying public speaking equips you to do this by enabling you to understand issues and evaluate claims. The processes of discovering, assessing, arranging, and presenting ideas will be valuable as you read and think about public issues, discuss them with others, and speak out when the issue and the occasion move you. You'll be able to make decisions even about matters that do not directly affect you. And when an issue does affect you, your involvement and participation will count.

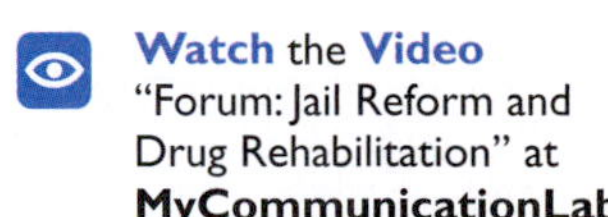

Watch the Video
"Forum: Jail Reform and Drug Rehabilitation" at
MyCommunicationLab

Ethics: Respect for Audience, Topic, and Occasion

OBJECTIVE 1.5

Even though we sometimes say that "talk is cheap" or that "words can never hurt me," we know better. Speech has tremendous power, and the person who wields it bears great responsibility. Public speakers, in particular, can affect others by altering listeners' knowledge, beliefs, values, or actions. Furthermore, the act of addressing an audience may alter the speaker's own beliefs and values in response to listeners' reactions. Given this powerful interaction in public speaking, both speakers and listeners should seek high standards of ethical conduct, so that they do not risk manipulating the other.

As a listener, you owe speakers your care and attention. Recognize and acknowledge the effort that went into preparing the speech, and appreciate that the speaker may be disclosing something personal. Assume that the speaker is sincere, and listen intently to the speaker's message. Do not engage in other activities that will distract you from the speech. Above all, listeners have the responsibility to think critically about the speech. Do not reject or refuse to consider the speaker's message simply because it differs from what you already believe. Nor, however, should you blindly accept the message. Assess the speech carefully to decide whether it merits your support. Whatever you decide, do so thoughtfully. Your agreement is especially valuable to a speaker when it reflects critical thought and you give it freely.

As a speaker you should demonstrate high ethical standards in four areas:

- Respect for your listeners
- Respect for your topic
- Responsibility for your statements
- Concern for the consequences of your speech

Respect for Your Listeners

Successful communication usually depends on evoking common bonds between the speaker and listeners. When a speech is effective, audience members feel both that the speaker cares about them and that they are not just passive spectators. Rather, they feel that they are actively involved in the speech.

Because a speech is presented to a specific audience in a specific situation, a high-quality speech is sensitive to listeners' perspectives. A speaker who carefully analyzes the audience at hand will select materials and strategies that are appropriate and effective. In particular, the following principles demonstrate a speaker's respect for listeners.

Meet Listeners Where They Are. One sign of respect is your willingness to acknowledge the audience's current position and to make it your point of departure—whether or not you agree with it. For example, in trying to convince opponents of capital punishment to rethink their position, student Mary O'Malley chose not to attack the audience's point of view right away but instead to begin by considering it:

> I understand that you have some reservations about the death penalty because you are worried that an innocent person might mistakenly be executed. This is certainly an important consideration. Death is final, and no one wants to be responsible for such a horrible mistake. Today I want to examine the possibility that a mistake might occur in the criminal justice system and to explore the consequences of such a mistake.

Rather than ignoring her listeners' views, Mary incorporated them into the speech, showing respect by meeting listeners on their own ground.

Don't Insult Listeners' Intelligence or Judgment. Besides starting her speech by acknowledging listeners' views, Mary also respected their judgment and intelligence by saying that she would examine their position in her speech. Likewise, when you prepare and present a speech, avoid patronizing or "talking down to" the audience. Don't devote the entire speech to repeating what listeners already know or believe, making them wonder why they took the time to hear you.

Also avoid suggesting that anyone who does not agree with you is somehow deficient in judgment. Steer clear of phrases that a listener might interpret as put-downs.

Public speakers make claims on their listeners' attention and beliefs. Speakers therefore have a responsibility to say something worthwhile, to respect listeners' judgment, and to respect the diversity of viewpoints and cultural background that listeners represent.

Make Sure Your Message Merits the Audience's Time. In general, although listeners could do other things with their time, they choose to attend your speech in the belief that you have something valuable and original to say. Recognize that you are receiving a gift of their time, and prepare a speech that deserves their gift.

Respect Listeners' Ability to Assess Your Message. Because you respect listeners, you want them to understand your message thoroughly and to give their approval freely. Do not mislead listeners about your purpose or conceal what you want them to believe, feel, think, or do. If you are urging them to make a choice among alternatives, do not try to manipulate them by hiding options or by casting any particular option in unduly favorable or unfavorable light. If it is your goal to advocate one option over another, you will best defend your position by explaining how it is superior to the alternatives, not by distorting or ignoring the options that you dislike.

As a general rule, you should assume that your audience is made up of critical thinkers and listeners, and your speech should aim for the approval of such an audience. Going about it in this way will reduce the risk that you will play upon the quirks or prejudices of any particular audience.

Respect the Cultural Diversity of Your Audience. Not all listeners share your perspective. An audience often includes people with many diverse cultural backgrounds, and these affect their attitudes and experiences. As society becomes even more diverse, all public communicators must expect that some listeners will have assumptions different from their own. The tendency to imagine that one's own views are typical of everyone else's is called *ethnocentrism*. It not only demeans listeners who have different cultural backgrounds, it also reduces the likelihood of successful communication.[10]

Ethnocentrism is usually unconscious. When student speaker Mary Winthrop concluded her speech on religion in American life by saying, "So in this country, it clearly doesn't matter where you go to church on Sunday," she thought she was celebrating religious freedom. She didn't realize that she alienated Muslims and Jews in her audience, whose religions focus on other days of the week and who do not call their houses of worship "churches," or that she had offended those who do not practice a religion. Likewise, when Patrick Dungan mentioned that "by eighth grade, everyone begins thinking about where to go to college," he probably didn't realize that in his audience were students who couldn't afford to go to college at all until after several years in the workforce.

Respecting cultural diversity requires being aware of one's own assumptions and resisting the temptation to assume that everyone else will share them. Although we will focus on audience culture in Chapter 5, respect for cultural diversity should influence every aspect of preparing and presenting a speech.

A Question of Ethics

Ethnocentric Assumptions

It is important for speakers to avoid making ethnocentric assumptions about the audience. However, sometimes you will know quite a bit about your audience that could help you to target a message to your listeners. For instance, your audience may be people of the same age group, from the same community, or with the same religious beliefs. If you tailor your message to take advantage of this knowledge, is that ethnocentric? Is it pandering to the audience? Is it acceptable to be ethnocentric if your audience is in fact homogeneous? How do you maintain a balance between appealing to your audience and being careful not to pander to their prejudices?

Respect for Your Topic

Presumably, you will be speaking about a topic that matters to you, and you will have something important to say. When you speak, you are putting yourself on the record; your words will outlast the actual speaking situation. You are also asking listeners to accept you as a credible source of ideas about the topic. To justify their confidence in you, and to meet your own high standards, you need to know what you are talking about in enough detail that you can present it clearly and fairly. You must demonstrate that you care enough about the topic to study it thoroughly. Otherwise, why should the audience take your ideas about the topic seriously?

Responsibility for Your Statements

A public speaker makes claims on the audience, and so you must take responsibility for the accuracy and integrity of your statements. This is every bit as important in speaking as it is in writing, and similar guidelines apply.

Particularly in speaking (because listeners cannot see the printed word), you need to distinguish between fact and opinion, being careful not to misrepresent one as the other. Additionally, whether you are presenting fact or opinion, a statement is made in a particular context, and you must represent that correctly; if not, you will mislead or deceive the audience. The film critic who writes, "Nothing could be better than this film if you are looking for a cure for insomnia," does not want to be quoted as saying, "Nothing could be better than this film." Likewise, stating that military spending has declined as a percentage of the gross domestic product over the past five years is not fair to the context unless you tell listeners that the source also said that actual military spending has *increased* by several billion dollars but that the economy grew at an even faster rate.

As in writing, one of the most irresponsible things you can do as a speaker is to present another person's words or ideas as though they were your own. Such **plagiarism** is nothing less than theft. Usually it results from carelessness rather than malice, but the problem is the same.

To avoid plagiarism:

1. Never present someone else's unique ideas or words without acknowledging it.
2. Specify who developed the ideas or said the words that you present ("As discovered by Professor Jones," "Socrates said," and so forth).

plagiarism
Using another person's words as if they were your own.

3. Paraphrase statements in your own words rather than quoting them directly, unless the exact wording of a statement is crucial to your speech.
4. Draw on several sources rather than on a single source.

Remember that it is also a form of plagiarism to present another student's speech as your own or to use the same speech in two different classes. Every speech you present should be your own original work.

CHECKLIST 1.1

Avoid Plagiarism

- ❒ Never present someone else's ideas or words without acknowledging it.
- ❒ Always give the source of the ideas or words that you present.
- ❒ Paraphrase statements in your own words instead of quoting someone directly, unless exact wording is crucial to your speech.
- ❒ Draw on several sources rather than only one source.
- ❒ Never present another person's speech as your own.
- ❒ Don't use the same speech for two different classes.

Concern for the Consequences of Your Speech

Recognizing that your speech has consequences is another important ethical responsibility. You cannot be indifferent to how your speech may affect others, even though you may not know what all the effects will be. A listener might repeat an amusing anecdote you told, might feel more closely connected to someone whose life you celebrated, might get a psychological lift from your upbeat tone, or might change health insurance based on the reasoning in your speech. The fact that others may repeat what you said in the speech is all the more reason to be sure that what you have said is true! You cannot be held legally responsible for such effects, of course, but high ethical standards should lead you at least to think about how your speech might affect listeners.

Moreover, in any rhetorical situation, speakers and listeners together make up a community united by experience, interests, and values. Speech is the glue that holds a community together by making us aware of our common bonds and by giving us a vision to which we might aspire. Ethical public speakers take their membership in this community seriously, and they accept their responsibility to sustain the community by adhering to high ethical standards.[11]

It is easy to state general ethical standards such as these, but ethical issues present themselves in almost every aspect of the speech. Often these are matters involving choices between competing ethical standards, and they often have to be resolved in the context of the specific case rather than by invoking general principles. For this reason, each chapter includes the feature "A Question of Ethics" to help you recognize ethical issues throughout the speech process.

Watch the **Video** "Mark Knapp on the Ethics of Deception" at **MyCommunicationLab**

What Have You Learned?

Objective 1.1: Identify the principal things you will learn in this course and how they will benefit you outside the classroom.

By studying public speaking, you will learn these essential skills:

- Reading, observing, and thinking critically
- Selecting what to say
- Using language effectively
- Presenting yourself skillfully
- Responding to others' reactions to you

Blending theory and practice will:

- Help you to be more articulate.
- Apply to a variety of everyday life and career situations.
- Enable you to participate more effectively as a citizen.

Objective 1.2: Describe public speaking as a communication process in which the speaker and listeners jointly create meaning and understanding.

Public speaking is communication:

- Communication is the joint creation of meaning by speakers and listeners.

- A speech is given in a specific rhetorical situation, determined by the audience, occasion, speaker, and speech.
- Listeners interpret a message and provide feedback.
- The speaker takes listeners into account both in developing the speech and in responding to feedback.
- Public speaking occurs in the public forum.

Objective 1.3: Name the elements of a rhetorical situation and explain the steps by which a speech affects the situation.

A rhetorical situation is constrained by:

- The audience
- The occasion
- The speaker
- The speech

Speakers can make choices regarding:

- Invention
- Arrangement
- Style
- Delivery
- Memory

Objective 1.4: Define the public forum and describe how studying public speaking will prepare you to participate effectively in it.

Characteristics of the public forum:

- An issue confronts people collectively as well as individually.
- Cooperative action is needed to address the issue.
- It is impossible to know for sure the best course of action to take.
- Nevertheless, a decision is required.

The health of the public forum:

- Depends on active participation.
- Is often weak, characterized by disengagement and apathy.
- May be changing in form and in location.
- Is aided by civic engagement.

Objective 1.5: Identify the principal ethical obligations of listeners and speakers.

High ethical standards reflect the mutual responsibilities of listeners and speakers:

- Listeners owe speakers their care and attention.
- Speakers owe respect for listeners, for the topic, for their statements, and for the consequences of their speech.

Listen to the **Audio Chapter Summary** at **MyCommunicationLab**

Discussion Questions

1. What is rhetoric? Why is it important to study rhetoric?
2. Watch a speech on television, and then identify the most important strategic choices made by the speaker. How would the speech be changed if these choices had been made differently?
3. Someone who is having trouble hearing a speaker usually leans forward to get closer to the sound. This is a cue to the speaker to increase the volume. What are some other common feedback cues that an audience might present? Discuss how a speaker might use each cue to modify either the message or the presentation. How much attention should you as a speaker pay to such nonverbal cues? When might paying attention to such cues become distracting or hinder your speech?
4. View a speech with your classmates, and then, as a group, evaluate the quality of that speech. Take into account its purpose; the degree to which the topic meets the requirements of the situation; sensitivity to cultural diversity; the meaningfulness and importance of the thesis; organization, support, and presentation; the way in which the speech builds community with the audience; and its ethical implications. Which of these characteristics are most helpful and most important to you in distinguishing a good speech from a bad one? Is this the same for all speeches, or do different speeches call for different evaluative emphases?
5. How do you define ethics? Discuss the ethical considerations that are most important to the class. What are the points on which the class as a whole agrees?

Activities

1. Using the diagram in Figure 1.2, identify the components of the rhetorical situation you will face when you give your first speech in class.
2. Watch a television program where people discuss public issues among themselves. Compare it to a program in which someone speaks to a live audience and a

television camera. How do these cases differ from each other? From the speeches you expect to deliver in class?

3. Watch a speech, and then write an evaluation of its quality. Consider both delivery and content of the speech.

4. Examine your reasons for taking this public speaking course. Beyond fulfilling requirements, what goals do you want to achieve? Based on your reading of this chapter, do you think this course will help you achieve your goals? Why or why not?

Key Terms

arrangement **15**
ceremonial **10**
communication **6**
critical thinking **5**
deliberative **10**
delivery **15**
entertaining **12**
exigence **11**
extemporaneous presentation **15**
facts **5**
feedback **7**
forensic **11**
identification **10**
informing **12**
invention **14**
manuscript presentation **15**
memory **15**
opinions **5**
persuading **12**
plagiarism **22**
public **15**
public forum **15**
rhetoric **8**
rhetorical situation **8**
situation **8**
strategic planning **5**
strategy **13**
style **15**

Study and **Review** the **Flashcards** at **MyCommunicationLab**

Notes

1 These skills will help you to succeed in college. See Ann Bainbridge Frymier, "Students' Classroom Communication Effectiveness," *Communication Quarterly* 53 (May 2005): 197–212.

2 For example, see the January 29, 2009, report of the National Association of Colleges and Employers, available at http://www.naceweb.org/press/display.asp?year=&prid=295.

3 An example of research demonstrating that people often tend to avoid the discussion of public issues is Nina Eliasoph, *Avoiding Politics: How Americans Produce Apathy in Everyday Life*, New York: Cambridge University Press, 1998.

4 For an excellent analysis of how the concept of citizenship has changed over time along with changing norms about public communication, see Michael Schudson, *The Good Citizen*, New York: Free Press, 1998. For more about how notions of citizenship are undergoing great change, see Russell J. Dalton, *The Good Citizen: How a Younger Generation is Reshaping American Politics,* rev. ed., Washington, D.C.: CQ Press, 2009.

5 For a discussion of this difference between literature and oratory, see Herbert A. Wichelns, "The Literary Criticism of Oratory," first published in 1925, reprinted in *Methods of Rhetorical Criticism: A Twentieth Century Perspective*, ed. Robert L. Scott and Bernard L. Brock, New York: Harper & Row, 1972.

6 See Lloyd Bitzer, "The Rhetorical Situation," *Philosophy and Rhetoric* 1 (Winter 1968): 1–14.

7 *Identification* is a rhetorical concept treated by Kenneth Burke in *A Rhetoric of Motives*, Berkeley: University of California Press, 1969.

8 The strategy of speakers who do not seek identification is examined in Robert L. Scott and Donald K. Smith, "The Rhetoric of Confrontation," *Quarterly Journal of Speech* 55 (February 1969): 1–8. For an argument that such confrontation may be necessary in certain rhetorical situations, see Corina Andone, "Confrontational Strategic Maneuvers in a Political Interview," *Controversia*, 7 (Spring, 2010), 74–90/

9 These three categories are described in Aristotle, *On Rhetoric: A Theory of Civic Discourse*, trans. George A. Kennedy, New York: Oxford University Press, 1991.

10 One way to begin breaking down ethnocentric views is to examine communication across cultures. See George A. Kennedy, *Comparative Rhetoric: An Historical and Cross-Cultural Introduction*, New York: Oxford University Press, 1998. The growth of the Internet makes such intercultural communication even more important. See Damien Smith Pfister and Jordan Soliz, "(Re)Conceptualizing Intercultural Communication in a Networked Society," *Journal of International & Intercultural Communication,* 4 (November, 2011): 246–51.

11 For more on ethical considerations in the public speaking class, see George Cheney, Steve May, and Debashish Munshi, ed., *The Handbook of Communication Ethics,* New York: Routledge, 2011; Richard L. Johannesen, Kathleen S. Valde, and Karen E. Whedbee, *Ethics in Human Communication,* 6th ed., Long Grove, IL: Waveland Press, 2008; and Ronald C. Arnett, Janie M. Harden Fritz, and Leeanne M. Bell, *Communication Ethics Literacy: Dialogue and Difference*, Los Angeles: Sage, 1999.

CHAPTER

2

Your First Speech

LEARNING OBJECTIVES

After studying this chapter, you should be able to:

Objective 2.1	Explain the relationship between understanding theory and gaining practical experience in learning how to speak.
Objective 2.2	Identify the principal goals of your first speech for this course.
Objective 2.3	Explain the functions of the introduction, body, and conclusion of the speech and arrangement strategies for materials within the body.
Objective 2.4	Explain and use outlines that will help in preparing and presenting a speech.
Objective 2.5	Use strategies to help you effectively practice and present your first speech.
Objective 2.6	Use strategies to manage nervousness to your advantage and overcome anxiety.

Listen to the **Audio Chapter** at **MyCommunicationLab**

OUTLINE

OBJECTIVE 2.1

Public speaking involves both learning theoretical knowledge and putting it into practice. We understand theory in large part by reflecting on our practice. And, because theory and practice interact, it's difficult to separate the two—to spend the first half of a course on theory, for instance, and then focus on practice during the second half. You become a more competent and experienced speaker by mastering theory at the same time you improve through practice. For this reason, Chapters 1 and 2 go together—whether your course begins with theory or with practice.

The goal of this chapter is to enable you to prepare and to present a simple first speech. Many of the concepts introduced here will be covered in more depth when you encounter them again later in the book.

OBJECTIVE 2.2

Goals and Strategies for Your First Speech

Most instructors assign a first speech early in the course. Whatever your specific assignment is, two goals are important for any speech:

1. Your message should be clear.
2. You should establish positive *ethos*.

Although these goals are highlighted for your first speech, they will continue to be goals for *every* speech you give. Subsequent speaking assignments will build upon them. This section examines what the goals entail and explores strategies for achieving them.

A Clear Message

First, your speech should have a clear purpose and thesis. The **purpose** is your goal for the speech, the response you are seeking from listeners. The **thesis** is a statement of your main idea; it summarizes the basic point you want the audience to accept.

Your Purpose.

Obviously, as a speaker you want listeners to pay attention to you and to think well of you. Beyond that, however, speeches can seek many different responses from the audience. Do you want to impart information, to teach listeners something new? Or do you want to remind them of something they already believe so they will be more aware of how it affects them? Is it your goal to make listeners see the humorous side of something they regard as serious—or perhaps to see the serious side of what they may otherwise view as a joke? Do you want them to pay attention to something that they may tend to ignore? Do you hope to change their beliefs or attitudes about something? Do you want listeners to take a specific action?

Questions like these illustrate the many possible purposes that a speaker might have, but not all of them are suitable for a brief first speech. You might want just to provide new information and ask listeners to think about it. For now, this may be a more realistic goal than aiming to change your listeners' beliefs or attitudes.

purpose
The goal of the speech; the response sought from listeners.

thesis
The main idea of the speech, usually stated in one or two sentences.

Your Thesis. After you have defined your purpose for speaking, you should clearly state the thesis, or main idea, that you want the speech to establish. After your speech is over, listeners should have little doubt about what you actually said or what you meant. If you find it difficult to state your main idea in a sentence or two, you may be trying to cover too much. Even complex technical claims should be reducible to simple, basic thesis statements.

For example, suppose your first effort to state your thesis results in a statement like

I'm going to talk about music.

In this case, you have not focused sharply enough on your subject; you have only identified a general topic area. A better statement might be

The iPod has changed how we listen to music.

Your thesis is now more specific about what the speech will seek to establish. Similarly, if the purpose of your first speech is to introduce someone

Broad: I am going to tell you about my classmate, Jack Green.
Focused: Growing up in Japan greatly affected Jack Green's life.

The first statement is too broad, whereas the revised, focused statement tells the audience exactly what your speech will claim.

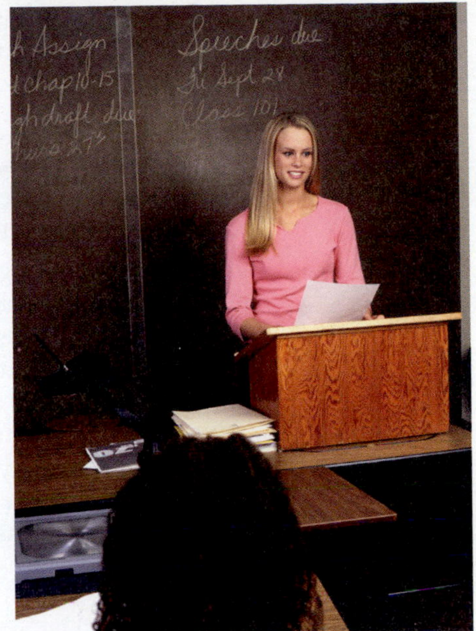

Maintaining good eye contact and using an informal tone will help you to establish a good relationship with the audience in your first speech.

In short, the thesis is not the general topic of the speech; it is a succinct statement of what you are saying *about* the topic. Stating your thesis in a single specific sentence will help ensure that you focus on the main idea rather than talk around it.

Positive *Ethos*

The second goal for your beginning speech is to establish positive *ethos* as a speaker. This Greek term was used by teachers of public speaking 2,500 years ago, and a rough translation is *character.*[1] But *ethos* does not refer to innate character traits, those at the core of a person's identity. Rather, ***ethos*** refers to the character that is *attributed to* a speaker by listeners on the basis of what the speaker says and does in the speech. *Ethos* is the character that you project when you are in a speaking situation. Some textbooks use the term *credibility* to describe this concept, but listeners make other judgments besides whether they should believe you. They also form impressions about what kind of person they think you are based on what you say and project as a speaker.

Assessing *Ethos*. Try the following experiment. Watch a video of a speech by someone you do not know; you can find one online or at MyCommunicationLab. Then, based only on the speech, jot down all the adjectives you can think of to describe this speaker. Your list might look something like this:

nervous	deferential	slick	committed
intelligent	concerned	friendly	tasteful
trustworthy	respectful	unsure	weak
funny	happy		

Watch the **Video** "Informative Speech/Self-Introduction: Bimal" at **MyCommunicationLab**

ethos
The speaker's character as perceived by the audience.

Even a list this long will not capture *all* the attributes you might perceive in a speaker upon hearing a short speech. What can we conclude from this simple exercise about *ethos* and its effects?

1. *An audience's judgments about a speaker's character can be quite detailed.* From this exercise, you seem to know quite a bit about the speaker, based only on a very brief speech. You have a sense of the person's intellect, emotions, judgment, relationships with others, power, confidence, and sense of self.
2. *Judgments about a speaker's character are made quickly.* The speech you watched probably lasted only a few minutes, and yet it gave you many insights into the person's apparent character. Whether the speaker walked confidently to the front of the room, looked at the audience, and then began speaking or whether the speaker seemed unsure, looked at the floor, and spoke even before reaching the front of the room may give you clues about the person. Your judgments may turn out to be wrong, of course, but you based them on the information you had. Listeners often only have superficial first impressions to guide them in assessing a speaker, and they form judgments quickly.
3. *Assessments of* ethos *are durable.* Listeners' first impressions not only shape how they judge the speaker but also affect how they interpret the speech. If the first impression you make is that you are very serious, it will seem out of character when you tell a joke later in the speech. The joke may cause listeners to revise their first impression ("Oh, that speaker's not so somber after all"), but it may also affect how they interpret the joke ("Such a serious person can't even tell a joke that's really funny"). If you already know some of your classmates, this knowledge also will affect your judgments of their *ethos*—and theirs of your *ethos*. In that case, assessments of *ethos* may be even more durable.

CHECKLIST 2.1

Goals for Your First Speech

1. Develop a clear message.
- ❒ Do you have a topic?
- ❒ What is the purpose of the speech?
  Informing?
  Persuading?
  Entertaining?
- ❒ Have you stated your thesis, or the main idea of the speech?
  Is the thesis succinct?
  Is the thesis specific?

2. Establish positive *ethos.*
- ❒ Recognize that an audience's judgments about a speaker's character are:
  Detailed
  Made quickly
  Durable
- ❒ Practice steps to establish positive *ethos.*
  Be confident.
  Make eye contact and show appropriate emotion in your facial expressions.
  Speak slowly and clearly enough to be understood.

Establishing Positive *Ethos*. Because an audience's assessments of a speaker are detailed, are formed quickly, and are durable, developing positive *ethos* in your first speech is just as important as having a clear statement of your purpose and thesis. If listeners do not perceive you as an honest and trustworthy person, they are not likely to take seriously whatever you have to say. For your first speech, there are several steps (discussed in more detail later in the chapter) you can take that will help listeners to form good first impressions of your *ethos*:

- Approach the front of the room confidently, not hesitantly.
- Plant your feet firmly on the floor so that you do not wander aimlessly.
- Make eye contact with audience members.
- Show appropriate emotion in your facial response so that listeners will realize that you are sincere about what you have to say.
- Speak slowly enough, and distinctly enough, that you can be understood easily.
- Pause for a brief moment after completing the speech, then walk confidently back to your seat.

In addition to *ethos*, the ancient Greeks identified two other resources of a speaker: *logos* and *pathos*. *Logos* refers to the substance and structure of a speech's ideas, and *pathos* refers to the speaker evoking appropriate emotion from the audience. These resources will be considered later in the book. However, because a listener's assessment of a speaker's character influences many other judgments about that speaker, learning how to establish positive *ethos* is important from the first speech you give.

Organizing Your Speech

OBJECTIVE 2.3

Once you have in mind the twin goals of presenting a clear message and establishing positive *ethos*, the next step is to think strategically about ways to organize the speech in order to achieve these goals. Every speech has three parts: the *introduction*, the *body*, and the *conclusion*. Chapters 9 and 10 will examine them fully. For your first speech, know that each part of a speech includes certain elements and performs certain functions.

Watch the Video "Informative Speech: Well-Done Introduction Speech" at **MyCommunicationLab**

The Introduction

Your **introduction** should be designed to (1) get the audience's attention, (2) state your thesis, and (3) preview how you will develop your ideas. Often the third function can be omitted in a short speech that has only one main point.

To get listeners' attention and put them in the right frame of mind, you might startle the audience with a significant but little-known fact. If your speech is about recycling, for example, you could begin by asking, "Do you realize that the trees of an entire forest are harvested each year to make paper for our textbooks?" Or, if your speech is about the benefits of technology, you might begin with a story that illustrates what it was like to practice law before the advent of digital databases. Your opening statement is the first impression of the speech that listeners will receive; you want to get their attention and focus it appropriately on your main idea. When people want to listen to you, your *ethos* also is enhanced.

The statement of your thesis further serves to put listeners in the right frame of mind by explaining how you want them to interpret what you are about to say. In speaking about recycling, for example, your thesis might be, "We need to get serious about conserving and replenishing our natural resources." If you identified your thesis clearly when preparing the speech, stating it in the introduction should be easy.

To preview how you will develop your thesis, the final thing the introduction should do is make a natural transition to the body of the speech by telling listeners what to expect. For example, you might follow your thesis statement with, "After examining how our forests have been reduced over the last 50 years, I will outline some simple measures that we can take to prevent further deforestation."

introduction
The beginning of the speech; designed to get the audience's attention, to state the thesis, and to preview the development of the speech.

The Body

The **body** is the largest portion of the speech; it develops your thesis statement and offers proof to support your claims. Sometimes the thesis will be a complex statement that must be broken down into smaller ones. In that case, preview

body
The largest portion of the speech; includes the development of supporting materials to prove the thesis and any subsidiary claims.

what the steps will be and make it clear how together they will support the thesis statement. For this first speech, though, the thesis should be simple and easily understood without the need for any further development.

Supporting Materials. **Supporting materials** are all forms of evidence that lend weight to the truth of your thesis, whether by explaining, illustrating, or defending it. The many kinds of supporting materials can be grouped into a few broad categories:

- Experience
- Narratives (stories)
- Data
- Opinions

You can draw on your own *experience* with a topic or problem to make it clear that you are familiar with and have been affected by the subject of your speech. For example, if your thesis is "On-campus housing is too expensive," you could tell the audience what percentage of your budget goes toward living on campus and contrast your experience with that of a friend living off campus. If your thesis is that volunteering is worth the time commitment, you could draw on your own experience volunteering on or off campus, detailing how much time you spend and describing the benefits you think the experience gives you. To support the thesis that everyone needs to know about self-defense, student Teresa Madera described how she escaped from an assailant:

> It was late, and I was returning to the dorm after studying at the library. When I was passing an alley, a stranger jumped out at me. Luckily, I was carrying this keychain. You'll notice that it has a small canister attached to it. This is mace, and it probably saved my life. I sprayed the guy who attacked me and then didn't wait around to see what happened.

Teresa went on to explain how her experience had convinced her that all students should be prepared to defend themselves.

You can use *narratives*, or stories, for supporting material; people often explain (and understand) situations in terms of a story. For example, in a speech about hazing, student Krupa Shah illustrated the impact of the problem by telling the story of a young college student named Chuck:

> Stuck in the trunk of a car with nothing to drink but a bottle of whiskey, a six-pack of beer, a quart of wine, and instructions to drink it all before the car stops—instructions given by a drunk and rowdy upperclassman—Chuck found out about hazing the hard way.

Krupa ended the speech—and concluded the story—by telling the audience what happened to Chuck during his car ride:

> The sensational nature of hazing can seem unbelievable, but it's true. Chuck would gladly tell you the dangers of hazing if he could. Sadly, he cannot. When Chuck was let out of the trunk he was taken to a house to complete the hazing ritual, and it was there that he spent the last moments of his life.

You can draw on *data* ("facts") for supporting material. If you claim that phones outnumber people in the United States, you could simply use statistical tables to report the two total numbers. Or, if the thesis is "Most American presidents have been lawyers," then naming all the lawyer-presidents would provide factual support.

supporting materials
All forms of evidence that lend weight to the truth of a claim.

CHOOSE A STRATEGY: Introducing Yourself to Others

The Situation

You have three minutes to introduce yourself at a local senior center where you wish to conduct a project for your sociology class. Recently there have been some traffic problems in the area caused by students from your college; therefore, audience members appear reluctant to cooperate. Three minutes is not enough time to describe everything there is to know about you or the worthiness of your project, so choices must be made.

Making Choices

1. How should you decide what you want to share about yourself? Should you consider: the members of your audience; your setting; your goals for the project; how much or how little you want the audience to know about you? What else might you consider?
2. What is the most relevant information to relay to your audience? Should you describe: your primary likes and dislikes; where you are from; what your hobbies and personal interests are; what your project is about; why your project is important to your audience? What other information might you want to include in your speech?

What If...

Let's assume you are given the same assignment but with a different audience and a different purpose. How would your decisions above be affected by the following conditions?

1. Your public speaking classmates are evaluating your speech for a grade.
2. Your speech of introduction assignment will not be graded.
3. Your audience is now the entire student body, and your purpose is to announce your candidacy for student president.
4. Your audience is the active members of a fraternity/sorority that you would like to join.

You also can use *opinions* to support your thesis. As noted earlier, opinions are subjective judgments based on a person's experience; unlike facts, opinions cannot be verified. But if you use the opinions of experts to support your claims, those judgments may be more likely viewed as authoritative, because they are based on expertise in the subject. Opinions are especially useful in situations where you cannot observe things yourself or when you want to support promises or predictions. For instance, to support a prediction that inflation will not worsen over the next six months, you could cite the opinion of the chair of the Federal Reserve Board. In offering an opinion, of course, you want to be sure that the person really is an expert in the field and that he or she is not biased.

Different cultures emphasize different supporting materials. In some cultures, storytelling carries great weight, whereas in others only data really matter. Partly for this reason, speakers addressing diverse audiences usually are advised to use a variety of types of supporting material. Varying the types of support is good advice for *any* speaker, because it will help to sustain the audience's interest and may enhance the speaker's *ethos* by suggesting that he or she has deep knowledge of the topic.

Using library sources as well as the Internet often will improve the quality of your research.

CHECKLIST 2.2

Decisions About Organization

1. Develop an introduction.
   - ❒ Does it include an attention-getting fact or story?
   - ❒ Does it state your thesis?
   - ❒ Does it preview what you will cover in your speech?
2. Assemble the body of the speech.
   - ❒ Which kinds of supporting material do you need to gather? Choose all that apply:
     Experience
     Narratives
     Data
     Opinions
   - ❒ How will you organize your supporting material? Choose one:
     Time order
     Spatial order
     Cause–effect order
     Problem–solution order
     Topical order
3. Prepare a conclusion.
   - ❒ Does it draw together the ideas in your speech?
   - ❒ Does it summarize or restate the ideas you've covered?
   - ❒ Does it repeat your thesis?
   - ❒ Does it provide a strong note of finality?

Organization of Evidence. Whenever you offer more than one piece of supporting material, you must decide in what order to arrange your evidence. Suppose, for example, that you want to use facts, narratives, and opinions to support the claim that prisons are seriously overcrowded. Which type of material should you present first?

Sometimes the decision about organization is just a matter of preference—of what seems instinctively to have the most natural "flow." You might decide to begin with a narrative, then state the facts about prison overcrowding, and finally conclude with the opinions of some prisoners and corrections officers. In cases like this, you should try several organizational arrangements to see which works best. You might ask some friends whether the thesis is clearer or more effective when you organize the supporting material one way rather than another.

At other times, the supporting material may suggest an organizational arrangement. If you are speaking about three times that your town was damaged by a flood, it makes sense to arrange the occasions chronologically—or in *time order*—either from first to last or from last to first.

Another natural organizational pattern is *spatial order*—arranging items according to their location. To discuss the varied geography of Texas, for example, you might proceed clockwise, beginning with the Panhandle in the far north, then describing the hill country of central Texas and the "piney woods" of the east, then dipping southward to cover the Gulf Coast and the Rio Grande Valley, and finally heading to western Texas and the Big Bend country.

Other common organizational patterns are *cause–effect* (beginning with conditions and then describing their causes, or vice versa); *problem–solution* (first explaining a problem and then pointing to the solution); and *topical structure* (mentioning all the economic facts, for example, before mentioning all the political facts). Strategies for using different organizational patterns will be explored in later chapters.

The Conclusion

The final part of the speech is the **conclusion**, which has two basic tasks. First, it should draw together the ideas in the speech so that they are memorable. This can be a brief summary of the argument, a restatement of the main points or ideas, or a repetition of the thesis. Second, the conclusion should give a strong note of finality to the speech. It might restate the idea in the introduction to suggest a completed circle. It might challenge the audience with an interesting question. Or it might draw on the claims in the speech to appeal for a specific belief or action on the part of the listeners.

conclusion
The ending of the speech; draws together the main ideas and provides a note of finality.

Strategies for Speaking to Diverse Audiences

Respecting Diversity Through the Preparation of Your Speech

When preparing your speech it is important to consider your audience members and to show respect for their viewpoints.

1. Be sure to pay attention to all sides of your topic when researching. For instance, if you are giving a speech about gentrification in your hometown, consider the fact that some people celebrate the renovation of run-down houses, whereas others bemoan being pushed out of their communities.
2. Think about the variety of ways in which bias may be present. How might your choice of topic, speech structure, or word choice reveal bias? Although bias cannot be removed completely, you should strive to make sure that it does not hurt your *ethos*.
3. Show respect for your audience by not insulting their intelligence and acknowledging their current position on your topic, or at least what you believe it to be. Even when acknowledging your audience, however, be sure not to rely on closed-minded assumptions and serve to treat both your topic and audience as fairly as possible.

Outlining Your Speech

OBJECTIVE 2.4

Sometimes speakers read a speech, word for word, from a fully written manuscript. On rare occasions, they commit the speech to memory.[2] These approaches may be helpful for highly formal speeches when every word matters and will be recorded for posterity. But for most of your speeches in this course, writing out and memorizing every word not only is a waste of time but may actually hinder your communication with the audience.

Neither is it usually a good idea to speak impromptu—without preparation, trusting that a flash of inspiration will strike you as you speak. Most successful speakers aim for middle ground with an **extemporaneous** speech, meaning that they have a clear sense of the main ideas and how to organize them, but they have not planned the speech in advance word for word and can adapt to feedback from the audience.

In speaking extemporaneously, two outlines are tremendously helpful: a preparation outline and a presentation outline.

Preparation Outline

Begin developing your speech with a **preparation outline**, which is more complete than the outline you will use when presenting the speech. The preparation outline helps you to identify your main ideas and to organize them sensibly, and it lists supporting materials and how you will use them.

For example, suppose your speech is designed to introduce a classmate, John Patterson. You've decided to highlight the fact that, unlike most students in the class, John has never lived outside of the town where you go to school. You think that his unusual history might give everyone insight into a sense of roots that people's ancestors had but that many lack today. The town is so much a part of John's identity that he cannot imagine himself apart from it. Key events in his life are associated with the town: growing up where everyone knew everyone else, participating in parades and celebrations, living as an adult in the same house he

extemporaneous
A mode of presentation in which the main ideas and structure have been worked out in advance but specific wording has not been developed.

preparation outline
An outline used in developing a speech; main ideas and supporting material are usually set forth in complete sentences.

occupied as a child, and watching things change around him as others moved into or out of town. You think John is a strong example of how some people can grow while staying rooted in one place.

A preparation outline incorporating these elements might look like this (notice that it is written in complete sentences):

ATTENTION GETTER:	Unlike most of us, John has never lived outside this town.
THESIS:	John has a clear sense of his roots.
SUPPORT:	A. He still lives in the same house in which he grew up.
	B. He has marched in the Fourth of July parade every year.
	C. He has never wanted to go anywhere else.
CONCLUSION:	Not everyone has to move in order to grow; John is a strong example.

Presentation Outline

Although the preparation outline is valuable in developing the speech, it is too complete to use while speaking. Your interaction with the audience will be limited if you are busy reading a fully elaborated, complete-sentence outline point by point. Instead, prepare a very brief outline of key words that will jog your memory and remind you of what comes next. You will use this **presentation outline** during the actual speech. Here is the previous example reduced to a presentation outline:

ATTENTION GETTER:	Never lived outside town.
THESIS:	Sense of roots
SUPPORT:	A. Same house
	B. 4th of July
	C. No desire to leave
CONCLUSION:	Can grow without moving.

Because you are familiar with the ideas of the speech, seeing the phrase "Same house" will remind you of the statement you want to make about how John still lives in the room he occupied as a child and how that experience has affected his perspective on life. You may never need to refer to the presentation outline while you are speaking, but if you do, a quick glance at the words "Same house" will remind you of the point you want to make.

You probably can reduce the presentation outline to fit on index cards, which are easier to handle than loose sheets of paper. For the first speech, you may need only one index card; three or four cards will usually be enough even for complex speeches.

OBJECTIVE 2.5

Practicing Your Speech

Because you are going to speak extemporaneously, practicing the speech is really a way to become familiar with the ideas by talking them through. You will not say exactly the same thing each time, but you will know the content of the speech well enough that the thoughts will come to you easily and you can express them naturally. To achieve this goal, use this sequence of activities:

presentation outline
An outline used while presenting a speech; typically consists only of key words written on an index card.

1. *Develop and talk through the preparation outline.* In your complete-sentence outline, fill in the explanation of your thesis and develop transitions

between ideas. Don't worry about awkward pauses that occur while you figure out what to say next. These will smooth out as you practice. After you have talked through the preparation outline once or twice to yourself, make an audio recording and listen to it. Ask yourself whether your main point is clear and easy to identify. If not, change your explanation or your transitions to present the thesis more effectively. You might also ask a friend to listen to you. Check whether your friend can identify the thesis correctly, and ask for suggestions to improve the speech. Ask, too, what listeners thought about the character you projected while delivering the speech. Does it match what you want the audience to think of you? If not, think about how you present yourself and what you might wish to change.

By maintaining good eye contact with the audience, the speaker will receive clues about how listeners are responding to the message, so she can adjust what she is saying if they don't appear to understand.

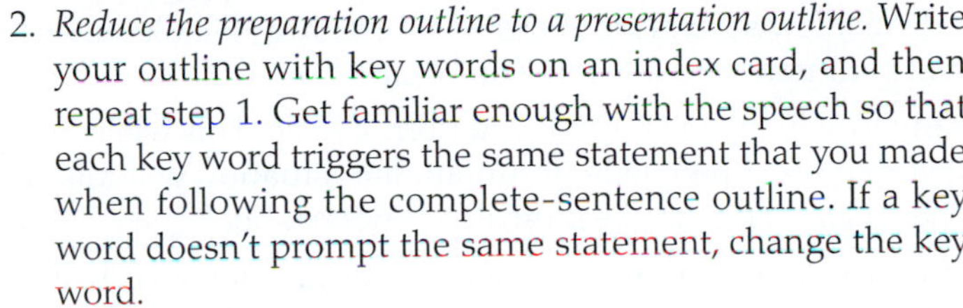

2. *Reduce the preparation outline to a presentation outline.* Write your outline with key words on an index card, and then repeat step 1. Get familiar enough with the speech so that each key word triggers the same statement that you made when following the complete-sentence outline. If a key word doesn't prompt the same statement, change the key word.
3. *Develop exact wording for the introduction and the conclusion.* Unlike the body of the speech, which will be more effective if presented extemporaneously, you may want to memorize the introduction and conclusion because of their importance in shaping the audience's first and last impressions. This is a good idea, especially when precise wording is needed to make your ideas clear. Knowing exactly how you will start should give you a sense of security, and you won't have to rely on inspiration for strong finishing remarks. Even so, you may not wish to recite the introduction and conclusion from memory. Although you may have specific wording in mind, you still are likely to speak extemporaneously.
4. *Simulate the conditions under which you will speak.* Find an empty room, and stand in the front—where you will stand when you present the speech. Imagine an audience present, and think about maintaining eye contact with them. (Don't present the entire speech looking either up at the ceiling or down at your notes.) Practice walking up to the front of the audience to speak as well as returning to your seat. Both before and after speaking, pause a second or two to "size up" the audience and to signal a sense of self-control and

CHECKLIST 2.3

Practicing Your Delivery

1. Develop and talk through the preparation outline.
   - ❒ Have you included all your main ideas?
   - ❒ Have you included all your supporting materials?
2. Reduce the preparation outline to a presentation outline.
   - ❒ Do your key words trigger the same statements each time you say them?
   - ❒ Have you written down your first and last sentences (see step 3)?
3. Develop exact wording for the introduction and the conclusion.
   - ❒ Introduction: Do you have an attention getter, a thesis, and a preview?
   - ❒ Conclusion: Do you have a summary, a link back to your thesis, and a final wrap-up of ideas?
4. Simulate the conditions under which you will speak.
   - ❒ Can you practice in the room or location where you will speak?
   - ❒ Can you imagine your audience?
   - ❒ Have you practiced your movements and eye contact?

Watch the Video "Professor Randy Cox Discusses Tips on Relaxing Before a Speech" at **MyCommunicationLab**

confidence. If you will be speaking at a lectern, practice using it (avoid the tendency to grip it and hang on for dear life). Finally, when you are familiar with the content of your speech, practice how you will position yourself and move around and gesture. The more you can imagine yourself in the actual speaking environment, the less threatening the environment will seem.

Presenting Your Speech

When beginners think about giving a speech, what often comes to mind are concerns about delivery: Where should I stand? Where should I put my hands? On whom should I focus my eyes? Is it all right to move or must I stand in one place? Should I try to disguise my accent? How fast should I speak? These are important questions, and yet giving them *too* much attention will distort your principal goals of conveying a clear message and establishing positive *ethos*. So, with a promise to return to delivery in the next chapter, here are the essentials you should know for your first speech:

1. Walk confidently to the front of the room, and do not begin to speak until you get there. Take a few seconds to stand comfortably and look out at your audience (not at your note cards) before you begin.
2. Speak a bit more slowly than you think you normally do. This will compensate for the fact that most people in an unfamiliar situation will talk more rapidly than they realize and may be difficult to understand.
3. Try to maintain eye contact with your audience. During your speech, look at different audience members or different parts of the room. Try not to look up at the ceiling, down at the floor, or at a spot on the back wall. Don't look at the same place for the entire duration of the speech. Help all audience members to feel that they are included.
4. When you don't need your hands to emphasize a point, let them hang naturally by your sides. When you do want to add emphasis to what you are saying, feel free to gesture, but be sure that you are raising your hands high enough so that listeners can see the gesture.
5. Make sure you are speaking loudly enough to be heard, but try not to shout. If you can, vary your pitch and rate so you do not appear to be speaking in a monotone.
6. Finally the most basic suggestion, which encompasses all the others: Think of what you are doing as communication with other people, not as a "performance." Don't worry if everything does not come out perfectly. Remember that your goal is to communicate naturally with your listeners. For the most part, address them as if you were in informal conversation. Some of your later speaking assignments may require a more formal posture, but this advice should work for now.

Watch the Video "Demonstration Speech: Blogs" at **MyCommunicationLab**

Remember that you are not trying to do everything at once and that perfection is not required. For this first speech, your two goals are to be clear in your message and to establish positive *ethos*. You can wait until later to add other goals.

Rhetorical Workout

Focus on Making Messages

In the everyday lives of most people, public speaking takes the form of informal presentations that communicate messages to a group, whether large or small. These kinds of audiences are focused more on the information, and less on you as the speaker. Your role is to make the messages clear and useful. The better the audience understands the information you give, the more effective you have been as a communicator—and the more they will view you this way.

Let's say you are in charge of a clean-up day for a small local park. About 20 volunteers have responded to an appeal to simply show up on that day and help. Your job is to organize them and distribute tasks, such as picking up trash, trimming weeds, planting flowers, and repainting playground equipment. You must also explain the tasks and convince the volunteers that each task is important to meeting the overall goal of finishing as much as possible in one day.

1. How might you address the group at the beginning of the day to give an overview of the tasks? How formal or informal do you think your presentation would need to be?
2. Would you expect to make eye contact with the volunteers as you talk to them? Why or why not? What effect do you think this might have on how well the volunteers understand what they need to do?
3. What kinds of feedback would you want to encourage from this audience? What would help you distribute the tasks?
4. You will be helping to paint equipment. Does your role as one of the volunteers make any difference in how you relate to the audience? Why or why not? Do you think it will make a difference in how the audience relates to you? Why or why not?
5. Suppose you feel a little nervous because you don't know any of the other volunteers, but you are committed to accomplishing all the clean-up tasks for a good cause. How can focusing on the messages and information help you overcome your nervousness in speaking to the others?

Strategies for Overcoming Speech Anxiety

OBJECTIVE 2.6

Even experienced speakers may be apprehensive when the time comes to speak.[3] In fact, researchers consistently report that most Americans fear public speaking more than anything—even more than death. As comedian Jerry Seinfeld has noted, that means that most people would rather be in the casket than delivering the eulogy! The term **communication apprehension** refers to fears and worries people have about communicating with others and can range from not wanting to speak up in a small group to worrying about talking on the phone. Anxiety about public speaking is a widespread example. People experience communication apprehension very differently, depending on such factors as their style of thinking and their general level of self-esteem and confidence. A few generalizations may be useful.

Explore the **Exercise** "Personal Report of Public Speaking Anxiety" at **MyCommunicationLab**

Being nervous is normal. You believe that what you have to say is important, and you value your listeners' judgment. Wanting to please your audience and to make a good impression, you may worry about making some innocent but colossal mistake.

In response to this emotional state, our bodies undergo numerous chemical changes. More blood sugar becomes available; insulin is secreted; blood pressure, respiration, and the conductivity of nerves all increase. In turn, these chemical changes induce feelings of anxiety or fear.[4] Most people find that the anxiety level

communication apprehension Fears and worries people have about communicating with others.

A Question of Ethics

Evaluating the First Speech

You have enrolled in a beginning public speaking class. One or two of the students appear to have had extensive previous speaking experience. They seem unusually confident when they speak. As you get to know them, you discover that they took public speaking in high school and that they have given many speeches before community groups and in competition. Is it ethical to evaluate their first speeches on the same criteria that are applied to less experienced students, those dealing with speech anxiety, or those for whom English is not their first language? Conversely, is it ethical to use different standards for different students? To what extent should evaluation be based on improvement and to what extent on the quality of a specific presentation?

recedes as they get into the speech. Although most people experience anxiety to a modest degree, around 15 percent of the population experience elevated levels of communication apprehension. Even they, however, usually are able to speak effectively. Nevertheless, even the old term *stage fright* falls short of describing the deep-seated fear that some people have of speaking in public.[5]

Explore the **Exercise** "Overcoming Nervousness" at **MyCommunicationLab**

Interestingly, though, the same chemical changes that cause extreme anxiety in some people bring others to a higher state of readiness and confidence. Many speakers get a boost of energy that, when properly channeled, causes them to feel "psyched up" for the speech and hence in a position to do well. The following six steps can help you tap into this extra energy and turn speech anxiety into an advantage:

1. *Acknowledge your fears, but recognize that you can overcome them.* Remind yourself that your listeners are not hostile; if anything, they will be supportive and sympathetic, especially for a beginning speaker. Also remind yourself that you have something valuable to say, that you know what you are talking about, and that it's important to share your ideas with the audience. This positive approach can convert nervous energy from a source of anxiety to a source of motivation.
2. *Think about what you are going to say and the effect you want to have on your audience.* The more you concentrate on your topic and on your relationship with the audience, the less anxiety you will feel—and the more likely you will do well. Becoming familiar with your outline through frequent practice will help boost your confidence.
3. *Act confident, even if you feel apprehensive.* Walk decisively to the front of the room, pause a moment to size up the audience, begin on a strong note, and maintain eye contact with your listeners. You may think of this as putting on a show, but remember that the audience has no idea of your nervousness. By acting confident, you will help listeners to feel positive about you, which, in turn, will help you feel more comfortable.[6]
4. *Visualize in your mind what it will be like to be a successful speaker.* As you are able to see yourself in this role, you can become more adept at overcoming the obstacles to it.
5. *Work carefully on the introduction so that you can start the speech on a strong note.* If you have written out the first few sentences of your speech and know exactly

what you are going to say, this will propel you into the body of the speech. As you get into the speech and focus on what you are saying, your nervousness is likely to subside.

6. *End the speech on a strong note and pause for a second before returning to your seat.* Even if you want to rush back to your seat, present a well-prepared conclusion in a deliberate manner; then pause to let your closing thoughts sink into the listeners' minds before you return slowly to your seat.

These simple steps will turn nervousness into an advantage for most speakers. In extreme cases of communication apprehension, however, nervousness becomes a pathological fear of relating to others in the public setting, and it may be necessary to treat the underlying anxiety through professional help outside of class—as is done with other phobias.[7] But such extremes are rare in a public speaking class. Even if you think that you are experiencing speech anxiety beyond the norm, remember this: You are in a relatively risk-free environment. Your classmates are likely to be friends and supporters because they are going through the same experience themselves. Your instructor's primary goal is to help you speak effectively, not to embarrass or intimidate you. Overall, there is probably no better setting in which to acknowledge your fears and then go ahead anyway. With practice, you are likely to find that speech anxiety becomes manageable and actually helps you.

CHECKLIST 2.4

Overcoming Speech Anxiety

- ❒ Acknowledge your fears, but recognize that you can overcome them.
- ❒ Think about what you are going to say and the effect you want to have on your audience.
- ❒ Act confident, even if you feel apprehensive.
- ❒ Visualize in your mind what it will be like to be a successful speaker.
- ❒ Work carefully on the introduction so that you can start the speech on a strong note.
- ❒ End the speech on a strong note, and pause for a second before returning to your seat.

What Have You Learned?

Objective 2.1: Explain the relationship between understanding theory and gaining practical experience in learning how to speak.

Theory and practice are interrelated; reflecting on practice helps you understand theory. The practical basics in this chapter will help you prepare and present your first speech, and we will more fully develop many theories and ideas later in the book.

Objective 2.2: Identify the principal goals of your first speech for this course.

Goals for the first speech:

- Presenting a clear message
- Establishing positive *ethos*

Topic: the subject of your speech—what it is about

Purpose: the specific goal of your speech—the listener response you seek

Supporting materials:

- Types: experiences, narratives, data, and opinions
- Functions: lend weight to thesis and help establish the claim

Objective 2.3: Explain the functions of the introduction, body, and conclusion of the speech and arrangement strategies for materials within the body.

Structure of a speech and functions of speech elements:

- Introduction: gets audience attention, states thesis, previews speech
- Body: develops thesis, offers support for claims
- Conclusion: draws together main ideas, gives note of finality

Arrangement strategies:

- Time order
- Spatial order
- Cause–effect
- Problem–solution
- Topical structure

Objective 2.4: Explain and use outlines that will help in preparing and presenting the speech.

Outlining:

- A preparation outline details structure and supporting materials.
- A presentation outline reduces to key words and offers cues while you speak.

Objective 2.5: Use strategies to help you effectively practice and present your first speech.

Practicing:

- Develop and talk through your preparation outline.
- Reduce to a presentation outline.
- Word the introduction and the conclusion.
- Simulate conditions under which you will speak.

Presenting the speech:

- Walk confidently to the front.
- Speak slowly.
- Maintain eye contact with audience.
- Let your hands hang by your sides when not in use.
- Speak loudly enough to be heard, but don't shout.
- Focus on communication, not performance.

Objective 2.6: Use strategies to manage nervousness to your advantage and overcome anxiety.

Speech anxiety:

- A natural reaction which can be turned to your advantage.
- Controls: acknowledge fears, remind yourself of the strengths of your speech, concentrate on topic and audience, carefully practice introduction and conclusion.

Listen to the **Audio Chapter Summary** at **MyCommunicationLab**

Discussion Questions

1. Develop two lists of adjectives, one describing what you consider to be positive judgments about a speaker's *ethos* and the other describing negative judgments. How might a beginning speech be strategically designed to develop positive judgments and avoid negative judgments? In answering this question, consider the following elements of strategy:

   Choice of topic

   Choice of purpose

   Presentation of supporting material

   Structure of the speech

   Delivery

2. Some teachers have suggested that a brief introductory speech has five steps:

   1. Wake up!
   2. This concerns you.
   3. Generally speaking
   4. For example
   5. So what?

   Why is this a good model for developing a short speech? Discuss the strategic purpose of each step and how it contributes to the goals of imparting a clear message and building positive *ethos*. Does anything seem missing from the model?

3. If you experience speech anxiety, compare your experience with your classmates. How do they manage and overcome speech anxiety?

4. Practice your speech according to the steps outlined in this chapter. Which steps do you find most useful? Do you believe that certain steps will become either more or less important as you become more comfortable with speaking?

Activities

1. For each of the following topics, devise a thesis statement that would be appropriate for a short speech.

   Affirmative action

   Date rape

   Solar energy

   Presidential debates

   Summer internships

2. Lay out three different types of supporting material for the thesis "Parking is a serious problem at most universities."

3. Following the recommendations in this chapter, develop both a preparation outline and a presentation outline for the following speech:

   When my parents went to college, they felt removed from their friends who went to schools in other parts of the country. They took time away from their books and wrote long letters, and then waited for a reply. Distant as they were from friends in this country, they couldn't imagine having strong friendships with people around the world. Like me, you may have had trouble explaining to your parents how you can keep up relationships with people abroad. But social networking has made it possible to build and maintain friendships around the globe. From our dorm rooms in the Midwest, we can use Facebook to "poke" a friend living in the Middle East. Business majors can secure summer internships in India by tapping into their peers' LinkedIn profiles. Aspiring musicians can promote their band's new album to a fan club in Germany using MySpace. The world is now a smaller place. And we can take advantage of its diminishing size. Web 1.0 was about the globalization of information, but Web 2.0 is about the globalization of relationships. We should learn more about people from far-off places and the events and rituals that mark their lives.

4. Outline a speech introducing someone, and present the speech to a few friends or family members. Pay close attention to their feedback, both during the speech and when you discuss it with them later. Then strategically modify your speech to accommodate their concerns and suggestions. In one page, explain how the changes you made to your speech responded to the feedback you received.

Key Terms

body **31**
communication apprehension **39**
conclusion **34**
ethos **29**
extemporaneous **35**
introduction **31**
preparation outline **35**
presentation outline **36**
purpose **28**
supporting materials **32**
thesis **28**

Study and **Review** the **Flashcards** at **MyCommunicationLab**

Notes

1 *Ethos* is discussed extensively in Aristotle, *The Rhetoric*, translated by George Kennedy, New York: Oxford University Press, 1991. See especially Book II. It has been suggested that, in forming judgments about public figures, *empathy* plays a greater role than the more traditional components of *ethos*. Audiences give more weight to speakers who appear to think and feel as they do. See Brooks Aylor, "Source Credibility and Presidential Candidates in 1996: The Changing Nature of Character and Empathy Evaluators," *Communication Research Reports* 16 (Summer 1999): 296–304.

2 A taste of how oratory was different in earlier U.S. history can be seen by reading Garry Wills's description of Edward Everett's address at Gettysburg in *Lincoln at Gettysburg: The Words That Remade America*, New York: Simon & Schuster, 1992, pp. 21–22, 33–34.

3 For a summary of research done in this area, see Daniel Goleman, "Social Anxiety: New Focus Leads to Insights and Therapy," *New York Times* (Dec. 18, 1984): C1. The increase of virtual social media has lessened the need to communicate face-to-face, as well. See Tamyra Pierce, "Social Anxiety and Technology: Face-to-Face Communication versus Technological Communication Among Teens," *Computers in Human Behavior* 25 (November 2009): 1367–72.

4 For a fuller description of the physical aspect of anxiety, see the table of physiological variables associated with anxiety in Raymond B. Cattell, "Anxiety and Motivation: Theory and Critical Experiments," *Anxiety and Behavior*, ed. Charles Spielberger, New York: Academic Press, 1966, p. 33; and Paul I. Witt, Kennaria C. Brown, et al., "Somatic Anxiety Patterns Before, During, and After Giving a Public Speech." *Southern Communication Journal* 71 (March 2006): 87–100.

5 For more about the study of speech anxiety, see I. Aly and M. Islam, "Factors Affecting Oral Communication Apprehension among Business Students: An Empirical Study," *Journal of American Academy of Business, Cambridge*, 6 (2005): 98–103; J. Butler, B. Pryor, and S. Marti, "Communication Apprehension and Honors Students," *North American Journal of Psychology*, 6 (2004): 293–96; H. M. Crandall and J. Ayres, "Communication Apprehension and the Spiral of Silence," *Journal of the Northwest Communication Association*, 31 (2002): 27–39; Flávia de Lime Osório, José Alexandre Crippa, and Sonia Regina Loureiro, "Experimental Models for the Evaluation of Speech and Public Speaking Anxiety: A Critical Review of the Designs Adopted," *Journal of Speech—Language Pathology & Applied Behavior Analysis* 3 (March 2008): 97–121; and Graham D. Bodie, "A Racing Heart, Rattling Knees, and Ruminative Thoughts: Defining, Explaining, and Treating Public Speaking Anxiety," *Communication Education* 59 (January 2010): 70–105.

6 Kenneth Savitsky and Thomas Gilovich, "The Illusion of Transparency and the Alleviation of Speech Anxiety," *Journal of Experimental Social Psychology* 39 (Novrmber 2003): 618–25.

7 Some colleges have programs to treat severe communication apprehension. See Jan Hoffmann and Jo Sprague, "A Survey of Reticence and Communication Apprehension Treatment Programs at U.S. Colleges and Universities," *Communication Education* 31 (July 1982): 185–94. There is extensive literature about different ways to overcome speech anxiety. For a recent example, see Joe Ayres, Tim Hopf, and Elizabeth Peterson, "A Test of Communication-Orientation Motivation (COM) Therapy," *Communication Reports* 13 (Winter 2000): 35–44.

CHAPTER

3

Presenting the Speech

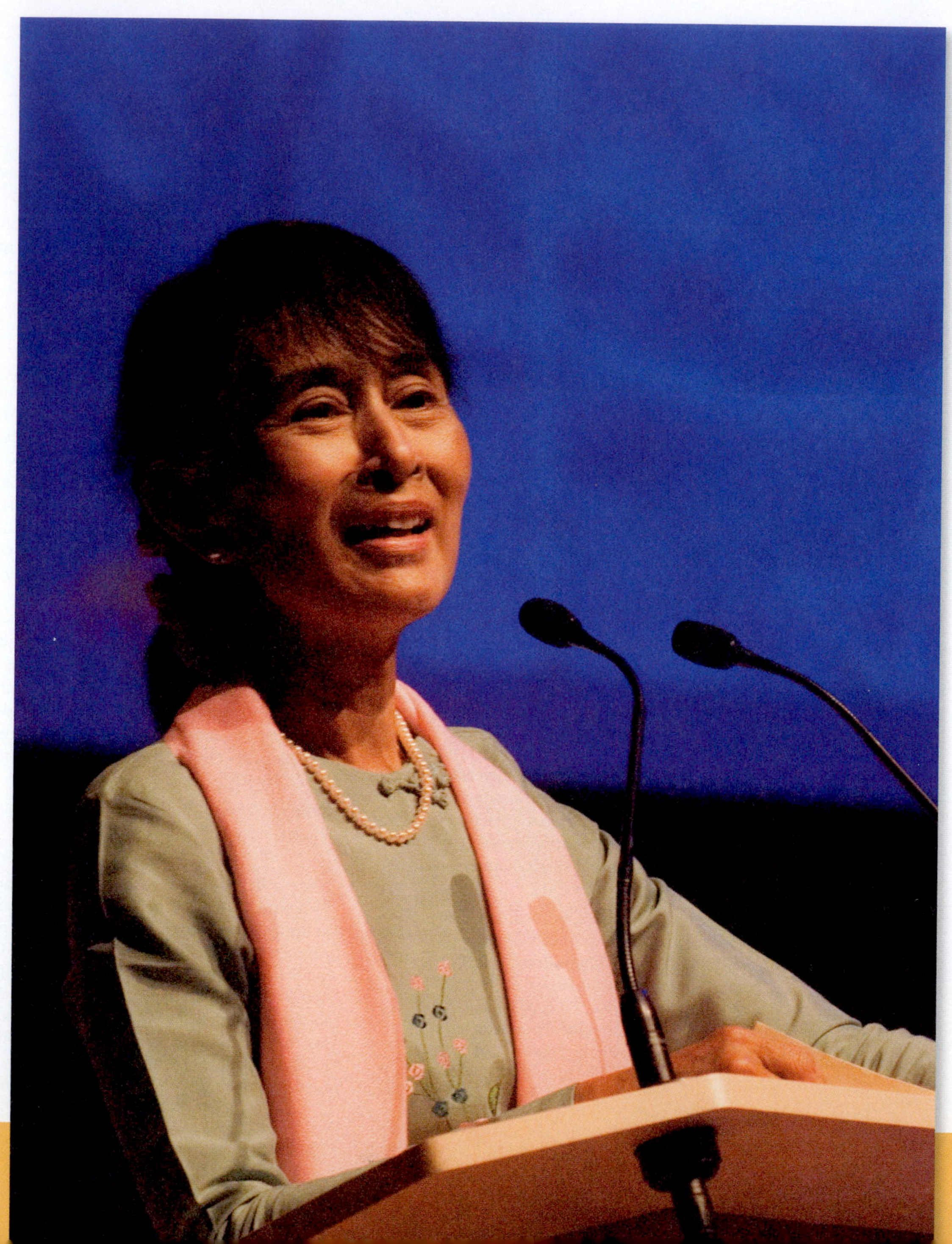

LEARNING OBJECTIVES

After studying this chapter, you should be able to:

Objective 3.1	Identify the characteristics of effective speech delivery.
Objective 3.2	Explain how the dimensions of a speaker's voice—volume, pitch, rate, pauses, articulation/enunciation, pronunciation, and inflection—can support the presentation, and how variety in each aspect enhances the speech.
Objective 3.3	Demonstrate how the speaker's body—physical appearance, movement, gesture, and facial expression—can help make the presentation effective.
Objective 3.4	Differentiate among four basic modes of speech presentation and identify the advantages and limitations of each.
Objective 3.5	Practice the speech before presenting it formally.

Listen to the **Audio Chapter** at **MyCommunicationLab**

OUTLINE

People who fear speaking in public are usually anxious about some aspect of oral presentation. "What will I do with my hands?" "What if I forget my speech?" "How will I know if I'm talking too fast?" "Suppose I start shaking and can't control it?" Concerns such as these often lead people to avoid public speaking altogether.

In some ways, it would make sense to defer a discussion of presenting the speech until after we had learned more about selecting and researching a topic, testing the reasoning, and organizing the speech. But since many beginning speakers are most concerned about presentation, it actually makes sense to focus on it first.

There is a potential drawback here. Strange as it seems, one of the *least* effective ways to improve your presentation is to concentrate on it directly. If you are self-conscious about what to do with your hands, for example, thinking about them will make you feel even more awkward—they'll suddenly seem like 50-pound weights. Worrying about using your hands will distract you (and your audience) from the subject of your speech. In fact, the best way to improve your presentation is to keep your attention on the speech and on the audience.

Why, then, should you study presentation now if it might make you even more self-conscious? Because, by learning about the aspects of presentation and by practicing certain strategies, you can train yourself to speak "naturally" and confidently even if you are nervous about facing an audience. You will be more effective at your own approach to speaking.

Presentation is also called **delivery**; the two terms are used interchangeably to refer to how the voice and body help create the effect a speaker wants. The same ideas, even the same words, can elicit different reactions from an audience, depending on how you present them. Delivery, then, is much more than simply a way to "embellish" a speech. *How* a speaker says something affects *what* is really said, and so it also affects what listeners actually hear and understand.

OBJECTIVE 3.1 Characteristics of Effective Presentation

A delivery style that contributes positively to the overall effect of your speech has three main characteristics:

1. *Effective delivery seems natural and uncontrived.* It does not call attention to itself or divert attention from the ideas in the speech.
2. *Effective delivery helps the audience to listen to, understand, remember, and act on the speech.* Listening carefully and critically to a speech is difficult; your presentation, if well done, can make it easier for your audience. For example, perhaps by lowering your voice, you can make the audience listen more carefully when you state your main idea. Or well-timed pauses may signal the transitions in your argument, making it easier to follow. Or a gesture that points to the audience may help you personalize your call for action in the conclusion of the speech.
3. *Effective delivery builds a sense of community between speaker and audience.* In most situations, the speaker wants to identify with listeners and symbolize that they are all members of the same speaking/listening community. In other words, the speaker wants to show **empathy** with listeners, to give them a sense that he or she knows what they think and can feel what they

delivery
The presentation of the speech, using the voice and body to create the desired effect.

empathy
Feeling what listeners feel and knowing what they think.

feel. Empathy is usually achieved through a presentation that invites audience members to listen and suggests that the speaker cares about them.

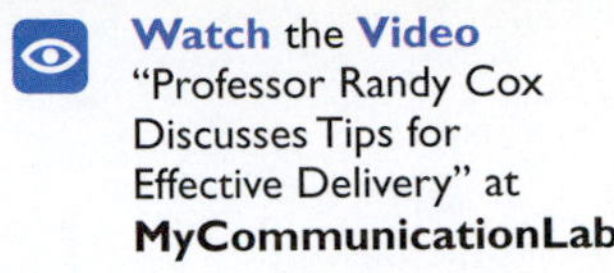
Watch the Video "Professor Randy Cox Discusses Tips for Effective Delivery" at MyCommunicationLab

This chapter looks closely at how both your voice and your body can enhance the presentation of your speech and to help you build the desired relationship with listeners.

The Voice in Presentation

OBJECTIVE 3.2

Unlike a singer, a speaker doesn't cultivate the voice as an end in itself, just to be expressive. Rather, a speaker uses the voice to advance the overall purpose of the speech.[1] Vocal cues are among the audience's earliest evidence in judging a speaker's *ethos*.

Seven dimensions of the voice can be drawn on to enhance your effectiveness as a speaker: volume, pitch, rate, pauses, articulation and enunciation, pronunciation, and inflection (see Table 3.1). Any vocal pattern—no matter how pleasant it first sounds—can easily become monotonous and distracting. Just as in conversation, to keep a speech interesting and to keep the audience listening, you want to create variety in the seven dimensions of your voice.

Table 3.1 Dimensions of vocal quality

Vocal Dimension	Description
Volume	Loudness
Pitch	Placement on the musical scale
Rate	Speed; number of words per minute
Pauses	Silences for emphasis or transition
Articulation and enunciation	Clarity and distinctness of individual sounds or words
Pronunciation	The accepted way to sound a given word
Inflection	The sound pattern for a sentence as a whole

Volume

Volume refers to loudness; the higher the volume, the louder the voice. But how loudly should you speak? That will depend on the size and the shape of the setting and on whether you use a microphone. As a beginning speaker, you probably should err on the side of greater volume rather than of less (as long as you don't scream), in order to help convey a sense of self-confidence. To check and adjust your volume in any setting, watch listeners' reactions carefully when you begin to speak.

Besides regulating the overall loudness of your voice, remember to vary the volume at key points in the speech. You can emphasize an idea either by speaking louder or by lowering your voice. In both cases, listeners renew their attention because the vocal variety signals that they should listen carefully. By changing your volume, you can either understate an idea or overclaim it, depending on your purpose and the situation.

volume
Loudness of voice.

Feedback. Most audiences will let you know quickly if they cannot hear you, and their feedback will help you decide how loudly to speak. Also pay attention to the volume of other speakers and to how the audience reacts to them.

Students Brad Cummings, Alicia Lee, and Rosa Dominguez all gave classroom speeches on the same day. Brad was first, and he began in a very soft voice. Listeners had so much trouble hearing him that they moved forward in their seats and even cupped their ears with their hands. Unfortunately, for the first two minutes of his speech Brad looked only at his notes, and he missed the signal from the audience that he should speak more loudly. Alicia noticed the problem and was determined to avoid it when she spoke. But she overcompensated, speaking in a booming voice that made some listeners so uncomfortable that they actually pushed their chairs farther away and covered their ears. When Rosa's turn came, she knew that her volume should be somewhere between Brad's and Alicia's.

Amplification. If the audience is large, you can choose to use a microphone to amplify your voice; this gives you the option of speaking at lower volumes. It takes some practice to use a microphone effectively, however. You need to speak more slowly and to articulate words more distinctly so that they will not become slurred through amplification. Position your mouth a few inches from the microphone, and speak directly into it. If you hear static or noises or your voice feeds back to you, move farther from the microphone and speak more softly. Don't wait until the time of your speech to test the microphone, and make sure that it is turned on if you plan to use it. You'll undercut the power of your introduction if you have to stop to ask, "Can everyone hear me?"

Because most classroom speeches are not amplified, you need to learn to project your voice adequately by controlling volume and the other dimensions of vocal quality. But because so many auditoriums, large meeting rooms, and outdoor rallies require the use of amplification, you also should look for opportunities to practice speaking with a microphone.

Pitch

When we say that someone's voice is "high" or "low," we are referring to its **pitch**—the placement of the voice on the musical scale. A soprano has a higher pitch than a bass. The pitch of a voice is determined by the speed with which sound waves vibrate. The faster the vibration, the higher the pitch—and voice.

As shown in Figure 3.1, the normal pitch for any speaker is within a fairly narrow range. But extending higher- and lower-than-normal pitch is a larger range within which both speaker and listeners will be comfortable. You can raise or lower your pitch within this range for emphasis, and listeners will still find it pleasant to hear you. The widest range that the speaker is physically able to produce includes extreme

Low	Medium low	Medium	Medium high	High
Possible but uncomfortable	Comfortable for variation	Normal	Comfortable for variation	Possible but uncomfortable

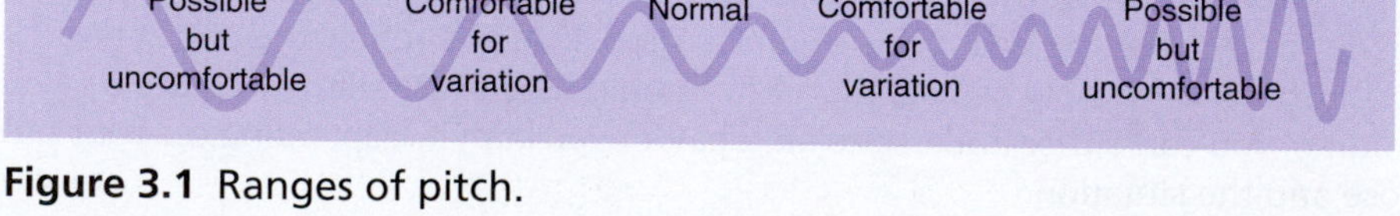

Figure 3.1 Ranges of pitch.

pitch
Placement of the voice on the musical scale, ranging from high to low.

pitches that are difficult for an audience to listen to. Extremely high pitches grate on the ears, like fingernails scratching a chalkboard; and extremely low pitches are distorted and too resonant, which most listeners also find displeasing.

Probably the most distracting pitch for listeners is a **monotone**—a very narrow, unchanging range that is used for the entire speech. Audiences quickly tire of it, and they tune it out; some people even fall asleep, lulled by the droning voice of the speaker. Because most people have a wider range of comfortable pitches than they customarily use, there's no reason to speak in a monotone. By varying your pitch, you can sustain the audience's interest, signal transitions in the speech, and emphasize important ideas.

If you record yourself delivering a speech, you may well discover that your pitch is higher than it sounds to you when you are speaking. Two factors account for this. First, your ability to hear your own voice is always distorted. Second, pitch rises under stress, and giving a speech is stressful for many people. The key to a pleasant pitch is to relax as much as possible. Control your breathing so that you have enough air to complete each sentence, relax your shoulder muscles, and project your voice from deep in your body rather than forcing it from your throat.

Rate

Rate is the speed at which a person speaks. The average rate is between 120 and 150 words per minute, but successful speakers vary considerably. John F. Kennedy typically spoke at a faster rate than did Ronald Reagan, and yet both presidents were immensely persuasive speakers.

Watch the Video "Informative Speech: Whatever Happened to Sisqó?" at **MyCommunicationLab**

Stereotype suggests that there also are distinct regional variations in rate—Southerners talk slower than Midwesterners do, and Easterners talk faster. In fact, regional differences in rate are much less dramatic than they used to be, partly because people move more often and partly because radio and television have created a national audience. Today, for example, many Southerners have just as rapid a speaking rate as anyone else.

Two factors that we considered in connection with pitch—stress and variety—also apply to rate.

Stress. Like pitch, rate goes up when a person is under stress. Students who practice their speech and time it to fill the 10 minutes required by the assignment may be surprised that the speech takes only 6 minutes when they deliver it in class. This happens not because they timed it inaccurately or forgot a large portion of the speech but because they sped up their rate under the stress of presentation.

Racing through your speech makes it difficult for the audience to follow and comprehend your ideas; listeners simply don't have time to process and react to what they hear. The remedy, as with pitch, is to control your breathing and relax. Pause frequently for breath, taking in enough air to complete each statement. And remember to watch for feedback from the audience since you also want to avoid speaking too slowly. A speech delivered at a very slow rate will tire listeners and will invite distractions by giving them time to think about things other than your ideas.

Variety. Just as a monotonous pitch can seem boring, so too a monotonous, unchanging rate can displease listeners. A speaker who utters every word and

monotone
A very narrow, unchanging pitch range.

rate
The speed at which a person speaks, measured in words per minute.

sentence at the same rate—no matter how significant or suspenseful the ideas are—gives no clues about what's really important. All ideas receive about the same treatment, and listeners tend to tune out.

Beginning speakers sometimes think that the only way to vary rate is to speed up at critical places in the speech. In fact, *both* speeding up *and* slowing down can convey movement or suspense and can compel attention and interest. Indeed, the choice of rate may itself communicate a message. Slowing down suggests that the speaker is serious and that every word matters; the audience had better pay attention. It may also create a mood such as calmness or sadness or may suggest that the speaker thinks the ideas are difficult to grasp. Speeding up may propel a narrative forward or may evoke feelings of suspense, excitement, or outrage.

Most speakers vary their rate less than they think they do, and most could benefit by cultivating greater variety. Exercises in which you read a sentence or a list of words at differing rates will help you see how variety in rate can enhance interest in the message. Record yourself reading part of a famous speech at different rates. The playback may surprise you by showing that changes in rate may change meaning as well. This exercise should also give you a sense of which "normal" rate is most comfortable for you personally.

Pauses

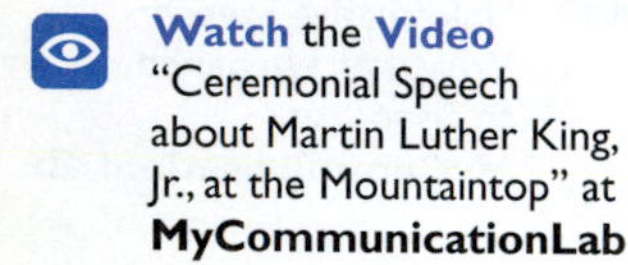
Watch the Video "Ceremonial Speech about Martin Luther King, Jr., at the Mountaintop" at **MyCommunicationLab**

Pauses are the brief silences within a speech. Although it may seem strange to include silence among the dimensions of voice, silence as well as speech can be highly communicative. The message in a pause is one of completeness and transition.

Properly used, pauses enhance a speech in two ways. First, they emphasize what the speaker said, providing a kind of nonverbal underlining. While the speaker is silent, listeners can think about what they have just heard, storing the thought in memory. A speaker who never pauses will move on to a new idea before listeners can make sense of the last one—and can unintentionally convey that all ideas are equally important or that none is really important. Without pauses, the audience will remember less and will be influenced less.

Second, pauses mark transitions in a speech. Because speaking doesn't have "punctuation marks," pauses—and variety in pitch and rate—can serve that function, telling the audience that the speaker has ended a section and is about to move on to a new topic or idea. This gives the audience time to absorb what was just said before switching again to active listening. It also gives speakers time to collect their thoughts before moving to the next idea.

Simple as the concept of pauses might seem, like the other dimensions of voice, pausing requires practice to be used effectively. You will want to avoid the following common problems.

Pausing too Often.

A pause can signal the end of a paragraph in a speech, but that signal will be undercut if you also pause for every comma or semicolon. Too many pauses make a speech jerky and make the speaker seem nervous. Use pauses sparingly for effect.

pauses
Periods of brief silence within a speech.

Pausing at the Wrong Places.

Because pauses are like punctuation marks, use them at the same places in the text as you would write the marks for which they stand. Pausing in the middle of sentences or ideas can confuse listeners and make comprehension difficult.

However, powerful effects sometimes can result from unusual pausing. One of the most memorable speeches of the twentieth century was delivered by Dr. Martin Luther King, Jr., on August 28, 1963. Standing in front of the Lincoln Memorial in Washington, D.C., he summoned his audience to work peacefully to attain civil rights for African Americans. He inspired listeners with his vision of the American Dream, closing with lines adapted from the song "America."

Instead of pausing after each sentence, Dr. King stopped briefly after each refrain of "Let freedom ring," building intensity and creating the musical effect of a crescendo. His midsentence pauses emphasized the repeating pattern in his examples and let the audience know what to expect next.

Not Pausing Long Enough. Uncomfortable with silence, speakers are notoriously poor judges of how long their pauses are; most imagine them to be much longer than is the case. Again an audio recording is a valuable aid. Time your recorded pauses, and compare them with how long you *thought* you paused when you spoke. All pauses should be relatively brief, of course, but the effects of a one-second pause and a five-second pause are considerably different.

Using Vocalized Pauses. Sounds such as "uh" and "umm" are **vocalized pauses**, meaningless sounds that a speaker produces during moments of silence. These almost always arise from nervousness and can be highly distracting to listeners. (Have you ever been in an audience that began to count the speaker's "uhs" and "umms"?) Sometimes vocalized pauses are words or phrases such as "like," "you know," "now then," "right?" and "okay?" Such repetition is a nervous response; the speaker is uncomfortable stopping for even a few seconds.

Whether syllables or words, vocalized pauses call so much attention to themselves that they interfere with the message. The remedy is easy to state but difficult to carry out: When you pause, *be silent*. Again, an audio recording is useful, because most speakers are not aware of their vocalized pauses. Listen to yourself, and discover how often you vocalize during a pause. If you do it frequently, make a mental note to *remain silent*.

Articulation and Enunciation

The related concepts of articulation and enunciation have to do with precise, distinct speech. **Articulation** refers to the clarity of *individual sounds*; **enunciation** refers to the distinctness with which *whole words* are sounded.

Articulation. For native speakers of English, common articulation problems include difficulty in forming the *th* sound (saying "dese" instead of "these") and dropping the final *g* from a word ("workin' " and "makin' "). Articulation can be improved through specific vocal exercises for particular sounds. The easiest way to diagnose articulation problems is to have someone else listen with you to a recording of your speech and to identify any sounds that call attention to themselves.

Not everyone articulates in the same way, of course. Speakers whose native language is not English, for example, often have difficulty with standard English articulation. Their goal should be not to articulate like native English speakers but

vocalized pauses
Pauses filled with sound, such as "uh" or "umm."

articulation
Precision and clarity in the production of individual vocal sounds.

enunciation
Precision and distinctness in sounding words.

Rhetorical Workout

Exercise Your Voice

Go to a space (your room, an empty classroom, etc.) where you can practice using the different dimensions of your voice. Use this sentence from President Franklin D. Roosevelt's first inaugural speech to practice: **"Our greatest primary task is to put people to work."** (The full text of this speech can be found at AmericanRhetoric.com.)

- **Volume:** First, speak the sentence at your normal speaking volume, as if you were talking to a friend just a few feet away from you. Then, speak it as loudly as you can without shouting. Now imagine what size of audience would fit in the space where you're practicing. Speak the sentence at a volume that would allow this audience to hear you clearly.
- **Pitch:** Speak the sentence using a fake, exaggerated high pitch—in a falsetto as if you had just inhaled helium. Then use a very low voice, an exaggerated bass, as if you were the announcer in a movie trailer. Try several levels in between, including your normal speaking voice. Is your normal pitch closer to the high end or the low end? What range of pitches do you think is most comfortable for your imagined audience to listen to?
- **Rate:** Say the sentence as fast as you can without skipping or slurring any words. Say it as slowly as possible without making it sound unnatural. Say part of the sentence quickly and the other part slowly. Try a few different rates and combinations. What rate or variety of rates makes the sentence sound best to your ear?
- **Pauses:** Say the sentence with a pause after the word "task." Say it again, pausing after "is." Does either sound better to you? Say the sentence with no pauses. How does this compare? If you pause after "greatest," does the pause make an interesting emphasis or does it sound awkward? Insert a vocalized pause such as "okay" somewhere in the sentence. How do you think your audience would respond to it?
- **Articulation and enunciation:** (a) Articulation: Change the sentence to "Our greatest primary task is putting people to work." Speak the sentence and drop the "g" in "putting"—say "puttin' people to work." Say the sentence again and articulate the "ing" precisely. How do these different ways of articulating the "ing" sound affect the impact of the sentence? (b) Enunciation: Try saying the sentence so it sounds like "Our greatest primary goal is taput people tawork." Now say it and carefully enunciate "to put" and "to work" as separate words. How do these different ways of enunciating words affect the impact of the sentence?
- **Pronunciation:** Practice pronouncing "our" in two different ways: (1) say "our" to rhyme with "are," then (2) say "our" to rhyme with "hour." Do you think either pronunciation is incorrect? Does either sound better to you? What if you were to pronounce "put" as "putt"? How would that change the meaning of the sentence?
- **Inflection:** Say the sentence with an inflection pattern that raises the pitch toward the end, as though it were a question: "Our greatest primary goal is to put people to work?" How does it change the meaning of the sentence? Now say the sentence several times, emphasizing a different word each time. Which words make sense to you to stress? What is the difference between stressing "our" and stressing "goal"?

to articulate clearly enough that they can be heard and understood. By the same token, listeners should make reasonable efforts to understand speakers whose articulation patterns are unfamiliar. In our increasingly diverse society, we all meet people who "speak differently." We should not allow cultural differences in articulation to block successful communication.

Enunciation. The distinctness with which *words* are sounded is another aspect of clarity that speakers need to consider. One specific problem is the tendency to slur words together. This is common in informal settings, where "I'm gonna," "Whaddaya know?" and "Howya doin'?" may replace "I am going to," "What do you know?" and "How are you doing?"[2] In a speech, however, such lack of enunciation will seem inappropriate; unless it is being used for effect, it is likely to influence negatively the audience's perception of the speaker.

The other extreme to avoid is being too precise in enunciation, saying each word so distinctly that you seem artificial and condescending to the audience. Speaking too distinctly not only distracts attention from the message but also may arouse negative feelings in listeners, who believe the speaker is either being snobbish or "hamming it up."

Pronunciation

Even when a word is familiar to the eye, we sometimes wonder how it should be sounded. Correct **pronunciation** refers to the accepted way to sound any given word. This includes such matters as which syllable to accent, whether to sound a vowel as short or long, and which optional consonant sound to use (for example, whether to give a *c* a hard sound, like a *k*, or a soft sound, like an *s*).

pronunciation
Sounding of a word in the accepted way.

dialect
A pronunciation pattern that characterizes a particular geographic area, economic or social class, or cultural factors.

The Importance of Proper Pronunciation.

First, the meaning of a spoken word may depend on its pronunciation, and mispronouncing it may prevent listeners from sensing which meaning you intend. The word *desert*, for example, means something different when you accent the first syllable (noun = "hot, dry place with lots of sand") than when you accent the second syllable (verb = "to abandon"). Second, like some of the other dimensions of vocal quality, mispronunciation calls attention to itself and may overshadow your ideas and message. Third, faulty pronunciation reflects negatively on a speaker's *ethos*; listeners may (mistakenly) get the impression that the speaker is ignorant or incompetent and hence is not to be trusted.

The phrase "proper pronunciation" may conjure up images of Eliza Doolittle, the British street vendor in *My Fair Lady* who could not speak "the king's English" and was stigmatized because of her lower-class **dialect**, or pronunciation pattern. Today in the United States, however, people are more likely to recognize and to accept that pronunciations vary according to geography (and according to economic and social class, among other cultural factors). We are more likely to hear speakers with a variety of dialects, and so we are less likely to view such differences as highly unusual.

On the other hand, just as slang is sometimes inappropriate, it remains important to speak standard American English in highly formal situations, where *any* sort of dialect may be seen as a distraction.

Pronunciation and Audience Analysis.

In thinking about pronunciation and dialect, analyze your audience in relation to yourself, asking the questions listed in Checklist 3.1. Depending on your answers, design a strategy for your speech as suggested in the checklist.

As you will learn in Chapter 5, cultural diversity is a feature of many audiences. Even though dialects have become more familiar and less distinct, the acceptance of cultural diversity may, at times, require overcoming strongly held preconceptions.

CHECKLIST 3.1

Pronunciation and Audience Analysis

Questions to Ask:

- ❐ Am I culturally different from most of my immediate listeners? If so, how might this affect their impressions of me and my speech?
- ❐ How do cultural differences affect my ability to achieve the goals of my speech?
- ❐ Does my pronunciation make me vulnerable to stereotyping by the audience? Conversely, is there a danger that I may stereotype the audience?

Strategic Decisions to Consider:

- ❐ Should I confront stereotyping, either directly or indirectly?
- ❐ How should I try to manage the impression that my pronunciation might give the audience?
- ❐ Should I modify my volume or rate, the amount of explanation I provide, or any of my supporting material?

Inflection

Articulation, enunciation, and pronunciation relate to the sound of individual syllables and words. **Inflection** is a similar concept except that it applies to the sentence as a whole. Appropriate inflection is important for the same reasons we have already discussed: Without it, you risk distracting listeners' attention, distorting your message, and damaging your credibility.

For example, one normal inflection pattern is to raise the pitch toward the end of a question and to lower the pitch toward the end of a statement. Speakers who reverse this pattern sound strange, and the audience may have trouble figuring out what they mean. Some speakers are so unsure of themselves that they raise their pitch after nearly every statement, hoping to discover whether the audience understands and agrees with their point. But this inflection pattern only makes ideas more difficult to follow, because they sound like questions rather than statements. In addition, the speakers appear to be unsure of themselves and overly tentative about whatever they say.

A given sentence may have more than one correct inflection pattern, and yet its meaning will change greatly depending on which pattern is used. Student Jordan Rivers, for example, was extolling the merits of a particular brand of breakfast cereal and confidently told the audience, "Nothing makes a better breakfast than this brand." He thought this statement was strongly positive, and so did most listeners. But Jordan was surprised to discover that a few audience members understood this remark differently, concluding that they really would be better off eating *nothing* for breakfast than eating this brand of cereal. Careful attention to inflection, taking care to stress the word *better* as well as the word *nothing*, would have given the audience a better clue about which meaning Jordan intended.

In general, think about the audience when you work on improving your speaking voice. Watch for feedback to ensure that your volume, pitch, rate, and degree of pauses are comfortable for listeners and to see that your enunciation, articulation, and pronunciation make your ideas clear. To avoid distracting from your message, aim for a presentation voice that has variety, that seems natural, and that captures and holds listeners' attention.

OBJECTIVE 3.3

The Body in Presentation

Just as the voice gives the speaker important *auditory* and *verbal* resources, the body provides equally valuable *visual* resources. Not surprisingly, the same general principles relating to the voice in presentation also apply to the body. The speaker's body is used to enhance the message, not to call attention to itself. The body and its movements influence listeners' first impressions of the speaker and, hence, their willingness to take the speaker seriously. And changes in body placement and movement can mark transitions in the speech and add enough variety to keep the audience interested in and focused on the message.

Physical Appearance

inflection
Pronunciation pattern for a sentence as a whole.

Even before you begin to speak, audience members are forming impressions of the sort of person you are. This happens quickly and on the basis of superficial judgments, but those judgments are durable. (See the discussion of *ethos* in Chapter 2.)

Consequently, you want to avoid doing anything that will make you seem unprepared, incompetent, or unreliable.

Before You Speak. Consider the physical arrangement of the speaking space before deciding such things as how to approach the podium and what to wear. Is the setting large and impersonal or small and intimate? How formal or informal is the setting (and occasion)? Will you be able to establish eye contact with listeners, or will you be far away from them and speaking with a microphone?

Your appearance to an audience at an outdoor rally will be far different from how you appear to the same audience in a cathedral. Similarly, the settings for a retirement banquet, a business meeting, a commencement address, and a medical lecture are all different and can influence how the audience perceives you. Whenever possible, then, you should examine the speaking space and practice in it before presenting your speech.

Approaching the Speaking Space. Your physical appearance begins to create impressions as you walk to the front of the speaking space. If you start speaking while you walk, before facing the audience, you may seem in a hurry to finish and so unsure of yourself that you won't look the audience in the eye. Likewise, if you shuffle uncertainly toward the front, the audience may think you lack confidence and don't know what you are talking about. Such assumptions may be wrong, of course, but they affect your *ethos* and can create a "credibility deficit" that you'll have to overcome.

No matter how you feel about speaking, create the best first impression that you can. Walk firmly and purposefully to the front, pause to collect your thoughts, look directly at the audience, and then begin with confidence. In Chapter 15, you will learn that your body acts as a visual aid for the speech—the audience will be looking at you. Try to make your body's message match and reinforce the message of your words.

Watch the Video "Special Occasion Speech: Tribute to Nike Founder" at **MyCommunicationLab**

Clothes and Grooming. What you wear and your personal appearance—everything from hairstyle to footwear—are the stuff of first impressions and will affect your *ethos*. A badly dressed, unkempt speaker easily becomes the focus of attention and distracts the audience from the message. If you constantly push hair out of your face, wear a baseball cap that makes eye contact impossible, or fiddle with keys or jewelry, you practically beg the audience to focus on the distractions rather than the speech. Sometimes clothing choices can even send messages that contradict your thesis and tarnish your *ethos*. For example, wearing army fatigues during a speech promoting pacifism or wearing a popular brand of running shoes during a speech about the shoe company's questionable labor practices could send mixed messages to your audience.

Typically, speakers dress a bit more formally than audience members do.[3] The general public may attend a speech in sports attire, but the speaker is a major figure and is expected to look the part. In recent years, this unwritten dress code has relaxed considerably, allowing our choice of clothes to adapt to a variety of situations more effectively. When President George W. Bush threw out the first pitch at a baseball game, it would have been odd to see him in a suit. Yet President Bush dressed in a suit and tie when addressing the public formally—when he wanted to project a serious image. So do many business and entertainment speakers.

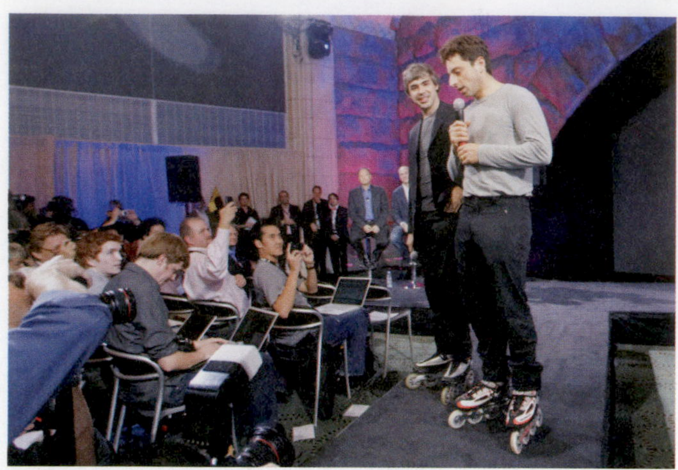

Usually a speaker wearing in-line skates will not be dressed appropriately, but if the speech is about how in-line skates work, the attire may be just right.

Sometimes, a speaker will want to make a cultural statement through unusual clothing and hairstyle and will resent any advice about adapting to the audience's expectations. For example, Sergey Brin, the founder of Google, frequently appears in public in jeans and tennis shoes. Other executives of technology companies may do the same, as a way to emphasize that their corporate culture is quite informal and that there is no hierarchy. You may be tempted to do this, too. But here, as elsewhere, audience analysis is critical; plan your personal appearance to advance your strategic goals.

Movement

How and where you position your body while speaking can also enhance or distract from the message. When student speaker Rachel Samuels stood behind the large, heavy podium in her classroom, only her head was visible. Recognizing the problem, Rachel stepped away from the podium to present her speech.

Even if the height of the podium does not affect your appearance this way, it's a good idea to step away from it occasionally. Many beginning speakers grip the podium tensely as though steering a car that is out of control. This may give you a sense of security, but it also puts a barrier between you and the audience. Instead, if you loosen your grip and step away from the podium at points in the speech, your body language will provide visual cues. For example, you can signal transitions in the speech by moving a step or two forward or to the side. And by moving toward the audience, you can show your trust and break down any imaginary walls between you and listeners.

The 1992 presidential debates among Bill Clinton, George Bush, and Ross Perot were the first that included one "Town Hall" format in which citizens in the audience asked questions. At one point, when Bill Clinton was asked how the federal budget deficit had affected him personally, he did not respond right away. First he took a few steps toward the questioner and established eye contact. Although he was actually speaking to a television audience of millions, Mr. Clinton seemed to be responding to this citizen one on one. The unstated message was that they had a common bond. And because Mr. Clinton had to face the cameras to answer his questioner, television viewers also felt that he was responding directly to them—and had a bond with them. Although this debate took place over 20 years ago, it still is the model for the "Town Hall" format. In contrast, in the 2008 "Town Hall" debate, the candidates seemed to move aimlessly on the stage and neither John McCain nor Barack Obama established a personal connection with members of the audience.

Although purposeful, planned movement will benefit your presentation, constant or aimless movement will be a great distraction. A speaker who moves all around the room for no apparent reason puts a burden on listeners; it's up to them to follow the movements and maintain eye contact. Many will simply stop trying—and stop listening as well. Speakers also should avoid shifting their weight from side to side, rocking on their feet. Like vocalized pauses, this nervous response calls negative attention to itself.

Just as you should not begin speaking until you have reached the front of the room and sized up the audience, do not gather up your notes and start returning to your seat while you are still speaking. The audience will not have a chance to absorb your final thoughts, and your conclusion will be weakened. You also will give the impression that speaking to them was painful and that you want to finish as soon as possible. Take your time, and take control of the situation. When you do return to your seat, walk confidently without calling attention to yourself.

Speakers who use natural and relaxed gestures while speaking can enhance listeners' interest in and comfort with the message.

Gesture

The term **gesture** refers to the movement of hands and arms during the speech as a means of emphasis. Many speakers are especially self-conscious about their hands and what to do with them while they speak. Some put their hands into their pockets—not to create an informal, conversational tone, but just to get them out of the way. These speakers usually seem tense, as though they are tightly clenching something buried deep in their pocket. Other untrained speakers fidget, moving their hands and arms aimlessly as a nervous reaction. One nervous student had a tendency to rotate his arms and hands in big circles so that he looked more like an orchestra conductor than a public speaker. Because such movements are not coordinated with the speech, they call attention to themselves and detract from the message.

In contrast, a well-timed, purposeful gesture heightens the power of both your text and your voice. But what is such a gesture like? Centuries ago, theorists of public speaking believed that certain gestures went naturally with particular words or ideas. They wrote manuals illustrating hundreds of gestures and their matching words so that speakers could learn the gestures by rote and perform them automatically when reciting the matching text.[4] Today, this approach is considered nonsense; such a presentation is so artificial and contrived that it seems funny.

Even so, not all speakers are naturally expressive with their hands. Whether you use many or few gestures does not matter; what matters is that your gestures support your message, and not draw attention away from it. If you made a video of yourself in informal conversation, you probably would discover gestures that you are unaware of—they simply come out naturally when you talk. A few possible uses of gestures are to emphasize the importance of a point, to suggest balance or opposition ("on the one hand," "on the other hand"), and to position ideas in space and time.[5]

Above all, gestures used in presentation should appear natural. Achieving this is less a matter of memorizing gestures than of becoming familiar with the general rhythm of gesture. It has three steps:

1. The **anticipation step**, in which you bring your hands to a position from which a gesture can easily be made. If you are gripping the podium or handling several pages of notes, gesturing will be difficult and awkward. You need to be in a position that lets you execute a gesture naturally.
2. The **implementation step**, the few seconds in which you execute the gesture. Typically, your hands will be somewhere between the waist and shoulders, an area that eases natural motion and is also visible to audience

gesture
Movement of hands and arms during the speech as a means of emphasis.

anticipation step
The first step of a gesture; involves bringing the hands into a position from which the gesture can be made.

implementation step
The execution of a gesture, raising the hand and moving it in the intended manner.

members. Perhaps most important in implementing the gesture is to *follow it through*. Untrained speakers often make a half-gesture, raising a hand partway without completing the motion. Such a gesture has little purpose or effect. It suggests that the speaker is nervous.

3. The **relaxation step**, in which you return your hands to their normal position—whether at your side, in front of you, or resting gently on the podium. Without this step, you risk being trapped in continuous gesture. If your hands are in the visual space where gestures take place and you haven't returned them to rest, you may find yourself gesturing repeatedly and in the same way for every word or idea. That, of course, dilutes the power of the gesture.

Finally, don't worry too much about gestures. Although "what to do with my hands" is a concern for many speakers, the issue is relatively unimportant. Gestures tend to take care of themselves as long as you avoid distracting mannerisms, practice the three steps of gesture, and concentrate on your message.

Facial Expression

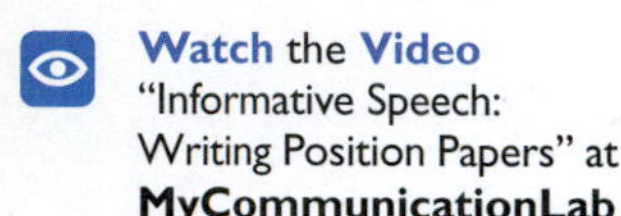

Watch the Video
"Informative Speech: Writing Position Papers" at MyCommunicationLab

The speaker's facial expressions are another powerful element of nonverbal communication that can heighten or detract from the speech. Obviously, a smiling speaker communicates something much different from a frowning one. But someone who smirks or grins throughout a serious presentation will seem out of place and hence not believable, as will a speaker who delivers a lighthearted message but shows no facial expression at all. Again, it is valuable either to record your speech or to have someone observe you practicing it. Discover whether your facial expressions are consistent with and support the message in your text.

Making Eye Contact. One aspect of facial expression, **eye contact**, deserves special attention. Speakers who do not look the audience in the eye may lose credibility. In mainstream American culture, not looking at someone is widely thought to mean that the person is lying or has something to hide. Speakers from cultures with different norms about eye contact may be misunderstood and misjudged by an American audience.

Another important point is that eye contact lets you see how the audience is responding to the speech; it provides feedback. Listeners' facial expressions often indicate whether the message is clear or needs explanation, whether claims seem persuasive or not, and so on. Such feedback helps you adjust your presentation to fit the audience while you speak. But if you stare at your notes or gaze at the back wall, you cannot engage your audience and take advantage of feedback.

Maintaining Eye Contact When Using Notes. How can you maintain eye contact if you are using notes? It takes practice, but the idea is to glance down at your notes during the brief moments when you pause and then to gracefully resume eye contact when you start to speak again. Having notes that are in large print and easy to read will help you. What you want to avoid are jerky movements of your head and eyes between your notes and your audience, and looking down at your notes while you're stating or explaining your main ideas.

Speaking to a Large Audience. Maintaining eye contact with a large audience presents problems. You can't look at everyone, but if you focus only on nearby listeners, those farther away will feel left out. And if you keep

relaxation step
Returning the hands to a normal relaxed position at the conclusion of a gesture.

eye contact
Looking directly at members of the audience.

turning your head mechanically from side to side, the constant sweeping movements will be a distraction, and you won't really make eye contact with anyone. The remedy is not to fix on particular audience members but to focus on general areas of the audience. Mentally divide listeners into three or four groups, and shift your focus among them to correspond to transitions in the speech. This lets all listeners feel—to some degree—that you are talking directly to them, and you can monitor the groups for feedback. At the same time, your shifting focus helps to signal transitions in the speech.

By resting your hands lightly on the podium rather than gripping it for dear life, you will be relaxed and your hands will be free for gesture.

Speaking for the Camera. Different problems arise when speaking either in front of a camera or for the camera. You *may* be addressing a much larger audience, but when you focus on the camera, you are speaking only to a single "listener" who provides no direct feedback through eye contact. If you are speaking to a group of people but are also being recorded on video, you must choose to give one audience priority over the other. For instance, if the immediate audience is more important, focusing on the camera will stifle your ability to distribute your eye contact effectively; the live audience may feel ignored. But if you are more concerned with the virtual audience, moving your eyes away from the camera may make you seem shifty, detracting from the recorded speech. Think about the difference between YouTube videos that were created for an Internet audience and the speeches you give in class. In the YouTube videos, the speaker purposefully addresses the camera, thinking of the audience watching the video online. But in class you will try to engage with your live audience precisely by not focusing exclusively on any one person. This is a trade-off. Moreover, trying to address both live and virtual audiences can detract from your appeals to either.

Being Dynamic. One important component of *ethos* is dynamism. A dynamic speaker is one who appears animated and enthusiastic. Eye contact, smiles, and especially variety in facial response are a few signs of enthusiasm. Although trained actors may be able to "fake" a sense of animation, most speakers cannot. The easiest way to convey the impression that you are animated and enthusiastic about your topic and about speaking to your audience is for you to actually feel that way. As we will see in Chapters 5 and 6, this is an important consideration in audience analysis and topic selection.

Explore the **Exercise** "Physical Delivery" at **MyCommunicationLab**

Modes of Presentation

OBJECTIVE 3.4

Most theorists identify four general modes of presentation: impromptu, memorized, manuscript, and extemporaneous. No matter which mode you choose, you can use voice and body to enhance the presentation, but the modes also involve choices that can strengthen or weaken the speech.

CHOOSE A STRATEGY: Presenting Your Speech

The Situation

You are a teacher at a grade school and your principal has asked you to present the new curriculum plan to the parents in your community and also to answer any questions they may have regarding these changes. There have been several major additions to the curriculum, and you want to make sure that each change is explained clearly to the parents. You will be presenting in the school gymnasium where a microphone and podium will be set up the evening of your speech—which is two weeks from today.

Making Choices

1. Which presentation mode do you plan to use? Why? What are the benefits and/or drawbacks of this mode?
2. How will you incorporate the podium into your presentation, if at all? Will you use the microphone? Why or why not?
3. How will you prepare for your speech? How will you prepare to answer the audience's questions?

What If...

How would your presentation strategies change if the following were true? Would your mode of presenting change? Would your practice strategies change? Why or why not?

1. You are presenting to a group of parents in a small classroom.
2. You have met each of the parents on an individual basis and know that they support the curriculum changes.
3. You have met with each of the parents on an individual basis and know that they do not support the curriculum changes.
4. Your principal planned to make this presentation but has become ill at the last minute. You need to give this presentation tomorrow.

Impromptu Presentation

When you have little or no time to prepare specifically for a speech, you make an **impromptu presentation**. Perhaps someone at a meeting says something that inspires you to respond, and so you raise your hand to offer your views. You thereby give a speech seemingly without any preparation at all. In fact, you may have "spent a lifetime" preparing for that speech. The issues are important to you, and you've thought about them a great deal. But you never imagined that you would be speaking about them on this particular occasion.

Structure an impromptu presentation as simply and clearly as possible. Because you do not have a chance to plan the speech in detail, you may become entangled in the web of your thoughts. The key is to focus on a very small number of main ideas, previewing and summarizing them so that listeners have no doubts about your thesis or how the ideas develop it. Impromptu speaking also often takes cues from previous speakers, referring to their specific points and suggesting how their message relates to yours.

impromptu presentation
A mode of presentation in which the speaker has done little or no specific preparation for the speech.

memorized presentation
The opposite of speaking impromptu; the speaker pays close attention to a prepared text and commits it to memory.

Memorized Presentation

A **memorized presentation** is the opposite of impromptu; you pay such close attention to your text that you commit it to memory. This mode of speaking was highly valued in the past. School children studied famous orations and recited them by rote. Great orators often wrote out their entire speeches and then committed them to memory.

Today few theorists advise anyone to memorize a speech. Besides the unnecessary investment in energy, speaking from memory has other problems. First,

Strategies for Speaking to Diverse Audiences

Respecting Diversity Through the Presentation of Your Speech

Your voice will affect how easily people will hear you, and your gestures will mean different things in different cultures. Here are strategies that will help you to consider audience diversity when presenting your speech.

1. **Volume:** Adjust your volume to your audience. Some cultures (such as people from Thailand) normally speak at a lower volume than do Americans. Yet if you are speaking to people with hearing impairments, you will need to speak louder.
2. **Gestures:** Consider how certain hand gestures may mean different things for different cultures. For instance, putting your forefinger to your thumb means "O.K." in the United States but can be offensive in Mexico or Syria.
3. **Stereotyping:** Using slang or false dialects that may stereotype your audience members can also be offensive.
4. **Speaker and audience:** Recognize that different cultures have different expectations about the physical relationship between speaker and audience.

you might not take feedback into account and adapt to the audience's needs. Second, if you write and then memorize a speech for oral delivery, the recital may be stiff and stilted. It will sound memorized, which quickly causes an audience to lose interest. Finally, a memorized text raises concern about what might happen if you forget a line. Some speakers can ad-lib and patch things up quickly, but many become flustered; having forgotten the memorized words, they don't know what to say.

Although memorized presentation is generally discouraged, it can be helpful to memorize the first few sentences of your introduction and the last few sentences of your conclusion. Then you will begin the speech confidently and end it solidly, without trailing off. And if you want to use a particular phrase or line in the speech, you might commit that to memory and plan where it would fit best. But the practice of memorizing an entire speech has fallen into disuse—deservedly.

Manuscript Presentation

Like a memorized speech, **manuscript presentation** also involves a text that is prepared word for word, but the speech is read rather than delivered from memory. This speaking mode is useful in highly formal situations, when specific wording is critical. The president of the United States uses manuscript presentation for the State of the Union address and for most speeches about major policies. The risk of saying the wrong thing is too great to rely on other presentation modes. Many leaders in business, labor, and community organizations use manuscript presentation when they speak in high-stakes situations where their precise wording is extremely important. Major presentations at corporate or academic meetings also are often read from manuscript.

Watch the **Video** "Section of the Classic Speech: Richard M. Nixon's Resignation" at **MyCommunicationLab**

Manuscript presentation also is useful when precise timing is important, as when speaking on radio or television. This was clearly illustrated in 1952, when vice presidential candidate Richard Nixon appeared on television to defend himself against charges of financial irregularities (the speech is discussed in Chapter 12). He ended by urging listeners to express support for him by writing to the Republican National Committee. But Mr. Nixon was not speaking from

manuscript presentation A mode of presentation in which the speaker reads aloud the prepared text of the speech.

manuscript, and he ran out of time as he was telling the audience where to write. Millions of listeners were able to respond anyway, but if you watch a recording of that speech, you will see how awkward the ending is.

Although manuscript presentation may be appropriate in these specific circumstances, as a general rule it is not the best mode. First, reading a paper aloud is not the same as speaking directly to an audience. As we will see in Chapter 12, it is very difficult to write in an oral style. Audiences recognize the difference and are less attentive; the manuscript interferes with direct communication between the speaker and listeners.

Second, very few people are well trained in the art of reading aloud. Even a text that is rich in imagery, that identifies with the audience, and that offers solid argument may be negated if it is read indifferently or with vocal patterns that do not match the intent of the message.[6]

Third, presenting a speech from manuscript makes it difficult to maintain eye contact and profit from feedback. Accomplished speakers sometimes can do it—taking in a sentence or two of their text and then gracefully looking up and speaking to the audience. But many speakers do this awkwardly, which is distracting at best, and they often lose their place in the text.

Extemporaneous Presentation

A speech that is prepared and rehearsed but is neither written out nor memorized is called *extemporaneous presentation*. This mode is recommended for most speakers and speeches, because it encourages a conversational quality and is flexible enough to permit adaptation to feedback. Extemporaneous speaking is not impromptu; the speaker has outlined and planned the speech carefully, has a specific structure in mind, and probably uses prepared notes during presentation. But no word-for-word text exists in advance of delivery, and the speech is not memorized or read aloud.

The advice in Chapter 2 that you develop a preparation outline and a presentation outline assumed an extemporaneous mode of presentation. The preparation outline helps you identify your main ideas, their relation to each other and to your thesis, and the order in which to present them. The presentation outline includes enough key words to help you keep the ideas straight and to present them as intended. As you practice the speech, you will try out different ways of verbalizing the ideas, getting a sense of how the speech sounds and what you mean. But you will not memorize or write down the specific wording (other than introductory and concluding sentences). Speaking extemporaneously lets you discuss ideas informally and conversationally. Your focus will be on ideas rather than on specific words, making it easier to maintain eye contact and modify your message in response to feedback.

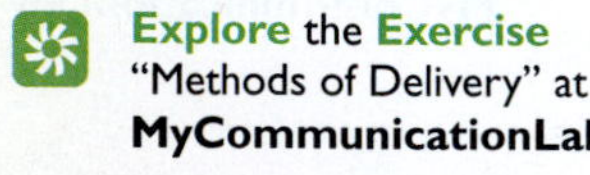
Explore the **Exercise** "Methods of Delivery" at **MyCommunicationLab**

OBJECTIVE 3.5

Practicing for Speech Presentation

The idea of practicing to appear natural may not seem quite so strange, now that we have explored how the speaker's voice and body can be used in a planned way to bring about that result. Yet the easiest way to fail at the goal is to focus too much on your voice or body rather than on what you are going to say and on what you are trying to achieve.

Thinking consciously about your strategic objectives—what you wish to share with the audience, how you want to affect listeners, or what you want audience members to believe or do after hearing your speech—should focus your attention on the purpose of the speech. If you keep content and purpose clearly in mind, then you can practice using your voice and body to *contribute* to those goals rather than to be ends in themselves.[7]

Explore the **Exercise** "Speech Delivery" at **MyCommunicationLab**

The most important advice about practice is to begin early. Skills of presentation take time to perfect, and you will learn them best when you are relaxed, not tense. Unless the assignment really calls for an impromptu speech, waiting until the last minute is never a good idea. Things will not seem to fall into place. The speech may seem disorganized or not artfully crafted; or the content and presentation may be out of sync; or the gestures, movement, and vocal variations may be distracting. Admittedly, the advice to start early on a task is easier to give than to follow, but it will pay great dividends in the case of speech presentation.

Each person takes a unique approach to practicing a speech, and you should find methods that work well for you. In general, however, a four-step process is likely to be effective:

1. Develop the presentation outline.
2. Mentally rehearse the speech.
3. Practice the speech orally.
4. Simulate the speech setting.

The Presentation Outline

Develop your presentation outline as discussed in Chapter 2, and talk it through several times. By referring only to the outline, you should be able to articulate your main ideas and the links in your thought. Each key word should trigger a more complete thought. If this does not happen, revise the presentation outline to include more key words, different words, or a different structure.

This is also the time to write out or memorize any portion of the speech for which exact language is essential, such as a few introductory sentences or your conclusion. You might include your thesis statement, if you want to have its precise wording in front of you. Although excessive memorization is discouraged, some parts of even an extemporaneous speech depend on exact wording, and this is the time to develop the words you plan to use.

Practicing in the room where you will speak can make you more comfortable—even if it is an empty auditorium.

Mental Rehearsal

Picture an imaginary audience, and run through the speech in your mind while holding this image. Try to see yourself in the speaking situation, and think through what you would say. As you rehearse mentally, you may hit upon a particular transitional phrase or may discover the most effective way to express an idea clearly. Speakers who skip the step of mental rehearsal often fail to consider the big picture of how the speech will look and sound when everything comes together. As a result, the speech may seem fragmented or unnatural to an audience.

Oral Practice

Practice the speech orally, several times, under a variety of conditions. Distributed practice (brief periods of practice spread over time) is likely to be more effective than massed practice (a few lengthy sessions shortly before you speak).

For the first few times, deliver the speech with no one else present. Although this will not give you feedback, you will become sensitive to the sound of the speech, to its length and timing, and to opportunities to enhance your use of voice and body. Because you are both speaker and listener, you'll want to satisfy yourself that everything fits together correctly.

Then practice with a small group of friends. Even two or three people are enough, if you trust them to give candid reactions that might improve the speech. This stage of practice will let you actually share your thoughts with others and see how the speech is affected by having an audience present. Use such "early reviews" to check whether the design of the speech will achieve your purpose. Ask especially whether listeners got a clear sense of your thesis, whether the speech moved clearly from one point to another, whether you spent too much or too little time on anything, and whether the speech seemed too slow or too fast. Raise any other specific concerns you have about the speech. One study found that speakers who practiced before an audience received higher evaluation scores on their speeches than those who did not.[8] The more feedback you get from these first listeners, the stronger your final presentation will be.

Record your presentation, if possible, and study it to see how the speech looks and sounds to others. This step makes many people uncomfortable, because they think they look and sound different from what the video reveals. But try to set aside such feelings, focusing instead on what listeners will see and hear. For example, if the video shows that you are looking only at your notes and are not making eye contact, you can correct this by the time you deliver the speech. The video also might reassure you about some aspect of performance, such as gestures—perhaps

A Question of Ethics

Ethics in Delivery

Speakers reveal how invested they are in their speeches by the way they present speeches to an audience. What responsibilities do speakers have with respect to performance? Is it ethical, for example, to assume a natural, conversational, informal stance if you really are hostile toward the audience? Is it ethical to badger or "browbeat" an audience when doing so can wear down their resistance? If an animated delivery leads an audience to accept a position the speaker knows to be weak, is that ethical? Is it ethical to mask your real anxieties by appearing to be confident? Similarly, when we are listeners, to what extent do we allow the presentation of a speech to affect our judgment of the speaker and the message? Do we trust a speaker who has memorized the speech more or less than a speaker who uses notes? More or less than a speaker who reads a manuscript? Does the effect of presentation on our judgments raise any ethical issues?

they appear more natural than you thought. Look for positive feedback as well as negative; the video can build your confidence even as it reveals areas that need improvement.

Simulation

Either practice the speech in the room where you'll speak, or simulate that setting as closely as possible. For instance, if you will be speaking in a large auditorium, practicing there or in a similar space will show you how much you should exaggerate gestures and movement so that they can be seen at a distance. If the setting will be smaller and more intimate, you may need to practice modulating your voice so that you don't seem to be shouting. And if you will be using a microphone, practicing with it will help you control and adapt your voice in ways that avoid distortion and slurring. Finally, this step will make you more comfortable with the setting so that, when the time comes, you can focus on your audience and your message.

CHECKLIST 3.2

Practicing the Speech

1. Develop the presentation outline.
   - ❐ Talk through the outline several times.
   - ❐ Write out or memorize any portion for which exact language is essential.
2. Mentally rehearse the speech.
3. Practice the speech orally:
   - ❐ With no one else present.
   - ❐ With a small group of friends.
   - ❐ On video if possible.
4. Simulate the speech setting.

What Have You Learned?

Objective 3.1: Identify the characteristics of effective speech delivery.

An effective delivery style should:

- Seem natural and not call attention to itself or detract from the message.
- Help the audience listen to, understand, remember, and act on your speech.
- Build a sense of community between speaker and audience.

Objective 3.2: Explain how the dimensions of a speaker's voice—volume, pitch, rate, pauses, articulation/enunciation, pronunciation, and inflection—can support the presentation, and how variety in each aspect enhances the speech.

The speaker's voice:

- Is a resource for the speaker.
- Gives the audience insights into the speaker's personality.
- When varied, keeps listeners interested and suggests emphases within the speech.

Dimensions of voice that can enhance a speech:

- Volume
- Pitch
- Rate
- Pauses
- Articulation and enunciation
- Pronunciation
- Inflection

Objective 3.3: Demonstrate how the speaker's body—physical appearance, movement, gesture, and facial expression—can help make the presentation effective.

The speaker's body and movements:

- Are visual resources for the speaker.
- Influence listeners' first impressions of the speaker.
- Can indicate transitions in the speech.

Resources of the body that can enhance a speech:

- Physical appearance
- Movement
- Gesture
- Facial expression

Objective 3.4: Distinguish among four basic modes of speech presentation and identify the advantages and limitations of each.

Modes of presentation:

- Impromptu
- Memorized
- Manuscript
- Extemporaneous (usually preferred)

Objective 3.5: Practice the speech before presenting it formally.

Speech presentation is improved by practice:

- Develop the presentation outline.
- Mentally rehearse.
- Practice orally with feedback.
- Simulate the speech setting as closely as possible.

Listen to the **Audio Chapter Summary** at **MyCommunicationLab**

Discussion Questions

1. How does delivery vary according to purpose? In what ways might delivery be different for a eulogy, an instructional speech, and a speech of dissent?
2. In what ways does delivery style contribute to or detract from a speaker's strategy? Discuss and compare the strategies and styles of some famous speakers—for example, Hillary Clinton, Michele Bachmann, Steve Jobs, Jesse Jackson, Jon Stewart, George W. Bush, and Barack Obama. Discuss both their manuscript delivery in formal televised speeches and their extemporaneous delivery in more informal settings.
3. In what ways might you improve your delivery? Each student should present a short introduction to a familiar person or thing, and classmates should then discuss the strengths and weaknesses of the presentation. Focus especially on aspects of delivery that the speaker is unlikely to recognize by examining a recording, such as articulation, enunciation, and pronunciation.

Activities

1. Select a passage from a speech that you can obtain in manuscript form. Record yourself presenting this passage first at a very slow rate, then at a moderate rate, and finally at a quick rate. Then vary the rate *within* the passage, slowing down or speeding up as needed to best convey the message. Repeat this process, varying the volume of your delivery. Listen to the recording of these variations, and identify how changes in rate and volume affected the presentation.
2. Write out the introduction and conclusion of your next speech. Before you practice the delivery of these sections, decide where you want to include pauses and which words you want to emphasize by changes in volume and pitch. Record yourself and listen to see if these decisions worked as you planned. If not, try to determine why.
3. Watch a video of yourself presenting a speech. Pay close attention to your delivery style—your volume, rate, and pitch variations; whether you use vocalized pauses; your eye contact, posture, and gestures; and so on. List the things about your delivery style that currently detract from your message and that you would like to improve. How might you go about improving them?

Key Terms

anticipation step **57**
articulation **51**
delivery **46**
dialect **53**
empathy **46**
enunciation **51**
eye contact **58**
gesture **57**
implementation step **57**
impromptu presentation **60**
inflection **54**
manuscript presentation **61**
memorized presentation **60**
monotone **49**
pauses **50**
pitch **48**
pronunciation **53**
rate **49**
relaxation step **58**
vocalized pauses **51**
volume **47**

Study and **Review** the **Flashcards** at **MyCommunicationLab**

Notes

1 For an excellent overview of the physiology of the voice mechanism and a wide selection of exercises to improve the speaker's voice, see Linda Gates, *Voice for Performance*, New York: Applause Books, 2000.

2 For a humorous treatment of the tendency to slur words, see William Safire, "Slurvian," *New York Times Magazine* (Sept. 17, 2000): 37, 40.

3 Studies have shown that a speaker's attractiveness has an influence on the persuasiveness of the message. Attractiveness can be achieved at least partly through clothing and grooming. See Shelly Chaiken, "Physical Appearance and Social Influence," *Physical Appearance, Stigma, and Social Behavior: The Ontario Symposium*, vol. 3, ed. C. Peter Herman, Mark P. Zanna, and E. Tory Higgins, Hillsdale, NJ: Lawrence Erlbaum, 1986, pp. 143–77.

4 For examples of this, see John Bulwer, *Chirologia: Or the Natural Language of the Hand*; and *Chironomia: Or the Art of Manual Rhetoric*, first published 1644, ed. James W. Cleary, Carbondale: Southern Illinois University Press, 1974; and Gilbert Austin, *Chironomia: Or, A Treatise on Rhetorical Delivery*, first published 1806, ed. Mary Margaret Robb and Lester Thonssen, Carbondale: Southern Illinois University Press, 1966.

5 For more discussion of gestures in informal conversation and in speeches, see Naomi Jacobs and Alan Garnham, "The Role of Conversational Hand Gestures in a Narrative Task," *Journal of Memory and* Language 56 (February 2007): 291–303.

6 Researchers Herbert W. Hildebrandt and Walter W. Stevens discovered this rather accidentally when trying to determine whether extemporaneous or manuscript delivery was more effective. See their "Manuscript and Extemporaneous Delivery in Communicating Information," *Communication Monographs* 30 (November 1963): 369–72.

7 It is important to remember that delivery should match the speaker's material, intent, and personality. See Harry W. Bowen, "A Reassessment of Speech Delivery," *Communication Quarterly* 14 (November 1966): 21–24.

8 Tony E. Smith and Ann Bainbridge Frymier, "Get 'Real': Does Practicing Speeches Before an Audience Improve Performance?" *Communication Quarterly* 54 (February 2006): 111–25.

CHAPTER

4

Listening Critically

LEARNING OBJECTIVES

After studying this chapter, you should be able to:

Objective 4.1	Distinguish between hearing and listening and explain why listening skills are important to speakers.
Objective 4.2	Identify obstacles to effective listening.
Objective 4.3	Listen carefully by mapping the central ideas of a speech and by taking notes.
Objective 4.4	Explain how critical thinking is applied in the speaking situation.
Objective 4.5	Evaluate speeches as a result of critical listening.

Listen to the **Audio Chapter** at **MyCommunicationLab**

OUTLINE

It's a standard scene in comic strips and television sitcoms: The husband sits at the breakfast table, face buried in the newspaper, seeming not to notice his wife seated across from him. The wife is trying to conduct a conversation about the day's events or about chores to be done around the house. Whenever she pauses, he mutters, "Mm-hmm"—never lowering the newspaper even to look at her. In desperation she finally grabs the paper and shouts, "You're not listening to me!" The husband calmly replies, "That's not true, dear. I heard every word you said."

OBJECTIVE 4.1 Are You Really Listening?

In this stereotypical scene, the husband and wife are both right, because hearing and listening are two different things. **Hearing** is a sensory process. Nerve endings in the ear receive sound waves and transmit them to the brain; the brain receives them, and we become conscious of sound. This is a physiological process.

Watch the **Video** "Melissa Beall Discusses the Difference Between Listening and Hearing" at **MyCommunicationLab**

In contrast, **listening** is a mental operation. It involves processing the sound waves, interpreting their meaning, and storing the interpretation in memory so that we can recall it, think about it, or act on it. The husband did hear every word, but he wasn't *listening*. His attention was focused entirely on the newspaper, and so he didn't interpret and store the information he heard. Now he can't repeat it, and he can't answer questions or make decisions about it.

Hearing comes naturally to most people (except for those with hearing disorders) and requires no special training. But listening is an acquired skill that takes practice. Even though people's ability to hear may be equally strong, some people are better listeners because they have trained themselves to:

- Focus attention
- Minimize distractions
- Process messages accurately
- Think critically[1]

In this chapter, you will learn how to develop and improve these skills. First, though, we need to explore two questions: (1) Why should we concentrate on listening in our study of public speaking? (2) What makes listening so difficult that we need training to do it well?

Why Listening Is Important

Checking for Accuracy. To begin with, we usually want to check the *accuracy* of what we heard, because the consequences of faulty listening can be far more serious than in the scene at the breakfast table. Students who don't listen to and correctly follow the professor's instructions could do the assignment but still get a failing grade. Employees who misunderstand the supervisor's instructions could jeopardize company profits—and their own jobs. Parents who don't really listen to a child's request for help could respond inappropriately, or not at all. And diplomats who don't listen carefully to each other could overlook an opportunity for a breakthrough in negotiations.

hearing
A sensory process in which sound waves are transmitted to the brain and someone becomes conscious of sound.

listening
A mental operation involving processing sound waves, interpreting their meaning, and storing their meaning in memory.

To avoid faulty listening, we often check that we have heard and understood correctly. Students and employees ask questions about instructions; parents try to find out what their child means; and diplomats "feel out" each other's statements before making a formal response.

Giving (and Getting) Feedback. Careful listening also enables hearers to provide **feedback** to speakers. We saw in Chapter 1 that even in formal situations the speaker and the audience both send and receive messages. The audience members' reactions are usually nonverbal—applause, head nodding, bored or distracted looks, and indications that they are having trouble following the speaker's argument. Such feedback enables speakers to modify their message and improve the likelihood of achieving their purpose. During the speech, careful listening makes feedback possible; after the speech, it helps listeners to remember and think about the speaker's ideas.

You will spend far more time listening to speeches than delivering them. By becoming a trained listener, you will provide appropriate feedback to other speakers. In addition, your reactions to a speaker whose voice is too quiet, or who ends too abruptly, or who seems to lack confidence will make you more determined to avoid such problems. You'll also pick up tips from classmates who perform well. You will develop ideas about what to do—or not to do—to make your own speeches successful.

Evaluating Messages. A third reason listening is so important is that you need to listen in order to *evaluate* and respond to what you hear.

You have a vested interest in paying close attention to a classmate's message so that you can decide how it relates to you and to others in a broader audience. You need to be able to assess how the speaker's beliefs and method compare with yours and whether they are models to follow when it is your turn to speak. Of course, when you listen to speeches given outside the classroom—whether by politicians, celebrities, people in business, or religious leaders—it is even more important that you be able to evaluate the message.

Finally—and unfortunately—not all speakers who seek our attention are scrupulous and ethical. Some urge listeners to do things that are unjustified or unacceptable. Be aware that their influence depends precisely on the fact that it is easy for people to hear without really listening. You need to know when a speaker is being unethical rather than just sloppy, insensitive, or misinformed. To protect yourself as a listener, you need to practice skills that will help you evaluate speakers and messages. Essentially, these are the skills of critical thinking, and you will learn to apply them to the speech situation later in this chapter.

Why Listening Is Difficult

What makes listening so difficult that we need training in it? Why are so many people poor listeners? At least four factors deserve close attention:

- Listener distractions
- Limited attention span
- Jumping to conclusions
- Situational distractions

feedback
Verbal and nonverbal audience response to a speech; usually taken seriously by a speaker and incorporated into the speech when possible.

Rhetorical Workout

Rate Your Listening Skills

Take the following quiz to rate your skills as a good listener. Answer the questions by grading your listening behaviors.

Read the question and think about whether the statements are always, sometimes, or rarely true of you. Check the appropriate box.

Listening Behavior	Always	Sometimes	Rarely
1. I listen for the speaker's main points.	■	■	■
2. I try to understand the speaker's expectations and needs.	■	■	■
3. I can remember the main ideas I have heard after listening to a speech.	■	■	■
4. I consider how the speaker's nonverbal behaviors relate to the message.	■	■	■
5. I indicate to the speaker that I am listening by nodding or, when appropriate, using listening noises such as "yes" or "I see."	■	■	■
6. I take notes to help me listen more effectively.	■	■	■
7. I listen with an open mind.	■	■	■
8. I concentrate on listening even when the information is complicated.	■	■	■
9. I can recognize when emotional appeals are backed up with facts.	■	■	■
10. I take into account the speaker's personal and cultural perspectives.	■	■	■
11. I ask questions, when appropriate, to be sure I understand the speaker.	■	■	■
12. I do not let distractions interfere with my listening.	■	■	■

1. Grade yourself: If you have mostly checked Always (10 or more times), you are an excellent listener. If you checked eight or nine statements as Always, you are a good listener but could improve in a few areas. If you marked Always for six or seven statements, you are a fair listener. If you marked Always for four or five statements, you are a poor listener. If you checked Always for fewer than four statements, this indicates that you are an extremely poor listener.
2. Based on your results, make a list of which skills are the most important for you to develop.
3. Identify strategies you will use in order to improve those skills.
4. Consciously practice these strategies in your classes over the next several weeks and take the test again. Where do you see improvement? Where do you need to do more work?

Sources: Based on "How Are Your Listening Skills? A Quick Self-Rating Quiz," Taft College Learning Resource Center, http://www.taft.cc.ca.us/lrc/quizzes/listtest.htm, and Judi Brownell, *Listening: Attitudes, Principles, and Skills*, 5th ed., New York: Pearson, 2013, pp. 31-34.

Listener Distractions. We can think faster than we can listen. Since listening does not fully engage the brain, it may be easy for our minds to wander, which distracts us from listening effectively.

Imagine a listener who is daydreaming during a speech, constructing a mental fantasy while listening. The fantasy may be more exciting and more personally relevant than the speaker's message. Gradually, without meaning to, this audience member will devote all energy to the daydream—still hearing, but not listening to, the speech. In fact, the distracting daydream may be stimulated by words in the speech. The word *movie,* for example, might trigger the thought, "I wonder what video we should watch at the party tonight," which in turn might lead to "I hope my roommate remembers to pick up the pizzas," and then to a mental checklist of preparations for the party. All these thoughts might lead to "I hope Ali Rickey is going to be there." Clearly, this is not careful listening.

Much of today's public communication is delivered in brief "sound bites" to which people only partially pay attention while engaged in other activities. As a result, many people have not practiced the skill of listening to a sustained statement or description, even when it concerns them directly. Notice how some of these listeners are distracted while others are paying attention.

Worse yet, the listener might be distracted several times during the speech before snapping to attention and thinking, "Oops! I'd better listen more closely to this speech." After tuning in again for a few minutes, the listener might then be distracted by some other word or phrase. The idea of "channel surfing"—of mindlessly switching among television programs without paying much attention to any of them—aptly describes how some listeners tune a speech in and out, seemingly at random. Although a speaker can't be held responsible for listeners' habits, a well-prepared, well-delivered speech is the best defense against listener distractions.

Limited Attention Span. Another factor that makes listening difficult is that most people's **attention span**—the length of time they will attend to a message without distraction—is short. In the past, audiences were prepared for (and expected) lengthy speeches, sermons, lectures, and debates. During the eighteenth and early nineteenth centuries, political orations went on for hours, sometimes days. But today's public messages are much shorter.[2]

Shorter messages are generally less complex and make fewer demands on listeners' powers of concentration. The speaker simply doesn't have time to try out many ideas, to develop them fully, and to suggest all their implications. Very short messages can present little, except slogans or sound bites. And frequent exposure to short messages—whether advertising jingles or political slogans—weakens listeners' capacity to process and evaluate longer, more intricate messages.

The trend to make messages "short and simple" has been accelerated by television.[3] Viewers are accustomed to changing channels frequently and may find it hard, even for entertainment, to pay attention for long. Also, the cost of advertising time (or ad space, in print media) has led to shorter, simpler messages. The brevity of e-mails and text messages and the speed of electronic communication further reinforce our limited attention spans. And, of course, experience with the Internet has increased our confidence in our ability to multitask. Many believe that they can check e-mail or text while simultaneously listening carefully, even if there is no reason to believe that this is the case.[4]

Watch the Video "Melissa Beall Discusses Listening Barriers" at **MyCommunicationLab**

Jumping to Conclusions. People sometimes assume that they "know" what the speaker is going to say, but jumping to conclusions is no basis for effective listening. Early in the semester, student speaker Smita Shah gave an impromptu

attention span
The length of time a person will attend to a message without feeling distracted.

speech about why society should enforce capital punishment. Later in the semester, she again chose capital punishment as the topic for a different speech. But after doing her research, she changed her opinion and decided that capital punishment should be abolished. Nonetheless, when she rose to speak, some audience members were so sure that she would again favor capital punishment that they misinterpreted everything she said. Here are some of the questions they asked after she spoke:

"How can you support state-sanctioned murder?"

"What about innocent people who might be executed by mistake?"

"Doesn't it cost more to execute someone than to keep him in prison for life?"

"Isn't it true that a disproportionately large number of those executed are black?"

These audience members thought they were asking hostile questions, but they had jumped to conclusions and showed instead that they hadn't listened carefully.

Most untrained listeners sometimes make such assumptions and misinterpretations. People who attend a speech as committed supporters of the speaker's cause already "know" that they will agree with the message and hence do not listen to it carefully. They sometimes find themselves endorsing a position that they don't really support. Other listeners who strongly oppose a speaker's cause almost instinctively reject every part of the message. In recent years, growing distrust of authority figures has led many listeners to reject cynically whatever a person in authority might say.

In both cases—instant acceptance and instant rejection—listeners jump to conclusions through **assimilation**; they blur the distinction between two similar messages and regard them as identical. If the speaker says something that in any way seems to confirm their position, they interpret that as the thesis of the speech. They also *disregard* any parts of the message that challenge their assumptions. They simply ignore those ideas. In both cases, hasty conclusions keep them from truly listening.[5]

Situational Distractions. Distractions in the specific speaking situation can also make listening difficult. Perhaps the wind blows the door shut while you are speaking, and listeners turn to look when they hear it slam. Or an audience member may arrive late, or some lights may go out, or loud laughter may erupt in the hallway. None of these events can be controlled, yet all can interfere with effective listening. The first thing a speaker can do in such cases is to try to offset the distraction by repeating or rephrasing the part of the speech that had to compete with it.

Because each of these obstacles to effective listening can lead to a bad listening habit, which careful listeners can overcome through concentration. Table 4.1 summarizes the obstacles, bad habits, and remedies for both listeners and speakers.

- Because *thinking is faster than listening*, your mind may wander and you may not pay attention. Some remedies are to concentrate harder on the speech and to take notes. As a speaker, you can offset this tendency by keeping the speech focused; rivet the audience's attention to each main idea by showing how it relates to your thesis.
- Because *your attention span is limited*, you may not be able to follow a long, complex speech. Besides concentrating and taking notes, you can stretch your attention span gradually by listening to longer speeches. As a speaker,

assimilation
The tendency to regard two similar messages as basically identical, blurring the distinction between them.

Obstacles	Listener's bad habit	Remedy	
		Listener	**Speaker**
Thinking is faster than listening.	Listener's mind may wander.	Concentrate on the speech; take notes.	Keep the speech focused; tie each point to main thesis.
Listener's attention span is short.	Not listening to speeches that are long or complex.	Practice gradually listening to longer speeches.	Divide speeches into small, compact segments.
Listener jumps to conclusions.	Missing speaker's point; judging by listener viewpoint only.	Try to set prejudices aside.	Careful audience analysis; extra effort on clarity.
Situations contain distractions.	Following the distraction rather than the speech.	Concentrate on the speech and on self-discipline.	Stay flexible; adapt to situation.

Table 4.1 Overcoming four obstacles to good listening

try dividing the speech into small segments that you can develop quickly and memorably; again, tie each segment to your thesis.

- Because *you jump to conclusions*, you may miss the speaker's point. You may think that statements you like are closer to your position than they actually are; and if you disagree with statements, you may magnify the differences between your views and the speaker's. The remedy is to set aside your prejudices and concentrate on the speaker's point of view. As a speaker, you can best overcome this obstacle through careful audience analysis, which is described in Chapter 5. If you analyze where listeners' preconceptions are likely to lead them, you can figure out exactly which points must be made especially clear.
- Because *elements in the situation distract you*, you don't listen carefully to what the speaker is saying. Again, try harder to concentrate; take notes, and exercise self-discipline. As a speaker, you can counteract distractions by remaining flexible, by adapting to the situation rather than being tied to your text. If you respond to a distraction quickly enough, you may even be able to turn it to your advantage.

As a speaker, the best defense against *all* obstacles to effective listening is your awareness that listening is difficult. Knowing this, you can compensate for listeners' bad habits by finding clear and interesting supporting material, by repeating points appropriately, and by varying your delivery to fit the circumstances. Speakers must make a whole range of strategic choices about how to design and present a message, and we will examine those choices throughout this book.

When you are an audience member, understanding the difficulties of listening should strengthen your resolve to concentrate and to listen carefully and critically. Try to identify any bad habits in how you listen, and strive actively to correct them. Some are easy to correct, such as putting away laptops and turning off cell phones in order to reduce the chances of accidental distractions. Other bad habits may require more concerted effort to overcome. In order to evaluate others' messages effectively, and thus improve your own messages, become more sensitive to the obstacles to listening.

Explore the Exercise
"Effective Listening" at
MyCommunicationLab

OBJECTIVE 4.3 Strategies for Careful Listening

Some people try to overcome the difficulties of listening by going to the other extreme of focusing on *each and every word* the speaker utters. This approach rarely works because the attempt to take in everything makes it less likely that you will think about, interpret, and assess what you are hearing. Similarly, students who try to take notes about every word in a professor's lecture often cannot explain what the lecture was about. They are so busy writing that they have little energy or time for thinking. It's a classic case of seeing the trees but missing the forest. Listening without thinking is just as flawed as hearing without listening.

Even careless listeners are quick to recognize the superficial strengths and weaknesses of a speech, such as whether the speaker tells an interesting story, mispronounces words, races through a quotation, or talks too loudly. Although these are important aspects of a speech, untrained listeners often fail to *think about* the ideas presented and whether those ideas support the thesis. They may be hearing the speech; they may even be listening to it; but they are not listening carefully.

Careful listeners avoid both of these extremes. They do not try to remember every word, and they do not attend only to superficial aspects of a speech. They focus instead on the thesis and the main ideas that support it. Two techniques that can help you do this—and thus become a more careful listener—are *mapping* and *note taking*.

Mapping

Careful listening is encouraged by the technique of **mapping**, in which the listener draws a diagram showing the relationship between the thesis of the speech and the main ideas that support it. This involves four basic steps:

1. Identifying the thesis
2. Identifying the main ideas
3. Assessing the main ideas
4. Deciding whether the main ideas support the thesis

Identify the Thesis of the Speech. Careful listeners should be able to identify not only the general topic of a speech but also its thesis, whether stated explicitly or not. For example, you should be able to say not only that a speech was about privacy protections on the Internet, but also that the speaker claimed that the current level of online privacy protection is inadequate. If the speaker states the thesis explicitly in the introduction, you can follow along and see how the claim is developed and supported in the body of the speech. But if the thesis is only implied by supporting material or is stated only in the conclusion of the speech, you have to listen carefully to extract the thesis and map its relationship to the main ideas.

Remember that your task in mapping a speech is not to reconstruct it word for word, but to identify its core elements. The thesis almost always can be expressed in one or two sentences; from this central point, the proofs and other supporting materials radiate.

mapping
Diagraming the relationship between the thesis of a speech and its main ideas.

Identify the Main Ideas that Develop the Thesis. Suppose, for example, that the thesis of the speech about online privacy was "The current level of online privacy protection is inadequate." To support the thesis, the speaker offered three claims as main ideas:

A. Hundreds of millions of people use the Internet.

B. Dot-coms have little incentive to regulate Internet commerce.

C. Consumers are left without protection of their personal information.

In this case, claims A, B, and C each represent a separate idea to support the thesis. A map of this speech would show each main idea as being connected to the thesis. Figure 4.1 shows two examples of how you might map this speech.

But suppose that the relationship among the main ideas was more complex, as in the following example:

A. Internet commerce is a relatively new industry.

B. New industries are notoriously complex and therefore difficult to regulate.

C. Absent regulation, each of the popular websites announces its own online privacy policies.

D. Many of these policies are contained in lengthy and tedious notices.

E. Cumbersome privacy protections will be ignored by consumers attracted to the efficiency of electronic commerce.

In this example, each claim follows from the one before it; only together—and not individually—do the main ideas support the thesis. As shown in Figure 4.2, a map of this speech would represent the relationship among the main ideas.

The structure of ideas in a speech map may or may not correspond to the actual organizational structure of the speech. Again, the goal for careful listeners is not to recall exactly what was said, but rather to be able to *reconstruct* the thesis and main ideas and to explain how they fit together.

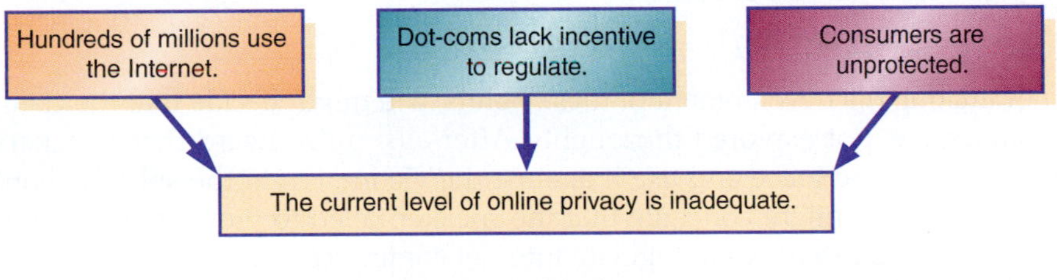

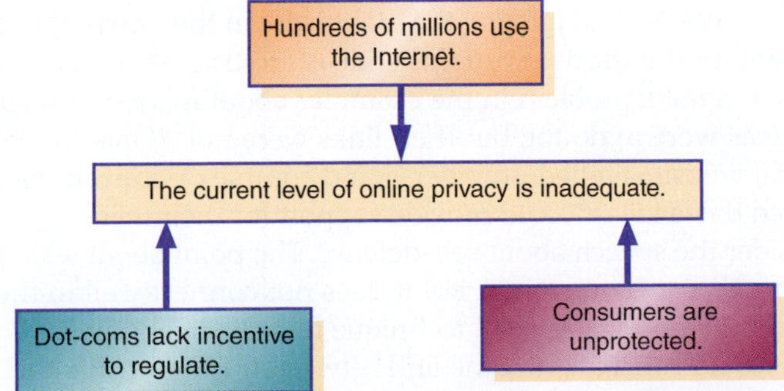

Figure 4.1 Mapping claims that separately support the thesis.

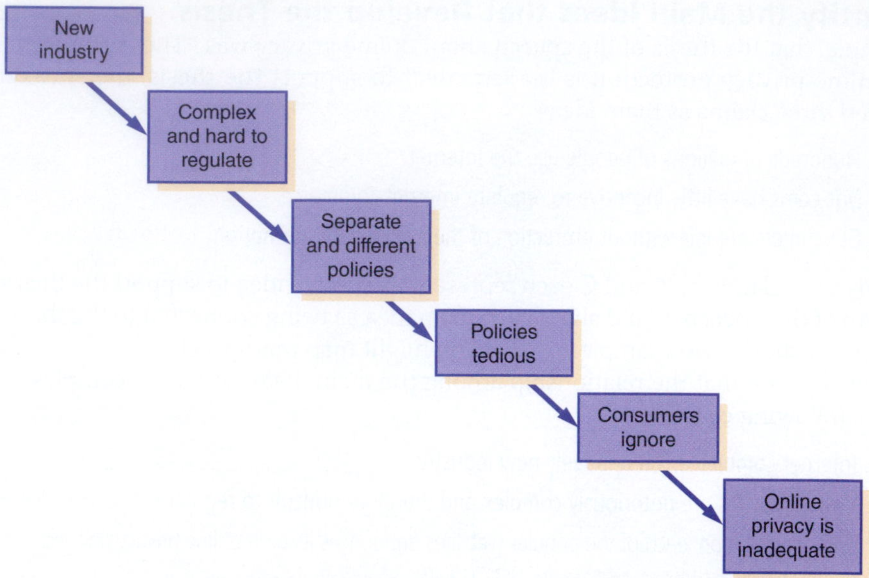

Figure 4.2 Mapping claims that only together support the thesis.

Assess the Adequacy of the Main Ideas. This is an evaluation step in which you judge whether the main ideas have been advanced solidly. For example, the thesis of a speech about techniques of self-defense might be "With knowledge of simple techniques, you can defend yourself if attacked." The main ideas that you diagram on your map are the following:

A. A victim can shout for help and run.

B. A victim can use mace to stop the attacker.

C. A victim can disable the attacker.

D. A person should walk only in safe neighborhoods.

In evaluating the development of these points, you might decide that the claim about mace was not explored thoroughly. After all, you've heard that attackers sometimes grab the mace and use it against the victim. Or, in the speech about online privacy, you might conclude that the speaker failed to prove that dot-com companies lacked incentives to regulate Internet commerce.

Decide Whether the Main Ideas Support the Thesis. This second evaluation step moves beyond judging the main ideas in their own right to judging whether they link to the thesis. Even if the ideas are true, they may not support the thesis. This was not a problem in the examples about mace and regulating the Internet; the ideas were in doubt, but their links were not. *If* mace were effective or *if* commercial websites relied on diverse and complex notifications of privacy protections, then those ideas would provide support for their theses.

Now reconsider the speech about self-defense. The point about walking only in safe neighborhoods may be sensible, but it does not connect well to the thesis. It describes a preventive measure, not a technique for self-defense when you are attacked. So you would conclude that the link between this main idea and the thesis is weak. Or, in the speech on protecting online privacy, suppose that the speaker convinced you that millions of people use the Internet but did not prove that this makes online privacy a significant problem. After all, many people who use the Internet do not buy things online and many who do buy are not worried about their privacy. The main idea itself is not in question, but the link between that idea and the thesis is not established.

Mapping a speech enables you to listen carefully, because you have a clear purpose: to discover and evaluate the thesis, the main supporting ideas, and the links between the thesis and the supporting ideas. One handy shortcut in mapping a speech is to use plus and minus signs to record your appraisal both of the ideas and of their links. For example, a plus sign next to a claim indicates that you think the claim was established, whereas a minus sign next to a link indicates that you believe the link was not supported. Obviously, every speaker wants the audience to make positive evaluations of *both* the claims and the links.

Note Taking

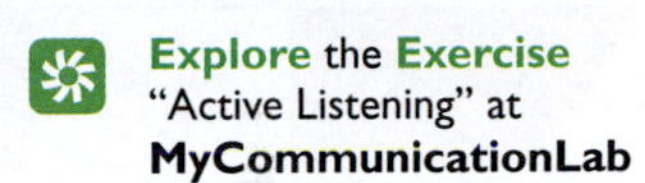

Explore the **Exercise** "Active Listening" at **MyCommunicationLab**

You may not be able to complete the speech map while the speech is being delivered. Even if the main ideas were previewed in the introduction, you may not fully grasp them or see how they link to the thesis until the speaker has finished. And you probably will not be able to evaluate them until you have had some time to think about them. Sometimes your preliminary understanding of the thesis may turn out to be wrong, and mapping during the speech may lead you to jump to (wrong) conclusions. But if you wait until after the speech to make the map, can you confidently remember the thesis and main ideas? Most listeners cannot; they need notes to remind them.

Note taking is not a substitute for thinking about the speech during its presentation. Instead, disciplined note taking is an essential tool for careful listening. The goals are to record as much *significant* information as possible and to do so as *efficiently* as possible. The following suggestions will help you:

1. *Focus on the thesis and main ideas.* Try to identify these critical elements, and take notes that will help you recall their relationship. Avoid being sidetracked by examples and less important points.
2. *Take notes quietly* on paper or an electronic device that is silent. Avoid typing on a laptop if the clacking of the keyboard is audible.
3. *Use key words rather than sentences.* Don't record every word; this is inefficient and distracting. In particular, prepositions, articles (*a, an, the*), and even verbs often can be omitted without losing the sense of the idea being communicated.
4. *Organize the notes as a rough outline.* You don't need a formal outline of the speech; the crucial thing is to identify major headings and subheadings (claims and supporting ideas). If you leave plenty of space in the left-hand margin and between items in your notes, you can insert headings, subheadings, and related points wherever they belong—whenever the speaker presents them.
5. *Abbreviate and use symbols whenever possible.* By establishing some consistent, memorable abbreviations and symbols, you can take notes quickly without missing anything the speaker says. For example, some common abbreviations and symbols are w/ for *with*, w/o for *without*, = for *is*, ~ for *is not*, < for *less than*, > for *more than*, and arrows pointing either up for *increasing* or down

for *decreasing*. Develop your own system of abbreviations and symbols for frequently used words and terms.

6. *Also make notes to help you evaluate the speech.* Because careful listening and evaluation are ongoing responsibilities, also write down comments that will help you prepare a critical assessment of the speech. If you think that the thesis was supported well, write "good support"; if the structure of the speech confused you, jot down "disorganized." Note these evaluative comments in the margin or in a different color, so that they don't interfere with your notes about what the speaker said.

The test of progress toward becoming a careful listener is whether, when a speech is over, you can reconstruct its basic form; not whether you have memorized the speech or can repeat it word for word, but whether you can identify the thesis and explain how it was developed.

OBJECTIVE 4.4

Listening Critically

The title of this chapter is "Listening Critically," which moves far beyond listening carefully. **Critical listening** results not only in an accurate rendering of the speech, but also in a personal interpretation and assessment of it. Basically, critical listening enables you to apply critical thinking to a speech.

Critical Thinking

You know from Chapter 1 that **critical thinking** is the ability to form and defend your own judgments rather than blindly accepting or instantly rejecting what you hear or read. *Critical* does not mean *negative, hostile*, or *adversarial*; but it does mean *reflective*. It is a conscious, systematic method of evaluating ideas wherever you encounter them—not only in speeches, but also in conversation, in print, on television, in films and plays, and so on. By reflecting on the ideas you hear or read, you can form judgments about which are strong and which are weak.

critical listening
Listening that enables you to offer both an accurate rendering of the speech and an interpretation and assessment of it.

critical thinking
The ability to form and defend your own judgments rather than blindly accepting or instantly rejecting what you hear or read.

facts
Statements that can be independently verified by others; they are either true or false.

opinions
Judgments that cannot be independently verified and that are not clearly true or false.

The Characteristics of Critical Thinkers.

Critical thinkers demonstrate at least six characteristics:

1. *Critical thinkers are reluctant to accept assertions on faith.* Unsupported assertions carry little weight with critical thinkers, who are skeptical and always imagine themselves asking, "What have you got to go on?"
2. *Critical thinkers distinguish facts from opinions.* In Chapter 1, we introduced this distinction. **Facts**, at least in theory, can be independently verified by others. They are either true or false, and their truth is not subject to interpretation. The number of people who don't have health insurance is a fact, as is the historical claim that "In fourteen hundred and ninety-two, Columbus sailed the ocean blue."

   Opinions are judgments that are *not* clearly true or false and so cannot be independently verified. For example, a person might hold the opinion that Paris is more beautiful than London or that the United States is the best country in which to live. Opinions may be highly individualistic, or they may be widely shared. Just because an opinion is widely shared, however, does not make it a fact—although it is not easily disregarded. Even so, remember that opinions *can* be changed. Often, the strength of an opinion depends on the *ethos* of the person who holds it (or who dismisses it).

Facts are not necessarily better than opinions, and both are well suited for particular kinds of statements. But you should understand the difference between them. Critical thinkers listen carefully to be sure that a speaker does not mistake an opinion for a fact or a fact for an opinion.

The audience members who are attentive and listening carefully will be able to remember and think critically about this speech.

3. *Critical thinkers seek to uncover assumptions.* **Assumptions** are unstated, taken-for-granted beliefs in a particular situation. For example, underlying the argument in 2012 that stronger United Nations sanctions were needed to prevent Iran from developing nuclear weapons are the assumptions that Iran plans to develop nuclear weapons and that doing so poses a serious threat to world peace.
4. *Critical thinkers are open to new ideas.* Although critical thinkers do not hold their opinions and beliefs lightly, they are willing to consider challenges to what they believe and are open to the possibility that they may have to change their minds.
5. *Critical thinkers apply reason and common sense to new ideas.* Critical thinkers ask whether a new idea makes sense, whether it seems internally consistent, and whether they can see and understand the links made by the speaker or writer in developing the idea. If reason and common sense tell them that everything is in order, they give the idea a good hearing—whether or not they expect to agree with it. But if reason and common sense tell them the idea is wrong, they are likely to reject it, even though it might support a conclusion with which they agree.
6. *Critical thinkers relate new ideas to what they already know.* They ask, "Is the new idea consistent with what I already think or know to be true?" If not, they ask how their existing attitudes and beliefs need to be modified and whether such modifications are justified. These steps enable them to put the idea into a broader context and to incorporate it into their constantly developing system of beliefs and attitudes.

What these six characteristics of critical thinking have in common is their emphasis on **reflective** judgment—neither blind acceptance nor automatic rejection of an idea, but a considered and thoughtful opinion about whether the idea and its support merit acceptance.

The Skills of Critical Thinking. From these six characteristics of critical thinkers, we can extract four basic skills that underlie critical thinking:

1. *Questioning and challenging,* both your own ideas and the ideas of others, so that you will neither accept nor dismiss an idea without thoughtful reflection. When a speaker puts forward an assertion or a claim, you should ask

assumptions
Unstated, taken-for-granted beliefs in a particular situation.

reflective
Considered, thoughtful (as opposed to automatic).

CHECKLIST 4.1

Critical Thinking

1. Characteristics of Critical Thinkers
   - ❐ Reluctant to accept assertions on faith
   - ❐ Distinguish facts from opinions
   - ❐ Seek to uncover assumptions
   - ❐ Open to new ideas
   - ❐ Apply reason and common sense to new ideas
   - ❐ Relate new ideas to what they already know
2. Critical Thinking Skills
   - ❐ Questioning and challenging
   - ❐ Recognizing differences
   - ❐ Forming opinions and supporting claims
   - ❐ Putting ideas into a broader context

yourself, "What does that speaker have to go on? Should I believe what he or she says?"

2. *Recognizing differences*—between ideas, between facts and opinions, between explicit claims and unstated assumptions, and between easily explained events and anomalies or puzzles. When hearing a speech about the selection of the national champion collegiate football team, for example, you will be alert to the differences between criticism of the Bowl Championship Series (BCS) formulas during the regular football season and after-the-fact criticism once the champion has been determined.
3. *Forming opinions and supporting claims* so that you can state and evaluate ideas. You can get beyond your vague uneasiness about the plan for health care reform and state that even if the plan increases the number of people covered, it may also hurt the quality of health care.
4. *Putting ideas into a broader context* by seeing how they relate to what you already know and by understanding what they imply about other things you might assert or believe.[6] After listening to a speech opposing affirmative action, you may realize that the speaker has not responded to most of the justifications of affirmative action that you had encountered.

Applying Critical Thinking to the Speech Situation

Earlier, we noted that listeners form judgments about the strength of a speaker's ideas and about their links to the thesis. Now we will consider *how* listeners form such judgments.

Some judgments are made uncritically. A statement "sounds right," so you decide it must be true; or it is at odds with your beliefs, and you conclude immediately that it is false. If a speaker *seems* personable and sincere, you might accept the claims without investigation; but if the speaker's delivery is unappealing, you might reject the content out of hand. Each of these is an *uncritical* judgment, one made without reason or reflection.

In contrast, **critical judgments** are those that you can articulate and defend by providing reasons for them. This does not mean that you are hostile or negative toward the speech. In fact, critical listening begins with the assumption that the speaker knows what he or she is talking about; but this assumption is balanced with skepticism, which is a reluctance to be pushed prematurely into conclusions.

Critical listening begins with mapping and is aided by note taking, but it adds the step of *reflection* before judgment. Reflective listeners think consciously about the speech and ask themselves questions about it.

Another way to say this is that critical listeners *elaborate* the message. Their minds are engaged, and they think actively about the speaker's ideas and how they might be answered. They carry on a kind of internal dialogue with the speaker about the speech. This tendency makes them skeptical, but in a healthy way. They are willing to accept a speaker's ideas, but only if those ideas satisfy the appropriate tests. We will discuss the *elaboration likelihood model* more fully in Chapter 14.

critical judgments
Judgments that can be articulated and defended by providing the reasons for them.

Here are some examples of questions that critical listeners might pose to test a speaker's ideas.

- Are the main ideas identifiable?
- Are the links among the ideas reasonable?
- Are the ideas supported where necessary?
- How does accepting or rejecting the thesis affect my other beliefs?

Are the Main Ideas Identifiable? As emphasized earlier, it is important to know not just the general topic of the speech, but also its specific thesis and the main ideas that support it. Critical listeners are especially concerned that the thesis be clear and precise.

Suppose you were listening to a speech about multiculturalism in U.S. education. You might recognize quickly whether the speaker thinks multiculturalism is good. But as a critical listener, you would ask yourself additional questions, such as:

- What does the speaker mean by multiculturalism?
- Does she mean the same thing each time she uses the term?
- Do others whom she quotes about multiculturalism mean the same thing that she does?
- Is she saying that multiculturalism is good in principle, as it is applied, or both?
- Is she saying that multiculturalism is good regardless of other values with which it may conflict? Or is she recognizing the conflicts and saying that multiculturalism is good on balance?

Notice that each of these questions is raised only to develop a precise understanding of the speaker's thesis, not to object to the thesis. Obviously, you cannot assess a speech critically until you know exactly what the speaker is trying to say.

Are the Links Among the Ideas Reasonable? When we addressed this question earlier, we asked only whether the links seemed to square with common sense. But critical listeners want to know more than that; they will ask whether the speaker has proved the claims in a reasonable way.

Suppose that in a speech about the global financial crisis of 2008 to 2009 the speaker claims that (1) irresponsible lending practices at banks and mortgage

Strategies for Speaking to Diverse Audiences

Respecting Diversity Through Critical Listening

Listening is a cultivated skill. Listening critically requires practice and respect for the speaker. Consider these ideas when practicing critical listening.

1. Is the speaker challenging one of your fundamental ideas, beliefs, or values? How can you listen carefully, keep an open mind, and frame your feedback if you do not readily agree with the position being taken by the speaker?
2. How should you react if the speaker's accent or pronunciation seems unfamiliar? How will careful listening help you?
3. How can you best avoid distraction if the speaker's physical appearance or clothing style are different from what you might expect? How might these physical differences potentially affect your ability to listen carefully?

companies were primary causes of the financial crisis and that (2) the crisis weakened the position of the United States in the world economy. As a critical listener, you would ask such questions as:

- *Does the speaker prove what he claims?* This speaker is claiming that one thing causes another. But if he can show only that, as the financial crisis worsens, our international economic position weakens, he has not proved a cause–effect relationship. He has only revealed a correlation. The decline in a country's global economic standing might result from some other factor or a combination of factors.
- *If the links are established, should you accept the speaker's claim?* Even though the speaker might convince you that irresponsible mortgage lending contributed to the financial crisis and that the financial crisis weakened the country's economic position, you still might not find the conclusion acceptable. For example, you may have just read in the newspaper that economists recently concluded that the U.S. economy was still outperforming European countries. Something does not add up: If the mortgage crisis was so harmful, why did the U.S. economy continue to excel over that of other wealthy countries? In raising this kind of question, you are recognizing that the speaker has not examined the topic completely. You want to know more about other factors that apparently are offsetting the effects of the mortgage crisis or, conversely, the factors that are negatively affecting other national economies.

Are the Ideas Supported Where Necessary? As we have seen, some statements are accepted at face value by most listeners, whereas other statements need to be supported by facts, narratives, data, or opinions. As a critical listener, you require a speaker to support ideas that need it, and so you would ask such questions as:

- *Does the idea need support?* Even critical listeners accept some statements at face value. Maybe the idea is clear intuitively, or perhaps the speaker's explanation makes it seem so obvious that no further support is required. For example, if the speaker clearly defines the subprime mortgage crisis as "the extension of credit to unqualified homeowners who began to default on their mortgages in record numbers," you might see no need for additional support. But you probably will not be so quick to accept an opinion such as: "The mortgage crisis threatens to cripple the U.S. economy permanently." Remember, though, that ideas may need support with one audience and not another. There is no standardized burden of proof.
- *Has the speaker offered enough supporting material?* For most listeners, one or two examples of uninsured people who cannot pay their medical bills will probably not be sufficient support for the thesis "Spiraling health care costs threaten to bankrupt the American people." The speaker doesn't offer enough examples to support a generalization about the entire population of the country. Insufficient support may lead listeners to conclude that there *is* no other support, and so they may not take the speaker's ideas seriously.

How Does Accepting or Rejecting the Thesis Affect My Other Beliefs? Critical listeners recognize that beliefs and values do not exist in isolation. Almost always, accepting or rejecting a speaker's thesis will have consequences for your beliefs about other matters. Believing, for example, that a national budget surplus would justify a tax cut may not square with another belief you hold—that there are significant needs for increased spending on education and health care that the surplus would make possible.

These four sets of questions are intended to help you develop a clear understanding of what a speaker is asking you to think about, to believe, or to do. They will help you to form a careful and reflective judgment about whether to agree with the speaker. But listening critically does not mean that you have to subject a speaker to an inquisition before accepting anything he or she says. Rather, it is a way to "trust, but verify"—to accept the *ethos* of the speaker but not to depend entirely on that in deciding whether the speech makes sense.

CHECKLIST 4.2

Critical Thinking About a Speech

- ❒ Are the main ideas identifiable?
- ❒ Are the links among the ideas reasonable?
- ❒ Are the ideas supported where necessary?
- ❒ How does accepting or rejecting the thesis affect my other beliefs?

Evaluating Speeches Critically

OBJECTIVE 4.5

So far, we have considered one dimension of critical listening: judging whether a speaker's ideas are sound. We saw that the basic skills of critical thinking are used as well in thinking strategically about the thesis and supporting ideas of a speech. Now we will consider a second dimension of critical listening: assessing the strength of the speech *as a speech*. This evaluation centers on three questions:

1. Did the speech demonstrate the principles and techniques of public speaking?
2. What was strong and what was weak about the speech?
3. How might the speaker improve the speech?

This dimension of critical listening is especially important in a public speaking class.

CHOOSE A STRATEGY: Listening Critically

The Situation

You and a small group of classmates are working together to practice your speeches for an upcoming presentation. Bansi has asked you to listen to a practice run of her speech on Iran's nuclear enrichment program and the threat it poses to world peace. You feel Bansi's speech is well organized, but you don't understand why she picked this topic or its relevance to you as a college student. Halfway through her speech you find yourself thinking about plans for the evening—your dinner date, finishing your own project, doing laundry, and preparing for class the next day.

Making Choices

1. What strategies could you use to help listen more carefully to Bansi's speech?
2. What questions could you ask to help better understand Bansi's topic and its relevance?
3. How can you use critical-thinking skills to provide useful feedback to Bansi? What recommendations might you have for her?

What If...

How would your listening strategies change if the following were true?

1. You are in the nuclear energy business.
2. You are critiquing Bansi's speech for a graded assignment.

Evaluation Standards

Watch the Video "Critique for Informative Speech: Brain Research of the Sexes" at **MyCommunicationLab**

Like judgments about the content of a speech, assessments of its quality can be made uncritically—as when an audience member says, "Wow!" or "That was a great speech!" without explaining why. But the goal is to make *critical* assessments, which depend on the four critical-thinking skills described earlier: questioning and challenging, recognizing differences, forming opinions and supporting claims, and putting ideas into a broader context.

As you apply these skills to speechmaking, remember that a speech is a strategic communication. It is presented in a specific situation to achieve a specific purpose. By focusing on these two concepts—*the rhetorical situation* and *the speaker's purpose*—you will develop evaluation criteria that turn careful listening into critical listening.

Rhetorical Situation. The discussion in Chapter 1 of the **rhetorical situation** made it clear that speeches are delivered not in a vacuum but in a specific context. Critical listeners thus realize that it is not fair to evaluate a speech without considering the situation in which the speaker prepared and delivered it.

Abraham Lincoln, to cite a historical example, has been criticized in recent years for not having come out more strongly against slavery in the period leading to the Civil War. Indeed, in his fourth debate with Stephen A. Douglas during the 1858 senatorial campaign in Illinois, Lincoln said:

> I will say then that I am not, nor ever have been in favor of bringing about in any way the social and political equality of the white and black races—that I am not nor ever have been in favor of making voters or jurors of negroes, nor of qualifying them to hold office, nor to intermarry with white people; and I will say in addition to this that there is a physical difference between the white and black races which I believe will forever forbid the two races living together on terms of social and political equality.

This position seems far from the popular image of Lincoln as the "Great Emancipator," but some of the criticism ignores the specific situation in which he spoke—especially the facts that very few white Americans in the 1850s could imagine the races as equal and that Lincoln was suffering politically because his opponents were labeling him an abolitionist. Nor did Lincoln have free rein about the content of speeches in these campaign appearances. Because his goal was to win the election, he could not antagonize listeners whose votes he was seeking. Any critique that altogether ignores the rhetorical situation in which Lincoln spoke would give a false impression of the realistic choices available to him.

The key questions, then, are:

- What was the specific rhetorical situation?
- What constraints and opportunities did it pose?
- How well did the speaker respond to the situation?

When evaluating a classmate's speech, consider *both* the constraints imposed by the immediate audience and the constraints imposed by the larger rhetorical situation. With respect to the immediate audience, ask whether the speaker adequately tailored the speech to the listeners' knowledge level. You also might consider whether the speaker's ideas and supporting material were interesting and effective for the specific audience. With respect to the larger rhetorical situation, ask if the speaker understands current attitudes, beliefs, and practices regarding the issue about which she spoke.

rhetorical situation
A situation in which people's understanding can be changed through messages.

Speaker's Purpose. Besides taking into account the speaker's rhetorical situation, also consider the speaker's purpose. It's easy to say that a speaker chose the wrong purpose and should have aimed for something else. Generally, however, you should evaluate a speech *in light of* its stated or implied purpose. To condemn a speech for not accomplishing what the speaker never intended to accomplish is neither rational nor fair.[7]

When you listen critically, you should ask yourself: What is the speaker trying to achieve? Should I accept what he or she says?

If you understand the purpose of the speech, then the next key question is "How well did the speaker achieve the purpose?" This focuses on the means used by the speaker and whether they were the best choices available. If the purpose is to introduce a complicated subject, then a speech that assumes prior knowledge on the part of the audience and that fails to explain key concepts would not be well adapted to the purpose. The speaker may not recognize any problems, but critical listeners can point them out.

Evaluating a speech in terms of its purpose raises a third important question: "Should a speech be judged by its effects or by its artistry?" If the **expediency standard** is the only measure of a speech, then whatever is most likely to accomplish the purpose should be done. By this standard, anyone would be regarded as a good speaker who was effective in achieving his purpose, without considering the ethical or moral dimension.[8]

Most theorists, however, reject effectiveness as the sole basis for evaluating a speech. As noted in Chapter 1, the goal is not only to achieve a stated purpose but also to achieve it while following accepted principles and observing ethical norms. Public speaking is a practical art. The **artistic standard** asks whether the speaker followed the principles of the art, and hence whether he or she did the best that could be done, consistent with ethical norms, in a specific rhetorical situation. For example, if a classmate speaks in favor of a controversial topic—such as abortion or gay rights—you should not fault the speech for failing to convince listeners who are already strongly opposed to the topic. The artistic standard does not ignore the issue of effectiveness, however, because the application of public speaking principles and the observance of ethical norms generally make a speech more effective than it otherwise would be.

Evaluating Classroom Speeches

To evaluate classroom speeches effectively, you and your classmates must listen carefully and critically to each other. By exchanging valuable feedback, you will help each other become better speakers, and you will all sharpen your skills as critical listeners.

Typically, a classroom speaking assignment does not highlight all the dimensions of public speaking at once but will focus on one aspect. When assessing a classmate's speech, be sensitive to the specific purpose of the assignment. If it is intended to focus on organization, for instance, that should be the focus of your critique. To concentrate exclusively on some other factor, such as the speaker's gestures, would be unfair, because the whole point of this assignment is to de-emphasize other aspects of speaking in order to put the spotlight on organization.

A constructive attitude is essential in evaluating classroom speeches, because that provides the best environment for learning from each other. If criticism is hostile or antagonistic, the speaker may become defensive and may ignore useful

expediency standard
Evaluation of a speech according to the effects it produced.

artistic standard
Evaluation of a speech according to its ethical execution of principles of public speaking without regard to its actual effects.

feedback. At the same time, listeners who are too eager to criticize a speech may not properly assess the speaker's situation and purpose. Don't overlook weaknesses in a speech, but remember that the purpose of the critique is to help your classmate improve the speech, not to undermine self-esteem. Emphasize what the speaker can improve and how to do that; and remember that the strengths of the speech need not be ignored in order to identify its weaknesses.

Critiques of classroom speeches take a variety of forms. The most common is informal discussion. After a speech is presented, the class may spend some time talking about its strengths and about how it might be improved. Students are sometimes reluctant to participate in these discussions. Some may fear hurting their classmates' feelings, or they may believe that, if they critique others, their own speeches will be evaluated more harshly. But vigorous evaluation—as long as your attitude is constructive—is one of the best ways to become more skilled in speaking.

Sometimes the feedback speakers receive will seem unhelpful. It might appear that a listener has missed the point entirely. Even if this happens to you, take the comment seriously, reconsider your speech, and think about whether you want to revise it to avoid "losing" additional listeners in the future. It's a good idea to take notes about listeners' comments. In the flush of energy right after you speak, you are unlikely to remember everything.

On some occasions, evaluation involves an *impromptu speech of criticism* in which the critic follows the speaker with a presentation that assesses the speech. This will sharpen your own critical skills and at the same time give you practice in speaking. Like any other speech, a speech of evaluation has a thesis and main ideas—in this case, whatever you think is most important to say in assessing a classmate's speech.

As a speaker, you also may receive unsolicited comments from classmates either after class or elsewhere on campus. If the comments are positive, express your appreciation. But realize that listeners are typically generous in their comments; the fact that classmates liked your speech does not mean that you did everything exactly right! Another classmate may express disagreement with your speech or want to argue about your conclusions. Listen carefully to the person's point of view and clarify your point if you were misunderstood. But don't feel that your success depends on the approval of every audience member. A listener who is dead set against your viewpoint is unlikely to change, no matter what more you might say. Be grateful that the person was honest and take whatever benefit you can from the criticism; however, do not think that you have failed if some members of the audience disagree with you.

CHECKLIST 4.3

Steps in Evaluating Classroom Speeches

- ❐ Focus your evaluation on the specific skills emphasized in the assignment.
- ❐ Make constructive suggestions that will improve the speech.
- ❐ Participate freely in discussion aimed to improve the speech.
- ❐ Take notes on the comments that you receive.
- ❐ If you use rating forms, see that they capture your critical judgments.
- ❐ If you give a speech of criticism, be sure it has a clear thesis and main ideas.
- ❐ Do not expect that everyone's assessment of a speech will agree.

Evaluating Speeches Outside of the Classroom

Most speeches are delivered outside of the classroom in a variety of public settings, such as banquets, commemorative celebrations, business meetings, churches and synagogues, political campaigns, and so on.

A Question of Ethics

Expectations and Critical Listening

In this chapter, we've discussed various obstacles to and motivations for listening to a speech. Because our own expectations of a speech topic or of a speaker can conflict with the speaker's purpose, how do we develop an appropriate listening strategy? How do we ensure that suspicious or cynical impulses on our part do not get in the way of clearly understanding a speaker? Conversely, is there a risk that we will listen less critically if a speaker sounds confident and pleasant? When should we give the speaker the benefit of the doubt, and when should we discount what he or she says?

Many of the principles of classroom evaluation also apply to speeches in daily life. In particular, you need to have a clear understanding of the rhetorical situation and the speaker's purpose. Speeches are presented in specific situations to achieve specific goals, and the critique must take these into account. As with classroom speeches, you need to decide which standards to use for evaluation, probably including such factors as the validity of the speaker's reasoning and assertions, any value judgments made consciously or unconsciously, and the ethical implications of the speech.

An advantage of assessing speeches outside the classroom is that they have more variety, because they don't all spring from the same assignment. No doubt you'll hear speakers who ignore some of the concepts and guidelines in this book or who give them a unique twist. By assessing speakers in the field, you will encounter a great range of speaking styles and can better develop your own distinctive approach to public speaking.

Rhetorical Criticism

Evaluating the speeches of others is an elementary form of **rhetorical criticism**—the analytical assessment of messages that are intended to affect other people. Careful, critical listening and evaluation of speeches will help you develop a mind-set for rhetorical criticism. It will give you experience in thinking rhetorically about speeches: asking yourself what the speaker's purpose seems to be, what opportunities and problems are presented by the speaker's situation, how the speaker has chosen to go about the task, whether other choices were available, and whether the selected means and ends were the best possible in that situation.[9]

Engaging in rhetorical criticism has two major by-products. First, it gives you insights into your own public speaking by providing a range of speakers to study and by drawing your attention to how they apply principles of public speaking. Second, it develops your sensitivity to public speaking and makes you more aware of how it works. Besides improving your own abilities as a speaker, this awareness should help you appreciate excellent public speaking and put you on guard against speakers who try to undermine listeners' critical abilities.

rhetorical criticism
The analytical assessment of messages that are intended to affect other people.

What Have You Learned?

Objective 4.1: Distinguish between hearing and listening and explain why listening skills are important to speakers.

Hearing is a natural physiological activity; listening is a cultivated skill. Listening is important in order to:

- Be sure you know what you heard.
- Provide feedback to the speaker.
- Protect yourself from unethical or unscrupulous speakers.

Objective 4.2: Identify obstacles to effective listening.

Listening is difficult because:

- People think more rapidly than they listen and therefore may be prone to daydream.
- People tune a speech in or out as they are stimulated by particular words and ideas.
- A limited attention span may make it difficult to take everything in.
- A commitment to listen to *everything* may impede reflective judgment.
- People may jump to conclusions because they agree or disagree with the speaker.
- Noise or physical disruption may interfere with listening.

Skills of careful listening include:

- Decoding the message by identifying the thesis.
- Mapping the links between the thesis and supporting ideas.
- Making a judgment about the content of the speech and the links within it.

Objective 4.3: Listen carefully by mapping the central ideas of a speech and by taking notes.

Mapping technique:

- Draw a diagram showing the relationship between the speech and its main ideas.
- Identify the thesis and main ideas.
- Assess the main ideas and decide whether they support the thesis.

Note-taking strategies:

- Focus on the thesis and main ideas.
- Use key words, abbreviations, and symbols.
- Create a rough outline.

Objective 4.4: Explain how critical thinking is applied in the speaking situation.

Critical listening involves application of critical-thinking skills to the speech situation. Characteristics of critical listeners:

- Open to new ideas and arguments.
- Assess ideas with skepticism and insist that they be explained and supported.
- Able to reconstruct thesis and main ideas.
- Able to form reflective, not hasty, judgment.

Objective 4.5: Evaluate speeches as a result of critical listening.

Evaluation of speeches should be guided by:

- Understanding of the rhetorical situation.
- Understanding of the speaker's purpose.

The artistic standard is more appropriate for most speeches than is the expediency standard.

You can practice rhetorical criticism by:

- Critiquing classmates' speeches.
- Evaluating speeches outside of the classroom, in everyday situations.

Listen to the Audio Chapter Summary
at MyCommunicationLab

Discussion Questions

1. We have all heard speeches that were interesting and speeches that were boring. What was it about the interesting speeches that grabbed your attention? What was it about the boring speeches that made them difficult to bear? Based on your answers, suggest some strategies for gaining and holding an audience's attention.
2. You are about to speak to a hostile audience. How do you get them to listen with an open mind rather than immediately discounting your position?
3. A major reason listening has become such a challenge for audiences today is the constant bombardment of media "noise" in our society. Name some of the cultural obstacles to effective listening that you, as a speaker, must overcome in order to connect with your audience.
4. You have just heard a speech that was particularly effective, but in your opinion it was ethically suspect. How would you evaluate the speech? Why?

Activities

1. Listen to a speech on television, in class, or at a lecture. Make a note of when your mind starts to wander and consider why this is the case.
2. Map a speech. Identify its thesis and main ideas, and evaluate its claims and links.
3. Write a three- to five-page essay to evaluate a speech. Analyze the rhetorical situation and the speaker's purpose; state and explain your evaluation standards; and apply rhetorical criticism to the speech.
4. Write a short review of an in-class response to a classmate's speech. How well does your reaction match up with the respondent's? In what ways did the respondent listen critically? How well did the respondent's comments address the speaker's purpose?

Key Terms

artistic standard **87**
assimilation **74**
assumptions **81**
attention span **73**
critical judgments **82**
critical listening **80**
critical thinking **80**
expediency standard **87**
facts **80**
feedback **71**
hearing **70**
listening **70**
mapping **76**
opinions **80**
reflective **81**
rhetorical criticism **89**
rhetorical situation **86**

Study and Review the Flashcards at MyCommunicationLab

Notes

1 The complexity of an individual's cognitive processes is also responsible for differences in listening comprehension. See Gary Buck, *Assessing Listening*, Cambridge: Cambridge University Press, 2001.

2 Neil Postman provides an extensive social critique of how television is responsible for this trend in *Amusing Ourselves to Death: Public Discourse in the Age of Show Business*, New York: Penguin Books, 1985. Doris A. Graber offers a more hopeful reading of the roles of television and the Internet in shaping public discourse in *Processing Politics: Learning from Television in the Internet Age*, Chicago: University of Chicago Press, 2001.

3 For a discussion of how television tends to simplify messages, see Jeffrey Scheuer, *The Sound Bite Society*, New York: Routledge, 2001.

4 See "Multitasking May Not Mean Higher Productivity," National Public Radio, August 28, 2009, http://www.npr.org/templates/story/story.php?storyId=112334449.

5 Charles Taber and Milton Lodge confront "motivated skepticism" when analyzing how individual citizens evaluate political interests in a biased manner, showing how previous attitudes importantly influence discussions of affirmative action and gun control. They discuss how messages that do not fit into previous attitudes or beliefs promote biased reactions. See Charles S. Taber and Milton Lodge, "Motivated Skepticism in the Evaluation of Political Beliefs," *American Journal of Political Science* 50 (July 2006): 755–69.

6 For more about critical thinking, see Brook Noel Moore and Richard Parker, *Critical Thinking: Evaluating Claims and Arguments in Everyday Life*, 2nd ed., Mountain View, CA: Mayfield, 1989; and Leonard J. Rosen and Laurence Behrens, *The Allyn & Bacon Handbook*, 2nd ed., Boston: Allyn & Bacon, 1994, pp. 1–9. Although these textbooks focus on essay writing and evaluation, many of their directives apply as well to public speaking.

7 According to Mikhail Bahktin, we automatically tend to judge all utterances—from sentences to completed speeches—by what we imagine the speaker wishes to say. See "The Problem of Speech Genres," in *Speech Genres and Other Essays*, translated by Vern W. McGee, Austin: University of Texas Press, 1986, p. 77.

8 Another example of why a speech should not be judged on effect alone is discussed in Edwin Black, *Rhetorical Criticism*, New York: Macmillan, 1965. For more about this debate in speech criticism, see Forbes I. Hill, "Conventional Wisdom—Traditional Form: The President's Message of November 3, 1969"; Karlyn Kohrs Campbell, "Conventional Wisdom—Traditional Form: A Rejoinder"; and Forbes I. Hill, "Reply to Professor Campbell," *Quarterly Journal of Speech* 58 (December 1972): 373–86, 451–60.

9 For more about rhetorical criticism, see James R. Andrews, Michael Leff, and Robert Terrill, *Reading Rhetorical Texts: An Introduction to Criticism*, Boston: Houghton Mifflin, 1998; Roderick P. Hart, *Modern Rhetorical Criticism*, 2nd ed., Boston: Allyn and Bacon, 1997; and Sonja K. Foss, *Rhetorical Criticism: Exploration and Practice*, 4th ed., Long Grove, Illinois: Waveland Press, 2008.

CHAPTER 5

Analyzing Your Audience

LEARNING OBJECTIVES

Listen to the **Audio Chapter** at **MyCommunicationLab**

After studying this chapter, you should be able to:

Objective 5.1	Explain how the success of a speech depends on the audience.
Objective 5.2	Describe how the audience demographics, cultures, and psychology affect listeners' receptiveness to a speech.
Objective 5.3	Identify both formal and informal methods of audience analysis.
Objective 5.4	Indicate how your *ethos* influences the audience and how you can improve your *ethos*.

OUTLINE

Checking Audience Demographics
Size | Heterogeneity
Voluntary Versus Captive Audience | Composition
Physically Present Versus Mediated Audience

Respecting Audience Cultures
Cultural Diversity | Self-Interest
Personal Interests | Beliefs and Values
Prior Understanding | Common Knowledge and Experience
Roles and Reference Groups

Understanding Audience Psychology
Selective Exposure and Selective Attention | Perception

Strategies for Analyzing the Audience
Formal Methods | Informal Methods
Simplifying Devices | Critical Appraisal

Analyzing Your Own *Ethos*
Audience Perceptions of You | Modifying Audience Perceptions

OBJECTIVE 5.1

Two students were presenting speeches to their classmates about the dangers of drunk driving. Both spent a great deal of time preparing, but they had strongly different attitudes about how to develop their speeches. The night before speaking, they met to compare their preparations. The first student said:

> There is so much statistical evidence on this topic, it was hard to pick only a few studies. I'll have lots of statistics. I had to trim my stories and anecdotes to stay within the time limit, but if I cite all this scholarly research, people will know that this is a serious topic and I'm well prepared to talk about it. Then I'll be more likely to get a good grade.

His classmate took a different approach:

> You're right; there is a lot of research on this topic. But our audience consists of students, and they're the age group at greatest risk of drunk driving. They don't believe anything will happen to them, so they disregard all those statistical studies. I'll refer briefly to the studies, but I'm going to concentrate instead on the tragic drunk-driving accident just off campus last year. I want to tell a story that students can relate to, so they'll know that my speech really concerns them.

The first student viewed the assignment only from his own perspective as speaker, worrying about how to include all the research and how to ensure a good grade. The second student considered the audience's perspective. She was determined to make the message interesting to classmates, and she carefully reviewed each bit of information from the viewpoint of someone hearing it in a short speech. Both speakers had the same general topic and goal, but to the audience the first speech was abstract, complicated, and dull, whereas the second was stimulating and full of common sense.

If these two students had been speaking at a scientific conference, the results might have been just the opposite. The first speaker would have established his credibility by grappling with the complexity of the research, whereas the second would have been criticized for oversimplifying difficult material. The fact that the two speeches could elicit such different reactions from different audiences emphasizes the importance of analyzing the audience and designing the speech with the audience in mind—the focus of this chapter.

You may be surprised that your attitude toward preparing a speech can create such a difference in the audience's reaction, but it's natural for listeners to give appreciation, attention, and support to a speaker who considers their comfort, interests, and beliefs. Even though this means your audience can constrain your freedom as a speaker, you can work with that constraint by careful audience analysis on three different levels: demographics, cultures, and psychology. All audience analysis requires judgment calls, and the three levels move from judgments about the objective characteristics of the audience as a whole to judgments about the subjective thought processes of individual audience members.

- By checking *audience demographics*, you will consider how your speech should respond to certain characteristics of the audience as a whole—such as its size, age range, and educational level.
- By respecting *audience cultures*, you will become aware of how listeners approach your speech in terms of their interests, beliefs and values, prior understanding, and common knowledge.
- By understanding *audience psychology*, you will realize that listeners are selective about what they attend to and perceive.

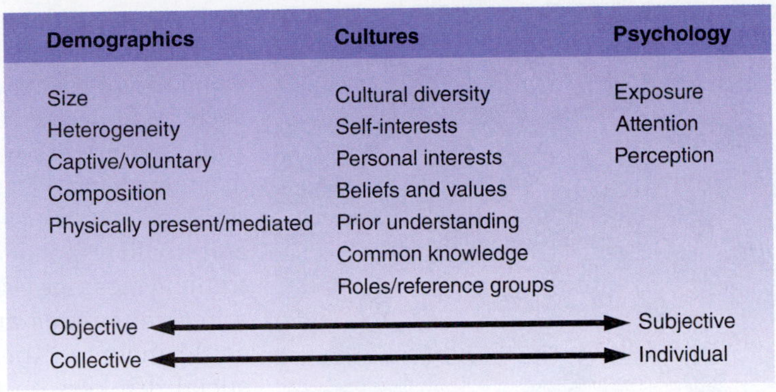

Demographics	Cultures	Psychology
Size	Cultural diversity	Exposure
Heterogeneity	Self-interests	Attention
Captive/voluntary	Personal interests	Perception
Composition	Beliefs and values	
Physically present/mediated	Prior understanding	
	Common knowledge	
	Roles/reference groups	

Objective ←——————→ Subjective
Collective ←——————→ Individual

Figure 5.1 Levels of audience analysis.

The relationships among audience demographics, cultures, and psychology are illustrated in Figure 5.1. After studying these three levels of audience analysis, we will examine strategies for learning about your specific audience and for assessing your own resources and *ethos* in relation to audience members.

Checking Audience Demographics

OBJECTIVE 5.2

Demographics refers to characteristics of the audience as a whole. The major demographic categories are the audience's size, heterogeneity, status as captive or voluntary, composition, and existence as physically present or mediated.

Size

How large is your audience? The more listeners there are, the greater your sense of distance from them, and, consequently, the more formal your presentation is likely to be. Someone speaking to a dozen people in a small room clearly faces a different situation than someone addressing a large lecture hall or a mass-media audience.

Classroom speakers probably have an audience of about 20 to 25 listeners, an audience size that is typical of many speeches to service clubs, neighborhood groups, and work-related organizations. This size lets you address a public without losing sight of individuals, and the setting is a middle ground between highly formal and extremely informal.

Heterogeneity

Heterogeneity refers to the variety or diversity of audience members—the degree of dissimilarity among them. The smaller the audience, the more likely that you will be able to notice similar assumptions, values, and ways of thinking among its members. Even a small audience may show marked differences in these criteria, but a large audience virtually ensures that members will have different values and assumptions as well as learning styles; such an audience is said to be *heterogeneous*.

heterogeneity
Variety or diversity among audience members; dissimilarity.

To hold the attention of his young audience, this speaker must relate his topic and ideas to their interests and experience.

The two students speaking about the dangers of drunk driving assumed that their audience of American college students would be like them, would learn about the subject in the same way, and would respond favorably to their message. However, a heterogeneous audience could include experienced social drinkers and stockholders of alcohol distributors who might oppose restrictions on drinking, as well as friends or relatives of alcoholics who might believe that restricting access is the best way to prevent alcohol abuse.

The more heterogeneous your audience, the more you need to find examples and appeals that will be meaningful to all kinds of listeners; or you might combine appeals that are relevant to different segments of the audience. Avoid materials that are significant only to some listeners but beside the point to others. The goal is to appeal meaningfully to a diverse audience without resorting to vague generalizations and **platitudes** (buzzwords or phrases that are devoid of specific content).

An audience can be heterogeneous even if its members share the same cultural background, but a culturally diverse audience is particularly likely to be heterogeneous. The audience for the speeches against drunk driving might include a student or two from countries where alcohol use is unrestricted or where few people drive, and they may not share their classmates' concerns about the safety risks of drunk driving.

Voluntary Versus Captive Audience

Under what circumstances has the audience assembled? In general, people who have chosen to hear a speech are more likely to be interested and receptive than are people who have been coerced into attending. A captive audience may resent having to hear the speech, and their resentment may undercut the speaker's *ethos* and message.

Students who are required to attend an assembly, employees whose jobs depend on participation in a seminar, and churchgoers who find themselves listening to a political message when they expected a sermon are examples of captive audiences. Speakers cannot assume that captive listeners have any interest in them or their subject, and they must work particularly hard to interest and motivate their listeners.

platitudes
Buzzwords or phrases that are devoid of specific content.

Some of your classmates may also be captive listeners, especially if the course is required or if individuals don't recognize the value of effective listening. With luck, you can turn them into voluntary listeners as they become interested in what you have to say and as they begin to see that they can improve their own speeches by listening carefully to yours.

If you assume that your audience is there voluntarily and you make no effort to motivate them, you could be setting yourself up for disaster. If you are wrong in your assessment and your listeners see themselves as captive, their feelings of boredom or hostility are likely to overwhelm any message you present. For this reason, when you don't know the status of the audience, it is best to assume that listeners are captive and that you need to motivate them.

Composition

Watch the Video "Informative Speech: Same Holidays, Different Customs" at **MyCommunicationLab**

Sometimes, if it will help you make choices about your speech, you can analyze the audience in terms of such demographic categories as age, gender, religion, ethnicity, educational level, or socioeconomic status. For example, it may be safe to assume that a young audience would be less interested in a speech about retirement planning than an older audience would be. Likewise, you might assume that listeners with a high level of formal education can think in figurative as well as literal terms and can deal with complex issues. And if an audience is made up mostly of members of a certain religious or ethnic group, you well may tailor your presentation to take advantage of their commonality by making brief reference to specific religious practices or by using phrases from another language that will be familiar to them.

These demographic categories may be useful in suggesting starting points for your speech. But giving too much weight to them may lead to false and unwarranted **stereotyping**—wrongly assuming that all members of a category are alike. For example, it is less true today than in the past that women and men differ in the likelihood of their being persuaded by a speaker. Nor do all people from rural areas think alike; and not everyone from a particular region has the same set of beliefs and values.[1] In short, demographic categories can provide important hints about an audience, but you should not assume that the hints apply to everyone.

Physically Present Versus Mediated Audience

Social media sites have become important means for public speaking. Although sites such as Facebook and Twitter offer a forum for expressing opinions, other sites such as YouTube and Vimeo cater more specifically to videos and are more likely to feature speeches. Such websites enable anyone to reach a potentially vast audience. It may be difficult, if not impossible, to analyze this audience with care, but you still can make informed choices about how to address it. Making your message stand out and easy to follow are still important guidelines, but remember that an Internet audience is likely to attend to your speech because of prior interest in your topic. They may care deeply about it, and this commitment means they are more likely to listen selectively to your speech and less likely to be open to different perspectives. Your message may be open to misinterpretation unless you are careful, clear, and precise. Think also about the *ethos* of the website to which you post, because that will affect judgments of your speech. What other videos are popular on the site, and what do viewers say about it? In sum, social media present you with additional opportunities but also with additional constraints.

stereotyping
Assuming that all members of a demographic category are alike in all respects.

Public figures often address both a physically present and a mediated audience. An example is first lady Hillary Rodham Clinton's 1995 address at the United Nations Conference on Women held in Beijing, China. Delegates at the conference were physically present but she was also indirectly speaking to the Chinese government, other nations, and women around the world. The combination of heterogeneous audiences made her choices about what to say especially important. (You can read this speech in the Appendix.)

Respecting Audience Cultures

As applied to audiences, the term *culture* has two different meanings. First, each individual listener represents one or (usually) more cultures—traditions that influence how people think, feel, believe, and act. Ethnic heritage, political orientation, and national identity are some components of culture in this sense. A heterogeneous audience is especially likely to be culturally diverse, but even an audience that is homogeneous on one factor may be quite diverse on others. For example, a campus audience might be alike in their devotion to the school, but highly diverse with respect to age, economic status, religion, and political ideology.

Second, if we can characterize a particular audience in terms of subjective factors, such as interests, beliefs and values, common knowledge and experience, and roles and reference groups, we can describe a distinct **audience culture**. This is likely to happen when the audience is relatively homogeneous. For example, because of his hobby of studying the stock market, Jon Koenig received several invitations to speak about investment strategies. In one week, he was asked to speak to a group of college seniors about to graduate, to a group of employed single women of various ages, and to a group of older workers interested in retirement planning. He tried to adapt his message to the culture represented by each of these different audiences, strategically planning his speech to increase his chances of success with each audience. To talk about audience culture this way is to recognize that an audience is more than the sum of its individual members. It will have certain norms and values as a result of common experiences, members' response to outside challenges, and their prior conversations and discussions.

audience culture
Subjective factors that characterize a particular audience and make its situation distinct.

Careful planning is needed for a speaker to be able to appeal to this culturally diverse audience made up of people with differing beliefs and value systems.

A thorough audience analysis considers audience culture in both of these senses. The following sections discuss how to recognize and respect the cultural diversity that characterizes many audiences today as well as several of the factors that can give an individual audience a distinct culture.

Cultural Diversity

Explore the **Exercise** "Culture" at **MyCommunicationLab**

The United States and many other nations are multicultural societies. Wherever you speak, it is important to remember that today's audience members represent a diversity of cultures and backgrounds. This is true of public speaking classes because schools, colleges, and universities have sought to attract international students and students from various racial and ethnic groups. It is also true of society at large, as racial and ethnic minority groups make up a growing proportion of the population.

Even within a single national, racial, or ethnic population, there are many types of diversity, including religious, gender, age, economic, and political diversity. Everyone, whether speaker or listener, must acknowledge and relate to people who reflect a wide variety of cultural backgrounds.

For example, conservative commentator David Horowitz discovered this basic truth during a speech at the University of Chicago. His topic—why financial reparations for descendants of slavery is a bad idea—was controversial and generated angry protests. One student stood with her back to Horowitz throughout the entire presentation of his speech. By calling reparations "racist" and arguing that no one group was responsible for slavery, Horowitz alienated his audience, which included African Americans. Arousing hostility in order to generate publicity may have been Horowitz's purpose in this specific case. Most speakers, however, prefer to obtain a hearing for their views. Controversial topics can and should be discussed in public, but they must be presented with clear acknowledgment of and sensitivity to cultural differences in order for the audience to receive the message.

Speaking to a multicultural audience challenges you to become aware of factors about the audience that you might take for granted, oversimplify, or mistakenly attribute to people universally. Here are a few of the most common examples.

Your Own Cultural Predispositions. People commonly assume that their own cultural values are universal ones although they generally are not. This is the extension of a tendency known as *egocentrism* to a cultural scale. Most people tend to pay attention to what is most interesting to them. Reflection and careful self-analysis can help you avoid seeing your own values as universal and thus seeming insensitive to cultural differences.[2]

For example, U.S. culture traditionally has valued youth, whereas Japanese culture has valued age. In speaking to an audience of both American and Japanese listeners, it would not be a good idea either to discredit something by labeling it "old" or to assume that our ancestors always understood things better than we do.

Gender Roles. Attitudes toward the role of women vary widely between more traditional and more modern cultures. Women's roles as professionals are not as widely recognized in some societies in the Middle East and Latin America as they are in the United States. So a speech about women in the business world might be planned and presented differently for an international audience composed mostly of men than for an audience of U.S. businesspeople.

However, even a speech on women in the business world to a group of women professionals needs to consider cultural diversity. Characterizing women professionals as engaged in "real" work as compared with stay-at-home mothers would most likely alienate many audience members, considering the number of women who work both inside and outside the home. A Democratic Party strategist suffered this problem when she suggested that Ann Romney, wife of the 2012 Republican presidential nominee and a stay-at-home mother, "had not worked a day in her life." The strategist forgot that cultural diversity is most likely present even in a seemingly homogeneous audience.

Who Can Speak. Cultures differ even with respect to who is eligible to speak in public. During the early 1800s, U.S. women often were not allowed to appear on a public platform because that would violate their "feminine" role. As recently as 1976, U.S. Representative Barbara Jordan, one of the most prominent African American politicians of the late twentieth century, began her keynote speech to the Democratic National Convention by observing:

> There is something different about tonight. There is something special about tonight. What is different? What is special? I, Barbara Jordan, am a keynote speaker.
>
> A lot of years passed since 1832, and during that time it would have been most unusual for any national political party to ask that a Barbara Jordan deliver a keynote address—but tonight here I am. And I feel that notwithstanding the past that my presence here is one additional bit of evidence that the American Dream need not forever be deferred.

Appropriate Language. Yet another example relates to people's attitudes about what is "correct" speech or language. Language is a tool for communication. You most likely do not want to use language that will alienate your audience and hinder the reception of your message. Generational differences sometimes can dictate the appropriateness of certain phrases or expressions. For example, slang such as "you guys" might be acceptable for an audience of your friends, but it is likely inappropriate for a group of older men and women. But cultural assumptions also can alienate people, as President George W. Bush discovered when he received much criticism for his use of the word *crusade* in a speech following the terrorist attacks of September 11, 2001. Although he may have meant a campaign to end global terrorism, his word choice suggested a Christian war against Muslims, which alienated American Muslims in his audience, among others.

Regional Differences. Culturally sensitive speech can also mean awareness of different ways of speaking. The United States includes many regional, ethnic, and social dialects. In some circumstances, these are perfectly acceptable ways of speaking; in others, listeners may regard them as substandard. If you plan to quote dialect in your speech, recognize that different language patterns are legitimate, and acknowledge the validity of "standard" patterns; yet do not disparage patterns different from your own.[3]

Regional differences in culture are also important. A student who grew up in the South and attends a university in the Northeast may not understand how classmates can survive winter. Likewise, those classmates may be surprised by this student's unhurried pace and "laid-back" lifestyle.

Strategies for Speaking to Diverse Audiences

Respecting Diversity Through Analyzing Your Audience

Audiences are never completely heterogeneous. Careful analysis will help you to identify how the audience is diverse. Then these strategies will help you to plan your speech with audience diversity in mind.

1. Avoid stereotyping by paying attention to cultural facts.
2. Employ examples from different cultures to appeal to your audience.
3. Consider the distinctive culture of a particular audience, the ways they are bound together by common identities or social roles. For example, if you know that your listeners share a common value or belief, you might mention that value and indicate your agreement with it (so long as you do, in fact, agree).
4. Pay attention to the multiple cultures of audience members (age, class, gender, ethnicity, etc.) and how these heterogeneous identities can both enable and constrain your speech. For example, do not assume that because all the members of your audience are young, they are all environmentally conscious or socially active.
5. Consider using universal appeals that transcend cultures.

Negative Stereotypes. Many beliefs about other cultures are based on negative, unflattering stereotypes, and it is particularly important to avoid these when addressing a multicultural audience. Stay away from any such belief as that one culture is hardworking and another is lazy, or that one is educated and another is ignorant, or that one is compulsive and another is relaxed. The reality is far more complex, and such simple-minded attitudes will rightly both insult and antagonize an audience.

Speakers adapt to a culturally diverse audience in three basic ways:

- Draw examples from many cultures so that all listeners feel that they are being addressed within the framework of their own culture. Even if some cultures are not mentioned specifically, your acknowledgment of diversity may make everyone feel more included.[4] This approach, of course, requires you to know which particular cultures are represented by audience members.
- Emphasize your own cultural heritage in a way that makes others feel that their distinctiveness is valued as well. For example, during the 2008 presidential campaign, Mitt Romney made frequent references to his Mormon faith and religious practices. He did so not only to appeal to the moral character of faith, but also to make the larger point that U.S. politics welcomes diversity, a point that encouraged members of other ethnic or religious minorities. (When he ran again in 2012, in a different political environment, Romney de-emphasized these references because he did not want to draw attention to his particular religious beliefs.)
- Resist culture-specific references altogether and search instead for appeals that transcend cultures. An appeal based on preserving the planet for the next generation, an appeal to the common interest in peace, or an appeal based on the beauty and wonder of nature may well transcend the limits of any particular culture.[5]

In the multimedia presentation *An Inconvenient Truth*, for example, former Vice President Al Gore says:

> You see that pale, blue dot? That's us. Everything that has ever happened in all of human history, has happened on that pixel. All the triumphs and all the tragedies, all the wars, all the famines, all the major advances…it's our only home. And that is what is at stake, our ability to live on planet Earth, to have a future as a civilization. I believe this is a moral issue. It is your time to seize this issue. It is our time to rise again to secure our future.

Self-Interest

Listeners have **self-interests**; they stand to gain or lose personally depending on what is done. For example, a proposal to raise students' tuition and fees would not be in the self-interest of those who are working their way through college, whereas a proposal to increase funds for financial aid *would* appeal to the self-interest of those same students. Or a speech that advocates limits on listeners' freedom or power or that casts them in an unflattering role also will be at odds with the audience's self-interest.

Watch the **Video** "The Process of Developing a Speech: Calling an Audience to Action" at **MyCommunicationLab**

Most listeners resist messages that clearly challenge their self-interest. If you feel that it is necessary to challenge your audience's self-interest, consider whether you can develop your message in a nonthreatening way while still being true to your beliefs. Perhaps you can plan the speech with a strong combination of appeals so that listeners will look beyond their self-interest to consider a broader concept of what is good.

As the United States began to recover from an economic recession in 2011 and 2012, for example, public attention was drawn to the growing inequality of income between the wealthy and the middle class. Many Americans were outraged at the large salaries and bonuses paid to the top executives of major companies. Although accepting this compensation was in their self-interest, several executives were persuaded that larger principles of equity and fairness were at stake. Those who were so persuaded urged that taxes be increased on the wealthy, even though this move would hurt their self-interest.

One common strategy for challenging listeners' self-interest is to suggest that their short-term sacrifices will bring long-term benefits (and so their self-interest will be satisfied in the long run). Business executives unaffected by appeals to equity and fairness might nevertheless decide to forego their short-term self-interest in being well paid, in order to avoid hostile public reaction or government regulation, which might be even more damaging to their self-interest in the long run. One student took a similar approach in arguing that course work should be more difficult. She began by admitting outright that her speech would challenge the audience's self-interest:

> Talk to any student at this college and you'll hear about how busy they are, how much work they have to do, how much time their classes take. I'm sure it's true, because many of us have never really been challenged to work hard before this. The last thing most students want is to hear someone say that classes should be made even harder. But if we can improve the academic reputation of this college, not only will it attract better students, but in the long run our own degrees will be more highly valued.

self-interests
Personal gain or loss resulting from an action or policy.

personal interests
What an individual regards as interesting or important.

Personal Interests

Listeners also have **personal interests**, and so you need to assess how likely it is that your topic will interest others. For example, you may be an avid student of military history, but you cannot assume that others will be captivated by a speech about battle planning. And although you may be thrilled by the details of auto mechanics, realize that many listeners only want to know how to start the car.

Sometimes listeners have strong passions and commitments about a topic. The successful speaker will meet audience members where they are, acknowledging and speaking about their convictions.

If you think that listeners will be strongly interested in your topic, a straightforward presentation may be fine. But if interest may be low, you should deliberately plan the speech in a way that captures the audience's attention and holds their interest. Startling statements, rhetorical questions, personal anecdotes, and narratives are especially good ways to involve listeners in your topic. And usually you should avoid technical language, jargon, and abstractions unless you know that the audience is familiar with the topic.

Sometimes listeners have a casual interest in your topic but do not regard it as important or of high priority. Then your task is less one of arousing initial interest and more a matter of impressing the audience with the urgency or significance of your message. By analyzing the audience's level of interest in your topic, you are better able to determine how to frame the speech.

Beliefs and Values

Beliefs are statements that listeners regard as true; **values** are positive or negative judgments that listeners make. For example, a listener might believe that homelessness is a serious problem (belief) and might also regard government aid for the homeless as a good thing (giving it a positive value). Another listener might agree that homelessness is a serious problem (belief) yet might object to government aid (giving it a negative value). Still another listener might not believe that homelessness is a serious problem and might think that its scope has been exaggerated. For the last listener, government aid is not an issue because no problem has been acknowledged.

As these examples show, an audience's beliefs and values are starting points for crafting the strategy of your speech. You will want to uphold your own beliefs and values, of course, but you can do that and also advance your purpose if you emphasize the connections between listeners' beliefs and values and your own.

Assume that you wish to advocate increased government aid for the homeless. For the first listener, your strategy might be designed to reinforce existing beliefs and values. For the second listener, you might briefly review the extent of the problem, but most of the speech would be designed to convince the listener that government aid works better than private solutions alone; your goal would be to

beliefs
Statements that listeners regard as true.

values
Positive or negative judgments that listeners apply to a person, place, object, event, or idea.

change the listener's value about government aid from negative to positive. For the third listener, it is pointless to consider whether public or private solutions are better unless you can demonstrate that homelessness really is a problem. In this case, much of your speech would be designed to illustrate the extent and severity of homelessness and the urgent need for action. Finally, if all three listeners are in your audience, your strategy should combine appeals in the hope that one thing or another would convince each listener.

Listeners also hold many general beliefs and values about a host of topics—about human nature, about their responsibilities to others, about the status of their nation in the world, about the significance of science or religion, and so on. For example, if an audience believes that things generally are better (or worse) today than in the past, speakers in a political campaign might exploit that belief by claiming that their party (or the opposing party) is responsible for the situation.

Prior Understanding

How much do your listeners already know about your topic? Have they heard about any of your points before? Do they have enough background information to follow your reasoning? Answers to questions like these can help you design a powerful speech without boring or confusing your audience.

Speakers sometimes mistake intelligence for knowledge, thus overestimating what the audience knows. Fearful of being **condescending** to listeners—of talking down to them and assuming that they can't think for themselves—some speakers cover complex material too quickly, omit important steps in an explanation, or relate events out of sequence. Another danger of poor audience analysis is telling listeners nothing that they don't already know. If the listeners believe a speaker is wasting their time and saying nothing new, they are less likely to pay attention. Worse, they may become angry or resent the speaker. You can avoid all these dangers by analyzing what the audience already knows.

President Ronald Reagan was dubbed "The Great Communicator" in part because he could render complex subjects in simple, understandable terms. In a 1983 speech seeking support for his Strategic Defense Initiative, he used simple terms to describe sophisticated military and strategic concepts, and he also overcame complex arguments about defense spending:

> But first, let me say what the defense debate is not about. It is not about spending arithmetic. I know that in the last few weeks you've been bombarded with numbers and percentages.... The trouble with all these numbers is that they tell us little about the kind of defense program America needs or the benefits and security and freedom that our defense effort buys for us.

In simple language, President Reagan then explained the importance of a defensive missile system:

> Wouldn't it be better to save lives than avenge them?

He admitted but downplayed the difficulties of developing this new system and called on the scientific community,

> those who gave us nuclear weapons, to turn their great talents now to the cause of mankind and world peace, to give us the means of rendering these nuclear weapons impotent and obsolete.

condescending
Talking down to an audience; assuming that listeners are not capable of thinking about a subject and reaching their own conclusions.

If President Reagan had focused only on technical and scientific issues in the belief that "everyone understood" the difference between offensive and defensive systems, his speech would have been far less effective.

Common Knowledge and Experience

What **cultural facts** in your listeners' general store of knowledge will be relevant to your speech? Surveys frequently report that embarrassing percentages of Americans cannot name their senator or representative, do not know when the Civil War was fought, or cannot locate a particular country on the globe. Such evidence does not prove that people are stupid. Rather, in recent years educators have been less concerned with teaching facts than with teaching students how to find information.[6] Thus, for a general audience, you may need to identify or explain cultural facts that are important to your argument. But if your audience is specialized—say a group of Civil War buffs—you can assume that listeners are familiar with basic information about your topic.

Speakers often make **allusions,** or brief references, to things that they assume listeners know about and understand. But if listeners don't "get" the allusion, they also will miss the point of the comparison. So you need to have a good sense of which allusions your audience will recognize. Well into the twentieth century, speakers could assume that most listeners were familiar with the Bible and with classic literature. Late in the century, however, popular culture—especially television—became the source of many allusions, especially in the United States. For example, during the fall of 1998, when President Clinton ordered the bombing of Iraq as Congress prepared to vote on his impeachment, his action was described as a "wag the dog" scenario—referring to a popular film in which a president creates a foreign crisis to divert attention from his domestic troubles.

Similarly, in a classroom speech about sexual harassment, one student alluded to an episode of the popular television show *The Office:*

> Sexual harassment first received prime-time coverage during the confirmation hearings for Supreme Court Justice Clarence Thomas in 1991, but we should not delude ourselves into thinking that a topic that garnered consistent attention two decades ago has now disappeared from our classrooms and workplaces. The reason Michael Scott's never-ending stream of sexist, homophobic, and generally inappropriate comments are so absurdly funny on TV is that they are rooted in the not-so-funny behavior and language that remain the norm for too many students and employees.

By analyzing and understanding his audience's shared cultural experiences, this student was able to allude to a character on *The Office* to build a strong introduction that captured interest and prepared listeners for his main point.

Roles and Reference Groups

Each listener occupies a variety of **roles**, or socially assigned positions, and these are an important part of an audience's culture. Consider, for example, an audience made up of Girl Scouts. A listener who is a Girl Scout is also a young woman, a student, and a daughter; and she may be a member of a church, the Honor Society, and the dance club. Depending on which role is dominant for her at any given

cultural facts
Facts that are commonly known among the members of a culture; common knowledge.

allusions
Brief references to something with which the audience is assumed to be familiar.

roles
Socially assigned positions, such as "parent," "student," "employee," and "citizen."

time, different topics and appeals are likely to be effective. If, while listening to a speech, she thinks of herself mainly as a Girl Scout, she may be more interested in physical adventure or social service than she would be if she thought of herself mainly as a dancer. In analyzing your audience, you need to decide which roles are most important to listeners while you speak.

Listeners also identify with many **reference groups**, whether or not they actually belong to them. Reference groups are also socially constructed categories. Because they serve as guides or models for behavior, they can influence listeners' beliefs, values, and actions. For example, a student may model his taste in clothes or hairstyle on the members of a popular band; he isn't a member of this band, but he likes people to think of him as sharing its characteristics. Another student may take cues about the importance of good study habits from older friends in her residence hall; they are a reference group for her because she likes to be thought of in reference to them. In other situations, however, each of these students will model different reference groups—family, friends, peers, public figures, and ethnic groups, for instance. By knowing which reference groups and values are important to your listeners, you can strategically plan effective appeals and supporting materials.

Understanding Audience Psychology

The final set of audience characteristics relates to psychology and the ways people understand and respond to the messages they hear.

reference groups
Groups with which listeners identify, regardless of whether they belong to them. Reference groups serve as guides or models for behavior.

Selective Exposure and Selective Attention

Each day, an infinite number of potential communication stimuli are available to us. We can converse with anyone we meet and can overhear the conversations of others; we can call, text message, or write to each other; we can read newspapers, magazines, and books; we can listen to the radio or watch television; we can see films or videos; we can attend speeches, listen to podcasts of lectures, hear sermons, or join group discussions. And while we're busy doing all this, we can connect to the Internet or use Facebook and Twitter to exchange messages and gather information.

Responding to audience psychology, this speaker tries to calm a hastily assembled and anxious audience in the wake of an emergency.

Even if we did nothing else except engage in communication, there is clearly too much for any of us to do. How do we choose which speeches to hear, which magazines to read, which television programs to watch, and which websites to visit? In short, how do we select the communications to which we will expose ourselves?

Selective exposure is the concept that our communication choices are not random; rather, we are inclined to expose ourselves to messages that are important to us personally and that are consistent with what we already believe. Few of us seek out messages that we do not think will be useful or pertinent to us; nor do we listen to speeches other than entertainment speeches merely for the pleasure of hearing them. And very few of us relish an attack on what we believe. Instead, we read magazines, listen to speakers, and choose friends whose views are similar to our own.

Although selective exposure governs which messages we will seek out, sometimes audience members are not given a choice. Your classmates, for instance, are captive listeners who do not have the option of not hearing you, even if they disagree with you. But both captive and voluntary audiences can exercise a second level of control over potential communications. They are selective about whether to focus intently on a message, to follow it, to absorb it, and to take it seriously. These choices, sometimes made unconsciously, are called **selective attention**.

As we discussed in Chapter 4, it takes effort and energy to listen carefully and critically to a speech. Listeners' minds tend to wander—to events of the day, people they want to see, things they need to do, problems they hope to solve. Making the effort to listen requires motivation, and the speaker can help to supply that for the audience.

Student speaker Scott Poggi overlooked this opportunity to motivate the audience when he decided to develop a speech based on his own special interests. On weekends, Scott worked as a stagehand for a production company, and his speech demonstrated his expertise in the subject. He told his classmates all about the backstage area, introducing them to the light designer, the head light technician, and the light crew; mentioning the "FOH" (footlights and overheads), the electrics, and the cyclorama; telling them about the necessity of "testing and gelling the lights"; introducing them to the sound crew and their equipment; and finally describing the stage manager's many duties. By the time Scott finished, many in the audience were half asleep. Not only did he provide too much technical information without explaining it (classmates still had to ask, "What is an 'FOH,' and how do you 'gel' a light?"), but he also never gave the audience any reason for wanting to know this information in the first place. By *assuming* that his listeners wanted to know all of these technical terms, he misunderstood the psychology of his audience. Better audience analysis might have shown Scott that he would have to motivate listeners to help them pay attention.

The speaker can motivate the audience in at least three ways:

1. Make the message personally important to listeners.
2. Make the message stand out.
3. Make the message easy to follow.

selective exposure
A tendency to expose oneself to messages that are important personally and that are consistent with what one already believes.

selective attention
Conscious or unconscious choice about whether or not to focus intently on a speech, absorb and process its contents, and take it seriously.

Make the Message Personally Important to Listeners.

Listeners are better motivated to pay attention if the speech is personally meaningful and important to them, affects them, offers new information and insights they haven't considered, solves puzzles or paradoxes, or tells a story or makes a comparison with something they already know. When you plan the strategy for your speech, focus on making it clear how your message relates to audience members personally. In effect, you are saying, "This concerns you. Sit up and take notice."

To apply these general principles, you might introduce your speech with an example that listeners will recognize or a story that describes an experience they might have had. Or you might translate statistics or abstract ideas into personal terms, as in the statement, "The percentage of people wrongly sentenced to death is so large that if all of us in this room were facing capital punishment, half of us would be taken off death row upon appeal." You might even announce explicitly that listeners will benefit from your speech: "I'm going to tell you how you can get better grades in every course."

Watch the **Video** "The Process of Developing a Speech: Audience Analysis" at **MyCommunicationLab**

Make the Message Stand Out.

The message may stand out because of a contrast between what the speaker is expected to say and what he or she actually says. Listeners will take notice if a student suggests that professors do not assign enough work, if an athlete maintains that physical fitness is unimportant, or if a known advocate of gender equality speaks in favor of some gender-based distinctions. Alternatively, the contrast might be between the speaker and other elements in the situation. If you were the fifth speaker after four classmates had all discussed similar topics in the same way, you might deliberately modify your speech to do something different. Or the contrast might be within the speech itself, such as changes in pitch, volume, or rate of delivery.

A word of caution: Any contrast effect you use should be closely related to the purpose of your speech; contrast for its own sake draws attention to itself and distracts from the message. Avoid attention-getting gimmicks, whether in the introduction or anywhere else in the speech. Even if you succeed in getting attention, the audience will remember the trick, not your message.

Make the Message Easy to Follow.

Paying careful attention is work for listeners. The more you do to minimize their task and to motivate them to make the effort, the more likely it is that they will be attentive.[7]

Speakers can do several things to make their message easier to follow:

- Strategically plan the organization of the speech in a way that makes your thesis and overall argument clear to listeners.
- State your main ideas explicitly so that listeners can easily identify them.
- Speak at a rate that sustains listeners' interest but is not so rapid that they have to struggle to keep up with you.
- Repeat your main ideas and key points, signaling to the audience that these are important.
- Use pauses to mark the transitions in the speech.
- Summarize your thesis and main ideas memorably.

Perception

perception
The interpretation or understanding given to a speech; the meaning it has for a listener.

An audience is asked not only to listen carefully to a speech but also to *interpret* it as the speaker intends. **Perception** is the particular interpretation or understanding that a listener gets from a speech. When listeners decide what a speech "means," they are perceiving it in a particular way. Unfortunately, a speaker cannot ensure that the audience perceives the meaning of the speech in the same way that the speaker does. Even individual ideas may be interpreted differently by speaker and audience.

Any message is open to different interpretations and can result in different perceptions. Suppose, for example, that early in an election year, the current president predicts economic growth over the next several months. Should you interpret that message as economic forecasting, or as a political appeal designed to win votes, or as wishful thinking by a candidate who does not really understand the economy? Or is it all of these?

Recall that perception, like attention, is selective; we interpret messages in ways that render them simple, stable, and consistent with our expectations. Complex or conflicting messages are simplified; qualifying statements and subtle distinctions may be lost. The following examples of how people perceive messages selectively are generalizations and obviously do not apply in every case. But they are based on research, and they can help you plan your speech. If applied *too* rigidly, however, they can result in stereotyping, which speakers should always avoid.

1. People tend to view their experiences as structured, stable, and meaningful rather than random, chaotic, or pointless. Seeking order, listeners are predisposed to accept patterns that the speaker can offer to explain seemingly unconnected facts.
2. People tend to view events not as accidental, but as having causes; they also tend to simplify the web of causal connections and sometimes even seek a single cause to explain complex effects.
3. People tend to view individuals as being responsible for their own actions and to assume that actions reflect a person's intentions.

CHOOSE A STRATEGY: Adapting to Your Audience

The Situation

Over the last few months, your town has seen a rise in accidents related to underage drinking. Your local government is starting a campaign to crack down on underage drinking. You have decided that you want to support this cause and volunteer your time. Your first job is to speak to a group of students at the local college about this community problem.

Making Choices

1. What assumptions do you make if you cannot formally poll your audience?
2. How else might you determine your audience's likely reaction to your message?
3. If you find that some of your audience members are hostile to your message, what strategies can you utilize to reduce the hostility of your audience and to gain their support and acceptance?

What If ...

How would your choice of strategies vary if you were speaking to the following audiences?

1. The local campus administration
2. The general audience at the next town meeting
3. The families of students who have been involved in drinking-related accidents
4. The high school PTA

4. People tend to view others as being basically like themselves. When a speaker discusses personal experiences, listeners often assume that the speaker thought and acted just as they would have in the same circumstances. And if the audience is heterogeneous, different kinds of listeners may perceive the speaker differently.
5. People tend to interpret things in the way that their reference groups do. The desire to fit in and to be accepted by important peers may cause some people to accept the group's perception as their own—without even being aware that they are doing it.
6. People tend to perceive messages within the framework of familiar categories, even at the risk of distorting the message. For example, if someone believes that athletes generally are weak students and that strong students do not respect athletic ability, that person is likely to perceive a strong student's speech praising the values of athletics as ironic or insincere.

Although the tendency of listeners to perceive selectively can distort the speaker's message, knowing about selective perception can help the speaker to plan the speech so that it will be interpreted as desired. Selective exposure, attention, and perception are characteristic of almost all listeners. Whenever you plan a speech, design strategies to overcome these tendencies.

Strategies for Analyzing the Audience

Knowing that audience analysis is so important to your success as a speaker, how do you go about it? Various methods are available, ranging from the highly formal to the frankly speculative.

Formal Methods

Companies developing a new product typically engage in market research. They conduct surveys to learn the needs and desires of consumers (their "audience"); they ask the target group to select adjectives to describe a concept or product; they may convene small discussion groups (focus groups) to probe people's feelings about a product. In principle, methods like these are available to speakers, too, and such formal analysis often is used in large-scale efforts such as a political campaign. Focus groups might also be used in a public speaking class if several speeches were going to address the same subject. But for most speeches this approach is impractical. You will have neither the time nor the resources to conduct formal surveys or in-depth interviews of classmates in preparation for a speech. Instead, a general audience survey like the one in Figure 5.2 can be invaluable. Your instructor might ask the class to complete such a survey early in the term and then might make the results available to everyone.

Informal Methods

Even if you can't conduct a formal audience survey, you still can learn quite a bit about your listeners. Here are some ideas:

Audience Survey

Age ______________ Gender ____________ Year of graduation ____________

Home town ____

High school attended: Public Private

Parents' occupation(s) ____

Taking course as: Requirement Elective

Politically, I would describe myself as:

strongly conservative	moderately conservative	middle of the road	moderately liberal	strongly liberal

In general, where do you fall along the following scale:

____

Prefer the familiar Prefer the new

What three adjectives most accurately describe you?

____

What three adjectives would you most like to describe you?

____

I regard college primarily as a time for:

____

What are the three most pressing problems confronting you in the next five years?

____

What are the three most pressing problems confronting the country or the world in the next five years?

____

[NOTE: The survey might well contain additional questions.]

Figure 5.2 Audience survey.

1. If your classmates gave introductory speeches, think back to what they said about themselves. They may have given you clues about their interests, their political leanings, their attitudes toward higher education, their family backgrounds, and other key aspects of audience culture.
2. In preparing to speak to an unfamiliar audience, ask the host or moderator some questions ahead of time. You may be able to find out which topics most interest audience members, who else was invited to speak to them recently, how attentive they are, and perhaps what their motives are for coming together to hear you.
3. If you know the demographic composition of your audience—its size, its average age, and the occupation of most members, for instance—interview people who represent this mix of variables. Although talking with just a few people is not a scientific sample, you may still get clues about the interests, beliefs, and values of the kind of people who will be in your audience.
4. If you know other speakers who have addressed an audience like the one you will face, talk with them ahead of time to learn what they encountered and what they think your audience will be like.

5. If you know which newspapers or magazines your listeners are likely to read, examine some recent copies before you speak. Besides getting a sense of what interests your listeners, you may locate allusions that will be especially meaningful to them.
6. Sometimes library or online research can help you analyze an audience. In Chapter 7, you will learn how to investigate your topic, and the same methods can help you investigate your audience. For example, you can find recent periodicals with surveys about the political attitudes of college students, or polls showing how older Americans feel about health care, or articles about how gender differences influence how people think or feel.
7. Don't overlook the most obvious method of audience analysis: direct observation. As your listeners assemble, size them up. About how many people are there? Are they all about the same age? What is the ratio of men to women? How are they dressed? Are they interacting or sitting apart? Do they seem enthusiastic? Such questions cannot give you perfect information about the audience, because they are superficial first impressions, but they often provide valuable insights that allow you to adapt your message appropriately and effectively.

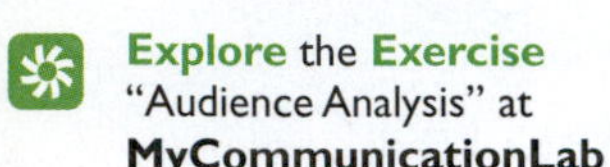
Explore the **Exercise** "Audience Analysis" at **MyCommunicationLab**

Simplifying Devices

Although it seems desirable to get all the information you can about an audience, having *complete* knowledge is impossible. After all, audiences are often composed of people who are strangers both to each other and to the speaker. Their common interest in the speech may be all that brought them together, and the speaker often does not know the specific audience members.

In these respects, speaking in the classroom is atypical. You and your classmates get to know quite a bit about each other by giving and hearing multiple speeches. You may even have conducted formal audience analysis through a survey like the one in Figure 5.2. Given this depth of information, it is not very difficult to craft speeches that recognize the audience's position. Outside the classroom, however, detailed audience analysis is much more difficult, and many speakers employ simplifying devices to make the task easier.

Focus on the General Public. For example, you might imagine your specific audience as the **general public**—listeners who share the characteristics of people in general, such as common sense, self-interest, sensitivity to others, and enthusiasm for a good story. The general public might be imagined as the readership of *Time* or some other mass-circulation magazine. In addition, this audience can be assumed to share whatever specific concerns or beliefs are reported in recent surveys of the population.

Focus on Audience Roles or Topic Fields. Another way to simplify audience analysis is to focus on the particular roles that you think your listeners play or on a particular field in which to place your topic. As we have seen, everyone occupies many different roles in society. A person may simultaneously be a parent, child, sibling, student, classmate, employee, coworker, manager, and so on. Each role may involve basic values and beliefs that are not as relevant to the other roles the person occupies. For instance, the standard of efficient

general public
Listeners who share the characteristics of people in general.

Rhetorical Workout

Learn About Your Listeners

You have been asked by the head of the non-profit organization where you volunteer once a week to give a presentation to several people who want to start their own non-profit organization on how to use the Internet for publicity. Before you prepare your speech, you want to understand more about your audience in order to decide what to cover.

1. What clues about your listeners have you been given so far, in the above description?
2. The head of your non-profit will be hosting the presentation. What are some questions you could ask her ahead of time that would help you prepare?
3. Which of the following audience demographics, if known, might affect how you approach your speech topic: audience size, diversity of views, age, gender, religion, ethnicity, native language, educational level, socioeconomic status? Choose one you think is important and explain how it could affect your speech.
4. You know a person who has spoken to a different group of people interested in non-profits on a different topic. What are some questions you could ask him that would help you?
5. You learn that all those who will be present receive a monthly newsletter via e-mail, and you are able to find the back issues online. How might this information help you analyze your listeners?
6. You do some research to learn more about people interested in starting a non-profit. How useful would each of the following be for you: (1) a national statistic that 75 percent of people who wish to start a non-profit have no experience with Internet publicity; (2) an article profiling people wishing to start non-profits in another state who have limited budgets for promotional activities; (3) the history of your own non-profit; (4) a list of people interested in starting non-profits and the businesses in which they previously have worked? Explain why.
7. If you prepared for an audience of 10 people and 30 show up, what are some ways you might have to adapt for this? If you assumed that your audience would be eager to learn how to create Internet publicity but observe that a few people seem skeptical of its value, how might you adapt for this?

communication that a woman uses at work is not the same standard that she uses as a wife or mother at home.

Similarly, we may think of speech topics as representing different **fields**, or subject-matter areas, with different norms and assumptions. For example, most of us regard religion, politics, science, and art as distinct fields. We would not expect an audience to listen to a political speech with the same standards in mind that they would use in assessing a religious discourse. Nor would we expect science and art to evoke the same standards of quality.

In using roles or fields to simplify audience analysis, you should emphasize the particular role or field that seems most relevant to your speech. When addressing an audience at your church, for example, focus on members' moral and religious commitments. When speaking at a rally for student government candidates, focus on the common field of campus politics. And when giving a speech to the local Parents and Teachers Association, focus on listeners' common concerns for children rather than on their highly diverse concerns as employees and taxpayers, men and women, and people of different ages.

In using simplifying devices to analyze an audience, keep in mind that generalizations often lead to stereotyping. Whether your assumptions about listeners' shared characteristics are true or not, you also want to show sensitivity to the many differences among audience members.

fields
Subject-matter areas with distinct norms or assumptions.

A Question of Ethics

Limits of Audience Analysis

Audience analysis tells us about the composition, beliefs, and values of the audience, and you are most likely to be successful as a speaker if you develop your message and appeal accordingly. However, a speech should be an expression of *your own* values and beliefs. What if the two are in conflict? Is it ethical, for the sake of gaining the audience's approval, for you to espouse a position that you do not personally believe or to urge an action that you personally would not take? Yet is it ethical to ignore the results of your audience analysis and express yourself regardless of whether anyone else would take your message seriously? What kind of equilibrium would you strike between these two different ethical positions?

universal audience
An imaginary audience made up of all reasonable people.

pandering
Saying whatever will please an audience even if it is not what the speaker really believes.

CHECKLIST 5.1

Strategies for Audience Analysis

1. **Formal methods:** Do you have time and opportunity to use a general audience survey?
2. **Informal methods:**
   - ❐ Has your audience previously given you information about themselves?
   - ❐ Is there a host or previous speaker you can ask about the audience?
   - ❐ Do you know any demographic information about your audience?
   - ❐ Do you know what kinds of publications your audience reads?
   - ❐ Can you find information about your audience in the library or online?
3. **Simplifying devices:** Focus on the general public, audience roles, or topic fields.
4. **Critical appraisal:**
   - ❐ How reliable is your audience information?
   - ❐ Can you craft your speech to fit the audience broadly?
   - ❐ Are you jumping to any conclusions about your audience?
   - ❐ How much can you adapt to your audience without sacrificing your beliefs and values?

Critical Appraisal

Much of the information you have gained from these methods of audience analysis is inexact, even though you have done your best. For this reason, you need to think critically about what you have learned. Ask yourself:

- How reliable, precise, and authoritative is my information about the audience? If the information seems questionable, how might I compensate for errors?
- Can I craft the speech so that it will be appropriate for listeners who are knowledgeable about the topic—and yet can be modified easily if listeners know less than I thought?
- Is my information about the audience really based on analysis, or might I be jumping to conclusions or relying on stereotypes?
- How much can I adapt to my audience without sacrificing my own beliefs and values?

One way to avoid jumping to conclusions is to view your listeners as representative of the **universal audience**—an imaginary audience made up of all reasonable people. No such audience exists, of course. The speaker constructs this image of an audience that accepts only those beliefs and values that no reasonable person would doubt.[8] Precisely because people are different, this is such a rigorous test that it could probably never be achieved. Yet it provides a norm or standard against which to assess your speech. It should prevent you from simply appealing to what you think are the audience's prejudices or indulging in false stereotypes.

You also want to guard against **pandering** to the supposed beliefs of your listeners and losing track of your own. One test is to ask whether your basic message to an audience that disagrees with some of your beliefs is consistent with what you might say to people who believe exactly as you do. Obviously, there will be *some* differences, because audiences are different, but the messages should not be contradictory. A speaker who is thought to be willing to say anything just in order to please an audience is not likely to be believed. Even Abraham Lincoln was accused of pandering to his audiences, speaking differently to committed antislavery listeners in northern Illinois than to more moderate audiences in the southern part of the state. Although there were obvious differences in tone and emphasis, Lincoln insisted that his basic message was the same. You should be able to reach the same conclusion about your speech.

Thinking critically about your audience analysis will also promote your strategic planning. It will help you determine what is useful to your speech and what questions remain unanswered. Although your knowledge of the audience will never be complete, critical thinking will help you decide whether you can afford to take chances and make guesses about the audience. And in planning strategies for presenting the speech, critical thinking will show you where you need to be especially sensitive to audience reactions.

You also have to be careful not to give *too* much weight to your audience analysis. The state of your audience before you speak may help to guide your speech preparation, but it is not an absolute constraint. This is because your speech may affect the audience's beliefs and values, as listeners are influenced by what you say. The audience analysis will not tell you what you definitely can and cannot say. Rather, it is a resource that will help you decide what to speak about, what to say, and how to construct your message. Audience analysis is more an art than a science; it offers a set of guidelines, not rules.

Analyzing Your Own *Ethos*

OBJECTIVE 5.4

In Chapter 2, we introduced the concept of *ethos*, the character that an audience attributes to a speaker. In thinking about your audience, you also want to think about how its members are likely to characterize you. Remembering what you know about the importance of *ethos*, you should want to have a realistic view of how audience members will regard you. Just like their demographics, cultures, and psychology, this factor will help you to plan your speech strategically.

Audience Perceptions of You

To begin with, you should determine similarities and differences between you and the audience with respect to demographics, cultures, and psychology. Are you older or younger than most of your listeners? Is your ethnic, cultural, or economic background different? Are your personal interests similar to theirs? Do you have different general orientations toward change? If listeners judge you to be very different from themselves, they may be less likely to respond positively to your message. You will want to plan the speech so that you either minimize perceptions of difference when that is appropriate or acknowledge and compensate for differences when that is desirable.

Knowing yourself and having thought about the similarities and differences between you and your listeners, consider how the audience members are likely to perceive you. Will they see you as knowledgeable and competent or as arrogant

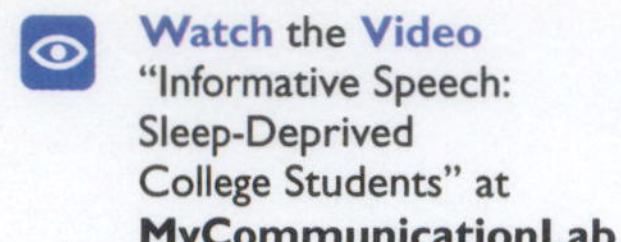
Watch the **Video** "Informative Speech: Sleep-Deprived College Students" at **MyCommunicationLab**

and condescending? In the first case, you can expect listeners to welcome your efforts to share information and ideas; in the second case, expect them to resent your seeming to tell them what to do.

Modifying Audience Perceptions

Thinking critically about yourself—and about how the audience is likely to perceive you—should point you to modifications that might improve your *ethos*. The goal is to remain true to yourself while also taking the audience's characteristics into consideration. Here are some strategies you can use.

1. Use wording that helps build a sense of community. Something as minor as "We all need to remind ourselves" may help connect you and your listeners better than using "I want to remind you," which can sound like you are emphasizing your superiority and their dependence. Attention to this aspect of *ethos* is especially important when your audience is culturally diverse. What seems like a straightforward presentation to listeners from a single cultural background may be seen as patronizing to listeners whose backgrounds are different.
2. Be careful not to assume that your own beliefs and values are universally correct and should be accepted by everyone. If audience members question or reject your values, they may also question or reject your message. For example, although *you* may believe that our society offers economic opportunities to all, listeners who have recently lost their jobs, are struggling to make ends meet, or are victims of discrimination will probably see things very differently. If you take your personal values for granted in this situation, your speech will fail. The audience will judge you as naive, if not misguided, and you will think they are ungrateful or unmotivated.
3. Consider whether you and your audience have different role models, different common knowledge, and different life-shaping experiences and how these differences may affect the way your audience perceives you. For example, are you addressing a rural audience although you have lived your entire life in cities? Or have you had a long period of unemployment while your listeners have been unaffected by a weak economy? Based on your audience analysis, determine whether to make any adjustments in how you present yourself. You can choose whether to establish eye contact, whether to smile or frown, whether to pause at the podium before returning to your seat, and so on. You can decide which supporting materials to use, how to organize them, and which words and gestures to convey. All these aspects of presentation are under your control, and you can use them to influence how the audience judges you.

You want listeners' assessments of your *ethos* to be positive, and not only because you like to have others think well of you. Your concern goes back to the belief, first articulated by Aristotle, that a speaker's apparent character may well be the most important resource to use in persuasion. How listeners perceive your *ethos* will affect what they think about your speech.

What Have You Learned?

Objective 5.1: Explain how the success of a speech depends on the audience.

The most important dimensions of audience analysis are

- Demographics
- Cultures
- Psychology

Objective 5.2: Describe how the audience demographics, cultures, and psychology affect listeners' receptiveness to a speech.

Demographic variables may correlate with how listeners think and act. These variables include:

- Size
- Heterogeneity
- Whether listeners are captive or voluntary
- Composition in terms of age, gender, occupation, religion, economic status, etc.
- Whether the audience is physically present or in a mediated setting

Cultural diversity characterizes many audiences today, and speakers need to be sensitive to how listeners from different cultures might regard a speech; this includes awareness of:

- The speaker's own predispositions
- Gender roles
- Who is permitted to speak
- Appropriate language
- Regional differences
- Negative stereotypes

Awareness of these factors will suggest strategies for adapting to a culturally diverse audience, such as:

- Deriving examples from many different cultures
- Emphasizing the speaker's own culture as an example of distinctiveness
- Resisting culture-specific references and searching for transcendent appeals

In addition to cultural diversity, audience cultures are characterized by their:

- Self-interest
- Personal interests
- Beliefs and values
- Prior understanding about the topic
- Common knowledge and experiences
- Roles and reference groups

Audience psychology is more subjective, involving listeners' tendencies toward:

- Selective exposure and attention
- Selective perception

In combating these psychological tendencies, speakers can try to:

- Make the message personally relevant and important to listeners.
- Make the message stand out.
- Make the message easy to follow.

Objective 5.3: Identify both formal and informal methods of audience analysis.

As important as audience analysis is, methods for doing it are imprecise, since the formal methods of large-scale campaigns are usually not feasible. Speakers therefore can:

- Use informal devices, such as reading what the audience reads, interviewing representative people, talking with other speakers about what to expect, and observing the audience as it assembles.
- Use simplifying devices, such as focusing on the audience as representatives of the general public or of specific roles and specialized fields.
- Think critically about their assumptions regarding the audience, and plan strategies that permit adjustments in the message.

Objective 5.4: Indicate how your *ethos* as a speaker influences the audience and how you can improve your *ethos.*

A final step in audience analysis is to examine realistically how the audience will perceive the speaker and then to take advantage of the speaker's opportunity to control many of the specific behaviors that affect audience judgments of *ethos*.

Listen to the **Audio Chapter Summary** at **MyCommunicationLab**

Discussion Questions

1. In preparing a speech about the dangers of smoking, how might your strategies differ for an audience of fourth-graders, an audience of college students, and an audience from a retirement community? Would you make different appeals to an audience of men and an audience of women? What changes would

you make in presenting this speech to an audience of Caucasians and to an audience of Mexican Americans? How might these modifications draw on stereotypes that could offend your listeners?

2. During the nineteenth century, our basic store of allusions came from the Bible and classical literature. From where does it come today? Does the difference really matter? Why or why not?
3. The Occupy Wall Street movement was the target of both strong support and criticism during 2011 and 2012. How did the larger public understand these protesters? To what extent did the Occupy Wall Street movement address a larger public successfully, and why does this matter? How might its message change depending on its audience? Does change in message present any ethical concern?
4. Identify some universal values that you could use in a speech to a diverse audience. Challenge your most fundamental beliefs as you and your classmates try to determine whether or not the values truly are universal.

Activities

1. In one page, explain how you would use the strategies of making the message personally important to listeners, making the message stand out, and making the message easy to follow to motivate your audience to pay attention to the message in your next speech. In what ways are you planning to appeal to the self-interest and personal interest of your audience?
2. Complete the audience survey in Figure 5.2, make copies of your answers for your classmates, and exchange them so that each person in the class has a booklet of questionnaire responses. Use this booklet to make a list of the commonalities and differences among audience members that you are likely to encounter when presenting a speech in this class.
3. As a follow-up to activity 2, compare your questionnaire answers to those of your classmates. In what ways are you similar to your audience members? In what ways are you different? How will this affect how your audience perceives you? After critically analyzing your own *ethos*, create a short speech designed to develop a positive *ethos* for you as a spokesperson for a particular topic.
4. Using more informal modes of audience analysis, answer the following questions
   a. What beliefs and values do your classmates hold regarding the topic you have chosen for your next speech?
   b. What do your classmates know about your topic?
   c. What common experiences do you and classmates share with regard to this topic?

   After answering these questions, write a short essay explaining the specific ways that you plan to use this information in developing strategies to maximize attention and to help the audience perceive your message in a way that advances your goal.
5. List the five most important values in your life. Share these with a classmate and discuss why you picked similarly or differently. Do each of you understand the same value to mean the same thing? Do you disagree with any of your classmate's values? Write a short essay describing your classmate's values and why they are important to him or her.
6. Identify several prominent public figures in entertainment, business, sports, politics, and the arts. For each figure, characterize the person's *ethos* and then identify the grounds on which you based your judgment.

Key Terms

allusions **105**
audience culture **98**
beliefs **103**
condescending **104**
cultural facts **105**
fields **113**
general public **112**
heterogeneity **95**
pandering **114**
perception **108**
personal interests **102**
platitudes **96**
reference groups **106**
roles **105**
selective attention **107**
selective exposure **107**
self-interests **102**
stereotyping **97**
universal audience **114**
values **103**

Study and **Review** the **Flashcards** at **MyCommunicationLab**

Notes

1 Joshua Meyrowitz makes the argument that traditional social differences between gender and age groups have been eroded in postmodern culture by the backstage information provided through television. See *No Sense of Place: The Impact of Electronic Media on Social Behavior*, Oxford, England: Oxford University Press, 1985.

2 Cultural differences may even influence expectations about the form and purpose of a speech. See Alessandro Duranti, "Oratory," *International Encyclopedia of Communications*, New York: Oxford University Press, 1989, vol. 3, pp. 234–36. Components of *ethos* are also understood differently in different cultures. See, for example, Masami Nishishiba and L. David Ritchie, "The Concept of Trustworthiness: A Cross-Cultural Comparison Between Japanese and U.S. Business People," *Journal of Applied Communication Research* 28 (November 2000): 347–67.

3 To get an idea of the different words and phrases used in regional dialects, see Eric Partridge, *A Dictionary of Slang and Unconventional English: Colloquialisms and Catch-Phrases, Solecisms and Catachreses, Nicknames, and Vulgarisms*, New York: Macmillan, 1984.

4 To gather examples that include the concerns of different cultural groups, you might want to examine speeches created by and directed toward members of those different cultural groups. One compilation of culturally diverse speeches is *Voices of Multicultural America: Notable Speeches Delivered by African, Asian, Hispanic, and Native Americans*, ed. Deborah G. Straub, New York: Gale Research, 1996.

5 Michael Osborn has written about how language is often used to appeal to universal themes. See "The Evolution of the Archetypal Sea in Rhetoric and Poetic," *Quarterly Journal of Speech* 63 (December 1977): 347–63. Todd Oakley offers an overview of recent discussions concerning how language is often used to appeal to universal themes. See "*The New Rhetoric* and the Construction of Value: Presence, the Universal Audience, and Beckett's 'Three Dialogues,'" *Rhetoric Society Quarterly* 27 (Winter 1997): 47–68.

6 See E. D. Hirsch, Jr., Joseph F. Kett, and James Trefil, *The New Dictionary of Cultural Literacy: What Every American Needs to Know*, 3rd ed., Boston: Houghton Mifflin, 2002.

7 Another list of guidelines for overcoming selective attention can be found in Howard W. Runkel, "How to Select Material That Will Hold Attention," *Communication Quarterly* 8 (September 1960): 13–14. Work also has been done on the importance of paying attention to visual cues. See Jan W. de Fockert, Geraint Rees, Christopher D. Frith, and Nilli Lavie, "The Role of Working Memory in Visual Selective Attention," *Science* 291 (March 2001): 1803–1806.

8 The concept of a universal audience is discussed in more detail by Chaim Perelman in *The Realm of Rhetoric*, translated by William Kluback, Notre Dame, IN: University of Notre Dame Press, 1982.

CHAPTER

6 Choosing a Topic and Developing a Strategy

LEARNING OBJECTIVES

After studying this chapter, you should be able to:

Objective 6.1	State when it is appropriate for you to choose the topic of your speech and when the choice is beyond your control.
Objective 6.2	Identify the characteristics of a good topic.
Objective 6.3	Proceed through the steps involved in choosing a good topic.
Objective 6.4	Define *strategic plan* and explain the steps for developing and implementing one.
Objective 6.5	Formulate statements of the specific purpose and thesis of your speech and illustrate how these statements will influence other strategic decisions.
Objective 6.6	Analyze your thesis statement to figure out which issues you need to discuss and which ideas need support.

Listen to the **Audio Chapter** at **MyCommunicationLab**

OUTLINE

OBJECTIVE 6.1

From your audience analysis, you know as much as you can about your listeners, and now you are ready to make the choices that will shape your speech. These choices involve *strategic* decisions; that is, decisions about what will best achieve your purpose. But first you need to know what your purpose is; and to decide that, you need to know what your **topic** is.

For many students, deciding what to talk about is the hardest part of a speech assignment. Fortunately, when you speak outside the classroom, elements in the situation will often make that decision for you. These elements may include:

- *Commitment to a cause.* Suppose, for example, that you are committed to a specific public issue, such as the fight against global warming. The issue itself defines your topic, and your personal commitment determines why it is important for you to speak.
- *Reputation.* Your experience and knowledge may lead to an invitation to speak about a specific topic. If you are an expert on Cascading Style Sheets (CSS), for example, a group of Web developers might invite you to speak at a meeting about new techniques for designing blogs. If you instead discussed U.S. foreign policy, or the pleasures of sailing, or the need for reform in the university, you would not be meeting your responsibility to the audience.
- *Occasion.* Many speeches are delivered on ceremonial occasions. If you are accepting an award, the award and what it represents will decide your topic. If you are delivering a eulogy, the achievements of the person who died become the subject of the speech. If you are roasting a coworker who is about to retire, your subject matter will be humorous traits or events involving that person.

Sometimes, a classroom-speaking assignment will specify the topic. More typically, in class the choice of topic will be left to you, with the understanding that you will address an audience of people your age, in your school. You probably will be more effective if you talk about something that interests you rather than an assigned topic that has been chosen by someone else.[1] In the classroom, it is particularly important that you size up the situation and then stand up for what interests you, for what you believe, and can share with others.

Outside of class, the primary occasion when you will have freedom in choosing your topic occurs when the audience is interested in hearing *you*, almost regardless of what you have to say. Such an open-ended invitation may arise out of respect for your achievements, interest in your experiences, curiosity about your personality or general approach, or the desire to learn whatever is on your mind.

Watch the **Video** "Professor Randy Cox Discusses Tips for Choosing a Speech Topic" at **MyCommunicationLab**

In short, selecting a topic is a complex matter. Sometimes speakers analyze the audience and then select a topic that will attract listeners. Sometimes they pick a topic first because it is important to them, and then analyze the audience so that the speech can be adapted to listeners. And sometimes topics are thrust upon them by the situation, in which case they can decide how to mold the speech in the most appropriate way.

OBJECTIVE 6.2

What Makes a Good Topic?

topic
The subject area of the speech.

If the topic of your speech is dictated by the issue, occasion, or audience, it is easy to decide what will make a good topic: whatever is pertinent and appropriate to the situation. You talk about what you were asked to discuss or about what the

Table 6.1 Sample speech topics

Public issues	Personal Experience	Significance of an Occasion
Stem cell research	Lifeguarding	Commencement
Health care costs	Snowboarding	Death of friend
Video game violence	Sign language	Wedding
Northwest logging	Yoga	School election
Gay rights	Poetry writing	Presentation of award
Internet privacy rights	International travel	Office party
Affirmative action	Volunteering at a homeless shelter	
Nuclear proliferation	Digital filmmaking	
AIDS epidemic	Political campaigning	
Third-World debt	Hot-air ballooning	
Dependence on fossil fuels	Tutoring	
Terrorism		

issue or occasion seems to require. You are not completely captive to the situation, because how you shape your speech will influence listeners' perceptions of the situation. But at the most basic level, your understanding of the situation will govern what you need to talk about.

But what should you talk about if you have complete freedom to select the topic? Table 6.1 identifies some potential speech topics, and the following criteria will help you to decide whether the topic you have in mind is a good one. (As you read, you might want to apply these criteria to the topics listed in Table 6.1.)

Importance to the Speaker

A good topic is one that matters to you. If you do not care about the subject, it will be very hard to make it interesting or important to the audience. Consider how the following three students used their personal interests to develop good speech topics:

- Melanie Nehrkorn listened to several of her friends complain that during city housing inspections, their landlord had to hide the fact that they lived off campus because a city ordinance limited the number of unrelated people who could share an apartment. Fearing that this might happen to her and others, Melanie used her public speaking opportunity to explain the city ordinance and why it threatened to hurt her fellow students who wished to live off campus. She wanted both to inform her audience about this controversial ordinance and to persuade them to campaign for its repeal.
- Elisabeth Pinkerton was at a movie theater with friends when someone's cell phone began ringing during the show. This was not the first time this had happened. Elisabeth was appalled by this person's rudeness and lack of consideration for others. She used her speech class to share information about cell phone etiquette with her classmates.

Rhetorical Workout

Estimate Audience Interest in Your Topic

You learn about a type of storm called a derecho (deh-REY-cho), a damaging straight-line windstorm that often occurs within a band of thunderstorms. Although you haven't heard of a derecho before, you find out that it has some similarities in scope and destructiveness to tornadoes. You wonder if this could be a topic of interest to your class for your next speech. Think about the following criteria:

- Does the topic provide new information to your class audience? Do you think they already know about the topic? Why or why not?
- You learn that derechos can occur in your region and that people can take certain measures to protect themselves from the storms. Do you think this information would be useful to your audience? Why or why not? What if derechos rarely occur in your area?
- Does the topic offer a solution to a puzzle or problem that affects your audience? Why or why not?
- Does the topic offer a way to connect something unfamiliar to what your audience already knows? Explain.
- You do some early research and find several stories about people who have been through derechos and what damage the storms did. Do you think these stories could relate to experiences of your classmates? Why or why not?

- Phillip Marcus was angry. During a closed-book exam in a sociology class, he saw another student sending a text message to his roommate seeking help on three of the questions. At first he was stunned by what he regarded as outrageous conduct; then he became upset that his work and the work of other honest students was devalued by this incident. He decided to give a speech in his public speaking class to make others aware of what was happening, to evoke in them similar feelings of anger, and to channel their emotions toward doing something about cheating. How Phillip chose his topic and developed his strategy will be seen throughout this chapter.

In choosing a topic of personal interest, you must be careful that your own interest does not harden into bias. You must be able to discuss the subject impartially and must recognize the value of other people's points of view.

Interest to the Audience

Even though the topic matters to you, you still must gain the interest of the audience. Audiences will be interested if your topic provides new information they can use, if it offers a solution to a puzzle or problem that affects them, if it connects what is unfamiliar to what they know, or if it reports stories or experiences similar to their own. Phillip Marcus decided that his story of the student who was cheating on the exam would interest others and also would arouse their anger.

Keep in mind as well that an audience's strong interest in the topic potentially may lead to *mis*communication as a result of selective perception. For example, when a manager addresses employees to describe the company's new policy about personal telephone calls and Internet use on the office's computer network, the audience has a strong interest in the message because it clearly will affect them. But there is also a risk that the audience will feel threatened or will believe that the company has become less friendly and may misperceive the message. Their personal interest may actually weaken their ability to listen critically.

A Question of Ethics

Appropriate Topics

In choosing a topic, it is important to think about the situation in which you will speak. Imagine that you will be speaking at a high-school graduation and that you feel very strongly about an upcoming gubernatorial election in the state. Is it ethical for you to engage in political advocacy on this occasion? Would your answer be different if the audience were voluntary instead of captive? How does the nature of the situation as a high-school graduation affect your answer? On the other hand, because you feel strongly about the matter, is it ethical to suppress your own feelings just because of the specific situation? How do you resolve a tension between articulating your own convictions and deferring to the expectations of the situation?

Worthy of Listeners' Time

A related criterion is that the topic should be something that listeners regard as worth hearing about. If the topic is frivolous or trivial, they may feel that they have wasted their time by listening to you, especially if they came voluntarily and could have been doing something else. Unless there is something unique about the approach, a topic such as "How to open a beer can" probably would not meet this test. This does not mean that your topic must be profound or deadly serious; lighthearted humor or new insights on familiar subjects can work very well in a speech. The question to keep in mind is whether the audience will feel that what you have had to say was worth their attention and time.

Appropriateness of Scope

A speaker has to cover the topic to an appropriate degree within the time available. A topic that includes a very large number of points that can be covered only superficially—for example, a five-minute analysis of U.S. foreign policy—should probably be avoided. Similarly, a very narrow topic that can be covered completely in a very short time—such as a description of how to stop when in-line skating—is probably not a good choice either.

Even in a five-minute speech, you might discover that you are repeating yourself several times. Although the topic of cheating on exams might invite a long philosophical discussion of ethics and morality, it also could be focused enough to be covered in a short speech. It is a good topic because it offers rich possibilities for the development of ideas without excessive repetition.

Appropriateness for Oral Delivery

Sometimes, a topic can be developed better in an essay than in a speech. Because readers proceed at their own pace, they can reread any passage that is difficult to understand. But a speech is delivered in real time and at the same pace to all listeners, some of whom will not be able to recall it after delivery. Listeners who miss a particular link in a speaker's chain of ideas cannot replay it; if the link was critical, the rest of the speech might become meaningless.

Topics that depend on technical formulas or elaborate arguments are usually better presented in print than in oral delivery. Still, if a speaker's main ideas and examples are planned carefully and presented clearly, even technical and complex topics can be understood by a nonspecialist audience.

Appropriateness to the Rhetorical Situation

Watch the **Video** "Special Occasion Speech: Grandmother Swanson, 'A Toast to You!'" at **MyCommunicationLab**

Even when the rhetorical situation does not completely determine your topic and you have a range of choice, still it is important that the topic fit the rhetorical situation. A humorous topic is not appropriate if the situation calls for solemnity; a secular topic is not appropriate at most religious functions; and a topic that does not present a problem is inappropriate if the situation calls for a problem–solution speech.

This does not mean, however, that it is inappropriate to discuss topics that are controversial. Topics that are faith based or that relate to personal or public morality are examples of these. They involve issues that many people regard as central to their identity, and people can be expected to disagree—sometimes sharply. The very fact that these topics are important and controversial makes them appropriate for the public forum. The question is not whether to select them but how to develop them. Even when you have strong convictions, your audience will likely be heterogeneous. You should remember that others will disagree with you. They are not likely to be swayed, and you are not likely to succeed, with a display of intolerance for competing views, bigotry, or closed-mindedness.

There also are topics that have been addressed so many times that—even though the subject may be important—it may seem that there is little new to be said. If that really is the case, these topics will not be appropriate to the rhetorical situation because speaking about them probably will not add to what listeners have heard already, and so will not inspire listeners to be attentive and interested. Examples include the dangers of smoking, capital punishment, whether abortion should be outlawed, and the abolition of the Electoral College. You should not necessarily avoid speaking on such topics, unless your instructor has ruled them out of bounds, but you should recognize that you will have a greater burden to offer a fresh perspective to your audience, not to just tell them what they already know. Speaking on hackneyed topics is not likely to be productive.

CHECKLIST 6.1

Characteristics of a Good Topic

- ❐ Importance to the Speaker: Does the topic matter to you?
- ❐ Interest to the Audience: Will the topic gain and hold the audience's interest?
- ❐ Worthy of Listeners' Time: Will your listeners feel the topic is worth their time to hear about?
- ❐ Appropriateness of Scope: Is the topic manageable within the time available?
- ❐ Appropriateness for Oral Delivery: Can the topic be understood from a speech or is it too complex?
- ❐ Appropriateness to the Rhetorical Situation: Does the topic recognize and respond to the constraints imposed by the rhetorical situation?
- ❐ Clarity: Is the topic one that your audience can easily identify?

Clarity

Finally, of course, the speaker should make the topic clear to all listeners. Speakers often fail to refine their topics sufficiently, and the result is a confused jumble of poorly connected ideas. If you are confused about the ideas in your speech, you can be sure that your audience will be confused, too. Even if you think you understand the topic, the fact that you know more about it than the audience does may lead you to present it in a way that is beyond comprehension. For this reason, you should always strive to understand and be sensitive to the audience's level of knowledge.

How to Choose a Good Topic

OBJECTIVE 6.3

What you have just read about the *general* characteristics of a good speech topic may still leave you wondering what the right topic is *for you.* This section offers some suggestions to help you identify a good topic.

Conduct a Personal Inventory

In Chapter 5, you learned how to ask questions to analyze your audience. Now it is time to ask some questions about yourself.

What Public Issues Do I Care About? Public issues are those that concern people generally. Because most audience members are likely to be affected by these issues, they often make good speech topics—but only if you yourself also care about them. It is important, then, to be aware of current events and to think about how you and others are affected by them.

Suppose you decide that the topics of animal rights, homelessness, child abuse, and shifting ethical standards really matter to you. But you are not very interested in international trade, health care financing, and school voucher systems. You probably could develop the first group of topics into effective speeches; the second group would probably not inspire you.

Which of My Experiences Might Be Generalizable? Everyone has had unique experiences, but these do not always make good speech topics. If audience members do not believe that your experience could happen to them, they may react to your speech with the same boredom that many people feel when watching someone else's home videos. However, if something about your experience can be generalized so that others can imagine themselves in the same situation, you may be onto a good topic.

The fact that you work a part-time job and cannot become full-time, so the company can avoid offering you full medical benefits, might matter only to you. But if you can generalize the experience—for example, to the anxiety that many people share about rising medical costs or to the advantages of health insurance that is not linked to employment—your experience might make a good topic. Audience members who don't care at all about your job might still become interested in a speech about a more general problem that they share. Likewise, Phillip Marcus's anger at seeing a classmate cheat could be generalized if he relates the experience so that listeners can imagine how they would feel if it had happened to them.

Which of My Interests Overlap with Those of the Audience? Another question to ask in your personal inventory is whether you share a common interest in any topic with your listeners. If so, you'll have a good match. You will have an incentive to speak about the topic, and they will be motivated to listen.

Sometimes, the match may be exact. For example, you may find that both you and your audience are interested in the Beatles because no musical group in the past 50 years has been so successful. At other times, you will have to match a specific interest with a more general category. For example, you are interested in the Beatles, and your audience is interested in rock stars of the past generation. In that case, you'll want to relate the more specific to the more general, explaining how the

Beatles exemplify the general subject of rock stardom. If you can do that, you have a good topic.

Brainstorm

If your personal inventory did not uncover a good topic for your speech, you can try **brainstorming**, a mental exercise in which you identify the first things that come to mind when you are presented with a given term or category. Do not censor your thoughts; just record them without evaluation. For example, you might divide a sheet of paper into columns with such category headings as "Heroes," "Places to Visit," "Hobbies," and "Favorite Books." (These are just examples, of course; pick whichever categories you want to explore through brainstorming.) Under each heading, jot down the first five things that occur to you. For example, you might list five heroes or five characteristics of a hero, or you might name five places you have visited or five places you hope to visit. Do not stop to evaluate your ideas; write down whatever first comes to mind. Then study the list to see whether you can find any patterns. You may discover, for example, that your lists of heroes, places to visit, hobbies, and favorite books all include items related to the Civil War. Because you seem to have an interest in the Civil War, some aspect of that could become your speech topic.

brainstorming
A mental free-association exercise in which one identifies, without evaluation, the first thoughts that come to mind when one is presented with a given term or category.

topoi
Common or typical categories for organizing subject matter.

Brainstorming works well when you can identify a group of categories, as in the previous example. ***Topoi*** (a Greek term meaning "commonplaces" or "common topics") can be used to form the categories in the first place. As the term suggests, *topoi* are general headings for subject matter. Among Aristotle's *topoi* were "war and peace" and "legislation." Today, the *topoi* of public life might include the economy, science and technology, public finance, social policy, education, and the environment, among others. The *topoi* of the college experience might include classes, residential life, social activities, extracurricular organizations, independent study, and community service. Under each of these categories you can identify potential topics for speeches.

You also can try casually browsing through newspapers, magazines, and the Internet, writing down notes about topics that interest you. Even if you have not given much thought to these topics before, perhaps now you can see how they could lead to a good speech. Being informed about current events and thinking about material covered in your other classes may also help you to brainstorm possible speech topics.

CHECKLIST 6.2

Steps in Choosing a Good Topic

1. Conduct a personal inventory.
   - ❒ What public issues do I care about?
   - ❒ What experiences have I had that might be generalizable?
   - ❒ Which of my interests overlap with those of the audience?
2. Brainstorm and browse through published or online materials.
3. Narrow the topic so that it can be covered adequately within the time available.

Narrow the Topic

The final step in selecting a good topic is to narrow it so that it fits the situation. If your speech is limited to only 10 minutes, for example, you could not begin to explore a topic like "America's Shifting Ethical Standards." But suppose that you narrowed the topic down to the specific standard of honesty, then narrowed that to cheating as an example of dishonesty, and then narrowed that to cheating by college students and finally to "Cheating on This Campus." *Now* you could cover the topic within the allotted time, and your topic would relate to the broader subject that caught your interest in the first place.

Narrowing the topic means sharpening your focus so you concentrate on only some part of a broad topic. It is like pouring

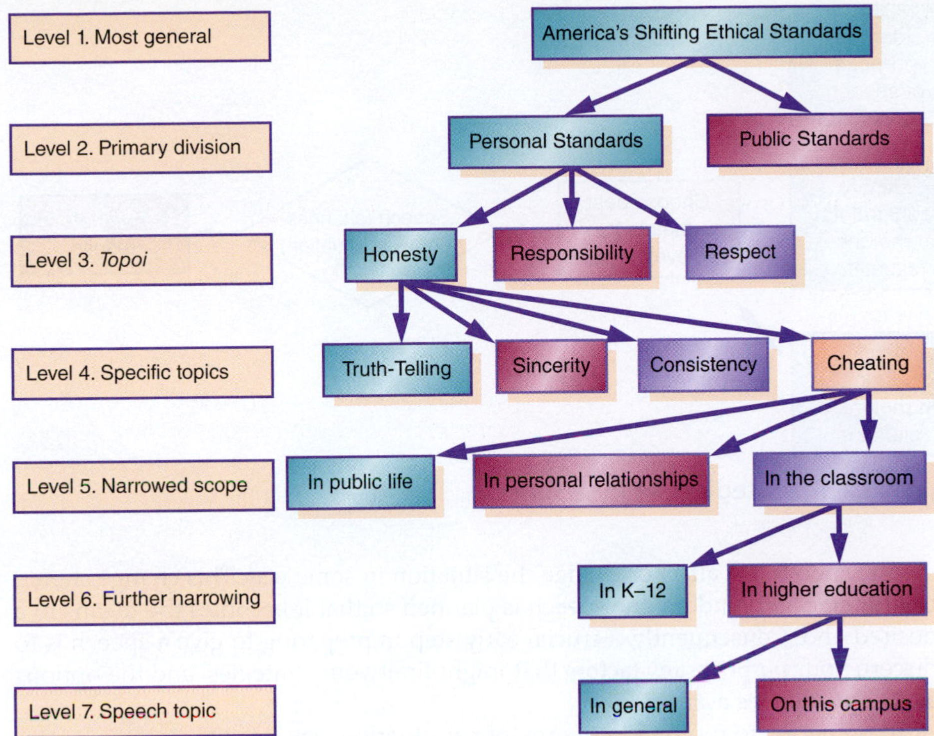

Figure 6.1 Narrowing a general topic.

the topic through a funnel: What goes into the large end is too much to manage, but what comes out the small end can be focused effectively. Time constraints are one obvious reason to narrow the topic. But you also should narrow it to be sure that you can learn enough about the topic before your speech is due and to be sure that the topic fulfills your specific assignment. You can still allude briefly to the topic's larger implications without attempting to develop them in depth.

Figure 6.1 illustrates one approach to narrowing a topic. Beginning with the most general statement, the speaker narrows through a series of steps, dividing the general topic until a topic of manageable scope is selected. For the sake of clarity, Figure 6.1 does not include all of the possible subdivisions; nor is the seven-step sequence in Figure 6.1 the only way to narrow this or any other topic. It is meant to illustrate the thought processes involved in narrowing a very general topic to manageable scope. It also shows how one very general topic can yield a large number of different specific topics for speeches.

Whatever else you do, resist any urge to postpone selecting a topic. If you wait until the last minute, you won't have time to inventory your interests, to brainstorm, and to narrow the topic appropriately.

Developing a Strategic Plan

OBJECTIVE 6.4

So far, we have examined the elements that *create* a rhetorical situation (audience, occasion, speaker, and speech). And now that you understand how to select a topic, it is time to consider how your speech will *respond* to the rhetorical situation.

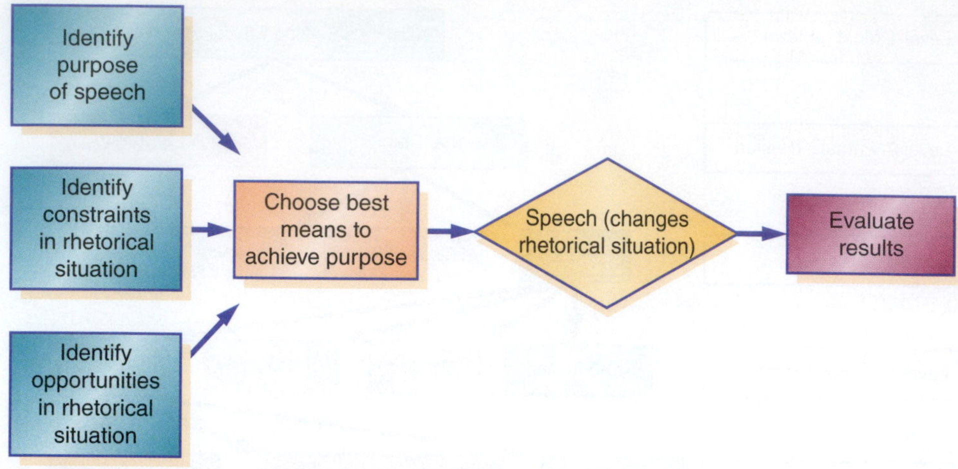

Figure 6.2 A strategic plan for a speech.

Any speech will affect or change the situation in some way. This change should be strategic, not random; the speech is planned so that it becomes the means to a desired end. Consequently, a crucial early step in preparing to give a speech is to discern your purpose, any factors that might limit your strategies, and the options and opportunities available.

In preparing to respond to the rhetorical situation, you need to develop a **strategic plan** that identifies the purpose of your speech, the constraints on it, and the opportunities it provides (see Figure 6.2). Then you select the best means to achieve your purpose, execute them, and evaluate the results.

Identifying the Purpose

The classroom assignment to "make a speech" may mislead you into thinking that fulfilling the assignment is an end in itself. This approach courts disaster, however, because strong public speeches have a clear sense of **purpose**. The speaker plans to achieve a particular goal and wants the audience to respond in a specific way. A speaker's purpose provides the criteria that determine whether the speech was successful or not.

We saw earlier that speeches traditionally are classified as ceremonial, deliberative, or forensic, depending on their purpose. Ceremonial speeches entertain but also celebrate shared values and strengthen commitments to them. Deliberative speeches explore what public policy ought to be. And forensic speaking seeks justice with respect to past events. In addition, recall that in Chapter 1 we described the general purposes of a speech as informing, persuading, and entertaining.

Both of these conceptions of purpose are useful, and yet both are limited. For example, many speeches combine deliberative and ceremonial elements, and it is not uncommon for a single speech to both inform and persuade. For the rest of our study, then, we will use a more precise classification that identifies seven common speech purposes.[2]

1. Providing new information or perspective
2. Agenda setting
3. Creating positive or negative feeling

strategic plan
An identification of the objectives to be sought in a speech and the means for achieving them.

purpose
The outcome the speaker wishes to achieve; the response desired from the audience.

4. Strengthening commitment
5. Weakening commitment
6. Conversion
7. Inducing a specific action

Providing New Information or Perspective. Sometimes, the audience generally knows about a topic but is unfamiliar with its details. Your goal as speaker may be to fill in such gaps by providing new information. For example, listeners may be aware that U.S. political campaigns are expensive, but they may not know that costs are escalating, or the reasons for this trend and its implications, or whether there are practical alternatives. Thus, the purpose of a speech about campaign finance might be "to deepen and enrich the audience's understanding of campaign costs."

Watch the Video "Ceremonial Speech: Tribute to Steve Prefontaine" at **MyCommunicationLab**

Alternatively, listeners may be accustomed to thinking about a topic only from a certain **perspective**, or point of view. For example, in his 2005 commencement speech at Stanford University, Steve Jobs, CEO of Apple Computer, spoke about getting fired at age 30. He said:

> I didn't see it then, but it turned out that getting fired from Apple was the best thing that could have ever happened to me. The heaviness of being successful was replaced by the lightness of being a beginner again, less sure about everything. It freed me to enter one of the most creative periods of my life.

Changing listeners' perspectives about a subject may alter beliefs and values relating to it. At the very least, it may convince listeners that the subject is more complicated than they thought and that how they think about the topic is affected by the perspective from which they view it.

Agenda Setting. One purpose of a speech is **agenda setting**, causing people to think about a topic that they previously knew little about or ignored. The goal of the speech is to put the topic "on the agenda," to draw attention to it. Many environmental threats, for example, were not taken seriously until advocates put them on the agenda by speaking about them.

Maria Rogers, a first-year college student, heard her parents rave about seeing Alaska glaciers "calve," or break off large chunks of ice into the sea. She was concerned that this beautiful sight might actually be a sign of global warming, and she gave a speech to encourage her listeners to think about this serious issue:

> My parents went on an Alaskan cruise last summer, and when they returned they kept raving about the spectacular "calving" of glaciers along the Alaskan coast. These enormous sheets of ice break off, or "calve," at the sea's edge, making a spectacular display as they splash and crash into the icy blue water to the delight of hundreds of cheering tourists. The passengers on deck responded with wild applause, but when I heard about it I listened with deep concern, and then I started doing some research into the causes and effects of global warming. I read scientific reports that, unfortunately, justified my concern. And today I want to encourage you to pay serious attention to this growing threat.

perspective
The point of view from which one approaches a topic.

agenda setting
Causing listeners to be aware of and to think about a topic that previously had escaped their attention.

Creating Positive or Negative Feeling. Sometimes a speaker's goal is more general: to leave the audience with a positive or negative feeling about the occasion, the speaker, or the message. Political candidates, even as they discuss specific policy issues, are often really more interested in making listeners generally feel good or bad about themselves or the world.

Student speaker Craig Hinners prepared a speech of this type when he took a short, nostalgic look at the Chicago elevated train, called the El by locals:

> On the El, you are always entertained. If you gaze out the window, you are treated to an intimate look at the lives of people whose backyards and windows face the tracks. If you set your sights inside the train, you can see and hear the stories of people from all walks of life—office workers, mothers with children, old men. You glance at the bright color of gum casually placed on the back of the seat by a teenager who no longer tasted its flavor, and hear the sound of old vehicles and snow-damaged tracks.

Craig's purpose was not to get listeners to do anything about the El, or even to change their beliefs about its run-down condition; rather, he wanted to share a wistful, comfortable feeling with them.

Likewise, many ceremonial speeches aim to evoke or strengthen common bonds by reference to a shared event or experience. The speakers wish to have the audience feel as they do, most often in a positive way. The audience's general attitude, not a belief or action, is the measure of success.

Strengthening Commitment. Many speeches are like "preaching to the converted"; they are delivered to listeners who already agree with the speaker. In such cases, the goal is to motivate audience members to become even more strongly committed. It is one thing to casually favor a candidate's election to office, but it is quite another thing to contribute money to the candidate's campaign, to display the candidate's poster on one's lawn, or to mobilize friends to vote for the candidate on Election Day. Increasing the intensity of listeners' commitment makes them more likely to act on their beliefs.

Narrowly defeated in the Democratic presidential primaries in 2008, then-Senator Hillary Clinton sought, even as she conceded victory to then-Senator Barack Obama, to strengthen the commitment of her supporters to their shared goals and vision of the future. She offered her supporters these words:

> I understand that we all know this has been a tough fight. The Democratic Party is a family, and it's now time to restore the ties that bind us together and to come together around the ideals we share, the values we cherish, and the country we love.
>
> We may have started on separate journeys—but today, our paths have merged. And we are all heading toward the same destination, united and more ready than ever to win in November and to turn our country around because so much is at stake.

This speaker needs a strong strategic plan to stay light-hearted while also addressing serious issues regarding gaming on Native American reservations.

These sentiments helped to convince Clinton's supporters to transfer their commitment to Obama and to see the man whom they had seen as an adversary now as an ally.

Weakening Commitment. Speakers also sometimes want to reduce the intensity of listeners' commitment to a belief—not so much to get them to change their minds as to acknowledge some sense of *doubt*. Recognizing that an issue has more than one legitimate side may be the first step in *eventually* changing people's minds. Even if listeners remain committed to their position, a reasonable but contrary argument may weaken their support for it. Although you may believe, for example, that higher defense spending is necessary, you may at least think twice about it after hearing a speech that argues that much defense spending is wasted.

Dorothy Hurst knew that her listeners strongly believed that the United States should withdraw all troops from Afghanistan immediately. She also knew that a single 10-minute speech was unlikely to change their belief. But she might be able to chip away at their position if she could show convincingly that an immediate withdrawal would endanger American troops and further destabilize an already fragile Afghan government. She focused not on whether to withdraw troops, but when.

> I know that most of you think that the United States should withdraw all of our troops from Afghanistan immediately. I do not stand here today to dispute the facts that our military is strained, our intelligence agencies have failed, and that our public is weary of war. Rather, I want to call your attention to another set of facts that receive less attention in our media. The Middle East remains a highly volatile region, as we saw during the 2011 "Arab spring," and I believe that maintaining a reasonable-sized force in Afghanistan would generate great strategic benefit to the U.S. Before you rush to judgment against this viewpoint, I ask that you at least consider the risks of leaving Afghanistan completely and immediately; they may be greater than the risks of staying a few years longer.

Conversion. Although it happens rarely on the basis of a single speech, sometimes listeners actually *are* persuaded to change their minds—to stop believing one thing and to start believing another. In short, listeners are converted. **Conversion** involves the replacement of one set of beliefs with another set that is inconsistent with the first. For example, a listener who believes that homeless people are to blame for their condition might be persuaded by a speaker that homelessness reflects faulty social policy, not faulty individuals.

Student speaker Rachel Samuels converted some of her audience by explaining the need for adult teachers to censor high school newspapers. Her classmates initially bristled at the idea of curtailing students' freedom of speech, but when Rachel demonstrated that libel lawsuits could bankrupt the public school system, they began to understand her position:

> The editing of high school newspapers is not government censorship of political or religious speech. Rather, it is editing by an authority to avoid the danger of libel lawsuits. In the world outside high schools, editors often keep journalists from printing the whole story in order to protect citizens' privacy. High school newspapers should be no different.

Inducing a Specific Action. The last purpose we will consider is the most specific and most pragmatic. Often, speakers do not really care about the beliefs and attitudes of individual listeners, as long as they can persuade people to take a specific action—to make a contribution, to purchase a product, to vote for a specific candidate, and so on.

When the goal is action regardless of the reason, the speaker may use widely different appeals. One listener may be induced to vote by the argument that it is a civic duty; another may favor a particular candidate's economic proposals; a third

conversion
The replacement of one set of beliefs by another that is inconsistent with the first.

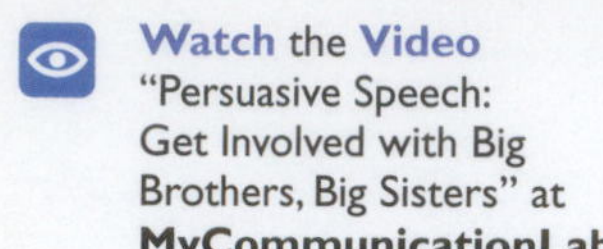
Watch the **Video** "Persuasive Speech: Get Involved with Big Brothers, Big Sisters" at **MyCommunicationLab**

may know one of the candidates personally. The speaker does not care whether listeners have the same reasons for voting; all that matters is that they be prompted to take the same action.

Sunny Lin, a student who was once stranded in inclement weather waiting for a campus shuttle bus, gave a speech urging students to organize a more effective shuttle system for the college campus. She started with an appeal to her audience's concern for public safety:

> While the current shuttle system is meant to transport students across campus at night in order to keep them safe from criminals and predators, 20 minutes between buses is too much time. It takes only a couple of minutes to be robbed or assaulted while waiting for a bus.

Although this was a strong argument, Sunny didn't think that it would motivate all the students. Knowing that others might be moved more by an appeal to the school's reputation, Sunny described the trends in campus shuttle systems at other colleges:

> Other colleges with campuses known for rough terrain, bad traffic, and poor weather have shuttles that run every 10 minutes and provide students with multiple routes to increase transportation options. It's about time our school implements a shuttle program on par with other colleges.

Sunny figured that still other listeners might petition for a better shuttle system if they thought a new system would benefit them directly:

> Some of the most important buildings on campus aren't even on the current shuttle route. A new schedule and the addition of more bus routes would make it possible, for instance, to get to the student union. Think of how much easier it would be to take advantage of the food and entertainment opportunities if you could take a bus to the student union instead of walking in the cold, wet weather.

Sunny's only real concern was whether audience members would participate in a push for a new shuttle system. She didn't care whether they were motivated by safety concerns, school spirit, or personal convenience. She used multiple appeals to achieve her purpose with as many listeners as possible.

These seven categories of purpose certainly do not exhaust the possibilities, but they illustrate some common reasons why people give a speech.[3] Identifying your purpose is a critical step that will help you plan strategies to accomplish your goal.

Identifying the Constraints

After you identify the specific purpose of your speech, the next step in developing a strategic plan is to identify the constraints within which you must maneuver. As noted earlier, constraints are factors beyond your control that limit your options. Constraints may arise from:

- Audiences in general
- Your specific audience analysis
- Your *ethos* as a speaker
- The nature of your topic
- The rhetorical situation

From Audiences in General. As we learned in Chapter 4, the attention span of most listeners is limited, and it has shrunk over the years. Today, most audiences begin to get restless when a speech exceeds 20 or 30 minutes. And even when listeners are generally attentive, the degree of attention varies. At one moment, your speech may be the most important thing on their minds; at another moment, something you say may trigger an unrelated thought; and at yet another moment, listeners may be distracted by something else altogether.

You can help the audience remember your main ideas by phrasing them simply, organizing them in a structure that is easy to follow, and repeating them during the speech. Another strategy is to use interesting examples and to choose language that captures attention.

Besides having limited attention spans, audiences tend to have a high opinion of themselves and naturally resist being talked down to. They may believe that they have exerted great effort or even done you a favor by coming to hear you speak. You should always show respect to the audience and recognize that they will be the ultimate judges of your speech.

From Your Specific Audience Analysis. You also will be constrained by the analysis you performed of your specific audience, as described in Chapter 5. Your audience analysis may tell you that some appeals are out of bounds and that others are far more likely to succeed. For example, the manager who speaks to employees about the company's strained economic conditions has many choices; to succeed, however, she or he *must* deal with the fact that workers are worried about losing their jobs. This fear, identified through audience analysis, is an important constraint on what the manager can say.

From Your *Ethos* as a Speaker. The audience's perceptions of the speaker's character, or *ethos*, are another important constraint. If listeners see you as competent to discuss the subject, as trustworthy, as dynamic and energetic, and as having goodwill toward them, you enjoy a positive *ethos*. As we saw in Chapter 5, you want to evoke positive assessments of your *ethos* because an audience's perceptions of your character strongly affect whether that audience will be influenced by what you say.

Even a generally positive *ethos* can constrain you, however, because then you must craft a speech that sustains or builds on the audience's high expectations. When, in a 2004 speech to the National Association for the Advancement of Colored People (NAACP), well-loved comedian Bill Cosby harshly criticized African Americans for a lack of responsible parenting, his remarks created a firestorm of controversy and debate. People had grown to expect lighthearted humor from this TV icon, and his serious tone surprised many who heard, read, or watched the speech. But Cosby's qualifications as a trained educator and his identity as one of America's most recognized fathers put him in a position to speak credibly on this important topic. Even though Cosby's cultural critique was vicious, he did not present a serious lecture but instead peppered the speech with dozens of jokes and witty observations about his own culture. Although Cosby's *ethos* is positive, he still must work within its constraints.

If, for whatever reason, your *ethos* is generally perceived as negative, then your challenge is either to change it or to overcome it. When President Bill Clinton acknowledged that he had been involved in an inappropriate sexual relationship with a White House intern, after having earlier denied it, he found subsequently that many people suspected him of dishonesty whenever he spoke. His negative *ethos* was a constraint on his effectiveness. He tried to overcome it by focusing his speeches instead on the strength of the economy and society during his administration.

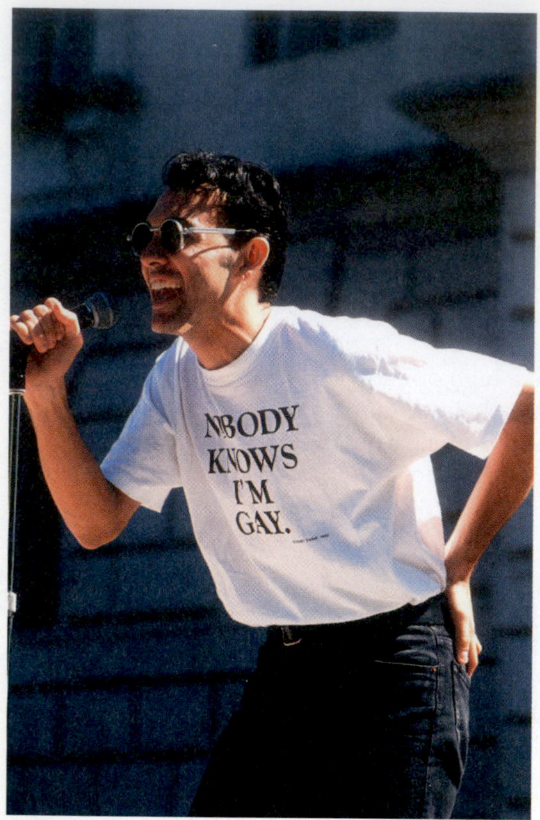

This speaker's strategic plan should recognize the constraint that his audience may be deeply divided and have strong emotions about his topic.

From the Nature of Your Topic. Some topics constrain a speaker more than others do. A highly technical subject that is difficult to make interesting challenges the audience's attention span even more than usual. And a topic that seems far removed from listeners' concerns is unlikely to spark and hold their interest.

In such cases, the challenge is to plan strategies that evoke and heighten interest. This is what student John Casey did in speaking about the research under way in the university's laboratories. Rather than droning on about details of antibodies and peptides, he made the topic interesting by describing the scientific community's quest for a "magic bullet" to cure cancer.

From the Rhetorical Situation. Every speech is a one-shot effort to influence the audience, but the occasions when a single message will change anyone's attitudes are few. For example, a classroom speech about abortion is unlikely to convince strong believers on either side to change their basic beliefs. Moreover, a speaker's range of stimuli is limited to only words and, sometimes, visual aids. Yet most cases of successful persuasion involve multiple messages and a variety of stimuli—verbal, visual, and experiential. Of course, a one-shot effort may be more likely to succeed when your goal is to reinforce the commitment that listeners already feel. Even so, a speaker should never overestimate the effect that a single speech can have on an audience.

We see, then, that a speaker cannot plan a speech with complete freedom. The constraints imposed by the audience, the audience analysis, the speaker's *ethos*, the topic, and the rhetorical situation must all become part of the strategic plan. Then the challenge is to be creative and find opportunities within these limits.

Identifying the Opportunities

Your opportunities as a speaker result from the assets that you bring to the situation and from the choices that you *are* able to make.

Your first and most important asset is that you should have an *information advantage* over listeners; you are likely to be better informed about the topic than they are. This may offset the constraints that the audience imposes. After all, you selected the topic because it matters to you, and you have researched it, as we will describe in Chapter 7. You have given the topic sustained attention, and so you should be able to awaken interest in it, to provide new information about it, and to explain difficult concepts.

A second opportunity arises from your *audience analysis*, as you learned in Chapter 5. It will tell you something about the composition and attitudes of your specific listeners. Furthermore, almost any topic can be presented in various ways; there is no single "correct" approach. Your audience analysis will enable you to plan the strategies that are most likely to succeed.

For example, suppose that you know that, despite threats of legal penalties, large numbers of college students share music files online. You want to persuade your fellow students that they should not share digital music files with each other because they may be doing so illegally, and you expect strong opposition from students who would see your proposal as a limitation of their freedom. So you might suggest that this limitation is justified:

> College students today are logged on and linked in like no generation in history. It requires no effort to rip, copy, download, upload, or send digital music files to each other. With a few clicks, we can enjoy the latest single from our favorite artists and bands. But where we get our music is not just a matter of convenience—it's also a matter of dollars and cents. When we share music downloads without obtaining the proper rights, then we are listening and distributing in direct violation of the artist's rights and, in more stark terms, we are breaking the law. Good music costs money to create, produce, and distribute, and illegal file sharing sabotages the very thing we are trying to enjoy.

Although these justifications seem reasonable, they depend on values such as sympathy for artists and respect for the law. This argument probably would be more effective in reinforcing the commitment of listeners who already believed in upholding copyright laws than in converting people who are not particularly bothered by this legal transgression but are disturbed by what they see as limitations on their

CHOOSE A STRATEGY: Identifying Constraints and Opportunities

The Situation

You are preparing a speech for your class on three things that people can do to improve or maintain their health. You want to pick three ideas that are significant and feasible for your audience to implement.

Making Choices

1. What do you know about your class audience that could constrain or limit the kinds of health measures you choose to talk about? How could their age, current health, level of activity, and economic status affect how they respond to your topic?
2. Suppose you personally follow the health measures you will talk about in your speech. How might this contribute to your *ethos*?
3. In your research, you learn that exercise can help prevent many more serious diseases than you realized. You assume that your audience already knows that exercise is good for them but that some people still don't do it. What opportunities for your speech does this information give you?

What If...

How would you change the way you choose which three health measures to discuss if your audience was:

1. A group of senior citizens
2. A kindergarten class

What are some constraints and opportunities you might encounter with each of these audiences?

freedom. To reach these listeners, a strategy of stressing the personal benefits of not sharing music files illegally might be more effective. For them, you might add:

> And not only that, we ourselves benefit from our restraint. How? First, a profitable music industry has the money to search out and develop new talent, expanding the pool of artists from which you can choose. Second, we avoid the potential nightmare of major lawsuits, confiscated computers, and network blackouts. And finally, since not every musician is a multi-platinum artist, we ensure that artists are paid fairly for their creativity, talent, and hard work. Asking that we refrain from illegal music file sharing is not really a curtailment of our freedom: it's an opportunity to show that we don't take our Internet access for granted and to show our support and desire for more music from innovative artists who will be secure in their ability to make music and make a living, too.

Selecting the Means

If you have been thinking strategically, by this point you have articulated the purpose of your speech and have identified your constraints and opportunities in proceeding toward that goal. The final step in strategic planning is to select the means that you will use to achieve your purpose. In many respects, this decision is the most important, because it touches on virtually every aspect of your speech.

- How will you lead your audience in reasoning through to the conclusions you want to establish?
- How will you structure the speech?
- What supporting materials will you use?
- What choices will you make about wording, emotional language, and repetition?
- How will you actually present the speech?

All these matters will be explored in later chapters, but here you should recognize that each of them involves a choice that can be made either by accident or by design. The essence of strategic planning is to avoid accident and to design means that are most appropriate for achieving your purpose.

Developing the Purpose Statement and the Thesis Statement

From this understanding of strategic elements—purpose, constraints, and opportunities—you can begin to construct the skeleton of your speech. You have already determined the topic. The next steps are to formulate a clear statement of purpose and a thesis for the speech.

general purpose statement
Statement of the overall goal of the speech: providing new information or perspective, agenda setting, creating positive or negative feeling, strengthening commitment, weakening commitment, conversion, or inducing a specific action.

The Purpose Statement

Our earlier discussion suggested seven general categories of purpose: agenda setting, providing new information, weakening commitment, and so on. Review those categories to determine which one best describes the overall purpose of your speech. That description is your **general purpose statement**. Then you need to develop a **specific purpose statement**. This focuses on the outcome of your speech by specifying what you want to achieve—or what you want the audience to take away from the speech—and for that reason it is audience centered. It follows from the seven general purposes described earlier; those general purposes are made more specific by relation to a particular topic.

For example, if you were going to discuss cheating at the university, you might proceed as follows:

TOPIC:	Cheating at the university
GENERAL PURPOSE:	To provide new information
SPECIFIC PURPOSE:	To inform listeners of widespread cheating on this campus

The thesis statement sums up what you most want listeners to remember. It should be possible to translate the thesis statement into a slogan for a poster.

The specific purpose is an instance of the general purpose, to provide new information. Notice that the specific purpose statement has three important characteristics.

1. It focuses on the audience rather than on the speaker. It identifies the outcome you seek, not how you will achieve that outcome.
2. It summarizes a single idea. Although some speeches are complex and have more than one purpose, you are likely to be more effective if you can state your purpose as a single succinct idea.
3. It is precise and free of vague language. It tells exactly what you are trying to achieve, so you can determine whether you succeed.

Next, think critically about your specific purpose statement. Remember that listeners are giving their time and energy to hear you speak, and ask yourself whether your specific purpose is worthy of their efforts. If you are telling them only things that they already know, if your purpose is too grand to be achieved in the time available, if the topic is too technical or seems trivial, listeners are unlikely to pay close attention. In that case, of course, you cannot achieve your purpose.

Watch the **Video** "Professor Randy Cox Discusses the Purpose of a Speech" at **MyCommunicationLab**

The Thesis Statement

The final step in preparing the overall design of the speech is to identify the **thesis**, a succinct statement of the central idea or claim made by the speech. Whereas the specific purpose statement indicates what you want the audience to *take from* the speech, the thesis statement indicates what you want to *put into* it. The purpose statement identifies the desired audience reaction; the thesis statement succinctly summarizes the content of the speech in a single sentence that you most want listeners to remember. Here is how the thesis statement about campus cheating might evolve:

TOPIC:	Cheating at the university
GENERAL PURPOSE:	To provide new information
SPECIFIC PURPOSE:	To inform listeners of widespread cheating on this campus
THESIS STATEMENT:	Far more students engage in cheating than most of us think.

specific purpose statement
Statement of the particular outcome sought from the audience; a more specific version of a general purpose.

thesis
The central idea or claim made by the speech, usually stated in a single sentence.

Notice how the topic (itself the result of a narrowing process) has been narrowed into a thesis statement that summarizes exactly what the speech will say.

Many of the tests of the specific purpose statement also apply to the thesis. Both should be stated in a single phrase or sentence. Both should be worded precisely. And both should fit the time available and other constraints in the situation.

Occasionally, a speaker does not state the thesis explicitly, relying instead on all the supporting ideas to imply it. There are advantages and disadvantages to letting the audience determine the exact thesis. If listeners participate actively in figuring it out, they are likely to stay interested in the speech and perhaps may even be more likely to accept the thesis. However, if the thesis is not stated, the audience might not identify it accurately, or different listeners might identify different theses. Even though accomplished speakers sometimes trust the audience to identify the thesis, students of public speaking are well advised to state it explicitly.

OBJECTIVE 6.6

Analyzing the Thesis Statement

The thesis statement governs various choices about the content of a speech. By analyzing your thesis statement, you can determine your choices.

Identifying the Issues

issue
A question raised by the thesis statement that must be addressed in order for the thesis itself to be addressed effectively.

First, you must identify the issues contained within the thesis statement. People often use the term *issue* quite loosely, as when they say, "Don't make an issue of it." But the term has a more precise meaning. An **issue** is a question raised by the thesis statement that must be addressed in order for the thesis itself to be addressed effectively.[4]

Strategies for Speaking to Diverse Audiences

Respecting Diversity Through Your Topic Selection and Strategy Development

Some topics work better than others for a diverse audience. Likewise, identifying your purpose and selecting a strategy are affected by the need to reach listeners with diverse backgrounds and perspectives. These strategies will help you to consider diversity at these key stages of speech planning.

1. Select a topic that is relevant to people of diverse interests rather than one that will be meaningful to only a narrow segment of your audience.
2. Emphasize points of commonality with your audience that do not rely on cultural stereotypes.
3. Keep in mind the diversity of your audience when identifying your opportunities and constraints. For example, "the role of faith in public life" will have a different mix of opportunities and constraints for secular than for evangelical audiences.
4. Remember that different levels of commitment may exist within the audience. Discussing certain issues may be more important for your audience's identity. For instance, discussing the issue of wearing headscarves in school will garner different levels of commitment from an audience of Muslim women than from secular U.S. men.

Issues are identified by posing questions about your thesis statement. Because the statement is so simple and brief, it always leaves much unsaid. By raising questions about the thesis statement, you'll discover what it seems to take for granted. Then your speech can flesh out these underlying assumptions and show that they are correct, giving listeners reason to accept the thesis statement itself.

Consider the thesis statement in the example above: "Far more students engage in cheating than most of us think." It seems straightforward. But notice what happens when we ask questions about the statement:

"Far more students"	→	How many? Is that number more than we think? Is it "far more"?
"Engage in cheating"	→	What is covered by the term cheating? And what must one do to "engage in" it?
"Than most of us think"	→	Who are "most of us"? What do "most of us" think? Why do we think this?

These questions identify the issues in the thesis statement. You may decide that some of the answers are obvious or that some can be covered together. You may decide not to take them up in the same order in the speech. But these essentially are the questions you'll need to answer if you want listeners to accept that "far more students engage in cheating than most of us think."

Now consider a thesis that is not yet well formed. Bill Goldman wanted to explore whether "voting in local elections is a worthwhile effort for me as a student." He had not yet framed an explicit thesis, but even this more broadly phrased statement can be questioned to discover the issues. Bill had to think about what "worthwhile" means for a student, whose stake in local elections is usually small; he also had to think about what "effort" is required to vote and why even that is an issue. He then began to question whether it was "harder" for him to vote than for others or harder than it "should" be. Gradually, he came to believe that low voter turnout can be explained by the fact that voting is inconvenient. This process of discovering issues helped Bill both to refine and to test his thesis statement.

Finally, consider the example of Angela Peters, who wanted to talk about the college admissions process to an audience of high school juniors. After doing some research, she might begin to develop her speech like this:

TOPIC:	The college admissions process
GENERAL PURPOSE:	Weakening commitment to a position
SPECIFIC PURPOSE:	To cause listeners to doubt their belief that admissions decisions are made rationally
THESIS STATEMENT:	Most colleges and students lack clear criteria for making admissions decisions.
ISSUES:	1. What are "most colleges"? Who are "most students"? How do we know? 2. What makes the criteria for admissions clear or unclear? 3. What are a college's or a student's criteria? Are they "clear" or not? 4. What are the admissions decisions about which we are concerned?

Now Angela can complete her research by looking for the answers to these specific questions. When she speaks about "the college admissions process," she will know what she wants to say, and she will have the supporting material she needs to weaken listeners' commitment to the belief that admissions decisions are made rationally.

Why Identify the Issues?

Analyzing the topic to identify the issues is important for several reasons. First, it enables you to determine what the speech must cover. Without knowing the issues, you risk giving a speech that listeners will dismiss as being beside the point.

Recall that Bill Goldman initially wanted to explore whether "voting in local elections is a worthwhile effort for me as a student." Through the process of discovering issues, he eventually came to believe that many students are dissuaded from voting in local elections because of the inconvenience of voting. At this point, his topic became "Why students don't vote," and his thesis was "Because voting is inconvenient, many students don't vote." He was able to document that, across the country, students are reluctant to vote in their adopted communities. He also was able to show that polling places may be in obscure locations, that lines are too long, and that paper ballots often are complex and tedious. He proposed as his solution that students be allowed to vote from their apartments or dorm rooms using the Internet. This solution seemed appropriate *as he described the problem*, but he did not really analyze the issues and causes fully. His thesis statement was too vague and did not consider alternative explanations.

After the speech, an audience member challenged whether Bill had really thought through the problem. The listener pointed out that, because people will endure inconvenience if they believe that the rewards justify it, perhaps the perceived benefits of voting in local elections do not outweigh the cost of inconvenience. The listener suggested that a more significant cause for students' failing to vote might be the lack of identification with a community that they do not regard as a permanent "home" but instead as a temporary "way station." They might prefer to register at home rather than at school. Students' lack of identification with the surrounding community perpetuates their disinterest in local politics, which in turn discourages students from learning more about the issues that are relevant to the community. Had Bill analyzed his thesis more carefully, he might have seen that the costs and benefits of voting were likely to be an issue, and he would have been prepared to address this.

A second reason to analyze the thesis statement is to direct your research, which otherwise could be endless. Combing your own experience and ideas, talking with others, and investigating library resources could go on indefinitely. A search of books and articles in just a single library will probably turn up hundreds of sources that have something to say about voting rates (and on the Internet, an unfocused search will yield truly unmanageable results).

One way to make your research task manageable is to focus your inquiry. By analyzing your thesis to determine the issues, you can better decide what and how to research. For example, in giving a speech about voting rates, you may decide that the key issue you want to explore relates to voting at state and local levels. As a result, you would not pay much attention to the vast literature comparing turnout rates among countries or turnout rates in national elections. Your research would focus on the issues you have identified.

A third reason to identify the issues is that doing so may lead you to modify your thesis. If your initial thesis is "Students are too busy to vote," analyzing the issues might convince you that your thesis should be "Students are too lazy to vote" or "Students are too confused to vote" or "Students feel that they have no reason to vote." The differences among these statements are obvious. Which one (or more) claim you try to develop and defend in the speech will be influenced by your analysis of what the issues really are.

Finally, as you will see in Chapter 9, analyzing your thesis is also helpful when you turn to organizing your speech.

What Have You Learned?

Objective 6.1: State when it is appropriate for you to choose the topic of your speech and when the choice is beyond your control.

You can choose your own topic if:

- A classroom assignment permits it.
- People are interested in hearing you, regardless of the subject you wish to address.

Topic choice is beyond your control if:

- Your commitment to a specific cause impels you to speak.
- Your reputation on a given subject leads you to speak out.
- The occasion calls for a speech on a particular topic.
- A classroom assignment specifies the topic.

The initial steps in preparing a speech are as follows:

- Choosing a topic, if the choice is up to you.
- Developing a strategic plan for designing the speech, reflecting a clear sense of purpose and identifying your constraints and opportunities.

Objective 6.2: Identify the characteristics of a good topic.

When you are able to choose your own topic, your speech will be more effective if

- The topic matters to you.
- You can make the topic interesting to the audience.
- The topic is worth the listeners' time.
- The scope of the topic fits the time available.
- The topic is appropriate for oral delivery.
- The topic is appropriate to the rhetorical situation.
- The topic is clear.

Objective 6.3: Proceed through the steps involved in choosing a good topic.

As aids in selecting a topic, you should

- Conduct an inventory of your interests and those of the audience.
- Use brainstorming and general reading.
- Narrow the topic so that it can be addressed adequately within the time available.

Objective 6.4: Define *strategic plan* and explain the steps for developing and implementing one.

Strategic planning—identifying objectives to be sought and the means for achieving them—develops an overall strategy for responding to the rhetorical situation, including

- Identifying the purpose
- Identifying the opportunities
- Identifying the constraints
- Selecting the means

Shaping your plan for the speech is guided by its specific purpose:

- Providing new information or perspective
- Agenda-setting (raising issues for consideration)
- Creating positive or negative feeling
- Strengthening commitment to a position
- Weakening commitment to a position
- Changing listeners' minds
- Inducing a specific action by audience members

Constraints limit what you can do in achieving your purpose; they result from

- Audiences in general
- Your analysis of the specific audience
- Your *ethos* as a speaker
- The nature of your topic
- The fact that a speech is a one-shot appeal that is primarily verbal

On the other hand, opportunities to achieve your purpose arise from the facts that

- You will know more about your topic than listeners do.
- You may draw on and respond to the audience's attention and values.

Objective 6.5: Formulate statements of the specific purpose and thesis of your speech and illustrate how these statements will influence other strategic decisions.

The process of formulating your strategic plan enables you to identify

- The general purpose statement
- The specific purpose statement
- The thesis statement

Objective 6.6: Analyze your thesis to figure out which issues you need to discuss and which ideas need support.

You might modify these statements as you learn more about the subject and refine your audience analysis, but they will influence the following strategic decisions:

- What you need to know about the topic in order to establish that the thesis is true
- Which main ideas you need to develop to establish the thesis
- Which inferences must be made to link the main ideas to the thesis
- How best to organize your development and support of the thesis
- Which elements in the design of the speech will make listeners most comfortable about accepting the thesis statement

We will focus on these important strategic choices in the next several chapters.

Listen to the **Audio Chapter Summary** at **MyCommunicationLab**

Discussion Questions

1. When a small liberal arts college decided to change its core curriculum, the issue of core requirements became important to students in a public speaking class, many of whom spoke about that topic. Discuss the issues in this rhetorical situation that seemed to call for speech.
2. How do the purpose of a speech and its subject matter relate to one another? Discuss the speech purposes described in this chapter, and identify some potential topics for each purpose.
3. Imagine that you are giving a six- to eight-minute speech to a group of fraternity members in which your purpose is to weaken their commitment to the idea that alcohol is desirable at parties. What constraints and opportunities do you face in this situation? How will you use those constraints and opportunities in your strategic plan for this speech?
4. Now imagine that you are giving a six- to eight-minute speech to a meeting of Students Against Drunk Driving in which your purpose is to strengthen their commitment to the idea that alcohol is dangerous at parties. How do the constraints and opportunities of this situation differ from those in item 3? In what ways would your strategic plan for this speech be different?
5. Think of a speech or other presentation that you have seen or heard that lacked a clear thesis. What are some of the common pitfalls of a speech without a well-defined thesis—from the perspective both of the speaker and of the audience?

Activities

1. Choose a good topic for a speech in this class. In doing so, conduct a personal inventory and use finding aids such as brainstorming and source browsing. Share topics with a classmate. In what ways does your classmate's topic appeal or not appeal to you? Is your classmate's topic narrow enough? Why or why not?
2. Produce a list of constraints and a list of opportunities for the topic you have chosen (in activity 1). Consider the audience, the occasion, the speaker, and the speech. In a few paragraphs, describe your purpose and how you are going to achieve it within the bounds of these constraints and opportunities.
3. Provide the following information about your speech:

   TOPIC:

   GENERAL PURPOSE:

   SPECIFIC PURPOSE:

   THESIS STATEMENT:

   Evaluate each of these decisions, explaining why you made the choices you did.
4. Make a list of topics that you think are hackneyed. What makes them hackneyed topics? Will such topics always remain hackneyed? If not, how might you apply a fresh perspective to them?

Key Terms

agenda setting **131**
brainstorming **128**
conversion **133**
general purpose statement **138**
issue **140**
perspective **131**
purpose **130**
specific purpose statement **139**
strategic plan **130**
thesis **139**
topic **122**
topoi **128**

 **Study** and **Review** the **Flashcards** at **MyCommunicationLab**

Notes

1 See Craig R. Smith and Paul Prince, "Language Choice Expectation and the Roman Notion of Style," *Communication Education* 39 (January 1990): 63–74.

2 This classification system is original. Although the broad categories served our purposes in Chapter 1, we will use this more precise system of purposes for the remainder of our study.

3 For another list of purposes, see Sonja K. Foss and Karen A. Foss, *Inviting Transformation: Presentational Speaking for a Changing World*, Prospect Heights, IL: Waveland Press, 1994, pp. 10–16.

4 Classical rhetoric addresses the subject of issue identification as "stasis theory." For more on modern approaches to classical stasis theory, see Sharon Crowley and Debra Hawhee, *Ancient Rhetorics for Contemporary Students*, 5th ed., New York: Pearson Longman, 2011; Richard Johnson-Sheehan, *Writing Proposals: Rhetoric for Managing Change*, 2nd ed., New York: Longman, 2007; and Allen H. Brizee, "Stasis Theory as a Strategy for Workplace Teaming and Decision Making," *Journal of Technical Writing and Communication* 38 (December 2008): 363–85.

CHAPTER

7

Researching the Speech

LEARNING OBJECTIVES

After studying this chapter, you should be able to:

Objective 7.1	Make strategic choices about research in light of your audience and your purpose.
Objective 7.2	Identify types of material that are available to support the ideas in your speech.
Objective 7.3	Use tools to locate supporting materials for your speech.
Objective 7.4	Describe several categories of sources you can use as supporting materials and when you might use each.
Objective 7.5	Explain the factors that can cause evidence to be deficient and the strategic questions you can use to evaluate Internet evidence.
Objective 7.6	Conduct research efficiently and productively.
Objective 7.7	Explain and use guidelines for how to cite sources and how to take notes about your research.

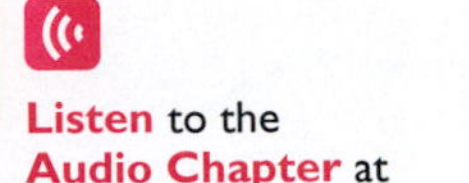

OUTLINE

In this chapter, you will learn how to investigate your topic so that you can speak about it intelligently. Because you are making claims on listeners' time and attention, both you and they will want to be confident that you know what you're talking about.

The process of finding supporting material for your speech is **research**. Just as you do research in order to decide which service plan is best for your cell phone or whether to buy a car, you look for material that will support the claims you want to make in your speech. Research is closely linked to the process of **analysis** that you studied at the end of Chapter 6. On the one hand, the available materials guide you in identifying the issues related to your topic. On the other, searching for material without knowing which issues you need to investigate is pointless.

Sometimes, analysis precedes research. This is the right sequence when you already know what your thesis statement is. You then determine which questions must be answered in order to make that statement, and you go to find the answers. Sometimes, though, you don't yet know your thesis statement; you know only the topic. Angela Peters wanted to talk about the college admissions process (topic), but she didn't know enough about it to be sure of what she wanted to say (thesis). In this case, she should begin not with analysis but with research. She needs a general understanding of the topic before she can frame the thesis statement. Then she should analyze her thesis statement as described in Chapter 6 and, finally, return to research for answers to the specific questions she identified.

OBJECTIVE 7.1 Strategic Perspectives on Research

Whether your research precedes or follows your analysis, you will want it to accomplish three basic goals:

1. To develop or strengthen your own expertise on the topic
2. To find the evidence that will support your ideas
3. To make your ideas clear, understandable, and pertinent to your audience

Keep in mind that these different goals may not all be achieved by the same kind of material. If you conceive of the research process too narrowly, you may find that you have obtained great background knowledge but have no specific material to include in your speech. Or you may find that your evidence is clear and meaningful in the context in which you found it, but it may mean little to your audience without that context.

Like every other aspect of public speaking, research involves strategic choices. You simply cannot find out all there is to know about every possible aspect of your speech topic. Consequently, you will have to decide the following:

- How much general background reading to do and what sources to select for this purpose.
- What issues in your speech will require specific supporting material.
- What types of supporting material you will need and where you should go to find it.
- How much supporting material you need to find.

research
The process of looking for and discovering supporting materials for the speech.

analysis
Exploration of a speech topic to determine which subordinate topics must be covered.

Unsuccessful speakers often make these choices haphazardly. For example, after an Internet search yields a large number of source citations, one speaker tracks down the first two or three she can find, and she stops as soon as she has enough to fill the speaking time she has been allotted. But she never considers whether she has the best kinds of support or the right amount of it. Or, because another speaker's personal experience is relevant to his topic, he does not bother looking for other types of supporting material. He doesn't think about whether an audience will find his personal experience adequate or credible.

To be successful, instead of acting in such an unplanned way, you should make these choices—like all others—in light of your audience and your purpose. What will your audience expect? What claims might listeners be expected to accept without evidence? Will examples or statistics be more likely to lead them to accept your thesis? At what point would you provide so much evidence that it overwhelms them?

In the classroom, this thought process may be simplified by the details of the speech assignment. You may be asked, for instance, to give a speech with at least five pieces of supporting material of at least three different types. These are arbitrary instructions, not an all-purpose formula. Their purpose is to expose you to the range of possible supporting material and to give you practice using it. But outside the classroom, you will have to make these choices based on the particular rhetorical situation you face.

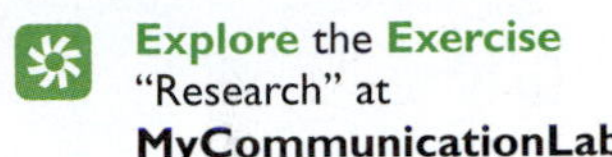
Explore the **Exercise**
"Research" at
MyCommunicationLab

Types of Supporting Material

OBJECTIVE 7.2

To do research for your speech, you first have to decide which types of supporting material you need. The following seven types illustrate the array of possibilities:

1. Personal experience
2. Common knowledge
3. Direct observation
4. Examples
5. Documents
6. Statistics
7. Testimony

Personal Experience

Sometimes, you can support your ideas on the basis of your own experience. Suppose your topic concerns the difficulties that first-year students have in adjusting to college life. You might well illustrate your main points by referring to your own first college days. If you were speaking about volunteerism, your experience in tutoring elementary school students or working in a soup kitchen would certainly be relevant. Student speaker Mitch Grissom used a personal story to introduce his speech about student protests against the continuing war in Afghanistan:

> Probably everyone in this class has an opinion on the war in Afghanistan. Some of you might think it was a good idea poorly executed, and others might think it was a bad idea tragically fabricated. I have my own ideas on Afghanistan, too. Last month, I participated

> in a student protest against the war, and a guy from my dorm came up to me afterward to say he didn't know I was a radical. I smiled and rolled up my left sleeve, exposing the shrapnel scars on my arm. I told him I wasn't a radical; I was just a veteran who had served in Afghanistan.

Mitch gained credibility—and the audience's attention—because he knew what he was talking about. He used his experience to illustrate his main points, and because his listeners could relate to him, they found his experience pertinent to them as well.

Watch the Video "The Process of Developing a Speech: Generating Credibility" at **MyCommunicationLab**

Those are the strategic benefits of using personal experience to support your ideas. Of course, audience members must be able to relate to your experience or they will not think it meaningful to them. For this reason, only rarely should a speaker rely on personal experience as the *only* type of supporting material.

Common Knowledge

An often-overlooked type of supporting material is **common knowledge**, the understandings, beliefs, and values that members of a society or culture generally share. Such beliefs are sometimes called "common sense." Some writers use the term *social knowledge* to emphasize that we know these things to be true on the basis of broad social consensus.[1]

Common knowledge is often expressed in the form of *maxims*, such as "what happens here, stays here," "this is no time for business as usual," or "if you want something done right, do it yourself." Sometimes, common knowledge takes the form of *generally held beliefs*. For example, whether correctly or not, most Americans believe that large government programs don't work, that taxes are too high and definitely should not be increased, that the Cold War is over, and that God plays a role in their lives. Common knowledge also is expressed in *value judgments*, such as the importance of protecting the environment, the commitment to a right to privacy, and a preference for practical solutions over ideological disputes.

One student speaker used common knowledge as supporting material when he said:

> Everybody knows that youth is a time for experimenting, for doing adventurous things. That's why you should consider signing up for study abroad.

When asked later, audience members agreed with the speaker's assertion that young people are adventurous and willing to try something new.

Common knowledge is not always correct, of course; people certainly can believe things that "ain't so." But common knowledge has the status of **presumption**—that is, we consider it to be right until we are shown otherwise. Precisely because the knowledge is "common" and widely shared, it can often be strategically useful as supporting material.

common knowledge
The beliefs and values that members of a society or culture generally share.

presumption
The assumption that a statement or claim is true until shown otherwise.

Direct Observation

Sometimes, you can support your claim on the basis of simple, direct observation—the heart of the scientific method. If you are speaking about whether drivers obey basic traffic laws, you can stand near a traffic light or stop sign and count how many drivers ignore these signals. If you are speaking about the widespread use of texting, you can keep track of how often you communicate with your friends by text rather than phone or e-mail (or in person). Student speaker Susan Anderson used direct observation to support her claim that students are taking unnecessary risks by not wearing bicycle helmets:

> You've seen them. They're big, oval-shaped, and odd-looking. And they sit on top of bicyclists' heads to reduce the risk of head injury in the unfortunate event of an accident. At least, that's what they're intended to do—but only if you wear them. Today I saw 27 students on bicycles, but only five—that's right, five—of them were wearing helmets. The other 22 students may not know this, but they were unnecessarily risking their lives.

This form of evidence appeals to the common cultural value that "seeing is believing." Susan's point gained credibility because she was reporting what she had seen with her own eyes. Direct observation is not just a recollection of personal experience; it can be verified by others. Usually, direct observation results from a deliberate decision to gather evidence that might support your point, but occasionally it is powerful because you saw something by accident—such as an act of crime—while you were doing something else.

Examples

When you offer an example, you make a general statement more meaningful by illustrating a specific instance of it. This form of supporting material helps to make an abstract idea more concrete. You can provide this kind of support for a claim by using a brief example, a hypothetical example, an anecdote, or a case study.

Brief Example. If you wanted to support the claim that the structure of the United Nations does not adequately reflect the current balance of power in the world, you might cite as an example the fact that Germany and Japan—despite their economic strength—do not have permanent seats on the Security Council. You might cite as another example the dominance of the General Assembly by Third-World nations. And you also might cite the United Nations' inability to compel member nations to pay their assessments. You would not develop any of these examples in detail; however, they are important to your speech because *together* they support your claim that the structure of the United Nations is outmoded.

Hypothetical Example. In using a hypothetical example to support a claim, you ask listeners to *imagine* themselves in a particular situation. You might say the following:

> Suppose that year after year you spent more money than you took in. What would you have to do about that?

Listeners might conjure up images of severe cuts in their budget, selling their home or car, or even bankruptcy. You then could use this example to help the audience understand the difficult choices Congress makes in fashioning the federal budget.

Referring to a specific example can help you to explain the claims you are making, as this speaker does when addressing members of the city council.

Anecdote. An anecdote, or story, allows you to develop an example in greater detail. If your topic is the frustration of dealing with a bureaucracy, you might tell a story about someone's failure to get a problem resolved within the system. You could describe the maze of telephone inquiries and form letter replies and your hero's trek to the appropriate agency, only to be directed to the wrong office. Finally reaching the appropriate official, the person is patronized by a clerk who says, "According to our records, you are dead." Such an extended, engaging story would illustrate your point and help the audience relate to the issues.

Case Study. You often can support a general claim by zeroing in on one particular true case and discussing it in detail. If your topic is about whether campus codes to regulate offensive speech can be effective, you might describe one or two campuses that have tried this approach and then argue that their experiences illustrate whether such codes are workable in general. If you believe that making Election Day a national holiday would increase voter turnout, you might support your claim by drawing on case studies of nations where Election Day is a holiday. During recent political campaigns, candidates frequently have used this form of support when they showcase specific families they said would benefit more from their tax and spending proposals than from their opponent's.

Notice that all these types of examples work by relating a part of something to the whole. By examining a particular instance of whatever is being discussed, you may be able to support claims about the topic as a whole.

Documents

Word processing programs often identify anything they produce as a document, and Web pages are also sometimes called documents. But as a type of supporting material, the term **document** has a more specific meaning. It refers to primary sources that can establish a claim directly, without the need for opinion or speculation.

A person's will is a document specifying what will happen to his or her possessions after death. This document takes priority over someone's opinion about what the deceased "really wanted." Likewise, a lawyer who wants to know what the copyright law is will not ask for a colleague's opinion; he or she will look up the text of the act passed by Congress. If you want to know who has the authority to set the dues for the campus film society, you'll consult the society's bylaws—another example of a document.

Documents can be a valuable source of supporting material. The Declaration of Independence is often quoted to support the belief that there are natural rights. For many people, the Bible is the document most often quoted. In the investigation of Watergate, the 1972 break-in at the offices of the Democratic National Committee in Washington, D.C., the key documents were tape recordings. Transcripts of news interviews, television shows, or court proceedings are also documents, as are contracts and loan agreements. Even a bus schedule or weather report is a document.

The student who spoke about cheating on campus referred to a university document to show that academic dishonesty would not be tolerated:

> According to the student handbook we got as freshmen, cheating is "a serious breach of our commitment to ethical behavior as students" and will be punished with "a failing grade in the class and possible expulsion from the university."

document
Primary source that can establish a claim directly, without opinion or speculation.

CHOOSE A STRATEGY: Using Research to Support Your Speech

The Situation

Residents and business owners in the town where you live have established a grassroots community organization to convince the city council to ban smoking in local restaurants and bars. Your state doesn't have smoke-free laws in force; therefore, it is up to you and your fellow committee members to prove to city government leaders and other business owners—especially bar owners, where smoking is commonplace—that such a ban will not result in a drop in revenue. You and other group members recognize that environmental tobacco smoke provides a serious health risk to nonsmokers and has been associated with increases in rates of cancer, respiratory conditions, and cardiovascular problems. Your group plans to present your case at the next city council meeting, and you have been appointed spokesperson.

Making Choices

1. What questions do you need to answer in order to provide evidence to back up your proposal?
2. What sources of information will you use to research your case?

What If . . .

Suppose that your research shows that a loss in revenue is possible.

1. With one of your key arguments lacking support, what additional information should you get to support your overall case?
2. What other arguments might you make based on the evidence, and how might you support them?
3. What will you do with information that does not support your case?

Documents can be a solid form of evidence if your audience regards them as trustworthy—and if you quote them accurately. The exact words of a document provide a record that is not skewed by the opinions and interpretations of others.

Statistics

Supporting materials presented in quantitative form, as statistics, are especially useful when the scope of the topic is vast. They make it possible to generalize beyond a few specific examples and hence to make a powerful statement about larger populations. If you are speaking about your family or your college class, the scope of the topic is narrow enough that you probably don't need statistical support; you can just provide a set of examples or case studies. When your topic involves the state or the nation, however, one or two examples are unlikely to represent the diversity of the population.

Statistics are numbers that record the extent of something or the frequency with which something occurs; they take such forms as medians, averages, ratios, indices, and standardized scores. Such numbers become meaningful when they are compared with a baseline or other pattern to show a relationship between the two. For example, you might support a claim by comparing the median family income for different professions or different ethnic groups or different nations.

Statistics can be misleading. If they sound too strange to be true, they may not be accurate. Therefore, you need to understand how they were derived and exactly what they mean. If your audience is likely to doubt the truth of a statistic, you will need to support it in the speech more than you will for a statistic listeners are likely to accept.

statistics
Numbers recording the extent of something or the frequency with which it occurs.

Although statistical statements take a great variety of forms, the following four types are especially valuable for supporting material in speeches.

Watch the Video "Tobacco Ordinance Public Hearing (Cardiologist)" at **MyCommunicationLab**

Simple Enumeration.

The most basic form of a statistic is a single number. For example

> A total of 35 faculty members on our campus have won teaching awards.

Such statistics have the virtue of simplicity, but they may be difficult to interpret without more knowledge of the context. Having 35 winners of teaching awards on the faculty means one thing at a small college with only 60 faculty members, but it means something different for a large public university with 3,000 people on the faculty.

Interpreting simple enumerations can be tricky. For example, in the spring of 2003, President George W. Bush said that under his tax cut proposal,"92 million Americans would receive an average tax reduction of $1,083," The figure for the average tax reduction—the mean—was mathematically correct, but the average was skewed by a small number of very large reductions. Indeed, 50 percent of all taxpayers would see a tax cut of $100 or less.[2] Because context shapes our understanding of simple enumerations, you want to be very careful not just to accept them at face value, but to place them in appropriate contexts.

Surveys and Polls.

Suppose your topic was about how most Americans regard the public education system. In theory, you or someone else could interview all Americans and then tabulate the results. But not even the Census Bureau has been able to find and count all Americans, and the time and expense involved would make the task impossible. Moreover, the data would be obsolete by the time you completed your survey.

Instead, you can *infer* the attitudes of people as a whole from the attitudes reported by a sample of the population, as long as the sample is representative of the whole. In the case of public opinion about the performance of the U.S. Congress, a 2011 Gallup Poll reported that 86 percent of the sample interviewed said that they were dissatisfied with the way Congress is handling its job. That statistic would be used like this in a speech:

> The Gallup Poll reports that 86% of its sample are dissatisfied with Congress. Since it used a random sample, we can conclude that about 86% of the whole country—six out of every seven people—give Congress a failing grade.

Surveys and polls are widely used in the physical and social sciences and to gain information about public opinion on matters of policy. Not all are equally reliable, however. Check how the sample was selected; a random sample is more likely to be representative of the whole population than is a sample in which people of any particular viewpoint are more likely to be included. Check the wording of the questions asked to make sure that they are not slanted to encourage one answer rather than another. Check the reported margin of error to see whether the results reported might have occurred just by chance. And check the organization sponsoring the survey or poll to be sure that it does not have a vested interest in the outcome.

Rates of Change.

Often, what is noteworthy about a statistic is not its absolute size, but its rate of change. For instance, it may be more important to know that the national debt more than doubled during the period from 2000 to 2013 than to know the total dollar amount of the debt. Similarly, knowing that medical costs have increased at a much faster rate than personal income since 2000 may be more useful than knowing either of the exact amounts. And knowing that the world's population is doubling faster and faster may have greater implications than knowing the total population. Speakers often can illustrate and emphasize such dramatic rate changes through visual aids.

Rates of change show what is happening and can help an audience compare the situation to a known benchmark. By themselves, however, statistics may not tell much and may easily mislead others.[3] For example, one student speaker supported the claim that the university was not promoting affirmative action by citing what seemed like an important statistic:

> Did you know that fewer African Americans were admitted to this school this year than last year? There's no excuse for that! It proves that this school has no commitment to diversity.

The speaker had fallen into a statistical trap, however, by failing to note that the *total* number of students admitted was lower this year than last. The percentage of African American students in the entering class was actually slightly higher and had increased for three years in a row.

Rhetorical Workout

Assess Types of Supporting Information

You are researching a speech about the safety issue of maple-wood baseball bats used in Major League Baseball (MLB). You know that a number of players and fans have been injured, some seriously, by sharp pieces of wood that hit them after a maple bat shattered during its use in a game. You learn that bats made of ash wood don't break as easily as maple. You also read that MLB and the Players Association, which represents professional baseball players, did a study in 2008 and came up with new recommendations in 2009. Your speech will look at the issues surrounding the problem of shattering maple bats, the safety solutions proposed in 2009, and whether the new recommendations have made a difference in safety.

What types of supporting material might be applicable to your speech?

1. **Personal experience:** Suppose you've played baseball for several years. Is this experience worth mentioning? Why or why not?
2. **Common knowledge:** Are there any kinds of common knowledge you could draw on? What about the topic might connect with the shared beliefs or values of a classroom audience?
3. **Direct observation:** How useful would the following experiences be for informing your speech: (a) You once watched a craftsperson make a baseball bat. (b) You were at a baseball game when a bat broke and flew across the field, although it didn't hit anyone. (c) Last summer you went to a Major League game.
4. **Examples:** What kinds of examples would help support your speech?
5. **Documents:** How useful would the following documents be for your speech: (a) a press release announcing the findings of the 2008 study; (b) a video of a bat breaking; (c) a brochure about collectible bats that aren't for game use; (d) a letter from a bat manufacturer protesting the new rules.
6. **Statistics:** You find a statistic that says 2,232 bats broke during Major League games from July to September 2008. What are some other types of statistics and information you might need to find in order to put this number in context?
7. **Testimony:** You find an article that quotes some bat makers who think the new rules have no scientific merit. What types of information about the article, the bat makers who are quoted, and the new rules might help you decide the credibility of this testimony?

CHECKLIST 7.1

Testing the Strength of Supporting Material

1. Personal experience
   - ❒ Are you sure your memory is reliable?
   - ❒ Is your experience generalizable?
   - ❒ Will others interpret it the same way?
2. Common knowledge
   - ❒ Are you sure the audience shares it?
   - ❒ Are you sure it is correct?
3. Direct observation
   - ❒ Are you sure of what you saw?
   - ❒ Do you have any bias?
4. Examples
   - ❒ Are they representative?
   - ❒ Are there enough of them?
5. Documents
   - ❒ Can they be trusted?
   - ❒ Are they properly interpreted?
   - ❒ Is the context made clear?
6. Statistics
   - ❒ Are appropriate measures used?
   - ❒ Are they reliable and valid?
   - ❒ Have they been interpreted properly?
7. Testimony
   - ❒ Does the person have access to the data?
   - ❒ Is the person an expert on the subject?
   - ❒ Is the person reasonably objective?

Experiments. Experiments are controlled tests of the effect of one thing on another. They are conducted by comparing situations that are essentially similar except for the factor being tested. A claim that secondhand smoke leads to lung cancer, for example, would be supported by comparing the cancer rates of two groups that were similar in all essential respects except that one had been exposed to secondhand smoke and the other had not. It could be used in this way in a speech:

> Two groups of people were basically alike—same city; same mix of age, race, and gender; same overall health; same income; in fact, alike in just about every way you can imagine, except one: One group was regularly exposed to secondhand smoke and the other was not. And the group that was exposed had significantly higher rates of cancer. Guess why.

Similarly, the claim that African American drivers are stopped by police officers in a particular neighborhood more often than are Caucasian drivers could be tested by sending the same model car through the same neighborhood at the same time of day at the same speed with drivers who differ only in the color of their skin.

Testimony

Testimony is information or an opinion that is expressed by someone other than the speaker. When using testimony, you rely on someone else's judgment, and so you need to assess that person's competence and credibility. You may also need to convince the audience that your source is knowledgeable and trustworthy.

Factual Testimony. *Facts* are pieces of information that can be proved true or false. Speakers often support ideas by reporting facts that were gathered by others, such as quoting the secretary of state about developments in the Middle East, or quoting a public health expert about the dangers of secondhand smoke, or quoting a campus security officer about the number of crimes reported last year. When you quote facts, you are implying that you cannot verify the information yourself but are willing to accept it because you think the source is credible.

Opinion Testimony. *Opinions* are beliefs formed from experience and judgment. When you offer another person's opinion to support a claim, you are indicating that someone whose judgment is trusted, whose expertise is valued, or who is in a better position to know than most people are has reached a certain conclusion. You are asking the audience to accept that conclusion because of the person's expertise, judgment, or knowledge. Thus, you might quote an expert in Middle Eastern politics to support a point about the peace process in that region, or you might quote campus security officers about whether the campus is a safe place to be after dark.

testimony
Information or an opinion expressed by someone other than the speaker.

When using opinion testimony for support, consider whether the audience will know and trust the person you are quoting. You may have to establish why your source's opinion is more valuable than the average person's.

Tools for Locating Supporting Material

OBJECTIVE 7.3

Now that you know about the *types* of supporting material, what tools can you use to find it? Some common research tools are search engines, electronic databases, catalogs, and indexes.

Search Engines

The easiest way to begin research is on your computer. Anyone with Internet access and a Web browser can conduct online research, but locating a specific piece of information tucked somewhere within the over 185 million active websites can be a daunting task. Most researchers therefore use search engines, such as Google, Yahoo!, or Bing to navigate this sea of data. Search engines employ slightly different algorithms, which are constantly being refined, so you may not want to limit yourself to only one search engine.

Search engines respond to the directions they are given, so you should be as precise as you can in directing the search. To generate more accurate results, it is helpful to use search commands, such as quotation marks around phrases or the command "AND" between related keywords. Different search engines may have different commands, and it is important to realize that a search engine is only as good as the questions you ask. Therefore, you may also wish to dig deeper into the "Advanced Search" functions of a search engine.

The search engine will generate lists and brief descriptions of websites containing the terms you entered. Usually these will be arranged in order of potential relevance to your request or else according to the frequency with which they are consulted (or "hit"). You then click on the link to the website and peruse it for the information you are seeking. Keep in mind, though, that advertisements and other "sponsored" sites may pop up. The sites that are "hit" most often are not necessarily the most credible.

Strategies for Speaking to Diverse Audiences

Respecting Diversity Through Research

Using a variety of research sources will help you to find and to recognize diverse perspectives on your topic. These strategies will help you to do appropriate research in light of the diversity of your audience.

1. Go beyond U.S.-based media sources, particularly if your topic is international in scope.
2. Be aware of the partisanship of your media sources. Include both "liberal" and "conservative" perspectives on your topic.
3. Consider the "voices" you quote in your speech. Are they all male? American? Over age 55? Be sure you are presenting diverse and relevant perspectives.
4. Consider how to treat radical or "fringe" voices. Should they be discredited because they attract few supporters? Does treating them in the same way as "mainstream" voices give them too much weight? Should they be excluded if they are hateful? Or does the pursuit of diversity dictate that *all* voices should be heard?

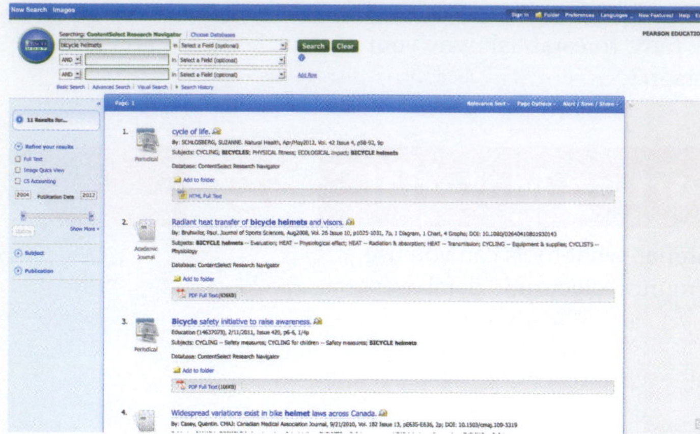

The search page of the EBSCOhost electronic database.

Electronic Databases

A search engine will direct you to websites that are available to anyone. Although these sites can be a good source of general information, you often can find more reliable, detailed, or pertinent information in subject-specific electronic databases. These provide full-text entries and abstracts from a wide range of academic and popular sources. Some databases are free and available to the public, like those listed in Table 7.1. Many, however, are available only on a subscription basis, and the cost of a subscription for an individual would be prohibitive. Fortunately, your college or university library most likely maintains subscriptions to many electronic

Table 7.1 Electronic databases

Source	Description	URL
ipl2 (*combines the Internet Public Library and the Librarians' Internet Index*)	Indexes online newspapers, magazines, and special collections.	www.ipl.org
Fed World Information Network	Index of local, state, and federal agencies.	www.fedworld.gov
Libweb	Links to library collections around the world.	www.lib-web.org
Bio.com	Database of famous people.	www.biography.com
American Rhetoric	Texts of famous American orators.	americanrhetoric.com
USA Services	Access to government documents.	www.usa.gov
THOMAS	Library of Congress site for learning about Congress and government.	thomas.loc.gov
State and Local Governments on the Net	Servers for each of the 50 states, with links to various branches of state government agencies, county or city servers.	www.statelocalgov.net
E-journals	Electronic journals organized by topic.	www.e-journals.org
White House	Links to White House documents.	www.whitehouse.gov
Fed Stats	Links to statistics from over 100 federal agencies.	www.fedstats.gov
Arts and Letters Daily	Media links, including magazines, newspapers, and wire services.	www.aldaily.com

databases in different fields of study. Some common databases are JSTOR, EBSCOhost, Project MUSE, and Lexis/Nexis. You may well be able to access these databases from your own computer by connecting to the library through the Internet; check with your reference librarian.

Catalogs

All libraries maintain catalogs of their collections, usually electronic catalogs that are searchable. If you have Internet access, you can likely connect to your college or university catalog and search by subject, author, title, or keywords to see what library resources are available. You may be able to connect to your local public library as well. In either case, you can contact a reference librarian if you need assistance.

In addition to the resources in your own library, you can check the holdings of more than 10,000 libraries worldwide by using WorldCat. This site (http://www.WorldCat.org) also offers varying degrees of access to databases, collections, library help, and other services.

Indexes

Newspapers, periodicals, and government publications publish indexes, many of which are available online and are searchable by author, title, subject, or key terms. These indexes will direct you to specific articles or reports on subjects of your interest.

Newspaper Indexes. Many major national newspapers have their own indexes, including the *New York Times* (probably the most comprehensive), the *Wall Street Journal* (especially good on business and economic issues), the *Christian Science Monitor*, the *Washington Post* (particularly on matters of national politics), the *Chicago Tribune*, and the *Los Angeles Times*.

Periodical Indexes. The most common index to periodicals is the *Reader's Guide to Periodical Literature*. This easy-to-use subject index can be found in virtually every library. With few exceptions, though, it indexes only popular, general-interest periodicals. More specialized indexes are also available. The *Bulletin of the Public Affairs Information Service* is useful for topics dealing with public policy issues. The *Social Sciences Index* and the *Humanities Index* can point you to journals and periodicals relating to these many disciplines. The *Business Periodicals Index* can help you research topics about the economy and business conditions, and the *Index to Legal Periodicals* covers law reviews and journals. The *Communication and Mass Media Index* includes hundreds of journals devoted to that topic. Finally, the *International Index to Periodicals* can guide you through journals published in other countries. Full-text versions of many periodical articles can be found through electronic services such as JSTOR and EBSCOhost.

Government Publication Indexes. The most comprehensive federal index is the *Monthly Catalog of U.S. Government Publications*, in which titles are arranged alphabetically under the government agency that published them. There also is a subject index, which usually would be the place to start. Although

At your library, you may be able to access digital material that is available only by subscription.

the *Monthly Catalog* is the most comprehensive index, it is not annotated. You will have to guess from the issuing agency and the title whether the document is of interest to you.

The *Congressional Information Service* is an especially valuable index to congressional publications because it includes abstracts, or brief summaries, of their contents. Again, the subject index lists entry numbers that you can use to look up the abstracts. The *Congressional Information Service* includes all publications of the legislative branch: hearings, committee reports, commissioned studies, and other documents. It does not index the executive or judicial branch, and it does not cover years before 1970. But for matters currently before Congress or that have been considered in the recent past, it is an invaluable index. Other indexes to federal government publications include the *Congressional Record Index*, the *American Statistics Index*, and the *Index to U.S. Government Periodicals*.

Supplementing the Tools

Even though most of the tools you will use can be accessed electronically, you may want to supplement them by physically going to the library. First, many sources are still not available electronically, and the library will have hard-copy versions of books, periodicals, and government publications. Second, if the library has open stacks (meaning that you can get the books you want rather than depending on library staff to get them for you) you can browse and discover material on your topic that is shelved near the book you want but that you might not discover otherwise. Third, you will be able to access digital materials that are available only by subscription if they can't be accessed from your own computer. And fourth, you will be able to consult with librarians who can give you valuable help on your topic and sometimes can direct you to reference materials of which you otherwise would be completely unaware.

Sometimes, the best source of supporting material is other people. Interviews enable you to ask the exact questions you need to have answered, and the give-and-take of the interview routine permits follow-up discussion. Moreover, people sometimes will make statements in an oral interview that they would not be willing to make in print or on the Internet. You will learn more about interviewing later in this chapter.

OBJECTIVE 7.4 Sources of Supporting Material

The tools described previously will lead you to the sources of your supporting material. These include periodicals, newspapers, books, reference works, government publications, other materials available online, and interviews. Many of these sources are available in both electronic and print formats, and they will be considered here without regard to the format in which you find them.

Periodicals

Periodicals (sometimes called *serials*) are published at regular intervals—usually weekly, monthly, or quarterly—and have the advantage of being more up to date than books.

General-Interest Periodicals. These are usually sold on newsstands and by subscription, and they thus circulate widely; examples include *Time, Newsweek, U.S. News & World Report*, and *People*. Periodicals such as these may have useful information about current events, but their coverage of issues is fairly brief and not deep, with the exception of feature articles. Given their mass circulation, they may be useful in identifying topics of interest and prevalent attitudes among many readers.

Other general-interest periodicals are more focused journals of opinion that delve more deeply into issues and often espouse a particular point of view. Examples include *The American Prospect* and *Progressive* (liberal) and *Commentary* and *National Review* (conservative). Consult sources such as these when you are interested in a particular political perspective on your topic. Other opinion journals, such as *Atlantic* and *Harper's*, tend to represent more diverse and eclectic viewpoints.

Special-Interest Periodicals. These are intended for readers who have particular interests, which may be as broadly defined as business (*Fortune* and *Bloomberg BusinessWeek*) or pop music (*Rolling Stone* and *Spin*) or may be as narrowly focused as snowmobiles, digital imaging, or coin collecting. Whatever your topic is, you probably can find a periodical that is devoted to it. Some are aimed at specific demographic groups—based on age, gender, ethnicity, and so on—and even cities, for that matter, are the focus of magazines named after them.

Technical Periodicals. These are written primarily for specialists in a given field. Scholarly journals are the obvious example, with one or more publications dedicated to most academic disciplines: *American Political Science Review, Journal of the American Medical Association, Journal of American History, American Bar Association Journal, Quarterly Journal of Speech*, and so on. Colleges and universities also sometimes publish scholarly journals, such as *Critical Inquiry* and *Yale Review*. Law reviews also fit into this category. Although journals such as these are intended mainly for subject-matter specialists, they sometimes include material that can be very helpful for a speech, such as the results of surveys, experiments, and historical and critical analyses conducted by experts in various fields.

Newspapers

Newspapers remain an important source of information that you can use for your speeches. Besides reporting the latest news, many newspapers analyze and interpret it and publish related feature articles, columns, and editorials. Your own daily newspaper will be a helpful source. Especially if you live outside a major metropolitan area, though, it's a good idea to consult newspapers that cover current events and opinions more comprehensively than your local paper does. This is particularly important if you are doing research on topics of national or international significance.

Books

Both general and specific books about your topic—as well as anthologies of essays by different authors—can be valuable sources of supporting material. If the book is not available electronically, its call number—which you can obtain from the digital catalog—will tell you where to find it on the library shelves.

Sometimes, particularly if your library is small, you may run across a citation to a book that your library does not have. Fortunately, most libraries can arrange an interlibrary loan, using specialized indexes to help you identify other libraries that have the book and borrowing it for you. Be aware, however, that this takes time. If you anticipate needing books that your library doesn't have, request them far ahead of when you will need them for your speech. The librarian in charge of interlibrary loans can explain the procedure and time frame to you.

Reference Works

Reference works are not intended to be read from start to finish; they do not develop a sustained argument or claim, and they usually are not written in narrative form. Rather, they are convenient collections of facts and information. In print form, they typically are shelved in a special section of the library, where a reference librarian can help you. Online, they are a convenient source for finding information quickly. Some of these sources will be familiar to you already; others may not be.

- *Dictionaries* not only tell you the definitions of a word but also trace its origin and usage. Besides general dictionaries, you can find specialized dictionaries that identify the terms and usage within particular fields, such as finance or medicine.
- *General encyclopedias* can sometimes be found in print form, but today many are accessible online. One of the largest and most viewed sites on the Web is the encyclopedia Wikipedia. Within general guidelines, anyone can contribute to it or revise entries, which makes the site accessible but also allows for easy corruption of data and misrepresentation of facts. That does not mean that all Wikipedia entries are inaccurate; many are comprehensive and adequately documented. You cannot be sure of the accuracy, so you need to verify facts, cross-check stories, and investigate the identity of the author. Wikipedia can be useful as a starting point to develop background knowledge, to locate primary sources, and to formulate research questions that you can try to answer by consulting other sources, even if you do not quote from it directly.

Watch the Video "Melissa Beall on Wikipedia as a Primary Source of Information" at **MyCommunicationLab**

- *Specialized encyclopedias and handbooks* are subject-specific and contain brief essays that will give you an overview of a subject. Examples include the *Encyclopedia of Philosophy*, the *Handbook on Race and Ethnicity*, the *International Encyclopedia of Communications*, and the *Handbook of the Supreme Court of the United States*. If you're looking up a subject that is not the main focus of your speech, the encyclopedia or handbook may be all you need. If you need a deeper understanding, the handbook or encyclopedia often will have bibliographical references that will steer you to other subjects.
- *Abstracts* are short summaries of articles or books related to a particular discipline. Many academic and professional groups publish abstracts of the articles appearing in their current journals. By reading abstracts instead of entire journals, you can discover which articles include material that may be useful.
- *Fact books* are compilations of statistical information that you can consult when you need specific data to support a point in your speech. Almanacs,

for example, are published every year and supply up-to-date facts about an enormous range of subjects.

- *Biographical references* identify particular individuals and outline their backgrounds and achievements. *Who's Who* is the best-known biographical reference, but a vast number of such sources can tell you about both contemporary and historical figures.
- *Compilations* and *yearbooks* are edited collections of material of a given type. For example, *Editorials on File* is a digest of selected newspaper editorials arranged by topic; it is published regularly and then compiled into a yearbook each year. Other examples of such compilations are *Facts on File* and *Congressional Quarterly Almanac,* an especially useful guide to the status of issues currently before the U.S. Congress. *Congressional Quarterly* also publishes a pamphlet called *CQ Researcher,* which examines a different issue of public interest each week. This compilation of facts and opinions includes background information, editorials about each side of the issue, and a bibliography of important books and articles to help you start researching the issue.
- *Atlases* provide geographical information, including the exact location and physical characteristics of specific sites, cities, and regions.
- *Collections of quotations* are useful both for tracking down the origin of popular sayings and for finding maxims or brief quotations related to a particular topic.
- *Book previews* will alert you to forthcoming books that may be relevant to your topic. You can find previews through such services as Amazon.com and books.google.com.

Government Publications

Many college and university libraries are government depositories, which means that they regularly receive copies of most federal (and sometimes state) government publications. Some also include the publications of foreign governments and of the United Nations.

Covering virtually every public issue, government publications include bulletins, reports, pamphlets, research studies, congressional deliberations, judicial opinions, and agency publications. Often, however, these are not indexed in the general digital catalog or in other online tools. If your speech topic is of concern to government bodies, you are well advised to visit the Government Publications section of your library and to consult with the librarian in charge.

Other Materials Found Online

Many documents that are hard to find otherwise are posted online and can be located through the use of search engines. These include papers presented at professional meetings, conference proceedings, position papers, working documents and archives of groups and organizations, and unpublished essays and manuscripts. These often can provide valuable background, lend a behind-the-scenes perspective on a topic, and give you access to specialized information. They should be viewed with some caution, however, because there often is no quality control in the selection of materials to post.

In addition, millions of individuals, companies, associations, professional organizations, and government agencies maintain websites to provide information and links to related sites. The home page for a university's website, for instance, might contain links to such topics as admissions, degree requirements, departments and curricula, events and activities, and recent news. Table 7.2 lists some examples of subject-specific websites. Also, many people maintain blogs on which they post their thoughts and invite comments from others. Blogs can permit extended discussion of an issue. Because websites and blogs are often self-published, they will vary greatly in quality and should be used with caution.

Table 7.2 Examples of subject-specific websites

Site	URL
Macworld	www.macworld.com
American Psychological Association	www.apa.org
Internet Movie Database	www.imdb.com
Susan G. Komen for the Cure	www.komen.org
U.S. Green Building Council	www.usgbc.org
Presidential Rhetoric	www.presidentialrhetoric.com

Interviews

It is not only national and international experts who provide valuable interviews. The manager of the local department store has a perspective on how economic conditions affect consumer confidence. Faculty members have expertise on a variety of issues in every academic discipline. And fellow students can tell you about all aspects of campus life, including, say, how changes in funding for student loans may affect their educational plans. The following guidelines will help make your interviews effective.

Prepare for the Person. Learn as much as you can about the people you plan to interview. How long have they held their current position? What experiences have they had with the subject? Are they prominently identified with an issue or aspect of your topic? Are they well known, or will you need to establish their credentials?

Prepare for the Subject. It is a waste of your sources' time if you ask them very general questions or seek information that you can get easily in other ways. Don't let the interview substitute for your own background reading and research. For instance, if you were interviewing a local banker about the influence of the national economy on your town, you should not need to ask such a basic question as "Can you tell me the definition of a recession?" Make sure that you understand basic concepts that are likely to come up in the interview so that you can focus your questions on unique information that your source can provide.

Prepare for the Format. An interview is a particular kind of communication event that proceeds through questions and answers. Before the interview, formulate your questions carefully so that they are not vague and not leading or hostile. Your questions should be simple and direct and should not anticipate answers or favor any particular viewpoint. Give your sources the opportunity to make their own judgments, to explain why they think as they do, and to comment on different points of view that others may have expressed.

Having specific questions prepared for your subject will help with the flow of the interview, but also be open to answers that may lead you in an unexpected direction.

Also be aware that different types of questions elicit different types of information. A **closed question** limits the respondent to a fixed number of choices, such as "Would it be more efficient for campus security to invest in (1) an escort system or (2) a shuttle bus?" This type of question directs the respondent to pick one option from those you have offered, which is helpful when you want to commit the person to a definite position. A closed question also allows you to count and compare the answers of different respondents, because they all choose from the same list of answers. However, closed questions do not reveal much about respondents' thinking and opinions.

In contrast, an **open-ended question** does not limit or direct the person's response, as in "What do you think should be done to enhance campus security?" Although an open-ended question does permit full expression of opinions, the answer may stray far from the information you most need for your speech, and you may have to refocus the interview.

Conduct the Interview Competently. Being a competent interviewer includes such basic matters as arriving on time, reminding the person who you are and the purpose of your interview, and thanking him or her for taking the time to help you. But competence also includes the ability to adjust your questions in response to the flow of the interview itself. The person may say something that answers several of your questions or parts of them, or a comment may bring up a question that you had not planned on asking. Do not regard your questions as rigid and inflexible; adjust them as the interview evolves. However, if the interviewee seems to ignore a question, you may need to ask it again, perhaps phrasing it differently. Or, you may need to ask a **follow-up question** that explores the implications of a previous response. Finally, you must take care to reach an agreement with the respondent about what information, if any, you can quote directly and what information is solely for your own use.

closed question
A question with a finite number of choices from which the respondent must pick.

open-ended question
A question that does not restrict the range of possible responses.

follow-up question
A question that explores the implications of a previous response.

Take Notes or Record the Interview. Don't assume that you will remember everything important that is said during an interview. Arrive prepared, with notebook in hand, so you can keep track of important points. If you prefer to record the interview, be sure to ask ahead of time whether that will be all right; no one should be recorded without permission. Think carefully about recording the interview, however. Although it does free you from the burden of note taking and ensures an accurate record of the interview, it also may make the respondent more guarded and less candid, knowing that every word is being "recorded for posterity."

CHECKLIST 7.2

Guidelines for Interviewing

- ❐ Prepare for the person.
- ❐ Prepare for the subject.
- ❐ Prepare for the format.
- ❐ Conduct the interview competently.
- ❐ Take notes or record the interview.
- ❐ Determine what information to use.

Determine What to Use in Your Speech. Not everything that you obtain in an interview will be useful in your speech; nor should the interview be your sole source of information. As you assemble materials for the speech, ask yourself which points can be supported most effectively by the interview and which points can be supported just as well by other sources. For example, you may decide to rely on printed sources for general or statistical information about your topic and then draw on the interview for opinion testimony and for real-world examples.

OBJECTIVE 7.5

Evaluating Evidence

From whatever source your supporting materials were obtained, you want to be sure that your evidence is credible—that it should be taken seriously and given weight by an audience of reasonable people. Unfortunately, not all supporting materials will meet this standard.

Potential Deficiencies in Evidence

Several factors can make evidence deficient. Poor evidence may be:

- *Unavailable for inspection*: In some cases, the evidence is kept secret and its quality cannot be assessed.
- *Inaccurate or uncertain*: Some evidence may be false or misleading. It may report inaccurately or out of context. The source of the evidence may be unknown.
- *Not credible*: The source may not be credible, whether because of inexperience or bias.
- *Not from a relevant expert*: The source may be speaking outside his or her field of expertise, as when a distinguished scientist offers opinions about the salary structure in baseball.
- *Inconsistent*: The evidence may be internally inconsistent—for example, one part of the evidence might assume that college students have significant discretionary income while another part of the evidence assumes that their budgets are strapped.
- *Contradicted*: The evidence may be contradicted by the best evidence from other sources.
- *Outdated*: The evidence may be out of date, supplanted by more recent evidence. Some matters are timeless, but for others recency is crucial. For example, in discussing how many nations in the world have the capability to develop nuclear weapons, it makes a difference whether the evidence comes from 2004 or 2014.
- *Irrelevant*: If the evidence is completely true but does not help to advance the speaker's main claim, then it is not strong evidence. The supporting material must be relevant to the point it claims to support.

You can use Checklist 7.3 to help test the credibility of your supporting material.

The Quality of Internet Evidence

There are additional concerns that relate to evidence obtained from the Internet. The Internet has been described as the most democratic means of publishing there is. Virtually anyone can post virtually anything on the Web. As a consequence, there is almost no editorial or quality control except whatever is exercised by the producer of the site. An online version of a printed publication—an electronic copy of a print journal article, for example—can be assumed to reflect the same editorial judgment as the printed publication itself. At the other extreme, an individual's personal website may not have been checked at all. And some organizations whose mission is to promote a particular viewpoint can be deceptive, presenting propaganda as if it were scholarship.

Search engines attempt to distinguish between reliable and unreliable websites, but they cannot do so perfectly. And whether the site looks "professional" is not a reliable indicator either, because it is easier to design a sophisticated-looking site than it is to produce a book. In fact, sophisticated websites that look like those of easily recognized organizations have been created for the purpose of coaxing individuals to reveal their Social Security and credit card numbers in order to facilitate identity theft. This, of course, is fraud.[4] Extra vigilance is needed to be sure that you take only reliable evidence from the Web. For these reasons, the responsibility to evaluate Internet evidence rests with you. We need, therefore, to note some special precautions about supporting materials from electronic sources. The following questions are especially pertinent:[5]

- **Does the site meet the basic standards of credibility?** At a minimum, a credible website should contain the name of the sponsor, identification of expert and believable author(s) or contributor(s), and information that is current, appropriate, and capable of being checked for accuracy.
- **Who set up the website?** If you cannot tell who sponsors the site, be suspicious of its contents. People or organizations with an ax to grind can disguise their motivations or identity, leading you to regard biased information as though it were neutral. One clue to a site's reliability is its *domain name*—the last portion of its URL. As a general rule, URLs that end in .gov (government agency) or .edu (educational institution) may be more reliable sites than those ending in .org (organization) or .com (commercial source).
- **What are the source's credentials?** To determine whether the author has expertise on the subject, you should check a credentials page. You may need to trace back in the URL (Internet address) to find one. If the author has a specific agenda or ideology, take that into consideration when you evaluate the source.
- **What is the purpose of the website?** If the goal is to sell a product or service or to campaign for an individual or a point of view, you should examine the content more skeptically than if the goal is simply to provide information. Sometimes the site's purpose will not be apparent from its title and the name of the source. You will need to read through the material on the site in order to form a judgment.

CHECKLIST 7.3

Testing the Credibility of Supporting Material[6]

- ❒ Is the evidence available for inspection?
- ❒ Is the evidence accurate?
- ❒ Is the source credible?
- ❒ Is the source making statements within his or her expertise?
- ❒ Is the evidence internally consistent?
- ❒ Is the evidence contradicted by the best evidence from other sources?
- ❒ Is the evidence recent enough?
- ❒ Is the evidence relevant to the point that it supports?

Watch the **Video** "Melissa Beall Discusses the Credibility of Online Sources" at **MyCommunicationLab**

- **Does the content appear to reflect scholarship?** Scholarly work generally provides documentation for claims, indicates where information was obtained, describes limits of the data and does not overstate claims, considers alternative viewpoints on matters of opinion and describes these alternatives accurately, honors context, and relies on critical thinking skills (such as those discussed in Chapter 1). If the site contains excessive claims of certainty, presents ideas out of context or without documentation, and suppresses alternative views, it is more likely to be biased advocacy or propaganda.
- **Can you confirm the information?** If you find information on the Web that seems to make your case airtight or to refute someone's ideas conclusively, be careful. A good general rule is to check electronic information against other sources. Even if you can't find the exact same facts or ideas, what you obtain from the Web should be compatible with what you learn from people or in print.
- **When was the site last updated?** One of the chief virtues of the Web is that it can supply up-to-the-minute information about current topics. Often, however, sites are not updated regularly, and the information becomes obsolete. If you cannot tell when a site was last updated, that may be a reason to be wary of its content.

OBJECTIVE 7.6 A Plan for Research

Researching for a speech can seem overwhelming. At first, the topic may seem so vast that you don't know where to begin. You may not be able to think of any people you should interview, or you may identify so many people that you don't have time to question them all. The resources of a major library can be daunting, and specialized indexes may only compound the problem by revealing an even larger mass of material to consider. Also, the Internet sources you checked might include thousands of citations. How can you possibly go through them all?

A research strategy can make these burdens manageable. Just as you need to understand your speech goals and the means to achieve them, you need to approach research strategically. The following suggestions will help you devise a research strategy.

Start Early. Don't wait until the last minute to begin preparing your speech. Research does take time and involves a certain amount of trial and error. The sooner you begin thinking about and working on the speech, the better.

Determine Where You Need to Go. Your topic may require you to do research on the Internet, in the library, in the field, or with a combination of these tools. The analysis of the issues related to your topic, described in Chapter 6, should help you determine which questions you need to answer and which kinds of research will help you answer them. Keep those questions in mind as you do your research.

Bring Necessary Materials and Supplies. It's frustrating (and often embarrassing) to arrive at the research site and discover that you don't have the

A Question of Ethics

Ethics and Research

Research is important to a speech because it ensures both that the speech is accurate and that you are credible. Using external sources, testimony, and data all increase your and the audience's knowledge of a topic. But the more you rely on others, the less room you have for your own analysis and conclusions. What is more, it may seem that you are just a conduit for other people's ideas. Is this ethical? Is there a point at which a speech suffers from too much information and citation? Do you have a responsibility to make sure your ideas are your own? Even if you appropriately cite every source in your speech, is it truly your speech if it is merely a well-crafted series of citations, quotations, and statistics gathered from other places? Conversely, is it ethical to expect any audience to accept your conclusions just on your own say-so? Why or why not?

materials you need. For example, if you are conducting interviews, you may need an audio recorder and batteries as well as a notebook and pen. In the library, you may need a laptop, a USB flash drive, notecards or paper, and pencils or pens. You also will need to be prepared to pay for the use of a copier. Think ahead.

Learn the Library's Layout. You do not want to waste valuable research time figuring out how the library is arranged and where things are located. You should know your way around. Learn where to find the digital catalog terminals, the reference room, and the stacks. Find out where periodicals, newspapers, and government publications are kept. Learn whether copiers and computer labs are available and what the library's hours and procedures are. If your library offers an orientation tour, arrange to take it before you begin intensive research for your speech. And do not be afraid to ask librarians questions, because they usually are knowledgeable about the library's resources and genuinely helpful.

Develop a Preliminary Bibliography. Consult the various indexes and reference works described in this chapter to develop a list of potential sources. To save time later, this preliminary bibliography should include the URL or other online locator, or the call numbers or other identifying numbers you will need to locate the material.

Set Priorities Within the Bibliography. The order of items in your bibliography probably will not reflect the order in which you want to read the materials. Decide what is most important to locate right away. It may be a particular aspect of the topic or a certain kind of source.

Read Progressively. If you are not yet very familiar with your topic, begin by reading general works to gain a background understanding of key terms, major issues, and the origins and development of the subject. This background will prepare you for in-depth reading about the specific issues that you will highlight in your speech. Finally, there probably are particular claims or arguments for which you will need support: a specific example, a particular statistic, or a certain piece of testimony.

As you proceed through your research, be clear about what level of understanding you seek. In general, if you find yourself reading about the same points repeatedly in different sources, it is time to move on to a more specialized level of research.

Read Selectively. Very likely, you will discover far more information than you can read—or even skim—in the time you have to prepare your speech. The key is to be selective in what you read. For example, check the dates of available sources. For some topics, such as how soon the economy may pull out of a recession, very recent material is crucial. For other topics, such as the origins of the Social Security system, older material may be more valuable. If the date seems inappropriate for your purpose, don't bother consulting that source.

Read Efficiently. Doing research is not like reading a novel; you want to read quickly and efficiently, not from start to finish. The goal is to identify which elements of a document or source are most pertinent for your speech. Skim material, looking for key words and a general sense of the context. Use guides—such as the subheadings and specific pages on a website, or a book's table of contents, index, and headings—to determine which sections to read carefully and which you may skim or skip. Stay alert, however; efficiency is not haste, and you do not want to make a wrong turn somewhere that causes you to misunderstand the context of key points.

Be Open to New Ideas. Even though you are researching with a particular goal in mind, keep open the possibility that your investigation may change your perspective or uncover something about your topic that you had not considered. You might discover issues that you did not originally anticipate, and you might even decide to change your thesis statement.

Watch the **Video** "Informative Speech: Fast Foods" at **MyCommunicationLab**

Use Multiple Sources and Evidence of Various Types. Your speech will be less credible if all the supporting material comes from a single source or is of one type. If you use a single source to support your claims, the audience may think that you are simply parroting the thoughts of someone else. For example, one student's speech about recycling presented the same information, in the same order, as did a pamphlet that had been distributed to every student on campus. Not only did this student bore the audience with information they already had, but she made them angry because they thought she was trying to avoid the work of amassing evidence from different sources, evaluating it, and arranging it creatively for their benefit.

Likewise, the speech will be less interesting if all your evidence is of the same type. A mix of examples, testimony, statistics, and other types of support not only will hold the audience's attention but also will add credibility to your claims by suggesting that the same conclusion was reached through several different methods.

Explore the **Exercise** "Avoiding Plagiarism" at **MyCommunicationLab**

plagiarism
Using someone else's words or ideas as though they were your own.

Protect Against Plagiarism. In Chapter 1, we were alerted to avoid **plagiarism**, which is usually thought of as the use of someone else's words as though they were your own. But the same warning applies to using someone else's *ideas* as though they were yours. In either case, the plagiarist both misrepresents himself or herself and steals the intellectual property of another.

Most people recognize that plagiarism is wrong. When it happens, it usually is unintentional. A student organizes her speech in exactly the same way as a magazine article on the same subject without identifying the article and either doesn't realize it happened or doesn't recognize that it is a form of plagiarism. Another student thinks he is paraphrasing his source, but in fact is engaged in almost direct quotation without saying so. Because he identified the source, he may not think this is plagiarism, or he may not realize how close his speech stays to the original. A third student gives a speech basically reporting what a single source said without identifying the source because the student's speech was not a direct quotation. He, too, has misrepresented another person's thinking by treating it as his own idea. Each of these examples is a form of plagiarism.

How can you protect against plagiarism while doing your research? First, don't limit yourself to a single source. The need to bring together several different sources should reduce any unconscious tendency to stick too closely to the text. Second, as you take notes, paraphrase except when the exact words of the source are important to quote. In this way, you'll cast your notes in your own words right from the beginning. Third, organize your notes without any of the sources immediately at hand, so you won't be tempted to follow someone else's organizational structure. Finally, whenever you draw upon one of your notes to use it in the speech, be sure you identify the source.

CHECKLIST 7.4

Research Strategy Checklist

- ❒ Start early.
- ❒ Determine where you need to go.
- ❒ Bring necessary materials and supplies.
- ❒ Learn the library's layout and the locations of various materials.
- ❒ Develop a preliminary bibliography.
- ❒ Set priorities within the bibliography.
- ❒ Read progressively.
- ❒ Read selectively.
- ❒ Read efficiently.
- ❒ Be open to new ideas.
- ❒ Use multiple sources and evidence of various types.
- ❒ Protect against plagiarism.
- ❒ Keep a speech material file.
- ❒ Know when to stop.

Keep a Speech Material File. Sometimes you will find materials that could be useful in a speech while you are doing something else—reading the newspaper, watching television, conversing with others, or studying for other courses. Don't lose track of this material or assume that you can find it when you need it. If you think that you may want to talk about a subject later in the term, begin now to save relevant material as you come across it.

Experienced speakers develop a **speech material file**. The file might be a notebook in which you jot down ideas, quotations, stories, poetry, or interesting examples. It might be a file of clippings from newspaper or magazine articles. More likely, it will be an electronic file that you keep on your computer with documents, images, and links that you find interesting or potentially useful. The form of the file is not as important as the habit of keeping one. You will be pleasantly surprised by how much easier it is to prepare a speech when you do not have to start from scratch, when you already have materials about topics that interest you.

Know When to Stop. Research is an ongoing activity, and you can always learn more about any topic—especially if you enjoy the subject and like doing research. But there comes a point at which you must stop collecting evidence and assemble the speech, which, after all, has limits of time and scope. Besides, you want to leave enough time for the other steps of preparation; further research will only tell you more about what you already know—and more than you can possibly tell the audience. Considerations such as these should help you to determine when it is time to move on to the other steps of speech preparation. As you develop the speech, you can return to research as needed to fill specific holes.

speech material file
A file of clippings, quotations, ideas, and other gleanings on a variety of subjects that may be used as supporting materials.

OBJECTIVE 7.7

Note Taking

No matter how thorough or extensive your research is, it will do you little good if you forget what you learned or where you learned it. Sometimes, something will seem so vivid or so obvious that you cannot imagine forgetting it, but most people remember far less than they think they will. Experienced speakers have learned to keep track of their speech material by establishing a system of note taking. Be guided by whatever works best for you, but the following suggestions should help you to establish an effective note-taking system.

Use a Flexible System. Recording each idea, statistic, example, quotation, and the like on an individual note card or sheet of paper is better than taking continuous notes about different topics or taking notes in a spiral notebook or other bound book. A flexible system is one that makes it easy to sort and rearrange material in organizing the speech, to locate related materials, and to discard items that you decide not to use. Taking notes on a computer may be the most flexible system, as long as you can rearrange the notes easily when developing the speech.

When taking notes from electronic sources, you can follow the same methods described here—copying material from the monitor onto note cards or sheets of paper. There are also programs that enable you to take notes electronically, such as EndNote and Zotero.

Include Full Bibliographic Citations. A "full" citation contains all the material needed to find the source from which you took notes. This step may seem time-consuming, but you can make it more efficient through careful use of abbreviations. In any case, it should not be omitted. First, you often will need to go back to the original source to verify your notes, to check their context, or to compare them with other sources. Second, the bibliographic information will often be helpful in evaluating the strength of evidence or in choosing among different sources of evidence. It takes far more time and effort to find the source a second time than to note its full bibliographic citation while doing research.

Standard guides for citing sources cover both print and electronic sources. Whatever citation system you use, it is important to use it consistently. (See Table 7.3 for some examples.)

The purpose of citation is to allow someone to obtain information from the sources you used. Unlike print materials, a document on the Internet can appear, disappear, or be revised without any warning. For this reason, you need to include information on when a source

Taking notes from different sources in your own words will enable you to integrate material from different sources and avoid the risk of plagiarism.

was posted on the Internet (if that is available) and, for some citation styles, on when you obtained the information. If you think that the Internet source may play a large role in your speech, it is a good idea either to print or to download the electronic document, preserving it in the form in which you consulted it.

Citing sources in notes or a bibliography is an essential part of your research. When you cite the source orally, during the speech itself, the process is a bit different. We will consider that issue in Chapters 9 and 11, when we discuss incorporating supporting materials into the speech and the presentation outline.

Table 7.3 Bibliographic formats

American Psychological Association (APA)—References

Type of Source	Sample Format
Book	White, R. C., Jr. (2009). *A. Lincoln: A biography.* New York, NY: Random House.
Chapter from an edited book	Hauser, G. A. (2008). Rethinking deliberative democracy: Rhetoric, power, and civil society. In T. F. McDorman & D. M. Timmerman (Eds.), *Rhetoric and democracy: Pedagogical and political practices* (pp. 225–264). East Lansing, MI: Michigan State University Press.
Magazine or newspaper article (online)	Stolberg, S. G., & Zeleny, J. (2009, September 10). Obama, armed with details, challenges Congress. *The New York Times.* Retrieved from http://www.nytimes.com
Magazine or newspaper article (print)	Stolberg, S. G., & Zeleny, J. (2009, September 10). Obama, armed with details, challenges Congress. *The New York Times,* p. A1.
Journal article (online)	Howell, B. W. (2008). Reagan and Reykjavik: Arms control, SDI, and the argument from human rights. *Rhetoric & Public Affairs, 11,* 389–415. doi: 10.1353/rap.0.0045
Journal article (print)	Bostdorff, D. M. (2009). Judgment, experience, and leadership: Candidate debates on the Iraq war in the 2008 presidential primaries. *Rhetoric & Public Affairs, 12,* 223–277.
Web page	Mehltretter, S. A. (2009). John F. Kennedy, "Inaugural Address," 1961. *Voices of Democracy.* Retrieved from http://www.voicesofdemocracy.umd.edu/documents/Mehltretter-Kennedy.pdf
Personal interview*	*Interviews are not listed in References. Cite in outline or text as: (O. Winfrey, personal communication, August 15, 2009).

(continued)

Table 7.3 Bibliographic formats (*continued*)

Modern Language Association (MLA)—Works Cited	
Type of Source	**Sample Format**
Book	White, Ronald C., Jr. *A. Lincoln: A Biography.* New York: Random, 2009. Print.
Chapter from an edited book	Hauser, Gerard A. "Rethinking Deliberative Democracy: Rhetoric, Power, and Civil Society." *Rhetoric and Democracy: Pedagogical and Political Practices.* Ed. Todd F. McDorman and David M. Timmerman. East Lansing: Michigan State UP, 2008. 225–64. Print.
Magazine or newspaper article (online)	Stolberg, Sheryl Gay, and Jeff Zeleny. "Obama, Armed with Details, Challenges Congress." *New York Times.* New York Times, 10 Sept. 2009. Web. 3 Jan. 2010.
Magazine or newspaper article (print)	Stolberg, Sheryl Gay, and Jeff Zeleny. "Obama, Armed with Details, Challenges Congress." *New York Times* 10 Sept. 2009, natl. ed.: A1. Print.
Journal article (online)	Howell, B. Wayne. "Reagan and Reykjavik: Arms Control, SDI, and the Argument from Human Rights." *Rhetoric and Public Affairs* 11.3 (2008): 389–415. *Project Muse.* Web. 10 Sept. 2009.
Journal article (print)	Bostdorff, Denise M. "Judgment, Experience, and Leadership: Candidate Debates on the Iraq War in the 2008 Presidential Primaries." *Rhetoric and Public Affairs* 12 (2009): 223–77. Print.
Web page	Mehltretter, Sara Ann. "John F. Kennedy, 'Inaugural Address,' 1961." *Voices of Democracy.* U of Maryland, 2009. Web. 3 Jan. 2010.
Personal interview	Winfrey, Oprah. Personal interview. 15 Aug. 2009.

Note: For citations of online sources, MLA lists two dates. The first is the date of online publication and the second is the date you accessed the source.

Decide Whether to Quote or to Paraphrase the Source. Unless an exact quotation is necessary, you can paraphrase, to summarize the gist of the idea in your own words. That way, you will be less likely accidentally to plagiarize. In any case, your note-taking system should signal to you at a glance whether a note is quoted or not. A good method is to enclose the words of others in quotation marks but to omit them from your own paraphrases or summaries.

Clearly Identify Deletions and Additions in Quoted Material. Sometimes, the quotation you want to use is interspersed with other material that is unrelated to your purposes or is longer than you want to quote. At other times, the quotation may not be clear unless you add some words—for example, to identify the reference of a pronoun in the quotation.

When you use a quotation, you must make certain that all deletions and insertions are faithful to the context of the original source. Your notes should identify any variations from the exact text of the quotation. The most common practice is to identify deletions in your notes with an ellipsis (a series of three dots, like this: . . .) and to identify insertions in notes with brackets (like this: [ ]). It is important to use brackets rather than parentheses, because parentheses would indicate that the inserted words were in the original source. (In the speech itself, use changes in pitch or rate to identify insertions or deletions.)

Take Notes Only Once. If you take notes in longhand, be sure that you write legibly so that you do not have to recopy or type the notes. Duplicate note taking is a waste of time. Increasingly, laptop computers are used for note taking at the library, which overcomes the problem of unclear handwriting. A computer also lets you take notes in continuous fashion and later print them out on separate sheets of paper, as recommended earlier. Or you may keep your notes in electronic files that you can search and manipulate as needs arise.

What Have You Learned?

Objective 7.1: Make strategic choices about research in light of your audience and your purpose.

Research is the process of locating the supporting materials to be used in the speech.

Objective 7.2: Identify the types of material that are available to support the ideas in your speech.

Types of supporting materials include the following:

- Personal experience
- Common knowledge
- Direct observation
- Examples
- Documents
- Statistics
- Testimony

Objective 7.3: Use tools to locate supporting materials for your speech.

Tools for finding supporting materials, in the order most people use them, are the following:

- Search engines
- Electronic databases
- Catalogs
- Indexes

These tools can be supplemented by visiting the library or by interviewing people.

Objective 7.4: Describe several categories of sources you can use as supporting materials and when you might use each.

Sources of supporting material, whether obtained electronically or in hard copy, include the following:

- Periodicals
- Newspapers
- Books
- Reference works
- Government publications
- Other materials found online, such as individual or corporate websites, conference proceedings, archives, and unpublished writings
- Interviews

Objective 7.5: Explain the factors that can cause evidence to be deficient and the strategic questions you can use to evaluate Internet evidence.

Potential deficiencies in evidence include the following:

- Evidence unavailable for inspection
- Inaccurate or uncertain evidence
- Evidence that is not credible
- Evidence not from a relevant expert
- Inconsistent evidence
- Contradicted evidence
- Outdated evidence
- Irrelevant evidence

Strategic questions to ask about Internet evidence are as follows:

- Does the site meet the basic standards of credibility?
- Who set up the website?
- What are the source's credentials?
- What is the purpose of the website?

- Does the content appear to reflect scholarship?
- Can you confirm the information?
- When was the site last updated?

Objective 7.6: Conduct research efficiently and productively.

The process of researching a speech can be managed by developing a plan for research. Such a plan includes the following:

- Beginning early
- Being clear about what is needed and where it can be found
- Setting priorities
- Reading progressively and efficiently
- Taking useful notes
- Keeping full bibliographic citations
- Maintaining a speech material file
- Knowing when to stop

Objective 7.7: Explain and use guidelines for how to cite sources and how to take notes about your research.

A full citation of a source contains all the material needed to find the source. This is important because

- You may want to go back to the original source.
- The bibliographic information may be helpful in evaluating the evidence or in choosing among different sources.
- Someone else may want to obtain information from the sources you used.

A note-taking system

- Should be flexible so you can rearrange notes.
- Should distinguish between quotations and paraphrases.
- Should clearly identify additions or deletions in quoted material.
- Should not require duplicative effort.

Listen to the **Audio Chapter Summary** at **MyCommunicationLab**

Discussion Questions

1. Which types of supporting material would you need to back up the thesis "Video games have too much violence"? Evaluate each type of supporting material, and determine which part of the thesis each type would best support.
2. What types of sources do you find most and least credible? Why?
3. With a group, discuss the pros and cons of the following sources of supporting material, including the situations in which each type would be most appropriate:

   Personal experience

   Interviews

   Library research

   Internet
4. In what situations might you want to use blogs as evidence? If a blog and a printed editorial say essentially the same thing, which is preferable? Why?

Activities

1. In researching a thesis of your choice, find an example of each type of supporting material. Test the strength of each type to determine which material would best support your thesis.
2. Conduct an interview, following the guidelines offered in this chapter.
3. Pick a clearly defined, narrow topic that you know little about. Brainstorm what research resources you would best consult. Use Internet search engines and your library to come up with an annotated bibliography of five sources that you would use in writing the speech, explaining how each source would strengthen your speech.

Key Terms

analysis **148**
closed question **165**
common knowledge **150**
document **152**
follow-up question **165**
open-ended question **165**
plagiarism **170**
presumption **150**
research **148**
speech material file **171**
statistics **153**
testimony **156**

Notes

1 Thomas B. Farrell,"Knowledge, Consensus, and Rhetorical Theory, "*Quarterly Journal of Speech* 62 (February 1976): 1–14.

2 The misleading statistics about the tax cut proposal are described in David E. Rosenbaum, "The President's Tax Cut and Its Unspoken Numbers, "*New York Times,* February 5, 2003, p. A23.

3 For more on the misuse of statistics, see Joel Best, *Damned Lies and Statistics: Untangling Numbers from the Media, Politicians, and Activists*, Berkeley: University of California Press, 2001.

4 For an example of this problem, see Ylan Q. Mui. "Justice Dept. cracks down on Cyber Monday scams,"*Washington Post,* November 28, 2011 (http://www.washingtonpost.com/business/economy/justice-dept-cracks-down-on-scams-on-cyber-monday/2011/11/28/gIQA1clz5N_story.html?tid=pm_business_pop.

5 Some of the problems with doing electronic research are explained in Steven B. Knowlton, "How Students Get Lost in Cyberspace," *New York Times,* "Education Life" section, November 2, 1997: 18, 21. There are also online sources offering good suggestions for evaluating Internet evidence. Two examples are wps.pearsoncustom.com/ph_hss_mycomplab_25/75/19245/4926917.cw/content/index.html and www.tarleton.edu/departments/library/library_module/unit8/8internet_lm.htm.

6 These tests for evidence are adapted from James A. Herrick, *Argumentation: Understanding and Shaping Arguments*, 3rd ed. (State College, Pa.: Strata, 2007), 73–80.

CHAPTER

8

Reasoning

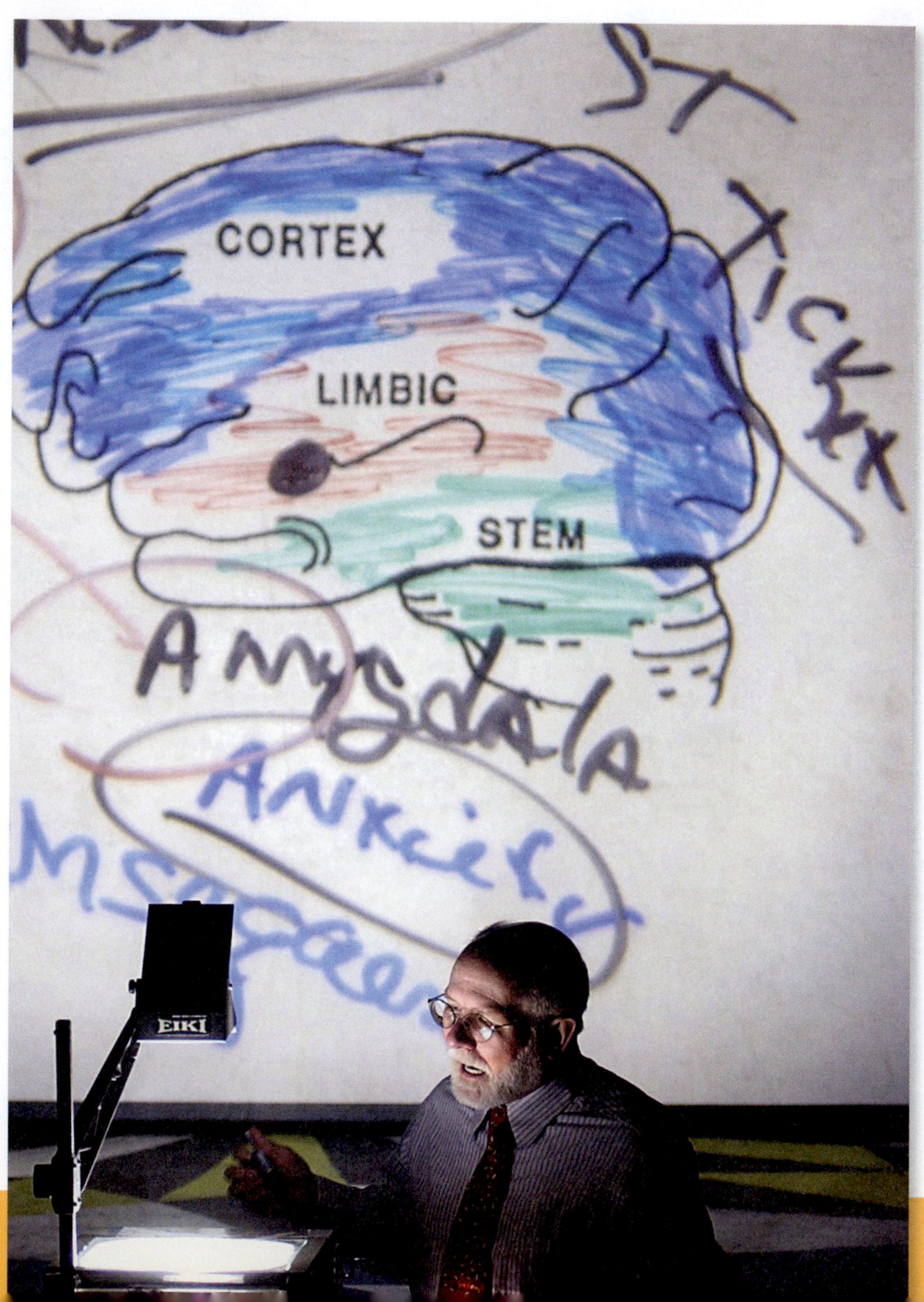

LEARNING OBJECTIVES

Listen to the **Audio Chapter** at **MyCommunicationLab**

After studying this chapter, you should be able to:

Objective 8.1 Explain the nature of rhetorical proof in public speaking and identify its three components.

Objective 8.2 Describe six basic patterns of reasoning, focusing on their types, appropriate tests of their soundness, and how to use them in a speech.

Objective 8.3 Define what a fallacy is and identify both general fallacies and fallacies that correspond to particular patterns of reasoning.

Objective 8.4 Explain how an understanding of reasoning processes helps in preparing and delivering a speech and in being an active, critical listener.

OUTLINE

Proof, Support, and Reasoning
Rhetorical Proof as Support | Proof and the Audience | Components of Proof
An Example of Rhetorical Proof | Using Rhetorical Proof in Your Speech

Example
Types of Inference from Example | Tests for Inference from Example
Guidelines for Reasoning Through Example

Analogy
Types of Inference from Analogy | Tests for Inference from Analogy
Guidelines for Reasoning Through Analogy

Signs
Types of Inference from Signs | Tests for Inference from Signs
Guidelines for Reasoning Through Signs

Cause
Types of Inference from Cause | Tests for Inference from Cause
Guidelines for Reasoning Through Cause

Testimony
Types of Inference from Testimony | Tests for Inference from Testimony
Guidelines for Reasoning Through Testimony

Narrative
Tests for Inference from Narrative

Avoiding Errors in Reasoning
Six General Tests of Inference

Reasoning in Public Speaking

By now, you have analyzed your situation, picked a good topic, and assembled some useful supporting materials. But how do you know whether these materials actually prove the point you want to make? In this chapter, you will learn about proof in public speaking and how to strengthen the reasoning in your speech.

Suppose that you are planning a speech on the ways that technological and economic forces are changing the newspaper industry. Using the methods of research discussed in Chapter 7, you have found examples of newspapers that have stopped publication altogether, statistics showing a drop in advertising revenue for large-city papers, and testimony from an expert who says that it may be that more people get news from the Internet than from the paper. You want to use this evidence to support the following claim:

> The daily newspaper as we have known it for generations is now a thing of the past.

Notice that this claim goes beyond what the evidence actually says. What enables you to make the claim on the basis of the evidence is *reasoning*—thinking through a connection between the evidence and the claim. This chapter examines various types of connections you can make and the factors that determine whether they are strong or weak.

OBJECTIVE 8.1 Proof, Support, and Reasoning

Consider the following claims:

- 2 + 2 = 4
- The sum of the angles of a triangle equals 180 degrees.
- Light travels at about 186,000 miles per second.
- The *Mona Lisa* is Leonardo da Vinci's most beautiful painting.
- The semester academic calendar is best for our university.
- The government's economic policy is bad for the country.

The first three statements are mathematical or scientific claims; they are based on a system of rules by which they can be proved with absolute certainty—as long as you operate within that system. The last three claims are different; they involve beliefs, values, and judgments. Although for any of these three you could find evidence that convinces *you* of their truth, someone else might be unimpressed by your evidence or might find counterevidence to argue an opposing point. Therefore, the "proof" of these claims is not offered with the same level of certainty that supports the first three claims.

The ideas in a speech almost never take the form of a fixed mathematical principle as in the first three claims above. Instead, the basic material of public speaking is like the last three claims, involving matters of belief or value, judgments about what ought to be, norms of conduct, or predictions about the future. Such statements require agreement between the speaker and listeners, not only about the truth of the claim, but also about what should count as proof in the first place.[1]

rhetorical proof
Proof established through interaction between the speaker and the listeners; provides support for a conclusion but not assurance that it is true.

Rhetorical Proof as Support

Rhetorical proof is established through interaction in which the speaker and listeners reason together. This type of proof does not *ensure* that a conclusion is correct, but it offers *support* for a conclusion. It gives listeners confidence that the conclusion is probably correct and that they can share it, make it part of their working knowledge, and act on it if they are able to do so. Rhetorical proof *justifies* claims. Although it does not establish that they are unquestionably true, it gives a critical listener good reason to accept them.

Suppose you are speaking to first-time employees about how they should save and invest their money. Research and analysis have convinced you that buying stocks is the best long-term investment, but you can't be absolutely certain of that conclusion because it involves value judgments, predictions, and speculations. Moreover, the substantial drop in stock values during the recession of 2008 and 2009—in some cases as much as half the value of a stock was lost—certainly would give pause to anyone investing in stocks. Therefore, to help listeners reach the conclusion that an investor thinking of long-term strategies should purchase stocks, your speech might draw on statistics, historical accounts of the growth of the stock market, examples of successful investors, and testimony from economists showing that by early 2012 the stock market had recovered from the losses it suffered during the 2008–2009 recession. These are called "supporting materials," precisely because their function is to *support* your conclusion. They do not guarantee that your conclusion is correct, but they give listeners good reasons to accept what you say and to act on it.

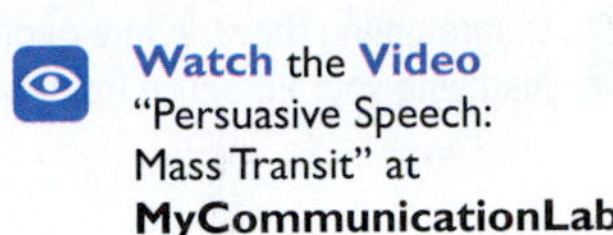
Watch the Video "Persuasive Speech: Mass Transit" at **MyCommunicationLab**

Unlike mathematical proofs, then, rhetorical proofs have degrees of support ranging from strong to weak. As a result, both speakers and listeners must evaluate rhetorical proofs critically, testing them rather than taking them for granted. Your goal as a speaker is to provide the strongest support possible for your conclusion. What factors make rhetorical proof strong?

Proof and the Audience

The overriding factor in supporting a claim is, of course, the audience. Listeners who pay attention to the reasoning in a speech are critical and active; they are willing to be convinced but are skeptical enough to ask whether the speaker's reasoning withstands scrutiny. Critical listeners will ask whether your causal links are valid, whether your comparisons are apt, and whether the people you quote are authorities in the subject—all tests that you will study in this chapter. Knowing that you will face a critical audience helps you as a speaker, because you will work hard to make your reasoning strong. In this way, you and your listeners work together to achieve the highest possible standard of rhetorical proof.

Audiences differ, of course, and so you might need different proofs to convince, say, an audience of Democrats that the current president's economic policy is flawed than you would need for an audience of Republicans. But if you focus too narrowly on the immediate audience, you could run into a serious ethical problem mentioned in Chapter 1: Yes, you may be *able* to convince the specific audience, but *should* you? Not all audiences are made up of critical listeners (as advertisers know only too well). Indeed, some listeners probably would accept just about any conclusion.

When many Americans accepted the U.S. government's call for the internment of Japanese and Japanese-Americans during World War II, did that prove the government's argument true? The answer to this difficult question turns out to be "yes and no." In a purely functional sense, yes: For those people in that situation, calls for Japanese internment could be considered proved; believers incorporated the government's claims into their working knowledge and acted on them. But in a

Diagramming the structure of proof can help you identify the warrants justifying your inference from evidence to claim.

larger sense, no: Regardless of what the supporters of the government's policies did or did not believe, they *should not have* accepted his claims, because the government's reasoning and evidence were flawed.

Speakers need to focus not only on proofs that listeners *actually do* regard as solid but also on proofs that they *ought* to regard as solid. Generally, a proof is **reasonable** if it would be taken seriously by a broad and diverse group of listeners exercising their best critical judgment.[2] Such an audience includes people who actually hear your speech as well as a larger, more culturally diverse audience who might "overhear" it through word of mouth or the media. When you offer rhetorical proofs, you are making strategic choices about the reasoning patterns that your immediate audience and this larger audience would accept. Think of a well-selected jury of peers in a well-run courtroom as your audience; if such a group of critical listeners would accept your proof, the inference is reasonable.

Even if your actual audience does not resemble such a group, do not abandon your standards. In offering a rhetorical proof, you must satisfy the immediate audience and also must meet a broader standard of reasonableness that would satisfy a larger imagined audience of critical thinkers.

Components of Proof

Any idea in the speech—whether a main point or a subordinate point—can be regarded as a *unit of proof* that has three principal components: the claim, the supporting material, and the reasoning.

Claim.

The **claim** is the statement that you want the audience to accept; it is what you are trying to prove. The claim could be your broad thesis:

> The shift to digital music formats has changed the nature of the recording industry.

Or the claim could be a specific subpoint:

> Because record labels can now distribute their music over the Internet without producing compact discs, they can affordably and efficiently offer consumers a wider variety of artists and genres.

Supporting Material.

This second component of a proof, examined in Chapter 7, provides *evidence* for your claim. To prove your claim, you must show that evidence supports it.

Reasoning.

It is reasoning that links the supporting material to your claim so that you and your listeners together can decide whether the evidence really does support the claim.

Usually, the claim and the supporting material are stated explicitly in the speech and are easy to identify. But the essential link, reasoning, is usually implied; it involves a mental leap from the supporting material to the claim. This leap is called an **inference**. The inference enables us to say that, even though we are going beyond

reasonable
Would be inferred by most people when exercising their critical judgment.

claim
A statement that a speaker asks listeners to accept and that the speaker tries to prove.

inference
A mental leap from the supporting material to the claim.

what the supporting material literally says, we feel justified in doing so because similar inferences in the past have usually led to acceptable results.[3] Exploring different kinds of inference and how they work is the primary purpose of this chapter.

An Example of Rhetorical Proof

After introducing a speech about the effect of tax increases on a family's budget, student Catherine Archer claimed

> Taxes have taken a bigger bite out of the average paycheck each year. Just look at the record. Our state sales taxes have gone up faster than our income. Local property taxes have gone through the roof. And now the federal government is proposing to raise gasoline taxes again. Where does it all stop?

After the speech, she invited questions from the floor. "What about Social Security?" one woman asked. Catherine replied

> Thank you. That's still one more example of a tax that has gone up faster than income. In fact, many people today pay more in Social Security tax than in their income tax.

Then a man in the audience said, "Since you mentioned income taxes, I want to remind you about the significant cuts in income tax rates that were passed by Congress and signed by President Bush in 2001 and 2003. Congress also has cut taxes on capital gains and on dividends. Many of these tax cuts were extended in 2004 and 2006, and President Obama's budget left many of these tax cuts in place, so it's not true that the government always raises taxes."

This man seemed to imply that Catherine had not considered all the possible taxes and had jumped to a conclusion. She didn't disagree with the man but restated her claim: "You're right about some of these specific cuts, but other taxes have gone up so much that my main point is still true. Besides, not all of these proposed tax cuts actually were enacted."

This example illustrates five important aspects of rhetorical proof:

1. Reasoning plays the crucial role in linking supporting material to the claim. Catherine's reasoning connected specific examples to her claim that taxes take a larger share of the paycheck each year.
2. Reasoning depends on an inference but cannot guarantee that the inference is "right." Nonetheless, we still can apply tests of soundness. In this case, for instance, do the examples really represent the overall tax picture, or has Catherine left out some important categories?
3. An inference often takes the form of an implicit statement that a general rule is being followed. Catherine's reasoning implied, "These examples of tax increases are significant and representative."
4. The speaker and listeners together decide whether the inference is sound. This audience participated by asking questions that helped to identify possible problems with Catherine's inference, and she had a chance to address their concerns. Together, speaker and audience probably became more confident about the inference. Even if audience members do not explicitly voice concerns, the speaker needs to think about what a critical audience might be asking and then build answers to those potential questions into the speech.
5. Nothing can guarantee that the inference of a rhetorical proof is correct, but tests have evolved over time to distinguish between good and bad inferences. Asking whether Catherine's examples represent all categories of taxes is one such test.

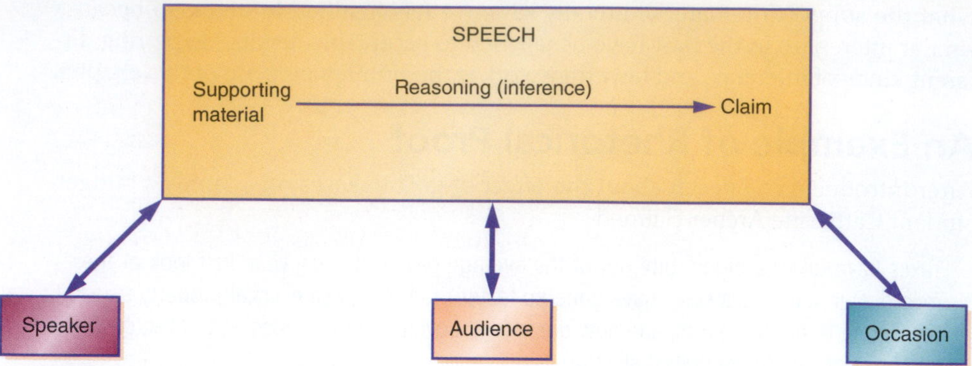

Figure 8.1 An enhanced view of the rhetorical situation: The inner workings of a speech.

Using Rhetorical Proof in Your Speech

Figure 8.1 shows the relationships among claims, supporting material, and reasoning. It shows the "inner workings" of the speech.[4] The other elements of the rhetorical situation are also shown, to remind you that the speech interacts with the speaker, the audience, and the occasion. Choices of reasoning patterns are influenced by each of these other elements.

The best time to construct effective reasoning relationships is after you research the speech. Your outline (discussed briefly in Chapter 2 and fully in Chapter 11) will help you to see what is used as supporting material for each claim. As Figure 8.2 shows, each Roman numeral in the outline identifies a main idea that supports your thesis statement, and each capital letter represents supporting material for that main idea. At a smaller level, each capital letter marks a claim that is supported by all the Arabic numerals under it, which, in turn, are supported by the lowercase letters, and so on.

Beginning with the smallest claims in your outline, identify the supporting material; then determine what kind of link (inference) will best connect the supporting material to each claim. This chapter presents practical methods to help you discover appropriate links and to test whether they will make the connection that you want to make with your audience.

To help you develop convincing rhetorical proofs, we will discuss six broad categories of reasoning: example, analogy, sign, cause, testimony, and narrative. For each category, the discussion first will focus on the variety of types, then on some tests to discover errors in reasoning, and finally on suggestions for using each reasoning pattern in a speech.

II. Lack of variety is not a valid complaint against Campus Food Service.
  A. You get more choices than you would at home.
    1. Each day, there are three main entrees and a vegetarian meal.
    2. There also are other options.
      a. A salad bar
      b. Cereals
      c. Breads
      d. Soups
  B. A special dinner is offered once each month.

Figure 8.2 An outline reveals links in reasoning.

It may seem confusing that some of the reasoning patterns have the same names as types of supporting material (reasoning through example, for instance). However, the reasoning pattern is not the same thing as the supporting material. Rather, it explains why the supporting material should count as support for the claim. Suppose you were to say, "Politicians are corrupt; just look at Smith, Baker, and Jones." The presumably corrupt politicians Smith, Baker, and Jones would be your examples (supporting material), and the inference that the three of them are representative or typical of politicians would be your reasoning (reasoning through example).

These categories were chosen because, at least in Western culture, they have been found over time generally to yield reliable results. Not all cultures will share all these norms of reasoning or give them the same emphasis. For example, some Eastern cultures are easily able to embrace contradictory positions. Western culture, however, usually adheres to the "law of noncontradiction": that something cannot have one feature (call it x) and its opposite (not-x) at the same time. Likewise, some cultures prize storytelling and therefore would give more weight to narrative inferences, whereas others are more concerned with prediction and control and hence give more weight to inferences from cause. When speaking to a culturally diverse audience, you will want to use multiple reasoning patterns in order to take these differences into account. Still, most of these reasoning patterns will be applicable across cultures, even if the emphasis differs.[5]

Example

OBJECTIVE 8.2

Probably the most common reasoning pattern in public speaking is inference from example. **Examples** are specific instances that are used to illustrate a more general claim; the inference is that the specific is typical of the general. For *example*:

- A tourist notices that three downtown streets are deserted at midday and infers that businesses in that town are generally not doing well.
- On four occasions, a student succeeds in visiting faculty members during their office hours and infers that most instructors are conscientious and accessible.
- A researcher discovers that 15 percent of the people in one community lack health insurance and infers that about 15 percent of the country's population has no health insurance.
- Believing that most politicians cannot be trusted, a citizen infers that neither of the candidates for mayor can be trusted.

In each example, someone has brought together a statement about a particular situation and a statement making a general claim and has attempted to relate the two. Whether proceeding from specific to general (the first three examples) or from general to specific (the last example), the inference is that particular cases are **representative** of the general category. To say that they are representative is to say that they are typical cases and that there is nothing unusual about them.[6]

A moment's thought shows why representativeness is important. Suppose that, although three downtown streets were deserted, traffic jams occurred near all of the city's shopping malls; then, the tourist would not be justified in drawing a general conclusion from the specific case observed. Or imagine that the student's four successful visits were all on days when faculty members were careful to hold office

examples
Specific instances used to illustrate a more general claim.

representative
Typical of the larger category from which a case is selected.

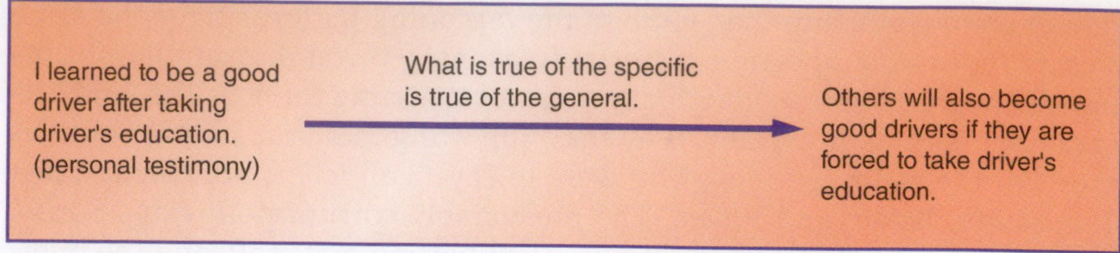

Figure 8.3 Inference from example.

hours because they were advising majors for next semester's registration; then, it would not be valid to infer that instructors are accessible at other times.

In short, if the particular cases are *not* typical (not representative), we cannot confidently infer that what is true of them is true in general. Again, inferences cannot be guaranteed as can mathematical proofs. But even if we can't be absolutely certain that examples are representative, we can still try to select them in a way that removes all known causes of distortion or bias.

The strategic advantage of inference from example is that it makes a general or abstract statement more concrete and tangible. The politician who says, "My economic program will benefit middle-class families," may help her audience to accept her claim by talking about specific families—preferably people with whom listeners can identify—who will gain from the program. Of course, the power of the appeal depends on whether the specific cases will be accepted as representative.

Figure 8.3 maps an inference from example, applying the general pattern shown in Figure 8.1. A student speaker says:

> I learned to be a good driver after taking driver's education. Others will also become good drivers if they are forced to take driver's education.

Notice something else about Figure 8.3. This student is offering herself as an example, but her supporting material is personal testimony. *Example*, as we have said, refers to *both* a reasoning pattern *and* a type of supporting material, but these are not exactly the same thing. *Any* type of supporting material could provide the specific cases you use when you reason from example.

Types of Inference from Example

Watch the **Video** "Business Presentation: Large Group" at **MyCommunicationLab**

Speakers use many different types of examples, depending on their purposes. The following three considerations are especially pertinent in selecting examples.

Individual Versus Aggregate Examples. Sometimes a speaker describes individual occurrences of an example. For instance, a speaker is friends with John, Martha, and Claude, all of whom had to interrupt their education for financial reasons; by talking about each of them, the speaker supports the inference that the cost of a college education is a serious concern.

At other times, individual cases will be less convincing than an aggregate statistical example. Because 50 percent of students in a national survey report that they have seen someone cheat on an examination, a speaker infers that probably half the students on campus have witnessed such behavior.

Factual Versus Hypothetical Examples. Factual examples are actual occurrences; whether individual or aggregate, they are "real." In contrast, a speaker may construct hypothetical examples, creating a vivid (but imaginary) illustration of something abstract. To describe the problems of homelessness, for example, a

CHOOSE A STRATEGY: Using Examples Strategically

The Situation

You are preparing a five-minute presentation to give to your city's planning commission, opposing a plan to build a big-box retail store close to a residential neighborhood. You are concerned about increased traffic and pollution, and you have also learned that the proposed building site includes a wetlands area that hosts 10 different rare and endangered bird species.

Making Choices

Which would be more effective to include?

1. An individual example of an endangered bird *or* an aggregate example of how many rare species live in the wetlands area?
2. A factual example of how much pollution increased in a different neighborhood after a similar store was built there *or* a hypothetical example of how much pollution could increase after the proposed store is built?
3. A brief list of neighborhoods that experienced increased traffic accidents and congestion after similar stores were built *or* an extended example of a fatal traffic accident in one neighborhood?

What If...

How would your choices be affected by the following?

1. A report by state engineers predicts that, due to water drainage issues, pollution increases at the proposed building site could be much greater than they have seen at past building sites.
2. Store officials have offered to install, at their own expense, a new traffic light and a bike trail to manage and reduce car traffic.

speaker might invent a hypothetical character whose daily experiences are typical of homeless people generally.

A speaker may have good reasons to offer a hypothetical example rather than a factual one, but the invention should be acknowledged and should never be treated as fact. One journalist received a Pulitzer Prize for a series of stories describing the plight of a child who was addicted to drugs; when it came to light that this child was hypothetical rather than a real person (as the stories had intimated), the prize was withdrawn.

Brief Versus Extended Examples. Sometimes a quick list of examples is effective because the speaker's emphasis is on the existence and number of cases rather than on their details. Thus, to establish that many students are worried about the cost of education, a brief mention of John, Martha, and Claude should support the claim.

But suppose the speaker wants listeners to understand what students go through when financial problems make them leave school. It would then be more effective to offer a more complete description of just one case. Better than to simply report that John had to leave school for financial reasons would be to describe the events that led to his decision—the conversations between him and his parents, how he broke the news to his friends, and what his life has been like since leaving.

Tests for Inference from Example

Inference from example will be accepted as reasonable if listeners have no good reason to doubt it. Ask yourself these questions when using inference from example to support your claim:

1. *Are there enough examples?* If the number of examples is very small, particularly in making a statistical generalization, the sample may not include

significant features of the population as a whole. If you claim that more students are graduating from high school than ever before because your high school graduated a record number of students, the audience may doubt your inference; your high school is only one of thousands.

2. *Do the examples represent the whole category?* If all the cases you cite are alike in some way that distorts your inference—say you use only fraternity members as examples to support some point about all college students—your claim will be weakened.
3. *Are the examples ambiguous?* Sometimes a single example can support different inferences, making it a poor example. If 70 percent of employees are dissatisfied with the company's new computer system, one speaker may claim that the new system is flawed; but another speaker may claim that employees need more training to understand the new system. Which claim is the audience to believe?
4. *Are the examples fallacious?* A **fallacy** is an inference that appears to be sound but that, on inspection, contains a significant flaw. In the case of inferences from example, which relate parts to wholes, the flaw is that the whole is not always the same as the sum of the parts. The **fallacy of composition** results from assuming that what is true of the part is automatically true of the whole. For instance:

fallacy
An inference that appears to be sound but that, on inspection, contains a significant flaw.

fallacy of composition
Assuming that what is true of the part is automatically true of the whole.

fallacy of division
Assuming that what is true of the whole is automatically true of the part.

> Each individual student will gain a better chance of getting into a popular course by registering for it at the very start of the enrollment period, so if all students register for it right away, everyone will have a better chance of getting in.

You should be able to spot the fallacy: If everyone tries to register for the same class at the same time, no one will have gained an advantage; instead, there will be a bottleneck in the registration system. What is true of the part individually is not true of the whole collectively. Conversely, the **fallacy of division** results from assuming that what is true of the whole is automatically true of the part. For example:

> The campus is excited about the homecoming game, and so each instructor must be excited, too.

CHECKLIST 8.1

Tests for Inference from Example

1. Are there enough examples?
2. Do all the examples represent the whole category?
3. Are the examples ambiguous?
4. Are the examples fallacious? Do any examples assume that:
   - ❒ What is true of the part must be true of the whole (fallacy of composition)?
   - ❒ What is true of the whole must be true of the part (fallacy of division)?

Guidelines for Reasoning Through Example

Here are suggestions for effective reasoning through example:

1. *Limit the number of examples.* You want enough examples to indicate a pattern that supports your inference, but you don't want to risk boring the audience with unnecessary examples. Consider your purpose and audience carefully; a single example may be enough.
2. *Make sure each example is believable.* Even one unbelievable example can undermine your inference—and your entire point.
3. *Avoid obvious, overused examples.* If you tell listeners what they already know, your inferences may seem trivial or trite. Seek novel examples that might surprise the audience. Arguing against censorship, for example, student Sarah McAdams skipped the standard example of book burning in Nazi Germany; instead, she surprised listeners by citing examples of U.S. censorship:

In 1925, anyone caught teaching Darwin's *Origin of Species* in a Tennessee public school was fined. In 1933, a young actor was arrested for smuggling an illegal item into the United States. That item was James Joyce's *Ulysses*—a book that is now considered a literary masterpiece. In 1980, some high school students were forced to read an edited version of Shakespeare's *Romeo and Juliet* because parents and teachers thought the original play was too racy.

And in the aftermath of September 11, there have been quite a few attempts to stop critics of the war on terror from speaking out.

4. *Match the details of examples to your purpose.* If your main point is the very existence of the example, few details are needed. But if you want to show the audience exactly how the example illustrates your inference, supply more detail about the example.
5. *Make the examples memorable.* After selecting enough believable, fresh examples, bring your inference to life for the audience by carefully selecting details and describing the examples vividly. We will pursue this goal in Chapter 12, "Achieving Style Through Language."

Analogy

An **analogy** is a comparison of people, places, things, events, or more abstract relationships. Whereas the key feature of inference from example is the link between the parts and the whole, the key feature of inference from analogy is a comparison between the known and the unknown.

An inference from analogy asks the audience to accept the idea that items that are basically alike in most respects will also be alike in the particular respect being discussed. For example, in a speech on gun deaths, a student speaker said:

The United States would have fewer gun deaths if it made guns illegal. Japan has few gun deaths and guns are illegal there.

Figure 8.4 offers a map of this analogy.

Analogical inferences are prominent in public speaking because they are psychologically appealing to an audience. They enable us to accept something that is unknown because it is similar to something that we do know.[7]

Types of Inference from Analogy

Depending on whether the comparison between things is direct or concerns their relationships, an analogy is either literal or figurative.[8]

analogy
A comparison of people, places, things, events, or more abstract relationships.

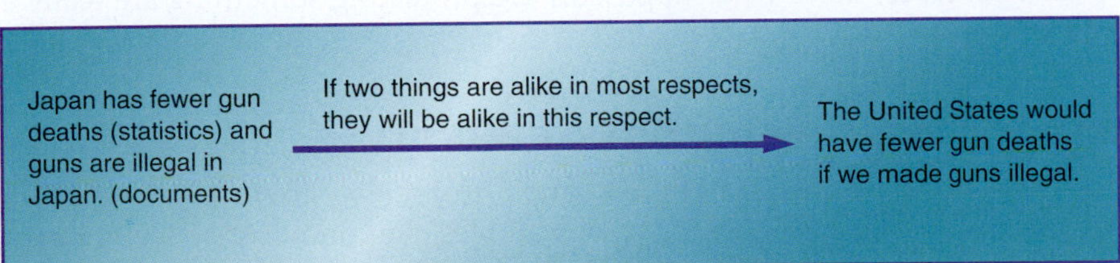
Japan has fewer gun deaths (statistics) and guns are illegal in Japan. (documents)
If two things are alike in most respects, they will be alike in this respect.
The United States would have fewer gun deaths if we made guns illegal.

Figure 8.4 Inference from analogy.

Literal Analogies. A **literal analogy** is a *direct* comparison of objects, people, or events. Suppose a speaker says:

> Illinois will not be able to escape the massive job cuts that have already hit Michigan—another midwestern industrial state.

This speaker is directly comparing Illinois to Michigan. The inference is that, because Illinois is basically like Michigan, it, too, will probably face a major loss of jobs.

Speakers often use literal analogies to suggest that one action or event is a precedent for another—that actual experience with one enables us to predict what will happen with the other. Former Senator Charles Robb of Virginia took this approach in arguing that a law to prohibit the federal government from recognizing same-sex marriages was discriminatory:

> Until 1967, 16 states, including my own state of Virginia, had laws banning couples from different races to marry. When the law was challenged, Virginia argued that interracial marriages were simply immoral.... The Supreme Court struck down these archaic laws, holding that "the freedom of choice to marry" had "long been recognized as one of the vital personal rights essential to the orderly pursuit of happiness by free men."
>
> Today, we know that moral discomfort—even revulsion—that citizens then felt about legalizing interracial marriages did not give them the right to discriminate 30 years ago. Similarly, discomfort over sexual orientation does not give us the right to discriminate against a class of Americans today.

Figurative Analogies. A **figurative analogy** compares the *relationships* between objects, people, or events in order to make complex or abstract statements more vivid and more concrete. Again, the comparison begins with something the audience already knows.

Suppose you wanted to claim that the Social Security System will face financial problems around the year 2020 as many "baby boomers" reach retirement age. You could support your claim with only statistics, of course, but that could be tedious and would work far better in print than in a speech. Instead, you might say:

> Depending on Social Security for your retirement income is like betting all of your money on one horse in a race.

Then your comparison would make the statistics—and your point—clear: Social Security is a gamble. Similarly, the speaker predicting major losses of jobs in Illinois might add:

> Trusting the politicians to find a way to avoid it is like putting the fox in charge of the chicken coop.

This speaker is not directly comparing politicians to foxes or job losses to a chicken coop. Rather, the comparison is figurative; it points to *relationships*. The politicians stand in the same relationship to the job losses that the fox does to the chicken coop. In both cases, those who supposedly are protecting something are really a grave threat to it.

literal analogy
A direct comparison of objects, people, or events.

figurative analogy
A comparison of the relationships between objects, people, or events.

Tests for Inference from Analogy

As we saw concerning inferences from example, things may be *similar*, but they are never completely *identical*. Thus, as with examples, we can never be sure that an analogy is completely valid. No matter how similar things are, they are also different in some respects.

For an analogy to be strong and compelling, listeners have to believe that the basic similarities between two items outweigh their basic differences. An analogy raises two closely related questions:

1. *Are there basic differences as well as similarities?* Suppose a speaker claims that Detroit and Chicago have similar economic concerns because they are alike in so many ways: Both are northern metropolitan areas, both have large populations, both are surrounded by suburbs that erode the city's tax base, and so on. Besides these similarities, however, there is an obvious and important difference between the two cities: Detroit's economy historically has depended on one industry, automobiles, whereas the economy of Chicago is more diversified.
2. *Do the differences outweigh the similarities?* The discovery of differences between items being compared is not, in itself, reason to question the analogy. One has to demonstrate that the differences really do matter. For instance, if a diversified economy protects a city better against recession because workers who lose jobs in one industry can find new jobs in another, then this difference outweighs the similarities between Detroit and Chicago, and the analogy is questionable. But if a weak national economy hurts cities in general—whether or not they have a diversified economy—then this difference between Detroit and Chicago would not matter much, and the analogy would stand.

CHECKLIST 8.2

Tests for Inference from Analogy

- ❒ Are there basic differences as well as similarities?
- ❒ Do the differences outweigh the similarities?

Guidelines for Reasoning Through Analogy

Here are suggestions for effective reasoning through analogy:

1. *Avoid analogies that are trite or farfetched.* An overused analogy will lose the audience's attention and make the entire speech seem stale, whereas an analogy with no basis in common sense may call so much attention to itself that it distracts from the point it is supposed to prove. A well-known televised public service announcement (PSA) compared the brain to an egg and heroin to a cast-iron frying pan that "smashes" the brain. The PSA also compared the heroin user's family, friends, job, and future to various kitchen utensils and appliances and implied that heroin also "smashes" the user's relationships and life. Though its shock effect gained it attention, the PSA was viewed by many as farfetched and trite. Its target audience of young people knew that their friends who use heroin did not immediately and irreversibly "smash" their brains and everyone and everything around them. The comparison was exaggerated and, consequently, the target audience dismissed it.
2. *Analyze what you are comparing.* Make sure that you understand the essential similarities and differences of the items in your analogy so that you can argue convincingly that their similarities outweigh their differences and will not be surprised if a listener suggests otherwise. The speaker who compared Detroit's and Chicago's economic outlooks must be ready to respond to a listener's observation that the cities differ in the important factor of economic diversification. If that difference wasn't important to the speaker's main point, the analogy could be defended.

A Question of Ethics

Ethical Issues in Reasoning

We employ reasoning to make our arguments and positions clear. One powerful mode of reasoning is analogy, because it compares something new to something that the audience already knows and understands. Analogy heightens similarities, but in doing so does it distort the items being compared? For instance, if a manager compares her company's precarious position in the marketplace to the United States' involvement in Vietnam during the 1960s and 1970s, is that a fair comparison? Does the manager trivialize the Vietnam conflict or, alternatively, make the company's position seem disproportionately dire? Do such comparisons properly respect the memory of the different events? Do they raise ethical issues?

3. *Use analogies sparingly.* Although analogies are a form of inference, they also are like ornaments (to use an analogy of our own). Too many ornaments may hide what they are intended to decorate, and too many analogies in a speech may obscure the main point. Governor Rick Perry of Texas, while seeking the 2012 Republican presidential nomination, used so many attention-grabbing figurative analogies that they probably overwhelmed his audience at times.[9]
4. *Use analogies sensitively.* The benefits of using analogy may be undone if the comparison strikes listeners as insensitive. This can happen if they focus on an embarrassing aspect of the comparison, one that the speaker did not intend. During the 2008 presidential campaign, for example, "change" was a key theme, so some messages presented Republican candidate Senator John McCain as the candidate of change. Democrats responded with a figurative analogy: "You can put lipstick on a pig, but it is still a pig." What they intended to suggest was that calling McCain a candidate for change did not make it so, just as another superficial change (lipstick) did not change the basic nature of a pig. But the analogy struck many as insensitive because Republican vice presidential candidate Governor Sarah Palin of Alaska, after referring to herself as a hockey mom, had joked that the only difference between a hockey mom and a pit bull was lipstick; thus, the "lipstick on a pig" analogy could be interpreted to suggest that Democrats were calling Palin a pig. Similarly, in early 2009 President Obama compared his skill at bowling to that of a contestant in the Special Olympics. His goal was to poke fun at his own low score, but the analogy easily could be misunderstood as belittling the Special Olympics, where some contestants in fact bowl very well.

Signs

sign
Something that stands for something else.

A **sign** is something that stands for something else—which is usually an abstraction or something that we cannot observe directly. The presence of the sign causes us to infer the existence of what it stands for.

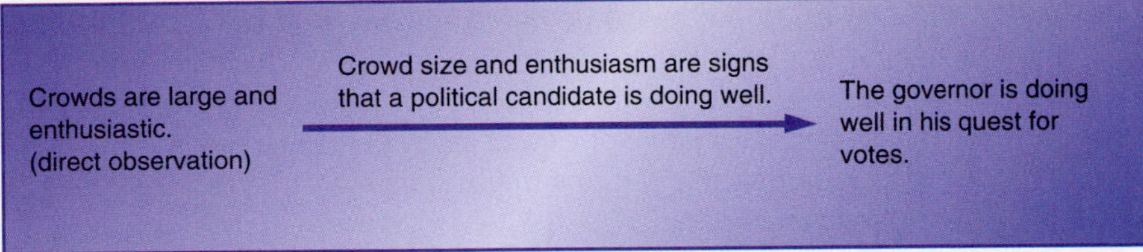
Crowds are large and
enthusiastic.
(direct observation)
Crowd size and enthusiasm are signs
that a political candidate is doing well.
The governor is doing
well in his quest for
votes.

Figure 8.5 Inference from signs.

If the number of students absent from class increases suddenly, that may be a sign of a flu epidemic. If today's average grades are higher than 10 years ago, that may be a sign that grading standards have changed. If homeless people are living on the streets, that may be a sign that public policies are not meeting the needs of the disadvantaged. If wages differ for male and female workers doing similar jobs, that may be a sign of gender discrimination. In each case, we infer that something exists based on something else that presumably is a sign of it. The strategic benefit of inferences from sign is that they enable listeners to reach a conclusion about something that they can't know directly, by linking it in this way to something that they do know. As another example, a newspaper reporter covering a political campaign writes:

> The governor is doing well in his quest for votes since his crowds are large and enthusiastic.

Figure 8.5 offers a map of this inference from signs.

Types of Inference from Signs

In theory, anything can stand for anything else. In practice, however, inferences from signs fall into several types:

- Physical observation
- Statistical indexes
- Institutional regularity

Physical Observation.

If the alarm goes off and you don't check the time but you look out the window and see a bright sun, you probably infer that the sun means it's morning. Similarly, through **physical observation** of a bulldozer on an empty campus lot, a student inferred that the university was about to construct a new building. The sun and the bulldozer were observable signs of other things that could not be observed.

Statistical Index.

Many statistical measures are taken as signs. High scores on exams, for instance, are widely accepted as a sign of intelligence. Similarly, the ups and downs of the Dow-Jones Industrial Average are seen to indicate the health of the economy, and a rising Consumer Price Index is regarded as a sign of inflation. Intelligence, economic health, inflation—these are all abstract concepts that cannot be observed directly. But in each case, a **statistical index** that we *can* see is regarded as a sign of something that we cannot observe.

Institutional Regularity.

Institutional regularity is an observable pattern that results from some norm or social convention. For example, because athletic competitions usually begin with the singing of the national anthem, if you turned

physical observation (as a sign)
Regarding something that can be observed as a sign of something that cannot.

statistical index (as a sign)
A statistical measure that is taken as a sign of an abstraction.

institutional regularity (as a sign)
A sign relationship that results from norm or social convention.

CHECKLIST 8.3

Tests for Inference from Signs

- ❒ Is an alternative explanation more credible?
- ❒ Can the alleged sign be found *without* the thing for which it stands?
- ❒ Is the sign part of a pattern, or a single unusual case?

on your TV and heard people singing it, you might infer that a game was about to begin. In the same way, because diplomatic disagreements often are described by such polite phrases as "They had a frank exchange of views," that phrase in a news story about international negotiations might be a sign that discussions had reached an impasse.

Tests for Inference from Signs

If a sign *always* stood for the same thing, then whenever we observed the sign, we could infer that the abstract concept was present as well. Thus, *whenever* someone scored high on a test, we could infer that the person was intelligent; and *whenever* we heard the national anthem, we could expect a sports event to follow. So certain a sign would be said to be *infallible*, meaning that it predicts with certainty the existence of the thing it signifies.

Reality offers few (if any) infallible signs. To say that something is a sign, then, means that it *usually* signifies something else, although in a given circumstance it might not. The high rate of absenteeism from class may well signify an epidemic, but are students suffering from the flu or spring fever? Because most signs are *fallible* and can be interpreted variously, critical listeners and speakers will subject them to the following tests of reasonableness:

1. *Is an alternative explanation more credible?* Is it more reasonable to suppose that today's higher grades signify harder-working students, or changes in grading standards, or changes in admissions policies? The question can be resolved by gathering other information. If the credentials of entering students have been similar for the past 10 years, then it is more reasonable to infer that the higher grades signify changes in grading standards. Examine alternative explanations for a sign before accepting inferences based on it.
2. *Can the alleged sign be found without the thing for which it stands?* Although the national anthem is often sung before an athletic contest, it also is sung on many other occasions—at the opening of a patriotic rally, for example, or at the beginning of a school day. A sign that can be found in a variety of circumstances is not a solid basis for an inference.
3. *Is the sign part of a pattern, or a single unusual case?* If only one instance of gender-based wage differences can be found, that is not a strong sign of pervasive, widespread discrimination. But if a pattern of wage differences can be identified, it is more reasonable to see that as a sign of gender discrimination.

Guidelines for Reasoning Through Signs

Here are suggestions for effective reasoning through signs.

1. *Use sign inferences to link the abstract with the concrete.* Keep in mind that the primary purpose of a sign inference is to predict the existence of something that cannot be observed on the basis of something that can be. Use sign inferences to convince listeners that something they cannot see does, in fact, exist.
2. *Explain the sign relationship clearly.* Make sure your listeners understand exactly what you are alleging to be a sign of something else and why you think

it predicts what you claim. A student speaker left her audience wondering when she said:

All we have to do is turn on the television set to see signs of the glory of modern civilization.

Was she referring to the technological achievements of broadcasting? Did she believe that the content of television programs showed the triumph of the human spirit? Or was she actually being sarcastic and preparing to criticize typical television fare?

Personal commitment combined with effective reasoning from evidence to claims makes this speaker's presentation convincing.

3. *Point to multiple signs of what you want to infer.* Student Roger Berkson used several signs in a speech. Alone, each sign could be fallible, but together they all pointed in the same direction and gave his inference more credibility:

   When I saw that many more students were absent from class lately, I wasn't sure that it meant that they were sick. After all, it was close to midterm exams, and everyone could use more time to study. But then I found out that visits to the infirmary went up, sales at the pharmacy were on the rise, and more beds were in use at the city hospital. Those signs suggest to me that we have a flu epidemic on campus.

4. *Do not claim more for a sign inference than it can establish.* A sign inference claims a predictable relationship between the sign and the thing for which it stands, but it does not establish that either one affects the other. Although a rise in the Consumer Price Index may predict inflation, it certainly does not influence, cause, or lead to inflation. This last point highlights an important distinction between sign inferences and our next form of reasoning: inference from cause.

Cause

Unlike a sign inference, a **causal inference** explains the relationship between things by pointing to the influence of one thing on the other.

Suppose the state legislature significantly raises the gasoline tax, which service stations pass along to consumers by raising the price of gasoline, and sales then decline. Is this chain of events a coincidence? We can never know for sure. But it may be reasonable to infer that the price increase affected consumption patterns—that as the cost of gasoline rose, more consumers decided to limit their driving and to conserve gasoline as well as their money.

A causal inference relates things by identifying one as the cause (higher price) and the other as the effect (lower sales). The cause must both precede and lead to the effect. Moreover, the speaker should provide reasons that the cause–effect relationship makes sense and that no alternative explanation is more plausible.

causal inference
A pattern of inference that suggests that one factor brings about another.

California has eliminated affirmative action in college admissions. (documents or common knowledge) → Affirmative action policies have been the cause of minority enrollment until now. → The number of minority students in California colleges and universities will decrease.

Figure 8.6 Inference from cause.

The strategic advantage of inferences from cause is that they enable listeners to see a pattern among what otherwise might be unconnected events. Recognizing the pattern, they can predict what will happen next or they can determine what must be done to avoid that outcome. Listeners are made to feel that they know "what is going on" and that they can do something about it.

Figure 8.6 maps an inference from cause. When California eliminated affirmative action in college admissions, some higher-education officials alleged that the end of affirmative action would drastically reduce the number of minority students.

Types of Inference from Cause

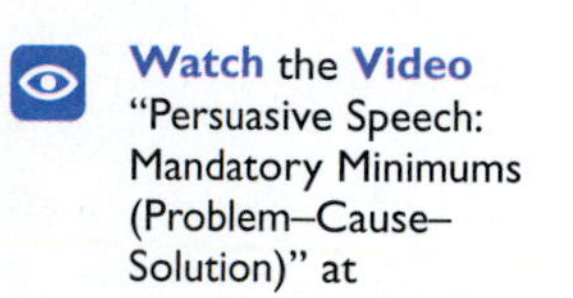

Watch the **Video** "Persuasive Speech: Mandatory Minimums (Problem–Cause–Solution)" at **MyCommunicationLab**

There are several types of causal inference. Among the most common are prediction, assignment of responsibility, explanation, and steps to a goal. Each of these types is a different use you can make of the inference from cause.

Prediction. Some causal inferences explain changes by predicting what leads to what. In a speech about energy efficiency, a speaker might say:

> When you replace a standard light bulb with a compact fluorescent one, you are not merely changing a light bulb. You are changing the world.

The inference is that the act of using energy-efficient compact fluorescent lightbulbs, if adopted on a wide scale, has the potential to make a major positive impact on the environment.

Assignment of Responsibility. Another common use of causal inferences is to assign responsibility for something, to tell why it occurred. Suppose you were asked to speak about the question "Why would someone run for president if there were no chance of being elected?" In thinking about the question, you may see other reasons to run for office: to get publicity, to establish political relationships, to add certain issues to the agenda for public discussion, to position oneself to run for vice president, to have a good time, and to be ready in case leading candidates falter. Through a causal inference, you could present these as reasons or motivations—as causes—for the decision to run.

Explanation. A causal inference also can be used to explain something that otherwise doesn't make sense. Consider this paradox: Why, in the richest nation on earth, are there shortages of funds for virtually every social program? Answering such a question involves finding an element—often unexpected or obscure—that explains the situation. If your inference explains that Americans strongly prefer private over public investment, you would have identified a possible cause of the paradox.

Rhetorical Workout

Reason Through Cause

You are researching a speech about the effectiveness of red-light cameras at intersections. You want to carefully assess the information you have to be sure you are making correct inferences.

Supporting material: You read an article about five major cities that installed red-light cameras. The cities reported fewer driver fatalities after installing the cameras.

Claim: You draft the following claim: Red-light cameras improve public safety.

Reasoning: Use the tests for inference from cause to evaluate your claim:

1. Has a *sign* relationship been confused with a *causal* relationship? Could either factor–(a) use of red-light cameras or (b) fewer driver fatalities–be a sign of the other, rather than a cause or effect?
2. Does some common cause of both factors make it seem that they have a cause-effect relationship? Suppose all the cities in the article also reduced speed limits in and around the intersections where they installed red-light cameras. How could this factor be a common cause of the two factors in your claim?
3. Does your claim contain a *post hoc* fallacy, assuming that one factor caused another only because the second factor occurred after the first? Why or why not?
4. Have important multiple causes or multiple effects been overlooked? What questions could you research to learn if your cause (use of red-light cameras) has more than one effect or if your effect (fewer driver fatalities) has more than one cause?
5. Is there likely an alternative cause? What questions could you research to learn if fewer driver fatalities were directly linked to the use of the cameras?

Steps to a Goal. A causal inference also can relate the means to the ends, as when we know our goals and want to determine the best way to attain them. This form of reasoning is used often in problem–solution speeches. If you advocated the development of solar power in order to avoid risking an energy shortage, you would be employing this type of causal inference.[10]

Tests for Inference from Cause

As with the other patterns of reasoning, the rhetorical proof in a causal inference is not ironclad. We may think we understand how one aspect of a situation influences another and yet we may be mistaken—as examples throughout this chapter have shown. In the case of Figure 8.6, for instance, some people have maintained that, except for an initial drop, the number of minority students did *not* decline after affirmative action was abolished. (There was considerable disagreement about whether this was true and what these results meant, but that is another story.) Any of the following analytical errors will make a causal inference less reasonable:

1. *Has a sign relationship been confused with a causal relationship?* Because we know that two things are somehow related, we mistakenly assume that one causes the other. Student Michael Leu, for example, let enthusiasm for his subject overpower his ability to test inferences when he made the following argument:

   Only the best professors on this campus teach their classes at noon. If Professor Walker really wanted to be a better teacher, he would change the time of his class so that it met at noon instead of 10.

Had Michael tested his inference carefully, he might have recognized a serious flaw in his reasoning. Teaching at noon might be a *sign* that one was a good teacher, because only the best professors teach at that hour right now. But there is no reason to believe that teaching at noon *causes* anyone to be a good teacher. Professor Walker's changing his class time won't make him a better teacher; instead, it will make Michael's first sentence no longer true.

2. *Does a common cause of both factors make it seem that they have a cause–effect relationship?* This reasoning error alleges that one factor is the cause of another, although in fact both manifest a third cause. If you fall prey to the **common cause fallacy**, you may mistakenly remove what you think is the cause of a problem, only to discover that nothing changes.

   For example, the fact that students in wealthy school districts generally score higher on standardized tests than do students in poorer districts may seem at first glance to prove that higher spending for education results in higher test scores. But some have argued that the real reason wealthy districts score better is that the families who live in them can afford to give their children reading and travel experiences and personal computers—and that this enrichment at home leads *both* to higher test scores *and* to pressure on school districts to spend more for education.

3. *Is there a* post hoc *fallacy?* In Latin, *post hoc* means "after this"; thus, a **post hoc fallacy** occurs if you assume that, because one event occurred after another, it was caused by the earlier event. This reasoning error comes up often in political speeches. Republicans observe that the Cold War ended after President Reagan took office and assume that he should get credit for it; Democrats point to a strong economy while President Clinton was in office and credit him for it. Can we reasonably infer that the end of the Cold War and the sustained economic growth at the end of the twentieth century were caused by these two presidents just because they were in office at the time?

4. *Have important multiple causes or multiple effects been overlooked?* If a problem has multiple causes, acting to remove a single cause is unlikely to solve the problem. Consider the disparities in educational achievement between urban and suburban schools. One important cause is the difference in budgets—suburban districts often are able to spend more on education. But simply equalizing budgets will not solve the problem, because other factors also contribute to the disparity: the preference of many talented teachers for suburban settings, the greater presence of books and other educational stimuli in suburban homes, and the greater involvement of suburban parents in their children's education.

   Likewise, a particular action may have multiple effects, some of which may be undesirable. Student speaker Demetris Papademetriou overlooked this when he used a causal inference to argue in support of economic globalization:

   > The globalization of business has produced tremendous benefits for the world as a whole. Stockholders receive better returns on their investment because of lower production and labor costs. Workers around the world are given new opportunities to earn a respectable living. The telecommunications and shipping industries have seen major growth as they work to connect producers and consumers in every place on the globe.

   Talking with classmates after his speech, Demetris found that he had not convinced them because he had neglected several *other* possible effects of

common cause fallacy
Assuming that one thing causes another when in fact a third factor really is the cause of both.

***post hoc* fallacy**
Assuming that, because one event occurred before another, the first is necessarily the cause of the second.

economic globalization that were not so pleasant. Besides the benefits he listed, globalization has led to the loss of millions of domestic jobs, the exploitation of some workers overseas, and other negative developments. These were multiple effects that should at least have been considered in the speech.

5. *Is there a likely alternative cause?* Sometimes what appears to be the cause really isn't. Things may be related, but for a reason different from the one the speaker suggests. Student Muhammad Gill pointed out this mistake in arguments that endorse racial profiling (the practice of making traffic or other investigative stops on the basis of a person's race or ethnicity):

> Some people argue that racial profiling is justified. And in rare cases, such as those involving suspected terrorists, it may be. But it is wrong when people look at the high arrest and conviction rates for illegal drug possession among African Americans and they infer that the reason that there are more blacks in court and more blacks in jail is that blacks are more likely to commit crime. The real reason our courts and jails are disproportionately black is that there has been long-standing racial discrimination in both arrests and sentencing.

CHECKLIST 8.4

Tests for Inference from Cause

- ❒ Has a sign relationship been confused with a causal relationship?
- ❒ Does a common cause of both factors make it seem that they have a cause–effect relationship?
- ❒ Does the fact that one event occurred after another falsely signify a cause–effect relationship?
- ❒ Have important multiple causes or multiple effects been overlooked?
- ❒ Is there a likely alternative cause?

Guidelines for Reasoning Through Cause

Here are suggestions for effective reasoning through cause:

1. *Analyze what the alleged cause is and how it exerts its influence on the effect.* A student speaker who ignored this advice argued that the position of the stars on a person's birthday causes that person to show certain personality traits. When listeners asked questions, though, the speaker was unable to explain the astrological cause or how it worked its influence.
2. *Realize that causal relationships are often complex and subtle.* A cause can have multiple effects, and an effect can have multiple causes. Be sure that your analysis of the cause–effect relationship is plausible and that your inference will be accepted as reasonable. For example, few people will accept that spending more money on a social problem, by itself, will solve the problem.

Testimony

When you rely on other people for the accuracy of supporting materials, their *testimony* stands in for your own direct encounter with the materials. You have confidence in their judgment and are willing to argue that the claim is true because they say so.

When a claim involves, for example, various economic indicators, or the long-term significance of a Supreme Court decision, or adequate safeguards for removing toxic waste, few speakers know enough to support the claim based on their own knowledge. In such cases, both speaker and listeners are usually willing to

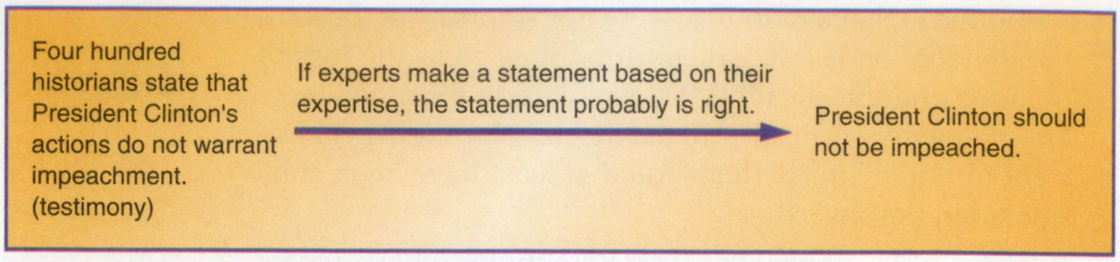

Four hundred historians state that President Clinton's actions do not warrant impeachment. (testimony) → If experts make a statement based on their expertise, the statement probably is right. → President Clinton should not be impeached.

Figure 8.7 Inference from testimony.

defer to the judgment of someone whose training, experience, or esteem might all be reasons to trust that person's judgment.

Using testimony, like any other form of reasoning, is a strategic choice. The benefit of inferences from testimony is that they make use of the source's authority in two ways: her expertise makes the audience more disposed to accept the claim and her *ethos* becomes associated with that of the speaker.

Figure 8.7 offers a map of an inference from testimony. It is based on an event that occurred in late 1998 when the House of Representatives was considering the impeachment of President Clinton. A large group of professional historians published a newspaper ad contending that the president's actions were not "high crimes and misdemeanors" as that term was understood in historical context and, therefore, that he should not be impeached. Citing this ad, Clinton's supporters urged that we take the historians' judgment seriously because of their professional expertise.

Types of Inference from Testimony

In Chapter 7, you learned that testimony can be either fact or opinion. Each of these forms of testimony can be classified further according to (1) the type of person who offers it and (2) whether it is quoted or paraphrased.

Expert Versus Lay Testimony. In most cases, we seek **expert testimony**—the support of someone who is recognized as an authority on a particular subject, who has studied the subject in detail, and whose knowledge and interest in the subject far exceed the average person's. It is not unusual, however, for an expert in one field to make judgments about another field, as when a sports figure endorses a breakfast cereal or an economist comments on fashion trends. When experts testify about matters outside their field of expertise, we should examine their claims closely.

Although expert testimony usually provides stronger support for a claim, speakers sometimes deliberately use **lay testimony**, citing the opinions of "ordinary people" to show what nonexperts think about the subject. Speeches urging teenagers to avoid drugs may cite reformed addicts, not because they are experts but because the audience can imagine these former drug abusers as not all that different from themselves. The speaker hopes that, for just this reason, listeners will learn from the mistakes of those who abused drugs.

expert testimony
Testimony from a person who is generally recognized as an authority on a particular subject.

lay testimony
Testimony from a person who is not an expert.

Quoted Versus Paraphrased Testimony. Quoted testimony repeats the exact words of the source, whereas paraphrased testimony gives only a general idea of what the source said. For example:

QUOTED: Police Chief Walters said, "The rate of burglaries in our town is an embarrassment to civilized society."

PARAPHRASED: Police Chief Walters said that the burglary rate was unacceptably high.

Although quoted testimony usually provides stronger support, at times a quotation is too long, too confusing, or too technical for listeners to follow. In that case, a paraphrase may allow you to cite what the source said without losing the audience's attention. The paraphrase, of course, must render the quotation accurately, or else you will *misquote* the source.

Tests for Inference from Testimony

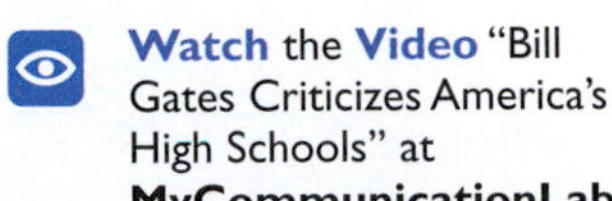

Watch the Video "Bill Gates Criticizes America's High Schools" at **MyCommunicationLab**

Enticed by fame or fortune, some people will say just about anything. Therefore, even the quoted testimony of an expert is not always strong support for a claim. Like other forms of reasoning, inferences from testimony must meet certain tests.

1. *Does the statement accurately reflect the source's views?* Imagine that a student, in arguing that the theory of intelligent design should be taught in public schools, paraphrased a well-known paleontologist as saying that Darwin's theory of evolution is wrong. Listeners could find this hard to believe, and their doubts would turn out to be well founded if the paleontologist actually said:

   Darwin was wrong. Natural selection is not the most important way in which evolution occurs. Other mechanisms that Darwin did not consider play a role just as crucial to the evolution of species.

   This exact quotation shows that the scientist would not have questioned Darwin's theory but only the importance of one proposed means of evolutionary change. The speaker's paraphrase of the statement as an attack on the theory of evolution would not be accurate, and the audience should reject the claim.

2. *Is the source an expert on the topic?* As noted earlier, an expert in one field sometimes offers opinions about other fields. A physicist is not necessarily an expert on international relations, nor is an actor the most credible source for a claim about nuclear energy. It is not enough that a source be regarded as *generally* well qualified; the source needs to be an expert in the *particular* subject about which you are making a claim. (This test was discussed in Chapter 7. Although it always applies to expert testimony, adapt it to assess lay testimony by asking, "Does this person have experience relating to the claim?")

   Student speaker Trisha Butcher gave a speech about the benefits of building more prisons as a way to reduce crime. She based many of her arguments on what she had heard from her father, the owner of a company that specializes in large-scale industrial construction projects and that had received several contracts to build new prisons:

   During a personal interview with my dad, I learned that building more prisons is an effective way to reduce the crime rates in our cities. My father also assured me that, compared to other methods of rehabilitation and punishment, prisons will prove the most economically feasible for the country in the long run.

   Listeners were unconvinced—as they should have been, because this testimony failed several tests. As the owner of a construction company, Trisha's father was hardly in a position to compare approaches to reducing crime;

nor was he qualified to make national economic forecasts. And because he earned money from industrial construction, and specifically from building prisons, his opinions were likely to be biased. But Trisha recovered when she revised this speech for her final class project. She found a criminologist to comment about how prisons might deter crime and an economist to assess the economic effects of prisons. Then she used her father's testimony to illustrate the personal experience of someone involved in building prisons—a point on which he *was* well qualified to speak.

3. *Is there a basis for the source's statements?* A speaker who offers judgments without providing any basis for them is said to **pontificate**. Unfortunately, experts as well as lay people can do this. But if the source is offering judgments, listeners need to be confident that he or she is familiar with all aspects of the topic and has reasons for making the claim.
4. *Is the source reasonably unbiased?* No one is completely free of bias, of course, but if a source has a vested interest in a claim, the pressure will be strong to offer testimony consistent with that interest. An environmental engineer who owns land at a particular site, for example, may be more likely to downplay hazards on the site than would an engineer who has no economic interest in the matter. Similarly, claims by industry experts—whether automakers, cigarette manufacturers, or health-care providers—should be scrutinized. Now, just because an expert stands to gain from the consequences of his or her testimony does not mean that the testimony itself is wrong. But when expertise and self-interest are mixed, you need to be a skeptical, critical listener.
5. *Is the testimony up to date?* Some issues are timeless, and so it will not matter when a person's testimony was offered. Moral and philosophical principles may be timeless matters, although even here advances in knowledge and technology may affect what once seemed settled matters. On most matters, though—and particularly when data and statistics are involved—recent testimony may be more valuable than older support.

Even when testimony meets all these tests, you still may have to choose among the conflicting claims of qualified experts who disagree. Do not simply pick what supports your thesis and ignore other testimony. Instead:

- Ask what each expert's record of previous statements may imply about the quality of judgment in this case.
- Ask which expert's testimony is closest to consensus in the field.
- Ask which expert's statement is most consistent with other things you already know or believe.

Guidelines for Reasoning Through Testimony

Here are suggestions for effective reasoning through testimony.

1. *Be sure you quote or paraphrase accurately.* Obviously, a direct quotation must be exactly what the source said. But it is equally important that a paraphrase be faithful to the context and meaning of the original statement and that it fairly reproduce its subtleties. For example, if the context suggests that the source favors an action but has reservations about it, you would not paraphrase accurately if you suggested that the source wholeheartedly supports the action.

pontificate
To offer judgments without providing any basis for them.

2. *Usually, draw on multiple sources of testimony.* If all your testimonial evidence comes from a single source, listeners may infer that no one else agrees or that your research is shallow; this could undermine even an authoritative source's credibility.
3. *State the credentials of your source.* Because an inference from testimony depends on listeners accepting the source as an authority, you should specify whom you are quoting or paraphrasing. Don't include every credential of the source, but list qualifications that support the claim in the quotation. Similarly, in selecting sources to quote, focus on people whose credentials are pertinent to your subject, and make sure that the audience understands why you are using the source. The endorsements of celebrities who lack subject-matter expertise carry little weight.
4. *Your own ethos affects the credibility of testimony you cite.* If listeners regard you as highly credible, they will be more likely to accept what you say; they will make inferences about the truth of your claims based on your own credibility. When basketball star Magic Johnson, after being diagnosed HIV-positive, urged others to avoid contracting the virus, he was a highly credible source because he was directly affected. Beyond that, if listeners love basketball and admire Magic Johnson, your use of his testimony will be more credible than it would be if they had no interest in him or the sport.

CHECKLIST 8.5

Tests for Inference from Testimony

- ❒ Does the statement accurately reflect the source's views?
- ❒ Is the source an expert on the topic?
- ❒ Is there a basis for the source's statements?
- ❒ Is the source reasonably unbiased?
- ❒ Is the testimony up to date?

When qualified experts disagree, ask:

- ❒ What does each expert's record of previous statements imply about the quality of judgment in this case?
- ❒ Which expert's testimony is closest to consensus in the field?
- ❒ Which expert's statement is most consistent with other things you already know or believe?

Narrative

This final category of inference, called *narrative,* comes into play when a speaker tells a story. A story is often more powerful than other ways of developing an idea. It is *personalized,* presenting a broad, general, or abstract idea as a specific situation involving particular people. Listeners become involved in the action and wonder what will happen; the story thus adds an element of suspense. A narrative works just like an extended example, and so *representativeness* serves to test the inference, just as it does for inference from example.

The dramatic structure of a narrative inference makes it powerful, which is apparent to anyone who reads novels or watches television and movies. The narrative structure consists of *characters,* a sequence of episodes or moves (often called a *plot*), the resolution of some sort of *conflict* (broadly defined), and an *ending* to which the resolution points. But the ending—the "moral of the story"—often is not stated explicitly. Audience members infer it for themselves.[11]

A speaker may use narrative reasoning to talk about hypothetical, real, or fictional events. To be effective, the story should be coherent, plausible, and consistent, and should resonate with the listeners.

Narratives take many forms in speeches and have many uses. They may be personal—a story in which

The Kansas–Nebraska Act, the president's statements, and the *Dred Scott* decision all prepared the way for the next advance of slavery. (examples) → A coherent story contains a pattern that enables prediction of what will come next. → The way is now being prepared for another *Dred Scott* decision that would make slavery legal everywhere.

Figure 8.8 Inference from narrative.

the speaker is the main character—or they may be about other people. They may describe real events or a hypothetical situation; fictional narratives are also common in speeches, as in the retelling of children's stories, fables, biographical accounts, and historical scenarios.[12]

Figure 8.8 maps a famous historical case of inference from narrative. During the 1850s, some Northern politicians, including Abraham Lincoln, believed that a group of Southern sympathizers were plotting to extend slavery over the entire country. In the "House Divided" speech, Lincoln arranged a series of recent events into narrative form so that they told a story of the work of this "slave power." Each of these events, such as the Kansas–Nebraska Act opening formerly free territories to slavery and the *Dred Scott* Supreme Court decision preventing Congress from outlawing slavery in the territories, prepared the way for more drastic action to extend slavery. Lincoln used the coherence of the story to predict what these plotters would do next: Bring about a second *Dred Scott* decision that would prevent *states* from outlawing slavery anywhere. Figure 8.8 paraphrases his argument.

We have referred to narrative as a kind of verbal storytelling, but narrative inferences can also be made from visual evidence. In interpreting a picture, for instance, one might reveal the "story" that the picture tells.

Tests for Inference from Narrative

To test whether a narrative inference is sound, examine various elements of its structure. Some important questions follow:

1. *Is the narrative coherent?* Does the story hang together and make sense? Is everything tied together at the end? Or do unexplained factors and loose ends make the story seem "unfinished" and its point unclear?
2. *Is the narrative plausible?* Is the story realistic, or is it farfetched? Because the narrative is offered to explain or support some claim, an implausible narrative will call that claim into question as well.
3. *Are characterizations consistent?* Do individuals in the story act as the audience has been led to expect? Just as you must be credible as a speaker and just as the experts you quote must be credible as authorities, so the characters in a narrative must be credible. If they are not, the audience will question the story—and the claim.
4. *Does the narrative have resonance?* **Resonance** is a feature that makes a narrative strike a responsive chord with listeners, allowing them to identify with the story and to relate it to their own experience. If your narrative has resonance, listeners will realize that you are telling the story not primarily for its entertainment value, but to speak directly to them and to make them understand your point.

resonance
The quality of striking a responsive chord with listeners, causing them to identify with what one is saying.

CHECKLIST 8.6

Tests for Inference from Narrative

- ❐ Is the narrative coherent?
- ❐ Is the narrative plausible?
- ❐ Are characterizations consistent?
- ❐ Does the narrative have resonance?

Avoiding Errors in Reasoning

OBJECTIVE 8.3

We have examined a variety of inferences and some tests for each of them. The best way to ensure that your reasoning is sound is to apply those tests to specific inference patterns. But there are also some general errors in reasoning. As we have seen, these also are called *fallacies*. The inference appears at first to be sound but, on inspection, it contains a major flaw. Although fallacies often seem persuasive, critical listeners quickly realize that the reasoning goes astray.

Sometimes the term *fallacy* refers very broadly to any claim that people disagree with or any statement that they do not like. At other times, the term refers very narrowly to defects in formal logic only. In public speaking, however, fallacies are inferences that would generally be regarded as unreasonable by a broad and diverse audience of listeners exercising their best critical judgment.[13]

Six General Tests of Inference

For any argument, regardless of the type of inference, these are important questions to ask:

1. *Does the claim follow from the supporting material?* This is the most basic question. Suppose a speaker stated:

   Because our school is 100 years old, it needs higher academic standards.

   We would be hard pressed to find any relationship between the supporting material (the age of the school) and the claim (that higher academic standards are needed). The claim might be correct, but it probably could not be inferred from this supporting evidence. The technical term for an inference in which the claim does not follow from the supporting material is **non sequitur** (Latin for "It does not follow").

2. *Does the claim advance our understanding beyond the supporting material?* Because we reason from what we already know (the supporting material) to what we wish to establish (the claim), an inference moves beyond the supporting material. Sometimes an inference has no real movement; the claim simply restates the supporting material in slightly different words. Such an inference is said to be a **circular argument**, as in this statement:

   Freedom of speech is for the common good [*claim*] because the expression of opinions is ultimately in the best interest of all [*supporting material*].

3. *Is the claim relevant to the issue?* Sometimes, a speaker makes a claim that is not pertinent to the topic at hand. Consider the following argument from a student who was claiming that the Scholastic Assessment Test (SAT) does not predict academic success:

   The test numbers do nothing to measure a student's potential for success in college. I am so tired of the way the modern world reduces us all to numbers. The college admissions process has become a clear example of this. When students want most of all to be seen as unique persons, they are instead reduced to an SAT score.

   By noting the dehumanizing effect of using test scores to assess college applicants, the speaker was making a claim about modern life, and supported it with reference to the SAT, but the claim had nothing to do with the issue

non sequitur
A claim that, on its face, is unrelated to the supporting material.

circular argument
Only restating the claim in slightly different words, rather than supporting the claim.

of whether the exam is a poor measure of students' potential. Whereas test number one (above) refers to the relationship between the supporting material and the claim, this test concerns the relationship between the claim and the issue. An inference that diverts attention from the issue is said to be **ignoring the question**. (More commonly it is called a *red herring*, from the practice in earlier centuries of dragging a smoked fish along a trail to confuse hunting dogs that were tracking the scent of a fox.)

4. *Is the language clear and unequivocal?* In Chapter 12, we will study the specific roles of language in a speech. The important point here is that the clarity of language may affect the quality of an inference. When the language of a speech can have multiple meanings, it is said to be **equivocal**; and any inferences based on that language will also be open to interpretation.

   Suppose that a politician promises "no tax increases." This sounds straightforward but can be interpreted in many ways. Is the politician promising that there will be no new taxes, or that the current tax rate will not increase? Or that the percentage of a family's income paid in taxes will not change? Or that the family will spend no more on taxes this year than last year? Furthermore, what is a "tax"? Is it limited to such obvious categories as income, sales, and property taxes, or does it also include fees for driving on toll roads or camping in national parks?

Watch the **Video** "Mark Knapp on the Accuracy in Detecting Deception" at **MyCommunicationLab**

5. *Has probability been clearly distinguished from certainty?* Speakers sometimes forget that inferences cannot be guaranteed, and they regard as certain what is really only probable. A speaker might argue, for example, that viewing violent television programs unquestionably inspires people to act violently. But this claim is hardly a sure thing; some researchers suggest that television violence may have little or no effect on behavior, and some even argue that television violence reduces aggression by providing a relatively harmless outlet for it. When a speaker suggests that all the evidence is clear-cut in one direction, listeners will do well to be wary that he or she is overstating the case.

6. *Is the speaker's emotional response appropriate to the situation?* Although over 20 years old, there is a still-famous example of what happens when the speaker's emotional response is not appropriate to the situation. During the 1988 presidential debates, Democratic candidate Michael Dukakis, who opposed capital punishment, was asked whether he would favor it were his wife raped and murdered. Dukakis virtually ignored the hypothetical situation posed by the questioner and proceeded in analytical fashion to restate his position on capital punishment:

   > I think you know I've opposed the death penalty during all my life. I don't see any evidence that it's a deterrent, and I think there are better and more effective ways to deal with violent crime. We've done so in my own state. And that's one of the reasons we have had the biggest drop in crime of any industrial state in America.

   Many viewers reacted negatively to this response because Dukakis seemed to show no emotion; nothing in his answer suggested the rage people might expect from a husband in this situation. As a result, many listeners both discounted Dukakis's views on capital punishment and decided that he was not credible. Both conclusions were reached by inference from the mismatch between Dukakis's emotional reaction and what would be expected.

ignoring the question
Making an inference that diverts attention from the issue at hand.

equivocal
Having multiple meanings.

As this example illustrates, appropriate emotional response sometimes is more important than the details of the inference. This point was made vividly in August 1998 when President Clinton spoke to the nation about his improper relationship with Monica Lewinsky. Although many people believed that an overzealous special prosecutor was the real cause of his problems, Clinton's use of that claim in his speech did not go over well. At that moment, the audience was expecting to see the emotions of contrition and remorse, not causal arguments.

The first key issue is the *appropriateness* of the speaker's emotional response. Some situations, such as the presentation of scientific research, call for straightforwardness and calm; others, such as the ones Dukakis and Clinton faced, call for a passionate response. But because the meaning of situations is not given and because inferences from emotions—like other inferences—cannot be guaranteed, the speaker should analyze the norms of appropriate emotional response as part of the audience analysis.

CHECKLIST 8.7

General Tests for Inferences

- ❒ Does the claim follow from the supporting material?
- ❒ Does the claim advance our understanding beyond the supporting material?
- ❒ Is the claim relevant to the issue?
- ❒ Is the language clear and unequivocal?
- ❒ Has probability been clearly distinguished from certainty?
- ❒ Is the speaker's emotional response appropriate to the situation?

Second, should speakers always respond in the "appropriate" way? At times, a speaker may deliberately violate listeners' expectations by making an "inappropriate" response, perhaps becoming emotionally aroused about a subject that the audience regards as "no big deal" or finding humor in a subject that the audience takes seriously. Usually, when a speaker violates norms of appropriateness, the purpose is to shock listeners, to make them pay attention, and to convince them to reexamine their ideas. But such a strategy is risky, because the discomfort produced by an inappropriate response may turn the audience against the speaker instead.

Finally, be aware that emotional responses are sometimes misused, as when a speaker labels ideas he or she does not like as "anti-American" or "sexist" or "racist." Unsupported appeals to fear, to prejudice, or to pride are actually devices to prevent inference, an attempt to substitute emotional reactions for substantial proof.

Reasoning in Public Speaking

OBJECTIVE 8.4

How can you apply the reasoning process to preparing, delivering, and listening to speeches? When preparing a speech, ask yourself why listeners should regard the supporting material as grounds for your claim. Then apply the tests for the particular kinds of inferences (Checklists 8.1 to 8.6) and the general tests for inferences (Checklist 8.7) to determine whether your reasoning seems sound. Then imagine a relatively skeptical listener—not someone hostile to the topic, but someone who really does need to be convinced. Would that person regard your reasoning as sound?[14]

Proceed to higher levels of claims and repeat this process. Finally, ask whether all the statements marked by Roman numerals in your outline taken together provide a basis for inferring your central claim. If so, then you have done a good job

Strategies for Speaking to Diverse Audiences

Respecting Diversity Through Reasoning

Not all individuals or cultures reason in the same way. The following strategies will help ensure that you do not unconsciously assume that all audience members reason in the same way that you do.

1. Think about how your audience may expect certain types of reasoning more than others. This is certainly true across cultures, where narrative (for example) may be expected in one case and scientific facts in another. But this is also true within U.S. audiences; a group of engineers would expect different evidence from that for literary scholars.
2. Be sure that your inferences (from example, analogy, sign, cause, testimony, and narrative) avoid stereotypes of individuals or cultural groups. Resorting to such stereotypes weakens your *ethos*. Not only does it potentially alienate your audience, but it also generally does not employ sound reasoning.
3. Pay attention to differences in the assumptions that your audience may have. Some things that you may consider so obvious that they require no explanation, may not be so obvious for others. Rhetorical proof relies on both audience and speaker, so keep in mind how reason and audience are linked.

in working with your speech materials. But if you find any questionable inferences, your listeners are likely to find them, too.

When presenting a speech, remember that the audience is a critical factor in establishing rhetorical proof; the speaker and listeners reason together. As we have seen throughout the chapter, your selection of one reasoning pattern rather than another is a strategic choice, because each pattern reflects a different aspect of how listeners think along with you. Moreover, you will not always make every step in your reasoning explicit; sometimes the supporting material or, more likely, the inference will seem to be assumed. This means that you are drawing on the audience's knowledge and expectations to establish the inference.

For example, audience analysis might suggest that your listeners believe that mergers of media companies threaten the ability of the press to be both a government watchdog and a guardian of democracy. You might never mention that inference explicitly in your speech, instead say:

> This week we heard news reports of yet another media corporation merger. We know what that means for the strength of American democracy.

Occasionally, of course, the audience analysis will be mistaken. Suppose that the last statement was met by blank stares—or, worse, by frowns. Such feedback signals that the audience is not ready to participate in this inference. Even while giving the speech, you may modify your strategic plan, deciding in this case to make the inference explicit—not only stating that media mergers threaten democracy, but also giving evidence to support your claim.

You can help listeners follow your reasoning process by signposting its steps and inferences. For instance:

> Let me provide three examples…
> An analogy is in order here…

Phrases like these will prompt listeners to anticipate the inference and its appropriate tests. Or you may ask (and later answer) such a question as:

How do we know that the statistical sample was representative?

This will suggest that you know the relevant tests of reasoning and are confident that your speech satisfies them. Even the use of reasoning terms (*consequently, therefore, the premise is, the implied conclusion is*, and so on) will help listeners understand where you are in reasoning through the speech. Your care in reasoning appropriately from supporting material will also help to promote your audience's critical thinking and listening skills—just as their critical listening will provide you with an incentive to reason carefully.[15]

What Have You Learned?

Objective 8.1: Explain the nature of rhetorical proof in public speaking and identify its three components.

Rhetorical proof in public speaking is different from proof in mathematics or science:

- Rhetorical proof depends on an interaction between the speaker and the audience.
- Although their joint conclusions cannot be guaranteed absolutely, they can be supported and shown to be probable.

A rhetorical proof includes three main components:

- The claim is the statement that listeners are asked to accept.
- Supporting material provides the foundation for the claim.
- Reasoning links the supporting material to the claim.

Reasoning involves making an inference:

- An inference is a mental leap.
- The leap is the judgment that the supporting material really does support the claim.
- Inferences cannot be guaranteed, but certain patterns of inference can be shown as generally reliable.
- An inference is reasonable if it would be made by most people when exercising their critical judgment.

Objective 8.2: Describe six basic patterns of reasoning, focusing on their types, appropriate tests of their soundness, and how to use them in a speech.

The major forms or patterns of inference include the following:

- Example
- Analogy
- Signs
- Cause
- Testimony
- Narrative

Each of these reasoning patterns has

- Several different types
- Specific tests to determine whether it is a strong inference
- Guidelines for use

Objective 8.3: Define what a fallacy is and identify both general fallacies and fallacies that correspond to particular patterns of reasoning.

In addition to the specific tests for each reasoning pattern, there are general tests of reasoning in order to avoid such fallacies as the following:

- *Non sequitur*
- Circular argument
- Ignoring the question
- Equivocal language
- Confusing probability with certainty
- Inappropriate emotional response

These are fallacies because the inferences appear to be sound but actually are seriously flawed.

Objective 8.4: Indicate how an understanding of reasoning processes helps in preparing and delivering a speech and in being an active, critical listener.

The chapter concluded with suggestions for using your understanding of the reasoning process in preparing, delivering, and listening to speeches.

Listen to the **Audio Chapter Summary** at **MyCommunicationLab**

Discussion Questions

1. In class, watch a recording of a recent political speech and discuss its reasoning process. What patterns of inference were used? Why do you think the speaker chose to use those patterns? Did they work? Did you recognize any fallacies?
2. If you knew that your audience would be uncritical, why would you still take time to test your inferences before speaking? With a group of peers, discuss the ethics of proper reasoning.
3. In what ways might emotion help someone or prevent someone from making a proper inference? Discuss situations in which particular emotions (love, fear, hate, anger, boredom) might advance or detract from the reasoning process.
4. As we have seen in this chapter, telling a story (narrative inference) is an effective way for speakers to make a point in very concrete terms. Share examples of speeches or other presentations where you have seen this technique used well. How in-depth were these examples?

Activities

1. In Chapter 4, you studied how to listen critically to a speech and to develop a map of what was said, evaluating each link between support and claim with a plus or minus sign. Now expand your evaluation of each link on that map. Identify each type of inference, and conduct appropriate tests to understand why each link is positive or negative.
2. Identify examples of each type of inference that you plan to use in your next speech. Which reasoning patterns are most appropriate for your topic? Which do you think will be most effective with your audience? How would your reasoning patterns need to be modified for a different audience, such as elderly veterans or mostly international students?
3. Using Checklist 8.7 as a guide, for the next few days, think critically about the everyday communication events around you. Identify claims in the wide variety of messages that surround you (TV commercials, newspaper editorials, or arguments with friends, for example). Demonstrate how at least three of these messages fail one of the general tests, and explain the fallacy of each.
4. Find a letter to the editor in the campus or local newspaper. Identify and analyze the inferences the writer makes. What patterns are employed? Are the tests for each pattern satisfied? Are there any general errors in reasoning?
5. Watch on television or listen on the radio to a highly partisan "news" and opinion show. List the fallacies and other lapses in reasoning you perceive the host or guests to be making, and supply examples.

Key Terms

analogy **189**
causal inference **195**
circular argument **205**
claim **182**
common cause fallacy **198**
equivocal **206**
examples **185**
expert testimony **200**
fallacy **188**
fallacy of composition **188**
fallacy of division **188**
figurative analogy **190**
ignoring the question **206**
inference **182**
institutional regularity (as a sign) **193**
lay testimony **200**
literal analogy **190**
non sequitur **205**
physical observation (as a sign) **193**
pontificate **202**
post hoc fallacy **198**
reasonable **182**
representative **185**
resonance **204**
rhetorical proof **180**
sign **192**
statistical index (as a sign) **193**

Study and Review the Flashcards
at MyCommunicationLab

Notes

1 Although scientists and mathematicians may argue about what counts as proof, their institutional standards for agreement are usually clearly defined. See Philip J. Davis and Reuben Hersh, "Rhetoric and Mathematics," *The Rhetoric of the Human Sciences: Language and Argument in Scholarship and Public Affairs*, ed. John S. Nelson, Allan Megill, and Donald N. McCloskey, Madison: University of Wisconsin Press, 1987, pp. 53–68. For a discussion of the similarities that may ground different standards of proof, see Stephen Pender, "Between Medicine and Rhetoric," *Early Science and Medicine* 10 (2005): 36–64.

2 See the discussion of "universal audience" in Chapter 4. See also Chaim Perelman and Lucie Olbrechts-Tyteca, *The New Rhetoric: A Treatise on Argumentation*, translated by John Wilkinson and Purcell Weaver, Notre Dame, IN: University of Notre Dame Press, 1969, pp. 31–35.

3 For a more detailed map of the reasoning process, see Stephen Toulmin, Richard Rieke, and Allan Janik, *An Introduction to Reasoning*, 2nd ed., New York: Macmillan, 1984. See also J. Ramage and J. Bean, *Writing Arguments*, 3rd ed., Boston: Allyn & Bacon, 1995; and Douglas N. Walton, *Argumentation Schemes for Presumptive Reasoning*, Mahwah, NJ: Lawrence Erlbaum, 1996.

4 This is an adaptation of a model developed by a contemporary British philosopher, Stephen Toulmin, in *The Uses of Argument*, Cambridge: Cambridge University Press, 1958. Toulmin's model includes some additional elements that need not concern us here.

5 For recent research on the influence of culture on reasoning patterns, see Erica Goode, "How Culture Molds Habits of Thought," *New York Times* (Aug. 8, 2000): D1, D4.

6 Also consult a theoretical discussion of inferences from example in speeches, such as John Arthos, "Where There Are No Rules or Systems to Guide Us: Argument from Example in a Hermeneutic Rhetoric," *Quarterly Journal of Speech* 89 (November 2003): 320–44.

7 For research detailing the persuasive effects of literal and figurative analogies, see Pradeep Sopory and James Price Dillard, "The Persuasive Effects of Metaphor: A Meta-Analysis," *Human Communication Research* 28 (July 2002): 382–419.

8 Our modern understanding of literal and figurative analogies developed from the classical tradition. For more on the genesis of analogical reasoning, see James S. Measell, "Classical Bases of the Concept of Analogy," *Argumentation and Advocacy* 10 (Summer 1973): 1–10. For an example of the prevalence of analogy in speeches, see David Hoogland Noon, "Operation Enduring Analogy: World War II, the War on Terror, and the Uses of Historical Memory," *Rhetoric & Public Affairs* 7 (Fall 2004): 339–65.

9 For more on the use of analogies in speeches, see James R. Wilcox and Henry L. Ewbank, "Analogy for Rhetors," *Philosophy and Rhetoric* 12 (Winter 1979): 1–20.

10 For a more detailed theoretical discussion of inferences from cause, see David Zarefsky, "The Role of Causal Argument in Policy Controversies," *Argumentation and Advocacy* 13 (Spring 1977): 179–91. Marketing and consumer research also depends heavily upon causal claims. See Elise Chandon and Chris Janiszewski, "The Influence of Causal Conditional Reasoning on the Acceptance of Product Claims," *Journal of Consumer Research* 35 (April 2009): 1003–1011.

11 According to some, storytelling is the most important aspect of speechmaking. See Walter R. Fisher, "Narration as a Human Communication Paradigm: The Case of Public Moral Argument," *Communication Monographs* 51 (March 1984): 1–22.

12 For a good practical discussion of the power of narrative in speeches, see Theodore F. Sheckels, "The Rhetorical Success of Thabo Mbeki's 1966 'I Am an African' Address," *Communication Quarterly* 57 (July 2009): 319–33.

13 Several books explore fallacies in detail. See Alex C. Michalos, *Improving Your Reasoning*, 2nd ed., Englewood Cliffs, NJ: Prentice-Hall, 1986; T. Edward Damer, *Attacking Faulty Reasoning*, 2nd ed., Belmont, CA: Wadsworth, 1987; Howard Kahane, *Logic and Contemporary Rhetoric*, Belmont, CA: Wadsworth, 1980; and Christopher W. Tindale, *Fallacies and Argument Appraisal*, Cambridge: Cambridge University Press, 2007.

14 It has been said that "arguments are found in people," meaning that listeners are responsible for making the inferential leaps between supporting material and claim. See Wayne Brockriede, "Where Is Argument?" *Argumentation and Advocacy* 11 (Spring 1975): 179–82.

15 For a more detailed discussion of how speakers (and audiences) develop skill in reasoning, see Dale Hample, "Arguing Skill," *Handbook of Communication and Social Interaction Skills*, ed. John O. Greene and Brant R. Burleson, Mahwah, NJ: Erlbaum, 2003.

CHAPTER

9

Organizing the Speech: The Body

LEARNING OBJECTIVES

Listen to the **Audio Chapter** at **MyCommunicationLab**

After studying this chapter, you should be able to:

Objective 9.1	Explain why the organization of a speech is important for both the speaker and the audience.
Objective 9.2	Identify criteria for selecting the main ideas to include in your speech and the characteristics that a main idea should have.
Objective 9.3	Arrange the main ideas into recognizable patterns and decide what patterns of arrangement to use.
Objective 9.4	Decide how much and which kinds of supporting material you need and how to arrange the support for each idea.

OUTLINE

If you have used all the strategies suggested in Chapters 6 and 7 for investigating your topic, you now should have a better understanding of the issues that are implicit in your thesis. You also should have located a variety of supporting materials for your ideas—examples, statistics, testimony, and so forth. You have probably investigated many more ideas than you can discuss in the time available, and you very likely have located far more supporting materials than you can use, even after applying the tests of reasoning that we examined in Chapter 8. For all this effort, your ideas and materials may show no evident pattern and may not seem to fit together well. What, then, do you do with all the ideas you have explored and all the evidence you have gathered?

Identifying and locating material for the speech is not enough; you also need to organize it in strategic ways that advance your purpose. **Organization** is the selection of ideas and materials and their arrangement into a discernible and effective pattern. This process is so crucial that we will discuss it in three chapters. Here, we will focus exclusively on the body of the speech. Then, in Chapter 10, we will consider introductions, conclusions, and transitions. Finally, in Chapter 11, we will learn how to apply the principles of organization in outlining your speech.

OBJECTIVE 9.1

Why Is Organization Important?

To help orient new students to the college, the counseling office offers a program in which seniors give speeches about how to develop good study habits. The first speaker, Burt Wilson, maintained that "good habits depend on several important factors. For one thing, you have to avoid procrastination. Good reading skills are also helpful to college students. Oh yes, and by the way, you also need to be self-motivated." The incoming students looked puzzled and unconvinced; they stopped taking notes, and no one asked questions. The very next speaker, Laura Simmons, covered the same ground, but she said: "Good study habits depend on a balance of skills plus motivation. On the one hand, you have to develop good reading skills; on the other hand, you need to overcome procrastination. You can do both if you focus on the priorities that motivate you to study." The audience responded very differently to Laura's speech; they took notes and asked a number of questions when she finished.

This example illustrates that audiences will understand, remember, and be influenced by an organized message more than by a disorganized one. The reason is obvious. Careful listening is difficult under any circumstances, and it is even more difficult when listeners cannot tell where the speaker is going or how the parts of the speech relate to one another. An idea or example that is not connected to anything else is easy to forget.[1] The mental energy that listeners use in reconstructing a confused or disorganized speech is not available for absorbing and reflecting on its main points.[2] Moreover, even critical listeners may resent this additional work of listening to a disorganized speech and may express their resentment by resisting the message.[3]

Beyond such basic considerations about the audience, a speaker should recognize that form itself is persuasive. The ability to follow a speaker's organizational pattern is important for several reasons:

- *Recall.* An audience can better remember the main ideas of a speech when the speaker presents them in a recognizable pattern. For example, the past/present/future pattern encourages listeners to remember the first idea if they can connect it mentally to the heading "past."

organization
The selection of ideas and materials and their arrangement into a discernible and effective pattern.

- *Active listening.* Effective organization engages listeners' attention and helps them to ignore or override distractions.
- *Personal satisfaction.* Being able to anticipate what's coming next makes listeners feel that they are "in the know." If the speaker has just discussed recent issues in intercollegiate athletics, for example, they may believe that the next natural step is to discuss the merits of a playoff system for college football. If that indeed is the next main idea, they are likely to feel personal satisfaction at having "called it right."[4]

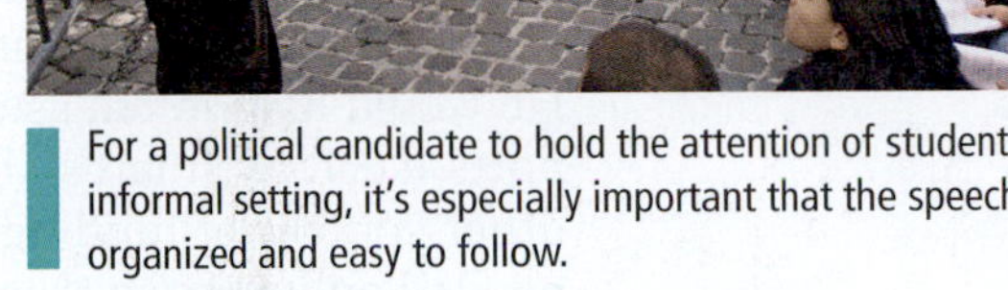

For a political candidate to hold the attention of students in an informal setting, it's especially important that the speech be well organized and easy to follow.

Organization is important for the speaker as well. In Chapter 6, you were introduced to the idea of *strategic planning* for a speech. In any rhetorical situation, the goal is to respond to your constraints and to take advantage of your opportunities to achieve your purpose. Organization is a major strategic resource as you make decisions about the number and order of ideas, how you group them, what you call them, and how you relate them to the audience.

Moreover, in planning your speech, organization can be a guide to check that you haven't accidentally left anything out. For example, noticing that your speech covers both the past and the present of your topic, you recognize that the audience will be likely to think, "But what about the future?" During your presentation, too, keeping the organization in mind can prevent the embarrassment of suddenly forgetting about the next point.[5]

Organization has two basic components: *selection* and *arrangement*. We will discuss each component with respect both to the main ideas of the speech and to the supporting materials.

Selecting the Main Ideas

OBJECTIVE 9.2

As you remember from Chapter 6, the thesis statement is the principal claim of your speech, the statement you want listeners to accept. When you ask questions about your thesis statement, you identify the issues that you must address in order to establish the thesis. **Main ideas** are the claims that address the issues in your thesis statement, and they are the major divisions of the speech. In Chapter 11, you'll see that main ideas are signaled in the speech outline by Roman numerals.

Identifying Your Main Ideas

The first step is to identify the main ideas in your speech. To do that, you must determine the possible main ideas from which you could choose. You can do so either (1) from your thesis or specific purpose or (2) from patterns in your research.

In either case, your answers will be affected by the current status of the topic in the public forum: what aspects or issues people generally are considering, which matters are accepted and uncontested and which are in dispute, which questions seem central and which seem peripheral.

main ideas
Claims that address the issues in the thesis statement; the primary divisions of the speech.

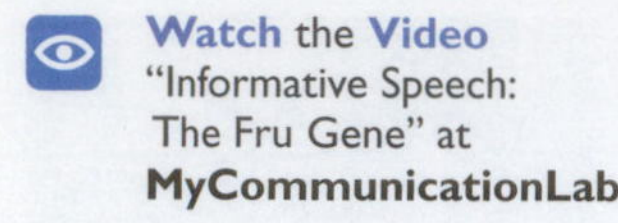
Watch the **Video** "Informative Speech: The Fru Gene" at **MyCommunicationLab**

From Your Thesis or Specific Purpose. Stuart Kim used this approach to identify his main ideas in a speech seeking to persuade the audience to contribute to the United Way. Like many college students, Stuart was a community-service volunteer; he tutored reading and math at an after-school center for children from low-income families who had no parent at home during the day. Stuart enjoyed the work and felt that he was really helping the children, but toward the end of the year he was startled to learn that the center would have to close. It was funded by the United Way, and contributions were down. Appalled that "his" children would have nowhere to go, Stuart decided to speak to community groups and urge them to support the United Way. He used his public speaking classmates as a test audience to practice the speech.

Because Stuart's purpose was to persuade the audience to contribute to the United Way, he thought immediately of several ideas that he needed to address. He would have to tell listeners what the United Way is, that the agencies it supports (such as Stuart's after-school center) were important and valuable, that other sources of funding were not readily available, and that the United Way needed and merited *their* support. If the speech failed to address any of these elements, the audience was unlikely to be persuaded to donate money. Stuart regarded these as the main ideas, and he divided the speech into corresponding sections:

I. The United Way is a federation of health, recreational, and social service agencies.
II. The activities of these agencies are important and valuable to our community.
III. These activities cannot be continued unless we support the United Way.

In this example, Stuart was able immediately to see the main ideas that derived from his thesis and purpose. But sometimes the connection is not so obvious. If Stuart had not identified his main ideas at once, he might have worked them out by quizzing his thesis statement, using the method you learned in Chapter 6:

TOPIC:	The United Way.		
GENERAL PURPOSE:	Inducing a specific action.		
SPECIFIC PURPOSE:	Convincing listeners to give money to the United Way.		
THESIS:	Everyone should contribute to the United Way.		
ISSUES:	1. Everyone	→	Why me?
	2. Should contribute	→	Why? What does it do?
	3. The United Way	→	What is it?
MAIN IDEAS:	1. The United Way needs and merits your support.		
	2. The United Way supports important and valuable programs.		
	3. The United Way is an umbrella organization to raise money for social service programs.		

Looking over this list, Stuart would probably decide to put main idea 3 first in the speech and to end with main idea 1. Why? Because listeners need to know what the United Way is before they can decide whether to support it and because the direct appeal in main idea 1 provides a strong conclusion. Applying these analytical steps, Stuart would derive the same main ideas that he was able to recognize instinctively.

Checklist 9.1 contains some of the standard questions to ask about a thesis statement in order to identify your main ideas.

From Patterns in Your Research. Another approach to identifying main ideas is to observe patterns in the research that you have completed. If the people you interview and the literature you read repeatedly mention certain subjects, those may well be the main ideas about your topic.

For example, suppose that almost everything Stuart Kim read about the United Way mentioned its low administrative costs and suggested that its reliance on volunteers meant that most of the money raised can be spent directly on providing services. This idea may not have emerged from Stuart's initial conception of a strategy, and yet it may be very important to include the idea in the speech. It suggests that it is better for people to contribute to the United Way than to support a host of individual charities that do not use their funds as efficiently.

CHECKLIST 9.1

Questions to Help Identify Main Ideas

- ❒ What does it mean?
- ❒ How to describe it?
- ❒ What are the facts?
- ❒ What are the reasons?
- ❒ How often does it occur?
- ❒ What are the parts?
- ❒ What is the reasoning?
- ❒ Why is it strange?
- ❒ What are the objections?
- ❒ Compared with what?

Choosing Among Main Ideas

Whichever method you use to identify main ideas, you are likely to have more ideas than you have time or energy to pursue—and more than your audience will be willing and able to consider.

Suppose, for example, that Stuart's research suggested all the following points:

- The administrative costs of the United Way are low.
- Organizations in the United Way must be nondiscriminatory.
- The United Way had its origins in charitable organizations of the late nineteenth century.
- Some groups within the public object to the programs of certain United Way organizations.
- The United Way is staffed largely by volunteers.
- It is not clear whether someone who lives in one community but works in another should support the United Way at home or at work.
- The United Way substitutes a single annual campaign for what otherwise would be continuous solicitation for each of the member agencies.
- The alternative to supporting the United Way is to expand the government's social welfare programs.

Each of these topics could be discussed at length, and each might be supported by a variety of materials. Yet no speech of reasonable length could address them all. Therefore, like most speakers, Stuart will need to select from among the possible main ideas which ones to use in his speech.

Criteria for Selecting the Main Ideas

Most speeches cover between two and five main ideas. Although there is no magic to these numbers, they do generally represent what an audience expects and can likely follow and remember.

If you have derived more than five main ideas from your thesis and purpose and from your research, you can reduce their number and select which ideas to include by asking two questions:

- Is this idea really essential to the speech?
- Can a more general statement combine several ideas?

Is This Idea Essential?

In researching a speech, you may discover many interesting things about your subject that are, frankly, sidelights. Although they may be fascinating to you, they distract from your specific purpose. For example, knowing that the United Way developed from nineteenth-century charitable organizations may reveal quite a bit about American attitudes toward charity or about how organizations evolve. But remember that Stuart Kim's purpose is to persuade audience members to donate money. Most people don't need to know about the United Way's origins and history in order to decide whether to contribute. Likewise, if Stuart's goal is only to persuade people to give, it may not matter whether they do so at work or at home.

This first criterion is often difficult to apply. Speakers are reluctant to omit ideas that interest them, and valuable research time seems wasted if the results do not find their way into the speech. Material that does not directly relate to your topic and purpose is nonessential. Including nonessential material may distract the audience and prevent you from achieving your ultimate purpose. It is necessary, then, to be hard-nosed and to subject all potential main ideas to this rigorous test: If an idea—no matter how interesting—is not essential to your specific purpose, it does not qualify as a main idea and should be excluded.

Can Several Ideas Be Combined?

When you find yourself considering a large number of main ideas, consider whether some of them are not main ideas at all but illustrations of, or support for, more general statements. You may be able to combine what you thought were distinct main ideas into one general statement, thereby reducing the number. Your thesis should suggest these more general statements into which you could combine elements.

In the United Way example, the low administrative costs, the nondiscriminatory policies, and the convenience of a single annual campaign might turn out not to be separate main ideas but examples to support a general statement such as "The United Way is the best way to contribute to charity." The three statements all answer the question "Once I've decided that it's important to make a charitable contribution, why should I do so through the United Way?" That question is a longer form of "Why me?" which was derived from the thesis statement. All these examples could support the main idea, "The United Way merits *your* support."

Audience members listen attentively to a presentation that is well organized and easy to follow.

Characteristics of the Main Ideas

Unfortunately, just cutting the number of main ideas—as difficult as that is—may still result in a speech that does not seem complete, coherent, or persuasive. It is also important that the selected main ideas have the following characteristics.

Simplicity. Because the main ideas serve as memory aids for both speaker and audience, they should be stated simply and succinctly so that they can be remembered. "The United Way is efficient" is a better statement of a main idea than is "The United Way has low administrative costs, economies of scale from combining campaigns, and simple distribution mechanisms." As a general rule, a main idea should be stated in a single short sentence.

Discreteness. Each main idea should be separate from the others. When main ideas overlap, the structure of the speech becomes confusing, and it is difficult to remember what was said under each main heading. For example, if one main idea is "The United Way supports agencies that meet social needs" and another main idea is "The United Way supports health and recreational agencies," the two ideas overlap; they are not discrete. After all, health and recreation are also among our social needs. Such a structure will not be clear to listeners, and the speaker will not know where to put supporting material.

Parallel Structure. When possible, main ideas should be stated in similar fashion. Sentences should have the same grammatical structure and should be of approximately the same length. This principle, known as **parallel structure**, makes the pattern easy to follow and to remember. For example, Stuart Kim might use this pattern:

The United Way is effective.
The United Way is efficient.
The United Way is humane.

In this example, *effective*, *efficient*, and *humane* are the key terms that listeners are asked to remember.

parallel structure
Structure in which phrases are of similar syntax and length.

coherence
Clear relationships among ideas and topics so that the speech appears to hang together as a natural whole.

Balance. Taken together, the main ideas should not be loaded toward one particular aspect of the subject. Rather, they should add up to a balanced perspective. In the preceding list, each of the three key terms refers to a different aspect of the United Way: what it accomplishes, what it costs, and what values it represents. These are three different factors that would affect the decision to contribute, and together they offer a balanced perspective. If, on the other hand, three or four main ideas related to the United Way's finances and only one dealt with its underlying values, the organization of the speech would appear unbalanced. Finances would be covered in detail, but other important aspects of the topic would be treated superficially or ignored.

Coherence. **Coherence** means that the separate main ideas have a clear relationship and hang together; listeners can see why they appear in the same speech. If Stuart Kim wished to persuade listeners to contribute to the United Way but offered one main idea about the origins of charitable organizations, another about efforts to extend the United Way to Eastern Europe, another about controversial agencies that the United Way supports, and another about accounting procedures, it is

CHECKLIST 9.2

Characteristics of Main Ideas

- ❒ Are my main ideas **simple** and succinct?
- ❒ Is each main idea **discrete,** or separate from the others?
- ❒ Are the main ideas stated in a **parallel structure**?
- ❒ Are the main ideas **balanced** in perspective?
- ❒ Are the main ideas **coherent** and clear?
- ❒ Do the main ideas, taken together, offer a **complete** view of my topic?

hard to imagine how the speech could be coherent. These topics are not clearly related to each other (except that they all involve the United Way), and they do not come together to support any conclusion—certainly not the ultimate claim that "you should contribute to the United Way."

Completeness. Finally, the main ideas taken together should present a complete view of the subject, omitting nothing of major importance. If Stuart wants to convince the audience to contribute to the United Way but fails to explain what the organization does with the money it receives, the pattern of main ideas would not be complete. Most people who make charitable gifts want to know how their contributions are used.

OBJECTIVE 9.3

Arranging the Main Ideas

After selecting the main ideas for your speech, the next step is deciding upon their order—which ideas to put first, last, or in the middle. We'll look at the factors you should consider in arranging your main ideas and then at a variety of organizational patterns that you can use.

Factors Affecting Arrangement

Are the Main Ideas Dependent? Ideas can be arranged in a pattern that makes them either *dependent* or *independent*.

Logically dependent ideas are like links in a chain, because the strength of each depends on all the others. If one link is broken, the chain is destroyed. Here is such a chain of logically dependent main ideas:

1. If we develop regulations for campus speech, they will necessarily be vague.
2. If regulations are vague, people will not know whether or not the regulations apply to them.
3. If people are unsure whether regulations apply to them, they will hesitate to speak out about controversial issues.
4. If people do not speak out about controversial issues, intellectual debate is undermined.

The links in this chain need to be arranged precisely as shown if the audience is to follow the speaker's reasoning.

Watch the Video "Demonstration Speech: Baking a Cake" at **MyCommunicationLab**

Logical dependence is common in telling a story. With obvious exceptions (such as flashbacks), you should relate events in the order in which they occurred so that listeners can follow the plot. Likewise, if you arrange ideas in a spatial pattern—talking, for example, about colleges in different regions of the country—then you need to maintain that pattern of geographical movement. You might move from east to west or from west to east, but you would not want to zigzag from New England to the Southwest and then to the mid-Atlantic states.

logically dependent idea
Cannot stand on its own but requires that another claim or statement be true.

logically independent idea
Does not require the truth of any other claim or statement as a condition for its own truth.

In contrast, **logically independent ideas** stand alone, and the truth of each in no way rests on the others. Again, using the example of a proposed code to regulate campus speech, here is a logically independent pattern of reasoning:

Campus speech codes are unacceptably vague.

Campus speech codes discourage the airing of controversial issues.

Campus speech codes bring bad publicity to the college.

This speaker also wishes to oppose campus speech codes, but notice the difference in the structure of main ideas. In this case, each idea bears *independently* on the conclusion. Any one of these claims by itself could give the audience good reason to oppose speech codes, regardless of the other claims. Speech codes are undesirable if they are too vague, *or* if they chill the discussion of controversial issues, *or* if they bring unfavorable publicity.

A dependent pattern of reasoning can be risky, because the defeat of any one link will cause the chain to break. But a dependent pattern also offers advantages. It is highly coherent and easy to follow. And if each link is established successfully, the force of the overall pattern may cause the whole chain to seem even stronger than the sum of its links.

The choice of a dependent or an independent pattern is influenced most strongly by your thesis statement. Use whichever pattern is more effective in establishing your claim for your audience. But one thing is certain: If your main ideas are dependent on each other, their arrangement is virtually decided. You can begin at either end of the chain, but you must connect the ideas in order, link by link. With an independent pattern, however, you do not have to present the main ideas in any particular order. In that case, additional questions will arise.

Are Some Main Ideas Relatively Unfamiliar? Because most people comprehend unfamiliar ideas by linking them to familiar ideas, you may wish to begin your speech with a main idea that is already familiar to listeners. This will attract their interest and get them thinking about your topic. Then you can move to the less familiar ideas, knowing that the audience is working with you.

Your audience analysis may suggest that most people realize that campus speech codes attract adverse publicity but that they may not be familiar with the vagueness of such codes and may not have thought about their effect on the airing of controversial issues. You therefore might begin with the familiar idea that campus speech codes attract negative publicity, making the point that this is just the tip of the iceberg. Speech codes also have two less obvious problems: They are too vague to be administered fairly, and—even worse—they stifle discussion of controversial issues. If your audience analysis is correct, you have succeeded in arranging the ideas from most familiar to least familiar.

There is another reason to begin with the familiar. If your first main idea were completely unfamiliar to the audience, it would be much more difficult for listeners to grasp. You might distract them by making them stop to think about what you mean by "the inherent vagueness of speech codes," and they might miss your next point. On the other hand, discussion of a familiar main idea can be used to explain a less familiar idea. For example, knowing that listeners might quickly recognize that campus speech codes cause adverse publicity, you might ask why the publicity is so adverse. This question would provide a natural transition into your second, less familiar idea.

When you have a strong idea that you plan to present emphatically, as this speaker does, should it be placed first or last in your speech?

Should the Strongest Idea Come First or Last? This question comes into play when two conditions are met: when the main ideas are independent and when they are not equally strong.

A "strong" idea is one that will seem compelling to an audience of critical listeners. An idea is not considered strong if it does not make much difference to listeners—even if it is true and well supported.

Should you present your strongest main idea first in order to make a strong first impression on the audience? Or should you present it last, to end with a bang and leave the audience on a positive note? Many researchers have studied the relative merits of a **primacy effect** (strongest idea first) versus a **recency effect** (strongest idea last), but the results are inconclusive because too many other factors also influence the impact of arrangement.[6] However, if one idea seems weaker than the others, you should present it in a middle position rather than either toward the beginning or toward the end.

Often, the strength of an idea depends not on any inherent feature of the idea itself, but on how well the idea sits with the audience. Therefore, your audience analysis is not finished when you first select a topic, purpose, thesis, and strategy; the audience affects all major decisions about speech preparation and delivery.

Patterns for Arranging Main Ideas

In theory, you can arrange main ideas in an infinite number of patterns, but several common patterns are easy for an audience to follow, and they work well for a variety of topics. You first should focus on these general patterns, which are described next. Then, if your topic, purpose, or audience seems to call for a different pattern, you can develop your own.

Chronological. The passage of time is the organizing principle in the chronological approach. The units of time (most often the past, the present, and the future) become the main ideas. For example, in discussing the topic of "Discrimination Against Female Sports Reporters," student Jordan Breal organized her speech this way:

I. Female sports reporters received little credit for their work until the 1930s.
II. Female sports reporters were not allowed into press rooms until the 1970s.
III. Female sports reporters were not allowed into locker rooms until the late 1970s.
IV. Treatment of female sports reporters leaves much room for improvement in the future.

Watch the Video "Informative Speech/ Self-Introduction: Martha Margaret Clark Cherry Gaines" at **MyCommunicationLab**

This example proceeds in normal chronological order, beginning with the past and ending with the future. But you can start at any point in the chronology. For example, you might decide that a speech about AIDS should begin with a discussion of the current crisis in Africa, then move backwards in time to examine the origins of AIDS, and conclude with a discussion of the future of AIDS research and possible cures.

Spatial. Whereas chronological order organizes main ideas according to time, spatial order arranges them according to place or position. A speech might begin with the aspects of the topic that are nearest and then proceed to the aspects that are farther away. This pattern might work well for a speech about the effects of a strong national economy, in which the main points include the following:

I. A booming economy increases the individual's spending power.
II. A booming economy supports state and local projects.
III. A booming economy improves the federal budget.

primacy effect
A tendency for what is presented first to be best remembered.

recency effect
A tendency for what is presented last to be best remembered.

Another common spatial arrangement would be to present ideas literally in geographic order:

I. A booming economy helps farmers in the South.

II. A booming economy helps manufacturing in the Midwest.

III. A booming economy helps the oil industry in the Southwest.

IV. A booming economy helps technology industries in the Northwest.

Categorical (Topical). In the categorical pattern, each main idea that you identified in analyzing your topic becomes a major division of the speech. For example, in researching the Hindu religion, student Anuj Vedak learned that Hindus hold many distinct beliefs, including a belief in karma as a guide to treating others ethically, a belief in reincarnation for those who have died, and a belief in Nirvana as the soul's act of attaining salvation. Each of these topics can become a major heading in a speech. Because a categorical pattern has no required order (e.g., from past to present or from left to right), it is important that main ideas be stated in parallel fashion and that they be easy to recognize and remember. The major headings for a speech on Hinduism might be the following:

I. Hindus believe in karma as a guide to ethical behavior.

II. Hindus believe in reincarnation as the process of rebirth for the deceased.

III. Hindus believe in Nirvana as the soul's act of attaining salvation.

This pattern is also called *topical* because it derives from the *topoi*. As we saw in Chapter 6, these are obvious or typical categories for organizing subject matter. They usually will have an obvious or standard structure."People, places, and events" is an example of a set of *topoi*, as is"economic, military, and political aspects."

Cause–Effect. In Chapter 8, you learned how to infer causes and effects. Cause–effect is also an organizational pattern, and it can proceed in either direction. You can focus on causes and then identify their effects, or you can first identify effects and then try to determine their causes. For example, a speech about global warming might proceed like as follows:

I. Factories, refineries, power plants, and cars emit vast amounts of carbon into the Earth's atmosphere.

II. Industrialized societies generate so much atmospheric carbon that they are effectively wrapping the Earth in a heating blanket.

III. As the Earth's surface temperatures rise, fundamental and irreversible shifts in our planet's climate patterns are occurring.

Or, rather than moving from cause to effect, you might proceed from effect to cause:

I. We are becoming more vulnerable to the effects of global warming and climate change.

II. This effect results from the release of carbon into the atmosphere from the world's factories, refineries, power plants, and cars.

III. Widespread use of carbon-based fossil fuels is a major source of the problem.

The choice between these two arrangements would be governed by which topics you wanted to present first and last, not by anything intrinsic to the cause–effect organizational pattern.

A Question of Ethics

Ethics and Organization

The desire to organize our thoughts and make them easily memorable for our audiences is natural. But what if our organizational patterns distort the subject matter of our speech? Suppose we would like to deliver a speech in a chronological pattern, explaining the historical development of the topic, but that history would not allow for some of the more critical information that might show up in a categorical pattern. For example, the history of the civil rights movement often focuses on major achievements since the 1960s rather than on the internal tensions within the movement or the extent and ferocity of resistance to it. Or suppose we select a categorical pattern but the categories are not really separate from one another. What are our ethical responsibilities to our subject, and how can these be reconciled with our strategic interest in effective organization? How do we negotiate these tensions?

Watch the **Video** "Persuasive Speech: Living Wills" at **MyCommunicationLab**

Problem–Solution. A variation of the cause–effect pattern is one that focuses on problems and their solutions. A speech using this pattern first lays out the dimensions of the problem and shows why it is serious; then it considers one or more potential solutions. It may simply report on the various possible solutions or it may proceed to explain why a particular solution is best. For example, a speech about the difficulties of the campus parking system might be structured like as follows:

I. There is a shortage of parking spaces near the main classroom buildings.
II. As a result, many students must walk almost a mile from their cars to their classes.
III. In the short term, expanding the campus bus service, and in the long term, building a central parking garage would solve the problem.

The development of the first two major headings would establish that there is a problem, perhaps by claiming that the current situation is unsafe for students attending evening classes. Possibly after considering other solutions, the speaker would claim in the third main idea that these problems can be overcome by a combination of expanded bus service and construction of a parking garage.

Often, problems are not self-evident to an audience. A speaker has to motivate listeners to feel that some important need is not being met before they will regard a situation as a problem. A variation on the problem–solution pattern, then, is to emphasize *psychological order*. The speaker first motivates listeners to perceive a problem and then provides the means to satisfy that feeling by identifying a solution. If Stuart Kim had chosen this approach in speaking about the United Way, his speech might have been organized as follows:

I. We all have a responsibility to others.
II. This responsibility includes financial support for the social service organizations that help others.
III. Giving to the United Way helps us to meet our responsibilities.

In this example, the first step is to arouse an attitude, motive, or desire among the audience members. Subsequent steps then refine that motivation and show how it can be satisfied by a particular action. In Chapter 14, we will examine an elaborated version of this organizational pattern, called the *motivated sequence,* that is especially useful for persuading.

Comparison and Contrast. Sometimes it is easiest to examine a topic by demonstrating its similarities to, and differences from, other topics with which the audience is likely to be familiar. From your studies of American history, for example, you know that women and racial and ethnic minorities have sometimes been subjected to prejudice and discrimination in the workplace. Your speech might be organized to compare the experiences among these groups:

I. Women often are not promoted to senior positions because executives do not think they will remain on the job while raising children.

II. Mexican Americans, in many parts of the country, are hired only for the most menial jobs.

III. Earlier, German Americans and Japanese Americans were fired from their jobs because employers thought they were unpatriotic.

IV. Today, immigrants from the Middle East are denied access to some jobs because they are categorically suspected of involvement in terrorist activities.

V. African Americans have been limited in work opportunities because many whites believe that they do not want to work.

Rhetorical Workout

Shape and Organize Main Ideas

You are working on an informative speech about zero waste and are ready to choose and arrange your main ideas. Your *general purpose* is to provide new information, and your *specific purpose* is to inform listeners of what zero waste means and what initiatives have been successful. You write this thesis: "Zero waste initiatives are making a difference for a better environment."

1. Use the criteria for selecting main ideas to assess the points below. Which ideas seem essential to your speech? Which can be combined into fewer general statements?
   - Zero waste initiatives have proven to reduce pollution.
   - Zero waste means eliminating waste in all stages of a product's life.
   - Initiatives are under way in nearly 20 countries.
   - Not creating waste is more environmentally friendly than recycling it.
   - The quantity of garbage in landfills has gone down in areas using zero waste initiatives.
   - At least five U.S. states have adopted zero waste initiatives.
   - A zero waste economy is based on recovering resources and can create jobs.
2. Using the principle of parallel structure, create three main ideas out of the above list. Is the grammatical structure of each main idea the same? Are the three main ideas approximately the same length? If not, revise the sentences to fit these requirements.
3. Does each of your three main ideas stand alone, as a *logically independent idea*, or are all three like links in a chain, as *logically dependent ideas*? Explain. If they are logically dependent, write them down in the order they need to appear in your speech.
4. Which organizational pattern would be best suited to your three main ideas: chronological, spatial, categorical (topical), cause-effect, problem-solution, comparison and contrast, or residues? Why? Apply the pattern to your three main ideas. Is the result logical and effective? Why or why not?

Now the question is whether you want to highlight the differences or the similarities among these groups. You might select either of the following as your last main idea:

VI. Although some groups have managed to overcome the effects of discrimination and have succeeded in the workplace, others have not been so lucky.

or

VI. Although the experiences of these groups are very different, they have one factor in common: Society's prejudice places an artificial ceiling on their economic opportunities.

In either case, the earlier main ideas are brought together in the last one, which shows either how differences outweigh similarities or the reverse.

Residues. A final organizational pattern is to arrange the speech by process of elimination. This pattern works well when there are a finite number of possibilities, none particularly desirable, and you want to argue that one of them represents "the least among the evils." For example, in a political campaign in which you find no candidate particularly appealing, you could use this pattern to rule out all but one candidate, whom you then support as being the least objectionable.

Student speaker Jennifer Aiello used organization by residues to get her classmates to consider seriously the proposal that gun manufacturers should be required to install locks on guns. She arranged her main ideas to rule out the other options available to society:

> No one wants freedom infringed upon. And no one wants to have to pay more for a gun. But let's consider the alternatives. Does anyone want more children to have access to guns that take virtually no effort to use? Does anyone want to attend more funerals of children shot dead while at school? Does anyone want to see more six-year-olds lying in critical condition in hospital beds because they thought their parents' handgun was a toy? Does anyone want to see parents, friends, and family mourning another unnecessary death?

By ruling out each of these other alternatives, Jennifer was able to convince many of her audience members that putting locks on guns was a proposal worthy of their reflection.

CHECKLIST 9.3

Basic Organizational Patterns

- ❒ **Chronological:** Can my topic be broken down into units of time?
- ❒ **Spatial:** Can my topic be organized according to place or position?
- ❒ **Categorical (topical):** Is my topic best organized according to my existing main ideas? If so, are my main ideas in parallel form?
- ❒ **Cause–effect:** Can my topic be organized around causes and effects?
- ❒ **Problem–solution:** Does my topic suggest a problem that can be organized around its possible solutions?
- ❒ **Comparison and contrast:** Can I examine my topic by showing similarities to or differences from other topics?
- ❒ **Residues:** Does my topic lend itself to a process-of-elimination pattern?

Choosing the Organizational Pattern

The organizational patterns described here do not exhaust all the possibilities, but they illustrate that you have many options from which to choose.[7] How should you decide which organizational pattern to use in your speech? Does it matter, for example, whether you use a cause–effect pattern or a comparison and contrast pattern? How do you know whether, say, the costs and benefits of voting are more important than the convenience of voting? Questions like these require you to think strategically. The answers are complex and must take into account your subject, your purpose, your audience, and your culture.

Based on Your Subject. Certain subjects lend themselves to particular organizational patterns. For example, because the collapse of communism in Eastern Europe is a historical event, it has a dramatic structure that would be emphasized by telling a story in chronological order. However, a speech about the components of air pollution would more likely suggest a topical pattern—unless, perhaps, it was being delivered to an audience of environmental historians who would be more interested in understanding when and how these components became serious national problems.

Based on Your Purpose. Your purpose or strategy also influences the selection of an organizational pattern. For instance, if you want to urge the audience to lobby for updated privacy laws that better protect consumers against online identity theft, an analytical pattern that emphasizes the problems and solutions will be especially appropriate because it will focus attention on the specific proposal for which you want listeners to lobby. In contrast, if your purpose is to show that the protection of a person's online identity is very different from the traditional practice of maintaining personal privacy, a comparison and contrast pattern probably would make more sense.

Based on Your Audience. Your audience is another influence on the arrangement of your speech. For example, listeners who have paid little attention to developments in relations between Russia and Ukraine probably would be more interested in an overview of events since the fall of the Soviet Union than in a detailed analysis of oil and gas supply agreements between the two countries. But an audience composed mostly of people with family origins in either Russia or

Strategies for Speaking to Diverse Audiences

Respecting Diversity Through the Organization of the Body of Your Speech

A sense of form is achieved in different ways for different cultures. Here are strategies to respect the diversity of the audience when organizing the body of the speech.

1. Acknowledge the presuppositions of your audience members. Analyze your audience, but be careful not to stereotype cultures by assuming that one's culture completely determines one's response to your speech.
2. Organize your ideas according to what you believe will appeal to the majority of your audience, but do not rely heavily on a structure that might alienate parts of your audience.
3. Consider whether cultures differ in their approach to space; for example, Hebrew and Arabic texts read from right to left. If you use spatial order in your speech, do not automatically move from left to right.
4. Consider whether cultures differ in their approach to time. For example, tradition remains an important source of authority for many, giving greater weight to the past, while some regard tradition as a hindrance to progress and give greater weight to the present.
5. Consider whether cultures differ in their approach to consistency. For example, Taoism celebrates *wu wei* ("action without action"), a concept that seems impossible to understand in the world of science, embracing opposites rather than regarding inconsistency as a logical error. You may not be able to assume that by identifying an inconsistency you have discredited an opposing argument.
6. Consider whether cultures differ in their dominant mode of reasoning; for example, prizing cause-effect thinking or prizing narrative and myth.

Ukraine might be strongly interested in hearing about developments in their "old countries." And listeners who are involved in foreign policy issues probably would be most interested in the implications of changes since the Orange Revolution and the political ascent of Vladimir Putin. These differences can help you decide which points to put first and last.

Based on the Culture. Finally, the culture will affect your organizational pattern. For example, mainstream American culture is strongly oriented toward pragmatism, and so a pattern that focuses on problems and solutions would resonate well for many listeners. But other cultures and subcultures have a much greater concern for ideology, for myth and ritual, for narrative, or for authority; the preference for these values would affect the pattern of analysis.

Joanna Watkins was about to address an audience with a high proportion of Asian students. She had studied some Roper Poll surveys about dominant values among various cultural groups in the United States and had learned that many Asians value family and group loyalty and mutual support more than such mainstream American values as competitiveness and individual achievement. Because Joanna's topic was about how to get ahead in college, she needed to arrange her speech carefully. In this case, a highly pragmatic cause–effect pattern—which might be just right in other situations—would probably be inappropriate.

Joanna chose to include material about the value of close friendships and the sense of community that often develops among Asian college students. At the same time, she was careful not to stereotype her audience or to assume that "all Asians think alike." She did not say, "Since most of you are Asian, let me talk about group loyalty," and she was careful also to include at least some appeals based on pragmatic values, too.

Clearly, no organizational pattern is automatically "right" for any given speech. You need to think critically about the implications and effects of any pattern and choose an arrangement that suits your strategy. Moreover, although we have considered these basic patterns as though they were mutually exclusive, you obviously can combine them. For instance, you could use a chronological pattern, but at each step in the chronology you might examine developments topically or by reference to causes and effects. Or you could organize your speech using both a topical pattern and comparison and contrast. In theory, the potential combinations of patterns are limitless. Particularly when audience members have different cultural backgrounds, value systems, and priorities, a creative combination may be most effective.

Explore the **Exercise** "Organization" at **MyCommunicationLab**

OBJECTIVE 9.4

Selecting and Arranging Supporting Materials

Most main ideas are sufficiently complex that they involve several supporting ideas or **subheadings**. The supporting material that you located following the guidelines in Chapter 7 will usually support these subheadings, which in turn will support the main ideas. Subheadings are chosen and arranged using the same methods that we have described for main ideas. Moreover, many of the same considerations also apply to the materials you will use to support your main ideas and subpoints. In Chapter 7, you studied research techniques to help you locate supporting materials; now, you should consider which materials to select and how to arrange them.

subheadings
Ideas that are components of or support for the main ideas in the speech.

Selection of Supporting Materials

Watch the Video
"Persuasive Speech: Secondhand Smoke" at
MyCommunicationLab

How Much? Probably the most important question, and the hardest to answer, is "How much support is enough?" You need to offer enough evidence to establish your claims but not so much that the speech becomes repetitive and boring. But how do you know what is the right balance?

The only all-purpose answer to this question is, "It depends."[8] It depends, most of all, on your audience analysis. In examining listeners' prior understanding of your topic, you may find that your main idea is one with which they are likely to agree. If so, a relatively modest amount of support will be enough. But if the audience is likely to find your main idea controversial, you will need more support to convince doubters.

For example, a speaker who tells a college audience that the legal drinking age should be lowered to 18 is probably "preaching to the choir." These listeners have likely already accepted the claim, and so the speaker needs only a few pieces of reliable supporting material. But a speaker who tells the same audience that the legal drinking age should be kept at 21 will probably need to supply much more evidence to convince listeners that the disadvantages of change would outweigh the benefits. In contrast, if the audience were composed of older people, the reverse would likely be true: The speaker who wants to raise the drinking age might need less supporting material than the speaker who wants to lower it.

Besides listeners' beliefs about the specific topic, their common knowledge and experience will affect how much supporting material you need. Also, if they are skeptical by nature, you will want to add more support. If they are impatient or are not good listeners, you will want to keep the speech short and the supporting materials simple. If they are accustomed to asking questions after a speech, you will want to anticipate their major questions and to incorporate supporting material that prepares you to answer them.

The general principle to follow is: The greater the distance between the audience's current views and the position you wish listeners to adopt, the more supporting material will be required. Yet you also must be careful not to stereotype or to assume that all listeners would identify their position on an issue in the same way.

CHOOSE A STRATEGY: Organizing Your Speech

The Situation

You and a number of other students are dismayed by your university's decision to limit Internet access to certain sites on campus. You've been attending rallies against the policy and have been invited to speak at the next student government meeting about your objections.

Making Choices

1. How should you decide what main points you want to relay to your audience, and in what order should you present them?
2. What do you know about the school board's position that would affect your organizational choices?
3. What kind of supporting material would be important to include—and where in the speech should you include it?

What If...

How would your organizational decisions change if the following were true?

1. There was evidence of illegal Internet activity among the student population.
2. The university had asked for student feedback before making the decision to limit Internet access.

CHECKLIST 9.4

Selecting Supporting Materials

- ❒ Does the supporting material meet tests of strength for its type? (These are given in Chapter 7.)
- ❒ Will the supporting material be easily understood?
- ❒ Is the supporting material vivid and interesting?
- ❒ Is the supporting material consistent with other things you know?
- ❒ Will the supporting material be efficient to present?
- ❒ Can the supporting material be easily cited in the speech?

In any case, supporting material should not be redundant; each piece of evidence should add something new to the speech as a whole. The testimony of three different people who say exactly the same thing is not likely to be higher in value than one person's testimony. Nor will you strengthen the speech by citing the same example from multiple sources.

What Kind? Regarding the types of supporting materials to use, the general goal is to aim for variety. The speech should not depend entirely on statistics, on testimony, on examples, or on primary documents. The reasons are simple. First, you are more likely to hold the audience's interest by varying the types of evidence you offer. Although it is important that the audience be able to anticipate your general pattern, too much repetition induces boredom. Second, different listeners will be persuaded by different kinds of evidence. If your audience is heterogeneous, then using a variety of support helps you to strike a responsive chord among many different listeners.

What Criteria? Having decided how much and what types of support you need, you still face other choices. For example, you may have decided that testimony is the form of support you need and that one quotation from an expert will be enough. But your research may have accumulated the testimony of four or five experts. How do you decide which one to use? Similarly, you may have found multiple examples, various statistical measures, or more primary documents than you might need.

What criteria can you use to assess these supporting materials?

1. *Apply the criteria for strength of supporting material that were given in Chapter 7.* For instance, with regard to testimony, you should ask which authority has the greatest expertise on the subject, which statement is most recent (if timeliness is a factor), and so on. With respect to examples, you want to use a case that is representative. And if you are choosing among pieces of statistical evidence, consider the reliability and validity of each.
2. *Select the supporting material that is easiest to understand.* If listeners have to work hard to understand and remember your supporting material, they will be distracted from the focus of your speech.

   This can be a special concern with respect to statistical evidence. Complicated or overly precise statistics may be hard to comprehend orally, and using them may require some minor editing. For example, rather than reporting that the federal budget deficit is projected to be $4,267,153,697,000 over a 10-year period, you might report the projection as "more than $4 trillion." Rather than "significant at the 0.001 level," you might say, "These are results we would get by chance only one one-thousandth of the time."
3. *Select vivid or interesting supporting material when you can.* Less interesting material requires the audience to give it greater concentration, which again will distract from your main ideas.
4. *Select supporting material that is consistent with other things you know.* If you use material that challenges commonly held beliefs, you should be prepared to defend it and explain why the audience should not reject it out of hand.

5. *Select supporting material that will be efficient to present.* In general, a short anecdote is better than a long narrative, if they make the same point. And a statistical measure with categories that are clear is more useful than one that needs lengthy explanations.
6. *Select supporting material that can be cited easily in the speech.* Unlike a written mode, you cannot supply a full bibliographic citation orally. But you do want to give enough information so that a listener knows where you got the material. An "oral footnote" that refers to "Secretary of State Clinton in last January's issue of *Foreign Affairs*" is a good example. Chapter 11 provides more guidance on creating oral citations to include in your presentation outline.

Arrangement of Supporting Materials

Just as the main ideas of a speech can be arranged according to a variety of patterns, so, too, can the supporting materials that establish each main idea. The same considerations—your purpose and your strategy—govern the arrangement of main ideas and of supporting materials.

Suppose, for example, that for a main idea you want to demonstrate that the percentage of deaths from car crashes linked to alcohol use declined over a certain period of time. Because your objective is to demonstrate a rate and direction of change, a chronological pattern might serve best. It would enable you to "take a snapshot" of how many crash fatalities were linked to alcohol at different points in

Table 9.1 Total traffic fatalities versus alcohol-related traffic fatalities, 1990–2004

	Total Killed in Alcohol-Related Crashes		Total Killed in All Traffic Crashes	
Calendar Year	Number	Percent	Number	Percent
1990	22,587	51	44,599	100
1991	20,159	49	41,508	100
1992	18,290	47	39,250	100
1993	17,908	45	40,150	100
1994	17,308	43	40,716	100
1995	17,732	42	41,817	100
1996	17,749	42	42,065	100
1997	16,711	40	42,013	100
1998	16,673	40	41,501	100
1999	16,572	40	41,717	100
2000	17,380	41	41,945	100
2001	17,400	41	42,196	100
2002	17,524	41	43,005	100
2003	17,105	40	42,884	100
2004	16,694	39	42,836	100

Source: National Highway Traffic Safety Administration FARS data.

time. You could show your audience that in 1990, 51 percent of accident fatalities were linked to alcohol; that it was down to 43 percent by 1994; and that by 2004 it was 39 percent (see Table 9.1). By arranging these "snapshots" in chronological order, you can convey the message of ongoing progress.

For another example, suppose you want to establish that alienation from politics is a nationwide occurrence. You might use a spatial pattern, drawing on examples from the East, the Midwest, the South, and the West. In yet another speech, you might want to emphasize trends in the training and preparation of popular music singers. You could use a topical pattern to focus on each singer you want to discuss or a comparison and contrast pattern that would let you demonstrate important similarities and differences among the singers.

You also can combine the patterns of arrangement in a single speech. In discussing the apathy of American voters, you might use both a chronological and a spatial pattern, as follows:

I. Voter apathy has become a growing concern.
   A. During the years before World War I, voter turnout was high.
   B. In the modern age, the height of voter participation came in 1960.
   C. Since 1960, there has been a slow but steady decline in political participation.
   D. By 1996, voter turnout was at the lowest level since 1924.
   E. Even in the razor-thin election of 2000, turnout rose only slightly.
   F. Even in 2008, although turnout among younger voters rose, the overall voter turnout remained a full 10 percentage points below its 1960 peak.

II. Voter apathy is widespread.
   A. It can be found in the East.
   B. It can be found in the Midwest.
   C. It can be found in the South.
   D. It can be found in the West.

Such a combination, aside from clarifying each main idea in the most appropriate way, also brings variety to the speech—a desirable objective in itself.

What Have You Learned?

Objective 9.1: Explain why the organization of the speech is important for both the speaker and the audience.

Organizing the body of the speech involves two sets of choices regarding main ideas as well as supporting materials:

- What to include
- What pattern of arrangement to use

Organization helps both the audience and the speaker, because

- Form itself is persuasive.
- A recognizable form makes content easier to remember.
- Listeners can anticipate what is coming next and feel satisfied when they are right.
- Structure is an aid in preparing the speech and in remembering what comes next.

Objective 9.2: Identify criteria for selecting the main ideas to include in your speech and the characteristics that a main idea should have.

Main ideas are chosen by reference to

- The speaker's strategy and purpose
- The themes most frequently identified in research

Main ideas should have these characteristics:

- Few in number
- Simple in phrasing
- Parallel in structure
- Coherent
- Complete in their treatment of the topic

Objective 9.3: Arrange the main ideas into recognizable patterns and decide what patterns of arrangement to use.

Arranging the main ideas raises questions such as the following:

- Their dependence on one another
- The value of beginning with the familiar
- The importance of first and last impressions
- The nature of the audience

Several of the most common organizational patterns are as follows:

- Chronological
- Spatial
- Categorical (topical)
- Cause–effect
- Problem–solution
- Comparison and contrast
- Residues

Objective 9.4: Decide how much and which kinds of supporting material you need and how to arrange the support for each idea.

Guided by audience analysis, speakers should select supporting material that is

- Tested for strength
- Easy to understand
- Vivid and interesting
- Consistent with what already is known
- Efficient to present
- Easy to cite in the speech

The same factors that govern arrangement of main ideas also affect arrangement of the supporting material.

Listen to the **Audio Chapter Summary** at **MyCommunicationLab**

Discussion Questions

1. In this chapter, we examined Stuart Kim's strategic plan to select and organize main ideas for a speech to convince listeners to donate to the United Way. But what would Stuart's speech be like if he faced a different rhetorical situation? Imagine that he is planning to speak to fellow volunteers at a year-end gathering to celebrate the United Way. Using the list of ideas that Stuart developed in his research, and drawing on your own imagination, discuss the selection and arrangement of appropriate main ideas for such a speech.
2. Which organizational pattern would you recommend for each of the following rhetorical situations? Why?

   To inform an audience of high school students about their college options

   To explain the history of your state capital to a group of German tourists

   To teach a group of coworkers how to use a new computer program

   To strengthen the commitment of fellow party members to a candidate's campaign

   To persuade an audience of restaurant and bar owners that smoking should be banned in public spaces

   To introduce an award-winning journalist who is about to give a lecture at a school assembly
3. What is the best organizational strategy for your next speech in this class? Gather in groups of four or five, and discuss your strategic plan with your classmates. Answer the following questions about each group member's strategy:

   a. Do the main ideas satisfy the criteria of simplicity, discreteness, parallel structure, balance, coherence, and completeness?

   b. Which other organizational patterns might be more suitable for the purpose and audience of this speech?

   c. Which type of supporting material is needed to develop each main idea in the speech?
4. Identify the basic organizational pattern used in a speech shown or presented in class. In small groups, discuss the benefit of a particular organizational pattern for this speech, and also think about alternative organizational patterns that might have worked well for that speech.

Activities

1. Select the main ideas for your next speech.
   a. Use Checklist 9.1 to generate a list of potential main ideas.
   b. Subject each idea in the list to the tests described in this chapter: Is the idea essential? Can a more general statement combine several main ideas?
2. Arrange the main ideas for your next speech.
   a. Choose an organizational pattern and explain why it is more fitting than the other patterns discussed in this chapter.
   b. Write a paragraph or two to justify the pattern that you have selected. In doing so, ask yourself the following questions:

      Are the ideas dependent on or independent of one another?

      Are you beginning with the familiar or with the unfamiliar?

      Are the first and the last ideas strongest?

      Why is this pattern most appropriate for your audience and purpose?
3. Select the supporting material for your next speech.
   a. Apply the general principle described on page 226 to determine how much supporting material you need.
   b. Choose the supporting material that you will use to develop each main idea in the speech.
   c. Using the criteria in Checklist 9.4, write a sentence or two to explain why you have chosen each piece of supporting material.
4. Using the presentation note cards from one of your previous speeches for this course, design a new organizational pattern. Since the content of your speech has remained the same, but the order is different, decide whether this reorganization affected the meaning or effectiveness of the speech. Try to imagine other audiences and situations in which your new organizational pattern might be desirable.

Key Terms

coherence **219**
logically dependent idea **220**
logically independent idea **220**
main ideas **215**
organization **214**
parallel structure **219**
primacy effect **222**
recency effect **222**
subheadings **228**

Study and **Review** the **Flashcards** at **MyCommunicationLab**

Notes

1 Experiments show that an audience retains more of a message that is organized than of one that is not. See Ernest C. Thompson, "An Experimental Investigation of the Relative Effectiveness of Organizational Structure in Oral Communication," *Southern Speech Communication Journal* 26 (Fall 1960): 59–69.

2 Research confirms that organized speeches are comprehended more fully than unorganized speeches. See Arlee Johnson, "A Preliminary Investigation of the Relationship between Message Organization and Listener Comprehension," *Communication Studies* 21 (Summer 1970): 104–107.

3 One study suggests that an unorganized persuasive message may actually produce an effect that is opposite to what the speaker intended. See Raymond G. Smith, "An Experimental Study of the Effects of Speech Organization upon Attitudes of College Students," *Communication Monographs* 18 (November 1951): 292–301. Another study simply concludes that an extremely unorganized speech is not very persuasive. See James C. McCroskey and R. Samuel Mehrley, "The Effects of Disorganization and Nonfluency on Attitude Change and Source Credibility," *Communication Monographs* 36 (March 1969): 13–21.

4 Rhetorical theorist Kenneth Burke envisions form as "the creation of an appetite in the mind of the auditor, and the adequate satisfying of that appetite." See "Psychology and Form," *Counter-Statement*, Berkeley: University of California Press, 1931.

5 One study demonstrated that speakers who have a plan and practice that plan have fewer pauses in their speeches. See John O. Greene, "Speech Preparation and Verbal Fluency," *Human Communication Research* 11 (Fall 1984): 61–84.

6 See Howard Gilkinson, Stanley F. Paulson, and Donald E. Sikkink, "Effects of Order and Authority in an Argumentative Speech," *Quarterly Journal of Speech* 40 (April 1954): 183–92; and Halbert E. Gulley and David K. Berlo, "Effect of Intercellular and Intracellular Speech Structure on Attitude Change and Learning," *Communication Monographs* 23 (November 1956): 288–97. For a more recent look at how these questions affect other aspects of our lives, see Jaime Murphy, Charles Hofacker, and Richard Mizerski, "Primacy and Recency Effects on Clicking Behavior," *Journal of Computer-Mediated Communcation*, 11 (January 2006), 522–35.

7 For a few more ideas, see James A. Benson, "Extemporaneous Speaking: Organization Which Inheres," *Argumentation and Advocacy* 14 (Winter 1978): 150–55.

8 Some researchers who have tried to determine experimentally the place of evidence in a speech have concluded that there are just too many variables (such as the prior beliefs of the audience members, the credibility of the speaker, and the different types of evidence) to draw deterministic conclusions. See Kathy Kellermann, "The Concept of Evidence: A Critical Review," *Argumentation and Advocacy* 16 (Winter 1980): 159–72; and Richard B. Gregg, "The Rhetoric of Evidence," *Western Journal of Speech Communication* 31 (Summer 1967): 180–89.

CHAPTER 10

Organizing the Speech: Introductions, Conclusions, and Transitions

LEARNING OBJECTIVES

Listen to the **Audio Chapter** at **MyCommunicationLab**

After studying this chapter, you should be able to:

Objective 10.1	Identify the main purposes and some common types of introductions.
Objective 10.2	Prepare an introduction.
Objective 10.3	Identify the main purposes and some common types of conclusions.
Objective 10.4	Prepare a conclusion.
Objective 10.5	Use transitions to connect the elements of a speech and give its structure a dynamic quality.
Objective 10.6	Recognize the elements of a transition, which may be either explicit or implicit.

OUTLINE

The body of the speech (Chapter 9) is certainly its most important part; it takes up the most time, and it expresses and supports the main ideas. But if a speaker launches directly into the first main idea and ends abruptly after the last, you probably would think something was strange, perhaps even insulting, about the speech. It would be like joining a conversation that was already well along, missing the beginning completely. The ending would seem abrupt, too—like reading a book that was missing its last few pages or walking out of a movie in its last minutes. You would be surprised that the speaker had stopped, because the speech would not seem "finished."

Listeners expect a beginning, a middle, and an end. They expect to be guided into a topic, not dropped in its midst, and they expect the discussion to conclude naturally. Audiences notice when a speaker departs from this customary sense of form; if they are not disturbed by it, they at least are likely to be distracted.

In this chapter, we will explore the two elements of a speech that surround its body: the introduction and the conclusion. We will focus on the purposes of these elements, some common types, and strategies for preparing them. Finally, we will look at how speakers use transitions to connect the introduction, body, and conclusion and thus give the speech a dynamic quality.

OBJECTIVE 10.1

Introductions: Beginning the Speech

Both daily life and studies in the psychology of persuasion tell us that first impressions are extremely important. When you meet someone new, you quickly form impressions about that person, often based on little more than superficial characteristics such as the person's clothing and hairstyle, or car, or way of speaking. Moreover, as we saw in Chapter 2, many first impressions are likely to prove durable; they will influence how you interpret what this person says and does.[1]

The Purposes of an Introduction

The **introduction** is the beginning of the speech, which affects listeners' first impressions of the speaker and prepares them for the speech. It gives the audience clues about the speaker's personality, intentions, style, and overall perspective. And it prepares the audience for the speech by giving clues about what will follow.

The overall purpose of using your introduction to prepare the audience can be broken down into four specific goals:

1. To gain the attention and interest of your audience
2. To influence the audience to view you and your topic favorably
3. To clarify the purpose or thesis of your speech
4. To preview the development of your topic

Watch the Video "Professor Jason Warren Discusses Tips for Effective Introductions" at **MyCommunicationLab**

Gaining the Attention and Interest of Your Audience. The introduction should make the audience want to hear what will follow. Accomplishing this goal is critical because, like someone switching television channels, listeners can choose whether to pay attention. Even when the audience cannot escape a speaker physically, individuals can decide whether to be active listeners.

introduction
The beginning of the speech, which affects listeners' first impressions of the speaker and prepares them for the speech.

The primary way to make listeners pay attention is to convince them that what follows will be interesting. An effective introduction suggests to listeners that they will be stimulated by the speech. A lively narrative, startling or unexpected information, or a personal experience that listeners can identify with will suggest that the speech will be interesting and thus warrants attention.

Influencing the Audience to View You and Your Topic Favorably. It is not enough merely to get the audience's attention. Indeed, a speaker can easily gain attention by appearing overbearing, pompous, or dogmatic.

The introduction aims to influence the audience to view you and your topic favorably so that listeners will be sympathetic and attentive. You can create a favorable first impression as follows:

- Be well prepared and confident, thereby establishing positive *ethos* (credibility) as we discussed in Chapter 2.
- Identify with the predispositions of the audience, which you will discover through the audience analysis described in Chapter 5.

Like most generalizations, this one needs to be qualified a bit. Sometimes, a speaker will choose deliberately not to gain the audience's favor. For example, a dissenter who feels the need to speak out against the majority opinion may intentionally make an audience hostile by, say, accusing them of denying rights to those who are less powerful. Even though the immediate audience is unlikely to be persuaded by such a direct attack, the dissenter may, in fact, be addressing those listeners primarily to gain the attention and favor of some other audience. The real intended audience is composed of people who will hear about the speech and conclude that the dissenter is a person of courage and principle for venturing into hostile territory. This audience, of course, will then be favorably disposed toward the speaker and the topic; the dissenter will have gained both their attention and their goodwill.

Clarifying the Purpose or Thesis of Your Speech. Listeners are more likely to follow your speech and be influenced by it if you clearly identify what you want them to believe or to do. Most introductions include an explicit statement of the speaker's thesis or purpose, as in the following examples:

Watch the Video
"Introduction: Voting" at
MyCommunicationLab

> I will argue that the United States cannot compete economically without strengthening public education.
>
> After you consider the facts, I hope you will call the Red Cross and volunteer to donate blood.

Speakers often state their purpose only after making introductory remarks that gain the audience's interest and make listeners favorably disposed. But, sometimes speakers can *assume* that the audience is interested and favorably disposed. For instance, a speaker addressing the student government, who discusses the benefits of student government, surely could assume interest and motivation on the part of the audience. In this case, the entire introduction might focus on an explicit statement of purpose.

Previewing the Development of Your Topic. Besides capturing the audience's attention, influencing them to view you and your topic favorably, and clarifying your purpose, the introduction also previews how you will develop your topic in the body of the speech. Classical theorists of public speaking refer to this step as the **partition**; the speaker divides the body of the speech into selected categories for discussion.[2] For example, a speaker might say:

> First I will explain how higher education got into financial trouble, then I will describe the consequences of this for students and faculty, and finally I will tell you what we can do about it.

Basically, the speaker has revealed the pattern for the body of the speech (in this case, a problem–solution pattern) and what the major headings will be. As we saw in Chapter 9, such a "road map" helps listeners to follow the speaker's thinking and to anticipate what will come next.

An Example of an Introduction

Only your own imagination and creativity limit you in devising an introduction that achieves the four primary goals. Let's look at how one student used her introduction to prepare the audience.

Michelle Ekanemesang was the third speaker in her public speaking class. To gain her listeners' attention (after all, they had already heard two speeches), she walked to the podium, paused, looked at the audience, and then suddenly dropped a large book on the floor. The resounding thud brought all eyes to Michelle as she began to speak: "Just as easily as that book fell to the floor, the innocence of a child can crash." Then, walking around to the front of the podium to retrieve the book, Michelle continued:

> However, unlike this book, a child's innocence cannot be picked up and placed back on the pedestal where it was. Children today encounter many experiences that challenge their innocence. Along with gangs, guns, and drugs, they also face another monster that is not so well publicized: sexual abuse. Approximately one child out of four is sexually abused by the age of 18. That would be four people in this classroom. Today, I want to discuss the causes and effects of childhood sexual abuse as well as to offer some tips about preventing it and what to do if you or a child you know has been a victim of sexual abuse.

Michelle's book-dropping trick could have turned into a resounding flop if she had not explained how it connected to her speech. She quickly and effectively gained her listeners' attention and then maintained it by saying that some of them might be victims themselves, thereby emphasizing the personal relevance of her topic. From the outset, it was clear that Michelle was going to talk about the horrors of child abuse. She took a serious tone of outrage and influenced the audience favorably toward her treatment of the subject. Her final statement in the introduction then clearly previewed which main topics the audience could expect her to cover: the causes, effects, prevention, and treatment of childhood sexual abuse.

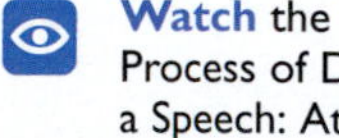

Watch the **Video** "The Process of Developing a Speech: Attention-Getting Devices" at **MyCommunicationLab**

Types of Introductions

Several types of introductions show up frequently in successful speeches, and you should be aware of them in order to decide whether they will be effective for your speech and audience.

In deciding which type of introduction to use, always try to relate the introduction directly to your speech, as Michelle did. If you quote someone famous or tell a story without showing how that connects to the speech itself, the introduction

partition
Division of the body of the speech among selected categories for discussion.

may soon seem out of place. The speech, after all, should be a unified whole. The introduction and the conclusion should work together with the body of the speech to create the response or action that you desire.

Identifying with Your Audience. One obvious way to build goodwill and capture the audience's interest is to draw on something that you share—a common experience, common acquaintances, common values, or common goals. If listeners perceive you as being basically like themselves, they usually form a good first impression of you. And their interest should be high because, in effect, you may be telling them something about themselves or be speaking on their behalf.

Student speakers often find it easy and effective to identify with their audience because, typically, they do share many common experiences with their listeners. One student began a speech about the disillusionment felt by many of America's less fortunate youth by making a reference to a popular Hollywood movie:

> Many of you may have seen the hit movie *The Matrix*. This high-budget film paints America as one huge computerized box in which we all are trapped, with no real control of our lives and no say in our futures. We are just digits in an artificially intelligent matrix—added, subtracted, multiplied, and divided at the will of a supercomputer. When my friends and I first saw the movie, we felt strangely numb and powerless, but the feeling only lasted a few minutes. But for many of America's less fortunate youth, this is the only feeling they know.

Having gained the interest and goodwill of the audience by identifying with them, and having stated the thesis, the speaker was then well positioned to complete the introduction by previewing how the feelings of disempowerment among America's disadvantaged youth would be developed in the speech.

Referring to the Speech Situation. Another way to establish common bonds with an audience and to strike an appropriate opening note is to refer directly to the situation. Many speeches are delivered on ceremonial occasions (for example, commencement addresses, wedding toasts, speeches of welcome or farewell), and these often are introduced effectively by an explicit reference to the occasion.

Similarly, speeches that happen to be given on a significant anniversary might make reference to the date. For example, a student speaking on September 11, 2013, might begin this way:

> Twelve years ago today, our generation and our country lost some of its innocence. Even though we were very young, none of us will ever forget the image of the planes crashing into the World Trade Center. That action started what President George W. Bush called a "war on terror." Twelve years later, do we feel safer or more secure? Can we deter or stop terrorists? In short, are we winning the war?

The speaker could go on to state the thesis and preview its development:

> I do not think we are. Our airports are safer, but our transportation system and our industrial base are vulnerable.

Similarly, Rachel Venegas used the beginning of final examination week as an opportunity to point out a disturbing trend in student study habits:

> With finals beginning, students all over campus will be frantically trying to absorb every bit of knowledge from their courses or putting the finishing touches on their papers. But during these cram sessions, students tend to put their academics before their own health,

especially by neglecting sleep. One way to bypass the urge to sleep, and an increasingly popular option, is the use of drugs meant to treat Attention Deficit Hyperactivity Disorder. Despite the serious side effects, many college students continue to take these drugs, prescribed or not, without knowing fully the risks of their misuse.

Telling an interesting story with enthusiasm is often a good way to dispose the audience favorably toward the speaker and the speech.

Other situational factors also can be the touchstone for an effective introduction. For example, the location of the speech might be important, as it was when Martin Luther King, Jr., began his famous address "I Have a Dream." Dr. King's introduction noted that he stood symbolically in the shadow of Abraham Lincoln; he was delivering his address from the Lincoln Memorial.

Referring to a previous speaker might be a natural introduction to your own speech. If your reference endorses or builds on something a previous speaker said, it creates a bridge between the two speeches and a seemingly logical flow to the discussion. And if the previous speaker was competent and credible, you even may inherit the audience's favorable disposition toward that speaker.

However, your reference does not have to support the previous speaker. In fact, that speech might provide the ammunition needed for you to disagree with something the speaker said. In this case, your introduction is both a bridge that maintains continuity and a stop sign that signals the differences between the two of you. For example, imagine that a student in a public speaking class just spoke about the ways in which Steve Jobs and Apple have revolutionized the personal computer, praising Jobs's vision and imagination. By coincidence, the next speaker had planned to condemn the overdependence by technology companies on foreign labor. Adapting the introduction to fit this situation, the second speaker could say:

> Many consider high-tech companies, such as Apple, to be ahead of their time, but in at least one respect they are dangerously behind the times: their dependence on exploited foreign labor.

Stating Your Purpose. Sometimes, an introduction that explicitly states your purpose can be very helpful, especially if the audience is captive or is known already to be favorably disposed to your ideas. This approach is also effective when your thesis is startling or unexpected:

> In the next hour, many children in this town will suffer from abuse and neglect. We will see why this happens. Then I want you to volunteer one day a week to help stop this.

Your direct challenge will probably make the audience take notice, because you've alerted them that you expect something of them, and so they are likely to pay attention in order to decide whether or not to grant your request.

Stating the Importance of Your Topic. Another effective opening device is to alert the audience to the significance of your topic before actually stating what the topic is. For example, a speech about preventing AIDS might begin with the statement "I have information that literally can save your lives."

Similarly, a speech about purchasing a home might begin with "Today, I want to discuss the most important financial decision most of us will ever make."

This type of introduction demands the audience's attention. Just by saying that your topic is important, you ask people to take notice. This strategy also has an element of mystery, which leads the audience to wonder just what it is that is so critical. Be aware, however, that this approach has been overused, and audiences sometimes react to such claims by being skeptical. A speaker who opens with "This speech could change the course of your life" may actually prompt listeners to think, "Oh, sure; I've heard that before."

If your speech has a formal title, be sure that its specific wording is accurate and complete. Then your introduction can "unpack" the title to forecast what will follow and to highlight your main points. In 1984, Governor Mario Cuomo of New York illustrated this introductory strategy in a speech at the University of Notre Dame:

> I would like to begin by drawing your attention to the title of this lecture: "Religious Belief and Public Morality: A Catholic Governor's Perspective." I was not invited to speak on "Church and State" generally. Certainly not "Mondale versus Reagan." The subject assigned is difficult enough. I will try not to do more than I've been asked.

Governor Cuomo then proceeded to state his perspective and to indicate how he planned to develop his ideas.

Citing Statistics, Making Claims. Listeners sit up in interest when a speaker cites startling statistics or makes a surprising claim. Their astonishment on hearing the information causes them to pay attention. For example, to introduce the topic of poverty in the Navajo Nation, a student might begin:

> The Navajo Nation is the largest Indian reservation in the United States. It has a population of 235,000 and covers an area of 16.2 million acres. But the largest Indian reservation in America is not thriving as well as some of the country's smallest towns. According to a recent Bureau of Indian Affairs report, the unemployment rate in the Navajo Nation is almost 58 percent. Only 22.5 percent of Navajo homes have any telephone service, and many of the lines are too old to support modern Internet communication.

This type of introduction works best when the statistics are accurate but not well known—when there is a gap between what listeners think they know and what is actually the case. Statistics can show that our common assumptions are not accurate, that a problem is greater than we know, that a condition we viewed as worsening is actually improving, and so on. But the risk with this approach is that listeners may become defensive about their predispositions. Rather than considering the possibility that academic dishonesty really is more serious than they thought, for example, they may react by doubting the statistics or by denying the claim. You certainly want to encourage listeners to think critically; but if their very first response to your introduction is to doubt what you say, it will be difficult to build goodwill and regain their interest.

Telling a Story. Speakers often begin with an anecdote—an extended illustration or example that is cast in narrative form. A speaker introduces the topic by relating a personal experience or something that happened to others. For example, when Elie Wiesel, Holocaust survivor, novelist, and Nobel Peace Prize winner, gave a speech at the White House in April 1999 on "the perils of

CHOOSE A STRATEGY: Weighing the Types of Introductions

The Situation

You are in charge of bringing a documentary about a charity to a local cinema. Before the movie starts, you will make a few comments about why you support the charity. You know that your main points will be that the charity directly benefits the community, it addresses a significant need, and it depends solely on donations. Now you want to create an attention-getting introduction.

Making Choices

1. Of the 10 types of introductions discussed in this chapter, what are some types that seem well suited to your topic and speech situation? Why?
2. You know the audience already supports the charity and you want to strengthen their commitment. Which type of introduction do you think would be more effective, (a) identifying with your audience or (b) stating your purpose? Why?
3. Suppose the charity has helped a member of your family through a tough time. What are the potential benefits and drawbacks of telling a story about your family member in your introduction?

What If...

How would your choices be affected by the following?

1. The film showing is to raise awareness for an audience that isn't familiar with the charity.
2. You are speaking at the end of a documentary festival and others have made similar introductions.

indifference," he began by relating the story of a young boy who had been rescued from a Nazi concentration camp by American soldiers:

> Fifty-four years ago to the day, a young Jewish boy from a small town in the Carpathian Mountains woke up, not far from Goethe's beloved Weimar, in a place of eternal infamy called Buchenwald. He was finally free, but there was no joy in his heart. He thought there never would be again.
>
> Liberated a day earlier by American soldiers, he remembers their rage at what they saw. And even if he lives to be a very old man, he will always be grateful to them for that rage, and also for their compassion. Though he did not understand their language, their eyes told him what he needed to know—that they, too, would remember and bear witness.

The power of an anecdotal introduction lies in its narrative form. The story is engaging, and the chronological sequence is easy to follow. A narrative is concrete—it involves specific characters in a particular situation—and therefore listeners can attend to it with less effort than is needed to follow something more abstract.

One potential drawback in using an introductory anecdote is that it may overshadow the preview of your topic or even the body of the speech. It may be so interesting that it distracts attention from your main points. To avoid this, use an anecdote that leads directly into your thesis statement and partition. Try to create unity between the anecdote and the main points so that each reminds the audience of the other.

Using an Analogy. Closely related to the anecdote is an analogy, which, as you learned in Chapter 8, is a comparison. An analogy draws attention to the similarities or the differences between two objects, events, or situations. A speaker can use an analogy to clarify an unfamiliar subject by comparing the subject with something else that the audience already understands. For example, a speech describing the pros and cons of school vouchers might compare public and private schools with retail stores and parents and their children with consumers. In this way, the unfamiliar issue of school vouchers can be explained in the more familiar terms of shopping.

Like anecdotes, analogies help to make abstract concepts concrete. They are especially useful in introducing technical material to listeners who are not specialists in the speaker's field. For example, to inform his audience, consisting of senior citizens unfamiliar with the Internet, about search engines, student Stan Barkers began with the following analogy:

> When borrowing a book from the public library, the first thing you do is consult the card catalog, which used to be housed in a large wooden cabinet but now is online and accessible with a computer. Whether the "cards" are typed on paper or captured electronically on a computer screen, the process still works the same: you use a catalog to find where the book is located, then you proceed along the shelf and get the book. A search engine uses a process very similar to the way in which you've always searched for a book in the library. Instead of looking up an author or title, the search engine identifies key words and looks for them in billions of documents that are posted on the Internet. So it may be helpful for us to think of a search engine like Google as the Internet's card catalog.

This analogy translated what could be an unfamiliar process—using a search engine to research on the Internet—into a process that the audience easily could grasp.

During World War II, President Franklin D. Roosevelt was gifted at using analogies to explain the complexities of foreign policy to average voters. Discussing why, in 1940, the United States should lend (rather than sell) war materials to Great Britain and its allies, he offered the analogy of a man whose neighbor's house was on fire. When the neighbor ran up to ask for a garden hose, the man did not first demand payment; instead, he gave the hose to the neighbor on the promise that it would be returned when the threat was past. In just this way, Roosevelt reasoned, the United States should approach lending supplies to cash-strapped allies. This simple analogy both explained and dramatized the president's perspective, and it helped make his case with the public.

Analogies are persuasive (and thus advance the purposes of an introduction) because most listeners find it easy to focus on similarities and differences. To be effective, though, an analogy should be fairly simple and direct, like Roosevelt's. A complex comparison will force your listeners to puzzle out just what it is that you think is similar about the two things, and they will be distracted from the body of your speech. And if your analogy is too farfetched, or if it assumes key similarities without considering significant differences, listeners' first impressions of you may be negative, and they may not take your main ideas seriously. For example, several people objected to Stan Barkers's analogy, because people use card catalogs to find specific books, not to see all the places that a particular word or phrase is used.

Watch the Video "Introduction: Van Gogh's Incredible Life" at **MyCommunicationLab**

Asking a Rhetorical Question. What's a rhetorical question? Like the sentence you just read, a **rhetorical question** is one that you do not expect listeners to answer (even if they could). You ask the question simply to cause an audience (or a reader) to think about the answer.

rhetorical question
A question for which no answer is expected but which encourages listeners to think.

A rhetorical question may prompt listeners to imagine themselves in some other time, place, or situation. For example, in urging white Americans to be sensitive to the role of race in the lives of African Americans, a student speaker might begin by asking,

> How would you feel if, at the time you were born, your earning capacity and life expectancy were automatically reduced for no reason but the color of your skin?

Then, to preview the development of the speech, the student might ask,

> Why is it that, more than 50 years after *Brown v. Board of Education*, educational opportunities still are not equal?

The first question gets the audience to empathize with African Americans, and the second question previews the development of the speech. Because the goal is to make the audience think, the speaker in this case would probably not state the thesis explicitly yet.

The pitfall in asking rhetorical questions is that speakers have overused or misused this device. Some may ask an introductory question merely to ask it, rather than to induce listeners to imagine a situation or to preview the speech. An even greater risk is that listeners will answer the question in their minds—with an answer that is different from what the speaker wants to discuss. In the worst case of all, someone in the audience may shout a response that undermines the entire introduction. One student began a speech about popular films of the 1960s by asking, "What do you think of when you hear the name 'James Bond'?" From the rear of the classroom another student called out, "A third-rate movie."

Sometimes you may ask a question that you *do* want listeners to answer orally, perhaps to get them actively involved in the development of your ideas or to start a pattern of questions and answers. In that case, you should pause after asking the question to give them time to reply. If they remain silent, you may even need to add a comment such as "This is not a rhetorical question" or "I really want to know your answer." The danger here is the reverse of the one above: your listeners may stay silent even though you want them to speak.

Quoting Someone. Starting with a quotation is especially common and useful in sermons; the scriptural quotation then serves as the text on which the sermon is based. In secular settings, too, speakers often open with a quotation that captures the essential idea they intend to develop. For example, student speaker Clayton Hottinger introduced a speech on AIDS in South Africa by saying:

> "Cry aloud for the man who is dead, for the woman and children bereaved. Cry, the beloved country, these things are not yet at an end." So said anti-apartheid activist Alan Paton in a time of hatred and strife for South Africa, but now that trouble is over, right? Sadly, South Africa still has reason to cry, not because of apartheid, but because of a growing infection that might be mankind's greatest enemy: AIDS.

Student speaker Andrea Richards introduced a speech on cultural diversity by saying:

> In a famous speech in 1963, President Kennedy said, "If we cannot now end our differences, at least we can help make the world safe for diversity." President Kennedy was talking about ideological diversity, but today we need to apply his insight to the growing issue of racial, ethnic, and cultural diversity.

The quotation does not have to come from a famous person. It might be a simple statement such as this one:

> My father once told me that when someone says, 'It's not about the money,' then it's about the money. This is how I feel about all the politicians who keep insisting that they won't use negative campaigning.

Quoting an opposing viewpoint is a variation of this type of introduction. Abraham Lincoln did this superbly in a famous speech he made at Cooper Union in 1860. He began by quoting what his political rival, Stephen A. Douglas, had said about the intentions of the country's founders; then Lincoln used the Douglas quotation to highlight and advance his own thesis and main points.

Beginning a speech with a quotation is such a common introductory device that whole books of short quotations are published for this purpose. The warning about introductory quotations, however, is exactly the same as for anecdotes and analogies: Your introduction must relate directly to what you plan to say in your speech. If the audience cannot see the connection clearly, the introduction will seem superfluous and, therefore, will be counterproductive. A good test is to ask yourself whether the quotation will lead naturally to your thesis statement and partition and then to the body of the speech.

CHECKLIST 10.1

Types of Introductions

- ❒ Identifying with the audience
- ❒ Referring to the speech situation
- ❒ Stating the purpose
- ❒ Stating the importance of the topic
- ❒ Citing statistics or making claims
- ❒ Telling a story (anecdote)
- ❒ Using an analogy
- ❒ Asking a rhetorical question
- ❒ Quoting someone
- ❒ Using humor

Using Humor. A very common introductory device is to begin the speech with a humorous reference or a joke. When it works, humor relaxes the audience, influences listeners to view the speaker favorably, and disarms skeptics. It also tells both the speaker and the audience to keep their perspective about the topic and not to take themselves too seriously.

Despite all these advantages of humor, the worst advice for preparing the introduction to a speech is that "every speech should start with a joke." Humor is not always appropriate to the subject (or the occasion or the audience), and the joke does not always relate directly to the speech. And sometimes a joke may not be as funny to your audience as it is to you. Especially with a culturally diverse audience, it is easy for a joke to backfire—to offend rather than to amuse. Despite the frequency with which accomplished speakers tell jokes, beginning speakers who have any doubt about them should avoid this type of introduction.[3]

This survey of the types of introductions is extensive, but it is not meant to be complete.[4] Anything can be used to begin a speech if it will achieve the four purposes of an introduction: gaining your audience's interest, influencing listeners to think well of you and your topic, clarifying your purpose or central theme, and previewing how you will develop the topic. The great variety and range of introductory devices, however, does not mean that you should select one hastily or without care. The introduction is clearly critical in making an effective speech, and you should prepare it as carefully as you do the body and the conclusion.

Strategies for Preparing an Introduction

OBJECTIVE 10.2

The multiple purposes of an introduction and the great variety of ways to achieve them may seem daunting, but the following strategies and suggestions should help you plan a successful introduction for your speech.

Prepare the Body of the Speech First. Just as this book explains how to organize the body of the speech (Chapter 9) before focusing in this chapter on introductions and conclusions, you should follow that same sequence in preparing your speech. After all, it helps to know what you are introducing. Having already prepared the body, you now know what your main ideas are and how you will develop them. That information will help you craft an appropriate introduction that prepares the audience effectively. Another good reason to follow this strategy is that you will be less likely to delay preparing the entire speech just because you haven't yet thought of the "perfect" introduction.

Relate the Introduction to the Body. Keep in mind that the introduction has to prepare your listeners and then lead them naturally into the body of your speech. The connection between the introduction and the body should be clear and direct. A particular anecdote, joke, or quotation might well arouse your audience's interest, but if it seems unrelated to your main points, it may not lead listeners in the direction you intend. Indeed, some introductions—no matter how engaging—may undercut your purposes, weakening the entire speech.

Keep the Introduction Brief. Remember that the focus of the speech is on the main ideas that you will develop in the body; the introduction should lead listeners to these ideas, not obscure them. A too-long, too-strong introduction could turn into the tail that wags the dog, running away with the speech and ultimately confusing your audience. Some speechwriters advocate that an introduction should take 10 to 20 percent of the total time for the speech. Although this text resists such precise measurement, the key point remains: Limit the length of your introduction so that it does not become a speech in itself.[5]

Make the Introduction Complete. Although exceptions exist, most introductions include the following elements: a device to gain your listeners' interest and to dispose them favorably toward you as a speaker, a statement of your thesis or purpose, and a preview of how you will develop the topic.

Keep a File of Potential Introductions. In developing an introduction, you will doubtless run across ideas, quotations, examples, and other materials that are not immediately useful but that you can imagine shaping into an introduction for a future speech. Keep track of such materials. Do not rely on memory to recall them or find them at just the moment you need them. You might keep a folder on your computer where you will enter introductory material arranged by topic, adding new entries as you find them. Perhaps you might even download audio and video clips. Just as you learned about keeping a speech material file to aid in your research (Chapter 7), you should keep track of potential introductions as well. Then, when you start preparing your next speech, you already will have resources and will not have to depend entirely on either memory or inspiration.

Be Guided by the Examples in This Book. In this chapter, you have studied the most frequently used types of introductions; the appendix and other speeches in the book also illustrate a variety of introductions. Consider these examples not as models to be followed blindly, but as guidelines to help you think creatively about the best way to introduce your particular speech.

Plan the Introduction Word for Word. Especially in the opening lines of the speech, you want to be sure that you say exactly what you intend. An extemporaneous opening is risky even for very confident, very experienced speakers, unless they have thought very carefully about the introduction first, because no one can entirely control the speech setting and circumstances. Nor is it wise to carry a written script to the podium, planning to read the introduction aloud. A good first impression is unlikely when your face is buried in notes. Instead, prepare and practice your opening words carefully so that you can begin speaking with confidence and good effect.

Preparing and practicing the introduction word for word will enable you to create the clearest, most compelling first impression on the audience. Moreover, knowing exactly what you are going to say at the beginning of your speech will give you greater confidence and a sense of security. So armed, you can overcome the anxiety that even experienced speakers feel when they stand to address an audience.

Conclusions: Ending the Speech

OBJECTIVE 10.3

Just as you want to begin your speech on the right note, so do you want to develop an appropriate, effective ending. A speech should neither end abruptly nor trail off into oblivion. As we did with introductions, we will approach conclusions by focusing on their purposes and their types and then looking at some strategies for preparing them.

The Purposes of a Conclusion

Like your introduction, your **conclusion** needs to accomplish several specific goals:

- Signal that the end is coming
- Summarize the main ideas
- Make a final appeal to the audience

Watch the Video "Professor Jason Warren Discusses Tips for Effective Conclusions" at **MyCommunicationLab**

Signaling That the End Is Coming. Perhaps the most basic function of the conclusion is to signal to listeners that the speech is ending. No doubt you have heard a speaker who seemed to be finishing several times before the speech actually ended. Such a speech has "false conclusions"—misleading signals that the end is near. Summary statements, the use of the word *finally*, and similar cues alert the audience that the speech is wrapping up. But if you send such signals prematurely, you will confuse listeners and may even arouse their impatience when the speech does not end as expected.

You probably also have heard a speaker who ended so abruptly that you were surprised. Suddenly, although you thought the speaker was still developing a major idea, he or she came to the end of a sentence, said, "Thank you," and sat down. Somehow, that approach did not seem right either.

In both cases, the speakers failed to provide a satisfying sense of closure. If you confuse listeners with false endings or surprise them by stopping abruptly, your conclusion has not completed the sense of form. Listeners do need to be signaled that it is time to draw together their perceptions about the speech, but you should send this signal only at the appropriate time.

conclusion
The closing of the speech, which draws together what the speaker has said and indicates what the audience should believe or do in response to the speech.

An effective conclusion will reward the audience's attention by completing the form of the speech, drawing the ideas together, and making clear what listeners should believe or do.

Summarizing the Main Ideas. A second important purpose of the conclusion is to draw together the main ideas in your speech in a way that helps listeners to remember them. Even trained and experienced listeners rapidly forget what they have heard. If you want the audience to remember what you have said, you need to issue reminders at appropriate points throughout the speech. And no place is more appropriate for a **summary** than the conclusion.

To end a speech about the messages embodied in popular music, for example, you might summarize by saying, "As we have seen, popular music tells us about our own values, about our relationships with others, and about our obligations to nature, society, and the next generation." A summary does not exactly repeat the main ideas, and it certainly does not reprise their development. Rather, it reminds the audience of key points, often by highlighting particular words or phrases in a way that listeners can remember—as in the parallel structure of the three "about" phrases in this example.

An effective summary, then, is an aid to memory. By including a summary in your conclusion, you will increase the chances that listeners will recall your main ideas correctly.

Making a Final Appeal to the Audience. The conclusion is also an opportunity to say exactly what response you want from the audience. It is your last chance to remind listeners about whatever you want them to think or do as a result of your speech.

Sometimes a speaker wants listeners to take a very specific action, such as signing a petition, donating money, writing to their legislators, or purchasing a particular product. At other times, the desired response is a belief rather than an action. For example, suppose you want the audience to agree that the current president and administration have set a correct course in foreign policy matters. You are not asking listeners to take any specific action, but you do want them to be favorably disposed toward the president's international policies. Your conclusion might say, "I hope I've convinced you that the president's foreign policy is on the right track." Although you are not asking for anything directly, you do want to intensify or to change your listeners' beliefs. Either response may lead to actions later.

Sometimes the response you seek may be even more general, as in these four examples of concluding remarks:

- The next time you consider buying running shoes from one of these companies, consider the people working in the sweatshops who make it possible for you to get an affordable deal.
- You may not agree with me that Michael Phelps is the world's best athlete, but I hope you will appreciate the dedication and perseverance of professional swimmers.
- There are strong arguments on both sides of the abortion debate. I ask that you think about what I have said and come to your own conclusion about what you believe.
- You may not decide to hop a plane to the slums of Bangladesh as I did, but maybe you will consider other spring break travel alternatives that will make a difference in the lives of the less fortunate.

summary
A condensed restatement of the principal ideas just discussed.

None of these concluding statements calls for action, and yet each of them asks listeners to "do" something: to become more aware of something they had not recognized or to think critically about something they had accepted.

Virtually any speech—whether or not it is billed as a "persuasive" speech—asks for some response from the audience. In developing the conclusion of a speech, your goal is to make the audience understand exactly what response you seek.

An Example of a Conclusion

Here's how Michelle Ekanemesang ended her classroom speech about online sexual predators:

> So remember that we must commit ourselves to keeping children safe from the scourge of online sexual predators. These psychologically damaged men and women use a bag of tricks to deceive, lure, and abuse their prey—innocent children who will bear emotional and physical scars for a lifetime. We can blunt the weapons of online sexual predators by equipping children in our community with the education and knowledge they will need to detect, report, and foil the plans of sexual predators. I hope the information I've shared with you today will not fall on deaf or apathetic ears; please mention the tools I've discussed to a young person in your life. Remember that prevention is always better than a cure!

Michelle's first concluding sentence hinted to the audience that her speech was coming to an end. The next two sentences summarized the points she had made in the body of her speech. Finally, she asked the audience to take action and help stop online sexual predators by passing on the information that children need in order to prevent this form of sexual abuse.

Types of Conclusions

You already know that the types of introductions can be developed in various ways to achieve your purpose. The same is true for conclusions. Indeed, some of the following types of conclusions mirror the types of introductions you have studied; others introduce new elements into the speech.

Summarizing. We observed earlier that one purpose of the conclusion is to summarize the main points of the speech. Sometimes, summary is the *dominant* purpose. In that case, the concluding summary would be more extended than in the preceding examples. It would remind the audience not only about major topics addressed but also about the details of your argument, even repeating some memorable thematic phrases. Such an extensive concluding summary may need a "miniconclusion" of its own, to avoid ending abruptly or trailing off into insignificance.

In contrast, sometimes a succinct, bare-bones restatement of key phrases may make the most rousing finish. Consider the following conclusion from a speech by President George W. Bush outlining his strategy for responding to the terrorist attacks of September 11, 2001:

> Fellow citizens, we'll meet violence with patient justice—assured of the rightness of our cause, and confident of the victories to come.

The first part of the sentence captures the essence of Bush's policy, and the two clauses after the dash (note their parallel structure!) are a brief but powerful reminder of the attitudes the president sought to represent and to evoke.

Watch the **Video** "The Process of Developing a Speech: Conclusions—Using Recapping/Summary" at **MyCommunicationLab**

Quoting Someone. Just as many speeches begin with a quotation, so many end with one. In both cases, remember to tie the quotation clearly to your speech. A concluding quotation, however, may also go beyond your central ideas and give the audience something to think about; the risk of confusing listeners is much lower at the conclusion, because they have already heard your main points.

Student speaker Kim Davis found a quotation that succinctly summed up her ideas in a speech about gays in the military. Quoting a gay soldier who had been discharged for his sexual preference, she read:

> "They gave me a medal for killing two men, and a discharge for loving one."

Closing quotations should be like this one—a few neatly balanced, memorable words that sum up your central idea or advance your main purpose.

Making a Personal Reference. Particularly if your speech is about impersonal or abstract issues, it may be appropriate in the conclusion to personalize the issues by making reference to yourself. Such a concluding device (1) illustrates your own identification with the subject—you embody the ideas and values in the speech—and (2) encourages the audience to identify with you. In this way, listeners might imagine that they have the same feelings you have about the topic.

Student Romila Mushtag used this type of conclusion effectively after arguing that hate speech should not be outlawed on campus. She ended the speech by showing the audience a handwritten racist note that had been taped to her locker door. By revealing that she had been victimized by hate speech and yet would defend someone's right to use such speech, she demonstrated a level of

Rhetorical Workout

Conclude Your Speech

You've written the body and introduction of your speech demonstrating how to ride a snowboard. Your purpose is to teach your audience a few basics about snowboarding. Think about some types of conclusions and how they could work with this speech.

1. *Summarizing:* How could an extended summary of your main "how-to" points benefit your listeners?
2. *Quoting someone:* Suppose you find three catchy quotations and you want to use one as a conclusion. How appropriate or interesting do you think each of the following might be: (a) a snowboarding instructor on how knowing the basics increases your safety; (b) a first-time snowboarder on how much fun he had learning; (c) a professional snowboarder on how much she practices.
3. *Making a personal reference:* How might concluding with a personal reference or story affect your audience?
4. *Challenging the audience:* How could you use your conclusion to challenge your listeners?
5. *Offering a utopian vision:* Suppose you chose this topic because you enjoy snowboarding and you find it to be good exercise. How could you turn these elements into a conclusion that offers a utopian, positive vision to your audience?
6. What are some potential strengths and weaknesses of each type of conclusion? Which type would you use for this speech? Why?

integrity that the audience couldn't help endorsing and trying to emulate. Her personal reference made listeners identify with her—and with the ideas in her speech.

CHECKLIST 10.2

Types of Conclusions

- ❐ Summarizing
- ❐ Quoting someone
- ❐ Making a personal reference
- ❐ Challenging the audience
- ❐ Offering a utopian vision

(In addition, many of the types of introductions in Checklist 10.1 can also be used as concluding devices.)

Challenging the Audience. Particularly when your speech asks the audience to do something, concluding with a direct challenge may be effective. This type of conclusion not only creates a common bond between speaker and audience but also transfers to the audience some of the responsibility for achieving the speaker's goals. For example, student speaker Todd McCullough, after summarizing his main ideas, ended a speech about the need for environmentally and economically responsible automobiles with this challenge:

> We need to use our power as consumers to purchase vehicles that are fuel efficient and to boycott the continued production of gas-guzzling vehicles. We are here at college to get an education so we can go out and make a living. We cannot afford to watch as our paychecks are devoured by our automobiles. It is time to rise up and demand fuel-efficient vehicles.

Offering a Utopian Vision. Closely related to challenging the audience is this type of conclusion, which offers an idealized, positive vision of what can be achieved if only the audience will work together with the speaker. Rather than focusing on the challenge itself, however, this approach emphasizes the results of meeting the challenge successfully. The vision is called "utopian" not to dismiss it, but to emphasize that it usually transcends the immediate, practical world. One of the most famous examples of a conclusion containing a utopian vision is Martin Luther King, Jr.'s "I Have a Dream" address, delivered in 1963 at the March on Washington.

Abraham Lincoln also used this type of conclusion often. After warning of the perilous situation facing the Union in 1861, at the time of his first inaugural address, Lincoln confidently predicted in his conclusion that "the mystic chords of memory, stretching from every battlefield and patriot grave to every living heart and hearthstone all over this broad land, will yet swell the chorus of the Union, when again touched, as surely they will be, by the better angels of our nature." Yes, clouds may darken the sky at the moment, Lincoln was saying, but he promised his listeners that together they could achieve positive results in the fullness of time.

Even speeches about less momentous topics may conclude by envisioning how things will be once a problem is solved or a goal is achieved. Offering a utopian vision is particularly effective when the speaker is calling on the audience to make sacrifices or to take risks to achieve a distant goal. By predicting ultimate success, the utopian vision assures listeners that what the speaker is calling for will be worth the efforts they make.

Besides these specific types of conclusions, notice that many of the introductory approaches discussed earlier also can be used for the conclusion, including narratives, anecdotes, and rhetorical questions.[6] In the same way, some types of conclusions can be adapted effectively for use in an introduction. A quotation or a personal reference, for instance, can be as powerful at the beginning of the speech as at the end.

Watch the **Video** "The Process of Developing a Speech: Conclusions" at **MyCommunicationLab**

Strategies for Preparing a Conclusion

Several of the earlier suggestions for preparing an introduction apply as well to preparing a conclusion:

- Work on the conclusion after developing the body of your speech; again, it helps to know what you are concluding.
- Connect the conclusion clearly to the body of the speech so that listeners will grasp how it relates to your main ideas.
- Keep the conclusion relatively brief so that it does not detract from the speech itself.
- Aim for a complete conclusion, including both a wrap-up of your major ideas and a clear indication of how you want listeners to respond.
- Summarize your argument memorably; then tell the audience what belief or action you seek.

The following additional guidelines and suggestions will help you develop an effective conclusion.

Be Sure That it Truly Is the Conclusion. This first principle is simple to state but no less important for that. As you begin to develop the conclusion, take care to put it at the end of the body, and lead the audience naturally into your summary and final appeal.

Recall once more that listeners get distracted or confused when a speech departs from customary structure. On the one hand, avoid any wording that might signal a false (premature) conclusion. You certainly do not want your audience to applaud when, after several false endings, you finally say, "In conclusion…," as actually happened to Arkansas Governor Bill Clinton at the 1988 Democratic convention. On the other hand, indicate clearly when you are ready to move from the body of your speech to its conclusion.

Return to Your Introductory Device When Possible. One way to enhance the sense of form and unity in a speech is to conclude by referring again to the device you used in the introduction. If you began with a quotation, you may be able to repeat that same quotation in your conclusion, teasing a different meaning from it now that the audience has heard how you developed your topic. If your introductory device was an anecdote or a rhetorical question, your conclusion might return to that same device and embellish it based on the ideas you developed in your speech.

Of course, this suggestion cannot always be followed. The ideas in the speech may have moved far beyond where they were in the introduction, and returning to the introductory device would seem jarring ("Isn't this where we came in?"). But when you can return to the introduction, listeners will feel that the speech hangs together well, that it has a satisfying sense of structure.

Practice the Conclusion. The inspiration of the moment is no more dependable at the end of a speech than at the beginning. Just as you developed your introduction word for word, so should you prepare a conclusion by writing out key phrases and sentences that summarize your ideas and make a strong appeal. In addition, practice the conclusion orally. Your speaking rate is likely to slow down by the end of the speech; you probably will pause briefly between the body and the conclusion; and specific words and phrases will need careful emphasis. Practicing the conclusion out loud a few times before you present the entire speech will help you craft both its content and its ultimate effect.

Transitions: Connecting the Elements of a Speech

OBJECTIVE 10.5

Introduction, body, and conclusion—these structural elements seem so static that, in planning one of them, you can easily forget how dynamic a speech actually is. From beginning to end, the speech represents movement. You begin with a set of ideas and a strategic objective; by moving through the ideas, you also move toward achieving the objective. Similarly, listeners begin with a certain level of understanding about the subject and a certain disposition toward you as speaker; careful listening and thinking move them through the speech as well.

This dynamic movement of both speaker and listeners is achieved by—and depends on—connections that the speaker provides to bridge any gaps between elements. **Transitions** connect the introduction to the body, connect the main ideas within the body, and connect the body to the conclusion.

The Purposes of Transitions

The most important purpose of transitions is to create this sense of movement. They also help listeners follow the speaker's movement and remember what the speaker said. Equally important, transitions keep the speaker from lapsing into nervous mannerisms that would accentuate the gaps between ideas.[7]

Even accomplished speakers sometimes neglect to think about transitions. They may organize the body of the speech carefully, labor to devise an effective introduction, and craft a compelling conclusion; yet they assume that transitions will spring up spontaneously. Facing the audience, however, their spontaneous connections may be as pedestrian as "My next point is…" or "Next, let me discuss…." The movement is halting; the sense of form is unclear.

transition
A connection, or bridge, between the main elements of the speech and between the main ideas within the body of the speech.

Strategies for Speaking to Diverse Audiences

Respecting Diversity Through Introductions and Conclusions

Introductions and conclusions are important places to recognize and adapt to the diversity of the audience. Here are some strategies that will enable you to do so:

1. Consider the variety of strategies for building goodwill with your audience. Strive to identify with them early in your speech, but recognize that you will have to make a conscious decision in your introduction about how to do so.
2. Humor is an excellent way either to build goodwill with your audience or to alienate them. Demeaning individuals or cultural groups through humor should be avoided.
3. Offer "utopian visions" that enable listeners to imagine themselves as you ideally want them to be, emphasizing common values or themes that transcend diverse cultures.

Even worse is a speaker who bridges gaps and moves forward on the basis of sheer nervous energy and repetition. You probably have heard a speaker who punctuated every pause with "Umm..." or "like...," or who completed every thought with "Okay" or "Right?" or who moved to each new point with "Now, then...." Such mannerisms can become so obvious and distracting that the audience starts counting them rather than listening to the speech.

From your experience as a listener, then, you know that an effective speaker understands the nature of transitions and includes them consciously to create movement and form. The rest of the chapter focuses on how to provide such connections in your speeches.

Explore the **Exercise** "Better Transitions" at **MyCommunicationLab**

OBJECTIVE
10.6

Elements of Effective Transitions

We cannot list and describe "types" of transitions, as we could with introductions and conclusions. Transitions have three basic elements: an internal summary of what has been completed, a link to what is coming next, and an internal preview of the new idea. These three elements sometimes will be found in isolation, but a complete transition will include them all.

Internal Summaries. Like a concluding summary at the end of the speech, an **internal summary** draws together the central points that were discussed within the body of the speech or even within the discussion of one main idea, serving both to aid memory and to signal closure to those points. The following are simple examples of internal summaries:

1. In a speech recommending that your college switch from a quarter to a semester system:

   So, as we've seen, abandoning the quarter system would permit students to take classes that last longer, allowing them to learn more about a particular subject and reducing the pressures they face.

2. In a speech arguing that both students and faculty would benefit if the school offered more sections of closed classes:

   I hope I've made it clear that one benefit of additional sections of closed courses is more individualized attention. The faculty will be able to answer more questions in class and students will get prompt feedback.

3. In a speech about current campaign finance laws:

   So the current campaign finance laws really do pose a serious problem, because they encourage influence peddling, because they encourage legislators to forego their legislative work to engage in time-consuming fundraising, and because they lessen public confidence in government's ability to represent the interests of ordinary working people.

4. In a speech about multiculturalism:

   As I see it, then, our commitment to cultural diversity came about through this and other key incidents that embarrassed us by showing the limitations of our perspective.

Each of these internal summaries wraps up one main idea of the speech. It gives the audience a brief reminder of the idea and also signals the point of completion.

internal summary
a summary within the body of the speech, drawing together one of the main ideas.

A Question of Ethics

Ethical Introductions and Conclusions

Introductions and conclusions are important because they set the tone for the speech and consolidate the ideas of the speech in a memorable way. Speakers should be creative in developing their introductions and conclusions. But what if the tone or nature of the introduction or conclusion is different from that of the body of the speech? For example, does a light-hearted or engaging story in the introduction distort the audience's response to the body of the speech that is the somber explanation of the latest economic crisis? Does the speaker have an ethical responsibility not to deviate from the body of the speech when crafting the introduction and conclusion? Is it ethical to create a tone in the introduction that gets the audience interested, and then to change the tone or nature of the argument within the speech? Or is this just a matter of artistic creativity and not ethics? What are the benefits, drawbacks, and ethical concerns raised by placing ideas in the introduction and conclusion that do not appear elsewhere in the speech?

Links. Links are connections from one idea to the next. Some links are subtle and are established through careful word choice; others are explicit.

The construction *not only...but also* is an example of a subtle link. It moves from the point that was just discussed to the one that is coming up next, as in "Not only are closed classes bad for the students but also they're bad for the faculty." The speaker thus links two ideas that previously were separate in the speech.

Conjunctions such as *in addition, furthermore,* and *moreover* have the same effect. They suggest the cumulation of ideas, linking the ideas by hinting that the one to come will build on the one just considered. In contrast, conjunctions such as *however, nonetheless,* and *on the other hand* signal that the speaker is going to move from one point of view to an opposing viewpoint or in some way will qualify or limit the force of what was just said.

Sometimes links are more explicit. The speaker who finishes one idea with an internal summary and then says, "But here's the proverbial fly in the ointment," is announcing that the point just made is about to be rendered troublesome or problematic or that something calls it into question. And the speaker who says, "It's not enough to focus on the cost of higher education; we also have to be concerned with quality," is telling the audience that they need to consider one more important factor.

How subtle or explicit should a particular link be? That depends on several factors. If the connection seems obvious and listeners can be expected to see it without help, an explicit link may be insulting. But if the connection between points is complex or seems to contradict common sense, an explicit link may be appreciated. Audiences can follow narrative and chronological links more easily than they can follow analytical links. Similarly, links based on "common knowledge" and general understanding do not have to be as explicit as links that require specialized knowledge or training.

Internal Previews. A preview is a compressed version of what the speaker is about to develop; it prompts the audience to anticipate what is coming. The introduction will probably preview your main ideas. Similarly, an **internal preview** will help prepare your audience to follow along every time you introduce

internal preview
A preview within the body of the speech, leading into one of the main ideas.

a new main idea. Here are some examples of how to do that, corresponding to the examples of internal summaries that you recently read:

1. In your speech on abandoning the quarter system, an internal preview might point out,

   One of the most important reasons is that in a semester system students will have a longer time to learn what is offered in each course.

2. In your speech arguing for more sections of closed courses, an internal preview between the first and second main points might tell the audience,

   The second reason to have more sections is that the faculty will be able to give each student more attention.

3. In your speech about campaign finance laws, the body of the speech might start with an internal preview of the first major argument:

   Some argue that campaign finance laws no longer pose a serious problem. I don't agree, and let me tell you why.

4. In your speech about multiculturalism, an internal preview might signal that you are going to tell a story about how cultural diversity became a concern on campus.

Watch the **Video** "The Process of Developing a Speech: Transitions" at **MyCommunicationLab**

Whether obviously or subtly, each of these internal previews tells the audience what to expect—each is a kind of early alert system for the audience. An internal preview signals that listeners should get ready to move on to a new aspect of the speech, and it provides clues about the nature of the movement or the new aspect itself.

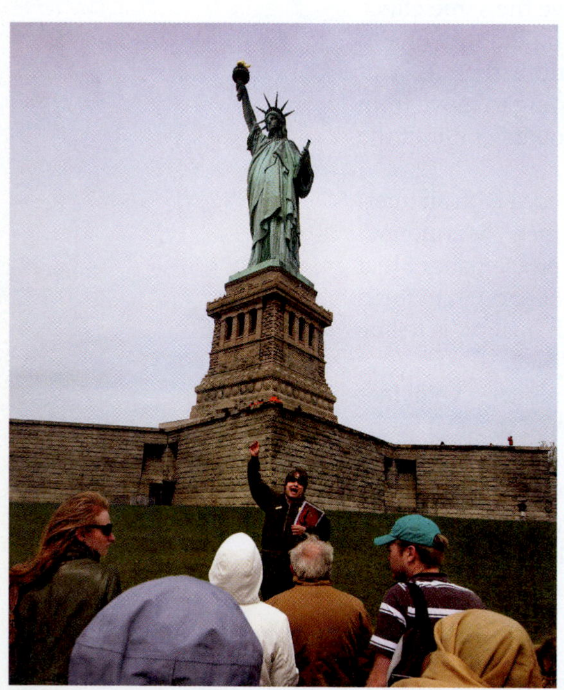

After discussing the history of the Statue of Liberty, the speaker signals a transition to considering its artistic features. Notice how the verbal transition is matched by gesture corresponding to the outstretched arm on the statue.

Whether previewing or summarizing the entire speech or just a part, you can use repetition and restatement to alert the audience that you are beginning or ending one of your key points. For example, the first internal preview described above might be elaborated as follows:

One reason to abandon the quarter system is that students will have longer to learn what is offered in each course. More time to learn means less rush. Let me explain why this is so.

Similarly, the second internal summary above might be drawn out in this way:

I hope I've made it clear that one benefit of additional sections of closed courses is more individualized attention. The faculty will be able to answer more questions in class, and students will get prompt feedback. Opening up more sections of closed courses will truly help our teachers to interact more with us and that, in turn, will benefit us.

Complete Transitions. As we have suggested, not every element of every transition need be made apparent. But a complete transition would include an internal summary of the point being concluded, a link to connect it to the next point, and an internal preview leading into the new point. For example, a complete transition in the speech about abandoning the quarter system might go like this:

So there's no doubt that students will benefit from the change. Abandoning the quarter system will give them more time to write papers and study for final exams and will reduce their level of pressure and stress. [*Internal summary*] But students aren't the only ones who will gain from this change. [*Link*] The faculty will gain two benefits as well. Let me tell you about them. [*Internal preview*]

If you think that such a complete transition somehow seems stilted or unnatural, think again after imagining how a speech would be hurt by a really awkward transition such as this one:

Uh, okay. Enough about that. Time to move on. Uh, okay. Oh yes, let me discuss...

This speaker completely sacrificed a sense of smooth progression of ideas, one of the most important contributions that transitions make to the speech.

Strategies for Preparing Transitions

Besides deciding how explicit to make each transition and whether to use repetition to emphasize the transition, consider the following brief suggestions.

Identify Main Ideas Succinctly. In internal previews and internal summaries, quickly and clearly identify the main idea being referred to; that will make it easier to remember. Rather than restating an idea completely, use a memorable word or phrase to highlight it in the transition.

Use Parallel Structure if Possible. When related ideas are identified in a similar or parallel fashion, that repeated pattern may make the link more memorable. Whenever possible, internal previews and internal summaries should use one of the organizational patterns described in Chapter 9.

Use Signposting. **Signposting** is the use of verbal cues to alert the audience to where you are in the speech. If you say that you will discuss three advantages of something, in previewing each advantage it will be helpful to identify it as "first," "second," or "third." Listeners will have no doubt that you have completed the discussion of one advantage and are about to talk about the next; and they also will clearly perceive the structure that you intended. Similarly, you can use pauses, repetition, and changes in speaking rate, pitch, or volume as signposting to guide the audience.

signposting
Using verbal cues to indicate to the audience where you are in the speech.

CHECKLIST 10.3

Transitions: Critical Thinking and Strategic Planning

1. Questions to ask yourself: At this point in my speech:
   - ❒ Do my listeners need a reminder or an alert about how far I've come?
   - ❒ Do my listeners need a reminder of how my last point relates to my next?
   - ❒ Do I need some verbal markers to help me and my listeners follow my outline?
   - ❒ Will my listeners follow my ideas better if I give them a brief preview?
2. If the answer is "Yes," here are some things worth doing:
   - ❒ Construct brief phrases that identify main ideas in the speech, and use them as markers and reminders at key intervals.
   - ❒ Set up your points in parallel structure whenever possible. Check your outline to help you do this.
   - ❒ Include verbal signposts that briefly show where you are and what comes next.

What Have You Learned?

Objective 10.1: Identify the main purposes and some common types of introductions.

The introduction shapes the audience's first impressions; its purposes are as follows:

- To gain attention and interest
- To influence the audience to view the speaker and topic favorably

- To state the thesis or purpose of the speech
- To preview how the speech will be developed

Some common types of introductions include the following:

- Identifying with the audience
- Referring to the speech situation
- Stating the purpose of the speech
- Stating the importance of the topic
- Citing statistics and making claims
- Telling a story (anecdote)
- Using an analogy
- Asking a rhetorical question
- Quoting someone
- Using humor

Objective 10.2: Prepare an introduction.

The introduction should be

- Prepared after the body of the speech is well in hand
- Related to the body
- Brief but complete
- Worded (and practiced) carefully

Objective 10.3: Identify the main purposes and some common types of conclusions.

The purposes of the conclusion are as follows:

- To complete the speech and signal to the audience that the end is near
- To summarize the main ideas
- To make a final appeal to listeners, asking them to adopt a particular belief or action

Among the common types of conclusions are the following:

- Summarizing
- Quoting someone
- Making a personal reference
- Challenging the audience
- Offering a utopian vision

Objective 10.4: Prepare a conclusion.

Guidelines for planning a conclusion are similar to those of the introduction. When possible, the conclusion should return in some way to the introductory device.

Objective 10.5: Use transitions to connect the elements of a speech and give its structure a dynamic quality.

Transitions serve to

- Give a sense of movement or progression to the speech by guiding listeners from one point to the next.
- Help the audience remember the main points and the structure of the speech.
- Reduce a speaker's distracting mannerisms in attempting to move from one idea to the next.

Transitions should have these characteristics:

- They should be succinct.
- They should use parallel structure if possible.
- They should provide signposting to guide the audience.

Objective 10.6: Recognize the elements of a transition, which may be either explicit or implicit.

A complete transition includes three elements:

- Internal summary
- Link
- Internal preview

However, not all elements are presented explicitly in every transition.

Listen to the **Audio Chapter Summary** at **MyCommunicationLab**

Discussion Questions

1. a. Which type of introduction would be most effective in each of the following speech situations?
    - A speech introducing the recipient of a lifetime achievement award
    - An informative speech to classmates about how to improve study skills
    - A speech to warn boaters about the dangers of "mixing water and alcohol"
    - A speech to strengthen volunteers' commitment to helping the homeless
    - A speech to reverse opposition to the death penalty

   b. In those same speech situations, which type of introduction would be least appropriate? Why?
2. What does an introduction need in order to prepare the audience effectively for the speech? Meet in small groups to answer this question. Each group member will present the introduction to a speech, and the other group members then will guess the speaker's purpose, the rhetorical situation, and the content of the speech. After everyone has made a guess, the speaker will reveal the actual purpose, situation, and content so that the group can compare intent and effect and then discuss ways to improve that introduction.

3. Which factors should a speaker consider when deciding how complete to make a particular transition? Discuss how the following constraints and opportunities might or might not influence your decision:
   - Your main points are organized in a dependent pattern.
   - Your main points are organized in an independent pattern.
   - You are moving between main ideas in the speech.
   - You are moving between subpoints within a main idea.
   - You are giving a speech that teaches a difficult concept to a group of students.
   - You are giving a speech to a group of protesters that enumerates well-known reasons to reinforce their commitment to the movement.

Activities

1. On a copy of a speech manuscript you have retrieved from the library or the Internet, do the following:
   a. Mark the passages in the text that make up the introduction, conclusion, and transitions. What do these markings tell you about the organization of the speech?
   b. Identify the strategies used in the introduction and in the conclusion.
   c. Closely examine at least one transition in the speech. Is it complete? Can you identify the internal summary, link, and internal preview?
   d. Evaluate the effectiveness of the introduction, conclusion, and transitions. What makes them effective or ineffective? How would you improve them?
2. Create three potential introductions and conclusions for your next speech. Choose the best one of each, and explain why you think it is best.
3. Follow the instructions in Checklist 10.3 to plan strategic transitions for your next speech.
4. Using the three introductions that you wrote for activity two, read each to a group of other students. Together, make a list of positive aspects (to repeat) and mistakes (to avoid).

Key Terms

conclusion **249**
internal preview **257**
internal summary **256**
introduction **238**
partition **240**
rhetorical question **245**
signposting **259**
summary **250**
transition **255**

Study and **Review** the **Flashcards** at **MyCommunicationLab**

Notes

1 Although first impressions may be durable, even such "first-impression bias" may be overridden. See Tanya Kraljic, Arthur G. Samuel, and Susan E. Brennan, "First Impressions and Last Resorts: How Listeners Adjust to Speaker Variability," *Psychology Science* 19 (April, 2008): 332–38.

2 Classical theorists often used words such as this, from the language of architecture, to describe the organization of speeches. See Leland M. Griffin, "The Edifice Metaphor in Rhetorical Theory," *Communication Monographs* 27 (November 1960): 279–92.

3 For more on the effects of humor in speeches, see C. R. Gruner, "Advice to the Beginning Speaker on Using Humor—What the Research Tells Us," *Communication Education* 34 (April 1985): 142–47. For a contemporary view on risqué humor and the varieties of interpretation open to an audience, see Lisa Glebatis Perks, "Polysemic Scaffolding: Explicating Discursive Clashes in Chappelle's Show," *Communication, Culture & Critique* 3 (June, 2010): 270–89.

4 For another list of introduction types, see Richard Whately, *Elements of Rhetoric*, Carbondale: Southern Illinois University Press, 1963, originally published 1828, pp. 170–72.

5 One early study found that, on average, introductions made up 9 percent of the total speech and conclusions made up 4 percent. See Ed Miller, "Speech Introductions and Conclusions," *Quarterly Journal of Speech* 32 (April 1946): 181–83.

6 For a discussion on the use of metaphor in conclusions, see John Waite Bowers and Michael M. Osborn, "Attitudinal Effects of Selected Types of Concluding Metaphors in Persuasive Speeches," *Communication Monographs* 33 (June 1966): 148–55.

7 Research shows that transitions make it easier for listeners to comprehend a speech. See Ernest Thompson, "Some Effects of Message Structure on Listeners' Comprehension," *Communication Monographs* 34 (March 1967): 51–57.

CHAPTER

11

Outlining the Speech

LEARNING OBJECTIVES

Listen to the **Audio Chapter** at **MyCommunicationLab**

After studying this chapter, you should be able to:

Objective 11.1	Explain why outlining is a valuable part of speech preparation and presentation.
Objective 11.2	Create a preparation outline that uses proper principles of subordination and coordination.
Objective 11.3	Adapt the preparation outline into a presentation outline that you can use in delivering your speech.

OUTLINE

OBJECTIVE 11.1

A speech **outline** is simply a display of the organizational pattern of the speech. If you already have selected one of the organizational patterns discussed in Chapter 9, the outline will record your choices and let you check that you have made them correctly. Sometimes, however, you may not have a specific organizational plan in mind. Developing the outline will enable you to decide which organizational plan is best. In either case, however, the outline serves several purposes. It helps you to:

- *Be sure that you have covered the topic adequately,* that you have not included irrelevant material, and that your ideas are developed in the right proportion so you don't spend too much or too little time on any one idea.
- *Clarify and choose the best organizational strategy* for your speech.
- *Check your organizational pattern* to see that it is sensible and consistent. It lets you determine easily whether the main ideas support your thesis statement, whether your reasoning is strong, whether the supporting materials are linked to your claims, and whether the overall design of the speech advances your purpose.
- *Become familiar with the claims you want to make* and the order in which you plan to make them.

From Ideas to Outline

Suppose that you've done quite a bit of research on your topic and have given it a good deal of thought, but you're not sure exactly how you want to organize it. A few basic steps will help you to develop the outline:

1. List the ideas you plan to develop in the speech. If you were discussing the drawbacks of the electoral college, for example, you might have a list like this:

   Exaggerates influence of small states
   Romney needn't campaign in Alabama in 2012
   Denies voice to the minority within each state
   Supports false stereotypes about states
   Excludes the campaign from much of the country
   Democratic votes in Texas didn't count for anything in 2012
   Denies democratic principle of majority rule
   Red states aren't dramatically different from blue states
   Harrison won in 1888 though Cleveland had more popular votes
   Obama could ignore Illinois in 2008 and 2012
   Red and blue states are not internally homogeneous
   Republican votes in California didn't count for anything in 2012
   Bush won in 2000 though Gore had more popular votes

   These are the ideas that have emerged from your research and thought about the topic.

2. Determine which of these ideas subsume other ideas. Rearrange the list so that you group together ideas that are closely related. For example, "Harrison

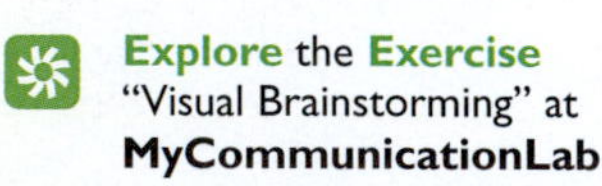
Explore the **Exercise** "Visual Brainstorming" at **MyCommunicationLab**

outline
A display of the organizational pattern of the speech.

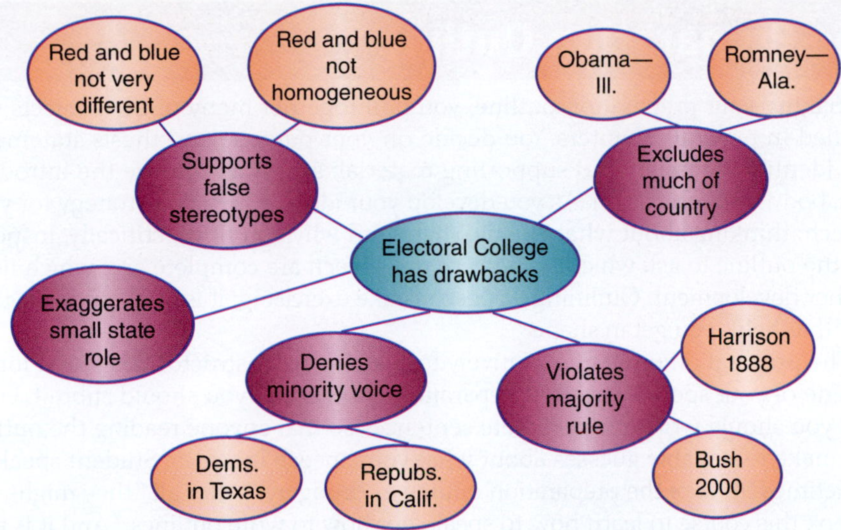

Figure 11.1 Mapping the main ideas.

won in 1888 though Cleveland had more popular votes" and "Bush won in 2000 though Gore had more popular votes" are both supporting points for the idea "Denies democratic principle of majority rule."

3. Diagram the relationships among the ideas. One excellent way to do so is by mapping, a technique you learned about in Chapter 4. A map of the above list is diagrammed in Figure 11.1. The circles connected directly to the thesis statement are the main ideas. Moving outward, the circles that are linked to them will be the supporting ideas. (If we proceeded to more subordinate levels of support, the map would continue to expand outward.)

   If you don't want to draw a concept map, you might simply draw lines among the ideas in your list, to connect those that go together. Either way, you will develop clusters that represent the main ideas of the speech. As noted in Chapter 6, most speakers will want to have between two and five main ideas, because having more will risk losing the audience's attention and comprehension. If you find that you have more than five main ideas, it may mean that you are trying to do too much in the speech. Or it may mean that some of your ideas still can be combined—that you haven't yet gone to the level of main ideas.

4. Determine the order in which you want to discuss the main ideas. You probably will want to use one of the organizational patterns in Chapter 9, because they are easy for listeners to follow, unless there is a good reason to develop a novel plan for your particular speech.

Now you are ready to translate the results of your mental exercise into the form of an outline. Speakers depend on outlines at two stages: when they put the speech together and when they deliver it. Each stage requires a different kind of outline. The **preparation outline** is used in composing the speech and is developed in enough detail to show how each idea and piece of evidence fits into the overall structure. The **presentation outline**, or speaking outline, is simpler and briefer and is used as a memory aid while you deliver the speech. Although the character and use of these outlines are different, the preparation outline should lead naturally into the presentation outline.

preparation outline
A detailed outline, usually written in complete sentences, used to develop a clear organizational structure during preparation of the speech.

presentation (speaking) outline
A brief outline, usually containing only key words, used as a memory aid during delivery.

OBJECTIVE 11.2

The Preparation Outline

In making your preparation outline, you pull together many of the subjects you studied in previous chapters. You decide on your purpose and thesis statement; you identify the issues and supporting material; and you organize the introduction, body, and conclusion. As you develop your ideas, you plan a strategy for your speech, thinking about what to put where and why. You think critically, inspecting the outline to ask which sections of the speech are complete and which need further development. Outlining a speech is like exercising; it is a "rhetorical workout" that helps you get in shape.

The preparation outline is relatively formal. If your instructor has asked for an outline of your speech, it is the preparation outline that you should submit. Usually, you should write it in complete sentences so that anyone reading the outline can make reasonable guesses about what your speech includes. Student speakers sometimes think of the preparation outline as drudgery. "After all," they might say, "I took this course to learn how to speak, not how to write outlines." And it is true that some very accomplished speakers can do without a fully developed outline. But for beginning speakers, the preparation outline is extremely important and you should approach it with care. It enables you to clarify your own thinking, to be sure that the structure of your speech is clear, and to rehearse on paper the main ideas you will develop and the relationships among them. On the other hand, once you have the structure of the speech in place, you should leave the preparation outline aside and work on the presentation outline. Be careful that you do not simply read the speech from the preparation outline. That could interfere with your ability to establish contact with, and receive feedback from, the audience.

What Does a Good Outline Look Like?

An outline indicates the hierarchy of importance of ideas within a speech. Typically, the main ideas are signaled by Roman numerals, and each successive level of less central ideas is designated first by capital letters, then by Arabic numerals, and finally by lowercase letters.[1] In short, you proceed from the ideas most central to your thesis to those least central, indenting each level appropriately. The overall structure of your outline would look something like this:

I. Main idea
    A. Supporting idea (subheading)
    B. Supporting idea (subheading)
        1. Supporting material (evidence)
        2. Supporting material (evidence)
    C. Supporting idea (subheading)
        1. Supporting material (evidence)
            a. Backing for the supporting material
            b. Backing for the supporting material
        2. Supporting material (evidence)
    D. Supporting idea (subheading)
II. Main idea

An outline may extend to additional detail, of course, with deeper indentations for each level of organization. But if the structure of a speech is that complex, the audience probably will not be able to follow it carefully. If your preparation outline needs more than four levels of importance, your thesis is probably too broad and unfocused.

Explore the **Exercise** "Using the Microsoft Outlining Tool" at **MyCommunicationLab**

Explore the **Exercise** "Practicing with the Microsoft Outlining Tool" at **MyCommunicationLab**

Outlining the Body of the Speech

The following principles will help you construct your preparation outline.

Statement of Topic, General Purpose, Specific Purpose, and Thesis. These elements, discussed in Chapter 6, should be displayed above the outline. By keeping them in view as you develop the outline, you can check the emerging plan against the goals it is designed to achieve. For a speech about the quality of Campus Food Service, you might precede the outline with the following:

TOPIC:	Campus Food Service
GENERAL PURPOSE:	Conversion
SPECIFIC PURPOSE:	To convince listeners that the often-criticized Campus Food Service is really quite good
THESIS:	Campus Food Service is vastly underrated.

Complete Sentences. One function of the preparation outline is to test the clarity and precision of your claims. Sometimes you may have a general idea of what you want to say but are unsure of the exact idea you want to express. By writing the outline in complete sentences, rather than just highlighting general topics, you will force yourself to specify exactly what claims you want to make. This will make you less likely to "talk around the subject" when you deliver the speech.

For example, if your outline simply says "Voting bad," you would have little idea what you really want to say—other than that there is something negative about voting patterns. In contrast, the complete sentence "Voting in presidential elections has declined over time" is much more precise and focuses your attention on your essential message.

Subordination. A primary purpose of the preparation outline is to map out the relationships between claims and supporting materials. The outline should clearly show **subordination**; supporting materials for a given idea should be outlined as indented under that idea. If you designate the main idea with Roman numerals, for example, then you should identify its supporting ideas (subheadings) with capital letters. It is easy to mistake subheadings for main ideas or for supporting material when your outline does not show their subordinate structure.

Look again at this fragment of an outline from Chapter 9:

I. Voter apathy has become a growing concern.
   A. During the years before World War I, voter turnout was high.
   B. In the modern age, the height of voter participation came in 1960.
   C. Since 1960, there has been a slow but steady decline in political participation.
   D. By 1996, voter turnout was at the lowest level since 1924.
   E. Even in the razor-thin election of 2000, turnout rose only slightly.
   F. Even though there were many new voters in 2008, the turnout rate did not change very much.

subordination
Designating the supporting materials for a main idea with the subordinate symbol and indentation system in an outline—for example, supporting materials, indicated by capital letters, indented under their main idea, indicated by Roman numerals.

II. Voter apathy is widespread.
    A. It can be found in the East.
    B. It can be found in the Midwest.
    C. It can be found in the South.
    D. It can be found in the West.

Details about the voting in different eras would be subordinate to a claim that voter apathy has increased over time. Likewise, information about voting rates in different regions of the country would be subordinate to a main idea about the geographic spread of the problem. Each subheading supports the idea under which it is indented. The distinction between main and supporting ideas helps to make the subordinate structure clear and easy for an audience to follow.

Coordination. Closely related to the principle of subordination is **coordination**: Ideas with the same level of importance should be designated with the same symbol series—all with Roman numerals, or all with capital letters, and so on. Items so designated are parallel, or coordinate, statements.

The preceding outline appropriately identifies the two statements "Voter apathy has become a growing concern" and "Voter apathy is widespread" as main headings. These are equally important ideas, and they are both parts of an overall topical organization that coordinates two aspects of the topic: chronology and geography. It would be a mistake to label as main headings "Voter apathy has become a growing concern" and "It can be found in the South." These statements are not united by a topical plan and might even be said to conflict, because the first statement implies a national problem and the second focuses on a single region. In the same way, it would be a mistake to label "Voter apathy has become a growing concern" as a main idea and "Voter apathy is widespread" as a supporting point, because the second point is on equal footing with the first, not subordinate to it.

It is easy to see in the abstract that these patterns are in error. But it is also easy to make these types of errors when you are not consciously thinking about outlining and organizational schemes—especially if, say, you happen to find compelling supporting material about voting rates in the South. As you compose your preparation outline, ask whether the ideas that you have designated with the same symbol series are really *coordinate*—whether they are of the same importance and (often) parallel in structure.[2]

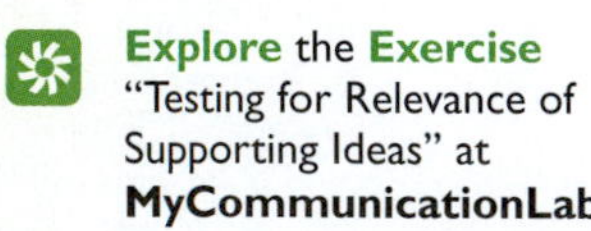
Explore the **Exercise** "Testing for Relevance of Supporting Ideas" at **MyCommunicationLab**

Activity 1 at the end of the chapter provides an opportunity to practice the principles of coordination and subordination.

Discreteness. Each element of the outline should express only one idea, so that you do not mix together themes that should be developed separately. "Voter apathy is growing and widespread" would not be a good entry in your outline because it combines themes that would be clearer for your audience if they were developed one at a time.

As a general rule, you should have at least two entries at any level of subordination—if there is a "capital A," for example, then there also should be (at least) a "capital B." The reason is that an idea cannot be subdivided into only one part. A single entry at any level of subordination usually is a sign either that something is missing in your analysis or that you have regarded as a subpoint what really is a main idea (in which case your "capital A" really should be "Roman numeral II."

coordination
Designating all ideas that are on the same level of importance with the same symbol series and level of indentation in an outline.

Rhetorical Workout

Format a Preparation Outline

Read Jaimie Sakumura's speech, "Immigration," in the Appendix. Then take apart the body of the speech and put it into the format of a preparation outline. For example, Jaimie's first main idea is at the beginning of her second paragraph. In a preparation outline, where you use complete sentences, the main idea would look like this:

I. Let me begin by telling you why treating illegal immigrants as felons is an inhumane and impractical way to deal with this problem.

Using the outline format under "What Does a Good Outline Look Like?" plug in the following items from Jaimie's speech. Be sure to write out the ideas in complete sentences.

- What are the other two *main ideas*?
- The first *supporting idea* for main idea number I is "Not providing illegal immigrants with the opportunity to obtain citizenship is, first of all, completely impractical." What *supporting materials*, or evidence, does Jaimie cite to back up this supporting idea? What other supporting idea(s) and supporting materials does Jaimie use in discussing her main idea number I?
- Fill in the supporting ideas and supporting materials for main ideas II and III.
- Look at the overall outline you have just created. Is each supporting idea *subordinate* to, or beneath, its main idea? Are ideas of equal weight designated as *coordinate*, or parallel, statements, with the same level of numbering?
- Is each element of the outline *discrete*, expressing only one idea?
- Based on the preparation outline, does the body of Jaimie's speech look balanced? Do the main ideas each have a similar number of supporting ideas? Does each supporting idea have supporting material (evidence) to back it up?
- How do you think creating a preparation outline as you write your speech could help you organize your ideas?

Some teachers of public speaking regard this general rule as an absolute prohibition against single entries, but there are cases in which an exception might be justified. For instance, you may wish to discuss a general idea and illustrate only one specific dimension. If you examine carefully the outline structure of this book, you will find a few cases where there is only one subpoint. Still, the general rule is a good guideline to follow when developing your first preparation outline. You can experiment with deviation later.

CHECKLIST 11.1

Principles for Outlining the Body of the Speech

- ☐ Complete sentences (in preparation outline)
- ☐ Subordination
- ☐ Coordination
- ☐ Discreteness

Outlining Introductions and Conclusions

Including the introduction and conclusion of your speech in the preparation outline is fairly straightforward. They are developed as separate sections of the outline, and the primary numerical divisions identify the elements of the introduction and conclusion. For the introduction, these elements typically include the following:

I. Attention-getting device
II. Statement of thesis or purpose
III. Preview of the speech

(The introduction also seeks to create a favorable impression, but that is an overall effect to achieve, not necessarily an individual component of the introduction.)

And for the conclusion, the key elements usually are as follows:

I. Summary of main ideas
II. Action desired from audience
III. Closure device

Here is how you might outline the introduction and conclusion of the speech about Campus Food Service:

Introduction

I. Attention-getting device: [*Take on persona of student going through food service line.*] "Oh great! Another meal at Campus Food Service. Let's see...what do I want? What is that? Uh...no mystery meat tonight, thanks. What? Chicken again. There's some pasta. Ugh, it looks like three noodles and a gallon of water. That's it. I'm ordering in tonight." This is a common but misguided student reaction.

II. Thesis: Campus Food Service, however, is vastly underrated.

III. Preview: By explaining how Campus Food Service keeps costs to a minimum, keeps offering a good variety, keeps a democratic system sensitive to the needs of the consumer, and keeps maintaining high-quality standards, I am going to show that Campus Food Service is the best meal program for students.

Conclusion

I. Summary: The Campus Food Service plan is a fair way for students at the university to eat. It keeps charging students a low price for meals, keeps offering a wide variety of food selections, keeps trying its best to meet the student's needs, and keeps maintaining freshness and taste standards.

II. Action step: The next time you hear people making ill-founded complaints about Campus Food Service, don't hesitate to set them straight.

III. Closure: We are just left with one problem, though. Now that we know all the benefits of eating at Campus Food Service, what are we going to complain about at dinner?

Outlining Transitions

The preparation outline will also help you check the flow of your reasoning and the structural "joints" of your message. Look over the outline to check that the sections naturally link to one another. Is it clear, for example, that B is the next logical step after A? Can you envision how you will wrap up the discussion of idea I and then move to idea II?

If you need to make the transitions of your reasoning explicit, incorporate them into your preparation outline. The easiest way to do this is to make parenthetical notes between the items in the outline that the transition will link. In the example about voter apathy, you might include an explicit transition between items I and II in the body of the speech. The relevant part of the preparation outline might look like this:

D.
(Transition)
II.

Citing Supporting Materials in the Outline

You also can use the preparation outline to fit supporting materials into the speech. You can do so physically, by sorting your note cards according to the designations on your outline. For instance, you could put in one pile all the notes that bear on item I-A in the outline; separate piles would contain notes that relate to items I-B, II-A, and so on. This process has two obvious benefits; you can:

1. *Evaluate the supporting materials* for a given idea in the speech and can select which evidence to include.
2. *Discover which ideas still lack supporting materials,* indicating that further research may be needed.

After you have selected supporting materials, incorporate them into the outline. The following three alternative ways to do this all have both benefits and drawbacks:

1. *Reproduce the supporting material immediately below the idea to which it relates.* This approach most closely resembles what you will do in the speech and is probably easiest for a reader of the outline to follow; but it will make your outline longer and may disrupt the clarity of its structure.
2. *Use footnotes in the outline, and then reproduce the supporting materials at the end.* This method preserves the clarity of your structure, but you'll have to flip back and forth between the outline and the supporting materials.
3. *Attach a bibliography indicating the sources of supporting materials.* This approach will keep your structure clear and will let a reader of the outline know, in general, where supporting materials came from; but it will not match up specific evidence with specific ideas.

Even if you cite supporting materials in the outline, you often will need a bibliography at the end. It will identify all the sources you consulted in preparing the speech, whether or not you cite or quote them directly. Several different guides offer information on how to cite sources, ranging from the *Chicago Manual of Style* to the style manuals of the American Psychological Association (APA) and the Modern Language Association (MLA). You may be instructed as to which guide to use or the choice may be left up to you. Whichever you use, however, use it consistently. As you take notes (discussed in Chapter 7), be sure to take down the information required by the style manual you use. Review the bibliographic formats discussed in Chapter 7 (see Table 7.3 on pages 173-174).

Sample Preparation Outline

Here is an example of a preparation outline for a speech by Christopher Chiyung, a student at Northwestern University. In the margin alongside the outline are comments, questions, and suggestions. As you review the outline, consider its strengths and weaknesses and how you might improve it in response to the marginal notes. This outline is not presented as "perfect," but as an actual student outline, with both strengths and weaknesses, for you to review and analyze.

Preparation Outline

Microlending in Evanston, by Christopher Chiyung

GENERAL PURPOSE: To persuade the audience to support microloans in Evanston, Illinois.

SPECIFIC PURPOSE: To get people who are unfamiliar with microfinance to begin thinking about it and to strengthen the commitment of those who already support it.

THESIS: Microlending in Evanston is crucial to allow depressed businesses to survive, institutions to be adequately funded, and the standard of living to rise.

Introduction

This may seem to be a trite attention-getting device, because the quotation is frequently used and because the speech really is not about teaching people how to do something.

I. **Attention-getting device:** "Give a man a fish, feed him for a day; teach a man to fish, feed him for a lifetime." This maxim relates directly to a sustainable practice that isn't as well known as it should be.

This step is not always included, but it is here because a technical term needs to be defined.

II. **Definition.** Microfinance is based on the premise that low-income individuals are capable of lifting themselves out of poverty if given access to financial services.

Building one's *ethos* is often done implicitly, but it is made explicit here because of the speaker's direct personal involvement with the issue.

III. **Personal credibility.** As a member of Northwestern's premier microfinance organization, Lending for Evanston and Northwestern Development (LEND), I have researched the microfinance model's feasibility and have seen its far-reaching and long-lasting positive impact in the community.

This is a clear statement of the thesis and suggests that the speaker will advocate a point of view, not just present both sides of an issue.

IV. **Thesis:** Microlending in Evanston is crucial to allow depressed businesses to survive, institutions to be adequately funded, and the standard of living to rise.

This is an unusually brief preview, suggesting that the structure of the speech will be simple and easy to follow.

V. **Preview:** First I will tell you why we all should support microfinance and then I'll show how you can become involved.

Body

There are only two examples here, but notice how they are varied: rural vs. urban, foreign vs. domestic.

Notice how Christopher combines examples with an analogy, and then uses another example to support the analogy. This is a strong combination of evidence and reasoning.

I. Microloans in poor areas have led to success.
   A. In Bangladesh, 48 percent of the poor using microcredit were able to rise above the poverty line, versus only 4 percent of those without access to microcredit. [CITE GLOBAL ENVISION STUDY]
   B. Microloans in St. Louis have also been successful. [CITE MARKETWATCH]
   C. West Evanston shares similar problems. [ANALOGY OF BARBERS & PAINTERS TO FARMERS & ARTISANS]
   D. There is a personal example of success in west Evanston [GIGI AT EBONY BARBERSHOP]

[TRANSITION: While these success stories are wonderful, they are few and far between, for one reason: there aren't enough microfinance institutions.]

Christopher is hoping that the 4 percent figure, being so small, will speak for itself. There is an implicit value judgment that this is nowhere near enough.

The visual aids become an additional form of support because the audience might not be able to remember the statistics.

II. Microfinance institutions need your support because they lack sufficient funding.
   A. The existing 10,000 microfinance institutions reach only 4 percent of the potential market worldwide. [WORLD BANK]
   B. Many small businesses and community organizations in the United States simply do not have access to credit or financing. [ANNIBALE—CITI MICROFINANCE & COMMUNITY DEVELOPMENT]
   C. These graphs illustrate how little funding is available.

Notice how this transition contains all the elements: internal summary of the previous idea, a link (reference to "other benefits"), and a preview of what is coming next.

[TRANSITION: In other words, microfinance institutions really need help in order to reach more people. But what other benefits are there besides growing small businesses? One is widespread financial stability from being employed.]

III. Microfinance brings up the standard of living and creates jobs.

   A. In Rwanda, a gas station owner was able to hire additional workers. [CNN CORRESPONDENT GAYLE LEMMON]

   B. In Sarajevo, a textile entrepreneur was able to start a company employing 20 people who could now afford to send their children to school. [GAYLE LEMMON]

   C. In St. Louis, microloans for appliances, car repairs, and college tuition allows repairmen and local businesses to thrive.

   D. There is a sort of unexplainable positive energy that surrounds microfinance and helps to reinvigorate communities. [CITE BRIDGET McDERMOTT FLOOD, INCARNATE WORD FOUNDATION]

Notice how the support for this main idea consists entirely of examples. Why might Christopher have made this choice? Is it a wise move? Do the examples meet the tests for this kind of evidence?

[TRANSITION: However, this is not to say that microfinance doesn't have its own set of criticisms.]

This transitional statement is a double negative. It might be confusing.

IV. The risks of supporting microfinance are not significant.

   A. Naysayers argue that microfinance institutions often fail to engage the communities where they work. [CITE foodfirst.org]

   B. Bringing people up to the poverty line is not enough; they need to be able to invest in themselves. [CITE HARVARD CRIMSON STUDY]

   C. Although microfinance cannot do everything, it still can make a significant difference.

If the audience is likely to be thinking critically, it can be advantageous to acknowledge that there are criticisms of your proposal. Are these representative of the objections that might be made to it?

Conclusion

I. **Summary:** Although the debate over microfinance continues, the most important facts to remember are that microfinance has proven successful in a decent number of cases, the institutions can use any means of financial support, and the positive effects aren't confined to just a small sphere.

A succinct statement of the main ideas in the body of the speech. This should make it easier for the audience to remember.

II. **Call to action:** Please donate to LEND and spread awareness of the organization. It is a great way to understand the economic divide between Evanston's lakefront mansions and those struggling to make it on the west side.

III. **Final plea:** The best thing you can do is to become a member next school year. In this way, we all could teach others how to fish, and we'd never have to just give the fish away.

Notice how the conclusion returns to the theme of the introduction, tying the speech together.

Bibliography

Baker, Meredith C. "Show Me the Money" [Opinion]. *The Harvard Crimson.* Web. November 9, 2011.

"Kiva—About Microfinance." *Kiva—Loans That Change Lives.* Web. November 9, 2011.

Lemmon, Gayle Tzemach. "Why Think Small When It Comes to Women in Poor Nations?" *CNN.com Breaking News, U.S., World, Weather, Entertainment & Video News.* Web. November 9, 2011.

"The Limits of Microcredit—A Bangladesh Case." *Food First/Institute for Food and Development Policy.* Web. November 9, 2011.

McFarland, Holly. "The Basics of Microfinance/Global Envision." *Global Envision/The Confluence of Global Markets and Poverty Alleviation.* Web. November 9, 2011.

"St. Louis Microfinance Conference Showcases Positive Impact of Providing Financial Services to Low-Income Families, Communities." *MarketWatch—Stock Market Quotes, Business News, Financial News.* Web. November 9, 2011.

Notice that all the sources came from the Internet and all were accessed on the same date. Is this a problem? Why or why not? Does the fact that there is a wide variety of types of sources make a difference?

Compare the format of Christopher's source entries to the citation style required by your instructor. What changes or corrections are needed to comply with that style?

A Question of Ethics

Ethics in Outlining

Because the presentation outline is always simpler than the preparation outline, you will be forced to make choices and edit out some information. How do you know what this crucial information is? What if you must trim your notes down anyway? What sort of ethical concerns might this pose? How can you minimize such concerns? If the audience is providing feedback suggesting that they are confused or need more information. Is it the speaker's responsibility to adapt to this audience response? Does having a presentation outline deter the speaker from being flexible? Can following the outline mean defaulting on one's ethical responsibility to the audience? How can the speaker negotiate responsibilities both to the outline and to the audience?

OBJECTIVE 11.3

The Presentation Outline

As important as the preparation outline is, you probably will not want to use it during your speech. It is cumbersome and wordy; and it may encourage you to read the outline as though it were a manuscript, rather than speaking extemporaneously and adapting to the situation. Therefore, when you are satisfied with the preparation outline, you should develop a presentation, or speaking, outline. This will be the main source of notes you'll use during the speech itself.

Guidelines for the Presentation Outline

Some basic principles will help you develop a useful speaking outline.

Match Structure of Preparation Outline. This first principle is the most obvious. The whole point of carefully developing the preparation outline is to devise a clear and meaningful structure for the speech. The outline from which you speak, therefore, should follow the same pattern.

Use Key Words. The complete sentences that you used in the preparation outline will distract you in the speaking outline; there will be too much to stop and read while you are speaking. Instead, the speaking outline should use key words that remind you of your ideas. For example, the preparation outline for the speech about voter apathy might be translated into this presentation outline:

I. Growing
   A. Before WWI
   B. 1960
   C. After 1960
   D. 1996
   E. 2000
   F. 2008

Explore the **Exercise** "Creating a Speaking Outline" at **MyCommunicationLab**

II. Widespread
   A. East
   B. Midwest
   C. South
   D. West

Each key word should recall to your mind the complete statement that appears in the preparation outline. If a key word does not reliably prompt your memory, change the key word.

Include Introduction, Conclusion, and Transitions.

Just as your preparation outline includes entries for the introduction, the conclusion, and transitions, your speaking outline can have separate sections for the introduction and the conclusion and can show transitions as parenthetical notes. In keeping with the key-word nature of the speaking outline, however, state these as briefly as possible, with only enough detail to ensure that you will remember them.

There are two exceptions to this general statement. Because the exact wording of your introduction and conclusion may be important to create the desired initial and final impressions, the attention-getting step in the introduction and the closure-developing step in the conclusion may be written out word for word or even committed to memory.[3]

Using small note cards is a practical way to keep simple cues in front of you as you speak.

Your speaking outline may refer to transitions in the form of parenthetical notes, such as "(Cause–effect link here)," "(On the other hand)," and the like. These will remind you of how you intend to signal transitions, thereby making the movement through your outline apparent to listeners.

Use of Note Cards

Most speakers find it better to use note cards than large sheets of paper for the speaking outline. Note cards are more compact, sturdier, easier to rearrange, and less distracting. You can set them on the lectern (if you are using one) or hold them in one hand without limiting your freedom of movement or gesture. You can outline each Roman numeral on a separate note card, or you can put your entire speaking outline on a single card. But be sure not to overload your note cards with overly small writing that will be hard for you to read while speaking. Some classroom assignments may limit you to a single note card so that you will make your key-word outline as simple as possible.

Reference to Supporting Materials and Oral Citations

The presentation outline should cue you about which supporting materials to use. If the actual materials are not simple enough to remember, put them on separate note cards. If you are speaking at a lectern, you can stack the cards in the order you'll use them. If not, you may want to hold them with your speaking outline cards.

CHOOSE A STRATEGY: Creating a Presentation Outline

The Situation

Choose a short speech from the Appendix or from the website http://americanrhetoric.com. Imagine that you have written it and will be delivering it to your class. Consider how you could create a presentation outline that would help you give the speech.

Making Choices

1. Choose an idea from the speech and identify if it is a main idea, a supporting idea, or supporting material (evidence). What are some key words you could use for this idea in your presentation outline?
2. Identify the speech's introduction and conclusion. Would you choose to include these in your presentation outline by using key words or by writing them out word for word? Why?
3. Of the supporting materials in the speech, what are some that you might want to include separate note cards for? Why?
4. Think about your delivery of an earlier speech or about presentation skills you want to work on. What kinds of stage directions would you include in your outline (slow down, pause, take a breath, gesture, eye contact, etc.)?

What If...

How would your choices be affected by the following:

1. You are limited to using three note cards for your speech.
2. Your speech contains many statistics.
3. You will be speaking without a lectern/podium.

Here is a simple illustration of how you might identify supporting materials in your speaking outline:

III. Voting not thought important
  A. Makes no difference—quote from Dionne book]
  B. No real choice—[on-campus interviews]

Point A would remind you to read the quotation that supports idea III (you can write the quotation on a separate note card or put it on a visual aid so that you don't need to handle a large book). Point B will similarly remind you to recount your informal talks with people on campus who said that there is no real difference between the major political parties and hence no reason to vote.

When you quote from source material, you need to cite the source, but an oral citation has less detail than a written bibliography entry. Exact dates, volume numbers of periodicals, lengthy titles and subtitles, and specific page numbers usually will not be necessary. Audience members will be unlikely to remember all of this information (though occasionally these elements will be necessary in order to put quoted matter into context).

The general guideline is that you should provide a full enough citation to enable an audience member to *evaluate* the quotation and to *find* it, should he or she so choose. In most cases, this will include the following:

- The name of the person being quoted
- A brief mention of his or her qualifications if they are not obvious
- The date, at least the year
- The title of the book, name of the journal or newspaper, or identity of other source

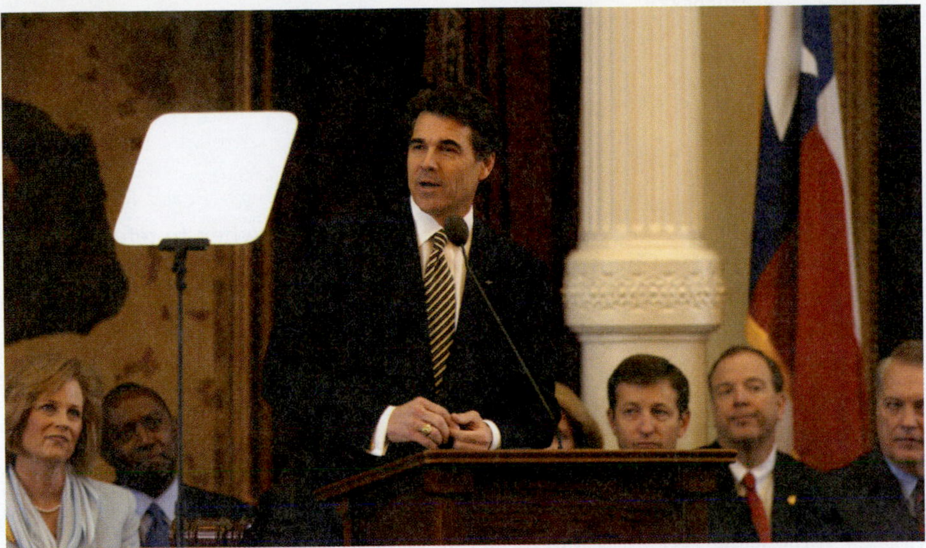

Governor Rick Perry of Texas reads his speech from a teleprompter. Since you will speak extemporaneously, use a presentation outline on note cards to remind yourself of the big ideas.

Here are some examples of oral citations:

1. "The columnist E.J. Dionne, in his 2004 book *Why Americans Hate Politics,* says..."
2. "Secretary of State Hillary Rodham Clinton was quoted in the July 1, 2012, *New York Times*..."
3. "Constitutional law scholar Erwin Chemerinsky, writing in the 2011 *Harvard Law Review*..."
4. "The Bureau of Labor Statistics unemployment rate, as reported on CNN on October 5..."
5. "According to the 1964 speech by protest leader Mario Savio archived on American-Rhetoric.com,..."

The easiest way to prepare oral citations is to put them on the note cards you will use with the presentation outline. Example 1 above might be put on the top of your note card as follows:

E.J. Dionne – columnist – 2004 – *Why Americans Hate Politics* (book)

Use of Stage Directions

Your speaking outline also can include reminders to yourself, as long as they are brief and don't interfere with the structure. Reminders like the following will alert you to things you plan to do during the speech:

I. Growing [REPEAT]
   A. Before WWI [SLOW DOWN]
   B. 1960
   C. After 1960
   D. 1996
   E. 2000
   F. 2008
   [SUMMARIZE/PAUSE]

II. Widespread [REPEAT]
   A. East
   B. Midwest
   C. South
   D. West
   [RESTATE POINT]

Your stage directions also can include cues to remind you when to refer to visual aids (to be discussed in Chapter 15). In this way, your presentation outline not only will remind you of the structural pattern of the speech, but also will help you to coordinate your actions during its delivery.

Using an Outline in Rehearsal

In Chapter 3, you learned how to practice presenting your speech. The speaking outline plays an important role in rehearsal. Be sure that its key words remind you of all the solid thinking you've done and the supporting material you've found. If a key word doesn't immediately prompt you to recall the details, change the key word to one that will. As you rehearse, it will become easier to see and remember the relationship between key words and the overall structure you have devised. Also, keep your preparation outline handy; you'll want to check during rehearsal that you are not leaving any gaps and that all your careful work is included in the speaking outline.

Sample Presentation Outline

Here is the presentation outline for Christopher Chiyung's speech on microfinance. If you compare it to the preparation outline, you will see how complete sentences have been reduced to key words, how essential stage directions have been included, and how key lines in the introduction and conclusion have been written out. As before, marginal comments are included alongside the outline. Study these to determine what is strong in the outline and what could be improved.

Presentation Outline

"Microlending in Evanston" by Christopher Chiyung

Introduction

I. **Attention-getter:** "Give a man a fish, feed him for a day; teach a man to fish, feed him for a lifetime." This maxim relates directly to a sustainable practice that isn't as well known as it should be.

II. **Thesis:** Microlending in Evanston is crucial to allow depressed businesses to survive, institutions to be adequately funded, and the standard of living to rise.

Some key words might be in order here so the speaker will recall the key points in the preview.

III. **Preview**

Body

I. Effectiveness
   A. Empirical evidence from Bangladesh [GLOBAL ENVISION]
   B. MarketWatch in St. Louis
   C. Businesses in west Evanston [ANALOGY]

[TRANSITION: Success stories are not as prevalent as they could be.]

II. MFIs lack sufficient funding
    A. 10,000 MFI's = only 4 percent of market [WORLD BANK]
    B. MFIs in United States lack access to credit or financing [ANNIBALE]
    C. Graphs

[TRANSITION: Other benefits as well]

III. Raising standard of living
    A. Creating jobs worldwide [LEMMON quote]
    B. Widespread benefits; health and education [SHERRADEN quote]
    C. Not just individuals; also communities [FLOOD quote]

[TRANSITION: Acknowledge limitations but outweigh]

Notice that there is no need to reproduce the content of the quotations so long as Christopher has their text easily at hand.

Again, some key words here would help Christopher to remember what limitations he plans to discuss.

Conclusion

I. Summary

II. Closure: Please donate to LEND and spread awareness. It's a great way to understand the socioeconomic divide between Evanston's lakefront mansions and those struggling to make it on the west side.

III. Final plea: Even better, join next school year. Then we could all teach others how to fish, not just give the fish away.

Do you think Christopher will remember the essential points of the summary? It might be helpful to include key words here.

Notice how the speaking outline follows exactly the structure of the preparation outline, while substituting key words for complete sentences and ideas. This is likely to be a valuable memory aid during the speech without getting in Christopher's way.

Strategies for Speaking to Diverse Audiences

Respecting Diversity Through Outlining the Speech

Even a seemingly mechanical process such as outlining reflects important strategic choices. These strategies will remind you how the diversity of the audience affects outlining and organization.

1. Use your outline to make sure that each of your points is treated fairly and uses balanced sources. If you discover any biases, make sure that they are intentional and chosen in light of your specific audience.
2. Pay attention to how well your speech holds together. Using your outline, consider whether your points will connect as obviously for your audience as they do for you. Do your connections or does your order depend upon implicit knowledge that your audience may not share?
3. Recognize that cultures may be differently sensitive to the order in which ideas are arranged. For example: Are points of disagreement valued more than consensus? Is analyzing problems more important than identifying solutions? Is linear progression expected more than indirect progression?

What Have You Learned?

Objective 11.1: Explain why outlining is a valuable part of speech preparation and presentation.

Outlines display the formal structure of the speech in terms of numbers and letters.

The outline allows you to do the following:

- Visualize the form of the speech
- Check your reasoning and organizational pattern

Objective 11.2: Create a preparation outline that uses proper principles of subordination and coordination.

The preparation outline:

- Is usually written in complete sentences.
- Includes separate sections for the introduction, body, and conclusion, each with separate numbering for the major divisions.
- Reflects coordination and subordination of ideas.
- Avoids overlap.
- Includes transitions as parenthetical comments.
- Includes citations within the outline or at the end in footnotes, a reference list, or a bibliography.

Objective 11.3: Adapt the preparation outline into a presentation outline that you can use in delivering your speech.

Because the preparation outline can be long and cumbersome, a presentation outline (sometimes called a *speaking outline*) is used during delivery. This outline:

- Follows the form of the preparation outline
- Is written in key words, not complete sentences
- Is reproduced on note cards
- Includes supporting material on separate note cards
- Includes information to be included in oral citations.
- May include notes about stage directions

The sample preparation and speaking outlines provided in this chapter show some of the issues to be addressed in order for the parts of a speech to come together into a well-planned, purposeful presentation.

Listen to the **Audio Chapter Summary** at **MyCommunicationLab**

Discussion Questions

1. Many speakers write speeches without first developing an outline. How does the construction of an outline help a speaker to prepare a better speech? What are the disadvantages of creating an outline?
2. When developing an outline, how do you determine which ideas are subordinate to others? How do you determine which ideas are coordinate? As a class, construct an outline of this chapter, and discuss how it demonstrates the principles of subordination and coordination.
3. In small groups, share the preparation outline for your next speech with your classmates. Discuss the following questions:
   - Do the main ideas support the thesis?
   - Are the main ideas parallel and on the same level of importance?
   - Do the subpoints support the claims made in the main ideas?
   - Are the subpoints parallel and on the same level of importance?
   - Are there places where transitions are especially needed?

Activities

1. Take an essay that you have written for another class and create an outline in order to turn this written essay into a speech. Switching outlines with a partner in class, use this chapter's discussion of outlines to critique the structure of your partner's outline.
2. Construct a preparation outline for your next speech. Then, annotate your outline, explaining why you made the decisions that you made. Model the page layout of your outline after the sample preparation outline at the end of this chapter, using marginal notes to describe your strategic choices.
3. Create a speaking outline for your next speech, and use it to rehearse. Practice and modify the speaking outline until your delivery becomes smooth.
4. Some of the marginal comments on Christopher Chiyung's outlines in this chapter identify problems with the outline. Modify the preparation and speaking outlines to correct these problems.
5. Examine the outlining features of any common word processing program. Explain how they reflect and how they differ from the principles discussed in this chapter. Is there any difference between writing an outline by hand and using a computer program?

Key Terms

coordination **268**
outline **264**
preparation outline **265**
presentation (speaking) outline **265**
subordination **267**

Study and **Review** the **Flashcards** at **MyCommunicationLab**

Notes

1 For another way of creating preparation outlines, see Collin Rae, "Before the Outline—The Writing Wheel," *Social Studies* 81 (July–August 1990): 178.

2 If you are having trouble with the mechanics of outlining, see James Gibson, *Speech Organization: A Programmed Approach*, San Francisco: Rinehart Press, 1971.

3 It has been shown that apprehensive speakers are less likely to follow the strategy that they had planned for the introduction of a speech. See Michael J. Beatty, "Public Speaking Apprehension, Decision-Making Errors in the Selection of Speech Introduction Strategies and Adherence to Strategy," *Communication Education* 37 (October 1988): 297–311. By including a detailed introduction in your speaking outline, you may be more likely to follow your plan, despite apprehension at the beginning of a speech. See, for example, Christina G. Paxman, "Map Your Way to Speech Success: Mind Mapping as a Speech Preparation Technique," *Communication Teacher* 25 (January 2011): 7–11.

CHAPTER 12

Achieving Style Through Language

LEARNING OBJECTIVES

After studying this chapter, you should be able to:

Objective 12.1	Elaborate a definition of style as the personal choices that distinguish or characterize speakers.
Objective 12.2	Identify the key differences between oral style and written style.
Objective 12.3	Illustrate how definitions affect the stylistic significance of individual words and phrases.
Objective 12.4	Achieve clarity, rhythm, and vividness.
Objective 12.5	Distinguish among levels of style and explain how variety, balance, and conciseness affect judgments of the overall style of a speech.
Objective 12.6	Enhance the stylistic quality of your speeches.

Listen to the **Audio Chapter** at **MyCommunicationLab**

OUTLINE

If you told your friends that a popular singer has an intimate style or that a politician displays a presidential style, they probably would know what you meant. Something about that person stands out and makes him or her easy to describe. There is a pattern in the person's behavior—conscious or not—that you can recognize and that may let you characterize the person as being, say, a folk-rock singer or a rising political star. Or the pattern may be unique, allowing you to distinguish that individual from all other singers or politicians.

OBJECTIVE 12.1

What Is Style?

These examples suggest a working definition of **style** as the pattern of choices attributed to a person by others to characterize or to distinguish him or her. A person's style, then, is what others perceive to be his or her manner of expression. We can elaborate on several aspects of this definition.

First, style is a pattern of *choices* that are not predetermined.[1] That is, the politician does not *have* to appear presidential. Nor does choice necessarily imply strategic awareness. The politician may or may not be conscious of all aspects of behavior that lead voters to regard one as seeming presidential. Even so, if you set out to cultivate a positive style, you *are* engaged in strategic planning, as we will see in this chapter.

Second, although we commonly say that a singer "has" a certain style, as though that style was possessed by him or her, in fact it is the fans who observe a pattern of choices, who label it as a certain style, and who then attribute the style to the singer. Style is perceived by others whose inferences and judgments attribute it to the person. Style does not exist in a vacuum. It is always audience dependent.

Third, style can be used either to set someone apart from others or to identify someone with a particular group. Some singers, actors, or politicians have a highly individualistic style; their patterns of choices make them unique among all other singers, actors, or politicians. In such a case, we say that the person's choices create a distinct **signature**. Just as your handwriting is slightly different from anyone else's and your actual signature is unique, so, too, can your speaking performance have a unique signature.

However, when a person's style is identified with a particular group, we say that the style is of a certain **type**. There are at least three ways in which a style may be of a given type:

- *Generic types* are styles that fit into a category, such as mysteries, jazz, or tragedy.[2]
- *Culture types* identify the basic styles of a culture, such as the pioneering spirit or the work ethic.[3]
- *Archetypes* are patterns of basic human experiences that recur across time and across cultures, such as the rhythm of birth and death or of struggle, defeat, and triumph.[4]

style
The pattern of choices attributed to a person by others to characterize or to distinguish him or her.

signature
An individual pattern of stylistic choices that characterizes a particular person.

type
A pattern of stylistic choices that characterizes a group with which a person identifies.

Style in a Speech

Even if we understand style in general, two common problems arise when we talk about a speaker's style. First, style is not always a positive attribute. If a politician has a bullying manner or a preacher is known for mumbling, style will hurt rather than help their effectiveness. The distinctive style of a speech can sometimes be negative, as when a speaker keeps saying, "uh," or peppers the speech with "like," or repeats "you know" so often that listeners start counting the repetitions. These are stylistic patterns, but they detract from the message rather than help it. For some speakers, the goal is to *remove* negative characteristics from a speech. In removing them, however, the speaker is not removing style, but is *changing* it from a nervous, unsure style to a smooth, confident one.

Careful word choice can help a speaker achieve a sense of balance between ideas, reinforced in this case by the gesture of extending each hand.

The other problem is that we often think of style in a speech as ornamentation that is added to the content rather than as part and parcel of the content. In this view, it is enough just to speak plainly and clearly without concern for style. Abraham Lincoln's Gettysburg Address is often cited as an example of a plain speech that is remembered far better than the highly stylistic two-hour address delivered on the same day by Edward Everett. The mistake is to think that Lincoln's speech was pure, distilled content, whereas Everett's had a great deal of added style. Lincoln's obvious stylistic features include plainness of structure, simplicity of wording, abstraction, and even brevity.[5]

If we avoid viewing style either as distracting mannerisms or as unnecessary ornamentation, we will see that the concept of style in public speaking is the same as in art, music, literature, and politics. With speeches too, style is a pattern of choices recognized and interpreted by the audience—that may categorize or distinguish the speaker. Like all other strategic choices, they are decisions about how to accomplish one's purpose in a given situation by taking advantage of opportunities and minimizing constraints.

Style and Language

Like other aspects of public speaking, style is best approached through strategic planning: identifying your resources and using them to achieve your purpose. The most significant resource for creating an effective speaking style is language, but speakers often take language for granted, paying little attention to the words they choose to express their ideas. This is a bad strategy because it surrenders control over a resource that can transform a dull speech into a memorable one. Language exerts such effects by influencing the audience's perceptions of both the speech and the speaker.

Perception of the Speech. A speaker's word choices direct listeners to view the message in one way rather than another. For example, consider these statements from two different speakers:

> The federal government is the engine of our economic strength.
>
> The federal government is a cancer destroying our independence.

Although both statements create a concrete image for the abstraction "the federal government," notice the difference in perspective. The first is a *favorable* evaluation; it urges us to view economic regulation positively. The second invites exactly the opposite reaction: The government is evaluated *unfavorably* and is viewed as a threat. The simple matter of word choice signals how each speaker feels about the subject and encourages us to evaluate it in the same way. Notice also that the word choices are inseparable from content; both statements make arguments and inferences implicitly as well as explicitly.

This brief example illustrates what happens repeatedly throughout a speech. Ideas have meaning for listeners only as those ideas are expressed in language, and the language chosen shapes the meaning of the ideas that are expressed.[6]

Perception of the Speaker. Additionally, language influences how the audience perceives the speaker as a person; that is, the speaker's *ethos*.

Again, consider some simple examples. The speaker who begins every other sentence with the word *now* will drive the audience to distraction. The speaker who needlessly uses obscure or highfalutin words may impress some listeners but also may seem distant, arrogant, or condescending. The speaker who uses words inaccurately or who mispronounces them may seem ignorant. And the speaker whose language offends listeners—as with racist, sexist, or ethnic slurs—usually loses credibility.

In contrast to these negative examples, if you effectively repeat a key word or phrase, you will actively involve listeners in your speech by helping them to identify what is important. If you use colorful, appropriate language, you can lead listeners to see things from a new perspective. If you can create a memorable "sound bite," listeners will more easily recall your point and will identify you with it. And if your wording avoids jargon, technical terms, and excess verbiage, you probably will be judged pleasing to hear.

OBJECTIVE 12.2

Oral Style Versus Written Style

A situation comedy on television requires different stylistic elements than an opera does, and the same characteristics that make a novel stylistically strong may be unacceptable in a newspaper column. In short, a style that is powerful in one medium may be ineffective in another.

In the same way, the stylistic goals that you might aim to achieve in an essay are different from the goals you would pursue in a speech. Try delivering as a speech what you have written recently as a term paper in another course. Your audience will easily recognize that this "speech" is inauthentic, difficult to follow, and perhaps even boring. Your term paper will not succeed as a speech because you have been trained to write for the eye, not for the ear.

Some differences between written and oral presentations are fairly obvious. You can read written material at your own pace, skimming some sections and reading other parts more closely. If something is unclear, you can go back and reread it. If there's an unfamiliar concept, you can stop and look it up. If you lose track of the author's main argument or organizational structure, you can go back and review it. And if you get tired, you can put the writing aside and return to it later.

A speech has none of these characteristics. Although you could record a speech and replay it later, this is rarely done. In most cases, a speech is ephemeral—it is delivered, and then it is gone. Listeners cannot control the pace of delivery; each of them must attend to the same idea at the same time. There's no "pause" button that makes the speaker wait while you consult a source to check something that you don't understand. If you forget the speaker's main points or structure, you can't review them. For all these reasons, listeners are much more dependent on the speaker than readers are on the writer. And because concentration is always important and always difficult, the speaker must make the speech as easy as possible for listeners to follow and remember.[7]

Rhetorical Workout

Write for the Ear

Writing for the ear in a speech is different from writing for the eye in a paper. The example sentence below was written for the eye. Practice rewriting it for the ear by using the factors for developing an oral style.

Example: The underground bomb North Korea detonated in May 2009 was equivalent in strength to those dropped by the United States on the Japanese cities of Nagasaki and Hiroshima.

1. *Simplicity:* Rewrite the sentence to simplify it. What could you say instead of "detonated"? How could you rewrite "was equivalent in strength" in more common language? How could you split the sentence into two shorter sentences? How does your result sound when you read it aloud?
2. *Repetition:* Rewrite the sentence so that you repeat "dropped by the United States." Split the sentence into two if needed. When you read your result aloud, is it easy to say? Does it emphasize this phrase effectively? If not, try a different version.
3. *Informality:* Rewrite the sentence to make it more informal. What would you say if you were simply telling your instructor this information? Write it down. In what ways does this look different from your previous versions? Read it aloud. How does it sound?
4. *Reflexivity:* Rewrite the sentence to refer to yourself and your classroom audience. Where could you use "I" or "we"? How does it affect the impact of the sentence?
5. *Putting it all together:* What parts of your previous versions sounded the best when read aloud? Was the information easier to follow if you used one sentence or two? Drawing from your earlier versions, rewrite the sentence as you would use it in a speech.

Given these differences between writing and speaking, you will want to consider the following factors when developing an oral style.

Simplicity. Oral style is simpler than written style. Speakers use shorter and more common words. Descriptions are briefer. Sentences are shorter and less complex. Jargon and technical language are avoided. The organization of the speech is clearly identified through summaries, transitions, and previews. All these features of oral style reflect the fact that, unlike the writer, the speaker must seek instant understanding. If listeners have to puzzle out the speaker's meaning or intention, they have less mental energy for concentrating on what comes next. This does not mean that you should "dumb down" the speech or talk down to your audience, but that your language choices should make your message easy for your listeners to understand.

Repetition. Oral style is more repetitive than written style. A speaker might repeat key ideas for emphasis or to ensure that listeners did not ignore them. A catchy phrase or refrain might recur throughout the speech. Even the structure of the speech might follow a repetitive pattern. (This element of oral style is found in print as well. Notice that each heading in this section is followed by the words "Oral style is …")

If not overdone, repetition serves several purposes. It can highlight your main ideas and provide emphasis, much like italic or boldface type in print. Similarly, repetition of a particular sentence structure can help listeners "see" the pattern of your speech, allowing them to follow and anticipate its organization. Repetition is also a memory aid for both speaker and listeners.

Watch the **Video** "Classic Speech: Franklin D. Roosevelt's New Deal (clip)" at **MyCommunicationLab**

Informality. Oral style is more informal than written style. Few of us always speak in complete sentences. Nor do we observe all the grammar rules of standard English. And we use contractions (such as "can't" and "don't") far more frequently than in writing. In fact, were you to transcribe and read one of your speeches, you probably would find a number of grammatical errors and incomplete sentences; yet when you deliver the speech aloud, these aren't noticed. Speeches often do not read well, just as essays often do not sound well.

Reflexivity. Oral style is more **reflexive** than written style, meaning that speakers often refer to themselves and to the audience and situation. In contrast, your English composition teachers may have told you to limit the use of *I* in your essays and to avoid statements that—although perfectly clear to you and your classmates—might be unclear to outsiders. Written material is often composed without a specific audience in mind; indeed, writers sometimes intend to transcend particular audiences. Speakers, on the other hand, usually intend to have an impact on a specific audience, which they analyze as described in Chapter 5.

Speakers are also more likely to make their organizational structure explicit, saying things like

Here's how I'm going to develop my idea . . .
Let me review my three main points.
Now, to conclude . . .

Because listeners cannot stop your speech to check its organization, or put it aside when their concentration wavers, you must help them follow your train of thought. You do this by referring explicitly to your outline and by such devices as signposting, using internal previews, and using internal summaries (see Chapter 10).

Potential for Clutter. Oral style is more likely to include clutter, because speakers are thinking on their feet and cannot revise their remarks as writers can. Sometimes the thinking and the speech get "out of sync," and—often unknowingly—a speaker may fill the gap with unrelated and unplanned words until the thinking and the speech are brought back into line. The result is clutter: vocalized pauses (*um, er, ah*), digressions, pointless repetition, and distracting words (*right, you know, okay*).

Because clutter usually occurs when you need some time to think about what you will say next, the remedy lies in your preparation. Before speaking, make sure that you have a strong sense of your outline, your main ideas, and how you will develop your thesis. Preparation helps you to avoid clutter and makes the speech flow smoothly.

Performative Versus Conversational Style

There is not just one "oral style." A recitation of a Shakespearean sonnet is very different from a speech at a protest rally, and a sermon is very different from a story—even though all of these messages are delivered orally. It is useful to distinguish between a *performative* and a *conversational* style. Performative style, as its name suggests, reminds listeners of a performance for which the audience consists of passive spectators. The performers are concerned primarily with expressing themselves and only secondarily with establishing a relationship with the audience members. In contrast, conversational style suggests that listeners are more active participants in a discussion with the speaker, who wants first and foremost

reflexive
Making self-reference to the speaker or situation.

to establish a connection with them. Giving a virtuoso performance is only a secondary concern, if it enters into the speaker's mind at all.

Until the television age, formal speeches at large public gatherings called for a performative style. Oratory was seen as a performance. Conversely, speeches to small groups or to one's peers were thought to call for a conversational style. But television has changed these norms. The small screen reduces the formal speech from a mass public event to a discussion in your living room. Contemporary politicians often speak with the informality and intimacy that fit a conversational style.[8] As President Reagan could, Presidents Clinton and Obama effectively establish bonds with listeners through a conversational style.

President Barack Obama uses gestures to add emphasis to his word choice in a speech at the G-20 economic conference in Mexico.

It is tempting to conclude that the day of the performative style has passed and that you should always speak informally, in a conversational style. Certainly most classroom speeches will be more effective if you speak informally and conversationally. But formal sermons, polished lectures, testimony in hearings and committees, and protest speeches are all examples in which a performative style usually is more appropriate. Even so, not all performative styles may be suitable. For example, in 2010 comedian Stephen Colbert was asked to testify before Congress. He performed as a comedian rather than an expert, which achieved his purpose of satirizing the congressional hearing but did not garner the goodwill of the members of Congress before whom he testified. You need to select the style that is most helpful to your strategic purpose and most appropriate to the opportunities and constraints of the situation.[9]

Basic Requirements for Effective Style

Before we examine some specific stylistic resources that are available to speakers, it is important to recognize two basic requirements for effective style in all speaking situations:

- The accuracy of what you say
- The appropriateness of what you say

Accuracy. Some philosophers think that there is no such thing as an "accurate" or "inaccurate" use of words, because the connection between a word and the thing for which it stands is just a matter of social convention, which changes. In everyday usage, however, it is meaningful to talk about using words accurately. Speakers who use a word in a way that is significantly different from common usage will appear not to know what they are talking about. Sometimes, this can be funny, as when a student speaking about medical research said,

> I know that there is a cadaver shortage, but we can train new ones in two weeks.

The student obviously didn't understand what *cadaver* meant. And although his slip delighted listeners, they were not just laughing along with a jovial speaker.

CHOOSE A STRATEGY: Using Appropriate Language

The Situation

You work part time for a local software company and have been asked by your boss to talk to a group of foreign visitors about your experiences working at the company, raising a family, and going to school—all at the same time. Your employer naturally wants you to emphasize the company's flexibility in helping you fulfill your other obligations and the benefits you have received working there. You're aware, though, that this English-speaking group of male and female visitors, from different countries and of different ages, does not necessarily share value and belief systems (either with each other or with you). They may not agree that a "balancing act" like yours is a good thing, or they may think you have divided loyalties. Unfortunately, you do not have the time to investigate all of their backgrounds to determine the best approach to the situation—but you do know that how you phrase the benefits and what language you choose will have an impact on their overall impression of you and the company.

Making Choices

1. How will you phrase the thesis of your speech to avoid any negative reactions from those who value obligation to family more highly than education?
2. What language strategies would you employ to make the speech sound appealing to the entire group?
3. How can you use language to establish a common ground with everyone in the group?

What If...

How would your language choices change if:

1. You were male instead of female or female instead of male?
2. You were a full-time college student without a family talking to the same group about the benefits of working at this company while going to school?

At the least, they were distracted. And the impression that the speaker was inept weakened his credibility.

Mrs. Malaprop, a character in an eighteenth-century play, repeatedly misused words and has given her name to another kind of inaccurate usage. A **malapropism** is the seemingly unintentional but possibly meaningful confusion of words or usages. While a presidential candidate, George W. Bush occasionally misspoke in this way. He referred to the danger that others might "hold this nation hostile" (he meant "hostage") and, in a speech on world trade, spoke about "terriers" (he meant "barriers"). An especially famous malapropism from over a generation ago came from Chicago Mayor Richard J. Daley. After the 1968 Democratic National Convention broke out in riots that some blamed on the aggressive conduct of the Chicago police, he told a press conference,

> The police aren't there to *create* disorder; the police are there to *preserve* disorder.

The mayor obviously meant something different from what he said. But his malapropism caused many listeners not to take him seriously and even to suppose that he had made a "Freudian slip" that revealed his "deeper" thoughts. Animated characters, such as Homer Simpson from *The Simpsons* or Peter Griffin from *Family Guy*, often use malapropisms. Although audiences are delighted by gross usage errors in humorous situations, a malapropism can be devastating to a speaker's credibility.

malapropism
Unintentional but possibly meaningful confusion of words or usages.

Appropriateness to the Audience and Situation. The second basic requirement for effective style is that your words be appropriate to the audience and situation. You want to show listeners that you are sympathetic and respectful.

If your words make them feel patronized, insulted, or taunted, your style will undercut your message.

Be especially sensitive to wording when your listeners have different cultural backgrounds, or you may easily offend someone. Also make sure that your overall tone matches what is expected in the situation. Vulgar language, for instance, would be jarring in a formal lecture. And although you may think you have an engaging dry wit, you might be surprised to discover that listeners perceive sarcasm that went beyond the bounds of acceptable irony.

Because every situation is different, it is hard to say what word choices will make your style seem appropriate, but the following general guidelines can help:

1. *Avoid sounding self-important or pretentious.* Do not use language that will make listeners think you are arrogant. The physics major who made fleeting references to "dark matter" and "superstring theory" without explaining what he meant was probably showing off rather than genuinely trying to communicate. Similarly, when a student speaker argued that the university should require more core courses, her language implied that her classmates were culturally illiterate:

   > A broad liberal arts background is essential for our generation to cope with the postmodern condition in which we find ourselves thrown. The fact that most of you cannot name the last 10 presidents and that many of you have no concept of even the most basic political, social, or literary theory signals an epistemological breakdown in our culture.

   Remember that you are seeking a favorable response from your audience. Usually, the most effective routes toward that goal are to establish common bonds and to stress significant points of similarity between you and the audience. No one enjoys being talked down to by a speaker. Listeners will resist your message if your language or attitude seems superior.

2. *Avoid signs of disrespect.* Racial slurs, sexist references, and ethnic jokes clearly fall into this category. Because such comments debase and degrade other people, most listeners regard them as inappropriate even if not directed at them personally. The best rule is the simplest: Don't use such language, not even to poke fun at yourself.

Explore the **Exercise** "Sexist Language" at **MyCommunicationLab**

3. *Avoid inappropriate emotion.* Just as you obviously would not choose the occasion of a funeral eulogy to speak badly of the deceased, neither would you prepare an after-dinner speech that is somber or gloomy. Cultures vary in what emotions are considered appropriate for a given occasion. Situational expectations also are not absolute, and speakers sometimes deliberately violate them in certain circumstances. But that should happen only for a clear purpose. As a general rule, analyze the nature of the speaking situation, and aim to keep your style and tone within the boundaries of what the audience expects.

Once you are certain that your speech meets these minimal conditions for effective style, you can consider various stylistic resources and make language choices that enhance your appeal. You can choose and arrange words to capitalize on their descriptive or persuasive power; to achieve clarity, rhythm, and vividness; and to create interest and balance in your speech.

As we examine the major resources available, understand that we will not even come close to the limits. Centuries ago, handbooks listed 200 or more variations in word usage that could be adapted by eager speakers.[10] Clearly, in this chapter, we are just beginning to scratch the surface.

OBJECTIVE 12.3

Defining Terms Appropriately

One of the most important stylistic resources is **definition**, the process by which you establish the meaning of a word for your audience. In defining a word, your choices range from neutral to persuasive, and your decisions should take into account all aspects of the rhetorical situation.

Neutral Definitions

Sometimes a speaker defines words in a fairly neutral way, with no goal other than being precise and clear. Although no definition is entirely neutral, in this case the speaker does not really want to change listeners' views about the thing described. The following definitional strategies are relatively neutral.

Replacing a Common Meaning with a More Technical Meaning.

A teacher of rhetoric might begin an introductory lecture this way:

> Many people, when they think about *rhetoric*, conjure up images of endless political speeches full of bombast and posturing which really don't end up saying anything. But to the Romans of antiquity, rhetoric was one of the seven liberal arts, a set of skills which was not inherently good or inherently bad, but capable of use for good or evil alike.

In this case, the teacher's goal is to invite students to equate the term *rhetoric* with classical antiquity rather than with contemporary popular usage. The common meaning is inadequate for the teacher's purposes because it distinguishes between rhetoric and content—precisely the distinction to which the teacher objects.

Defining by Similarities and Differences. You can convey to listeners a more precise meaning of a term if you can both distinguish the term and compare it with something the audience already knows. Someone speaking about the Internet might say,

> Not all people who have access to the Internet access it at the same pace. Internet bandwith determines how fast we can access information. Bandwidth is a data highway, and with higher bandwidth, more data can travel because there are more "lanes." But because the speed limit is set by the laws of physics, not by society's laws, data do not "speed" as a motorist might. Rather, data are less likely to get caught in other people's Internet traffic.

Thus the term *bandwidth* is defined both by comparing it to a highway and by showing how it is different.

Operational Definitions. An abstraction can often be defined by an **operational definition**, which explains the meaning of the term by identifying specific operations to be performed. A speaker might ask, "How will we know when we have dealt effectively with worldwide famine?" The answer to the question—"When we have doubled the amount of food aid and when the rate of death by starvation is cut in half"—makes the abstract concept of "effective famine reduction" concrete by defining it in terms of what must be done to achieve it.

In each of these neutral examples of definitions, any shift in the audience's perceptions and attitudes about the topic is incidental to the speaker's goal of clarifying meaning and usage. Often, however, as shown in the next two sections, speakers use definition *precisely* to change listeners' perceptions and judgments.

definition
The process of establishing meaning for a word or phrase.

operational definition
Explaining what a term means by identifying specific operations to be performed.

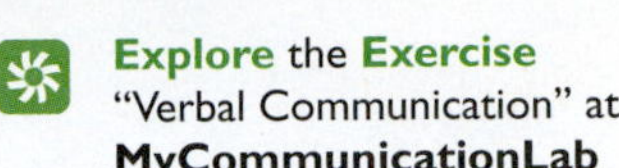
Explore the **Exercise** "Verbal Communication" at **MyCommunicationLab**

Denotation and Connotation in Definitions

Words have meaning on at least two levels. A word's **denotation** is what it refers to, or "denotes"; its denotation is similar to its dictionary definition. For example, the denotation for *chair* is "a seat with four legs and a back intended for one person." At the same time, a word also evokes feelings. This second dimension of meaning is **connotation**. The connotation of *chair* is relatively neutral. But if a speaker referred to this object as a "throne," listeners might respond with feelings of respect or dignity (unless, of course, the speaker was being ironic or sarcastic).

Moving from physical objects to abstractions, the influence of connotation is even stronger. *Liberal* denotes a person who adheres to a particular political philosophy, but its connotation has changed considerably over the years. During the 1930s, and again during the 1960s, *liberal* typically had positive connotations, suggesting farsightedness, vision, and idealism. Since the 1980s, however, the same word with the same denotation took on quite different connotations, suggesting poor judgment, impracticality, and waste. Because of these shifts in connotation, someone who might have been proud to be called a liberal in 1965 would probably have preferred a designation such as "moderate" or "progressive" in 2012.

As a speaker, you naturally will want to use words whose connotations are consistent with your goals—positive connotations if you want to praise or advocate, negative connotations if you want to condemn or dissuade. But you want to be sure that your listeners share what you regard as positive or negative connotations. Otherwise they will be less likely to accept your viewpoint and may accuse you of simply assuming what you really need to prove.

Consider, for example, the connotations in student Zana Kuljanian's speech about why the death penalty should be abolished. She never used the term *capital punishment*:

> There is no reason why we should sanction state-sponsored murder. State-sponsored murder is immoral, unconstitutional, and dangerous. Nevertheless, we allow these organized public assassinations to proceed at an alarming pace.

Because Zana used words such as *murder* and *assassinations*, she was not very successful at persuading listeners who didn't already agree with her. Similarly, the white student who called capital punishment "justice for barbaric criminals" was not well received by black listeners, who saw racism rather than justice behind the fact that black prisoners are executed in disproportionately large numbers. However, if either speaker had faced an audience of people already in agreement with the message, these connotations would have reinforced their agreement.

Persuasive Definitions

The shifting connotation of *liberal* since the 1980s illustrates the persuasive power of definitions. Its connotation changed not by accident, but by the deliberate choice of "conservative" politicians to make *liberal* a word of criticism rather than of praise. To do this, they associated the previously positive word with phrases that have negative connotations, such as "big government," "special interests," and "tax and spend." These new associations allowed them to shift the commonly accepted connotation of *liberal* while preserving its denotation.

denotation
The referent for a given word.

connotation
The feelings or emotional responses associated with a given word.

Persuasive definition can take two forms. In this example, the denotative meaning of *liberal* remained the same while its connotative meaning changed. The word identified the same people as liberals, but its connotation changed from positive to negative. Alternatively, connotative meaning can stay the same while denotative meaning changes. Consider the phrase "special interests." Its connotations are negative because "special interests" are seen in contrast to the general or public interest. Throughout much of the twentieth century, "special interests" were associated with big business and with people of great wealth. During the 1990s, however, they came to be associated with advocates for women's rights, for multiculturalism, for labor, or for abortion rights. Although the phrase retained its negative connotations, the people to whom it referred were considerably different.

Freedom is a good example of a term that is susceptible to persuasive definition. Unlike "special interests," its connotation is positive. Not surprisingly, it has been used to characterize a variety of objects speakers wanted their audiences to favor, ranging all the way from the Iraqi war of 2003 ("Operation Enduring Freedom") to the purchase of consumer goods and services that promise to give you freedom from drudgery, worry, or limits on your lifestyle.[11]

You may be wondering how one goes about persuasive definition. Connotations, after all, are not easily abandoned. How does one break the connection between a word and what it "means"? Often, it's done by finding a different connotation that people will respond to. Affirmative action programs came under assault during the early 2000s because critics called them "reverse discrimination"—suggesting that, far from helping the goal of equal opportunity, they were counterproductive. In 2009, Sarah Palin referred to a proposal to reimburse physicians offering end-of-life counseling as "death panels" in order to arouse opposition to health-care reform legislation. Because of public concern, the proposal was removed from the legislation, but "death panels" continued to offer a shorthand way for people to signal their disagreement with the larger piece of legislation.[12]

Persuasive definition occurs not only in public life but also in the public speaking classroom. Student Jon Peterson wanted to convince listeners that licensed deer hunting was not a bad thing. Unfortunately, most of his audience had the image of Bambi's mother in mind whenever he uttered the word *deer*. To alter this connotation, Jon created a different vision of what deer are like:

> The Disney cartoon version of a deer is touching. But the innocent creature portrayed in *Bambi* is just as inaccurate as Disney's version of a mouse called Mickey that stands on two feet and wears gloves. To farmers trying to protect their crops, suburbanites trying to grow shrubbery, even nuns trying to tend their garden, overpopulated deer have become large rats with hooves. They eat everything in sight and leave a wake of destruction in their path.

Every speaker has important resources of definition. If your topic is an unpopular proposal to increase students' tuition and fees, you will induce very different reactions in listeners by characterizing the proposal as "extortion" rather than as "fair pricing." Likewise, even though you cannot affect how the whole society views an issue such as health care, you *can* affect how your audience will view it—by deciding, for instance, whether to define national health insurance as "cost containment" or as "socialized medicine." Your ability to use language in defining a situation will affect how your audience perceives and reacts to it.

persuasive definition
A shift in connotation applied to the same denotation or a shift in denotation applied to the same connotation.

Achieving Clarity, Rhythm, and Vividness

OBJECTIVE 12.4

Just as you can affect the style of a speech by making persuasive definitions, so you can affect its style through language that creates clarity, rhythm, and vividness. Table 12.1 lists the strategies that we will consider to achieve these three goals.

Clarity

Because listeners usually cannot replay your speech, you should make the speech as easy to comprehend as is appropriate for the situation. The following stylistic resources can increase the clarity of your message.

Concrete Words. If listeners have to puzzle out the meaning of your words, they will be distracted from your train of thought. And if they don't decipher your meaning correctly, your message will not get through to them. Because most people process images more easily than abstract concepts, your message will be clearer if you use concrete words and images. The speaker who tries to help listeners grasp the magnitude of "a trillion dollars" by calculating the length of a line of dollar bills laid end to end may be offering a trite example, but the effort is sensible. Concrete, clear images help an audience grasp and remember a message; as a result, listeners are more likely to be swayed by it.

Watch the Video "Classic Speech: Harry S. Truman's Decision to Drop the Bomb (clip)" at **MyCommunicationLab**

Maxims. **Maxims**, or aphorisms, are short, pithy statements—often in the form of proverbs—that are familiar to most people and can be used to describe a situation or idea. Maxims contribute to clarity by offering listeners a memorable phrase that encompasses a larger argument or theme. The speaker who wants to downplay the fears of critics who have suggested obstacles to his plan to reform the fraternity system might say, in the words of a popular commercial for athletic apparel, "Just do it." This maxim succinctly expresses a thought that most people will grasp intuitively: An idea can be talked to death; sometimes, one just has to act. Another speaker who wants to inspire confidence that a difficult goal can be accomplished might refer to a popular slogan from the 2008 presidential election, assuring the audience,

> Some say we can't solve this problem, but I say: Yes we can.

In this case the maxim says that hope should prevail over doubt.

Table 12.1 Achieving clarity, rhythm, and vividness

Clarity	Rhythm	Vividness
• Concrete words • Maxims • Limiting jargon and defining technical terms • Word economy • Active voice • Careful use of irony • Purposeful ambiguity	• Repetition • Parallel wording • Antithesis • Inversions of word order	• Description • Stories • Comparisons: simile and metaphor • Vivid sounds: alliteration and onomatopoeia • Personification • Reference to hypothetical people: dialogue and rhetorical questions

maxim
A concise statement of a principle, often in the form of a proverb; also called an *aphorism*.

Limiting Jargon, Defining Technical Terms. Virtually every field of knowledge has **jargon**—specialized or technical terms that outsiders find difficult to understand. Lawyers, for example, speak of "torts," "probable cause," and "incompetent testimony," but few who are not trained in law will know exactly what these terms mean. Similarly, when student Tracy Hocutt gave a speech about artificial turf, she tossed around such terms as *turf burns* and *staph infections*. Although this is common language for athletes, Tracy was talking over the heads of most of her audience.

Science, athletics, religion, medicine, music, accounting, and even public speaking have specialized languages that make it easier for people within the field to discuss issues and to understand each other. But because specialized terms and jargon may confuse outsiders, you should avoid using them in a speech. The reason is simple: Unless all your listeners are familiar with the specialized meanings, such terms will make your speech difficult to comprehend. And unless *you* are very familiar with the field and its specialized language, you run the risk of using the terms inaccurately or inappropriately.

Even places can generate a specialized language. Every college campus, for example, has its own terms to designate campus landmarks, types of courses, procedures and rules, and the like. If you're speaking on campus or addressing an alumni audience, you can use these terms freely, especially to help establish common bonds with your audience. Jargon can be useful when everyone knows what it means. But if you're speaking to a general audience, you should avoid specialized terms for the same reason that you avoid professional jargon—to make your meaning clear.

It's not always possible to rid your speech of every last **technical term**. There may be no easily understood equivalent for the term, or it may be important to distinguish the technical term from a more general, popularized concept. In such cases, use technical terms as needed, but be sure to define them clearly and carefully. Some good strategies are to repeat the definition, to restate it differently, or to offer examples that illustrate it.

Word Economy. You can increase the clarity of your message through **word economy**—using words efficiently and avoiding unnecessary words. Listeners find it difficult and tiresome to follow a speech that beats around the bush, that is cluttered with digressions, extraneous ideas, inexact wording, and nervous asides such as *like, okay, now*, or *right* in nearly every sentence. They also have trouble understanding overly complex sentences, excessive use of adjectives and adverbs, and needless hedging terms or qualifiers.

Active Voice. In writing and speaking, we can distinguish between the **active voice**, which focuses on *who did what* ("John hit the ball"), and the **passive voice**, which focuses on *what was done* ("The ball was hit by John"). The passive voice is much less personal than the active voice.

For clarity, you generally should use the active voice. It makes clear who does what, and it usually requires fewer and simpler words to express an idea. Use the passive voice only when focusing on the person might distract attention from the act or consequences you want to emphasize.

How Clear Should You Be?

We began this section by observing that you want to be as clear as is appropriate. That is not always the same thing as saying "exactly what you mean" and being so clear that the speech is transparent. Here are two uses of language that enable you, when circumstances call for it, to be a bit more subtle than that.

jargon
Specialized or technical terms within a given field of knowledge.

technical term
A term that may or may not be widely used in ordinary conversation but that has a specific meaning within a particular field of knowledge.

word economy
Efficiency in the use of words; avoidance of unnecessary words.

active voice
A word pattern that focuses on who did what and prominently features the agent.

passive voice
A word pattern that focuses on what was done and largely ignores the agent.

Careful Use of Irony. Speakers use **irony** when they say the opposite of what they mean, often with a shift in vocal tone or another nonverbal clue that they do not intend to be taken literally. If you recite a long list of complaints about the quality of the campus food service and then conclude by saying, "No one, it seems, can find fault with the food on our campus"—while really meaning the opposite—you have made an ironic statement. Listeners may chuckle as they realize the great gulf between what you're saying and the reality that you have just described. The reason to use irony in this situation is that you might not want your criticism to be too harsh. You don't want to seem like you are whining or that you are impossible to please, because either of those reactions would cause the people in charge of food service to dismiss your complaints without acting on them. So you coat what you say in an ironic expression that is like a disarming smile. Listeners hear what you say, figure out what you really mean, and realize that you remained in good humor even while being critical.

The listener has just one chance to understand the speaker's message. The successful speaker can help to make that happen by seeking to achieve clarity, rhythm, and vividness while speaking.

Likewise, a speaker once referred to a group of tabloid publications at the supermarket checkout counter as "learned journals" in order to make the point that the information in these publications should not be given much weight. Carefully used, irony also can be a way for speakers to signal to the audience that they take their ideas seriously but don't take themselves too seriously.

Be aware, however, that irony can make a speech less clear if listeners cannot recognize it as irony. Student Mark Nielson tried to mock animal rights activists in a speech ironically "praising" them:

> We have come here to praise those brave souls, standing out in the rain with their dogs shivering in the cold, as they stand up against the inhumane treatment of animals.

Mark thought that his use of irony was clear; to his dismay, however, he learned that most listeners thought he was sincere in commending the activists. If you decide to use irony, be certain to provide enough clues so that listeners will not be in doubt about what you really mean.[13]

Purposeful Ambiguity. Words or phrases that can be interpreted in more than one way are said to be **ambiguous**, and speakers striving for clarity generally avoid them. If you use the word *conviction* in a context in which some listeners think you mean "deeply held belief" and others think you mean "judgment of guilt," you probably will not have everyone understand you. But there are some cases in which a speaker deliberately and purposefully uses ambiguity.

The presidential election of 2000 turned on the vote in Florida, where the outcome was a virtual tie. In contesting the award of the state to George W. Bush, Al Gore alleged that thousands of votes had not yet been counted. Bush insisted that they had been both counted and recounted. The disagreement turned on what it meant to "count" a vote. The ballots in question had been run through counting

irony
Saying or writing the opposite of what is meant.

ambiguous
Capable of being interpreted with more than one meaning.

machines, but the machines recorded no presidential vote. Bush thought they had been counted, because they had been processed; Gore thought they had not, because they had not been tallied for anyone. But each found it advantageous to leave the term *count* ambiguous. Bush could portray Gore as persisting beyond reason in his challenge, and Gore could portray Bush as disregarding the wishes of thousands of Floridians. Meanwhile, each speaker could act as though the audience clearly agreed with his interpretation of the term, even though he never made that interpretation explicit.

Public speakers often engage in purposeful ambiguity when they use language to provide a rallying point for listeners who have different interests and agendas. In this case, the ambiguous reference is called a **condensation symbol**, because it condenses harmoniously in one word or phrase a variety of attitudes that might diverge if the reference were more specific.[14]

The phrase "family values" is a good example of a condensation symbol. Virtually everyone can be expected to value families, but "family values" may conjure up an array of very different themes. For example, both pro-life and pro-choice supporters believe that their position on the abortion issue better promotes "family values." Most people—whether loggers protesting the loss of jobs because of laws that protect forests or environmental activists concerned about the future of "the human family"—may view their own position as the one that most values families. Recently, "family values" has been invoked both to support and to attack proposals to legalize gay marriage. Without ambiguity, it would be impossible to enlist the power of family imagery to draw support from listeners with so many different opinions and interests.

Condensation symbols are especially useful when addressing an audience that is culturally diverse. They are **multivocal**, meaning that they communicate on many different levels at once. Diverse audience members hear a condensation symbol as having different denotations but a common connotation, whether positive or negative. For example, one educator supports "No Child Left Behind," meaning expanded special education programs. Another also supports "No Child Left Behind," meaning increased support for underperforming school districts. A third agrees, calling attention to disparities in educational achievement based on race. And a fourth also agrees, having in mind the testing and achievement requirements contained in the "No Child Left Behind" federal education law. The term means something different to each listener, although the meanings are not in conflict. And all four agree that they support "No Child Left Behind." The multivocal term enabled the speaker to embrace different levels of meaning. The goal, then, is not always to avoid ambiguity altogether but to limit it to the appropriate level for your specific audience and situation.

condensation symbol
A word, phrase, or thing that harmoniously accommodates (condenses) diverse ideas or references within a single positive or negative connotation.

multivocal
Speaking simultaneously with different "voices" or on different levels of denotative meaning but with similar connotations.

rhythm
The sense of movement or pacing within a speech.

Rhythm

Because a speech is heard, not read, the sound of the message contributes greatly to its stylistic effect. Language choices that affect the **rhythm**, or pace, of the speech can help to convey a mood—of loftiness, of momentum, or of equilibrium, for example. Moreover, listeners who grasp the pattern of the rhythm can anticipate what is coming next. These effects of rhythm on listeners make clear that it is not just embellishment for the speech; it is integral to the speaker's achieving his or her purpose. The following stylistic resources are especially useful in affecting the rhythm of a speech.

Repetition. Repeating a key idea, argument, or theme is a way to emphasize its significance. The speaker who says,

> The incarceration rate in the United States is astonishingly high—higher than Canada's, higher than England's, higher than Singapore's, higher even than China's.

has left little doubt that the central point is the magnitude of the U.S. incarceration rate. Properly used, repetition acts like bold or italic type in printed material. It tells the audience, "Here is a really important idea." Use repetition selectively, however, or its power will diminish.

Another kind of repetition is a refrain that the speaker begins and the audience joins in or completes. Knowing that the speaker will be pausing for the refrain holds listeners' attention, and shouting out the refrain involves them actively in the speech. Political speakers often use such a repetitive refrain to rally support, and it is also common in protest rallies. Preachers, too—particularly in some mostly African American communities—are fond of using this pattern of **call and response** with their congregations.[15] This form of repetition helps the speaker and listeners bond as they jointly create the rhythmic pattern.

Parallel Wording. A speaker who uses one of the familiar organizational patterns described in Chapter 9 will find that listeners are following along and can guess what will come next. Assume that your topic is unemployment. If you begin by saying, "Here's how unemployment developed in the past," and then you ask, "What's the nature of unemployment in the present?" a careful listener will guess that your next major organizational unit will have something to do with the future. You can further emphasize this pattern, and heighten its effect, by using parallel wording:

> Unemployment has been a tragedy in the past.
> Unemployment is a tragedy in the present.
> Unemployment will continue to be a tragedy in the future.

Parallel wording is stylistically useful even at levels lower than the statement of main ideas. The challenging candidate who insists that the incumbent is "out of luck, out of touch, and come November will be out of office" has created a parallel pattern that listeners can follow easily and in which many can participate. By the time the speaker says, "come November," most listeners can probably figure out that the last item will be "out of office." The rhythm of the three-part pattern is catchy and easy to remember, and being involved in creating it will make listeners more likely to accept it.

Antithesis. Another rhythmic resource is **antithesis**, the pairing of opposites within the speech. Besides suggesting to listeners that the speaker is clever, antithesis also creates a kind of equilibrium, or balance, in which competing views are weighed and taken seriously. As was mentioned earlier, President John F. Kennedy was noted for his stylistic effectiveness as a speaker, and most particularly for his use of antithesis. In his inaugural address, for example, he said,

> Let us never negotiate out of fear. But let us never fear to negotiate.

In promoting individual responsibility and voluntarism, he said,

> Ask not what your country can do for you—ask what you can do for your country.

call and response
A pattern in which the audience responds to a speaker's questions or prompts, often with a repetitive refrain.

antithesis
The pairing of opposites within a speech, often to suggest a choice between them.

The first parts of these statements acknowledge that there are concerns; the second parts transcend them. The use of antithesis suggests that the speaker is aware of the concerns but is prepared to deal with them.[16]

Sometimes antitheses are more subtle. A tourist destination may advertise, "Come for the weather; stay for the people," using the terms *come* and *stay* as opposites. Or a business executive facing a crisis might say, "The question isn't how we got into this problem, it's what we do now." Although these are not as precisely balanced as some of President Kennedy's antitheses, they are similar in their comparison of opposites.

Inversions of Word Order. Variations from normal word order, even if they are not antitheses, may cause listeners to sit up and take notice because an unusual phrase is memorable. In spoken English, the normal word order is subject–verb–object. A variation on this, if not overdone, will attract notice simply because the sound of the speech is different from what is expected. In Kennedy's speech, the phrase "Ask not" differs from the more normal word order, "Do not ask." This inversion attracts extra attention to the sentence.

Vividness

Watch the **Video** "Informative Speech/Self-Introduction: My Twenty-First Birthday Party" at **MyCommunicationLab**

Beyond clarity and rhythm, a third stylistic resource is the ability to make sentences or paragraphs **vivid**—to present in words what are really compelling visual images, pictures that listeners can see in their mind's eye. Not only does vividness add color and interest, but also it makes the speech easier to understand. Again, a variety of stylistic resources are available to make your speech vivid.

Description. Probably the most common way to paint mental pictures is by **description**, by giving specific details. Nearly every day we describe someone in terms of gender and age, height and weight, color of eyes and hair, occupation and interests, style of dress, characteristic attitudes, relationships with others, and so on. The composite of all these details creates the mental picture or image of that person.

Similarly, a speaker can use an accumulation of details to describe an event, a place, or a situation. Student speaker Jennifer Frantz used that strategy to set the tone for an antidrug speech; she began by describing a Swiss park called the Platzspitz:

> It was once a tranquil park, where families could picnic and children could play. Now it is covered with syringes, infested with rats, and inhabited by addicts who no longer have hope. When you see a mother, a father, and a small child lying on the ground and suddenly the mother wakes up, reaches out, and violently shoves a needle into her leg, you begin to wonder what the world is coming to.

Stories. A story has power not only because of its familiar narrative form, but also because it permits listeners to "see" what is going on and to identify with it. An issue such as homelessness, for example, is much more compelling to listeners when the speaker tells a story rather than discusses it in the abstract. The speaker might describe a typical day in the life of a particular homeless person: the contempt in the eyes of passersby, the daily search for food, the difficulty of bathing and grooming, and the cold and dangerous night on the street. The story will make vivid for the audience what it is like to be homeless even for one day.

vivid
Graphic; easy to picture. A speech is vivid if its language enables listeners to develop mental pictures of what is being said.

description
Accumulation of details that suggest a mental picture of a person, event, or situation.

Comparisons: Simile and Metaphor. In Chapter 8, we saw that analogy is a powerful form of reasoning; a comparison can help people to accommodate a new idea or new information by deciding that it is similar to what they already know or believe. Comparisons can be made vivid by using similes and metaphors.

A **simile** is an explicit statement that one thing is like another. Responding to a proposal that the drinking age be reduced to sixteen, a speaker might say,

> That's *like* giving a stick of dynamite to a baby.

The simile clearly invites the audience to see the new or the unknown in familiar terms. Knowing the obvious absurdity of giving a stick of dynamite to a baby, listeners can see that the proposed lower drinking age is a bad idea.

A **metaphor** discusses one thing *in terms of* another. Rather than stating that one thing is *like* another, it assumes as much and names the thing as though it actually were the other. A speaker who refers to a new dormitory as "the Taj Mahal" is not explicitly saying that the dorm is like the Taj Mahal but is assuming so and is inviting listeners to see it in terms of the Taj Mahal. The metaphor thus makes more vivid the disparity between the new dorm and older, less luxurious housing. Similarly, suppose a college admissions officer says,

> Transfer applicants are our safety net.

The officer is not speaking literally. Transfer applicants are people, not netting. The point of the statement is to emphasize that unexpected drops in regular admissions can be offset by admitting more transfer students, thereby keeping the overall enrollment at its target number. Referring to potential students as a "safety net" helps to make the point more vivid.

These examples illustrate how metaphors work. Audiences are familiar with and easily able to visualize one of the terms of the metaphor (called the *vehicle*)—the Taj Mahal in the first example, a safety net in the second. The thoughts and emotions that listeners associate with this term are then transferred to the other term (called the *tenor*)—the new dormitory or the college admissions process.[17]

Vivid Sounds: Alliteration and Onomatopoeia. You also can create vividness in a speech through patterns of sound.

Alliteration is a repetitive consonant sound, as in "Tiny Tim" and "Big Bang." Former Vice President Spiro Agnew reveled in such phrases as "the nattering nabobs of negativism." Another politician called for reform "in our communities, our countryside, and our classrooms," repeating the hard *c*. The value of alliteration is that it makes it easier to remember the words in the series.

Onomatopoeia is the use of sounds that resemble what they describe. In the phrase "the hissing of the snake," the *s* sounds simulate the very hissing that the speaker wants listeners to imagine. Similarly, people often describe the slow passage of time simply by saying, "tick-tock, tick-tock."

When used sparingly and purposefully, both alliteration and onomatopoeia add sound to mental images, making them more vivid.

Personification. A powerful means of achieving vividness is through **personification**, the discussion of abstract or complex ideas in human terms. In a speech about unemployment, talking about "how Sam Walters spends his days out of work" is likely to be far more vivid than talking about national unemployment statistics or about unemployment in the abstract.

simile
An explicit statement that one thing is *like* another.

metaphor
Naming one thing *in terms of* another; discussing one thing as though it were another.

alliteration
Repetitive consonant sounds.

onomatopoeia
Use of sounds that resemble what they describe.

personification
Discussion of abstract or complex ideas in human terms.

A Question of Ethics

Ethics and Style

Choices about style in speeches might seem to be a matter primarily of taste. But sometimes a speaker might choose an oral style that, although not necessarily inappropriate for the particular audience, might not fit entirely with the situation. For example, suppose a person speaks in a casual and conversational tone about "hot-button" topics such as abortion or capital punishment. How would such a stylistic choice affect the speaker's relationship to the topic? To the audience? How do these choices affect the audience's relationship to the topic? In this example, would the speaker be inviting the audience to view abortion or capital punishment as a light-hearted matter? When do stylistic choices raise ethical issues? What are the potential ethical dilemmas facing a speaker as he or she tries to find the right style for the audience and the topic?

Presidential candidate Barack Obama used personification in his March 2008 speech on race. Speaking about the pervasiveness of racial prejudice, he referred not only to his pastor (who was the focus of heated controversy) but also to his white grandmother who loved him but nevertheless occasionally made prejudiced statements about blacks. (You will find this speech in the appendix.) By using these personifications, Obama was able to depict the complexity of racism far more vividly than he could have done through a general discussion of race relations in the United States.

Reference to Hypothetical People. The charge is often made that speeches are one-way communications in which listeners are passive and don't participate in the give-and-take of ideas. A speaker can combat the sense that a speech is unexciting by incorporating hypothetical people into it, either through dialogue or by asking rhetorical questions.

Dialogue draws the audience in by reproducing a conversation within the speech, including what both dialogue partners said. Here's how student Beverly Watson used dialogue in a speech about student government:

> I was discussing campus elections yesterday with my roommate. She said, "People don't vote because the elections are a mockery." But I insisted, "The problem is just that there isn't enough publicity." She said, "You're very naïve." I said, "And you're far too cynical." Then she began to defend her position.

Although the listeners are still spectators, to be sure, dialogue lets them witness a lively interaction between people. The "overheard" conversation gets them more involved in the speech.

Sometimes, a speaker uses dialogue to refer to opponents' objections—usually anonymously—and then to answer them. Comments such as "There are those who say . . ." or "And then you might ask . . ." or "I hear it said. . . ." allow the speaker to state and refute a variety of arguments. Richard Nixon's famous "Checkers" speech of 1952 (when he was a senator running for the vice presidency) took this approach to respond to charges that he had benefited personally from a secret fund established by his political supporters. Nixon admitted there was a fund but

dialogue
Reproducing a conversation within a speech.

insisted that "Not one cent of the . . . money of that type ever went to me for my personal use." To more fully satisfy his critics, he then engaged in hypothetical dialogue: "But then some of you will say, and rightly, 'Well, what did you use the fund for, Senator? Why did you have to have it?' " Nixon speaks as though "some of you" were actually present, talking with him. He states "your" concerns and then proceeds to answer them, and "you" as a listener hear both sides of the dialogue. If the speaker has analyzed the audience well and identifies the real concerns on listeners' minds, this can be an effective way to respond to them.

The use of **rhetorical questions** is another way to involve others hypothetically. As you learned in Chapter 10, a rhetorical question is one for which you do not really expect an answer. You ask the question solely to make the audience think about an issue and to quickly reach the obvious answer, which you already know. The "Checkers" speech illustrates this approach to vividness as well. To talk about why the secret fund was necessary, Nixon first asked listeners some questions:

> Do you think that when I or any other senator makes a political speech, has it printed, [we] should charge the printing of that speech and the mailing of that speech to the taxpayers?
>
> Do you think, for example, when I or any other senator makes a trip to his home state to make a purely political speech that the cost of that trip should be charged to the taxpayers?

Nixon raised these questions because he assumed that listeners would agree that the answer is "No." That set the stage to say that a special fund was needed because these expenditures should not be "charged to the taxpayers."

Stylistic Choices in Combination

We have been discussing these stylistic choices individually, but they often are found in combination. For example, here is the conclusion of a speech by a student, Monica Crane, concerning the crisis in Darfur:

> Knowing the history, recent developments, and possible resolutions of the genocide in Darfur, you are now aware of the terrible cost of our global ignorance. You have witnessed the bodies of men, women, and children forced to suffer rape. You have witnessed graphic images of horrific mutilation. And finally, you have witnessed death at the hands of those who live for hate. University students around the globe are the only remaining hope for these people, and for our country. We are the future, and it is up to us to decide whether all people should be afforded certain rights as human beings, or just some. Whether all people deserve the right to live, or just those with our skin color. Whether we can afford to wait, as 6,000 more die every month, for the United States to take responsibility, or whether we must act now. Ultimately, the choice is ours.

The sentences beginning "You have witnessed..." exhibit parallel wording and vivid description. The "whether" clauses also reveal parallel wording. The metaphorical use of "cost" in "the terrible cost of our global ignorance" helps listeners to see that the United States somehow is responsible. The phrase "death at the hands of those who live for hate" contains an implied antithesis between death and life. "We are the future" is a maxim that shows how students can help to correct the situation. The "whether" claims also pose a series of antitheses, contrasting the desired outcomes with the outcomes that will result from doing nothing.

rhetorical question
A question for which no answer is expected; it is asked to get listeners thinking so that they quickly recognize the obvious answer.

Monica's combination of stylistic choices magnifies the impact of her conclusion. She is careful, however, not to make the mistake of including so extravagant or so many unusual linguistic choices that they call attention to themselves and distract from the speech.

OBJECTIVE 12.5

Style and the Entire Speech

Having examined a variety of stylistic resources relating to word choice and arrangement, it is time to step back, change our perspective, and consider the style of the speech as a whole.

Choosing the Right Level of Style

Classical writers on public speaking distinguished among three levels of style: The *grand style* is majestic, lofty, and formal; the *plain style* is simple and colloquial; and the *middle style* falls somewhere between those two poles.[18]

Our society has largely abandoned the grand style, but not entirely. African American preachers often employ the grand style, with extensive use of repetition, parallel wording, and antithesis. Similarly, speakers from some Latin cultures may use indirection or flowery language that characterizes the grand style, and some speakers from Eastern cultures may use a style that relies more on embroidered narrative than on logical demonstration.

Still, most people in mainstream U.S. society overwhelmingly favor the plain style, viewing the grand style as a relic of nineteenth-century orations that often lasted several hours. Most of us prefer understatement to overstatement. We use figures of speech and other stylistic resources not so much for ornamentation as for how they contribute to the clarity of an argument. It is a serious mistake, however, to confuse plainness with artlessness. The "plain" style is not as plain as it sometimes seems. Nor is it achieved naturally, without work. Rather, it is carefully crafted of simple sentences, familiar words, the active voice, and a clear progression from one idea to the next.

Finding the Right Pace and Proportion

Variety. Using all the stylistic resources we examined in connection with words, sentences, and paragraphs at once—or using the same few over and over—will call attention to your style rather than to your ideas. This detracts from the audience's perception of the speech as a unified whole. The alternative is variety—in the resources you use, in how often you use them, and so on. Stylistic variety will keep any particular technique from calling attention to itself and will contribute to a pleasing overall impression of the speech.

Balance. A speech that is uniform in style may not sustain the audience's attention and interest. If the entire speech is concrete and anecdotal, listeners may miss the larger point that the examples are trying to make; but if the speech is completely abstract and theoretical, they may not see how it relates to their own experience. If the speech is entirely intense and gripping, listeners may experience "emotional overload"; but if it is completely dispassionate and low key, they may decide that the speaker does not really care about the subject. A speech loaded

Strategies for Speaking to Diverse Audiences

Respecting Diversity Through Style and Language

Because language is so powerful, it sometimes can marginalize or offend listeners even though that was not the speaker's intent. These strategies will help you to avoid this mistake.

1. Avoid language that is vulgar, offensive, or patronizing. Keep in mind that what you think is acceptable might not be so considered by your audience. Use your analysis of the audience to help determine acceptable language.
2. Define technical terms so everyone knows what you are talking about and no one will feel ignorant. Some in your audience may be experts while others are not, so you must figure out how to address both segments of the audience without talking down to either.
3. In choosing between performative and conversational style, consider the cultural backgrounds and expectations of your audience. Employing the same strategies for speaking at a motivational seminar and at a scientific conference might leave either audience stunned. Although purposely defying conventions can sometimes be effective, it should always be a deliberate choice.

with alliteration and antithesis may call attention to these devices rather than to the purposes for which they are used, but a speech that has no interesting turns of phrase may strike listeners as dull. In these cases and in all matters of style, an effective balance among available resources will enhance the overall style of the speech.

Conciseness. Many writers say that it is easier to write a long book than a short one, because editing one's own thoughts is so difficult. In the same way, it often is easier to speak for 30 minutes than for 10. (Although that may surprise you, it's true. As you research your topic, you'll find more and more material that you want to include, and deciding to omit any of it will be difficult.) Particularly in modern American culture, however, speeches that go on for too long or that lack a clear, compact thesis and structure usually will not be judged as exhibiting good style. Today's audiences tend to value messages that are brief, stripped of adornment, to the point, and concise.

Memorable Phrases

Many classic speeches are remembered because of a particular line or phrase. Examples include Abraham Lincoln's "House Divided" Speech; William Jennings Bryan's "Cross of Gold" speech; and Martin Luther King, Jr.'s "I Have a Dream" speech. A pithy phrase or quotable quote that somehow captures the essence of the speech is today called a **sound bite**, because it is often the only part of the speech that receives media coverage. The 2002 State of the Union address by former President George W. Bush is remembered for the phrase "axis of evil," and his 2003 speech announcing the end of major combat operations in Iraq is known for the premature use of the phrase "mission accomplished." In 2008, presidential candidate Barack Obama became known for his use of the refrain "Yes we can," and his opponent John McCain for his frequent references to "Joe the Plumber." Similarly, the phrase "We are the 99%" is a popular culture sound bite from the Occupy Wall Street movement of 2011 that conveys both solidarity and dissatisfaction. But whether you are addressing 25 classmates or a national television audience, a memorable phrase prevents listeners from forgetting your speech and also enhances their judgment of its style.

Watch the Video "Classic Speech: Martin Luther King, Jr., 'I Have a Dream' (clip)" at **MyCommunicationLab**

sound bite
A memorable phrase that is recalled from a speech and used to identify the speech.

Congruence of Language and Delivery

Finally, the language of the speech should match your delivery (examined in Chapter 3). If your topic and language are serious and formal, your delivery should not be casual and informal, and vice versa. Generally, classroom speeches are informal in both style and delivery. But you may sometimes speak in a more formal situation, and it is important that your choice of language and style of delivery match.

OBJECTIVE 12.6

Achieving Good Style

We have been talking about stylistic choices that involve careful planning and forethought. But if you deliver a speech extemporaneously and cannot labor over each word, how can you possibly pay so much attention to language? And isn't it better, anyway, to focus on the content of your message and just talk naturally? Is it realistic to expect any speaker these days, especially a beginning student speaker, really to focus on style?

These are good questions, and you probably have thought about them. Obviously, no one expects you to attain the stylistic talent of Winston Churchill, Ronald Reagan, or Barack Obama, at least not right away. But you have to start someplace. And lurking behind those questions are two erroneous assumptions about speeches. If you can correct those errors, you will be on the way to understanding how to develop a good style.

Erroneous Assumptions About Speeches

One mistaken assumption about speeches might be called the "plain-style myth"—the belief that people naturally speak in the plain style and have to exert effort only to achieve the grand style. Far from being impromptu, however, the plain style may require several outlines and hours of preparation. Few of us speak extemporaneously as clearly or as precisely as we would like. (To test this claim, record an impromptu speech and play it back; you may be surprised that your language usage is unclear or awkward.) Most of us have to force ourselves to simplify, to consolidate, to focus, and to delete language in order to make the speech artfully plain. *Any* style requires preparation.

Equally mistaken is a second belief: that a focus on style is somehow at odds with attending to the content of the speech. As we've seen in this chapter, "content" and "language" are not completely separate categories. Content becomes meaningful as it is expressed in language, and speakers' choices about style and language affect listeners' perceptions of the content. When we talk about what a speaker "said," then, we are talking about both content and language. So yes, it pays for speakers—even beginning speakers—to focus on achieving style through language.

Suggestions for Developing and Improving Style

1. Review your preparation outline and your presentation outline from the standpoint of style and word choice. Incorporate key phrases and stylistic choices into the preparation outline so that you won't lose track of them when you speak.

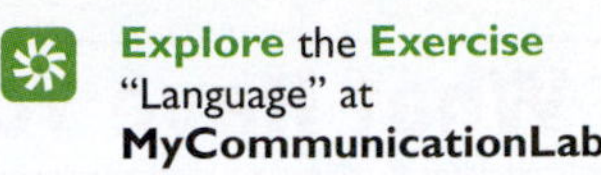
Explore the Exercise
"Language" at
MyCommunicationLab

2. Practice composing speeches in writing. Although you will seldom speak from manuscript, actually writing out a speech can help you focus on style; it creates a specific text that you can examine and revise to improve your style. This exercise also will help you make stylistic choices when you speak extemporaneously.
3. Be your own toughest critic when revising your outline or manuscript for style. Are key ideas and arguments worded as effectively as possible? Does your language make the message easy or difficult for the audience to remember? Does the speech seem interesting or tedious? Use the stylistic resources discussed in this chapter to modify your speech and enhance your style.
4. Practice your speech, not only to become more familiar with its contents and to gain self-confidence but also to listen to its overall rhythm. Does the speech "move" in the way you would like? Does the climax occur at the place in the speech where you intend it to be? If the answers to these questions are negative, you can revise the speech to make appropriate adjustments.
5. Choose your words with your audience in mind. An audience of older adults, for example, might be uncomfortable with large amounts of slang and informal language, and an audience of non-specialists might be uncomfortable with jargon and technical language. You also want to be careful to avoid gender-specific language when the audience or topic calls for gender-neutral or inclusive language.
6. Consider how your speech might incorporate the stylistic resources discussed in this chapter. For example, identify any similes or rhetorical questions that you might use. Then practice the speech, and ask yourself whether the stylistic devices really enhanced the overall quality. If not, be ruthless in omitting them. But if a device seems to work, don't be afraid to keep it in. You can apply this process to each of the stylistic devices in this chapter: Invent alterations, try them out, and assess their contributions to the speech.
7. Raise your awareness of other speakers' styles. Read some classic speeches, and try to identify how each speaker achieved the style for which the speech is known. Watch videos of contemporary well-known speakers and analyze their stylistic choices. Many videos of speeches are available on social media sites such as YouTube. Listen carefully to classmates' speeches, and try to characterize each person's style. Listening critically to speeches of the past and present will make you more sensitive to the whole idea of stylistic choices—and also occasionally may give you ideas about how similar choices might enhance your own speeches.
8. Don't work on too many things at once. One advantage of giving several speeches in a course on public speaking is that you can focus on different skills in different speeches. It's unrealistic to expect solid research, flawless reasoning, perfect organization, and effective style all in the same beginning speech. But it's also true that all these elements work together to produce an effective speech. By focusing on and practicing a few skills at a time, you will make gradual progress toward integrating all of them.

CHECKLIST 12.1

Strategic Language Choices

1. Questions to ask yourself: After outlining my speech...
   - ❒ Am I sure this will sound like a speech, and not an essay?
   - ❒ Will my key terms have the connotations I want?
   - ❒ Does the language suggest momentum for the speech?
   - ❒ Is the language vivid and interesting?
2. If the answer is "No," here are some things you might want to consider:
   - ❒ Review your key-word choices, and put them in the speaking outline so you won't lose sight of them.
   - ❒ Record as you practice the speech; review the recording, and modify word choices to make the speech more clear and more oral.
   - ❒ Identify alternative ways to express your main ideas, and test whether they improve clarity or rhythm.
   - ❒ Insert appropriate figures of speech into the outline to make the speech more vivid.

What Have You Learned?

Objective 12.1: Elaborate a definition of style as the personal choices that distinguish or characterize speakers.

Style is attributed to speakers by listeners, based on the distinctive pattern of language choices made by speakers to express themselves.

The basic requirements for effective style are as follows:

- Accuracy
- Appropriateness to the audience and situation

Objective 12.2: Identify the key differences between oral style and written style.

Oral style differs significantly from written style in its:

- Simplicity
- Repetition
- Informality
- Reflexivity

Performative style also differs from conversational style, based on whether listeners are seen mainly as spectators or as participants.

Objective 12.3: Illustrate how definitions affect the stylistic significance of individual words and phrases.

The speaker's powers of definition are a considerable stylistic resource, especially the following:

- Choice of denotations and connotations
- Persuasive definitions

Objective 12.4: Achieve clarity, rhythm, and vividness.

Clarity—to the degree desired—is achieved through the following:

- Use of familiar and concrete terms
- Use of maxims
- Limiting the use of jargon and defining technical terms
- Removing clutter
- Employing the active voice

Rhythm includes attention to the following:

- Repetition
- Parallel wording
- Antithesis
- Inversion of normal word order

Vividness is a matter of the following:

- Clear and compelling description
- Use of narratives
- Employing similes and metaphors for comparisons
- Using words with vivid sounds (alliteration and onomatopoeia)
- Personification
- Reference to hypothetical people through dialogues and rhetorical questions

Objective 12.5: Distinguish among levels of style and explain how variety, balance, and conciseness affect judgments of the overall style of a speech.

For the speech as a whole, the important criteria are as follows:

- The stylistic level (grand, middle, or plain)
- Variety
- Balance
- Conciseness
- Memorable phrases
- Congruence of language and delivery

Objective 12.6: Enhance the stylistic quality of your speeches.

Conscious efforts to improve style may seem at odds with a natural or conversational tone, but even achieving the plain style requires effort, and is not an off-the-cuff presentation as it sometimes may seem.

Listen to the **Audio Chapter Summary** at **MyCommunicationLab**

Discussion Questions

1. What does it mean to say that content and style are interconnected? Try rewording the following statements. Do they have the same impact when you rephrase them? Discuss the ways in which word choice helped to convey the meaning in these passages.

a. "The mystic chords of memory, stretching from every battlefield and patriot grave to every living heart and hearthstone all over this broad land, will yet swell the chorus of the Union when again touched, as surely they will be, by the better angels of our nature."—Abraham Lincoln, First Inaugural

b. "I remember: It happened yesterday or eternities ago. A young Jewish boy discovering the kingdom of night. I remember his bewilderment, I remember his anguish. It all happened so fast. The ghetto. The deportation. The sealed cattle car. The fiery altar upon which the history of our people and the future of mankind were meant to be sacrificed." —Elie Wiesel, Nobel Peace Prize Acceptance Speech

c. "Freedom and fear are at war. And we know that God is not neutral between them."—George W. Bush, Address to Joint Session of Congress after Sept. 11, 2001, terrorist attacks

2. What is the variety of connotations possible for the following words? Which connotations might be more common among your classmates? If you wanted to draw on the positive connotations for these words, what terms would you use?
   - Technology
   - Rhetoric
   - School
   - Marriage
   - Rap music
3. As a class, watch a video of a great orator. Discuss that orator's style. In what ways does he or she use language to achieve clarity, rhythm, and vividness? How do the language choices of that orator help achieve the purpose of the speech?
4. Books, papers, and essays are written *for the eye*, whereas speeches are written mainly *for the ear*. How does that difference affect the way you approach the composition of a speech?

Activities

1. Adapt a written form to an oral form, and vice versa. (Note: To complete this activity, you will need a video or audio recorder.)
   a. Read an essay that you wrote for another class. Then put the essay aside, and with a video or audio recorder capturing the event, describe the information in that essay as though you were making an oral presentation before a class. Do not look at the written essay when you make the presentation. When you are done, play the recording, and compare the written essay to your oral presentation. In what ways are they different?
   b. Record yourself giving an extemporaneous speech. Listen to the recording and transcribe that speech, word for word. Then transform that transcription into a form that is appropriate for a written essay. What did you have to change, and why?
2. Read the manuscript of a speech, and seek to discover which language devices are used to develop the style of the speech. Identify the use of at least five stylistic resources (such as persuasive definition, maxim, irony, purposeful ambiguity, repetition, parallel wording, antithesis, metaphor, alliteration, rhetorical question, and dialogue; see Table 12.1 for a complete list). What effects do these resources have on the audience? How do they create those effects? Why does the speaker use these resources in the way he or she does?
3. Using the speech above, what stylistic changes would you propose for speaking to the following audiences? How and why does your choice of stylistic resources change depending on the audience? To what extent might changing the style of the speech affect its overall message?
   - A group of Iraq war veterans
   - A group of PTA parents
   - A group of senior citizens
   - A group of high schoolers
4. Write the following sentences on the board at the front of the classroom:

   I like a cold drink on a hot day.

   The girl walked to the school.

   The man was very strong.

   Happy children were dancing.

   Using the principles in this chapter, brainstorm alternative sentences that you could use to convey the same or a similar meaning with more vivid language.

Key Terms

active voice **296**
alliteration **301**
ambiguous **297**
antithesis **299**
call and response **299**
condensation symbol **298**
connotation **293**
definition **292**
denotation **293**
description **300**
dialogue **302**
irony **297**
jargon **296**
malapropism **290**
maxim **295**
metaphor **301**
multivocal **298**
onomatopoeia **301**
operational definition **292**
passive voice **296**
personification **301**
persuasive definition **294**
reflexive **288**
rhetorical question **303**
rhythm **298**
signature **284**
simile **301**
sound bite **305**
style **284**
technical term **296**
type **284**
vivid **300**
word economy **296**

Study and **Review** the **Flashcards** at **MyCommunicationLab**

Notes

1 For more about style as choice, see Geoffrey N. Leech and Mick Short, *Style in Fiction: A Linguistic Introduction to English Fictional Prose*, 2nd ed., New York: Pearson, 2007; especially Chapter 1, "Style and Choice." Also see Jeanne Fahnestock, *Rhetorical Style: The Uses of Language in Persuasion,* New York: Oxford University Press, 2011.

2 For more about generic types, see Kathleen Hall Jamieson, "Generic Constraints and the Rhetorical Situation," *Philosophy and Rhetoric* 6 (Summer 1973): 162–70.

3 For more about culture types, see Michael Calvin McGee, "The 'Ideograph': A Link between Rhetoric and Ideology," *Quarterly Journal of Speech* 66 (February 1980): 1–16. For a recent look, see Brent Allen Saidon, "Debating Michael Calvin McGee's 'Critical' Shift in Rhetorical Theory," *Contemporary Argumentation and Debate* 29 (September 2008): 88–117.

4 For more about archetypes, see Michael Osborn, "Archetypal Metaphor in Rhetoric: The Light–Dark Family," *Quarterly Journal of Speech* 53 (April 1967): 115–26. A contemporary application is Laura C. Prividera and John W. Howard III, "Masculinity, Whiteness, and the Warrior Hero: Perpetuating the Strategic Rhetoric of U.S. Nationalism and the Marginalization of Women," *Women & Language* 29 (Fall 2006): 29–37.

5 The style of Lincoln's Gettysburg Address is discussed in detail in Garry Wills, *Lincoln at Gettysburg: The Words That Remade America*, New York: Simon & Schuster, 1992.

6 Since classical times, rhetorical theorists have commented on the connection between ideas and language. See Marcus Tullius Cicero, *De Oratore*, translated by H. Rackham, Cambridge, MA: Harvard University Press, 1982, pp. 23–24.

7 For a more thorough examination of the differences between written and oral forms, see Marcia Irene Macaulay, *Processing Varieties in English: An Examination of Oral and Written Speech Across Genres,* Vancouver: University of British Columbia Press, 1990.

8 For an example of this argument, see Kathleen Hall Jamieson, *Eloquence in an Electronic Age: The Transformation of Political Speechmaking,* New York: Oxford, 1988.

9 This analysis disagrees with the conclusions of Todd S. Frobish, "Jamieson Meets Lucas: Eloquence and Pedagogical Model(s) in *The Art of Public Speaking,*" *Communication Education* 49 (July 2000): 239–52, which represents the conversational style as being more universally applicable.

10 Modern handbooks of such stylistic tools also exist. See Arthur Quinn, *Figures of Speech: Sixty Ways to Turn a Phrase,* Salt Lake City: Gibbs M. Smith, 1982; Richard A. Lanham, ed., *A Handlist of Rhetorical Terms,* 2nd ed., Berkeley: University of California Press, 1991.

11 The use of the term *freedom* as a persuasive definition is considered in Geoffrey Nunberg, "More Than Just Another Word for Nothing Left to Lose," *New York Times*, March 23, 2003, sec. 4, p. 6. See also Eric Foner, *The Story of American Freedom*, New York: W.W. Norton, 1998.

12 For an analysis of how definitions can affect the course of a controversy, see Douglas Walton, "Persuasive Definitions and Public Policy Arguments," *Argumentation and Advocacy* 37 (Winter 2001): 117–32.

13 For more about irony, see Wayne Booth, *Rhetoric of Irony*, Chicago: University of Chicago Press, 1974.

14 However, it should be noted that ambiguity can have positive immediate effects that are followed by negative long-term effects. See David Zarefsky, *President Johnson's War on Poverty: Rhetoric and History*, Tuscaloosa: University of Alabama Press, 1986.

15 See Maggie Sale, "Call and Response as Critical Method: African-American Oral Traditions and *Beloved,*" *African American Review* 26 (March 1992): 41–50.

16 Kennedy's phrasing also illustrates the rhetorical technique of *chiasmus*—a reversal of phrasing as well as of content (for example,"country for you"/"you for country"). See James Jasinski, *Sourcebook on Rhetoric,* Thousand Oaks, CA: Sage, 2001, pp. 545–46.

17 Much has been written about the way in which metaphors work. For a start on this subject, see I. A. Richards, *The Philosophy of Rhetoric,* New York: Oxford University Press, 1965, Chapters 5 and 6; Max Black,"Metaphor,"*Proceedings of the Aristotelian Society* 55 (1954–1955): 273–94; and George Lakoff and Mark Johnson, *Metaphors We Live By,* Chicago: University of Chicago Press, 1980.

18 For example, see Marcus Tullius Cicero, *Orator*, translated by H. M. Hubbell, Cambridge, MA: Harvard University Press, 1939, pp. 69–111.

CHAPTER

13

Informing

LEARNING OBJECTIVES

After studying this chapter, you should be able to:

Objective 13.1	Distinguish between informing and persuading as purposes for a speech while recognizing that they often overlap.
Objective 13.2	Identify which speech purposes are achieved primarily through informative strategies and explain why.
Objective 13.3	Illustrate the strategies of defining, reporting, describing, explaining, demonstrating, and comparing.
Objective 13.4	Explain how you can design your speech in order to increase the chances that essential information will be remembered.

Listen to the **Audio Chapter** at **MyCommunicationLab**

OUTLINE

Now that we have explored delivery, audience analysis, research, reasoning, organization, and language, we are ready to bring these skills together into a complete speech. To do so, we should revisit two related concepts: purpose and strategy. A speech is designed to achieve a purpose, and strategic planning is the process of deciding how your speech can best do that.

In Chapter 6, we examined seven different kinds of purpose:

- Providing new information or sharing a perspective
- Setting the agenda
- Intensifying or weakening a feeling
- Strengthening commitment to a position
- Weakening commitment to a position
- Converting the audience away from one belief and toward another
- Inducing a specific action

Now the question is which strategies are most appropriate for achieving these purposes?

OBJECTIVE 13.1

Planning Your Strategy

Broadly speaking, speech goals are achieved through the strategies of informing, persuading, and entertaining. These are sometimes mistaken as resulting in three fundamentally different kinds of speeches. In fact, though, because successful sharing of information also affects people's attitudes, informing and persuading occur together. Likewise, a successful persuasive speech is also entertaining and enjoyable to listen to, and an entertaining speech usually also conveys new information.

The broad strategies overlap, then, and they do not exclude each other. So if your assignment is to present "an informative speech," this does not mean that you should avoid saying anything entertaining or persuasive. Rather, you should achieve your purpose primarily through strategies of informing.

Defining Your Specific Purpose

What happens if the assignment does not specify a purpose? Or what if you are speaking outside the classroom setting? Then you must decide what you want to achieve (for example, to teach people something new, to get them to contribute money to a cause, or to make them laugh). You will need to assess how the audience and the occasion create opportunities or constraints. Finally, based on this analysis, you will define your specific purpose.

For example, suppose that many of your listeners believe that the Internet should be regulated to protect children from indecent material. Your own opinion is exactly the opposite, and you would like to change their minds. But you know (or will learn in the next chapter) that people do not usually make major changes in their beliefs because of a single speech. You also realize that although most of your listeners use the Internet frequently, they lack a basic grasp of the decentralized and transnational structure of the Web that makes regulation of the Internet so difficult. Finally, you will be speaking at an educational conference that is exploring how better to use the Internet in elementary school classrooms. All of these factors lead you not to try to convert your audience but to seek the more realistic goal of providing new information about the Internet. You hope that this new information, in turn, will weaken the audience's commitment to the view that the Internet should be regulated, but that is not your goal for this speech. Believing that your audience must be informed before it can be persuaded, you have chosen to provide new ideas or perspective.

Informing her audience about the extent of child labor practices, this speaker draws on information from the Department of Labor.

However, sometimes an audience must be persuaded before it can be informed. Consider another example. During the Cold War years, most Americans approached foreign policy issues from the premise that the world was locked in a mortal struggle between freedom and communism. Information about world events was understood within the framework provided by this dominant assumption. For a speaker even to discuss independent nationalism in Eastern Europe, it first was necessary to challenge the prevailing view that all of Eastern Europe was a monolith dominated by the Soviet Union. In order to share information effectively, it first was necessary to change listeners' attitudes.

Informing Your Audience

In this chapter, we are concerned with informing. **Informative strategies** presume that a principal goal of the speech is to share ideas with the audience. They rely on the metaphor of the speaker as teacher and the speech as a lesson. The speaker is expected to be clear, accurate, and interesting. Listeners are asked to be attentive, to understand what is being said, and to modify their knowledge and belief systems to take this new information and perspective into account. Informative speeches share information about objects, processes, events, and concepts.

Watch the Video "Informative Speech: The Use of Plastics in Vascular Surgery" at **MyCommunicationLab**

In a speech about the microscopic world around us, Kimo Sanderson made his classmates think about something they had previously ignored:

> There are millions of living creatures in your house right now. They crawl through your carpet, reproduce under your bed, and snack in your closet. When examined under a microscope, they look like creatures from your worst nightmares. They are dust mites, and we live with them every day.

In her speech about pharmacists and the idea of a "conscience clause," Krupa Shah introduced her audience to a developing controversy:

> Every day, every hour, every minute, someone steps inside a pharmacy that holds the medicines to fill nearly every prescription a doctor can write. I say "nearly," of course, because there may be times when the pharmacy runs out of a certain drug or maybe the pharmacist just doesn't want to give it to the patient. Wait! Running out of a drug seems legitimate, but the latter seems odd. However, it is possible, and it is possible because pharmacists have what is called a "conscience clause," which allows them to refuse certain prescription requests based on their own moral concerns.

informative strategies
Approaches to preparing a speech in which the overall goal is to share ideas with an audience.

Informative strategies do not explicitly ask listeners to believe or do any particular thing. Rather, they ask that listeners alter their understanding of a subject. Sometimes this can be done by taking new information into account, such as when one learns that the local community was founded by immigrants 150 years ago. At other times, listeners' understanding is changed because they see the subject in a different light, such as when confusing instructions for filling out a tax form are made clear, or when the speaker explains the counterintuitive fact that the Panama Canal is farther east on the Pacific side than on the Atlantic side (the canal mainly runs north–south).

Of course, learning something new might stimulate listeners to take action. For example, imagine that you heard a speech about fuel economy standards for automobile manufacturers, knowing very little about the scientific, ecological, and economic details of this important issue. The speaker's purpose was to share information about the significant global decrease in oil consumption that could be achieved by a modest increase in the average fuel efficiency of American cars and trucks. The speaker did not actually call on you to do anything; the goal was only to make you aware of an issue you previously had neglected. But it would not be surprising if, after hearing such a speech, you paid more attention to how many miles per gallon your car gets. The speech might also prompt you to take fuel economy into consideration the next time you buy a car, and even to urge legislators to support tougher standards for automakers. In the next chapter, we will contrast informative strategies with strategies of persuasion, which seek to influence listeners' beliefs, values, or actions.

Informative speeches come within the public forum for two reasons. First, they provide information enabling audiences to think and decide about matters that affect people generally. Second, having the information may enable the public to decide what to do about these matters. The speech on fuel economy standards illustrates both of these points.

OBJECTIVE
13.2

Clarifying Your Informative Goal

Watch the Video "Informative Speech: Peer Mentors" at **MyCommunicationLab**

Two of the speech purposes discussed in Chapter 6 rely primarily on informative strategies: providing new information or perspective and agenda setting. Information is essential if you are to induce listeners to think about something new, to view it from a unique perspective, or to take into account something they had previously ignored. In addition, the purpose of creating positive or negative feelings relies heavily on both informative and persuasive strategies, as well as on entertaining.

Providing New Information or Perspective. Common knowledge about a subject is often quite general. It is widely acknowledged, for example, that many eligible voters in the United States do not vote. But most people have little understanding of what lies behind this statement—whether the percentage of voters has been increasing or decreasing, how participation varies among different groups, factors that tend to increase or limit participation, the relationship between registration and voting, and so on. One informational goal for a speech would be to enrich the audience's common knowledge about voting rates, moving listeners from a broad understanding to a more detailed awareness of the issue.

Sometimes a speaker's objective is not merely to supply more details but to update and revise the audience's common knowledge. Part of what people generally believe may be mistaken, and social knowledge changes with the times. There is probably no clearer example than what people in the United States "know" about

Rhetorical Workout

Keep Your Informative Goal in Mind

You are working on an informative speech about the International Space Station (ISS). You assume it is common knowledge that the ISS is a research laboratory in space with an international crew, even if most of your audience may not know any more details. Think about the informative goals presented in this chapter.

1. If your goal is to *provide new information or perspective*, how useful or interesting might each of the following be: (a) a list of countries that have contributed to the ISS; (b) a demonstration of how to look up NASA's website; (c) data on the size of the station and what kinds of equipment are aboard; (d) information about which countries built each part of the station? Explain why.
2. If your goal is *agenda setting*, how useful might each of the following be: (a) a report that the life span of the ISS is due to end in 2015; (b) information that experiments on the station are vital to understanding how living in space affects humans; (c) figures for how much funding for the ISS comes from the United States? Explain why.
3. If your goal is to *create positive or negative feeling*, how useful might each of the following be: (a) a poll showing that few Americans are interested in the ISS; (b) information about recycling innovations tested on the station; (c) an anecdote about how NASA named a treadmill on the station after comedian Stephen Colbert? Explain why.

Russia. For most of the period from 1945 to 1990, people "knew" that the Soviet Union (which included Russia) was engaged in a deadly economic and political struggle with the United States. But in the years after 1990, people came to "know" that this was no longer the case. Since the rise to power of Vladimir Putin in the early 2000s, Americans have once again modified what they "know" about Russia. If not a deadly adversary of the United States, that nation is now seen as an economic and diplomatic rival.

The question of what Americans "know" about Russia came up again during the 2012 presidential election campaign, when Republican presidential hopeful Mitt Romney alleged that Russia was the number-one security threat and ideological adversary of the United States. His claim was vigorously denied by both the Russian president and the Obama administration, who assigned that ranking instead to the international terrorist network al-Qaeda.

You probably will not be able to alter your listeners' perspective so dramatically as in this example. But if your speech about the Internet gives listeners information that leads to a new way of thinking about "indecency," you probably will have accomplished a similar purpose.

Agenda Setting. A speaker whose purpose is **agenda setting** wants to create awareness of a subject that listeners did not know about or think about before, thus putting it on the agenda of topics that warrant their concern. Until fairly recently, for example, the majority of Americans simply didn't think about whether there was a pattern to the race or ethnicity of drivers who are stopped by police officers and searched in an effort to reduce crime. Most Americans went about their errands, assuming that if a person was stopped and searched by an officer, that person was rightly suspected of engaging in illegal activity. But many African American drivers who have been pulled over and searched without reasonable cause have protested against "racial profiling," the practice of making traffic or other investigative stops on the basis of a person's race or

agenda setting
Creating awareness about a subject that listeners did not know about or think about before.

ethnicity. As a result, the subject now warrants our attention, and increasing numbers of people are becoming aware of the problem. Speakers and writers focused attention on a topic that had been ignored, and at some point it was put on the agenda. The September 11, 2001, terrorist attacks added yet another dimension to the issue, as people who had not thought one way or another about profiling during security screening at airports had to consider how it was being used to combat terrorism.

Creating Positive or Negative Feeling. It borders on cliché to say that information gives people power. Knowledge and understanding enable people to perform competently and to make intelligent choices. Providing information empowers listeners to feel better about their ability to control their lives. Ellen Benson, for example, did not think that she was good at managing her time. She never seemed to have enough time to get everything done; tasks took much longer than she thought they should, and she often forgot what she needed to do. But then she attended a speech about time management skills, and the speaker's information helped Ellen to understand her problems and gave her some techniques to manage time better. After the speech, she told a friend, "I feel like this speech has given me a new way to take control of my own life." The speech had created a positive feeling.

The ability to make intelligent choices is also a source of power. Informative speeches do not tell the audience which option to choose. But if they lay out the costs and benefits of alternatives, they may help listeners to form criteria for making a decision. By resolving a difficult question, people feel better both about the subject and about themselves.

To provide new information or perspective, set the agenda, or create positive or negative feeling, you will rely on informative strategies. We now will consider some of the primary informative strategies, most of which can be used to achieve any of the three goals.

CHECKLIST 13.1

Speech Purposes and Strategies

1. Purposes achieved primarily through informative strategies
   - ❐ Providing new information or sharing a perspective
   - ❐ Agenda setting
2. Purposes achieved through a combination of informative and persuasive strategies
   - ❐ Creating positive or negative feeling
3. Purposes achieved primarily through persuasive strategies
   - ❐ Strengthening commitment to a position
   - ❐ Weakening commitment to a position
   - ❐ Converting the audience away from one belief and toward another
   - ❐ Inducing the audience to perform a specific action

OBJECTIVE 13.3

Informative Strategies

For ease of explanation, we examine informative strategies one at a time, as though speakers used only one strategy in a given speech. Although that is possible, most speeches combine a number of strategies to achieve the speaker's purpose and to make it more likely that listeners will remember the information.

Defining

In Chapter 12, we discussed definition as the process of giving meaning to a word. The strategy of **defining** uses this process to clarify a term or concept that is vague or troublesome. Or definition may be used to introduce a new or unexpected way of viewing the subject, so that the speech can develop the details and implications of this new approach.

defining
A strategy to clarify a term or concept that is vague or troublesome, or to introduce a new way of viewing the subject.

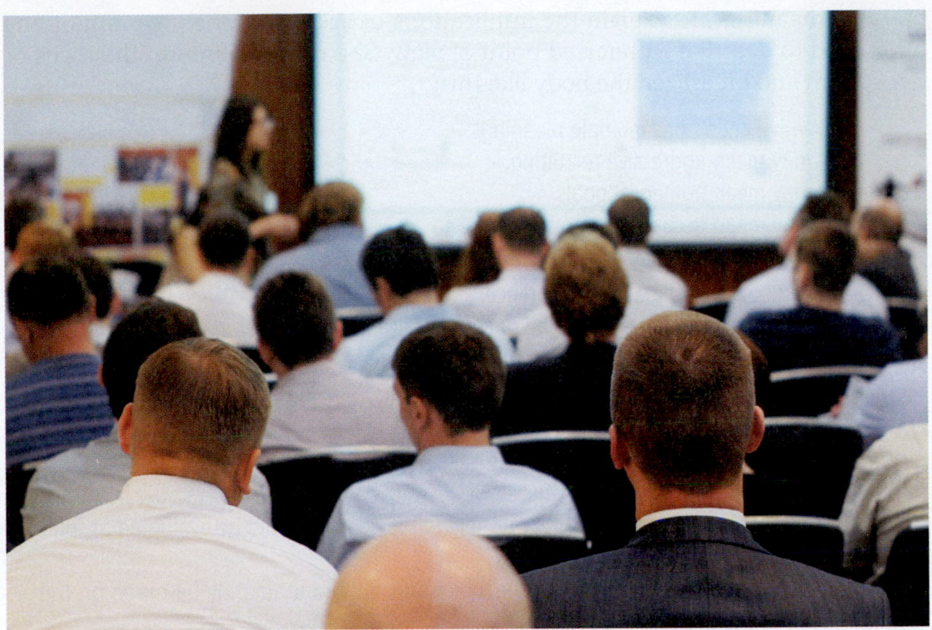

When the subject about which you are informing listeners is complex, charts, drawings, and pictures can aid in the explanation.

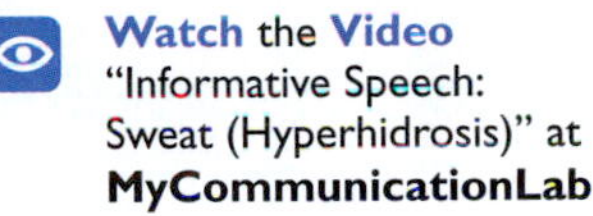

Watch the Video "Informative Speech: Sweat (Hyperhidrosis)" at **MyCommunicationLab**

Definition is unnecessary when a term's meaning is clear-cut. It is necessary, though, when a concept is not clear at all, as when new technical terminology makes its way into general usage. In the early 2000s, when computer-mediated interaction came into widespread use, most people suddenly needed to learn a new vocabulary: texting, Facebook, social networking sites, friend (as a verb), tweeting, and so on. A speech entitled "Deciphering Social Networking"—which included definitions of such terms—would have been well received. In this case, defining would serve as the means to provide new information or perspective. In the example about racial profiling, definition serves as a means of agenda setting, because understanding the meaning of the term helps audiences to think about the problem.

At other times, definition is used to create a positive feeling. Student Sonia Rubenstein, for example, believed that many of the unfortunate racial incidents and cases of "hate speech" on college campuses arose partly because the key concept "affirmative action" was misunderstood. She used the strategy of definition to clarify the concept and to establish a preferred meaning:

> Mention the term *affirmative action*, and some people will tell you that it means special recruiting efforts to attract minorities and women. Others say it means identifying a specific goal for the number of minorities and women to be hired. Still others think it means reserving a specific number of places for minorities and women. And people speak so often of the mechanics of affirmative action that they lose sight of the goal: We all benefit from the perspectives offered by a culturally diverse student body. If we keep track of that goal, then the best way to think of affirmative action is as special efforts to seek out qualified students who will enable us to achieve the goal.

Intelligent discussion is unlikely when the participants have different ideas of what they are talking about. For that reason, Sonia's goals were to identify different possible meanings, to explain the implications of accepting one meaning or another, and to describe a preferred point of view. She made definition the focus of her speech and organized the body like this:

I. Affirmative action has multiple meanings.
  A. It may mean aggressive recruiting.
  B. It may mean numerical goals.
  C. It may mean tie-breaking preferences.
  D. It may mean quotas.
II. Selecting a meaning makes a difference.
  A. It will influence how actively the government takes an interest in the question.
  B. It will clarify whom affirmative action seeks to help.
  C. It will determine whether it is fair to place at a disadvantage people who have not caused previous discrimination.
  D. It will influence how actively committed we should be to the goal.
III. Affirmative action really means aggressive recruiting.
  A. This meaning is consistent with our belief that people should be evaluated as individuals, not as groups.
  B. It is consistent with our belief that decisions should ultimately be made on the basis of merit.
  C. It recognizes the historical underrepresentation of minorities and the fact that qualified minority candidates may not be identified through normal means.

In this example the speaker uses definition to identify and explain a preferred meaning. As we saw in Chapter 12, however, such definitions are not neutral; they shape how we view or think about a subject. In educating listeners about a definition, the speaker is also influencing them to think about the topic in a particular way, and to prefer one definition over another. This illustrates why the purposes of informing and persuading cannot be strictly separated. Although the strategy of definition is intended mainly to be informative, definitions also are persuasive.

Reporting

Watch the Video "Informative Speech: History of the Circus" at **MyCommunicationLab**

Reporting is journalism in the oral mode. It answers the question "What happened?" and usually does so in strict chronological order with little overt analysis or interpretation. Select this strategy if your analysis of audience, occasion, and purpose suggests that you need to explain a complex event by identifying each of its components.

If you were giving a speech about the recent trip to India by a group of students to build a house for a low-income family, and your goal was to share what happened, the body of the speech would report the major events of the trip:

I. Travel to India
  A. Who was part of the group
  B. Arrival at airport
  C. Coping with jet lag
II. Meeting charity organizers
  A. Why the low-income housing is needed
  B. Who will benefit from the housing
  C. Understanding cross-cultural differences

reporting
A strategy to relate what happened with little analysis or interpretation.

CHOOSE A STRATEGY: Using Informative Strategies

The Situation

You are preparing an informative speech for your class on how immigration reform might affect your classmates. In your research, you have found several studies and personal stories that speak to economic, political, and social impacts. Your informative goal is to place the issue of immigration reform on the agenda and raise the awareness of your audience about this complex issue. Now think about the informative strategies presented in this chapter.

Making Choices

1. Would defining be an appropriate informative strategy for your topic? Why or why not?
2. Which of the following strategies seems well suited to your topic: reporting, describing, or explaining, or some combination of these? What are the potential benefits or drawbacks of each strategy?
3. If you wanted to include a demonstration of some aspect of this topic, what might you be able to include? What would you need to do to your larger topic in order to include such a demonstration?
4. What might you compare your topic to in order to help your audience understand it better?

What If...

How would your answers above be affected by the following conditions?

1. Your audience is a group of recent immigrants. Or your audience is a group of anti-immigration activists.
2. Your informative goal is to provide new and updated information for your audience.

III. Building the house
   A. Where the house is located
   B. What materials were used
   C. How long it took to build

IV. Arrival of the new occupants
   A. What the new occupants thought of the house
   B. What the charity organizers thought of the house

V. Returning to campus
   A. What student participants thought of the experience
   B. How to participate next year

Reporting is primarily a means to provide new information or perspective, but it can also contribute to other goals. Knowing about this trip might lead listeners to think about sponsoring others. Moreover, although the image of reporting is that it is purely factual, usually far more has occurred than can be conveyed in a relatively short speech. Selecting which items to include and which to leave out therefore involves the speaker in making subjective judgments; in turn, these can influence what listeners think about the topic. Even reporting, then, is not a purely informative strategy.

Describing

Many passages in novels use words to try to paint a picture of the scene. When readers can "see" the characters, setting, and action in their minds, they become more actively involved in the novel.

Painting a mental picture involves description. The strategy of **describing** can benefit a speech as well as a novel.[1] In a speech about travel to the French Riviera, we are unlikely to hear a set of arguments about why we should go. Rather, the

describing
A strategy in which a cumulation of details characterizes, or evokes a mental image of, the subject.

Strategies for Speaking to Diverse Audiences

Respecting Diversity Through Informing

Information is not neutral. How people understand information is affected by their backgrounds and perspectives. These strategies will help you in presenting information to a diverse audience.

1. Consider how your audience members' beliefs and experiences influence what can be considered informative. For instance, speaking about evolution for an audience of biologists may be considered informative, whereas speaking for an audience of creationists may require persuasive strategies.
2. When providing new information or perspective, recognize that anyone's perspective on a topic is influenced by one's culture. Speaking about women's rights to an audience raised in a male-dominated culture requires awareness of your audience's expectations. You cannot assume that the audience shares your perspective.
3. Acknowledge that cultures may differ with respect to what topics legitimately can be placed on the agenda. Sometimes the topic itself may alienate the audience. In order to assure good will, remember that some topics may require greater sympathy than others.
4. Do not knowingly bias audience members' views. Insofar as possible, present all sides of an issue.

Watch the **Video** "Informative Speech/ Self-Introduction: Lady with a Gun" at **MyCommunicationLab**

speaker will develop so appealing an image of the Riviera that we will *want* to go. Similarly, a speech about the 2011 earthquake and tsunami that hit Japan might mention not only the fact that the earthquake was magnitude 9.0 or that more than 15,000 people lost their lives, but could also describe the fear and destruction caused by tsunami waves that were over 130 feet high, in order to convey a sense of what it was like rather than just reporting what happened. In this way, description achieves the purpose of creating positive or negative feeling.

A mental picture becomes vivid through its details. Instead of a general reference to a person, an effective speaker describes the color of the eyes or hair, whether the person was standing erect or leaning against a post, the expression on the person's face, and so on. But a steady stream of details quickly becomes tedious, so the speaker selects details that evoke a larger picture. The expression on the person's face, for example, might convey a certain attitude. In a speech about the professor who had the greatest influence on her life, student Janet Wickstrom described many such details to her audience:

> I walked into Professor Alvarez's office and immediately noticed her desk. Or, rather, I noticed that I couldn't *see* her desk. One corner was piled high with new books. The telephone was covered with reminder notes. Students' papers and memos were strewn across the desk. There was yesterday's newspaper opened to the crossword puzzle. A napkin with crumbs from a leftover bagel was on top. Somewhere nearby was a coffee cup. Class notes were piled on top of the computer. A grade book was buried underneath a stack of paper. "What a desk," I thought. Yet I soon would discover that behind that desk was the most organized woman I ever have met.

Describing is an especially useful strategy when you believe that listeners will share your appraisal of the details, once you mention them, and that they will regard them as signs or examples of some characteristic that you could not observe or report directly—such as, in this example, the generalization that first appearances can be deceptive. Stated directly, the claim would seem a cliché. But if it is developed indirectly through detailed description, listeners' interest in the details will help them to appreciate the generalization.

Explaining

Beyond simply defining a term or making an idea precise, speakers sometimes want to share with an audience a deeper understanding of events, people, policies, or processes. This is done through explanation, which goes beyond reporting to consider different views of what happened, to ask how or why it happened, or to speculate about what it means or implies.

For example, if you wanted to explain the 1962 Cuban missile crisis to listeners who were not yet born and who don't really understand that event, you would not simply report what took place from October 16 to October 28, 1962. You would discuss such topics as how and why Soviet missiles were placed in Cuba, why Americans regarded them as so threatening, what options for a response were weighed by President Kennedy and his advisers, how the crisis was resolved, and what it meant for U.S.–Soviet relations at the height of the Cold War. If your explanation is successful, listeners not only will know more of the facts but also will grasp the significance of the crisis and will appreciate why the issues it raised have fascinated people for over 50 years. In this example, you would be both providing new perspectives on the missile crisis and setting an agenda by encouraging listeners to think critically about what they might otherwise have regarded as just a series of facts.

Speeches that explain events or people often begin simply and then build toward greater richness or complexity. In contrast, speeches that explain policies or processes generally proceed in the opposite direction. Ever since 1980, for example, the diplomatic relationship between the United States and Iran has been either poor or nonexistent. A speaker who wants to explain why the United States does not have diplomatic relations with Iran in 2012 would have to break this simple concept down into its components: the 1979 overthrow of the U.S.-backed shah, how Israel is both a friend of the United States and an enemy of Iran, how nuclear development is understood as an aggressive act to the United States and an act of national sovereignty for Iran, and so on. Only by understanding these components well could listeners really understand why the United States and Iran do not have diplomatic relations in 2012 and what types of barriers stand in the way of future relations.

Speeches explaining a difficult concept should distinguish between its essential meaning and other meanings that may be associated with it but that are less central.[2] Similarly, speeches that explain a process proceed by breaking down complex operations into a simple sequence of steps. For example, because public opinion polls are reported so often in the news, you might want to speak about how such polls are conducted. You would explain all the steps in the process: the framing of the questions, identification of the population to be sampled, procedures for obtaining responses from the sample, recording and coding of responses, performing statistical analyses, and interpreting significant results. After hearing your speech, listeners will not be able to design and conduct polls themselves but they will recognize and understand the key steps in the polling process.

Demonstrating

Sometimes, it is not enough to explain a process; it is necessary as well for the audience to see it. Or sometimes, the goal is not just for listeners to understand something; the object is to enable them to do it themselves. In such a case, a speaker may offer a demonstration, describing a seemingly mysterious

Sometimes explanation is not enough—the speaker must show listeners how to do something. The speech of demonstration enables listeners to view a process so that they may be able to repeat it themselves.

or complicated procedure as a series of fairly simple steps performed in a particular order. Such a speech that demonstrates how to cook a meal, how to wallpaper a room, how to prepare a simple tax return, or how to organize a cluttered desk demystifies the topic for listeners, so that they learn to do something that they could not do before. The speech obviously provides new information; in making the subject less mysterious to listeners, it also helps to create a positive feeling.

Demonstration could be the only focus of a speech, or it could be part of a speech that employs other strategies as well. In either case, as you prepare the demonstration, the following considerations are particularly important:

1. Do listeners really need to see the process to understand it? If not, a demonstration may seem superfluous or boring; but if so, a demonstration will be strategically essential.
2. Is the subject precise enough that it can be demonstrated in the time available? Complicated operations, such as rebuilding an automobile engine, can't possibly be covered in a single speech. And even without a time limit, it's unlikely that an audience will attend to, much less remember, a long demonstration about how to rebuild an engine. However, such topics as how to make an apple pie, how to plan one's study time, and how to pack a suitcase efficiently lend themselves well to brief demonstrations.
3. Are the steps of the process clear, distinct, and in proper sequence? Listeners will not understand what they are supposed to do if your instructions are vague or incomprehensible or if you demonstrate the steps out of order. Start at the beginning, and go through all the steps leading to the finished product. Do not skip any necessary steps, and do not duplicate steps.

4. Are your actions and your verbal instructions coordinated? Avoid any long gaps in the speech while you are doing something or waiting for something to happen. You will lose both the continuity of the speech and the audience's attention if you must pause and wait for results. This problem often weakens a demonstration of how to cook something.

Demonstration speeches usually benefit from visual aids, which will be examined in Chapter 15.

Comparing

Watch the Video "Informative Speech: Fear of Public Speaking" at **MyCommunicationLab**

The final informative strategy is comparing, which seeks to clarify for listeners the similarities and differences between the items compared. It can be used to make things seem more similar than an audience had imagined. For example, computer platforms are often thought to be quite different from one another, but a speech comparing features of two leading systems, PC and Mac, could convince the audience that they are so similar that anyone who knows one can learn the other quickly. Alternatively, a comparison might heighten awareness of differences between things thought to be alike. If listeners think that all systems of parliamentary procedure are basically the same, they might learn otherwise by hearing a speech that compares different systems. Or the strategy could accomplish both of these purposes. A speech comparing the curriculum in engineering with that in liberal arts could make listeners aware of both similarities and differences that they had not recognized.

Another use of the strategy of comparing is to decide in what category something should be placed. Deciding whether Social Security is basically an insurance program or basically a welfare program could be helped by a speech exploring its similarities to and differences from each of those concepts.

Finally, comparing can provide listeners with a basis for making a choice. The speaker does not tell them what to do or urge them to accept one perspective over another but instead identifies the options available and compares the benefits and costs.

The public debate about affirmative action in university admissions policies provides a good example. In 2003, the Supreme Court heard arguments in two separate cases from two students who believed that they were denied admission to the University of Michigan as a result of reverse discrimination. Opponents of affirmative action have suggested some alternatives to it, such as focusing on economics rather than race, and adopting "affirmative access" that guarantees state university admission to top high-school seniors from any high school in the state. Other opponents have called for race-neutral admissions policies. Supporters of affirmative action believe that it is still necessary to take race into account in order to achieve a truly equal educational opportunity. A speech of comparison might increase public understanding by identifying the problem, describing the proposed options, and determining the strengths and weaknesses of each. The purpose of the speech would not be to urge any particular choice, but to make the alternatives clear so that listeners could apply their own criteria in deciding and forming a judgment about what action should be taken once the Supreme Court announced in the spring of 2012 that it would re-examine the issue. The body of such a speech might be organized this way:

I. Subjective individual review of each applicant is a possible solution.
   A. It offers certain benefits.
   B. It poses certain drawbacks.

II. Race-neutral admissions is a possible solution.
    A. It offers certain benefits.
    B. It poses certain drawbacks.
III. Admissions focused on economic diversity is a possible solution.
    A. It offers certain benefits.
    B. It poses certain drawbacks.
IV. "Affirmative access" guarantees of admission to all top students is a possible solution.
    A. It offers certain benefits.
    B. It poses certain drawbacks.
V. Race-conscious admissions for a limited time period is a possible solution.
    A. It offers certain benefits.
    B. It poses certain drawbacks.
VI. Summary: The choices that we must consider are subjective review of individual applications, race-neutral admissions, admissions focused on economic diversity, "affirmative access," and race-conscious admissions for a limited time period.

The principal purpose of this speech was to provide new information for listeners unfamiliar with alternatives to affirmative action. A secondary purpose might well be to create a positive feeling of sympathy for the complex nature of the issue.

Finally, remember that speakers often combine these informative strategies. A speech may both report what happened and attempt to interpret what it means, or may both explain and compare, or may both define and describe, or may both demonstrate and explain. Always, however, the goal is to share understanding and insight in order to provide new information or perspective, set an agenda, or create a positive or negative feeling.

OBJECTIVE 13.4 Encouraging Retention

It might be said that the true test of learning is not how much knowledge or insight one takes in but how much one retains. There are cases in which the speaker seeks only an immediate response. If the purpose of the speech is to convince people to donate to a fund-raising effort, then the immediate response—Did people actually give money?—may be the sole test of success. But with informing, it is different. Speakers want the audience not only to attend to and understand what they said but also to remember it.[3]

forgetting curve
A curve that displays the rate at which something learned is forgotten over time.

Over a century ago, psychologists explained what is called the **forgetting curve**. This concept is applied to public speaking in Figure 13.1, where the horizontal axis represents the amount of time after the speech and the vertical axis shows the percentage of content that is remembered. As you can see from the fast-falling curve, a large portion of the speech is forgotten quickly; the line begins with a sharp negative slope and then levels out later. The forgetting curve applies both to the main points of the speech and to the sources of information. Over a short period of time, listeners quickly forget what was said. We might say that the information conveyed in a speech typically has a short half-life. Indeed, this is the biggest constraint on the effectiveness of informative strategies.

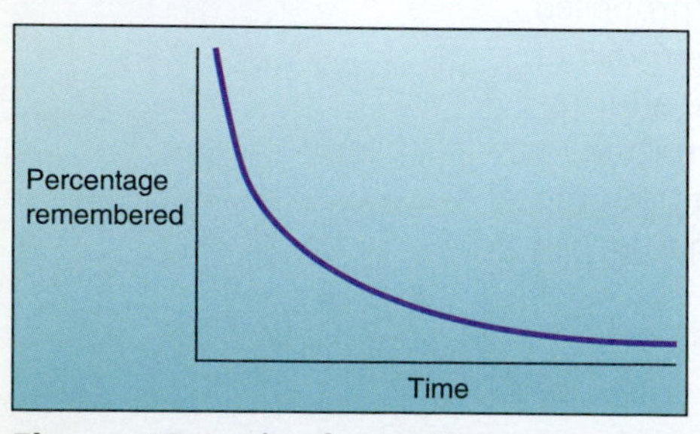

Figure 13.1 The forgetting curve.

A Question of Ethics

The Ethics of Informing

If information is empowering, even more empowering is the opportunity to present information. The speaker chooses what information to share and what to omit, how to describe the information, and how to explain what it means. Under what conditions can the exercise of this power result in unethical manipulation of the audience? Can any speaker be truly neutral in presenting information? If not, is it ethical to distinguish informing from persuading? Why or why not?

Although the forgetting curve typically takes the shape shown in Figure 13.1, the sharp decline does not have to appear at the same place on the graph. It is possible to "shift the curve upward," to increase the likelihood that listeners will remember more content at any given time:

1. In Chapter 5, we examined ways to gain and keep an audience's attention, such as making the speech personally relevant to listeners, making the message stand out, and making it easy to follow. Fortunately, the methods used to increase attention apply to retention as well.
2. In Chapter 4, we learned the importance of active listening, which occurs when the speaker challenges listeners to think, to role-play situations mentally, and to ask and answer questions. Compared with passively receiving information, active listening requires a higher level of participation. And because participation enhances motivation, it should be no surprise that active involvement by listeners (rather than just passive hearing of the speech) increases the chances that they will remember the message.
3. Retention is also strengthened through **reinforcement**, a response by the speaker that rewards the listener and thereby strengthens the listener's positive attitudes toward the speech. In the public speaking classroom, listeners often reinforce speakers. If audience members nod their heads in agreement whenever a speaker expresses an opinion, the speaker is likely to increase the number of opinion statements.

As a speaker, though, you also can use reinforcement strategically to ensure that the audience remembers the message. As you learned in Chapter 9, if your organizational pattern enables listeners to anticipate what will come next and the subsequent development of your speech confirms their guess, then by confirming their expectation you reward their shrewd judgment.

You can also reinforce audience members by how you refer to them. Saying "we" instead of "you" conveys the message that you identify with listeners and regard them as your equals; you signal that you respect their thoughtful judgment. In his historic speech on election night in 2008, Barack Obama repeatedly avoided referring to himself, and focused on "we" rather than "I." This usage reinforced the beliefs of listeners that they were in the know and had participated actively in making the election result possible. Explicit references to them within the speech may have the same effect. A speaker whose transition says, in effect, "Since you've followed this complex topic so far, I'm sure you can see why the next point is valid,"

reinforcement
A response by a speaker that rewards the listener to strengthen the listener's positive attitude toward the speech.

is speaking well of the audience and providing reinforcement. This, along with strategies that draw attention and encourage active listening, will shift the forgetting curve and improve the odds of ensuring retention.

Finally, some of the stylistic elements discussed in Chapter 12 also encourage retention. Parallel wording makes it easier to remember ideas, vivid language will keep a description in the listener's mind, and simple sentences enable a listener to follow the message and focus more easily on what is being said. These elements help to make ideas not only more readily understood, but also more likely to be remembered. They are strategic resources that can be used to achieve any informative purpose.

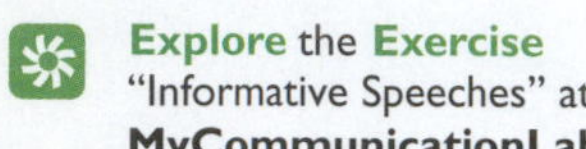

Explore the Exercise
"Informative Speeches" at
MyCommunicationLab

What Have You Learned?

Objective 13.1: Distinguish between informing and persuading as purposes for a speech while recognizing that they often overlap.

Speeches that rely mainly on informative strategies do not seek directly to influence listeners' actions, yet it would be unfair to say that they have no persuasive effects.

Objective 13.2: Identify which speech purposes are achieved primarily through informative strategies and explain why.

Informative strategies achieve several speech purposes:

- Provide new information or perspective
- Agenda setting
- Create positive or negative feeling

Objective 13.3: Illustrate the strategies of defining, reporting, describing, explaining, demonstrating, and comparing.

Based on analysis of the audience, occasion, and purpose, you can select appropriate informative strategies, including a combination of the following:

- Defining: clarifying a term or concept or introducing a new way to view the subject
- Reporting: relating what happened with little analysis or interpretation
- Describing: characterizing or evoking a mental image of the subject
- Explaining: sharing a deeper understanding beyond reporting
- Demonstrating: showing a process as steps in a particular order
- Comparing: clarifying similarities and differences between items

Objective 13.4: Explain how you can design your speech in order to increase the chances that essential information will be remembered.

Listeners quickly forget much of what was said in a speech, so you will want to encourage and reinforce retention by doing the following:

- Providing information that draws attention
- Using an organizational structure that allows listeners to anticipate what is coming next
- Making complimentary references to the audience
- Making strategic choices about style

Listen to the Audio Chapter Summary
at MyCommunicationLab

Discussion Questions

1. In the public speeches that you've heard lately, were informative strategies or persuasive strategies dominant? Consider speeches from outside the public speaking classroom, such as the following:
    - A presidential address
    - A speech at a protest rally
    - A lecture in your history class
    - An oral research report presented by a student in another class
    - The closing argument in a trial

Were any of these speeches completely devoid of persuasive strategies? Were any completely devoid of informative strategies? Can a speaker inform listeners without influencing them in some way? Can a speaker persuade listeners without providing information?

2. Speakers encourage retention by reinforcing listeners, by drawing their attention, and by encouraging them to listen actively. Two strategies for doing these things are (a) to provide a clear organizational pattern and (b) to refer to "we" instead of "you." What other strategies help a speaker to encourage retention in a speech with a primarily informative goal? Discuss the strategies that in your experience were most effective in making you remember the message long after the speech was over (e.g., visual aids, audience participation, etc). Do the means of making the speech memorable distract from its message?

3. The lectures of a college professor are a form of informative speech. Discuss what distinguishes a good lecture from a poor one. Might other factors, such as class size or topic, create different requirements for an effective informative speech?

Activities

1. Watch a news report on television. In what ways is it like a speech to inform? In what ways is it different? Can you take anything from this model to help you create speeches with informative strategies?

2. Create one of the following:
   a. A speech of explanation about the process of developing informative strategies in speeches
   b. A speech of comparison that discusses informative and persuasive strategies
   c. A speech of definition about the concept of "strategic planning" in speech preparation
   d. A speech of explanation about five strategies that you plan to use in your next speech to increase the audience's retention of information.

3. Outline a speech describing one side of a controversy, and then outline a speech detailing the other side. Put these two together to create a speech, informing your audience about the complexity of a particular controversy. If your purpose is to inform without bias, to what might you need to pay attention? Where might bias potentially lie? At the level of words, sentences, overall structure, etc.?

Key Terms

agenda setting **317**
defining **318**
describing **321**
forgetting curve **326**
informative strategies **315**
reinforcement **327**
reporting **320**

Study and **Review** the **Flashcards** at **MyCommunicationLab**

Notes

1 For more about description in speeches, see Gerard A. Hauser, "Empiricism, Description, and New Rhetoric," *Philosophy and Rhetoric* 5 (Winter 1972): 24–44. Fear can be instilled through description as well. For one example, see Brian Jackson, "Jonathan Edwards Goes to Hell (House): Fear Appeals in American Evangelism," *Rhetoric Review* 26 (2007): 42–59.

2 For a fuller discussion of explanatory discourse, see Katherine E. Rowan, "Informing and Explaining Skills: Theory and Research on Informative Communication," *Handbook of Communication and Social Interaction Skills*, eds. John O. Greene and Brant R. Burleson, Mahwah, NJ: Erlbaum, 2003, pp. 419–430.

3 For more about retention, see Robert L. Greene, *Human Memory: Paradigms and Paradoxes*, Mahwah, NJ: Lawrence Erlbaum, 1992. For retention in visual media, see John J, Hale, "The Visual Superiority Effect: Retention of Audiovisual Messages," *International Journal of Instructional Media* 36 (2009): 275–86.

CHAPTER

14 Persuading

LEARNING OBJECTIVES

After studying this chapter, you should be able to:

Objective 14.1	State the differences between informative and persuasive strategies for speeches and identify the speech purposes that are achieved through persuasive strategies.
Objective 14.2	Describe how determining the target audience and analyzing the audience's motivation and the speaker's purpose can help the speaker plan for persuasion.
Objective 14.3	Explain the Elaboration Likelihood Model and what it implies for persuasion.
Objective 14.4	Describe how audiences resist persuasion and what resources help a speaker overcome resistance.
Objective 14.5	Identify strategies that speakers can use for each specific purpose and in general.
Objective 14.6	Use two basic structures for persuasive speeches: the problem–solution structure and the motivated sequence.

Listen to the **Audio Chapter** at **MyCommunicationLab**

OUTLINE

Dominique Crain, a student at the University of Kansas, was proud of her school, its traditions, and its mascot, the Jayhawk. She felt a lump in her throat when she heard the alma mater played at sporting events, and she even befriended the Jayhawk mascot on Facebook. She planned to give a speech explaining the culture and history behind the university's special customs, dances, and mascot's costumes.

As she was planning her speech, Dominique realized that she would be incensed if students from rival schools were to mock Jayhawk customs or ridicule the mascot at games. But this realization got her thinking that Native Americans would feel the same way, if not worse, about school mascots that mock their own cultures. Imagining herself in their shoes, she decided that, rather than telling her audience about Jayhawk traditions, she should instead urge that the use of Native American mascots be banned. She would use her own feelings about the Jayhawk as a starting point, but her goal would be to convince her listeners to support a proposal to ban Native American mascots.

As Dominique discovered, informative goals are sometimes insufficient. They do not require listeners to commit themselves to any belief or action. Sometimes, a speaker may want not only to make listeners think about something but also to influence what they think about it; or may want to move listeners beyond having a belief to taking action; or may want listeners to change their minds, to abandon one belief and accept another. In all these cases, the speaker's goal is to persuade the audience, to prompt listeners to feel, act, or believe in a particular way.

When you ask listeners to make a particular choice about believing or doing something, you are asking listeners to eliminate other possible choices and commit themselves to your choice. For this reason, you must be sensitive to your ethical responsibility not to manipulate listeners. A speaker can so "load the deck" that the audience has an illusion of choice even though the speech predetermines what that choice will be. If a speaker moves listeners to action by persuasive but unsound appeals, or withholds crucial information or arguments because they might lead to an unwanted conclusion, or rushes listeners to judgment by pronouncing an issue more urgent than it actually is, then the audience has been manipulated. In Dominique's case, she presented her arguments, supported by sound evidence, and let her audience decide whether they were persuaded to agree with her. Many of the persuasive messages we encounter every day fall short of this high ethical standard. But as Dominique realized, influencing listeners by presenting a case and asking them to support it after thinking carefully about it is the goal for which speakers should strive.

OBJECTIVE 14.1 Purposes for Persuasive Strategies

Chapter 6 introduced seven specific speech purposes, and we saw in Chapter 13 that both agenda setting and providing new information or perspective are achieved mainly through informative strategies. The goals of strengthening commitment, weakening commitment, conversion, and inducing specific action all depend primarily on persuasive strategies.

The term *persuasion* is sometimes misunderstood as referring only to situations in which a speaker *reverses* an audience's beliefs. According to this view, if your roommate is strongly opposed to taking a public speaking course and you talk him or her into taking one, only then have you persuaded your roommate. But this is an overly limited view of persuasion. A person's commitment to a position is not just a matter of yes or no; there is a range, and listeners can become either more committed or less committed to a position. By reasoning with audience members, the speaker seeks to move them from one point to another along a scale reflecting degrees of commitment.

- The speaker might want to *strengthen commitment* to a belief, moving listeners farther along the scale in the direction toward which they are already headed. Your roommate might be thinking about taking public speaking, and your advocacy leads him or her to feel more strongly that it would be a good idea. In this case, you would be trying to move the listener from a positive position on the scale to an even more positive position. (Or, if your roommate were opposed and you wanted to strengthen his or her opposition, you would be trying to move the listener toward an even more negative position.)
- The speaker might want to *weaken commitment* to a belief, moving listeners closer to the middle of the scale. Your roommate might be strongly opposed to taking public speaking, and your message leads him or her not to rule out the idea completely. The option is "back on the table" even though your roommate is still leaning against it.
- The speaker might even want to try to change listeners' minds, moving them from one side of the scale to the other—a process of *conversion* that seldom results from a single speech. (This is what we mentioned as the reversal of positions, and it's a mistake to think of it as the only situation in which persuasion occurs.)
- The speaker might try to shift the entire scale, aiming to move listeners from a strong belief to approval of a *specific action*. Your roommate has been thinking seriously about taking a public speaking class for some time, but after hearing your remarks, he or she finally goes to next semester's registration and signs up for the course.

As you know from Chapter 13, informing and persuading are not entirely separate goals, and both create positive or negative feelings in the audience. If you want listeners to remember new information, you need to persuade them that the information is important. And to persuade them to take action, you need to be sure that they understand what the action means. Nevertheless, there are differences between informative and persuasive strategies. Both seek to change the audience's perspective, but informative strategies do so by enlarging the audience's scope of awareness and concern, whereas persuasive strategies do so by altering the audience's position.

Strengthening Commitment

Speakers often address audiences that already agree with them. Why, then, do listeners need to be persuaded?

Suppose that you believe your town should hire more policemen to increase community patrols, even if that means an increase in taxes. You suspect that your audience favors a more visible police presence in the community, but you also know that most citizens dislike paying higher taxes. Concerned that opposition to taxes might outweigh the commitment to a larger police force, you seek to strengthen the audience's commitment to hire more police. In this way you will insulate their commitment from possible objections. The body of your outline might look like this:

I. A more visible police presence would benefit the community.
   A. It would make people feel safer.
   B. It would provide additional employment and economic stimulation to the town.
   C. It would lower the crime rate.

II. The risks of a tax increase are slight.
   A. Only a very small increase will be needed to fund this program.
   B. The safety and economic benefits will attract new business to the community.
   C. Our town's overall tax rate still would be lower than that of other towns in the area.

Your listeners may have been vaguely familiar with these arguments but had not considered them carefully. Therefore, you succeed in *strengthening their commitment* to the belief that the benefits of additional police are worth the possible tax increase.

Is this really a form of persuasion? Yes, because your attitude about the subject differs after the speech as a direct result of the speech. The speaker has influenced you to believe more strongly about the subject than you did before. Strengthening commitment is a very common approach to persuasion because it takes advantage of people's tendency to seek out and accept messages with which they already agree.

Weakening Commitment

Sometimes a speaker will face a **hostile audience**. This does not mean that audience members are personally unfriendly, but that they have strong commitments that are opposed to the speaker's view. Suppose, for example, that the zoning board in your town has recommended that businesses be allowed to locate in certain residential neighborhoods in order that the town might gain more tax revenue. Residents of the affected neighborhoods are strongly opposed to this idea. They fear that increased traffic, noise, and litter will reduce their quality of life. You support the zoning proposal and plan to speak in its favor to several neighborhood groups. In this situation, you will be trying to weaken the commitment of your audience to the belief that residential and commercial uses of property should be kept completely separate.

A speaker who tries to weaken the audience's commitment to a position is not asking them to abandon it completely. That is usually too much to hope for, and it may not even be what the speaker wants. In speaking to the neighborhood groups, for example, you do not expect them to give up their commitment to protecting residential property. Nor is that your goal. Rather, you want to make them less sure of their commitment and willing at least to consider making an exception for the edge of the neighborhood. If you imagine a scale ranging from strictly separating residential from business use (at one extreme) to opposition to all zoning (at the other extreme), your goal is to move listeners from their current position closer to the *middle* of the scale, the point that represents no commitment. An audience member who said after the speech, "I certainly believe in strong zoning, but we should at least think about whether the edge of the neighborhood is an exception," would have been persuaded to weaken his or her prior commitment.

hostile audience
An audience that is strongly committed in opposition to the views of the speaker.

conversion
Abandoning one belief or value and replacing it with another.

Conversion

Far more difficult than strengthening or weakening a commitment is *changing* it. Speakers who attempt **conversion** aim to alter listeners' beliefs, either by convincing them to accept something they had previously rejected or to reject something they had previously accepted.

Because people defend themselves against persuasion, no speaker is likely to achieve conversion through a single speech, unless listeners' opinions about the subject are not deeply held in the first place. The most obvious case of conversion is old-time religious revivals in which the emotion of the situation and the magic of the preacher's words cause listeners to feel in a flash the seriousness of their situation and the need for reform.

Presidential candidate Mitt Romney tries to persuade undecided voters to support him and to encourage his supporters to come out and vote.

Conversion also occurs at times in the secular realm. During the 1960s, for example, many people completely changed their views about the role of African Americans and women in American life from what they had thought at the beginning of the decade. Many others changed their views about foreign policy and the Cold War as a result of the war in Vietnam. And many changed their views about family lifestyles, dress and grooming, and taste in music as a result of exposure to alternatives. For some people, the terrorist attacks of September 11, 2001, had a similar effect, completely changing their view of U.S. foreign policy, or of the importance of homeland defense compared with the protection of civil liberties. For still others, the economic downturn starting in 2008 led them to abandon their opposition to deficit spending or to government's involvement in the marketplace.

Even in the classroom, there are occasional cases of conversion. Students who have previously denied that they harbor any racial prejudice might come to see that, at least subconsciously, they do. Or a student who was convinced that the administration's policy on scheduling final examinations was unfair could be led to the opposite position.

Inducing a Specific Action

Watch the **Video** "The Process of Developing a Speech: Building a Persuasive Argument" at **MyCommunicationLab**

Finally, there are situations in which modifying belief is not enough. The speaker wants audience members actually to do something as a result of the speech. The most obvious examples are the candidate who is seeking votes, the charitable organization seeking contributions, the advertiser who is trying to sell a product, and the neighborhood organizer who is seeking signatures on a petition. They will not achieve their purpose if listeners simply say they like the message or that they agree with it. Listeners have to take the next step and act on the message.

Moving from belief to action is sometimes difficult. In part, it is a matter of inertia. It is usually easier to say that you agree with a message than it is to exert yourself to do something in response. Beyond that, there is sometimes a discrepancy between people's attitudes and their behavior. They may agree that they ought to modify their eating habits (attitude) without actually altering what they choose to eat (behavior). Or they may say what is socially desirable—what they think others wish to hear—and then act otherwise. This is illustrated by the case of the smoker who is convinced by an antismoking message and yet continues to smoke, or by the person who denies that he or she has any religious or racial prejudice but will not vote for any minority candidate for office. Conversely, listeners might be induced to modify their behavior without changing their underlying attitudes. Thus, a speech decrying racial slurs might persuade listeners to avoid them when speaking with members of other racial groups and yet not change in any way how they feel about race. Surely that is a start, but is it enough? In such a situation, you will need to decide whether achieving a change only in behavior is sufficient for your purposes or whether you need to alter the underlying attitude as well.

OBJECTIVE 14.2

Plan Your Strategy

Throughout our study, we have emphasized speechmaking as strategic planning. Being able to analyze the audience, to size up the situation, and to determine its constraints and opportunities—the basic skills you learned in Chapters 5 and 6—will enable you to make the best use of persuasive strategies. Because you seek an altered commitment from listeners when using persuasive strategies, you need to perform a more detailed audience analysis aimed at identifying your target audience and at assessing that audience's motivation.

Determine Your Target Audience

If your audience is diverse and you are not seeking unanimity, the first step is to determine as precisely as possible which members are your **target audience**. Although you would be happy if you could persuade everybody, these are the people you really seek to influence. They may be the key decision makers or their own prestige and credibility might help to influence others. For example, suppose you are speaking at a corporate meeting attended by upper management and by the heads of all departments that might be affected by your presentation—even though any decisions ultimately will be made by only the president and the chair of the board. It would be nice to influence the department heads by your speech, but your real target audience is the president and the board chair. They are the decision makers, and it is they whom you want to persuade.

Assess Your Audience's Motivation

Listeners will be *motivated* to let your speech influence them if they perceive that your appeal is linked to their own motives and needs.

Psychologists have offered many different accounts of the nature of human **motivation**. What is the incentive for people to do something that requires effort, such as considering a persuasive message? At the most general level, people seek to attain pleasure and to avoid pain. This motive is the basis for persuasive speeches about everything from the dangers of air pollution to the benefits of good nutrition—as student speaker Michael Masdea demonstrated in urging his audience to stop drinking so much caffeine:

> Caffeine can help us stay up during those frequent student all-nighters. But it can also cause severe headaches, stomachaches, and insomnia. The psychological and behavioral effects of caffeine are frightening. It is a highly addictive drug, and it may be the cause of many problems you are experiencing right now.

Another general account of human motivation was offered by psychologist Abraham Maslow, who theorized that human beings have a *hierarchy of needs;* we first seek to satisfy biological and safety needs, which include food, clothing, shelter, and protection from harm, and then proceed to higher-order needs, such as identity, meaningful relationships, and self-actualization.[1] (See Figure 14.1.) Maslow argued

target audience
Within a larger audience, those individuals whom a speaker especially wants to address, usually people whose response will determine whether the speech succeeds.

motivation
The incentive to do something that requires effort, such as considering a persuasive message.

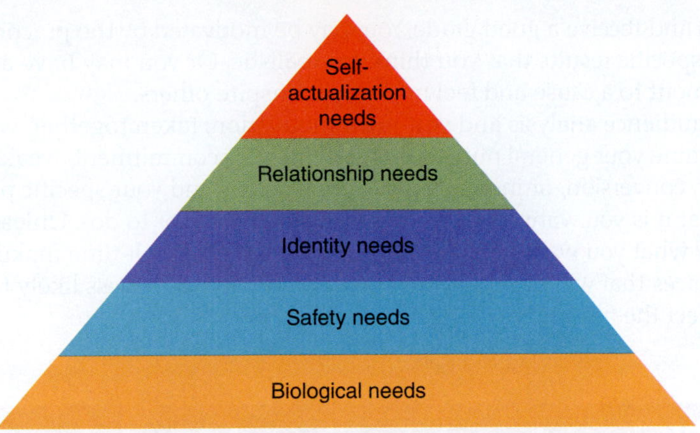

Figure 14.1 Maslow's hierarchy of motivation.

that a person's higher-order motives become important only after lower-order needs are satisfied. It is useless, for instance, to discuss abstract ideals with someone who doesn't know from where his or her next meal is coming. On the other hand, people who have been able to satisfy their lower-order needs often find that they are not truly fulfilled; then higher-order needs and motives become important. According to this view of motivation, the persuasive speaker's task is to determine approximately where in Maslow's hierarchy listeners are and then both to arouse the appropriate motive and to show how it can be satisfied by the recommended action or belief. Often, of course, different members of an audience will have different kinds of motivation, and the speaker accordingly will include appeals to different levels in the hierarchy.

In a class with many student-athletes, student speaker Kevin Krebs appealed to motives on different levels of Maslow's hierarchy. Speaking in favor of the NCAA policy of enforcing stricter rules about athletes' minimum grade-point averages and test scores, Kevin first appealed to the athletes' basic need to make a living:

> How many of you really think you're going to get a job playing professional sports? If you do, the odds are stacked against you. Only a small percentage will actually make a living playing the game. Chances are, when you get out of college, you're going to need the education being forced upon you by the NCAA rules.

Then, turning his attention to athletes and sports fans alike, Kevin appealed to the higher need to enjoy winning:

> The policy at this university is already stricter than the NCAA rules. By accepting these guidelines, some of our competitors with lower academic standards will be eliminated from the field. Our school will finally get a chance to win a game or two!

Determine Your Purpose

We have been speaking about the *audience's* level of motivation, but the *speaker* also can have different motives for speaking. At the most obvious level, you may want to fulfill an assignment in

CHECKLIST 14.1

Strategic Planning for Persuasion

1. Ask yourself these questions:
   - ❒ Who is my target audience?
   - ❒ What is the audience's motivation?
   - ❒ What specifically do I want to achieve?
   - ❒ What means of audience resistance might be present?
2. Decide whether your specific purpose is realistic in light of your answers. If not, modify it. If so, then determine:
   - ❒ Which of the purpose-specific strategies will be most useful.
   - ❒ Which general strategies represent resources you can use.
   - ❒ How to organize the overall speech.

the class and receive a good grade. You may be motivated by the practical desire to achieve specific results that you think are realistic. Or you may have a passionate commitment to a cause and feel impelled to inspire others.

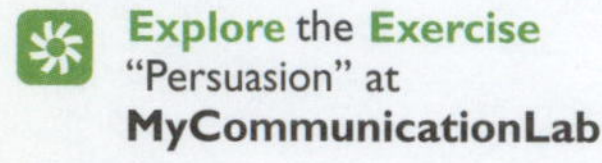
Explore the Exercise
"Persuasion" at
MyCommunicationLab

Your audience analysis and your own motivation, taken together, will help you to determine your general purpose—strengthening commitment, weakening commitment, conversion, or inducing a specific action—and your specific purpose (exactly what it is you want audience members to believe or to do). Unless you know explicitly what you want to achieve, you will have a difficult time making the strategic choices that will develop your speech and you will be less likely to recognize and respect the free choice of your listeners.

OBJECTIVE 14.3

The Elaboration Likelihood Model

In thinking through your strategic purpose, it may be helpful to know more about how people are persuaded. One answer to that question is offered through the *elaboration likelihood model*. This model reflects the communication process described in Chapter 1, especially the fact that speakers and listeners cooperate jointly to develop meaning and understanding.

Components of the Model

Elaboration refers to listeners' tendency to think about information related to the topic of the speech. The likelihood of elaboration varies among people, and for any given person it varies among topics. With relatively high elaboration, a person will be persuaded—if at all—by systematic thinking about the message and the topic. This is the result of critical listening, which was discussed in Chapter 4, and includes careful assessment of the speaker's arguments in light of other things the listener knows. Messages that hold up under such scrutiny will be persuasive.

In contrast, with relatively low elaboration, a person is more likely to be persuaded as a result of "short-cuts" that simplify thinking (for example, whether the speaker is attractive or whether the delivery is animated). These are easier bases for decision because they are triggered more by intuitive reactions than by detailed analysis.

Put another way, the more that listeners are likely to elaborate, the more persuasion will depend on the message's arguments, and the less that they are likely to elaborate, the more it will depend on intuitive judgments that suggest simple decision rules. In principle, critical listening is a sounder basis for persuasion, but no one has the time or energy to listen critically to every message on every topic. In fact, listeners will position themselves at points all along the range of elaboration, from high to low, and each listener is likely to use a mix of critical listening and simplifying devices.

Implications of the Model

For the speaker, it is important to know what factors will make a listener more likely to elaborate, and then to determine whether these factors are present in the particular audience. Helpfully, many of the same factors that influence attention and perception work here as well. If the topic is personally relevant, or if the listeners generally enjoy thinking about things, or have prior knowledge about the topic, or if there are few distractions, they are more likely to elaborate the message.

Of course, the fact that listeners think critically about a message is no guarantee that they will be persuaded by it. That will depend on the outcome of their thought. When elaboration is high, speakers who follow the standards of evidence and reasoning discussed in Chapters 7 and 8 are more likely to be persuasive than those who do not. When elaboration is low, speakers who follow the advice we have offered in Chapters 2, 3, and 5, to establish positive *ethos*, to appear likable, and to seem interesting are more likely to be persuasive than those who do not. Although the paths are different, either central or peripheral processing can result in acceptance of your message.

Finally, it's not the case that a person's elaboration likelihood is firmly fixed in advance; it can be affected by the speech itself. Listeners who don't think that a topic affects them personally can begin to feel differently during the speech, or a person who thinks he or she knows a lot about the topic already may discover otherwise. If the message can encourage listeners to elaborate, and if it succeeds in persuading them, it is more likely that their attitudes will persist over time and that their attitudes will correspond to their behavior.

What the elaboration likelihood model implies is that persuasion is complex and that there is more than one route to the goal. For the speaker, it suggests the need for careful audience analysis to determine the specific purpose, and selection of strategic resources that recognize the multiplicity of ways in which people are persuaded.[2]

Constraints on Effective Persuasive Speaking

OBJECTIVE 14.4

As you know well by now, the strategic plan for a speech requires that you identify the constraints in the situation and that you use your resources to take advantage of opportunities. When you seek to persuade, the constraints are often greater than when you seek to inform or to entertain. Listeners often resist attempts to persuade them. They do so because their identities may be tied closely to their opinions; thus, an appeal to change their opinions might threaten their identities. The nature and strength of such resistance varies significantly among listeners and situations, and it often takes one of the following forms:[3]

- Selective listening
- Selective perception
- Selective influence

These patterns were introduced in Chapter 5. They are described here in slightly different terms in order to highlight the constraints that are especially significant for persuasion.

Selective Listening

As we have seen, audiences typically attend to messages, interpret them, and remember them selectively. But a message that reinforces what the audience already believes does not arouse defensive reactions, perhaps because it is less threatening or because it offers reassurance. For example, if you already support single-payer health care, you are more likely to attend to, understand, and remember messages that also support it. But selective listening goes beyond selective exposure and paying attention to messages with which you agree. It also includes how you listen to messages. If the focus of a speech is vague or unclear, listeners will "clarify" it by interpreting it in a way that supports what they already believe. Odd as it seems, a speech that decries the cost of health care and demands reform but does not propose a specific solution might be seen by both supporters and opponents of single-payer health care as "really" agreeing with their views.[4]

Because these barriers to persuasion are potentially powerful, it is important to plan strategies that surmount them. One often-used approach is to begin with areas of agreement and gradually move to areas of difference. If your listeners are known to favor single-payer health care but you oppose it, you could start by agreeing with them that costs are out of hand, that reform is needed, and that government must play a role. Only then would you make the case that single-payer health care is an undesirable solution. The audience will react more favorably to this strategy than if you broadly attack single-payer health care without acknowledging the positive aspects of the issue or the intensity of their feelings.

However, when you acknowledge common ground in a persuasive speech, you have to be careful. Selective listening may lead the audience to hear the common ground but to ignore your message. For example, one student speaker thought that she was being considerate of opposing viewpoints when she began a pro-life speech by acknowledging, "A pregnancy at this point in my life would be a disaster." Somehow, half the audience failed to hear her later statements that abortion would make the disaster even worse and that adoption would make it bearable. The speaker did not move clearly enough from common ground to her own thesis; as a result, her confusing speech was made even more confusing by the selective listening of the audience.

Selective Perception

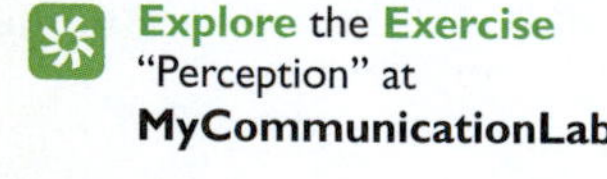
Explore the **Exercise** "Perception" at **MyCommunicationLab**

Even if your persuasive message urging listeners to change gets past the filters of selective listening, audiences may selectively perceive and respond to the message in still other ways that result in their not being persuaded.

Denial. Listeners sometimes refuse to accept a message that challenges them to change, no matter how well that message is supported or defended. Wanting to believe otherwise, they simply will not accept the truth of the message; they are in **denial**.

For example, at various times since the mid-1970s, some speakers have maintained that there are limits to what the United States can do in the world. Even when this message has been clearly explained, well supported, and articulately presented, it usually has not been well received. Many Americans—influenced by a two-century tradition that views the United States as a land of unlimited opportunity and promise—simply will not accept that there are limits to what they can achieve.

In a public speaking class, Christy Verneuil learned just how powerful a constraint denial can be. Her persuasive speech urged that gay couples be allowed to serve as adoptive parents. Christy presented study after study proving that children of homosexual parents are as happy and well adjusted as children of heterosexual parents. After the speech, the audience questioned her extensively about those studies. Yet, even though Christy answered every question, her classmates' strong beliefs about this issue kept them from accepting her proposal.

denial
The refusal to accept the claim in a message no matter how strong its justification is.

A Question of Ethics

The Ethics of Persuading

Probably no speaker is so arrogant as to think that merely presenting an excellent speech will automatically cause audience members to change their minds or their conduct. Persuasion is not a unilateral activity, but a negotiation between speaker and audience. What are each party's ethical responsibilities in this transaction? Should a speaker adapt to the audience even if it means concealing or denying the speaker's own beliefs? Is it ethical to persuade an audience to believe or do something that the *speaker* is not also willing to believe or to do? Should a speaker ever attempt to convert an audience, knowing that the attempt at conversion will fail? When attempting to induce a specific action, should the speaker care about the reasons that the audience would choose to act, or just that they act? Conversely, are audience members ethically obligated to be suspicious of speakers who support their own views, or to take seriously ideas with which they disagree? Is it ethical to assume in advance that a speaker is motivated by self-interest and that attempts at persuasion should be resisted? Why or why not?

Dismissal. A second way that audiences may selectively perceive an unfavorable message is to dismiss it as not really applying to them. Unlike denial, in which they refuse to accept the *general* truth of the message, in **dismissal** they dispute that the truth applies *specifically* to them.

Dismissal is a common response to unsettling messages about health. A smoker, for example, may hear a speech that describes the harmful effects of nicotine and urges smokers to quit, may conclude that the speech was well reasoned and probably correct in its claims, and yet light a cigarette after the speech because, "It won't happen to me." If you can imagine reasons why your audience might dismiss the message, plan strategies that respond directly to those reasons. One strategy might be to address such a possible dismissal directly ("You may think this will never happen to you, but…"), although you should be careful not to alienate your audience. You may have to accept, however, that dismissal is sometimes purely self-delusion—and insurmountable.

Belittling the Source. A third way of selectively perceiving a threatening message is to attack the credibility of the source. If your persuasive appeal relies almost entirely on a single source, you run the risk that listeners might discredit the source and thereby avoid your message.

An example of belittling the source occurred during the early months of 2009, when impeached Illinois Governor Rod Blagojevich maintained that he had been removed from office only so that state lawmakers could raise taxes without the governor's objection. Many of the governor's critics responded by suggesting that he had lost touch with reality since he ignored the mounting evidence of corruption in his office, which they were sure was the reason for his ouster. They attacked Blagojevich's *ethos,* insisting that he should not be trusted as a source. This was an effective way to belittle his statements as well.

Compartmentalization. If a message challenges what listeners already believe, they may avoid its influence by keeping it separate from their conflicting

dismissal
Disregarding a message (even if it is generally true) because one disputes that it applies to oneself.

belief, so that the two ideas do not seem at odds. This defense against persuasion is called **compartmentalization** because it is like putting the conflicting ideas into separate mental boxes. It usually is not a conscious decision by audience members to compartmentalize their beliefs, but the effect is the same as if it were.

People often have different compartments for their general beliefs and their specific beliefs. For example, some people who say they are environmentalists nevertheless buy sport utility vehicles with lower fuel economy and higher air pollution levels than smaller cars.

One approach to influencing people who are sustaining an inconsistent position is simply to make apparent to them that they are defending something in the abstract which they are unwilling to apply in practice. Student Robert Myers, for example, believed that everyone should have the right to speak; yet he was agitated when a campus group scheduled a speaker who claimed that white Americans were responsible for poverty in the Third World and who urged U.S. minority groups to revolt. Robert, like many white students on campus, resented the college giving this speaker a platform.

Classmate Susan Martinson decided to discuss this issue in her next speech. She began by identifying with her listeners, noting that they all shared the value of freedom of speech. She then argued that we diminish this value by applying it only to easy cases and supporting free speech only for those whose messages we approve. The real test, she said, is whether we are secure enough in our own beliefs to extend freedom of speech to "disreputable" speakers whose ideas we hate. By focusing on this criterion for what makes freedom of speech really meaningful, Susan convinced Robert and her classmates to reexamine their opposition to allowing this controversial person to speak on campus.

In exposing listeners' inconsistencies to them, it is important to be gentle and sympathetic. If you are too direct and accuse your audience of hypocrisy, they naturally could become defensive and even deny that there is any inconsistency. Instead, you want to inspire them to recognize that they have not fully embraced their own ideals.

Selective Influence

In addition to selective listening and perception, which we first encountered in Chapter 5, audiences also may be selective in how they are influenced by the message. Two conditions that can prompt selective influence are a polysemic message and the boomerang effect.

Multiple Meanings: Polysemy. It is a characteristic of many messages that, depending on what a listener emphasizes, they can be understood in more than one way. Such messages are called **polysemic** (pronounced pol-i-SEEM-ic). It is not that audience members actively distort the message but rather that the message interacts with listeners' different prior experiences, beliefs, and expectations in different ways.[5]

For a simple example of how a message can be polysemic, consider the famous speech by Dr. Martin Luther King, Jr., "I Have a Dream." This speech was delivered at the conclusion of the March on Washington in 1963. As you read the text, which can be found on the Internet, ask yourself whether this speech is a call for militancy or for moderation on the part of the African American community. You'll find evidence in the text to support both views. It is not hard to imagine how different listeners could think they were accepting different messages: for

compartmentalization
Keeping two conflicting beliefs separated so that one need not be conscious of the conflict between them.

polysemic
Capable of being understood in more than one way.

one person, the speech might be accepted as a call to action; for another, it might be accepted as a call for caution and patience.

A more recent instance of polysemy can be found in President George W. Bush's address to Congress following the terrorist attacks of 2001. At one point, President Bush stated,

> We are in a fight for our principles and our first responsibility is to live by them.

Many listeners interpreted this statement as calling for protection of civil liberties and avoidance of racial prejudice. Others, however, viewed it as a call to live by the principles of patriotism and national unity.

In Chapter 12, we discussed condensation symbols. These are symbols, like the American flag, that are highly valued although people value them for different reasons. They condense a wide range of divergent viewpoints in a common expression. By their nature, condensation symbols are polysemic. They are used principally to bring people together around a common symbol or meaning, as Dr. King sought to do with his unifying symbol of the dream. But they also can foster selective acceptance, if people understand the symbol-laden message in different and conflicting ways.

The Boomerang Effect. A final defense of listeners against being influenced is called the **boomerang effect**, because the message turns back on the speaker. This can happen if an appeal is so powerful that it overwhelms the audience. Concluding that nothing they can do will help matters, listeners may actually do the opposite of what the speaker has urged, thinking, "What I do won't matter anyway."

Julie Richardson knew that the presence of trans fats in the American diet was a serious public health issue. In trying to convince listeners of the issue's importance, she explained that food manufacturers began to use hydrogenated oils containing trans fats in their packaged foods to preserve shelf life and to lower production costs. Specifically, Julie wanted her audience to stop consuming foods containing trans fats, because those foods have been shown to adversely affect cholesterol levels and increase the risk of heart disease.

boomerang effect
The opposite effect from that which a speaker intends.

Several classmates reacted as Julie had hoped; they were persuaded to stop eating packaged foods containing trans fats. But Jeff Martin had quite a different reaction. Julie's speech showed him that many of his favorite foods contained trans fats; to stop eating trans fats would require a major overhaul of his eating habits. Moreover, Jeff found Julie's comment, "If you have half a brain, you will never put this stuff in your mouth," to be off-putting and overzealous. If she was going to draw such a hard line and not allow any exceptions, why bother? Why not continue to eat the foods that he enjoys and can buy at low prices at the grocery store? Julie's speech boomeranged and had the opposite effect on Jeff from what she desired. Hoping to persuade Jeff to stop consuming trans fats, she actually convinced him that he had little hope of avoiding them, so he might as well enjoy them.

To avoid the boomerang effect, you must assess carefully just how much to arouse the audience about an issue. Obviously, you want to convey a sense of seriousness or urgency when discussing a significant problem. At the same time, however,

CHECKLIST 14.2
Audience Constraints on Persuasion

1. Selective listening
2. Selective perception
   - ❒ Denial of the message
   - ❒ Dismissal of the message as not personally applicable
   - ❒ Belittling the source
   - ❒ Compartmentalization
3. Selective influence
   - ❒ Multiple meanings (polysemy)
   - ❒ Boomerang effect

your speech should leave listeners optimistic about their ability to contribute to the problem's solution and confident that concerted efforts along the lines recommended in the speech really can make a difference.

Fortunately, these methods by which audiences resist persuasion—selective listening, perception, and acceptance—are not absolute. Speakers can overcome them by making wise use of their resources and opportunities.[6]

OBJECTIVE 14.5

Strategic Resources for Specific Purposes

In reviewing the constraints facing speakers who wish to persuade, we hinted at some of the ways in which the constraints can be overcome. Now, we want to focus more carefully on the strategic resources available to the speaker. In the last chapter, we discussed a variety of strategies—defining, reporting, describing, explaining, demonstrating, and comparing—that applied across a range of informative goals. With persuasion, it is a bit more complicated. Some of the strategies pertain to a particular purpose, whereas others are more general in their application. This section of the chapter will focus on the former category, and the next section will deal with the latter.

Strengthening Commitment

Here are several common approaches that speakers use to strengthen commitment.

Consciousness Raising. You undoubtedly have beliefs or values that you are barely aware of because you take them for granted. Only when you deliberately focus attention on those values will you acknowledge and reaffirm support for them. For example, people often don't realize how important families and loved ones are until they are separated from them or someone becomes ill.

In the 1970s, the emerging women's movement used the term **consciousness raising** to refer to the process of making people aware of values and commitments that they had taken for granted.[7] Consider the issue of sexual harassment in the workplace. Prior to the movement toward public awareness, many people believed that sexual harassment was wrong, but they were not aware of how this general belief applied to everyday occurrences at work. By bringing such values to the surface and applying them to a specific situation, a speaker can cause listeners to identify with them consciously, thereby strengthening their convictions.

Watch the Video
"Persuasive Speech: Preventing Child Abuse" at MyCommunicationLab

Moving from Education to Commitment. Informative strategies might provide listeners the background that they need to understand an issue. For example, listeners need to be informed of the causes of homelessness to recognize that it is not just a matter of people temporarily not having a home, but that it also is a systemic problem. An informative speaker might choose to focus on "chronic homelessness" to show how emphasis on those who suddenly became homeless during the 2008 financial crisis can obscure others who are consistently homeless: racial minorities, veterans, those with mental health problems, and those suffering substance abuse issues. A persuasive speech would go further, building on listeners' intellectual awareness of the issue and seeking to convince them that the problem is serious and urgent, and that recovery from the financial

consciousness raising
Making people aware of values and commitments that they previously took for granted.

crisis will not take care of it. The speaker's goal might be to convince listeners to give time or money to a local homeless shelter or maybe even to lobby for the passage of laws that would deal with homelessness more comprehensively.

This speaker is trying to raise the consciousness of an audience, hoping then to move his listeners from belief to action. These are two of the most important specific goals in persuasion.

Increasing the Sense of Urgency.

Political campaign managers face the difficult problem of convincing a candidate's supporters that their ongoing support really matters. Tracy Baxter saw the need to fire up supporters when she was managing a political campaign for her neighbor, Martha Scott, who was running for the city council. Martha was well known in the neighborhood for such projects as increasing crime patrols, beautifying parks, and encouraging parents to volunteer at their child's school. She seemed certain to win the election—and that's what troubled Tracy. She was worried that Martha's supporters might think their efforts weren't needed and wouldn't bother to contribute to the campaign or even to vote. If enough people felt that way, Martha could lose the election. So Tracy addressed a rally of Martha's supporters, stressing that the race could go either way and that their efforts, money, and votes were essential to victory.

Tracy was worried that a **self-fulfilling prophecy** might derail Martha's campaign. If supporters believed that their efforts weren't needed and thus didn't contribute, the campaign wouldn't have the resources to advertise and mobilize voters; Martha's chance of winning would be reduced. Then, if Martha were defeated, supporters would conclude that they were right not to waste their money and time. To break this circular, self-fulfilling reasoning, Tracy needed to establish a sense of urgency among listeners. She convinced listeners that each person's action would make a real difference in averting defeat and ensuring victory. Her speech carefully balanced how serious the problem was and how easily listeners could be effective in solving it.

In such situations, speakers typically argue that (1) the issue is important, (2) it could be decided either way, (3) it will be decided soon, and (4) the listener's action could tip the scales. Properly crafted, such a message will jolt listeners out of complacency and intensify their commitment to the cause.

Weakening Commitment

There are two general approaches to weakening commitment. You can try to qualify or limit the audience's commitment, or you can try to disprove or dispute the claims that support it. The former approach involves finding a critical distinction; the latter involves refutation.

Finding a Critical Distinction.

One way to weaken commitment to a principle is to deflect it by invoking a different principle. Think again about the example of the speech about zoning. The audience believed strongly that the zoning board should insist on a strict separation between residential and commercial uses of property, even if the result was a loss in jobs and in tax revenue. You might have made a distinction between the *core* and the *periphery*

self-fulfilling prophecy
A prediction that comes true because of actions that people take upon hearing the prediction.

of the neighborhood, denying any interest in changing zoning in the core while maintaining that the periphery should be treated differently. In this way, you would weaken the audience's commitment to the belief that current zoning should be left intact, without challenging their core belief in the value of separating residential and commercial land use.[8]

What makes this strategic move possible is that audiences' commitments are complex. They may *seem* simple, but upon inspection they usually can be found to contain multiple perspectives, not all of which work in perfect harmony. For example, a person may believe in the death penalty and also believe that it should be imposed only in cases in which there is absolute certainty of guilt. A speaker might weaken the commitment to capital punishment by using the second belief to argue for mandatory DNA testing of defendants, for provision of highly qualified defense counsel, or even for a moratorium on executions until doubts about the fairness of capital punishment could be resolved. In some cases, the accumulation of these qualifying principles eventually can cause the first principle to collapse. That is what happened in the process that convinced the Supreme Court to declare segregated public schools unconstitutional. The constitutionality of "separate but equal" schools was not challenged directly until a series of cases had established that there was no way that segregated facilities really could be equal.

To employ this means of weakening commitment, you should identify the audience's commitment as precisely as you can and then ask what considerations might limit or qualify the commitment. Mentally explore these possibilities until you find one or more that would compete with the original commitment for the approval of your listeners.

Refutation. If finding a critical distinction serves to *deflect* the audience's commitment, **refutation** is an approach that *challenges* it directly. It tries to disprove or dispute the arguments or appeals made by others. Of course, if you convince listeners not to be persuaded by someone else, you actually have persuaded them yourself.[9]

Before you can refute an argument or appeal, you first need to be sure that you understand what it says. This is where the tests of reasoning that were offered in Chapter 8 are important. Once you have decided why the other person's argument is weak and should be refuted, you can use either or both of the following strategies:

- *Object to the claim itself, and develop a contrary claim.* This form of refutation does not target the internal workings of the argument; instead, it suggests that the conclusion is mistaken and offers an alternative conclusion. For example, on hearing a speaker maintain that only private industry will stimulate economic growth, you decide to refute the speaker by presenting your own arguments that government spending will stimulate the economy more effectively. Your arguments are independent of the other speaker's. You develop them not by analyzing the internal workings of the speaker's argument, but through your own careful and independent thought.
- *Object to the speaker's inferences, and thereby refuse to accept the conclusion.* In this case, you do analyze the internal workings of the other person's argument, applying the same tests of reasoning (see Chapter 8) that you used in

refutation
The attack or defense of a challenged statement or claim.

developing your own speech. If the speaker employs hasty generalization, confuses cause with sign, develops a faulty analogy, or commits any other error in reasoning, the conclusion may well be faulty even if supporting evidence is true. You will want to point out these deficiencies in reasoning if your goal is refutation.

Whether you want to refute a particular argument or an entire speech, the basic steps in developing your own message are similar. You must specify what you are refuting, make your refutation convincing, and explain to listeners what the refutation has accomplished. To achieve these goals, the following steps are recommended:

1. *Identify the position to be attacked.* State the position as clearly and as fairly as you can. It is especially important to state the position in a way that its supporters would accept. Advocates who fail to do this usually end up speaking past each other rather than truly refuting each other's positions.

   For example, if you opposed abortion and began to refute a pro-choice speech by stating,

   > Pro-choice speakers support the killing of innocent babies.

   you would not be stating the position fairly. You may regard the fetus as an innocent baby, but pro-choice supporters do not. In fact, that is probably the essential difference between those who oppose and those who support legalized abortion. A fairer statement of the position might be,

   > Pro-choice supporters don't think the fetus is a human being, but I believe we must assume that it is.

2. *Explain the significance of the position you are attacking.* This often-omitted step lets the audience know why your refutation is important. Most people dislike hearing disagreement for disagreement's sake. If your refutation can be granted and yet do no real damage to the opponent's position, then listeners will probably not take your speech seriously.

   Consider the abortion example again, but this time imagine that the speaker is pro-choice and is refuting the statement that protesters stayed 10 yards away from the entrance to an abortion clinic, instead insisting that they were within 5 yards of it. In this case, the refutation is probably not very important; it is hard to imagine why the difference between 5 and 10 yards would matter. But suppose that the speaker were to say, "Pro-life supporters violated a local ordinance by entering the 10-yard radius and blocking the entrance to an abortion clinic," and then went on to explain,

   > This is important because the law was designed to balance the rights of protesters with the rights of women seeking abortions. If the 10-yard rule is too difficult to maintain, then it should be changed by the City Council, not by protesters.

   Now the speaker has both identified the argument to be refuted and explained why the refutation matters.

3. *Present and develop the attack.* State your position, and support it with appropriate materials. This step will probably take the most time. The process is basically the same as if you were developing a constructive position of your own. Pay special attention to the tests of evidence (Chapter 7) and reasoning (Chapter 8). You might say, for example,

CHECKLIST 14.3

Steps in Refutation

1. Decide on the grounds for refutation.
   - ❐ Can you object to the claim? If so, what contrary claim can you develop? If not …
   - ❐ Can you object to the inferences, and thereby refuse to accept the conclusion?
2. Develop the refutation.
   - ❐ What is the position to be attacked?
   - ❐ How can you explain the significance of the position you are attacking?
   - ❐ How can you present and develop the attack?
   - ❐ How can you explain the impact of the refutation?

> The fetus has recognizable human characteristics very early in its development, according to studies reported in the *New England Journal of Medicine* last year. This means that the fetus appears to be far more human than not, so we should presume its humanity even if we are not completely sure.

4. *Explain the impact of the refutation.* Having presented and supported your own claim, do not assume that the significance of your achievement is self-evident. Include a sentence or two to explain exactly what your refutation has accomplished. If you are refuting the argument that the fetus is not a person, and show that it has recognizable human characteristics early in its development, you may believe that you have been very clear about what you've accomplished. But the audience often still needs help. Draw the argument together by saying,

> So it's far more reasonable to conclude that the fetus is a person than to conclude the reverse. Even though it might be nice to wait for all the evidence, we never will have all the evidence we need. And despite the uncertainty, we have to decide *something.* I have offered the most reasonable assumption for us to make.

Rebuilding Arguments. Refutation is not solely a process of criticizing arguments; it is also a means of rebuilding an argument that has been attacked. You can rebuild an argument by responding to criticism against it—either by showing that the attack was flawed or by developing independent reasons for the audience to believe the original claim.

Conversion

We have observed that conversion is difficult, yet it does take place. People do change their minds, do abandon positions that they have held and replace them with others. How does this happen? Typically, a speaker attempts conversion through the following strategies.

Chip Away at the Edges of Beliefs. Rather than attack beliefs head-on, where they are most strongly defended, work first on the periphery. During the civil rights movement of the 1950s and early 1960s, for example, many resistant Southerners who did not abandon racial prejudice were nonetheless convinced by marches and demonstrations that inhumane treatment of blacks was wrong. That was often the first step toward conversion because it aroused sympathy for the demonstrators and led listeners to examine whether other aspects of the treatment of blacks were also wrong.

One effective way to chip away at the edges of beliefs is to defend a value that initially coexists with the value you want to challenge but that eventually will undermine it. Again, the civil rights movement furnishes an example. Many who believed in racial segregation also revered the Constitution. These two values could coexist as long as the Constitution was not seen as prohibiting segregation; indeed, many opposed integration based on the belief that it violated the Constitution. When laws and court rulings indicated that it was segregation that was unconstitutional, President Lyndon Johnson appealed to many Southerners not so much by discrediting racial prejudice (although he attempted that as well) as by appealing instead to reverence for the Constitution. Suddenly, the two values were in opposition, and one was used to undermine the other.

Identify a Pattern of Anomalies. People change beliefs when their old beliefs no longer explain things adequately. *Anomalies* are puzzling situations that an explanation does not fit. When we first discover them, we tend to dismiss them as freak coincidences or point to them as exceptions to the rule. But if anomalies continue, and especially if they intensify, they eventually call a position into question. Then, the old view may collapse of its own weight and the listener might convert to a new belief.

Such a pattern has been used to explain why many Democrats during the 1980s converted their support to Republican Ronald Reagan. Believing in the effectiveness of government programs, they watched through the 1960s and 1970s as those programs grew; yet, in their view, social problems worsened rather than improved. At first, this was just a puzzle for them. But as evidence (and their taxes) continued to mount, they eventually came to believe that government was not a solution to social ills but was part of the problem. This, of course, was the position advocated by President Reagan. Likewise, many who were committed to unrestrained free-market principles and were opposed to government regulation changed their minds when the economic crisis of 2008 and 2009 revealed the dangers of inadequate regulation of financial institutions and the subsequent federal regulations proved to be effective.

Employ Consciousness Raising. Besides being a means of strengthening commitment, consciousness raising can be used when a speaker wants the audience to change. Let's look again at the example of the women's movement. Early advocates of consciousness raising maintained that women had accepted their subordinate role because they had never regarded their role as subordinate. By raising women's consciousness about the dominant/submissive pattern in many of their existing relationships with men, advocates were able not only to sensitize them to their situation but also to evoke an alternative toward which they might strive.

Watch the **Video** "Citizens for Community Justice (Hal Taylor, Episcopal Priest and Ph.D.)" at **MyCommunicationLab**

In another example, student speaker Laura Davisson gave a speech to raise listeners' consciousness about their daily acts of discrimination against overweight people:

> You might just laugh at them behind their backs. Perhaps you call them names like "whale" or "pig." Maybe they are the butt of your jokes. Or maybe it's something much more subtle than that. Maybe you just assume that fat people have no self-control, that they eat too much and too often, or that they get no exercise.

By pointing out the existence of listeners' discriminatory feelings and actions, Laura was able to begin altering them. Consciousness raising made listeners sufficiently uncomfortable with their own actions that they could be induced to change.

Seek Incremental Changes. Usually conversion comes about slowly, in a series of small and gradual steps. Knowing that people typically change their views incrementally rather than radically, keep your goals modest. Don't ask for too much too soon.

Rhetorical Workout

Practice Persuasive Strategies

You are preparing a speech on food safety in the United States. You want to persuade your audience to support new legislation that would tighten regulations on food manufacturers and require more safety inspections. Let's explore a few of the many persuasive strategies discussed in this chapter:

1. *Consciousness raising:* Explain how the following information could focus your audience's attention on their values related to food safety: (a) food-borne illnesses can be fatal; (b) contaminated foods from mass producers can be distributed widely before the problem is discovered. Write a sentence about one of these items that you could use in your persuasive speech.
2. *Increasing the sense of urgency:* Explain how the following information could mobilize your listeners: (a) the legislation comes up for a vote next month; (b) widespread food-borne illnesses have increased rapidly in recent years. Write a sentence about one of these items that you could use in your persuasive speech.
3. *Seeking incremental changes:* Suppose that your audience wants to do something more personal and direct than writing to legislators. Explain how the following information could persuade them to make a small step toward taking a greater interest in national food safety: (a) locally grown food from small farms is less likely to cause widespread disease; (b) an area restaurant called Paunch publicizes all the locations from which it buys its ingredients. Write a sentence about one of these items that you could use in your persuasive speech.

Imagine, for example, that your goal is to defend public funding for the arts, even though you know that the audience is hostile to it, considers most contemporary art unnecessary or even perverse, and sees public funding as a waste of tax money. Successful persuasion will probably require several steps, beginning with asking the audience to acknowledge the importance of art both in fostering self-expression and advancing culture; then perhaps moving to the position that one need not like or support all examples of art to believe strongly in the value of the arts; then explaining why it is in the public interest to support art; then defending the overall administration of public funding programs and establishing that errors and mistaken judgments are few; and only then moving to the question of whether the government should reduce funding for the arts. Getting to this point might require several speeches, over a long period of time. But a frontal assault on the audience's values is likely to fail, whereas a gradual, incremental approach has at least a chance of success. People often accept in small doses a belief that they would reject outright if it were presented all at once.

Use Reluctant Testimony. Your statements will be weakened if listeners think that you have something to gain by stating them. If your audience believes that you have a vested interest—whether economic, political, or ideological—in a particular outcome of the speech, listeners will tend to discount what you say. However, if you make a statement that is at odds with your own interest, that statement is considered to be **reluctant testimony**. Because you are working against your own interests by making this statement, listeners presume that you would not make it unless it was true.

Likewise, if you quote sources who are widely known to favor your position, the audience you are seeking to convert may simply dismiss the sources out of hand. However, using sources who generally support the audience's position but disagree with it in this case will give their words added credibility.

reluctant testimony
Statements that are not in the speaker's self-interest.

Consider how reluctant testimony has worked in the political world. Only Ronald Reagan, for example—who had called the Soviet Union an "evil empire" and whose anticommunist credentials were secure—could really begin to seek arms reduction agreements with the Soviet Union. If someone else had attempted this, it might have seemed like a cave-in to Soviet demands. But President Reagan was trustworthy because people believed that he would not betray conservative interests. Similarly, George W. Bush, although he had opposed the use of U.S. military forces for "nation building," was able to convince many Americans that this was an appropriate, even necessary, use of U.S. troops in Afghanistan and Iraq. And when the actor Charlton Heston, well known as a political conservative, supported public funding of the National Endowment for the Arts, his words were reluctant testimony that helped convert some conservatives in Congress to support continued funding for the endowment.

Because reluctant testimony generally is more credible than evidence reflecting the source's self-interest, you should look for it when conducting your research. Reluctant testimony is the opposite of **biased evidence**, which you should try particularly hard to avoid.[10]

Reluctant testimony enhances the credibility of classroom speakers, too. Western State University had a tradition of strong social fraternities, a system that had come under fire because several recent initiation rituals clearly had been excessive. A vocal group of faculty members charged that all fraternities were anti-intellectual, and the campus newspaper called them "social clubs for the privileged rich." Two students of public speaking addressed this issue, arguing that major changes were needed if fraternities were to survive on campus. Ben Peters was an independent who was known to dislike fraternities. Although his speech was well prepared, it had little impact on his classmates; it said exactly what everyone expected Ben to say. But when Charles Thompson, a fraternity president, acknowledged that the system had serious problems, listeners noticed. If a prominent fraternity man criticized the system, his views had to be taken seriously.

CHECKLIST 14.4

Strategies for Specific Purposes

1. Strengthening commitment
   - ❒ Consciousness raising
   - ❒ Moving from education to commitment
   - ❒ Increasing the sense of urgency
2. Weakening commitment
   - ❒ Finding a critical distinction
   - ❒ Refutation
3. Conversion
   - ❒ Identify a pattern of anomalies.
   - ❒ Employ consciousness raising.
   - ❒ Seek incremental changes.
   - ❒ Use reluctant testimony.
4. Inducing a specific action
   - ❒ Identify the desired action precisely.
   - ❒ Make the action as easy to perform as possible.

Inducing a Specific Action

Two strategies will be especially helpful if your goal is to induce a specific action.

Identify the Desired Action Precisely. A speaker who says, "So I urge you to do something about this," is not likely to accomplish much. The action is so general that no one will know what to do. Identify the specific behavior that you want listeners to perform—to stop using the car for trips of fewer than five blocks, to contribute money to a charitable organization, to write legislators in support of a pending bill, and so on.

Make the Action as Easy to Perform as Possible. Audiences are subject to inertia. If a difficult action is requested of them, they are less likely to go to the trouble of performing it. So, for example, if you want your listeners to

biased evidence
Statements that are suspect because they are influenced by the self-interest of the source.

sign a petition, have a copy of the petition with you. If you want them to write a legislator, provide the specific address (and maybe even hand out stamped, self-addressed envelopes if you are seeking letters rather than e-mails). The easier you make it for the audience to do what you ask, the more likely you are to succeed.

General Strategic Resources

In addition to the approaches that are tailored to specific persuasive goals, there are resources available to all persuasive speakers. The earliest theorists of public speaking, during classical times, identified three general means of persuasion: *logos, ethos*, and *pathos. Logos* referred to the speaker's argument; *ethos*, to the speaker's apparent character and credibility; and *pathos*, to appeals to appropriate emotions. In different combinations, these resources are employed whenever speakers try to persuade. Without always using the classical terms, we have discussed many of these resources in earlier chapters, so it is appropriate to review them briefly here.

Select Appropriate Supporting Materials

In Chapter 7, we explored the various forms of supporting material, and in Chapter 9, we considered how to select supporting materials for the speech. Astute selection is particularly important when persuasion is the goal.[11] A startling statistic, for example, might move listeners to take notice of an issue that is far more vast than they might think. Student speaker Mitchell Johnson, a Chicago native, talked about the fact that many ballots cast in an election are not counted:

> In 2000, the country focused on uncounted ballots in Florida. But did you know that over 120,000 ballots were discarded as uncountable in Cook County, Illinois, my home? In fact, across the country there were *millions* of punch-card ballots that could not be counted by machine readers.

He then pointed out that this total easily could be larger than the winning margin in a close election. Insisting that every legally cast vote should be counted, Mitchell sought to persuade listeners that all states should replace punch-card voting systems with a more reliable instrument.

A personal narrative also can be a potent form of supporting material, making an abstract problem concrete and showing its effects on the lives of real people. If you discuss how "taxpayer resistance has squeezed the public sector of the economy," the problem may seem distant, removed, and impersonal. Instead, you can make the issue more vivid and immediate by telling listeners, "The local elementary school has been forced to close its library, depriving children of books and the librarian of a job."

Of course, startling statistics and personal narratives are not the only types of supporting material to use in persuasion. *Any* type of supporting material can work well if it is carefully chosen and clearly related to the speaker's purpose.

Use Sound Reasoning

Watch the **Video** "Persuasive Speech: Untreated Depression (Well-Done Version)" at **MyCommunicationLab**

Because in a persuasive speech you are asking the audience to believe or to do something, it is particularly important that you offer good reasons for your claims. Good reasons are those that meet the tests of reasoning we developed

CHOOSE A STRATEGY: Persuading

The Situation

The local homeless shelter where you volunteer is running out of money, and you want to rally support from your campus and community. You've compiled a list of organizations to approach and have contacted your local city administrators to ask what support they might be willing to offer. After some consideration, you've decided that a two-pronged strategy would be best: first, to raise supplies of food and other donations for the short term; second, to organize a series of cost-cutting measures and long-term donations to prevent such a problem in the future. You schedule your first appointment with your campus student union and ask to speak at their meeting.

Making Choices

1. What resistance do you expect to encounter, and what strategies will you use to overcome it?
2. What basic persuasive speech structure will be most effective for realizing your goals?

What If...

The type of audience will most likely affect your specific speaking goals and how you structure your speech to achieve these goals. Decide what purpose and motivation you will emphasize in the following situations:

1. You are speaking to the local chamber of commerce, whose membership is made up of business managers and small business owners.
2. You are speaking to a group of retired persons at a local senior center.
3. You are speaking to your campus organization of volunteers.

in Chapter 8. They will show listeners that you have used inference patterns that generally yield reliable results. People who are confident about your reasoning will be more likely to accept your conclusions and less likely to quarrel with your thinking.[12]

Follow Appropriate Organizational Patterns

Not only does being organized itself enhance persuasiveness but also the choice of one organizational pattern over another can make a difference. Review the organizational patterns we developed in Chapter 9. Many speakers find the problem–solution pattern to be particularly effective for persuasion. It makes listeners aware of a problem and then advocates its solution. But other patterns can be effective too, especially cause–effect and comparison–contrast.

A slight variation on the problem–solution pattern is to identify the criteria that a solution would need to satisfy and then to argue that one's proposal best satisfies them. For example, on the subject of diversity in college admissions, a speaker might first establish that a good policy was one that admitted a diverse student body, did not grant preferences based on race or ethnicity, and did not incorporate a quota system. Then, the speaker could suggest that the best way to meet these criteria was to guarantee admission to the top 10 percent of each high school graduating class.

Other organizational patterns also can be strategically valuable. For instance, narrative sequence lets you tell the story of how the problem developed, topical structure allows you to examine various dimensions of the problem, and biographical structure enables you to focus on key individuals in the evolution of the problem.

This speaker is using strategies to strengthen listeners' commitment to her cause.

Not only are organizational choices important in individual sections of the speech but also organization is an important strategic resource for the speech as a whole. In the next major section of this chapter, "Organizing Persuasive Speeches," we will identify two common organizational plans for a speech in which persuasion is the principal goal.

Establish Positive *Ethos*

Your *ethos* is a powerful resource in persuasive speeches. If listeners trust you, they will be more inclined to give your ideas a fair hearing. Particularly important among the many factors that engender trust are a speaker's previous record and association with trustworthy sources.

Previous Record. A speaker who has established a record of being trustworthy is likely to be trusted in the specific situation at hand. Warren Buffett, CEO of the investment firm Berkshire Hathaway, enjoyed positive *ethos* when he spoke about tax reform in 2011, because he was viewed as a seasoned expert with a long track record of success; he was even called the "Wizard of Omaha" because of his shrewd investments and understanding of the market. Of course, right now you do not hold a position of such influence. Still, if in earlier speeches you've convinced the audience that you are careful, faithful to the evidence, and critical in reasoning, and that you don't make claims beyond what the evidence supports, you have created a strong presumption that what you say in this speech will be trustworthy as well.

Association with Trustworthy Sources. If you are not an expert on your topic, you need to draw on the statements of people who do have expertise in the subject. If your sources have a reputation for trustworthiness, your association with them will suggest that you are trustworthy too. George W. Bush followed this advice during the 2000 presidential campaign. When he spoke about foreign policy, with which he had little previous experience, he often mentioned that he received valuable information from General Colin Powell, former Stanford provost Condoleezza Rice, and former Defense Secretary Richard Cheney, all of whom were quite experienced and were held in high regard at the time, and all of whom he brought into his administration and assigned significant roles. During the 2008 campaign, Barack Obama likewise consulted with foreign policy experts, although he was less likely to publicize their names.

Encourage Retention Through Reinforcement

We saw in Chapter 13 that the slope of the forgetting curve is steep, particularly when the message involves new, unfamiliar, or uncomfortable ideas (see Figure 13.1). Unless your persuasive goal is very specific and can be achieved through the speech itself, you should think creatively about how to reinforce what you want listeners to believe or to do. Your strategies might range from the simple act of thanking the audience for hearing you out to the extreme of asking listeners to participate actively in encouraging others to accept the view you propose.

Student Margaret Orsinger used an interesting metaphor to reinforce her message that bicyclists and motorcyclists should wear helmets:

> We do more to protect the melons in our grocery stores than we do to protect our own heads! Every time you see a cyclist without a helmet, take a good hard look at these "melon-heads." They are people in need of a good, solid crate around their ears.

There is no magic recipe for reinforcing a persuasive message. In general, though, you are more likely to succeed if you give listeners opportunities to rehearse and remind themselves of your conclusion and how you arrived at it and if you can make acceptance of your position seem to enhance listeners' self-worth.

Achieve Identification

 **Watch** the **Video** "Persuasive Speech: Preparing for a Job" at **MyCommunicationLab**

Establishing common bonds between speaker and audience is referred to as **identification**.[13] The more that listeners believe themselves to be basically like the speaker and to share the same values or experiences, the more willing they are to be influenced by what the speaker says. Speakers can develop common bonds explicitly, by stating the features they share with the audience. Or bonds can be developed implicitly, when the speaker relates a personal experience that many listeners also have had. Common bonds can even be developed with no mention at all. For example, the fact that a college student speaks to an audience of college students about concerns of college students is a source of common bonds. Not surprisingly, listeners are more likely to be persuaded by a peer than by a more distant figure with whom it is difficult to identify.

Identification with the audience helps to create a good feeling. It is, in a sense, an emotional connection, suggesting that you understand and share the emotions you have aroused in the audience. Your speech can evoke emotions (such as happiness, anger, relief, satisfaction, or fear) that match your own emotions and that you believe are appropriate to your topic. Together with good reasons and good character, good feeling helps you to persuade.

identification
Establishing common bonds between speaker and audience so that the speaker appears to be at one with listeners.

To keep identification from being perceived as pandering to the audience or telling listeners whatever they want to hear, apply the test you learned in Chapter 6: Use appeals that will satisfy not only the specific audience that is immediately present but also the broader audience of unseen critical listeners whom you might imagine as your court of appeal.

Even facing a potentially hostile audience, speakers employ some level of identification. The common bond that leads an audience at least to listen attentively to ideas with which they disagree might be a shared procedural value, such as a belief in fair play or a willingness to hear the speaker out. Or the bond might be respect for a speaker who has the courage of his or her convictions.

Do not conclude, then, that you can't disagree with your audience. In fact, a speaker who always tailors the message to what listeners believe is suspect. But when you cannot achieve identification with the audience on the basis of your content, try to do so on the basis of an overarching value.

CHECKLIST 14.5

Generally Applicable Strategies

- ❒ Select appropriate supporting materials.
- ❒ Use sound reasoning.
- ❒ Follow appropriate organizational patterns.
- ❒ Establish positive *ethos*.
- ❒ Encourage retention through reinforcement.
- ❒ Achieve identification.

OBJECTIVE 14.6

Organizing Persuasive Speeches

As we have seen, persuasion can be accomplished in any speech. Often, however, the principal purpose of the speech is to persuade. In this section, we will consider two very common patterns for structuring the persuasive speech: the problem–solution pattern and the motivated sequence. These two organizational patterns attempt to trigger a sequence of cognitive changes that correspond to the experience of being persuaded. (Note, however, that some researchers do not believe that persuasion always occurs in such a neat sequence.) These patterns are offered as guidelines for organizing your persuasive appeal well, but they do not exhaust the possible organizational patterns for persuasive speaking.

The Problem–Solution Speech

As its name suggests, the problem–solution speech establishes a serious problem and then identifies what should be done about it.[14] Problem–solution speeches can be organized in a variety of ways, but they generally apply to an entire speech the four-stage structure that you learned in Chapter 9:

1. Describe the situation.
2. Evaluate the situation as a problem.
3. Propose a solution.
4. Argue for the solution.

Watch the Video "Childhood Obesity and the Need for Physical Education Classes (clip)" at **MyCommunicationLab**

Describe the Situation. This part of the speech is primarily informative. Your goal is to make listeners aware of the magnitude or importance of the problem. For example, in discussing the use of tobacco among teenagers, you might report how many teenagers use cigarettes, smokeless tobacco, and cigars; how teenagers feel about tobacco use; and the relationship between teen smoking and adults' use of tobacco. The outline for this part of the body of your speech might be:

I. Tobacco use among teenagers is significant and high.
   A. Rates of tobacco use among teenagers are high.
   B. Teenagers continue to believe that using tobacco enhances their image.
   C. Most adults who use tobacco began when they were teenagers.

Evaluate the Situation as a Problem. The second stage is to convince listeners that the situation you described really does represent a problem—that it is cause for genuine concern. People will endure all sorts of inconveniences without taking action; they become concerned only about what they regard as serious problems.

To establish that a situation is a problem, you need to show that it violates a value that is important to your audience. In the case of teenage tobacco use, for example, you might establish that the use of tobacco products is strongly associated with premature death. In addition, tobacco-related diseases add billions of dollars to the cost of health care. These conditions probably will be accepted as problems in their own right. They also might lead people to question the quality of life not only for tobacco users but also for those who live, work, and play with them. They might also call into question whether it is economically just for society at large to bear the costs of tobacco-related illnesses. Because people care about these values, they are likely to be disturbed by the high rate of tobacco use among teenagers.

Values are rooted in emotions, and so persuasive strategies must be concerned with emotional appeals. In Chapter 8, you learned that an inappropriate appeal to emotions is an error in reasoning. The key word here is *inappropriate*. Although emotional appeals can be misused, there is nothing irrational about responding to an appropriate appeal. When you decide not to go out alone at night because of safety concerns, when you try to mend fences with parents or siblings because family harmony is important, or when you strive to do your best in response to competition, your choices are perfectly reasonable and sensible.

The second part of the speech's body might be outlined like this:

II. High tobacco use among teenagers is a serious problem.
  A. Use of tobacco products is strongly associated with premature death.
  B. Tobacco-related diseases add billions of dollars to the cost of health care.
  C. The quality of life is diminished for smokers and others.
  D. It undermines economic justice to burden society with the costs of tobacco-related illness.

Many students are tempted to text while driving, but doing so is a major safety risk. What strategies would you use to persuade fellow students to refrain from texting while they drive?

A speaker cannot create in listeners an emotion that they do not feel. However, the speaker can make audience members aware of their emotions and indicate the importance of those emotions. When you evoke fear, pride, anxiety, or any other emotion, you also create a need to satisfy that emotion. Some emotions can become highly disturbing if they are left unrelieved. Your power as a speaker lies in the ability not only to arouse the emotion, but also to satisfy it by providing a positive course of action. We have seen that arousing too much fear can cause a boomerang effect. But if you arouse an appropriate level of fear in the audience and you then offer the means to relieve the fear—by talking to a school counselor, by taking advantage of over-the-counter aids to stop smoking, or by joining a community organization that works to reduce teenagers' use of tobacco products—the speech is likely to be persuasive.

Propose a Solution. Your solution might be simple (a single option) or complex (a range of options). You might identify it at once, or you might first rule out alternatives. But your solution should be detailed enough to address the problem as you have described it. If you have presented three separate dimensions of the problem, for instance, each should be addressed by your solution.

In the example of teenagers' use of tobacco, few listeners would feel that a statement such as "We have to have faith and hope that things will turn out for the best" is an appropriate solution. It is too vague, and the outcome is too uncertain, to match the speaker's detailed analysis of the problem. You are more likely to be persuasive if a section of the body of your speech details the solution, such as:

Watch the **Video** "Childhood Obesity: Statistics and Solutions (clip)" at **MyCommunicationLab**

III. A successful solution to the problem has several components.
  A. It includes efforts to eliminate the root causes of teenage tobacco use.
  B. It includes more effective enforcement of laws regarding the purchase of tobacco.
  C. It includes creating more persuasive appeals to tobacco companies.

Strategies for Speaking to Diverse Audiences

Respecting Diversity Through Persuading

Successful persuasion meets listeners where they are and adapts to the opportunities and constraints of a situation. These factors are all more complex when an audience is diverse. Here are strategies for success in persuading diverse audiences:

1. With diverse audiences, identification is both more important (since it cannot be taken for granted) and more difficult (since you must acknowledge the variety of your audience members' beliefs and commitments). Identify with your listeners before moving them to a new commitment.
2. Consider the diversity of values and commitments. For instance, "family values" in Mexico include the expectation that children live with their parents until they are married, whereas this is much less common in the United States.
3. Consider how different cultures may present you with different constraints or opportunities. If your emotional appeal relies on a culturally specific value, then you may need to plan ahead and think about other possible strategies you might use.
4. Suggest actions that are appropriate and "do-able" for your specific audience. Calling on an audience to solve the Israel-Palestine conflict not only is asking for too much but may alienate certain audience members who think you are trivializing the issue.
5. Establish a positive *ethos* that invites trust from members of a diverse audience.

Argue for the Solution. The final step in the problem–solution speech is to convince listeners that your solution really works—that it resolves the problem, is feasible, and produces benefits that outweigh its costs. Speakers too often neglect this final step, as though the value of the solution were self-evident. But if that were so, the solution would probably have been tried already!

Instead of taking the value of your solution for granted, give listeners reasons to believe that your solution is the best option. In the tobacco example, this final section of the body of your speech might be organized in the following way:

IV. The comprehensive solution I have proposed is the best way to deal with the use of tobacco among teenagers.
  A. It will stop tobacco use at the source when possible.
  B. It will deter the sale of tobacco products to teenagers.
  C. It will improve the quality of life for both smokers and nonsmokers.

From this example, you can see that the basic problem–solution organizational pattern adapts easily to persuasive speeches. Although each step of the structure includes informative elements, the principal purpose of the speech is to affect the audience's beliefs, attitudes, values, or actions—in other words, to persuade.

The Motivated Sequence

motivated sequence
A persuasive message that is organized in terms of steps in the audience's motivation rather than in terms of the specific subject.

A sequential scheme for achieving persuasion in a speech was developed many years ago by Alan H. Monroe.[15] His **motivated sequence** is similar to the problem–solution speech, but it is organized with respect to the audience's motivation, not the specific subject matter of the speech. The sequence has five steps (see Figure 14.2).

Attention Step. As its name suggests, this step is intended to engage listeners' attention. It serves as the introduction to the speech and includes such appropriate devices as visual narratives, engaging anecdotes, and startling statistics.

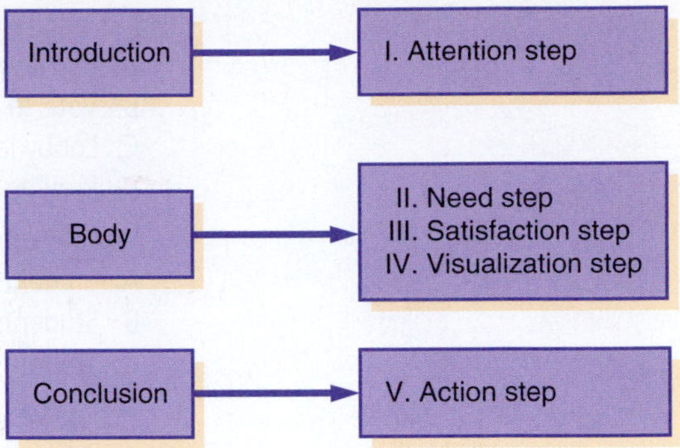

Introduction → I. Attention step

Body → II. Need step, III. Satisfaction step, IV. Visualization step

Conclusion → V. Action step

Figure 14.2 Organization according to the motivated sequence.

Need Step. This step is intended to convince the audience that something is amiss. The goal is to arouse listeners to believe that an important value is being lost, an opportunity is being wasted, or an objective is not being met. This belief will motivate them to take corrective action if they know what to do.

Satisfaction Step. This step provides listeners with the means to fulfill the motivation that the need step aroused. People seldom respond to broad and abstract generalizations, however, and so slogans such as "Stimulate the economy" or "Affirmative action: mend it but don't end it" are unlikely to satisfy listeners. To avoid this problem, the speaker goes on to explain how the solution will work and how it will affect listeners personally.

Visualization Step. This step is intended to give the audience a mental picture of the solution. Instead of saying, "Stimulate the economy," the speaker shows what the solution will mean:

> Putting an extra $1,000 saved from taxes into the hands of the average family will make it easier for them to buy the things they need. Increased demand for those products will create millions of new jobs, so that even more people will be better off.

Action Step. In the final step, the speaker asks the audience to do specific things to bring about the solution that they have visualized: change one's personal behavior, sign a petition, patronize some stores but not others, write to senators and representatives, make a donation, and so on. The action step resembles the final plea that is one of the traditional functions of the conclusion of a speech.

An outline based on a persuasive speech by student Sarah Crist on the problems of the commercialization of America's classrooms could be organized into the motivated sequence as follows:

I. Attention Step
   A. Description of fondness for Coke products, but school sells only Pepsi because of an exclusive contract.
   B. Statistics showing percent of school day spent watching commercial "information" video programs.
   C. Statistics documenting the profits of commercialized education companies.
   D. Translation of these statistics into the probability that a younger relative is being treated as a consumer, not a student, by his or her school.

II. Need Step
   A. Commercialized education promotes consumerism, not education.
   B. Commercialized education exploits schools' financial problems.
   C. Commercialized education benefits advertisers, not students.
   D. Commercialized education promotes unhealthy food and beverage options.

III. Satisfaction Step
    A. End contracts with commercialized education companies such as Channel One.
    B. Vote to pass school levies to alleviate financial problems.
    C. Lobby lawmakers to pass laws prohibiting exploitation of students as consumers.
    D. Provide healthy food and beverage alternatives at school.

IV. Visualization Step
    A. Students will not be held captive to advertisers.
    B. Students will spend more class time learning, not consuming.
    C. Students will eat healthier and live healthier.

V. Action Step
    A. Write a letter to school board officials urging them to end contracts with commercialized education companies.
    B. Support your school by voting in favor of school levies.
    C. Participate in school fundraisers as an alternative to commercialized funding.

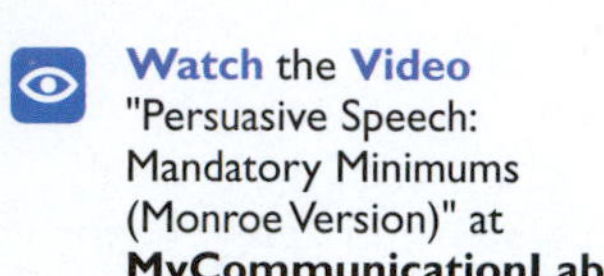
Watch the **Video** "Persuasive Speech: Mandatory Minimums (Monroe Version)" at **MyCommunicationLab**

Criticisms have been raised against the motivated sequence. First, these steps are not always completely separate. It's possible, for example, that visualizing a solution is what alters the perception of a need. Second, not all listeners experience the steps in precisely the same order. Someone might be attracted to the satisfaction step, for example, without having grasped the full dimensions of the need. But even if the motivated sequence is not a universal account of human motivation, it still can provide a clear, coherent, and compelling way to organize speeches when the goal is persuasion.

What Have You Learned?

Objective 14.1: State the differences between informative and persuasive strategies for speeches and identify the speech purposes that are served through persuasive strategies.

Persuasive strategies are more ambitious than informative strategies:

- They aim not only to provide information but also to affect audience members' attitudes and behavior.
- They ask for a greater degree of commitment from listeners, although no speaker can motivate an unwilling audience.

Through persuasive strategies, the following purposes are achieved:

- Strengthening commitment
- Weakening commitment
- Conversion
- Inducing a specific action

Objective 14.2: Describe how determining the target audience and analyzing the audience's motivation and the speaker's purpose can help the speaker plan for persuasion.

To be successful at persuasion, speakers must know clearly the purpose they wish to achieve, determine the target audience they are trying to influence, and understand that listeners must

- Be motivated
- Comprehend and agree with the message
- Incorporate the message into their overall system of beliefs and attitudes

Objective 14.3: Explain the Elaboration Likelihood Model and what it implies for persuasion.

The elaboration likelihood model explains how people are persuaded:

- Elaboration is the listener's tendency to think about the message and the topic.
- When elaboration is high, persuasion is likely to result from systematic analysis of the speaker's argument.
- When elaboration is low, persuasion is likely to result from intuitive judgments about the speaker.
- When elaboration is at moderate levels, listeners are likely to use a mix of these bases for judgment.

Objective 14.4: Describe how audiences resist persuasion and what resources help a speaker to overcome resistance.

Listeners are often resistant to persuasion and may selectively listen to, perceive, and be influenced by the message. They may resist persuasion by

- Regarding an ambiguous message as "really" supporting their own position
- Denying the message
- Dismissing the message as inapplicable to them
- Belittling the source
- Compartmentalizing the message in their minds so that it affects beliefs without affecting values or behavior
- Understanding the message to mean different things from what the speaker intended
- Actually doing the opposite of what the speaker recommends, through a boomerang effect

To attain results, speakers draw on the following:

- Their ability to analyze the audience and the situation
- Their own credibility
- The effective use of evidence, reasoning, and emotional appeals

Objective 14.5: Identify strategies that speakers can use for each specific purpose and in general.

To strengthen commitment, the speaker might try the following:

- Move from subconscious to conscious values
- Move from education to commitment
- Move from belief to action

To weaken commitment, the speaker might try to do the following:

- Draw a critical distinction
- Engage in refutation

To achieve conversion, the speaker might try to do the following:

- Chip away at the edges of beliefs
- Draw on a pattern of anomalies
- Use consciousness raising
- Seek incremental changes
- Employ reluctant testimony

To induce a specific action, the speaker might try to do the following:

- State clearly just what is to be done
- Make the action easy for listeners to perform

Whatever the speaker's purpose, persuaders might try to do the following:

- Achieve identification by establishing common bonds with the audience
- Call on listeners to be true to their own beliefs
- Give listeners a sense of trust that they can draw on to support their message
- Use an appropriate organizational pattern
- Make an appropriate choice of supporting materials
- Provide listeners with opportunities not only to say that they agree but also to perform some action.

Objective 14.6: Use two basic structures for persuasive speeches: the problem–solution structure and the motivated sequence.

The problem–solution speech

- Describes a situation
- Evaluates the situation as a problem
- Proposes a solution
- Argues for the solution

The motivated sequence aims to arouse and satisfy the audience's motivation; the parts of the message are the following:

- Attention step
- Need step
- Satisfaction step
- Visualization step
- Action step

Listen to the Audio Chapter Summary
at MyCommunicationLab

Discussion Questions

1. What are the most urgent issues of controversy in the public forum of your classroom? List issues that most interest your community and your generation. Which of those topics would be good for a persuasive speech that
   - Strengthens commitment?
   - Weakens commitment?
   - Converts opponents?
   - Calls for a specific action?
2. When a speaker has strong beliefs about a controversial issue, how can that speaker achieve identification with an opponent without compromising his or her own beliefs? What common bonds might be established between the opposing sides on the following highly controversial topics?
   - Immigration restrictions
   - The death penalty
   - Stem cell research

   How could a speaker use those common bonds as an aid to persuasion?
3. What, if any, differences are there between persuasion and manipulation? For many people, the image of a slick used-car salesman defines persuasion. Given what you have learned in this chapter about persuasion and throughout this course about the ethics of communication, do you think that is a fair characterization? Why or why not?
4. In what ways do persuasive strategies differ for the various speech purposes? As a class, create a chart based on the one below and fill in the boxes to describe what you think would be likely differences in organization, choice of supporting material, and style for the following persuasive goals.

	Organization	Supporting Material	Style
Strengthening commitment			
Weakening commitment			
Conversion			
Inducing a specific action			

Activities

1. Identify a topic and develop a thesis statement for each of the persuasive goals in the chart for Discussion Question 4. In a sentence or two, explain why you think each of these would be a good topic and thesis statement for a speech aimed at your target audience.
2. Choose one of your thesis statements from activity 1, and develop an outline for a persuasive speech. In a short essay, explain how you intend to motivate your audience. To which values do you plan to appeal? How do you plan to use emotional appeals?
3. From an opponent's perspective, examine the issue that you have chosen for your persuasive speech. Honestly try to step into the shoes of someone who disagrees with, and might refute, you.
   a. Which argument is most important for your opponent?
   b. What concerns would your opponent have if your position is argued successfully?
   c. How will your opponent view the supporting material that you plan to use in your speech?
4. Watch a debate. It can be a campaign debate, an academic debate, or a debate between two friends. In a short essay, answer the following questions about each speaker:
   a. Did the speaker fairly identify the opponent's position?
   b. Did the speaker refute the claims or the inferences being made by the other side?
   c. Did the speaker explain the significance of the position being attacked?
   d. Did the speaker explain the impact of the refutation?
   e. Who do you think won the debate, and why?
5. a. Identify a topic on which you and your classmates hold strong opinions and on which your classmates do not all agree. Then prepare and deliver a short speech arguing *in favor* of a position that you personally *oppose*. Afterwards, discuss what you learned about your own strongly held views regarding the topic and about the views of those with whom you disagree.
   b. Listen to your classmates as they complete the same activity. How effectively were they able to develop arguments against their previously held opinions? As a class, discuss how well you were able to relate to opposing views.

Key Terms

biased evidence **351**
boomerang effect **343**
compartmentalization **342**
consciousness raising **344**
conversion **334**
denial **340**
dismissal **341**
hostile audience **334**
identification **355**
motivated sequence **358**
motivation **336**
polysemic **342**
refutation **346**
reluctant testimony **350**
self-fulfilling prophecy **345**
target audience **336**

Study and **Review** the **Flashcards** at **MyCommunicationLab**

Notes

1 A. H. Maslow, "A Dynamic Theory of Personality," *Psychological Review* 50 (July 1943): 370–96.

2 For a more complete review of the elaboration likelihood model and research supporting it, see Daniel J. O'Keefe, *Persuasion: Theory and Research*, 2nd ed. Thousand Oaks, CA: Sage, 2002, pp. 137–67.

3 A review of the psychological literature about persuasion further explains the resistances discussed in this chapter. See Joseph P. Forgas, Joel Cooper, and William D. Crano, ed., *The Psychology of Attitudes and Attitude Change*, New York: Taylor and Francis, 2010; and Gerd Bojhner and Michaela Wanke, *Attitudes and Attitude Change*, New York: Taylor and Francis, 2002.

4 The tendency to make ambiguous messages seem closer to one's own position than they actually are is one of the major conclusions of social judgment theory. For more on social judgment theory, see Carolyn W. Sherif, Muzafer Sherif, and Roger E. Nebergall, *Attitudes and Attitude Change: The Social Judgment–Involvement Approach*, Philadelphia: W. B. Saunders, 1965.

5 For an excellent overview of the concept of polysemy as it applies to the analysis of speeches, see Leah Ceccarelli, "Polysemy: Multiple Meanings in Rhetorical Criticism," *Quarterly Journal of Speech* 84 (November 1998): 395–415. On the strategic deployment of polysemy, see Stefano Puntoni, Jonathan E. Schroeder, and Mark Ritson, "Meaning Matters," *Journal of Advertising* 39 (Summer 2010): 51–64.

6 For more discussion of persuasive strategies, see Herbert W. Simons and Jean G. Jones, *Persuasion and Society*, 2nd ed., New York: Routledge, 2011.

7 Consciousness raising often occurred in group discussions but could also be the result of a more formal speech. See Anita Shreve, *Women Together, Women Alone: The Legacy of the Consciousness-Raising Movement*, New York: Viking Press, 1989.

8 The technical term for this kind of distinction drawing is *dissociation*. For a thorough treatment of the concept, see Chaim Perelman and L. Olbrechts-Tyteca, *The New Rhetoric*, translated by John Wilkinson and Purcell Weaver, Notre Dame, IN: University of Notre Dame Press, 1969, pp. 411–59.

9 Research has shown that messages which provide both arguments for a position and refutation of the opposition are more persuasive than messages that simply present arguments for a position. Mike Allen, Jerold Hale, Paul Mongeau, et al., "Testing a Model of Message Sidedness: Three Replications," *Communication Monographs* 57 (December 1990): 275–91.

10 One study of communication questions whether reluctant testimony is more persuasive than neutral testimony. See William L. Benoit and Kimberly A. Kennedy, "On Reluctant Testimony," *Communication Quarterly* 47 (Fall 1999): 376–87. Both reluctant testimony and neutral testimony, however, are clearly more persuasive than biased testimony.

11 See John C. Reinard, "The Empirical Study of the Persuasive Effects of Evidence: The Status after Fifty Years of Research," *Human Communication Research* 15 (Fall 1988): 3–59.

12 The relationship between good reasons and attitudes or behavior is established by the theory of reasoned action. For a discussion of this theory, see O'Keefe, *Persuasion: Theory and Research*, pp. 101–13.

13 See Kenneth Burke, *A Rhetoric of Motives*, New York: Prentice-Hall, 1950. For a discussion of Burke's theory of identification, see Dennis G. Day, "Persuasion and the Concept of Identification," *Quarterly Journal of Speech* 46 (October 1960): 270–73.

14 A message that first arouses a need and then attempts to satisfy that need is more persuasive than a message organized in the reverse order. See Arthur R. Cohen, "Need for Cognition and Order of Communication as Determinants of Opinion Change," *The Order of Presentation in Persuasion*, New Haven, CT: Yale University Press, 1966, pp. 79–97.

15 Alan H. Monroe, *Principles and Types of Speech*, Glenview, IL: Scott Foresman, 1935. The book has multiple editions with various authors. In the most recent edition, the lead author is Bruce E. Gronbeck.

CHAPTER 15

Speaking with Visual Aids

LEARNING OBJECTIVES

After studying this chapter, you should be able to:

Objective 15.1	Enumerate the main benefits and possible drawbacks of using visual aids in a speech.
Objective 15.2	Identify major categories of visual aids and how each might contribute to the effectiveness of the speech.
Objective 15.3	Describe how to make visual aids using a variety of materials and how to choose which materials to use.
Objective 15.4	Explain the principles of preparing visual aids and of using them during the speech.

Listen to the **Audio Chapter** at **MyCommunicationLab**

OUTLINE

Benefits of Using Visual Aids
Interest | Credibility
Comprehension and Retention | Argument

Types of Visual Aids
Charts | Graphs | Representations | Objects and Models | People

Visual Aid Media
Computer-Generated Slides | Audiovisual Media | Multimedia
Transparencies | Flip Charts and Posters | Handouts

Preparing Visual Aids
Choosing Ideas for Visual Aids | Designing Visual Aids
Planning for Technical Difficulties

Using Visual Aids in the Speech
Avoid Distraction | Do Not Obstruct the Audience's View
Speak to the Audience, Not to the Visual Aid

In a classroom speech about the benefits and harms of a popular diet plan, Sarah McGonigle used her computer to project cartoons that she had scanned and arranged to relate to each point in her speech. Similarly, in a speech about diabetes, Dimitra Apostolopoulos showed her listeners a blood-sugar tester and a syringe, explaining how each is used by a diabetic. And in a speech arguing that the legal drinking age should be lower, Justin Whitney presented a graph to show the relationship between age and drunk-driving accidents. All three speakers enabled their listeners to see as well as hear by using one or more **visual aids**, which are any materials shown to the audience during the speech. Such materials are "aids" because they help the speaker by adding a visual dimension to the verbal message.

Each of these speakers carefully selected visual aids by keeping the audience and specific purpose in mind. Sarah knew that her audience regarded a diet as a formidable problem, and so she thought that humorous cartoons would serve her purpose of making it seem less imposing (so long as she chose cartoons that did not make fun of obesity or threaten listeners' self-esteem). Dimitra decided that her speech would be clearer if listeners could see the instruments she described. And Justin believed that the information in his speech would be more memorable if the audience could picture the relationship rather than just hear about it.

Watch the Video "The Process of Developing a Speech: Using Presentation Aids" at **MyCommunicationLab**

OBJECTIVE 15.1 Benefits of Using Visual Aids

Not every speech calls for visual aids. Sometimes the message and its structure are so simple that visual aids aren't needed. Sometimes a speaker prefers to achieve an effect through voice and personality alone. And sometimes visual aids may even distract the audience from the message. Moreover, using visual aids makes you dependent on the available equipment and technology, and there is always the risk that the equipment may break down. Nonetheless, visual aids often can be used to good effect. Technology and software have made the preparation of sophisticated visual aids much easier than before. And as visual media play a growing role in our culture, knowing how to design and construct images are increasingly vital skills.

In some speaking situations, such as a sales presentation or a business proposal, visual aids are required; audiences expect to see them and will regard the speaker as unprepared without them. Visual aids also play a growing role in the public forum. In early 2003, Secretary of State Colin Powell made the case for war in Iraq with a multimedia presentation to the United Nations Security Council. In addition to his verbal text, Powell utilized photographs, objects, and tapes of conversation to support his thesis. Likewise, the documentary film *An Inconvenient Truth*, released in 2006, shows former Vice President Al Gore explaining the dangers of global warming through the use of charts, graphs, pictures, animation, textual graphics, and video.

There are four main benefits of using visual aids:

1. Visual aids make the speech more interesting.
2. Visual aids enhance the speaker's credibility.
3. Visual aids improve comprehension and retention.[1]
4. Visual aids can advance your argument in the speech.

visual aids
Materials that the speaker shows to the audience during the speech.

Visual aids can make a speech much more interesting and immediate.

Interest

Throughout this text, you have seen how a speech is strengthened by variety—in the speaker's voice, gesture, and movement, for example. Similarly, visual aids can enhance listeners' interest by adding variety to your message. When you stop to point to a chart or graph, or to show a slide, you alter your delivery pattern. Moreover, adding visual to aural stimuli is a means of making the speech interesting. Because listeners must "switch gears" to look at a chart or a map, they are less likely to fall into the trap of passive listening and more likely to attend to the message. By attracting attention, gaining interest, and possibly generating emotion, visual aids enhance the affective dimension of understanding.

Credibility

A speaker who prepares and uses visual aids well often makes a better impression on the audience.[2] Carefully prepared and appropriate visual aids suggest to the audience that you know the subject and think highly enough of them to do extra work. Again, careful audience analysis is the key to knowing how visual aids might enhance your credibility. When Sarah McGonigle used cartoons to illustrate her speech about a diet plan, she knew that these aids were appropriate for an audience that expected to be entertained. But had her audience been nutritionists who anticipated a technical presentation, or people for whom dieting posed serious issues of self-esteem, the cartoons might have backfired and caused listeners to downgrade Sarah as a speaker.

In some cases, the absence of visual aids can undermine a speaker's *ethos*. For example, if you were making a presentation to a board of directors and the norm was for such presentations to include computer-generated slides and video, your failure to use visual aids might suggest that you hadn't done the necessary preparation, didn't have your speech ready ahead of time, or weren't taking the audience seriously.[3]

Comprehension and Retention

A critical benefit of visual aids is that they often make it easier for listeners to understand and remember the speech.[4] Words by their nature are abstract; listeners have to translate them into mental images. But visual aids are concrete. They make it easy for listeners to see what you are talking about and to remember what you said. Listeners may remember a map, a graph, or a picture and associate it with a particular idea in your speech. In this way, visual and aural stimuli work together to affect audience members' cognitive understanding by making ideas clear and easily remembered. They also affect information processing by providing previews and summaries, making it easier for audiences to follow the speech.

For instance, you might effectively illustrate a point you are arguing about the inadequacy of Americans' diet by using a graph showing diagnosed cases of diabetes over the past decade. You can strengthen a statement such as "The rise in adult-onset diabetes is tied largely to inadequate nutrition and excessive carbohydrates among our nation's poorest citizens" by using two side-by-side charts, one listing the poorest states and one listing the states with the greatest incidence of adult-onset diabetes, and pointing out the high correlation between the two lists. Similarly, listeners may not immediately grasp a verbal description of highway directions from Chicago to Detroit; however, showing them a simple map is an effective way to strengthen the message.

Even in printed messages—when readers have the luxury of proceeding at their own pace and can go back over the text—complex material is often accompanied by visual aids. In public speaking, when the message cannot be slowed down or replayed, the variety achieved through visual aids is even more important.

CHECKLIST 15.1

Strategic Planning for Visual Aids

1. In making decisions about visual aids, ask yourself these questions:
   - ❐ Does the audience expect me to use visual aids, making their absence distracting?
   - ❐ Would my speech be clearer if I illustrated important points?
   - ❐ Can I retain the audience's interest through visual aids?
   - ❐ Can visual aids make it easier for listeners to remember and understand my important points?
   - ❐ Can I prevent visual aids from distracting from my message?
2. If any answer is "Yes," then proceed to:
   - ❐ Decide which type of visual aid would best serve your purposes.
   - ❐ Determine the appropriate size and material for the visual aid, based on the audience and the circumstances.
   - ❐ Design the visual aid.
   - ❐ Practice the speech including the use of the visual aid.

Argument

Sometimes visual aids do not just embellish your ideas; they may actually make an argument themselves. Al Gore's film *An Inconvenient Truth*, noted previously, is an interesting example. It is the experience of observing the visuals that makes the argument that dramatic climate changes are under way. Another example is a visual presentation called "The Civil War in Four Minutes" at the Abraham Lincoln Presidential Library and Museum in Springfield, Illinois. (This presentation is available for sale; you do not have to travel to Springfield to see it.) Without using any words, the rapidly shifting colors on a computer-projected map, and the mounting count of casualties, establish the claims that certain places had great strategic significance in the Civil War, that control of these places sometimes shifted back and forth, that the winning strategy divided the Confederacy, and that after a very slow start the casualty rate mounted very quickly. Both of these multimedia presentations are cases in which a picture truly is worth a thousand words.[5]

Some speakers will give their speeches in "smart" classrooms that are equipped with up-to-date technology; these settings may resemble those of business or professional presentations. Others will speak in rooms equipped only with an overhead projector, if that. Such settings are more like those of neighborhood organizations or simple meeting rooms. Because you must adapt to the situation, this chapter describes a mixture of "high-tech" and "low-tech" visual aids and considers some of the design principles common to both.

Types of Visual Aids

OBJECTIVE 15.2

The varieties of visual aids can be grouped under five headings: charts, graphs, representations, objects or models, and people.

Charts

A **chart** simplifies complex material by arranging it visually according to an obvious principle. The listener is helped not only by being able to see as well as hear the information, but also by the way in which the chart organizes the material.

Statistical Charts. One common type of chart is the *statistical chart* (see Figure 15.1). Because statistics are abstract, they are often hard to comprehend or remember when heard; displaying them on a chart makes them easier to grasp. But remember that the purpose of a statistical chart is to *simplify* complex information. All too often, statistical charts used in speeches contain too much information, making them difficult to read and hard to grasp. The energy that the audience spends trying to decode them is a distraction from the main point of the speech. Generally, a statistical chart should illustrate only one point or support only one conclusion. A series of simple charts is easier to understand than a single complex table that includes all the information. See Figure 15.2 for an example of a chart that contains too much information for use in a speech. The value of this chart will be further reduced if, as often happens, it is projected onto a screen for

Child Mortality Rates (per 1,000 live births)

	1960		2000
1. Afghanistan	360	1. Angola	260
2. Angola	345	2. Afghanistan	257
3. Haiti	253	3. Iraq	133
4. Bangladesh	248	4. Haiti	123
5. China	225	5. Bangladesh	82

Source: UNICEF, available at www.childinfo.org/cmr/revis/dbz.htm.

Figure 15.1 A statistical chart should show important relationships clearly. Here, the figures are contrasted in parallel columns and arranged in order of decreasing rates.

chart
A visual arrangement of words or numbers according to an obvious principle.

Top 20 Religions in the United States

Religion	1990 Est. Adult Pop.	2001 Est. Adult Pop.	% of U.S. Pop., 2000	% Change 1990–2000
Christianity	151,225,000	159,030,000	76.5%	+5%
Nonreligious/Secular	13,116,000	27,539,000	13.2%	+110%
Judaism	3,137,000	2,831,000	1.3%	−10%
Islam	527,000	1,104,000	0.5%	+109%
Buddhism	401,000	1,082,000	0.5%	+170%
Agnostic	1,186,000	991,000	0.5%	−16%
Atheist		902,000	0.4%	
Hinduism	227,000	766,000	0.4%	+237%
Unitarian Universalist	502,000	629,000	0.3%	+25%
Wiccan/Pagan/Druid		307,000	0.1%	
Spiritualist		116,000		
Native American Religion	47,000	103,000		+119%
Baha'i	28,000	84,000		+200%
New Age	20,000	68,000		+240%
Sikhism	13,000	57,000		+338%
Scientology	45,000	55,000		+22%
Humanist	29,000	49,000		+69%
Deity (Deist)	6,000	49,000		+717%
Taoist	23,000	40,000		+74%
Eckankar	18,000	26,000		+44%

Source: Data from adherents.com, 2001.

Figure 15.2 An extensively detailed chart such as this one contains too much information to use on a single presentation aid.

Source: Data from Barry A. Kosmin, Egon Mayer, and Ariela Keysar, *American Religious Identification Survey* (ARIS, 2001). Institute for the Study of Secularism in Society and Culture, Trinity College, Hartford, CT.

only a few seconds. (If, for some reason, you have to use a chart containing too much information, you can highlight the relevant sections, either on the chart itself or by pointing.)

Also, charts should not present information that is *too* precise to grasp. And generally, order-of-magnitude numbers (those that are rounded off) will be better than numbers that are precise but complicated and hard to remember. For example, rather than showing the U.S. population as 308,745,538, you can just use 309 million.

Sequence of Steps. Another common chart is one that shows the *sequence of steps* in a process. Many speeches give instructions about how to do something, or they describe the evolution of a process. For example, a speech telling high school students how to apply for college might cover the steps of (1) determining which criteria are most important—such as size, cost, distance from home, or the presence of special curricular programs; (2) assessing your aptitudes and interests; (3) determining a range of schools that satisfy your criteria and match your interests; (4) obtaining literature about those schools and eliminating some

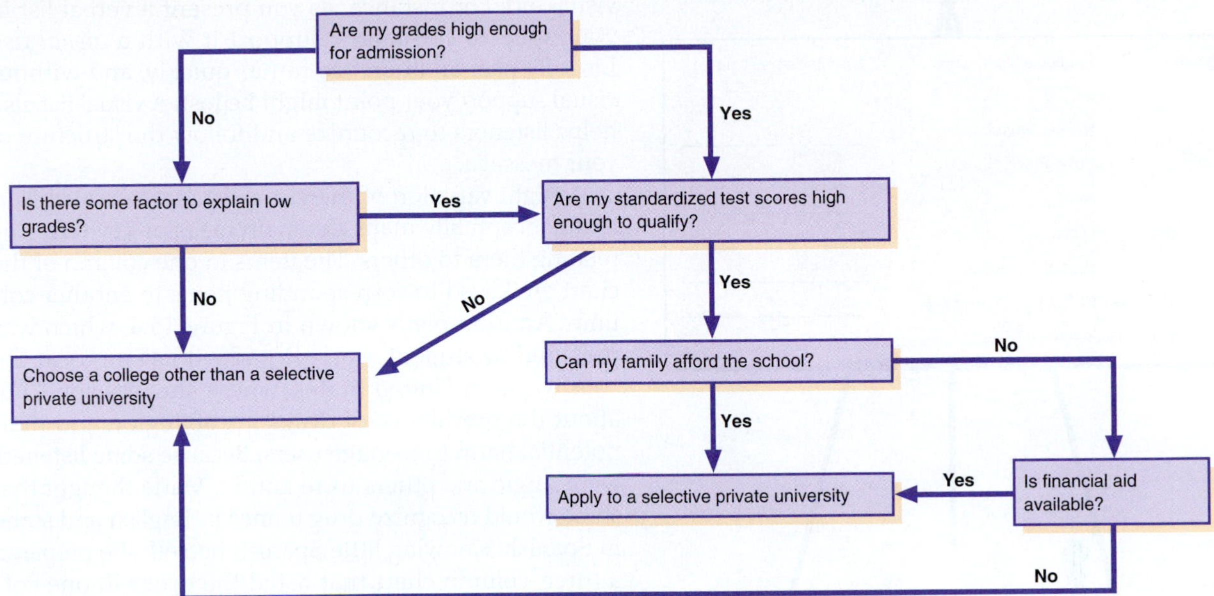

Figure 15.3 A sample flowchart.

as options; (5) arranging to take whatever standardized tests are necessary; (6) obtaining application materials; and (7) filling out the application forms and submitting them online or mailing them. These seven steps might form the subheadings of the speech. A chart listing the seven steps in order would help listeners to remember the steps and to keep track of where you are in the speech. The chart would make clear not only what the steps are, but also the appropriate sequence to follow in completing them.

Although the entire sequence of steps in a process might be listed on a single chart, consider whether you could heighten interest in the speech by developing the chart gradually. You could use a *series* of charts, with each one revealing additional new information. For example, in a speech about how the territory of the United States expanded beyond the original 13 colonies, you might start with a chart listing only the Northwest and Southwest Territories. After discussing those acquisitions, you might then show another chart that lists those territories and also adds the Louisiana Purchase as a second stage in the sequence. By using a series of charts, you can control the information so that it evolves as your speech progresses, and listeners will not be distracted by items that you have not yet discussed. Presentation programs such as PowerPoint make it easy to add material to charts so that they can be shown in a series.

Flowcharts. Another common type of chart is a **flowchart**, which suggests how each decision "flows." The chart consists of labeled boxes connected by arrows; at key points, one decision flows in one direction, and a different decision leads in a different direction. Figure 15.3 shows a flowchart on the topic of "How to choose whether to apply to a selective private university."

flowchart
A chart showing the "flow," or progress, through several steps, with alternative paths showing the outcome of different decisions.

Visual Lists and Columnar Charts. Even when you are not presenting a series of statistics or describing a sequence of events, a chart can be a helpful

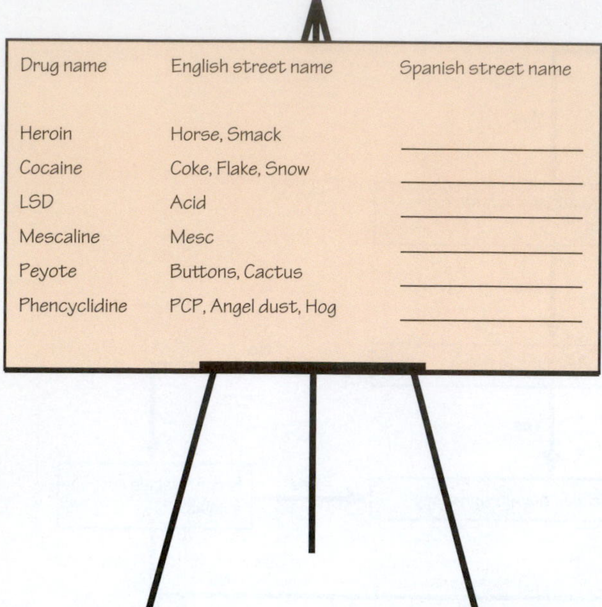

Drug name
English street name
Spanish street name
Heroin
Horse, Smack
Cocaine
Coke, Flake, Snow
LSD
Acid
Mescaline
Mesc
Peyote
Buttons, Cactus
Phencyclidine
PCP, Angel dust, Hog

Figure 15.4 A columnar chart for discussing drug names.

visual aid. For instance, as you present a verbal list in your speech, you might support it with a *visual list.* Lists fly past an audience rather quickly, and without visual support your point might be lost. A visual list also helps listeners to recognize and follow the structure of your message.

A slight variation of the visual list is a *columnar chart* that conceptually maps the main ideas or key terms by relating them to others. The items in one column of the chart are keyed to corresponding items in another column. An example is shown in Figure 15.4, which was prepared by student Maria Rosado at a campus in the southwestern United States, where she was speaking about the prevalence of drugs in the region and their potential harm to teenage users. Because some listeners were Anglo and others were Latino, Maria thought that some would recognize drug names in English and some in Spanish. Knowing little Spanish herself, she prepared a three-column chart that listed the drugs in one column and their English street names in the adjacent column. The third column she left blank. Then she asked the audience to help her fill the blanks by providing the Spanish street names. (Figure 15.2 is also a columnar chart, but, as you can see by comparing it with Figure 15.4, it contains too much information—and probably too many columns—to be very useful.)

Graphs

A **graph** is a visual display of relationships that shows how change in one thing is related to change in another. The most common types are line graphs, bar graphs, and pie graphs (see Figure 15.5).

Line Graphs. A **line graph** charts one variable as a function of another. The values for one variable are shown on the horizontal axis, and those of the other variable are shown on the vertical axis. Any pair of values can thus be represented by a point on the graph. A line connects the various points to show the relationship between the variables.

For example, suppose you wanted to demonstrate that the crime rate increases in hot weather. The two variables might be "temperature" (on the vertical axis) and "average reported crimes per hour per 1,000 population" (on the horizontal axis). At 60 degrees Fahrenheit, you find that there is an average of 25 reported crimes per hour per 1,000 population, so you would find the point on the chart where a horizontal line from the "60 degrees" mark and a vertical line from the "25 crimes" mark intersect. Suppose that at 80 degrees Fahrenheit, there is an average of 40 reported crimes and at 100 degrees Fahrenheit, there is 65. These points could also be located on the graph. Then a line could be drawn to connect all three points. The line would show clearly that the crime rate goes up as the temperature increases. The relationship between the crime rate and the temperature will be clear and memorable.

graph
A visual display of relationships, showing how change in one thing is related to change in another.

line graph
A graph in which a line connects points, each of which represents a combination of the two items being compared.

Sometimes, however, things are more complicated. The trend will go one way up to a point, but then it will reverse. For example, grades have been shown to

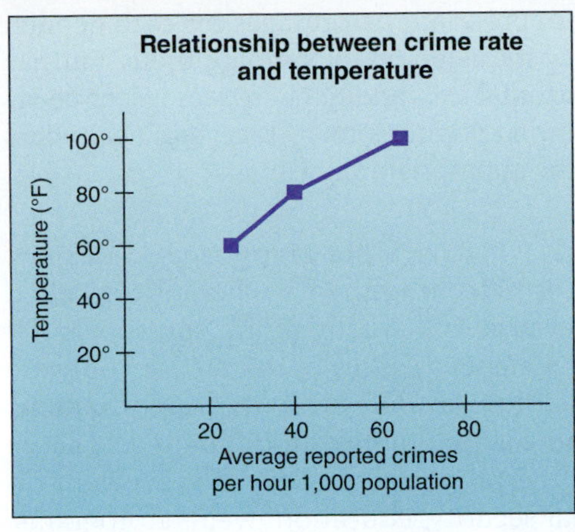

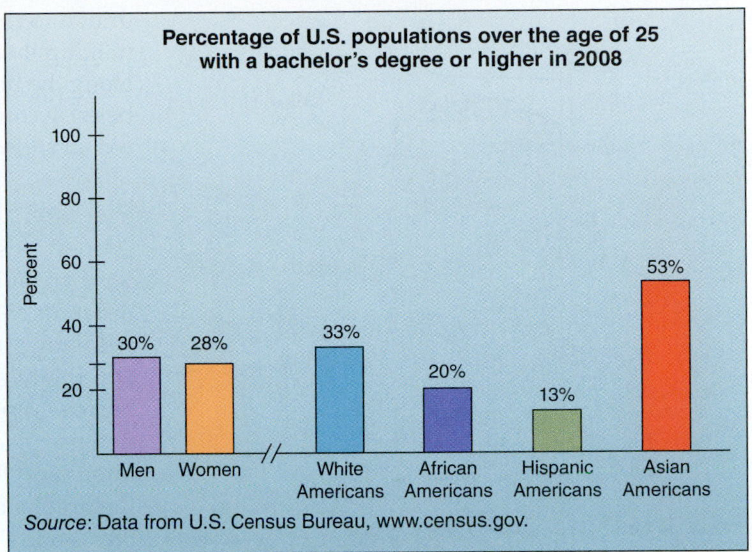

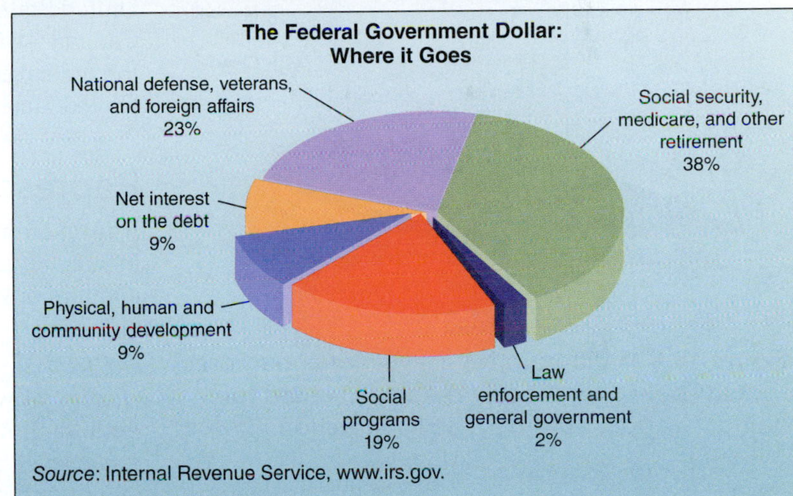

Figure 15.5 Graphs should be kept as simple as possible, with all elements labeled and a minimum number of variables displayed. Clockwise from left: line graph, bar graph, pie graph.

motivate improved student performance. Up to a point, a teacher who gives more as may prompt students to do better work. But if it becomes clear that large numbers of students will receive an *A*, there is *less* incentive to do better work because students know that grades will be high anyway. Line graphs can show complex relationships as well as simple ones.

Bar Graphs. Unlike a line graph, a **bar graph** shows units of measurement on only one axis; the other axis identifies the categories to be assessed. Then, for each category, a bar is drawn to the appropriate value. The relative lengths of the bars permit easy comparison.

For instance, you might wish to show how gender and race affect the likelihood of completing a college degree. In this graph, the two genders and the various races are the primary variables. The vertical axis could show percentages from 0 to 100. The horizontal axis is labeled with the variable categories. One space would be labeled "Men," and another would be labeled "Women." Then bars would be

bar graph
A graph in which the length of bars indicates the amount or extent of items being compared.

drawn to the appropriate percentages for each gender, making it easy for listeners to compare them. Further along the horizontal axis, additional spaces might be labeled according to populations by race, and again bars would show the appropriate values.

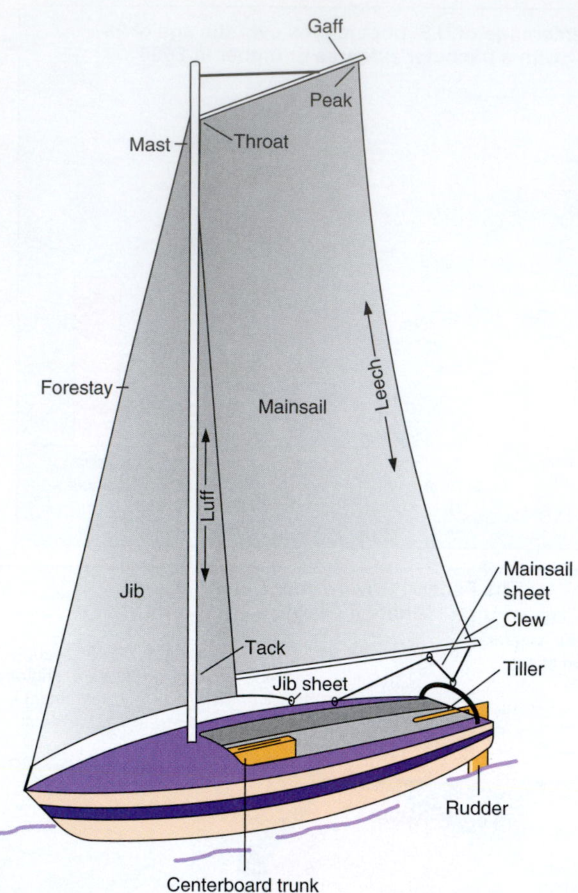

Figure 15.6 A diagram for instructional purposes should show only the key features needed for demonstration, as in basic sail instruction.

Pie Graphs. Finally, a **pie graph** is used to show proportions, or percentages, of a whole. (It is called a *pie graph* because it is usually round and shows the different components as slices of the pie.) If you were speaking about how tax dollars are spent, for example, you might show a pie graph with different size slices representing the proportions of tax money spent on defense, social security, education, welfare programs, interest on the national debt, and so on. Like bar graphs, pie graphs can be used to illustrate two variables. Two pies—one showing the distribution of the budget of the United States and the other showing its distribution in Canada—will make it clear that a larger percentage of the federal budget has been required for defense in the United States.[6]

Representations

Representations are visual portrayals of reality. They include textual graphics, diagrams, maps, photographs, and film or video.

Textual Graphics. A **textual graphic** is a display of words. It is used so that the audience can simultaneously see and hear the words. At the most basic level, a teacher is using a textual graphic when he or she writes an unfamiliar word on the chalkboard. Seeing the word helps students to learn it. In speeches, textual graphics may be used to show a simple outline of the main ideas, to show the central thesis of the speech, or to show the action the speaker wants the audience to take. If you are asking listeners to write to their senator, for example, you could use a textual graphic that shows the senator's contact information.

pie graph
A graph in the shape of a circle in which the various components of the whole are shown as portions of the circle, like various-sized slices of a pie.

representations
Visual portrayals of reality.

textual graphic
A display of words so that the audience can both see and hear them.

diagram
A simplified drawing or sketch that represents a more complex object.

Diagrams. A **diagram** is a simple drawing or sketch that represents a more complex object. A diagram is more abstract than a photograph, and because it leaves out many details, you can emphasize the parts of the object that you think are most important. If you were describing how to raise a sail, you might display a diagram of a boat in order to refer to its parts as you proceed (see Figure 15.6). The diagram will not look exactly like a boat, as a photograph would, but it will let listeners know what the principal parts are and how they are used in the process of raising the sail.

Maps. *Maps* can be particularly useful visual aids if the speech focuses on directions to, or relationships among, places. For example, a speech about the

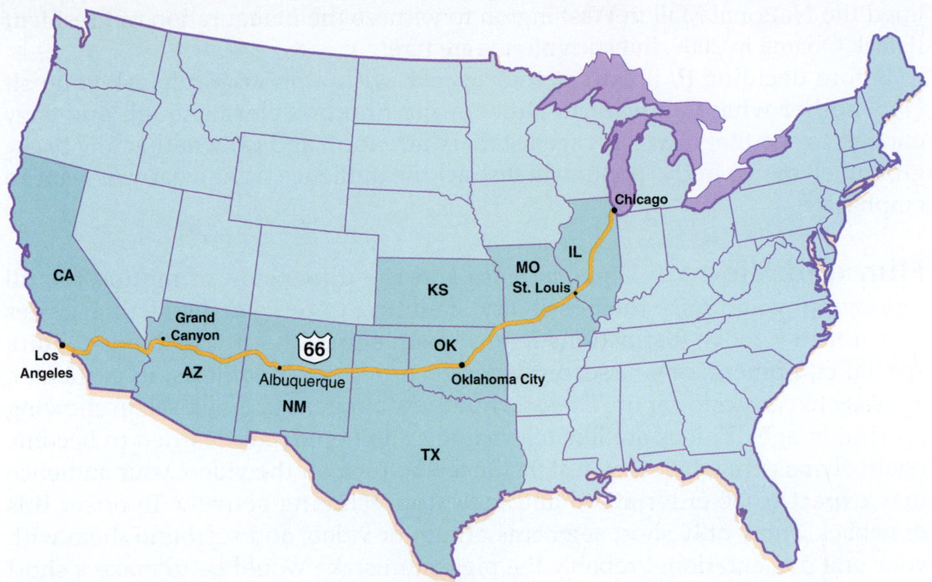

Figure 15.7 Maps should be simplified to display only the key features needed for the presentation—in this case the states and main stopovers on Route 66 from Chicago to Los Angeles.

history of U.S. Route 66 would be aided by a map showing the major points on the famous highway that, in the years before interstates, stretched from Chicago to Los Angeles. But a map almost always needs to be simplified for a speech. Even an enlarged Rand McNally map would not be effective in this case, because it would include so much detail that the audience would not be able to see or focus on Route 66. A much simpler map, showing only the outline of the states and the approximate path of Route 66, would be much more useful (see Figure 15.7). Nor should the map identify all the points of interest along this famous road; it should show only the points featured in the speech—perhaps three or four. Finally, the map need not be drawn to scale or provide an exact representation, because you are using it primarily to help listeners picture the relationships among the places on Route 66.

Photographs. *Photographs*, too, should be used cautiously as visual aids. Because a photograph portrays reality in all its complexity, it may contain far more information than is important to the speech. What you wish to emphasize may not stand out from the background, and background elements may distract the audience from your intended focus. For example, if you show a photograph of a traffic accident to support your speech about safe driving, your point will be obscured if the audience instead pays attention to the unusual billboards near the scene of the accident.

Some photographs, however, clearly capture the essence of their subject. They are called *iconic* photographs because virtually everyone recognizes what they show and what they symbolize.[7] Examples include such famous photos as the soldiers raising the U.S. flag at Iwo Jima in World War II; the hooded detainee standing on a box at Abu Ghraib prison in Iraq in 2004; or the enthusiastic crowds that lined the National Mall in Washington to witness the inauguration of President Barack Obama in 2009. But such photos are rare.

Before deciding to illustrate your speech with a photograph, ask yourself (1) whether what you want to show in the photo is clear enough and easy enough to see that it will engage listeners' attention and (2) whether any background elements in the photo will distract the audience from what you want to emphasize.

Film and Video. *Film and video* add the dimension of motion to still photography and raise the possibility of editing to remove distracting scenes (but not to remove distractions in any given shot). These visual aids require special equipment, of course, but video recorders and monitors, in particular, are easy to carry and set up. There is, however, a potential drawback in showing moving images. Videos are like television, and people have learned to become relatively passive when they watch. Once you turn on the video, your audience may expect to be entertained and may stop listening actively. To offset this drawback, show only short segments of film or video, and surround them with your oral presentation. Probably the biggest mistake would be to make a short introduction and then just turn the presentation over to video. Active listening will decrease markedly.

Objects and Models

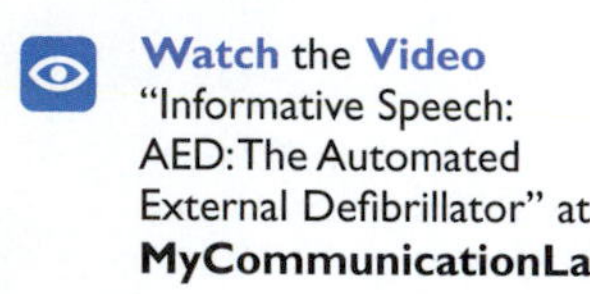

Watch the Video
"Informative Speech: AED: The Automated External Defibrillator" at
MyCommunicationLab

Sometimes, the best visual aid is the actual object you are talking about—as when a lawyer holds up key evidence for the jury to see. Chefs on television, for instance, usually explain recipes by using real ingredients, real pots and pans, and real ovens. Student Ezra Wexler, speaking about how Lego instills creativity, brought in Lego pieces to demonstrate the variety of shapes and figures that he could make from a few pieces. Be aware, though, that objects require you to use your hands more extensively than if you were just pointing to a diagram.[8] You will need to hold things, to manipulate them, and to move them around. All this may solve the problem of what to do with your hands, but you must be careful. Hold the objects firmly and steadily, avoid accidentally knocking them over with sweeping gestures, and be sure to put them away when you are finished with them so that they will not distract the audience.

If it is not feasible to use the actual object, either because it is too large or because it is not portable, you may be able to use a model of the object. For example, a developer who is making a presentation about how a mixed-use building would improve the downtown area might find it useful to prepare a scale model of the development to refer to during the talk. Similarly, lawyers trying to fix responsibility for an accident might find it useful to refer to a scale model of the accident scene. The one general principle to follow in using a model is that it must be large enough for listeners to see easily. If they have to strain to see the model or you have to apologize because some feature of it is not visible to everyone, it will not be an effective visual aid.

Use good judgment in deciding what to use as objects or models. A little bit of common sense will go a long way. For instance, you should think twice about bringing in animals, and it is definitely a bad idea to bring in objects that are illegal or dangerous.

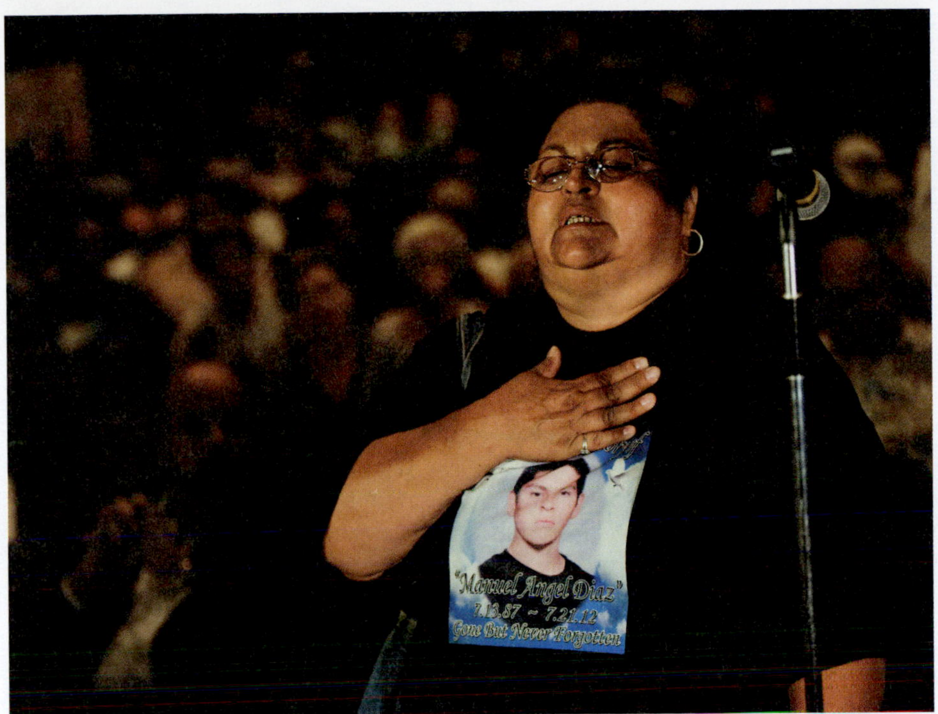

Clothing can serve as a visual aid and make a speaker a part of the presentation. Can you think of topics in which a speaker might use him- or herself as a visual aid in the speech?

People

It may seem odd to think of yourself or others as visual aids; it may even sound demeaning at first. But your own body can serve as an effective visual aid. For example, if your topic is "Power Walking," you can demonstrate the high-intensity movements involved in this type of walking. The demonstration not only will show listeners how to do it, but also will help make credible your claim that power walking is vigorous exercise.

Your appearance and grooming can also serve as a visual aid. It obviously makes a difference whether you arrive for a business presentation in a suit or in a sweatshirt and jeans. Your clothing either reinforces or undercuts your message that you are seriously interested in obtaining the account. This is not to say that you always have to wear a suit to make a good impression as a speaker. If your speech is about lifeguarding, a pair of shorts and a Red Cross T-shirt may be the most effective clothing. The critical thing is to match your appearance to the situation.

For example, when giving a speech blaming the Greek life for limiting social opportunities on her campus, Paige von Achen came in dressed in baggy sweatpants and a sideways hat, showing the logo of a sorority, using her appearance to frame her opponents. Such a tactic, although it may help orient your audience, does risk stereotyping and mocking opponents, thereby hurting your *ethos*.

For many people, dress is an important means of asserting cultural identity. Covering your head, wearing non-Western clothing, or dressing in dark colors may be ways to express your heritage and values. At the same time, however, less conventional styles of dress may lead listeners to stereotype you and perhaps to be distracted from your message by your unfamiliar (to them) appearance. Should you dress to accommodate the expectations of your audience? Or should you "be yourself" and deliberately assert your different cultural identity? The answers to these questions should reflect your analysis of the audience and your specific purpose.

Watch the Video "Demonstrative Speech: Preventing Sexual Assault" at **MyCommunicationLab**

Other people can also serve as visual aids. The obvious example is a speech in which someone helps you demonstrate something. If you plan to use the help of others, it is best to make arrangements with them ahead of time. You will avoid being embarrassed if no one responds when you ask for a volunteer, and you will also be able to coordinate the presentation so that the "volunteer" doesn't seem surprised and you don't seem poorly prepared, or so that the volunteer does not upstage you and draw attention away from your speech.

Of all these different types of visual aids, which is the best to use? Charts? Graphs? Representations? Objects and models? People? By now, you know, of course, that there is no "correct" answer to such questions. The decision depends on your topic, on where you are speaking, on the size of the audience, on what the audience is likely to expect, and on how comfortable you are with using visual aids. Any visual aid can be used well or badly. The important thing is to choose it knowingly and with a specific purpose in mind.

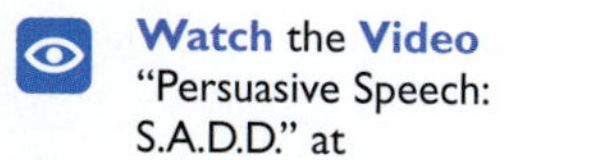

OBJECTIVE 15.3 Visual Aid Media

Besides your decisions about the types of visual aids to use, you have many options about the media in which they can be made. Some involve the use of readily available technology, whereas others are distinctly "low tech."

Computer-Generated Slides

Watch the Video "Persuasive Speech: S.A.D.D." at **MyCommunicationLab**

Computers are commonly used to generate visual aids that are projected directly onto a screen or printed as handouts for distribution to the audience. Almost any word-processing program can help you make attractive charts, tables, and textual graphics. With the use of a scanner, you can retrieve photographs, maps, or documents electronically and incorporate them into the slide as well.

An obvious advantage to using the computer is that you can experiment with different sizes and shapes, and you can correct errors easily. You can vary the size and font (type style) of textual graphics and can modify the color, proportions, background, and other elements of an image. In fact, it is tempting to use too much of the computer's capability, leading to visual aids that ignore the principle of simplicity—and have too many colors, too many fonts, and too much information. The following suggestions should help you to resist this temptation with regard to text.

1. *Choose a basic design and color scheme for the entire presentation.* You might repeat a word, symbol, style, or font throughout your visual aids, or maintain a consistent color scheme, or use consistent spacing. Any of these will help to create a sense of unity for your presentation.
2. *Select fonts carefully.* Graphic designers usually divide typefaces into four basic classes of fonts: serif, sans serif, script, and decorative. *Serif* fonts, like the one you are reading, have little lines (serifs) at the tops and bottoms of letters, and the letters are usually made up of both thick and thin lines. *Sans*

CHOOSE A STRATEGY: Using Visual Aids

The Situation

Your school will be renovating the student center, including the commons, and you are on the student advisory committee. Most students know only what the school and the architect have told them about the new amenities. However, you have seen the proposed floor plan for the updates and you don't think the architect's plan meets the needs that students have conveyed to you. You're preparing to present a case to the student advisory committee for considering your additions. You've put the final touches on your speech and are considering using visual aids to supplement your case.

Making Choices

1. In articulating your concerns to the architects and designers, what types of visual aids should you use? Why?
2. How should you determine what visual aids would be most appropriate and most useful for this speaking situation?

What If...

Your choice of visual aids will be affected not only by the type of information available to you, but also by the audience to whom you are speaking and your purpose. Decide what type(s) of visual aids you might use and why you would use them in the following situations:

1. You are speaking to an entire group of student government members instead of the board.
2. You are speaking to all 10,000 students on campus.
3. You are speaking to members of the administration.

serif fonts do not have the extra lines at the tops and bottoms, and all lines in the letters are usually the same thickness. Although serif fonts are used often for longer passages of text (the serifs create a continuity, leading the eye from one letter to the next), sans serif fonts often are preferred for headlines and brief snippets of text where visual clarity is at a premium. *Script* fonts imitate handwriting but are far more precise and uniform. They can be very fancy and complicated, which can make them hard to read. *Decorative* fonts are designed not so much for ease in reading as to convey a particular feeling or tone. Figure 15.8 shows examples of each class of font.

Most designers agree that you should use no more than two typefaces on a single visual aid and that they should be from two different font categories. The most common combination is to use a sans serif font for displayed titles or headings and a serif font for text passages. Of course, designers sometimes violate these guidelines to achieve special effects.

3. *Choose an appropriate type size.* Visual aids are of little use if the type is not large enough for everyone in the audience to see. Designers at Microsoft recommend using 44-point type for titles, 32-point type for subtitles or text if there is no subtitle, and 28-point type for the text if there is also a subtitle. (To give a sense of what this means, there are 72 "points" in an inch.) The smallest sizes recommended are 36-point type for titles, 24-point for

Route 66 – Key Dates
1926: Officially designated as U.S. highway
1956: Acts signed to create Interstate highways
1985: Decommissioned
Source: www.nps.gov

Choose a basic, unifying design for your entire presentation. Stick with a simple and straightforward theme and layout—especially if you are new to a slide-creating program or new to making slides for your speeches.

Serif	Sans Serif
Palatino	Arial
Times New Roman	Officina Sans
Courier	Century Gothic
Century Schoolbook	Kabel

Script	Decorative
Linoscript	Whimsy
Caflish Script	LITHOS
Brush Script	Metropolis
	Wonton

Figure 15.8 Typefaces grouped by font type.

subtitles, and 18-point for text. Figure 15.9 shows how these sizes look in print. In any case, avoid using capital letters for emphasis except in short titles. Long stretches of all-capital text are hard to read, because our eyes rely on contrasting letter shapes to decode quickly.

4. *Limit the amount of text on each slide.* Too much text on a slide can be difficult for the audience to read, understand, and remember. A common guideline is to use no more than six lines per slide, with no more than six words per line.
5. *Use color to create a mood and sustain attention.* Graphic designers have long known that warm colors (oranges and reds) appear to come forward and have an exciting effect, whereas cool colors (greens and blues) seem to recede and have a more calming effect. When you choose colors, think about how you want your audience to react to your visual aid. Your topic, occasion, and purpose should influence this decision. For example, in a business setting, you might use cool colors to convey disappointing news and warm colors to convey good news.

   It is also important to choose colors for backgrounds and for text or graphics that contrast with one another but do not conflict. Figure 15.10 provides examples of an effective and an ineffective color combination. Using yellow against a blue background is effective; the colors contrast yet are harmonious. Using purple against a blue background, however, is not effective; both colors are dark, and so the purple letters do not stand out from the background. Be cautious about combining red and green. Some audience members may have a type of color blindness that makes these two colors indistinguishable. Even for those without color blindness, this combination is not effective because it is difficult to read.

Title set 44-pt. or 36-pt.
Subtitle set 32-point or 24-point
Text (with a subtitle) 28-point or 18-point

Figure 15.9 Variations of a typeface.

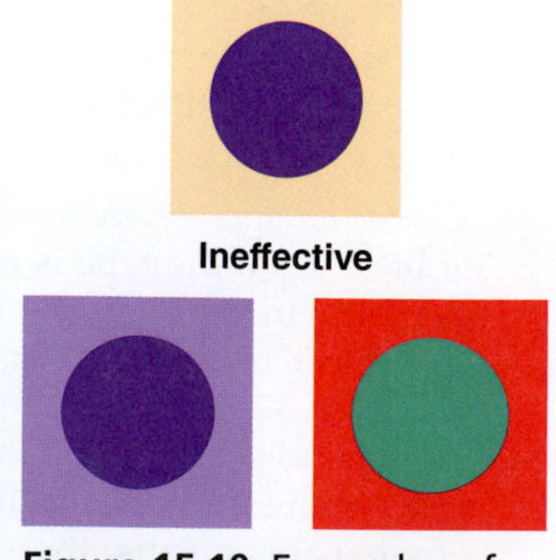

Figure 15.10 Examples of effective and ineffective color combinations.

CHECKLIST 15.2

Tips for Using PowerPoint

- ❒ **Identify the mood you want to establish with your speech and presentation slides.** Your topic, occasion, and purpose should influence this decision. Are you trying to motivate or persuade your audience? To entertain or inform them? To reassure them? Keep your speech goals in mind as you create your slides.
- ❒ **Choose a basic unifying design for the entire presentation.** If you are choosing from the built-in slide themes and slide layouts, pick something simple and straightforward—especially if you are new to the program or new to creating slides for your speeches. Don't use a different theme for each slide.
- ❒ **Choose a simple color scheme for the entire presentation.** Using too many different colors will distract your audience from the content. If you have chosen a simple built-in slide theme that uses only two or three colors, you can then pick from built-in color schemes without worrying about having too many colors.
- ❒ **Select font styles and colors carefully.** Avoid using more than two different font styles in the entire presentation and getting too fancy with options like 3-D styles. Choose font styles and colors that are easily readable, such as black or dark fonts on a white or very light background. White type on a black background can be more difficult to read.
- ❒ **Choose an appropriate font size.** Be sure your audience can see the type from anywhere within your speaking venue. As a general guideline, use a font size of at least 18 points.
- ❒ **Choose appropriate slide transitions.** Overdoing transitions like fades, blurs, wipes, and dissolves can distract from your speech. Use them strategically, which may mean minimally or not at all.
- ❒ **Match your slides to your speech.** For example, don't list only two points on a slide if you're going to talk about three points while the slide is showing.
- ❒ **Remember that less is more.** Use only a few lines, key words, or a single image on each slide. Don't be afraid of white space, which helps focus your audience on the content of your slide.
- ❒ **Don't over-rely on your slides.** Use them to supplement your speech, not replace it.
- ❒ **Use a tutorial.** Many free tutorials for PowerPoint and other programs can be found online. Search for "PowerPoint tutorial," and choose from sites such as the manufacturer (Microsoft) or an educational organization (.edu).

Audiovisual Media

Video makes it possible to present moving images as visual aids. You'll want to record more material than you can use, to ensure that you get the most effective images. Because you can show only short segments of video, review and edit it carefully before the speech. Remove whatever is not directly relevant to the point you want to make.

If you use PowerPoint, Prezi, Keynote, or other presentation software, you may choose to embed visual images or short video clips in the slideshows. Google Images and YouTube are excellent resources for students wanting to access and import these digital files. Be careful, though, that the "bells and whistles" of the technology do not "hijack" your agenda and the audience's attention. As with all visual aids, make sure that they really do aid your presentation.

Digital music players such as the iPod can also be used in your speech. An iPod can run presentations developed in PowerPoint or Keynote. The iPod will need to be attached to a projector or a television so people can see the presentation, and attached to speakers if you have a soundtrack.

Similarly, some of the functions of the computer can be performed using smartphones or other personal data assistants (PDAs). Such handheld devices often are able to present your visual aids, and some may even be used to develop multimedia presentations. Because smartphones and PDAs are even more portable than laptop computers, they make it even easier to access advanced technology.

Even if you are planning to use a laptop, having your presentation on a USB flash drive, iPod, or PDA gives you a convenient backup option if you run into computer problems.

Multimedia

Programs such as PowerPoint, Prezi, Keynote, and others allow you to incorporate drawings, photographs, video segments, animation, and sound into your visual aids, along with charts, graphs, and text. Such a combination is called a **multimedia presentation**. Many presentation software programs can also assist you in making more traditional, professional-quality visual aids, including transparencies, handouts, and even posters.

Most of the professional software programs provide tutorials and templates to help you get started. Using these templates, you can input the text for your graphics in outline form and the program will automatically format it into slides for a presentation. The programs often incorporate design elements discussed in this chapter, such as font size and color coordination, which makes preparing the graphics even easier.

For a very small audience, you may be able to display the finished presentation on the computer monitor, but for most speeches you will need to project the visual aids onto a larger screen. You can set the computer to advance the visuals automatically at the pace you choose—to match where you expect to be in the speech—or you can advance the visuals manually. You can also use the "build" feature to control the information the audience sees. The presentation will begin with the first major bullet point on your slide and then display progressively more information as you speak about the various points. You can also vary the transitions between slides (how they move on and off the screen), such as making the slides fade in and out or move across, up, or down. For most audiences, however, it is a good idea to choose simple transitions, because a dizzying variety of fades, dissolves, and swirls tends to distract from your ideas and to make the presentation look juvenile.

Think carefully about how you will switch between slides in order to advance the presentation. If you must return to your keyboard or mouse, you may find it difficult to maintain the flow of your speech or your eye contact with the audience. You may be able to use a remote device, but then you will need to consider whether to hold the remote throughout the speech or whether to place it nearby and pick it up only when needed.

Although you may prefer to deliver a multimedia presentation using your personal laptop computer, in the classroom and in many other speaking situations (such as conferences and business presentations) it is more convenient for multiple presenters to use the same computer. It is wise, therefore, to keep a copy of your multimedia presentation on a portable storage device, such as a USB flash drive from which the presentation files can be uploaded to a computer or a digital projection device. An e-mail account or "cloud" storage may also serve as backup, though keep in mind that Internet access may not be available at your speaking location—or may not work when you need it.

multimedia presentation
A presentation using a combination of different media, such as video, animation, sound, drawings, photographs, charts, graphs, and text.

Transparencies

If you are not using a computer, you may want to make **transparencies**, which are acetate sheets that are projected onto a screen with the use of an overhead projector or document camera. The acetate sheets are inexpensive, you can easily prepare them with markers or print them from a word processing program, and the projector enlarges the transparency and makes it easily visible to the audience. The room does not have to be completely dark in order to view transparencies with an overhead projector, so the flow of the speech need not be disrupted by turning lights off and on.

Transparencies are effective only with an audience of about 50 or fewer people. With larger audiences, transparencies have to be enlarged so much to fit the screen that they lose their focus and impact. In those circumstances, using computer-generated slides will be better, especially if you can use the "zoom" feature to magnify portions of the slide.

Document cameras, another type of projection equipment, achieve the same benefits as transparencies while allowing you to project from opaque materials. They are even easier to prepare for and to use.

Flip Charts and Posters

A **flip chart** is a writing tablet made of large sheets of paper, usually newsprint, that rests on an easel; you can "flip" each sheet over the binding at the top of the tablet after you have used it. You can create a flip chart by using markers that let you write large enough, wide enough, and dark enough for the audience to see without difficulty.

Anything you can draw on a flip chart can also be prepared on posterboard. Posterboard is as firm as stiff cardboard, making it easier to hold and to handle than a flip chart. The most basic kind of poster is a drawing on the white board (or dry erase board). Where do you put the posterboard? It, too, can rest on an easel, and like other visual aids, it should be concealed when you are not referring to it. Just be sure that your means of concealment does not make the posterboard hard to reach and uncover when you are ready to use it.

Watch the **Video** "Informative Speech: Transcranial Magnetic Stimulation" at **MyCommunicationLab**

Handouts

The logical extension of the presentation slide, flip chart, or poster is the **handout**—one or more sheets of paper that you or an assistant literally hands out to audience members to refer to during the speech.

Teachers of public speaking disagree about using handouts. On the positive side, handouts make it easier for a speaker to present complex information, because listeners have their own copy of key terms and definitions or can follow the details of a diagram or the text of a slide. Handouts reduce the need for audience members to take detailed notes, which *may* permit them to concentrate more fully on the substance of the speech. And in some situations—such as a sales presentation—leaving a handout with prospective customers is a highly desirable way to reinforce the message.

But handouts are also a potential source of distraction. The audience may pay more attention to the handout than to what you are saying. This is especially likely to happen if you distribute a handout at the very beginning of the speech but do not refer to it until several minutes have elapsed or do not refer to it explicitly at

transparencies
Celluloid sheets that are projected onto a screen with the use of an overhead projector.

flip chart
A writing tablet made of large sheets of paper, usually newsprint, the pages of which can be flipped over after they are used.

handout
One or more sheets of paper given out to audience members before or during the speech; at some point the speaker refers to the handout.

all. The difficulties with handouts are magnified if you do not have enough copies for everyone. Although some people will share, others are likely to be left out. The worst situation is to pass photographs or a book around the audience while you are speaking. Listeners' attention will lapse in waves as the material reaches them and they focus on it rather than on your speech.

OBJECTIVE 15.4

Preparing Visual Aids

Whatever materials you use in creating visual aids, the most important strategic consideration is that visual aids should be carefully matched to the contents of the speech.

Choosing Ideas for Visual Aids

Watch the **Video** "Persuasive Speech: Drinking and Driving" at **MyCommunicationLab**

The first decision to make is which ideas in your speech will be aided by the presentation of visual material. Sometimes a class assignment may require you to use a certain number of visual aids, but ordinarily it is up to you to decide whether to use visual aids and, if so, how many and at what points in the speech. Like all choices discussed in this book, it should be made strategically, with an eye on your purpose.

The general principle is: If an idea can be made easier for an audience to understand or accept with a visual aid than without one, you should use a visual aid in your discussion of that idea. If you follow this principle, you will use visual aids when:

- An idea is complicated and the visual aid will make it seem simpler.
- Presenting an idea orally will seem dry but visual aids will add interest.
- Words alone cannot capture the idea but seeing a visual aid will make it clear.
- Listeners may forget your words but the visual aid will help them to remember.

On the other hand, you should not use a visual aid just because it is available. Visual aids that do not contribute to the audience's understanding of your speech are likely to be seen as a distraction.

A related question is how many visual aids to use. Because it is easy to make presentation slides on the computer, for example, the temptation is often to make too many of them, with the result that the speech is just a series of slides joined together by loose transitions. When this happens, the visual aids have run away with the speech. Rather than making an important presentation, your role has become that of a master of ceremonies introducing the slides. Not every idea needs to be illustrated, and you should give the audience enough time to absorb what you show and to listen carefully to what you say before you make them shift attention to another image. Speeches of 10 or 15 minutes' length ordinarily will call for just a few visual aids, at most.

Designing Visual Aids

The following design principles will help you to prepare effective visual aids that support your presentation. Also revisit the suggestions regarding design, color, and

Rhetorical Workout

Choose Images for Visual Aids

Suppose you are giving a speech about the traditions of Taos Pueblo and you want to find images (whether photos, maps, videos, or other images) to use in your visual aids.

1. Search for **Taos Pueblo** online.
2. What types of images can you find through a primary source like the Taos Pueblo website? What types of images can you find through secondary sources like Google Images or YouTube? If you do a general search for "Taos Pueblo images" or "Taos Pueblo video," how do your results differ?
3. Select one image—still or moving—and assess its usefulness as a visual aid:
   a. Does the source you're looking at include enough information that you know exactly what the image is showing and when it was created?
   b. How might the image add interest to a speech? How might it be a distraction?
   c. Does it illustrate something that's difficult to describe in words?
   d. Is it memorable?
   e. How good is the quality?
   f. Will important details be visible to an audience?
   g. If it's a video, how long is it? How might you use some or all of it in a 15-minute speech? In a 10-minute speech?
4. How would you cite the source of the image in each of these places:
   a. In your speech?
   b. On your visual aid?
   c. In your bibliography?

type styles for computer-generated slides on pages 378–381, which can be applied to many types of visual aids.

Visibility and Clarity. Visual aids must be seen easily by members of the audience. If people must strain to see, if the visual aid is too small, or if it is too complex, the benefit of using the visual aid is lost. This principle dictates that visual aids be *simple*. Each visual aid should illustrate only one idea in the speech, and each should be as uncluttered as possible. Pay attention as well to the size and proportion of visual aids. For example, the lettering in textual graphics should be large enough to ensure that people who are seated in the back of the room can read it without straining. Also, you should select the kind of visual aid that is appropriate to the situation. A flip chart or a whiteboard drawing might work perfectly for an audience of 25, but for an audience of 200, you probably need projected images or video to ensure that everyone can see well.

Portability. Visual aids should be easy for the speaker to handle. Your aids should be portable, not heavy or cumbersome, and they should not restrict your movements or gestures during the speech. In addition, you should be able to set up and remove them quickly, because it is unlikely that the room will be available for any great length of time either before or after your speech. Finally, design the visual aids with an eye toward how they will be kept in place during your presentation. If the aids need to be placed on an easel, be sure that one is available. If you plan to mount your visual aids on the wall or to hand them out to the audience, consider carefully how best to do this and at what point during the speech you will need to use them. If you plan to hold the visual aids, be sure that their size and materials permit you to do so easily.

CHECKLIST 15.3

Designing Visual Aids

Keep in mind the following principles:

1. Visual aids should be carefully matched to the contents of the speech.
2. Visual aids should be easily seen by members of the audience.
3. Visual aids should be easy for the speaker to handle.
4. Visual aids should be aesthetically pleasing without distracting from the speech.

Appeal. Visual aids should be aesthetically pleasing without distracting from the speech. Determine what the central element of the visual aid is and what elements are in the background. You might use color to heighten the appeal and focus of your aids and to make points clearly. Color is more vivid than black and white and usually will grab the audience's attention. To make your meaning clearer, you might use variations of a single color (shades of green, for example), colors that are close to one another on a color wheel (to suggest similarities), or colors that are usually thought of as opposites (to emphasize distinctions). Aesthetic considerations might also lead you to choose, for example, whether to use a chart or a graph and whether a bar graph or a pie graph is a more compelling way to illustrate a central idea. For additional help and ideas, take advantage of resources such as online tutorials or design guides like *Slide:ology: The Art and Science of Creating Great Presentations* by Nancy Duarte and *The Non-Designer's Presentation Book* or *The Non-Designer's Design Book* by Robin Williams.[9]

Be careful that elaborate visual aids do not run away with your speech, causing listeners to remember your attractive charts and graphs rather than what you said. You do not want your speech to be like the movie that is remembered primarily for its special effects. Follow two key principles: Restrict your visual aids to those that really are crucial, and keep the design of each visual aid as simple as possible. Although visual aids will help make your ideas clearer, remember that the speech is ultimately about those ideas, not about the visual aids.

Planning for Technical Difficulties

There is a familiar saying called Murphy's Law: If anything can go wrong, it will. You hope, of course, that your speech will not prove this principle to be true. The best way to avoid it is to imagine the technical problems you might confront and to have alternative solutions in mind.

You always should rehearse the presentation on the equipment that you will actually use when you deliver the speech. Then you can deal in advance with any technical mishaps. For example, the presentation that you have created on a computer may appear different when projected. Also be sure to bring backup files with you (if you are using a computer) or to protect your posters, charts, or transparencies from physical damage. If you will not be using your own computer, be sure that the computers at the speaking site are compatible with your software. If you think that you might need extra batteries, chargers, or other equipment, remember to have them available.

Additionally, you may want to have a backup plan in case of technology problems. For example, you may wish to store your files on a flash drive rather than using a method that requires you to access the Internet. You might use computer slides to make a set of transparencies that could be shown on an overhead projector in an emergency or print copies of the slides that could be distributed as handouts if necessary. Having multiple ways to access and present your electronic material will reduce the risk of technological failure.

If you anticipate technical difficulties and have backup options available, you can use the time right before your presentation to collect your thoughts, knowing that the technical aspects of your visual aids are under control.

Strategies for Speaking to Diverse Audiences

Respecting Diversity Through Visual Aids

In preparing visual aids, it is important to make them accessible to all members of the audience. The following strategies recognize that members of diverse audiences may process visual aids differently.

1. Because some members of your audience may be visually impaired, be sure that the visual aids supplement but do not replace verbal content. Do not rely too heavily on the multimedia aspect of your presentation.
2. Remember that your images may not mean the same thing to your audience as they do to you. Certain pictures or symbols may be more confusing than clarifying, and some may even be offensive. For example, showing a picture of a woman in a bathing suit in order to talk about your vacation may cause others to feel uncomfortable.
3. Realize that cultures may differ in how they process different kinds of visual information such as statistics, flow charts, graphs, and the like.

Using Visual Aids in the Speech

To plan the effective use of visual aids, you must be sensitive to your audience, your purpose, and the physical circumstances. The composition and culture of the audience will affect your decisions about which visual aids are appropriate, and the size of the audience will affect how large or how complex the visual aids should be. You also need to think about how to use the aids during the speech—and to practice the speech including them.

Avoid Distraction

Although there are many benefits to using visual aids, they can be a powerful distraction, drawing attention to themselves rather than to the heart of your speech. If listeners begin to notice how frequently you project pictures or that you have misspelled a word on a PowerPoint slide, then they are not paying attention to the main idea of your speech, and they will be far less likely to remember what you said.

Usually, when visual aids distract, it is because the speaker did not prepare or use them properly. The audience will be distracted if the visual aids are too complex, if the print on them is too small, if you use too many, if you present them out of order, or if you change them too rapidly. These problems can be avoided. The fault lies not in the decision to use visual aids, but in how they are used. In planning your visual aids, then, the first principle is to make sure that they do not distract from your speech.

Do Not Obstruct the Audience's View

One of the first decisions is where to place the visual aids. Will they be in the center of the room or to the side? Will they be mounted or free-standing? Will they be visible throughout the speech or concealed except when you refer to them? Make these decisions consciously, not by accident. Then gather whatever materials you need—a laptop, USB flash drive, extension cord, easel, thumbtacks, tape, and so on. Also, scout the presentation space to make sure you have everything you need, and have a strong backup plan in case anything fails to work.

Position the aid so that, when you stand to speak, listeners will be able to see it as well as to see you. Otherwise, there is no point in preparing the visual aid. For example, if you plan to stand at the center of the room, place the visual aid to the side. If you are using a projection screen, try placing it in one of the front corners of the room rather than in the center.

Consider carefully the details of the room. If your audience is in tiered ("stadium style") seating, you can display your visual aid at your own eye level. But if audience members are seated at the same level (at banquet tables or in an ordinary classroom, for instance), you will need to position the visual aid above your head so that everyone can see it. If you are speaking in a wide room, place the visual aid far enough from the front row that people at the sides can see it; if the room is long and narrow, be sure that the visual aid is large enough that people seated at the back can see it.

Remember, though, that you need to have access to the visual aid. If you plan to point to it, you must stand close enough that your pointer will identify the specific spot you want to highlight. If you plan to turn flip charts, you have to be able to reach them. If you need to be near the overhead projector, that should govern where the projector is placed.

If possible, experiment with the placement of your visual aids in the room where you will speak. If you can arrive early, try out different locations for the visual aids, and find out what works best. If you can't do that because the room is occupied or because you must speak immediately after others, at least think ahead of time about what placement will make the most sense. If you have seen others speak in the same space, think about where they have placed their visual aids and whether that placement has been effective.

If the visual aid is positioned some distance from you and you will need to point to it, select the type of pointer that will work best in the situation. You could consider using your hands, although some find that awkward or even impolite. You might use a ruler or a yardstick, or you could buy a retractable pointer. Laser pointers throw a beam of light onto the screen, but these must be used with care. They are hard to hold steady, and the audience may think you are nervous if the pointer

A Question of Ethics

Ethical Issues in Designing Visual Aids

When data are converted into visual images, a speaker has a variety of choices to make. For example, suppose the Dow Jones Industrial Average, which measures the price of selected stocks, falls from 11,000 to 8,000 during the course of a month. The speaker could show that change on a graph in which the range is from 12,000 to 8,000; it will look like a catastrophic loss. Or the speaker could show the change on a graph in which the range is 15,000 to 0; now it will look like a more modest fluctuation. Additionally, the speaker easily could change the graph to represent only the past year, or a longer time span, which would provide other perspectives. What ethical issues are posed by such choices? What responsibilities, to both the audience and the topic, does the speaker have when converting data into visual aids?

moves back and forth. With a laser pointer, it is usually best to circle the object you want to highlight rather than focusing directly on it; then turn the light off so it won't be distracting.

Speak to the Audience, Not to the Visual Aid

Many speakers forget to whom they are speaking. They face the screen or the whiteboard, pointing to the visual aid, moving their arms around, but with their back to the audience. This is obviously ineffective—first, because it prevents listeners from seeing the visual aid and, second, because the speaker cannot maintain eye contact with the audience. When you turn to the visual aid, do so briefly, to highlight or point out certain features, and then be sure to turn around to face the audience again.

These three considerations suggest the importance of practicing the use of visual aids. Plan where to put them, how and when to refer to them, how to use your hands, and how to put the visual aids away. If you practice these steps several times, the visual aids will become a natural part of the speech rather than a distraction.

Explore the **Exercise** "Presentational Aids" at **MyCommunicationLab**

What Have You Learned?

Objective 15.1: Enumerate the main benefits and possible drawbacks of using visual aids in a speech.

Visual aids offer significant benefits. They can provide the following:

- Enhance interest
- Sustain the speaker's credibility
- Improve audience comprehension and retention
- Make arguments visually

The main potential drawback of visual aids is that they can distract attention from the speech.

Objective 15.2: Identify major categories of visual aids and how each might contribute to the effectiveness of the speech.

There are many types of visual aids:

- Charts
- Graphs
- Representations
- Objects and models
- People

Objective 15.3: Describe how to make visual aids using a variety of materials and how to choose which materials to use.

Both "high tech" and "low tech" media are used for visual aids:

- Computer-generated slides
- Audiovisual media
- Multimedia
- Transparencies
- Flip charts and posters
- Handouts

Objective 15.4: Explain the principles of preparing visual aids and of using them during the speech.

Visual aids should be used if they will make an idea clearer or more convincing to an audience than if there were no visual aid.

Visual aids should be designed with an eye to the following:

- Visibility and clarity
- Portability
- Appeal

Use of visual aids in the speech should be guided by a commitment to the following:

- Avoid distraction
- Leave the audience's view unobstructed
- Speak to the audience rather than to the visual aid

Listen to the **Audio Chapter Summary** at **MyCommunicationLab**

Discussion Questions

1. In early 2003, Secretary of State Colin Powell went before the United Nations Security Council to present a case that Iraq was not disarming as required by a U.N. Security Council resolution. Powell used presentation software in this address. Examine Powell's speech as a prominent example of a multimedia presentation, rather than for its political import. Locate both a transcript of the speech and a reproduction of the slides, and then do the following:
   a. Briefly evaluate the speech and determine where Powell was most effective.
   b. Evaluate the slides. Are they composed appropriately? Are they effective?
   c. Evaluate the relationship between the speech and the slides. Do they work well together? How could they be improved?
2. Seventy-five years ago, people listened to the radio for news and entertainment. Today, most young people are raised on the visual medium of television, and on personal computers with sophisticated graphics capabilities. How has the rise of television and the computer altered expectations about visual support in speeches? How in turn do these considerations affect the strategic decisions you make about your speech?
3. What type of visual aid would be most appropriate for the following purposes? Could the speaker get away with not using a visual aid? What would visual aids add to these oral discussions?
   - Describing your trip to Paris
   - Informing your audience about the length of sentences for certain crimes and the length of time that criminals actually serve for those crimes
   - Explaining the technique of crab picking
   - Teaching an audience how to fill out a 1040EZ tax form
   - Teaching the Heimlich maneuver
   - Describing the change in expected life spans over the last 500 years
   - Getting your audience excited about a new use of the Internet
4. Sometimes visual aids not only increase interest, credibility, and memory but also add to the persuasiveness of a message. Can you think of any examples of visual aids (in speeches, newspapers, advertisements, or the courtroom) that would have an especially powerful persuasive impact?

Activities

1. Take some statistics from one of your speeches, and try to display those statistics in the following forms:
   - Chart
   - Line graph
   - Bar graph
   - Pie graph

   Which form seems to best communicate the information that you want to get across in your speech? Why?
2. Evaluate each piece of support in your speech to determine whether or not a visual aid will contribute significantly to the message. In making this determination, be sure to consider the many types of visual aids that you might use.
3. Using the visual aids that you have chosen in activity 2, practice your speech in the room where you are going to give it. Note the potential pitfalls (for example, lack of an easel for the poster, unfocused overhead projector, low volume on audio equipment), and be prepared to avoid them in the actual presentation.
4. Create a visual aid that is distracting and poorly constructed. Exchange visual aids with another student. Critique each other's visual aids and compile a list of what needs to be fixed and how. Were you both in agreement about what needed to be fixed and how to fix it? Was there something that you found distracting and your classmate did not, or vice versa?

Key Terms

bar graph **373**
chart **369**
diagram **374**
flip chart **383**
flowchart **371**
graph **372**
handout **383**
line graph **372**
multimedia presentation **382**
pie graph **374**
representations **374**
textual graphic **374**
transparencies **383**
visual aids **366**

Study and **Review** the **Flashcards** at **MyCommunicationLab**

Notes

1 For more about these three benefits, see Virginia Johnson, "Picture-Perfect Presentations," *Training and Development Journal* 43 (May 1989): 45–47.

2 William J. Seiler, "The Effects of Visual Materials on Attitudes, Credibility, and Retention," *Speech Monographs* 38 (November 1971): 331–34. In the classroom setting, visual aids also can help to involve your audience more than if you simply were lecturing to them. See Yiannis Gabriel, "Against the Tyranny of PowerPoint: Technology-in-Use and Technology Abuse," *Organization Studies* 29 (2008): 255–76.

3 Visual aids are often the norm in business speeches. For a good discussion of the minimal standards for visual aids in corporate presentations, see Michael Antonoff, "Presentations that Persuade," *Personal Computing* (July 1990): 60–68; and Dale Cyphert, "The Problem of PowerPoint: Visual Aid or Visual Rhetoric?" *Business Communication Quarterly* 67 (March 2004): 80–84.

4 William J. Seiler, "The Conjunctive Influence of Source Credibility and the Use of Visual Materials on Communicative Effectiveness," *Southern Speech Communication Journal* 37 (Winter 1971): 174–85. See also Paul Brett, "A Comparative Study of the Effects of the Use of Multimedia on Listening Comprehension," *System* 25 (March 1997): 39–53. Because of such increased comprehension, the health care industry has turned to multimedia presentations when discussing complicated medical procedures with patients. See Melissa Bekelja Wanzer, Ann M. Wojtaszczyk, et al., "Enhancing the 'Informed' in Informed Consent: A Pilot Test of a Multimedia Presentation," *Health Communication* 25 (June 2010): 365–74.

5 There is an extensive scholarly literature on visual argument. For a good review, see Lester C. Olson, "Intellectual and Conceptual Resources for Visual Rhetoric: A Reexamination of Scholarship Since 1950," *Sizing Up Rhetoric*, ed. David Zarefsky and Elizabeth Benacka, Long Grove, IL: Waveland Press, 2008, pp. 118–37.

6 For more about the mechanics of constructing charts and graphs without the aid of a computer, see Robert Lefferts, *Elements of Graphics: How to Prepare Charts and Graphs for Effective Reports*, New York: Harper & Row, 1981.

7 For a detailed analysis of how iconic photographs are persuasive, see Robert Hariman and John Louis Lucaites, *No Caption Needed: Iconic Photographs, Public Culture, and Liberal Democracy*, Chicago: University of Chicago Press, 2007.

8 Lawyers often use objects in their persuasive messages. For a description of one lawyer who was particularly skilled at the use of visual aids, see Edward Palzer, "Visual Materials with a Point," *Today's Speech* 10 (April 1962): 15–16. For additional suggestions regarding the use of visual aids by lawyers, see Ronald Waicukauski, Paul Mark Sandler, and JoAnne Epps, *The Winning Argument*, Chicago: American Bar Association, 2001, pp. 94–102.

9 For more ideas about the effective use of PowerPoint, see James Katt, Jennifer Murdock, Jeff Butler, and Burt Pryor, "Establishing Best Practices for the Use of PowerPoint as a Presentation Aid," *Human Communication* 11 (Summer 2008): 193–200.

CHAPTER

16 Occasions for Public Speaking

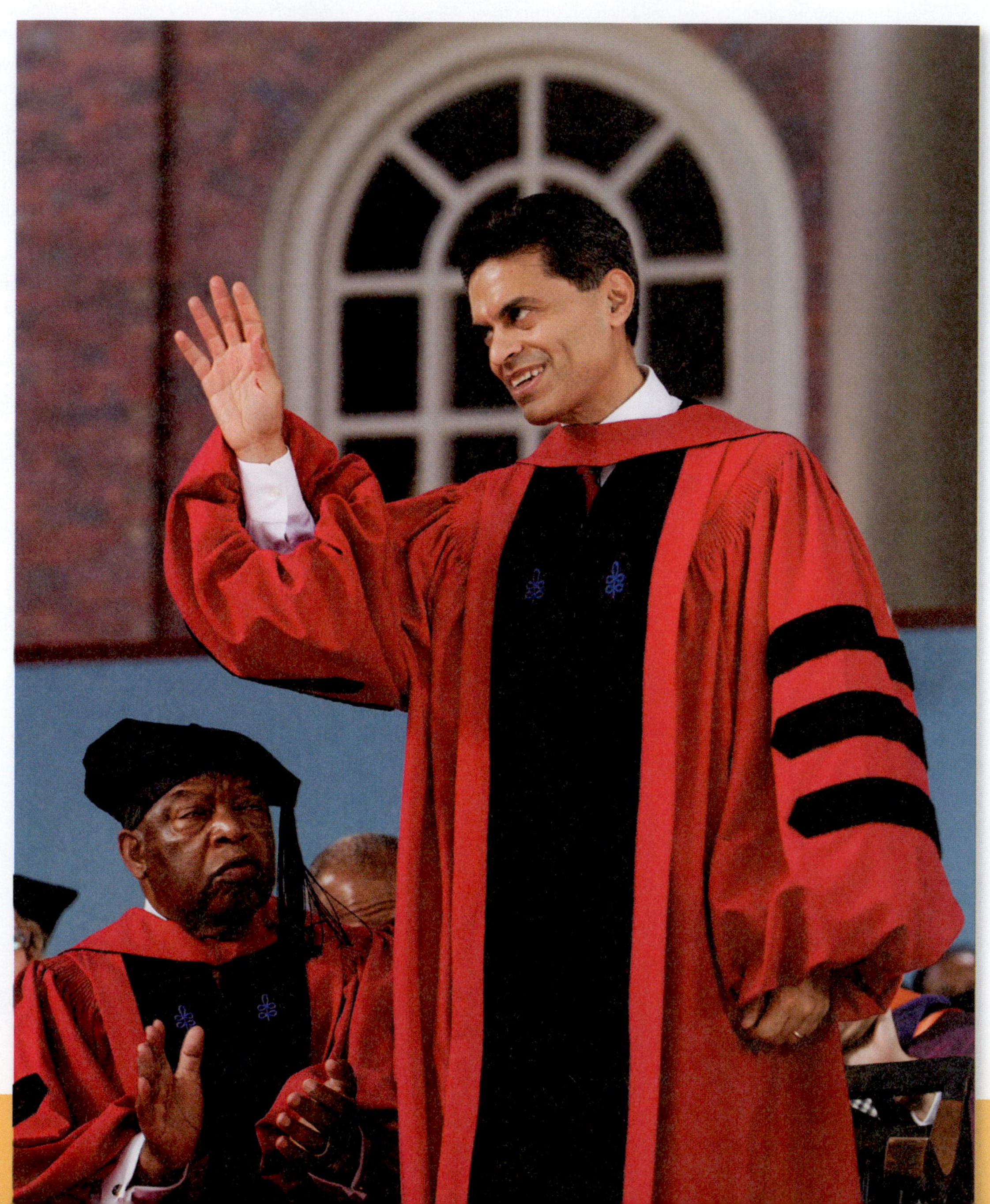

LEARNING OBJECTIVES

Listen to the **Audio Chapter** at **MyCommunicationLab**

After studying this chapter, you should be able to:

Objective 16.1 Explain how the nature of the speaking occasion and the purpose influence the speech.

Objective 16.2 Prepare a speech characterized by decorum, or "fittingness to the occasion."

Objective 16.3 Explain the nature of deliberative speaking and develop various kinds of deliberative speeches.

Objective 16.4 Explain the nature of ceremonial speaking and develop various kinds of ceremonial speeches.

Objective 16.5 Develop types of speeches that combine deliberative and ceremonial elements.

OUTLINE

In preparing classroom speeches, you probably have been careful to follow specific instructions. If the assignment was to demonstrate a process, you made certain that your speech did that. If you were supposed to include three different types of supporting material, you probably paid extra attention to that aspect of preparation. And if the speech could not be longer than eight minutes, you most likely worked carefully with your outlines to be sure that you could cover the topic in that time.

OBJECTIVE 16.1

Fitting Your Speech to the Occasion

Although the requirements of an assignment may sometimes seem arbitrary, they help you to focus on your goals for a speech, and they make the point that all speeches—whether inside or outside the classroom—are given in specific situations. Strategies of informing and persuading are selected and combined so that you and your listeners will have the greatest chance of achieving your goals in a particular situation. (Although we have not focused specifically on them, the same is true of strategies of entertaining.)

What's needed in one situation is different from what's needed in another. Just as an hour-long lecture is out of place when an eight-minute speech is expected, so is self-congratulation inappropriate in a speech to accept an award. However, just as including a variety of supporting material makes a persuasive speech effective, so does well-intentioned humor play an enhancing role in a "roast."

Influence of the Occasion

So far, we have examined the *speech*, the *speaker*, and the *audience*, as well as the relationships among them. It is time to consider the final dimension of any rhetorical situation—the *occasion*. The concept of the occasion was introduced briefly in Chapter 6 when we explored the components of a rhetorical situation. Now it is time to consider more carefully how the occasion influences the development of a speech. Then we can examine types of speeches that are appropriate to different occasions.

We begin with three premises: (1) speeches are presented for specific occasions, (2) occasions create constraints, and (3) constraints are not absolute.

Speeches Are Presented for Specific Occasions. At its best, literature is meaningful regardless of the circumstances in which it is written or read. Speeches, however, achieve their power by responding effectively to a particular occasion.

Even an occasion that is as formal and well defined as a president's State of the Union address can be influenced by specific circumstances. In 1986, for example, President Reagan's speech responded to special circumstances. His address was his first televised speech since the astronauts died in the *Challenger* explosion, so he changed the address into a tribute that reflected the occasion. Had he ignored the circumstances and delivered his original State of the Union address, that response would have been far less appropriate. Similarly, in 1998, President Clinton believed that the occasion called for statesmanship, and he delivered his State of the Union address without commenting on allegations that he was involved in a personal scandal. Although the two presidents had the same "assignment," their responses were quite different. Yet both were appropriate to the occasion.

Some speeches—such as Lincoln's Gettysburg Address and Martin Luther King, Jr.'s "I Have a Dream"—retain great force and power long after delivery, largely because they both responded to the specific occasion and also made that response more universal.

Occasions Create Constraints. Certain expectations arise on any occasion. If you attend a commencement speech, for instance, you expect that it will do certain things and not others. Undoubtedly, it will pose a challenge to the graduates; most likely, it will not criticize their parents and families. At a funeral or memorial service, you expect speakers to talk about the noble character of the deceased and to recall significant events in the person's life; you do not expect anyone to urge the audience to see an important new movie.

Constraints Are Not Absolute. Satisfying the expectations of a particular occasion still leaves the speaker much room for making creative and strategic choices. Not only are there many different ways to meet expectations but also a speech might go beyond them. In the process, it could change listeners' understanding of a situation.

Consider the example of the commencement speech again. Once it has posed a challenge to the graduates, it might proceed to discuss an important issue of public policy. Secretary of State George Marshall used the 1947 Harvard commencement address to announce what became known as the Marshall Plan to rebuild Europe after World War II. When First Lady Barbara Bush spoke at commencement at Wellesley College in 1990, she used the occasion to focus on lifestyle choices of women. And speakers in 2002 and 2003, after noting that the graduates' lives were affected by the September 11, 2001, terrorist attacks, often proceeded to predict how their experience and the country's future would be different because of this tragedy.

In each of these examples, the speech not only responded to but also altered the situation. It met the audience's expectations for what they should hear, and yet it transformed those expectations. Each speaker presented a commencement address but also announced or proposed policies or placed significant public issues on the nation's agenda.

Moreover, experienced speakers sometimes choose deliberately to violate the audience's expectations. For example, in a series of speeches thanking teachers and parents, one speaker might choose to be humorous to set the speech apart from the others and to entertain the audience. Deliberately violating the expectations of the occasion can sometimes be an effective strategy. But beginning speakers are wise to understand and fit a speech to the expectations of the occasion before breaking these informal rules.

In any situation, speakers both respond to and actively shape the rhetorical situation. That is why any occasion for public speaking requires not that you follow a prescribed formula but that you make strategic choices while also recognizing the constraints imposed by the occasion.[1]

Town hall meetings allow citizens to express their views to their public officials.

The Concept of Decorum

Centuries ago, theorists of public speaking developed the concept of **decorum** to identify "fittingness to the occasion."[2] Decorum implies more than common courtesy. A *decorous* speech is one that conforms to the expectations of a particular occasion, such as the following:

Formality. Some occasions are highly formal, such as the inauguration of a president or the keynote address at a conference. These may call for a carefully worded speech delivered from manuscript. Other occasions are informal and call for a conversational delivery, use of familiar maxims, and plain language. Although neither approach is right or wrong in the abstract, either one can be successful or disastrous in the context of a specific situation.

Length. Some occasions call for lengthy remarks; others demand brevity. If your campus organization spends thousands of dollars to present a distinguished guest speaker who talks for only two minutes about the topic and then asks, "Any questions?" the audience will feel cheated. In contrast, a nomination speech should not go on for more than a few minutes because the speaker would eclipse the nominee. For most occasions, brevity is preferred. Speeches that are too long challenge the audience's attention, undercut the import of the occasion, and may even expose the speaker to ridicule.

Intensity. If you are speaking at a dinner to honor a retiring faculty member, how lavish should your praise be? If you are extravagant, the honoree may be embarrassed, and the audience may not take you seriously. But if your remarks are perfunctory, listeners may think that you don't really know or care about the person. Determining just how intense to make your remarks is a particularly difficult challenge. As you gain experience in speaking, however, you should develop an almost-intuitive sense of what an occasion calls for.

Supporting Material. In a speech of introduction, you may decide to highlight an incident from the person's early life to characterize him or her for the audience. As supporting material, that anecdote should truly represent the person. Other occasions call for different types of supporting materials. Formal arguments might be appropriate in congressional testimony, narratives in a speech of tribute, and examples in a pep talk.

Identification. Most speakers try to evoke a sense of common bonds among listeners and between the audience and themselves. Sometimes, the bonding is explicit, as in a speech that commemorates an important occasion and seeks to draw attention to the community. At other times, the bonding is implicit, as when the chair of a meeting summarizes a discussion. To be decorous, a speech also matches expectations about identification.

The most general standard for decorum is the answer to the question "Does the speech capture the thoughts and emotions appropriate to the occasion?" Every aspect of the speech—selection of materials, arrangement, language, and delivery—should help to express the sentiments which, if they thought about it, listeners would agree were the things that ought to be said on the occasion. This doesn't mean that

decorum
Fittingness or appropriateness to the occasion.

audience members would necessarily agree with everything the speaker said, but rather that they would agree that the speaker, given his or her standpoint and purpose, selected the right topics and presented them in the right way.

Identifying Your Purpose

Some theorists believe that the only purpose of speeches for special occasions is to entertain, but this position is misleading. First, entertaining is sometimes not the goal at all. An oral report or a small-group deliberation is likely to focus on presenting information or on reaching a decision, not on entertaining. Second, speeches that are entertaining often serve other purposes as well. They have a deeper underlying message. Just as we saw that no speeches are purely informative or persuasive, the same is true for entertaining. Even accomplished comedians often use humor in order to make an important point, believing that they can be more effective if they do so gently and disarmingly. In fact, speeches that have no purpose other than entertaining for its own sake will often appear to listeners as silly or shallow.

Recall once again the seven speech purposes identified in Chapter 6. Speeches on special occasions often serve to strengthen commitment. For example, an anniversary commemoration allows audiences to reexperience their common past, strengthening listeners' commitment to a person, group, or organization. Special-occasion speeches also create positive or negative feeling. A speech to present an award, for example, may describe the awardee and narrate his or her life in order that listeners may feel good about the person and the values for which he or she stands. Other occasions, such as group presentations, may have the goal of inducing a specific action.

When giving a speech to mark an occasion, therefore, you need to know just what your purpose is and then to make strategic choices so that the speech will be designed to achieve it. Don't just follow a standard formula or pattern that you think covers speeches of a particular kind.

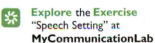

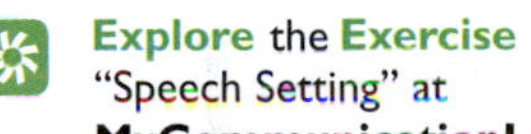
Explore the **Exercise** "Speech Setting" at **MyCommunicationLab**

Deliberative Speaking

OBJECTIVE 16.3

In ancient Greece, the earliest theorists of public speaking distinguished among three types of occasions: forensic, deliberative, and ceremonial (also called epideictic).[3] **Forensic speaking** occurs in a court of law and is concerned with establishing justice. Because this type of speaking is highly specialized and is largely the province of lawyers, judges, and legal panels, we will not examine forensic speaking here. But both deliberative and ceremonial speaking warrant our close attention. Also, many occasions, including pep talks, political campaigns, commencement speeches, and inaugural addresses, call for combinations of deliberative and ceremonial speaking. We shall examine some of these situations as well.

forensic speaking
Speaking in a court of law; concerned with establishing justice.

The Nature of Deliberative Speaking

Just as the law court is the model setting for forensic discourse, the legislature is the model for deliberative speaking. Actually, though, it occurs in any formal or informal decision-making group. **Deliberative speaking** aims to answer

deliberative speaking
Speaking in a decision-making assembly; concerned with matters of expediency; addresses the question "What shall we do?"

the question "What shall we do?" Its focus is on action, and it occurs when two conditions arise:

1. The answer to "What shall we do?" is not self-evident. Matters are uncertain, perhaps because they deal with the future, because they involve questions of value, or because the information needed for certainty is simply not available.
2. A decision is required. Action cannot be deferred until everything is known and the outcome is self-evident. Either that may never occur, or, if it does, it will happen too late.

Many of the examples discussed throughout this book involve deliberative speaking occasions. For instance, suppose you were addressing the topic "How the government should regulate the financial sector." The topic itself is oriented to action and implies that you might choose among potential actions or at least review your solution options. Not everything about the topic can be known. Even if you know how the financial sector currently works, you obviously will not know the results of untried alternatives. Yet a decision must be made because many have blamed irresponsible lending for the economic crisis that began in 2008, and economic recovery depends upon responsible financial decisions. Needing to make a decision under uncertain conditions, listeners turn to you for help in answering the question, "What should we do?"

It should be apparent from this description that deliberative speaking uses the strategies of informing and persuading, which we examined in Chapters 13 and 14. By providing needed information or by giving good reasons to favor one choice over another, a deliberative speech helps the audience to determine what should be done. Following are some of the most common occasions that call for deliberative speaking.

Community Service and Involvement

As you become active in your community, there will be many occasions for you to speak in deliberative settings in the public forum. You may represent your point of view in speeches to service clubs, neighborhood groups, the Chamber of Commerce, or the PTA. In the process, you will help to make people aware of the public dimensions of issues they might not have recognized previously. You will both inform and persuade, pursuing goals that range from agenda setting to inducing a specific action.

For example, for some years, there had been a disparity in the academic achievement of students of different races in the Oak Grove public schools. For some, this had been accepted as a "fact of life," and for others, each student's achievement was an individual and private matter. But George Rivers and Linda Sanchez decided to draw people's attention to this situation. They thought it had larger consequences for the school district. Property values would decline if the school district had a reputation for poor performance by students of different races. Even more important, this differential was not encouraging for the future of race relations in Oak Grove, which was becoming increasingly multiethnic and multicultural. George had children in the Oak Grove schools; Linda did not. But they both insisted that the issue affected the entire community, and their speeches to

CHECKLIST 16.1

Deliberative Speaking Occasions

1. Community service and involvement
2. Oral reports and presentations
3. Group presentations
   - ❒ Group reports
   - ❒ Speaking in small groups
   - ❒ Chairing a meeting
4. Public hearings and debates
   - ❒ Giving testimony
   - ❒ Participating in debates
5. Responding to questions

neighborhood associations, church groups, and PTAs caused the school district to acknowledge the issue and recognize it as a priority.

George and Linda's situation is like many that you will face. They did not regard themselves as "politicians" in any way. Their major concerns were personal—their families and their careers. But they became aware of an issue that affected the general welfare of the community and about which they felt strongly. That issue prompted them to speak in public, and doing so brought them into the public forum.

Community service and involvement is the way in which you are most likely to be an active participant in the public forum. What is more, if the issue engages you and you become strongly committed, you are likely to find that becoming involved by speaking out can be personally meaningful and rewarding.

Watch the **Video** "Grant Proposal Presentation (Joel Rekas, Shalom Community Center)" at **MyCommunicationLab**

Oral Reports and Presentations

Staff members in businesses and government agencies often have to brief their supervisors about important issues and situations. Such a briefing is simply an oral report in which the staff member identifies the topic or issue and gives background information to help the supervisor reach a decision. Similarly, when you describe a problem facing the company or explain to coworkers how to perform a task, you are presenting an oral report.

You probably have made oral reports in some of your classes. Although your purpose might not have been to help someone make a decision about what to do, such reports are much like the oral briefings expected in business and government settings. In preparing an oral report, the organizational pattern that you select is particularly important because you want to present the material in an order that is appropriate and easy to understand. If you are describing a process, for example, you want to be sure to list its specific steps in the right order. If you are proposing a solution, you want to be sure that the problem is explained first.

Laura Winston was the project manager responsible for developing new information systems for her company. She and her staff were experts in handling the technical aspects of databases, networking, and data security, but these systems also were used by managers who did not understand them well. So when Laura was asked to describe a new system at a meeting of company executives, she wisely began with a clear forecast of her speech:

> The company will soon develop a new information system. Let me describe its key features, explain the major differences from the old system, and show you how it will benefit us all. I know that change is sometimes difficult, but once we get used to this new system, I think we'll find it to be a big improvement. So please follow along, and be sure to ask questions if there's something you don't understand.

Laura might have met the expectations for a briefing even without this careful preview. But by including it, she altered the occasion to make it also a time for reassuring her listeners in the face of uncertainty.

Laura's presentation was primarily informative, but sometimes a speech's goal is to be persuasive, not just to present information but to urge decision makers to select your proposal over others. Persuasive presentations are common in the sales environment, where they emphasize how the benefits of your proposal are most in line with the decision makers' values.

For example, if you know that a corporation's decision makers will select the advertising campaign that most appeals to the values of youthfulness and creativity, you will make primary reference to those values in presenting and defending

CHOOSE A STRATEGY: Preparing an Oral Presentation

The Situation

You work at a marketing firm and have prepared three different presentations to pitch to a client who will choose only one. Your client wants the final marketing campaign to appeal to a young demographic and have a distinctive aesthetic but also wants the costs to stay low. You will present the three campaigns to the client and explain the demographic appeals, aesthetic features, and costs of each.

Making Choices

1. Is the purpose of your presentation to inform, to persuade, or both? Explain.
2. Which of the basic organizational patterns would you choose for this presentation: chronological, spatial, topical, cause-effect, problem-solution, comparison and contrast, or residues? Why?
3. Based on the information you are given, what analysis can you make of the self-interests, beliefs, and values of your audience (your client)? What are some strategies you can use to reinforce these in your presentation?

What If...

How would your answers and strategies change under the following conditions?

1. The campaign that you think has the best aesthetics also costs the most of the three.
2. The campaign that best appeals to a young demographic is not as distinctive aesthetically but costs the least.
3. Your client is also considering designs from other companies.

your proposal. If you know that the city council will select the parking plan that makes parking easiest in the downtown area, you will point out that your proposal creates the greatest number of spaces at the lowest cost. In cases like these, the principles of audience analysis and persuasion that we examined in earlier chapters will be of great help.

Jon Hobbs applied these principles when he was president of New Images, a student group that made films and videos. Appearing at a meeting of the Student Activities Funding Board, which was responsible for allocating all student activity fees, he made a convincing presentation. He emphasized the large number of students involved in New Images, the artistic merit of the group's previous work, the fact that the group had won production awards that brought prestige to the college, and the group's track record in attracting outside donors and staying under budget. These themes matched the values of the funding board, whose members were interested in benefiting large numbers of students, bringing favorable recognition and publicity to the college, and stretching its resources as much as possible. Although several other student organizations left the budget meeting unsatisfied, Jon's effective presentation resulted in full funding for New Images.

Group Presentations

Group Reports. It is quite common for people to join groups that investigate an issue, propose solutions, and then present the results of their work to others, either in a small group or in a larger setting. Group reports are often presented orally, as the starting point for discussion by a larger public audience. For example, a citizens' panel might be asked to propose ways to improve public education in the community. When the group presents its findings for public discussion, one member might talk about curriculum, another might talk about extracurricular programs, another might discuss cultural diversity, another might stress the significance of parental involvement, and yet another might address matters of school finance.

An example of a group report on campus is one that focused on how fraternities and sororities were making the transition to alcohol-free rush as required by their national organizations. The report's purpose was to inform fraternity and sorority members of their responsibilities and options under the new plan. One panelist outlined the new regulations, a second talked about alcohol-free events being organized by her sorority, and a third discussed the values that would lead students to affiliate with fraternities and sororities in the absence of alcohol.

When a group report is presented in this fashion, the occasion is called a **symposium**. As in the example of the citizens' panel, the organizational structure of a symposium is usually topical. All participants in a symposium should understand how the issue has been divided into topics and what will be discussed under each topic heading. That will make them less likely either to repeat each other's points or to omit an important dimension of the issue. Each participant should present only a limited number of main points, being careful that these relate to his or her portion of the larger discussion.

Speaking in Small Groups. Although this discussion has emphasized formal occasions, people are far more likely to engage in deliberative speaking when they participate in small groups. The task of the group is to reach a decision or to propose a solution to a particular problem, and participants advocate specific suggestions in a collaborative effort to find the best solution.

Watch the **Video** "Business Presentation: Team Meeting" at **MyCommunicationLab**

In the previous example about an alcohol-free rush, the symposium was preceded by group meetings in the individual fraternities and sororities. Members discussed whether they should challenge, ignore, or observe the new regulations. They talked about the benefits and drawbacks of alcohol-free events. And they reflected on whether alcohol played any role in their own decisions to join a fraternity or sorority. As the groups worked through these issues, members made short speeches advancing ideas and arguments for their point of view.

By participating in a group, members gain access to the thinking of many other people about the question at hand. Because the audience is small and often intimate, the speech can be tailored to the values and interests of specific audience members. Speakers can draw on more information in reaching a decision, and those who participate in problem solving tend to have a better understanding of the issues and to be more committed to the group's solution. On the other hand, a member who has a particularly strong personality may dominate the discussion and influence others to go along unthinkingly. And people sometimes propose more extreme solutions within a group setting because they do not feel personally responsible for the outcome. Be especially alert in a group, and avoid these dangers, sometimes labeled **groupthink**. Make sure that in advocating a position you do not close the door to other possibilities, that you listen as carefully to other people's ideas as you want them to listen to yours, and that you do not urge the group to adopt any course of action that you would not adopt personally. The idea is to take advantage of the assets that a group offers while minimizing the risks.[4]

symposium
A group presentation in which a subject is organized topically and each speaker addresses a limited portion of the subject.

groupthink
The tendency for groups to approve more extreme solutions than would an individual because no one is personally responsible for the group's decision.

Chairing a Meeting. Deliberative decisions are often made during a meeting, whether small and informal or large and public. Unless the occasion is very informal or spontaneous, someone will act as the **chair**, or presiding officer,

chair
The presiding officer of a meeting.

of the meeting. This person may be appointed or elected or may simply assume the role by performing its functions. Some of the chair's functions are themselves deliberative in nature, particularly stating the issues, summarizing what group members have said, and identifying the issues to be decided.

Chairing a meeting is an important skill in its own right. **Parliamentary procedure** is a set of rules for a public meeting to ensure that the majority will reach the most effective decision while protecting the rights of the minority. It involves **motions**, or statements, that propose what the group should do. But even in informal meetings, the chair has the following responsibilities:[5]

1. Ensuring that the physical space is set up appropriately—that there are enough seats, that they are arranged in the best pattern for the meeting (circle, theatre style, and so on), that lighting is adequate, that noise is controlled, and that the temperature is comfortable.
2. Previewing what will be discussed or decided—the equivalent of preparing an agenda for formal meetings.
3. Stating the issues precisely.
4. Summarizing major points that emerge in discussion and indicating how they are related.
5. Stating clearly what has been decided.

People chair meetings far more often than you might think. You may emerge as the leader of an informal study group that is deciding on the best way to prepare for an examination. You may function as the moderator of a current-events discussion group. Or you may be elected or appointed to a leadership position in student government. Experienced public speakers are often selected to chair meetings because their skills of analysis and argument are of great value in these situations as well as at a podium.

Public Hearings and Debates

Sometimes, you may wish to speak out by providing testimony at public hearings or participating in debates.

Providing Testimony. A development firm is proposing to build a major shopping center in your neighborhood. The plan offers great potential economic benefits to the town, but it's likely to increase neighborhood traffic and will create a commercial presence in a residential area. The development firm seeks a zoning variance to build the center even though it will not comply fully with regulations. The zoning board holds a public hearing at which interested citizens can testify.

Individuals who testify in public hearings present deliberative speeches; their goal is to persuade those conducting the hearings to their point of view. Because many people testify at a hearing, each statement must be brief. An analysis of the decision makers helps a speaker to determine which points to emphasize and how best to be persuasive in the situation.

Janet Carpenter and Richard Brinkley were both well informed about the proposed shopping center. They both knew that the city would welcome the additional tax revenue from the center, especially because citizens had recently voted against higher taxes. But they were also aware that the shopping center might damage the residential character of the neighborhood. They both

parliamentary procedure
Rules for the conduct of public meetings.

motion
A statement proposing what an assembly should do.

testified before the zoning board that would have to approve the project. Janet favored the development and began by saying

> This shopping center will revive the sagging economy of our town. That's worth a lot. It will strengthen the value of our homes and make money available for schools and parks without our tax rates having to go up. Now, I know that the residential character of this area is important, but tough zoning regulations will still protect that, even after the shopping center is built.

Richard opposed the project. In his testimony, he argued

> We must be careful to avoid being lured too strongly by money. Sure, we all recognize the need to bring more money into the town, and let's find better ways to do that. But this shopping center will change the quality of our lives forever. That's a far more harmful effect, even though it can't be measured in dollars.

Watch the **Video** "Tobacco Ordinance Public Hearing (Shirley Lindsey Sears, respiratory therapist and tobacco educator)" at **MyCommunicationLab**

Both Janet and Richard focused on a small number of arguments and made each as clear and concise as possible. Those are excellent goals to strive for if you are called upon to provide testimony.

Debates. Sometimes an organization will sponsor a debate about a controversial issue. You may be invited to advocate one side of the issue while someone else supports the other side. Debaters not only present speeches they have thought about in advance but also respond to the statements of their opponents. The purpose of a debate is to enable the audience, by hearing the opposing positions at the same time, to understand the issues better and to decide which side they wish to support.

Some debates are highly structured, with rules prescribing the number of speeches and the time limits. Other debates are loosely structured; one advocate presents a speech, the opponent responds, and then the speakers alternate their responses until everyone feels that the issue has been exhausted. Debates employ all the techniques of informative and persuasive speaking, with special emphasis on testing reasoning. Participants not only develop their own arguments but also refute opposing arguments.

In election campaigns, candidates appear in debates to enable voters to decide whom to support. In legislative bodies discussing a proposal, members engage in debates both to make a record for their constituents and to clarify issues to influence their undecided colleagues' votes. In local communities, civic organizations hold debates so that people will be informed about important issues and can decide what they believe. Although it may be some time before you participate in debates that will affect your community, school or campus organizations may give you practice in debating issues ranging from the nation's foreign policy to the allocation of student funds for campus activities.

Responding to Questions

One situation that calls for deliberative speaking does not seem like a prepared speech at all. After you speak, listeners may ask questions. Or, in an informal situation such as a campaign rally, they may interrupt your speech to ask questions. Sometimes, as in a press conference, the entire point of speaking is to respond to questions.

Answering questions can be a way to share information. After a speech, you may be asked to explain an idea in greater detail or to develop an interesting point further. Sometimes, a questioner will confront you with an alternative or even an opposing view of your topic, and you will have the opportunity to defend your position.

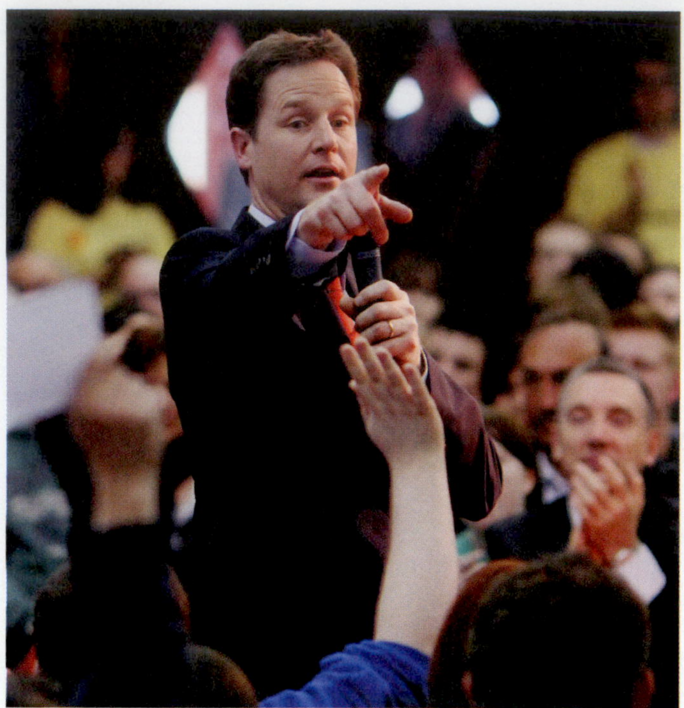

When you take questions, listen to them carefully so you know exactly what is being asked.

Sometimes, questions may not be so straightforward. Skeptics or critics may try to discredit your speech under the guise of asking a question. The classic example is the **loaded question**, one that presupposes an adverse value judgment. The reporter who asks the president of a company, "Have you stopped harassing your workers?" has loaded the question because the president can't answer it satisfactorily if it is taken at face value. A "yes" answer would imply that the company president had been harassing workers in the past; a "no" answer would imply that the president is doing so now. Instead, the president should identify the unsupported assumption of the question, that he or she had ever been harassing the workers.

Another trick question is one that poses a **false dilemma** by identifying two unacceptable options and assuming that they are the only alternatives. Ellen Williams faced such a question after a speech urging her classmates to spend their vacations in the United States rather than abroad. She had pointed out the many natural wonders and historical sites that many Americans have never seen, and she had argued that domestic tourism could strengthen the U.S. economy and improve the balance of payments. After the speech, she was immediately confronted by another student who asked, "Well, Ellen, if you don't support foreign travel, aren't you saying that we should all be ignorant of the rest of the world?" Obviously, these are not the only alternatives available, and a speaker should identify the false dilemma rather than being trapped by attempting to answer such a question.

If a listener asks multiple questions or a complex question that requires multiple answers, it is usually wise to divide the question and respond to its parts separately. Doing so will keep your organizational structure clear and make it easy for listeners to follow you. Sometimes humor or even obvious evasion can deflect an inappropriate question without antagonizing the audience. One lecturer, after speaking about changes in political campaigns over the years, was asked, "Did you vote for Obama or Romney in 2012?" Believing that his personal political choices were irrelevant to the discussion but not wanting to offend the questioner, he answered, "Yes." Chuckles from audience members signaled their recognition that the lecturer had answered the literal question but chose not to provide the information the questioner sought. Because the lecturer smiled and obviously was in good humor, listeners interpreted his response to mean that the question was inappropriate rather than that the lecturer was evasive.

loaded question
A question that presupposes a value judgment adverse to the speaker.

false dilemma
Identifying two unacceptable options and assuming that they are the only alternatives.

Although no speaker can anticipate every possible question, it's a good idea in preparing a speech to think about what listeners may ask. Try particularly to imagine questions that will challenge your position, and be ready to answer those. People who hold press conferences often prepare in advance by asking others to act as hostile questioners; then, they rehearse the answers they plan to give. Thinking about possible questions will allow you to plan your answers mentally and to select among different ways of responding.

During the question-and-answer session itself, remember that you are both answering questions and giving listeners more evidence of your *ethos*. If you become defensive, they may decide that you are not really confident about what you said in the speech. If you become aggressive or hostile, they may conclude that you are not being fair to your questioner. If you take advantage of a vague or unclear question, you may seem to be playing a game rather than being genuinely committed to your topic. As a general rule, use question-and-answer periods to enhance your image as being fair, genuinely interested in your subject, and committed to the goals of sharing information and making intelligent decisions.

Ceremonial Speaking

OBJECTIVE 16.4

The third type of speaking occasion identified by ancient theorists was called **epideictic** (ep-uh-DIKE-tik), but **ceremonial** is a more contemporary term. Epideictic speeches are delivered at ceremonial occasions. Speeches of tribute at a retirement dinner, speeches introducing a distinguished guest, speeches upon receiving an award, and speeches commemorating a significant event are all examples of ceremonial speaking.

The Nature of Ceremonial Speaking

Although ceremonial speeches have informative and persuasive elements, their basic purpose is different from deliberative speeches. Instead of sharing information and guiding decisions, ceremonial speeches strengthen the bonds between speaker and listeners and among listeners themselves, building a sense of community. Epideictic speakers often use humor to entertain listeners and to make them more aware of their common bonds. To achieve that sense of community, they usually create a sense of **presence** for particular ideas and values, bringing them to the forefront of consciousness. Although deliberative speeches also may emphasize values, they do so to guide an audience in decision making. Ceremonial speeches tend to focus on values to draw people closer together.

By recalling events or stories that are important to the group, the speaker enables the audience to relive its history vicariously. By explicitly reminding listeners of the principles or values they share, the speaker knits them together as a community. By giving a particular interpretation to events, the speaker may place them within a frame of reference that draws the group together. And by referring to people the audience reveres, the speaker may draw upon their unifying power and add emotional force to the issue being discussed.

The strength of a ceremonial speech does not depend primarily on its informative or persuasive dimensions, as a deliberative speech might, but on the speaker's ability to craft words and images that capture the occasion. The speaker's ability to articulate the audience's unexpressed feelings is called **resonance**, because the speaker's words echo listeners' feelings. This, of course, also enables the speaker to better identify with the audience.

The speaker chooses a mix of stories, images, and arguments to use in responding to the occasion and enjoys great flexibility in the selection of specific purposes. But the tone must be appropriate for the occasion; the speech should build to an

epideictic
Ceremonial.

ceremonial speaking
Speaking at ceremonial occasions; it reaffirms a community's common bonds and values, strengthening ties between individuals and the group.

presence
Conscious awareness, salience.

resonance
Articulating the unexpressed feelings of listeners, who then conclude that the speaker's message rings true with them.

emotional climax; its length has to be controlled carefully; and humor must contribute to, rather than weaken, the presentation. Do not leave these elements and other key decisions to chance.

Speeches of Greeting

Introductions. Early in this course, you may have delivered a speech of introduction, either of yourself or of another student. This is a common type of ceremonial speech. When a group invites a speaker to address it, a member of the group usually introduces the speaker. The goals of such a speech of introduction are to make the speaker feel welcome, to give listeners relevant information about the speaker, and to contribute to the speaker's *ethos*.

These general purposes suggest guidelines for the speech of introduction. It should be selective, because a lengthy list of all the speaker's achievements may embarrass the speaker and bore the audience. Mention only significant accomplishments that are directly related to the occasion, carefully avoiding any incidents or information that might digress from the point. Also avoid overly lavish praise, which either might be embarrassing or raise the audience's expectations to an unattainable level. Listeners who are told,"Our special guest is simply the most captivating speaker you will ever hear," are likely to be disappointed, which can only undercut the speaker's efforts.

A speech of introduction should not be read, because a manuscript suggests that the introducer doesn't really know the speaker. If you are to introduce a speaker whom you don't know well, learn about him or her in advance. In particular, be absolutely certain that you use and correctly pronounce the speaker's preferred name. Finally, never anticipate or try to summarize what the speaker will say; besides stealing attention from the speaker, you might be mistaken. Few things weaken the introducer's *ethos* more than being corrected immediately by the speaker.

Here is how student Jonathan Cherry introduced a guest speaker on campus:

> Welcome, and thank you for coming tonight. Our guest has been called socially conscious, family oriented, and a business wizard. She has served on planning commissions under the last three mayors of our city and has been responsible for innovations in housing, human relations, and education. Her many years of practical experience, combined with her undergraduate degree in sociology and her master's degree from Eastern State in urban planning, make her especially qualified to discuss "The Future of the City." Please join me in welcoming to our campus Laura Westerfield.

Speeches of Welcome. A visiting individual or group is often greeted on arrival with a speech of welcome. This aims not only to introduce the guest to the host but also to make the guest feel comfortable and at ease. Your tone should be upbeat and optimistic. You should explicitly express greetings to the guest, identify a common bond or interest between you and the guest (such as "We look forward to learning more about each other"), and honor the guest by saying how pleased you are by the visit.

Speeches of Tribute

Testimonials. One of the most common ceremonial speeches is the **testimonial**, a speech to honor someone. Testimonials are presented on many occasions, such as a significant wedding anniversary, a transition to new responsibilities, an outstanding achievement, retirement from a career or profession, and, of course, death.

The honoree's accomplishments are the organizing principle for a testimonial speech. You should discuss achievements that are significant in their own right as well as representative of the person's general character. To keep listeners interested, mention specific incidents and describe them vividly. If possible, select at least some incidents that might not be known to the audience. Be cautious about focusing on incidents or situations in which you played a part, because the point of the testimonial is to focus on the honoree rather than on you. Although your goal is to praise the person, you again should be careful not to exaggerate. Doing so could embarrass the honoree, cause listeners to doubt your sincerity, or suggest that you are so enthralled by the person that you cannot exercise independent judgment.

Weddings and engagement parties are common occasions for public speaking. Toasts to the couple often involve celebrating the joining of two individuals and wishing them a lifetime of happiness together.

Eulogies. A **eulogy** is a special form of testimonial speech that is concerned with praising the dead. Eulogies are often delivered at funerals or memorial services or on special occasions such as the birthday of the deceased. Eulogies typically celebrate the essential character of the person, so the organizing principle is the person's virtues rather than specific accomplishments. Cite examples that illustrate the virtues. A caring individual, for example, might have donated much time and money to various charity organizations. Someone who was "ahead of her time" might have recognized a cultural trend before it became popular.

A eulogy is positive in tone, magnifying the person's strengths and minimizing weaknesses. Still, if it praises too lavishly, it may become maudlin or sound insincere. The goal is to help listeners recall the honoree's personality and character. As in a testimonial, in a eulogy you should limit personal references so that the focus remains on the honoree.

Earlier in this book, we briefly mentioned President Ronald Reagan's eulogy for the astronauts killed in the 1986 explosion of the space shuttle *Challenger*. (You will find this speech in the appendix.) President Reagan spoke again five days later at a memorial service in Houston. His remarks on that occasion illustrate many of the characteristic features of a eulogy:

> We come together today to mourn the loss of seven brave Americans, to share the grief that we all feel and, perhaps in that sharing, to find the strength to bear our sorrow and the courage to look for the seeds of hope....
>
> Their truest testimony will not be in the words we speak but in the way they lived their lives and in the way they lost their lives—with dedication, honor, and an unquenchable desire to explore this mysterious and beautiful universe.
>
> The best we can do to remember our seven astronauts—our *Challenger* Seven—remember them as they lived, bringing life and love and joy to those who knew them and pride to a nation.[6]

This excerpt combines praise for the dead with advice for the living, the two most common components of a eulogy.

testimonial
A speech honoring a person.

eulogy
A special form of the testimonial speech, honoring someone who has died.

President Clinton likewise delivered a public eulogy for the victims of the Oklahoma City bombing in 1995. There were many eulogies for the firefighters and rescue workers who died while trying to save the victims of the September 11, 2001, terrorist attacks, just as there were many eulogies for the victims themselves. And, President Obama spoke movingly on behalf of the victims of an attempted assassination in Tucson in early 2011.

Watch the **Video** "Special Occasion Speech: A Wedding Toast" at **MyCommunicationLab**

Toasts. A **toast** is a miniature version of the testimonial speech. It is usually delivered in the presence of the honoree and often concludes by raising a glass to salute the person.

The toast usually should celebrate one key characteristic of the honoree; supporting materials should include one or two incidents which illustrate that characteristic, talent, or virtue. A toast at a wedding reception, for example, might emphasize the devotion of the newlyweds by referring to an eight-year engagement that spanned three different states and two time zones. After stating the key characteristic and providing the examples, the person giving the toast should recognize the honoree, wish for continued strength and success, and conclude.

Here is a simple example of a toast given at a retirement celebration:

> When offered a job that paid more money, Bob Howlett turned it down because he was loyal to this company and he didn't want to move. When an employee made a mistake, he took the responsibility for it himself. When offered a higher position that would require him to work longer hours, he said that his family came first. Ladies and gentlemen, please join me in honoring Bob Howlett, a man who always has his priorities straight.

toast
A brief testimonial speech, usually delivered in the presence of the person honored and accompanied by raising a glass in the person's honor.

Rhetorical Workout

Give a Toast

Imagine that one of your friends is getting married and you are one of a few people who will give toasts at the reception. About 100 people—family, friends, and coworkers of the couple—are expected to attend.

1. How long do you think your toast should last? Why?
2. Think about the demographic features of an audience that you have learned about in this book, such as size, diversity of views, age, gender, religion, ethnicity, native language, educational level, and socioeconomic status. What are some things you might know about your audience for the toast? What might you *not* be able to know? How will these things affect what you choose to say in your toast?
3. How appropriate do you think each of the following would be for a wedding toast: (a) an inside joke that only you and your friend will understand; (b) a family-friendly story about a funny incident involving your friend; (c) a story about a time your friend was embarrassed; (d) a reference to the couple's future children or grandchildren; (e) a quotation about the joys of marriage. Explain why.
4. It is likely that not everyone will know you. How might you introduce yourself? Write a brief sentence that you could use in your toast.
5. What is one key characteristic, talent, or virtue of your friend that you could talk about in your toast? Write a sentence that describes this key characteristic in general terms. What one or two supporting examples or stories could you talk about to illustrate this characteristic of your friend? Write a sentence or two for each example that you could use in your toast.
6. What could you say to conclude your speech on a positive note and lead the guests in the toast? Write a short sentence that you could use.
7. What key words or other aids could you write on a note card to help you give this speech?
8. Suppose you feel a little nervous about the upcoming event. What are some speech preparation and delivery strategies you have learned that can help you feel confident when you give your toast?

Roasts. A slightly different variation on the speech of tribute is the **roast**, which both honors and pokes fun at a person. When you roast someone, your deft handling of the humor is essential to the success of the roast. Yet, the humor can backfire. Humor is used to put listeners at ease and also to demystify the honoree, suggesting that he or she is "just one of us." But it should never embarrass the person, nor should it distract from the fact that you and the audience are engaged in a tribute.

Like other forms of the speech of tribute, a roast should focus on only one or two key themes or incidents in the honoree's life. Select incidents that poke fun in a good-natured way and yet also have an underlying positive message. For example, the person you are roasting may have done something that seemed unusual or silly at the time, yet revealed a positive character trait. Avoid humor that could be misunderstood as prejudice. Although the roast may begin humorously, it should always end by pointing to the honoree's strengths. Like the toast, the roast should be relatively brief.

Commemorative Celebrations

Commemorative celebrations are speeches that remember important events. Often, they are delivered on the anniversary of the event. The most common example is the Fourth of July oration, a patriotic speech delivered annually on the anniversary of American independence. Other major historical events are also commemorated. For example, in 1994, President Clinton delivered an address to mark the fiftieth anniversary of the D-Day landing during World War II, just as President Reagan had done on the fortieth anniversary in 1984. Referring to D-Day, Clinton said

> My fellow Americans, we have gathered to remember those who stormed this beach for freedom who never came home. We pay tribute to what a whole generation of heroes won here. But let us also recall what was lost here. We must never forget that thousands of people gave everything they were, or what they might have become, so that freedom might live.

Commemorative celebrations share common features. First, the speaker typically refers to the event being remembered, perhaps recounting it as a narrative and perhaps emphasizing a few key points. This reminds listeners of their historical roots in the event. Second, the speaker may abstract certain virtues or special characteristics from the event. The Fourth of July orator may highlight the selflessness and farsightedness of the nation's founders, much as President Clinton noted the courage and dedication of those who landed at Normandy on D-Day. These virtues are discussed to remind listeners why the event is celebrated and to show that the event has continuing significance beyond its historical details. Third, the speaker relates these features to listeners' lives, perhaps challenging the audience to adhere to the standards evidenced in the event, to behave as nobly today as their predecessors did in the event commemorated, or to keep the memory of the event alive as it recedes into history. Through these steps, the anniversary celebration combines tribute to the past with a challenge for the future.

Speeches Marking Awards

Presentation Speeches. Suppose that an organization to which you belong sponsors an award for a student who has done an outstanding job of community or volunteer service. The award is presented at a dinner at the end of the year, and your job is to present the award. On most occasions the presentation of an award calls for a speech.

roast
A speech of tribute that both honors and pokes fun at a person.

commemorative celebration
A speech of remembrance delivered on the anniversary of an important event.

The **presentation speech** typically has two basic elements, and there are choices to make about each. First, it establishes the importance of the award itself. You might say something about the values it represents—in this case, community or volunteer service. If the award is named after someone, you might say a word or two about that person, to pay continuing tribute and to remind the audience of how he or she is connected to the award. Or you might emphasize the award's importance by stating how it relates to other awards that the organization presents—perhaps it is the oldest award, the most prestigious award, or the most competitive award.

Second, the presentation speech establishes the winner's fitness to receive the award by sharing with the audience the actions or achievements that render the person particularly qualified. Often, this step can be linked directly to the preceding part of the speech. For example, if you have shown that scholastic achievement and participation in extracurricular activities are the qualities honored by the award, you then could describe the winner's accomplishments in these respects. This step of the speech symbolically links the winner with the award.

Besides these two basic elements, presentation speeches may include other components. It may be appropriate to explain the selection process for choosing the recipient. If the choice reflects the subjective judgment of a committee, for instance, you might want to discuss some of the criteria the committee used. If a large number of applicants or nominees were considered for the award, you might describe how they were screened down to the finalists. There is no need to describe the selection process if the criteria for the award are purely mechanical, such as an award to the student with the highest grade-point average.

If the finalists who did not win the award are known to the audience, it may be appropriate to praise them as well. You might indicate that anyone in this strong group could have received the award, that the choice of the selection committee was especially difficult, or that the judges wished they could have made multiple awards. Make such statements only if they are true, of course; insincerity can seldom be concealed. But if the competition for the award really was keen, it takes nothing away from the winner to suggest that other candidates were also highly qualified. If anything, winning may magnify the recipient's achievement.

If your speech concludes with the physical presentation of the award, manage your gestures carefully to avoid any awkwardness. Present the award with your left hand into the recipient's left hand so that you can use your right hands to shake.

Watch the **Video** "Video Acceptance Speech: 2007 Clarion Award, Kevin Spacey, actor and artistic director of the Old Vic" at **MyCommunicationLab**

Acceptance Speeches. The recipient of an award is usually expected to say a few words. An honoree who just says, "Thanks," and sits down quickly may seem not to value the award or the audience very much. Such a brief acknowledgment is successful only when the recipient is genuinely overcome with emotion and cannot put his or her feelings into words.

Like the presentation speech, the **speech of acceptance** has certain basic elements. First, you should express gratitude for the honor that the award represents. Be modest; it is always more appealing to say that you are surprised by the award than to say that you know you deserve it. Thank those who presented the award for the honor they have shown you. If it is appropriate, praise the runners-up, or indicate that you are accepting the award on behalf of all the candidates. (This courtesy may be especially diplomatic if the selection process was close or if the runners-up are good friends or are highly regarded by the audience.)

presentation speech
A speech marking the issuance of an award.

speech of acceptance
A speech presented when one receives an award or a nomination for office.

Second, when appropriate, thank those who helped make it possible for you to receive the award. Few people are solely responsible for their own achievements; most have been helped along the way by parents, teachers, friends, and colleagues. Worthy recipients usually seek to share the honor with those whose influence has led to their success. Yet this seemingly simple step has potential dangers. Mentioning a very long list of people not only might bore the audience but also might imply that no single person made a significant contribution to your success. And if you are too specific in identifying helpful people, you may omit someone unintentionally. Sometimes references to people in categories, such as "my parents, my teachers, and my coworkers," may be the safest approach, unless the influence of certain individuals truly was exceptional.

Third, you should indicate your understanding of the values that the award represents. This step not only makes it clear that you know why you are being honored but, more important, also makes the point that you appreciate and pay tribute to those same values in accepting the award.

Probably the most prestigious award of all is the Nobel Prize, given annually in several different fields for distinctive achievement. Accepting the 1986 Nobel Prize for Peace, Elie Wiesel began by speaking about the significance of the award:

> It is with a profound sense of humility that I accept the honor you have chosen to bestow upon me. I know. Your choice transcends me. This both frightens and pleases me.
>
> It frightens me because I wonder: Do I have the right to represent the multitudes who have perished? Do I have the right to accept this great honor on their behalf? I do not. That would be presumptuous. No one may speak for the dead, no one may interpret their mutilated dreams and visions.
>
> It pleases me because I may say that this honor belongs to all the survivors and their children, and through us, to the Jewish people with whose destiny I have always identified.

Wiesel chose to put his selection for the Nobel Prize in the broader context of the survivors of the Holocaust.

Like most ceremonial speeches, a speech of acceptance should be brief. Audiences want to hear a few words of thanks, not a long speech. Indeed, an overly long acceptance speech may suggest that you are using the receipt of the award as a launching pad for a presentation of your own. Usually, a few minutes will be quite enough for an acceptance speech. Then, quit while you are ahead, and return to your seat.

CHECKLIST 16.2

Ceremonial Speaking Occasions

1. Speeches of greeting
   - ❒ Introductions
   - ❒ Speeches of welcome
2. Speeches of tribute
   - ❒ Testimonials
   - ❒ Eulogies
   - ❒ Toasts
   - ❒ Roasts
3. Commemorative celebrations
4. Speeches marking awards
   - ❒ Presentation speeches
   - ❒ Acceptance speeches

Speeches Combining Deliberative and Ceremonial Goals

OBJECTIVE 16.5

We categorize speeches to help recognize differences among them. Some speeches clearly fit into the deliberative category (such as proposal presentations and oral reports); others clearly fit into the ceremonial category (such as introductions and roasts); and some speeches share the basic characteristics of both categories. This should not be surprising. A single speech may well attempt both to guide decision

Facebook founder Mark Zuckerberg gives a keynote speech to a meeting of developers.

making and to celebrate values in a community. In fact, on certain occasions, the two goals are expected to come together, and the speech should be designed to achieve both deliberative and ceremonial purposes.

Keynote Speeches

Meetings of business, academic, professional, or political organizations often feature a speaker near the beginning of the program to set the tone of the event. You may find yourself inviting a keynote speaker for a meeting that you organize, or you may be asked to deliver a keynote speech yourself.

Coming near the beginning of a meeting, the **keynote speech** has two special purposes. First, it draws together and defines the diverse members of the audience as a community. The individual delegates at a state convention of a civic organization, for example, have come from cities and towns that have diverse issues and concerns. The fact that the delegates all belong to the same organization may not seem important to them individually. But when they assemble at the convention, the keynote speech helps to focus their attention and energy on what they share.

Second, the keynote speech helps to set the meeting's thematic agenda. This refers not to the listing of specific items of business but to the larger matters of topics, themes, or issues that will dominate the meeting. Sometimes a meeting has a designated theme, for example, "achieving unity through diversity," and the keynote speaker is asked to address that theme. On other occasions, the meeting may have no theme; the keynote speaker, if successful, will help to determine what listeners will be thinking and talking about for the rest of the meeting. It also serves to rally or inspire listeners, presenting them with a challenge and the motivation to meet it.

Although a keynote speaker has considerable latitude, some cautions are appropriate. Remember that the purpose of the keynote is to open, not close, discussion. A successful keynote address poses issues or questions for delegates to ponder; it does not offer dogmatic proclamations. Stating your own views too strongly, unless you know that the audience holds the same views, can hurt the keynote speech. Recognize that the audience is likely to be diverse, at least on some dimensions. Design the keynote so that it seems to speak to everyone without excluding significant segments of the audience. This means that the speech has to be somewhat **multivocal**, including terms and phrases that individual listeners can interpret in light of their own experiences and concerns. A reference to "the American dream," for example, will mean different things to different listeners, and yet it can be a positive symbol for everyone. This is an example of a *polysemic* message, which we described in Chapter 14, because there are different layers or dimensions of meaning that will appeal to different people. Polysemic messages are multivocal, and vice versa.

keynote speech
A speech presented near the beginning of a meeting to guide its thematic agenda and to help set its tone.

multivocal
Capable of being heard in different ways by different listeners, all of whom find the term or concept positive.

Pep Talks

A **pep talk** is virtually any speech that is intended to motivate and inspire, ranging from a seminar presentation for sales executives to a coach's locker-room address to professional athletes. This speech has two basic purposes: (1) to heighten a sense of community, so that listeners believe that they are "all in this together" and are working for one another, and (2) to increase motivation, so that listeners will put forth extra effort willingly.

To inspire enthusiasm, you need to be enthusiastic yourself. In a pep talk, your emotional tone, intensity, and body language will communicate at least as much as your words do. You should remind listeners of shared goals, both to strengthen commitment to the goals and to move listeners beyond belief to action. To help unify the audience, you may remind everyone of past successes. Recalling a shared experience in narrative form will bind the group together. Reference to past successes will suggest that future successes also are possible and are called for, to honor the successes of the past. Sometimes a pep talk will remind the audience of their shared sacrifices, suggesting that their efforts will be justified if success is forthcoming. Finally, the speech should end on a strong, positive note. Indicate that success is possible in the task at hand, and directly exhort every listener to perform as well as possible, not only for personal gain but for the achievement of the group's goals.

After-Dinner Speeches

The **after-dinner speech** is so named because it typically follows a banquet or other meal, which could be anything from a continental breakfast to a state dinner. This type of speech is deceptively simple. On the surface, it has no serious content but aims primarily to entertain. Like the roast, however, it is delivered with serious intent and ultimately does challenge listeners. It is a speech of celebration that also contains a serious message.

Watch the Video "Special Occasion Speech: After-Dinner Speech—Emergency Preparedness" at **MyCommunicationLab**

The theme of the after-dinner speech should be easy to state and easy for listeners to grasp. The speech's development should be lighthearted and humorous. Again, though, be careful in how you use humor. It cannot be forced; your stories or anecdotes must be genuinely funny. Your use of humor cannot involve religious, racial, gender, or ethnic jokes. Although all were commonplace in the past, today they are offensive to most audiences and will reflect negatively on you as a speaker. And humor should not become an end in itself, or the point of the speech will be lost. As a general rule, the safest humor is that which seemingly comes at one's own expense. Poking fun at yourself may cause listeners to see their own situations in a more lighthearted vein.[7]

The well-known television personality Stephen Colbert delivered an after-dinner speech at the White House Correspondents' Dinner in 2006. Although the speech was delivered with humor and was entertaining, its underlying message was criticism of then-President George W. Bush. The speech was controversial; some people praised it and others thought it was inappropriate to the occasion and hence a violation of decorum.

Commencement Speeches

Few speaking occasions are more common—or more the object of satire and ridicule—than are graduation ceremonies. Although a formal speech is not essential, custom is strong enough that the absence of a commencement speaker is noted, usually negatively. Much energy goes into identifying just the right speaker, for the

pep talk
A speech that is intended to motivate a group and inspire enthusiasm for a task.

after-dinner speech
A speech presented following a ceremonial meal, usually humorous in tone but with a serious message.

ethos of the speaker is somehow thought to transfer to the graduates. Yet most commencement speeches are eminently forgettable. Only a few—such as the speeches by George Marshall and Barbara Bush mentioned in this chapter—outlive the occasion.

The obvious purpose of the commencement speech is to challenge the graduates, urging them to go out into "the real world" and dedicate themselves to a task that is larger than them. Yet the speech cannot be that simple. First, although it is directed primarily to the graduating students, it somehow must acknowledge the presence of others, particularly the parents and families of the graduates, who may be of different generations and who have had different experiences; for them, the same basic message may not be appropriate.

Second, although the speech is intended mainly for this specific occasion, it also needs to suggest a broader scope without sounding "canned." Presumably, the commencement speaker at Eastern State University would not give a dramatically different speech at Western State; and yet something must be said to the graduates of Eastern that distinguishes them from their counterparts at Western.

In 1997, United Nations Secretary General Kofi Annan spoke at the Massachusetts Institute of Technology commencement about the importance of the United Nations and America's role in a globalized future. His remarks were significant because they offered advice and encouragement to the graduates while challenging all Americans to think of their role in the world in a different way:

> All of you in the Class of 1997, wherever you go from here and whatever you do in the future, will participate in a world that is becoming increasingly globalized. . . . As you enter this new world, I call upon you to remember this: as powerful and as progressive a bond that market rationality constitutes, it is not a sufficient basis for human solidarity. It must be coupled with an ethic of caring for those whom the market disadvantages, an ethic of responsibility for the collective goods that the market under-produces, an ethic of tolerance for those whom the market pits as your adversary.

Some commencement exercises include a student speaker. If you perform this role, you will face additional challenges. You will appear presumptuous if you seem to have more experience or expertise than your classmates. You want to issue a challenge, and yet you do not want to talk down to an audience of your peers. Student speakers are most successful when they do not try to issue a challenge themselves but rather discover and articulate one that is already "out there"; it also helps to speak frequently in the first person rather than the second person, referring to challenges facing "us" rather than "you" and indicating what "we," not "you," must do to meet those challenges.

Speeches Marking Candidacy and Election

Important moments in the process of selecting candidates for public office are marked by speeches. These include nominating, acceptance, and inaugural speeches. Although the most obvious place for these speeches is in national politics, you may find that they also are used in the public forum in which you participate, whether on campus, in your community, or in organizations to which you belong.

nominating speech
A speech in which a person is named for an office or honor.

Nominating Speeches. Every four years in the United States, each major political party holds a national convention to nominate its candidates for president and vice president. Especially when there is a contest for these offices, the **nominating speech** becomes a centerpiece of the convention. Each candidate is nominated by a delegate who makes a speech on his or her behalf, concluding by formally placing the person's name in nomination. Candidates select their nominating speakers with care, and delegates who are chosen for this task consider it a great honor and prepare their speeches with equal care. Nominating speeches are also made in student government, in housing units, and in civic and religious organizations of all kinds.

Watch the Video "Special Occasion Speech: Nomination Speech" at **MyCommunicationLab**

Although a nominating speech attempts to guide and persuade people in choosing a leader, it is usually presented at a formal celebration and is meant to draw an audience together in support of common values.

A nominating speech has three basic goals:

1. To make the importance of the office clear. A speaker usually does this by alluding to the responsibilities of the office, describing the issues that the victorious candidate will have to confront or explaining the traits and attitudes that a successful office holder must demonstrate.
2. To show the fitness of the candidate for the office. If certain traits and attitudes are important, then the candidate should be shown to have them. The goal is to link the candidate with the office so that listeners can imagine that outcome and will consider it natural. For example, if previous experience is important, you might emphasize the candidate's record in other positions. If the candidate shares your beliefs about important issues and how to handle them, it will be helpful to note that you have similar priorities.

   To demonstrate your candidate's fitness for the office, you may find it desirable to say something about other candidates. Here, you need to be careful. Several recent national elections have been marked by negative campaigns that emphasized the opponents' weaknesses rather than the candidate's strengths, and voters have begun to resist this approach. In any case, negative campaigning is almost always inappropriate in a nominating speech. Appeals that compare your candidate with others will be more effective if they are generic and emphasize the candidate's positive features without attacking specific opponents. Your own conviction and enthusiasm

A Question of Ethics

Ethics in the Public Forum?

When working in groups, members sometimes have conflicting responsibilities. They want to advance their individual ideas, but they also want the group to be cohesive and successful. When speaking in a group, how do members balance these conflicting responsibilities while protecting against the risk of groupthink?

***

Has technology changed the public forum, reducing the opportunities for most of us to engage in deliberative speaking? Are we, in practice, limited to speaking when a keynote lecture or a toast or a eulogy or an introductory remark is in order? If so, how can we meet our ethical responsibilities as members of a public and a democracy? How can we preserve or revitalize the opportunities for deliberative speaking in the public forum?

will convey a strong positive message about your candidate; attacks on others may suggest that you lack confidence about your choice and see your candidate simply as the least of evils.

3. To formally place the candidate's name in nomination. Speakers sometimes save this formality for the end of the speech, to build to a dramatic climax. At national political conventions, for instance, nominating speeches often avoid mentioning the candidate's name because it might set off a demonstration by the audience that would compete for attention with the speaker's intended message. Even when everyone already knows which candidate you will nominate, saving the formal step of the nomination for the very end focuses listeners on why you think your candidate is best suited for the job.

Acceptance of Candidacy. Sometimes, the nominating process selects the person who will actually occupy the office. In that case, election to office is similar to receiving an award. But when the nominating process determines only who will run for office in an upcoming election, then the acceptance speech needs to be slightly different.

First, of course, the candidate should formally accept the nomination, pledging his or her best efforts in the subsequent campaign and, if elected, in office. It is appropriate to acknowledge the supporters who made it possible to gain the nomination. Particularly if the contest for the nomination was hard fought, the winning candidate should appeal to the losers for support in the race ahead and should express appreciation for their campaign and principles. If at all possible, incorporation of elements from the losers' positions into one's own campaign will help to draw the community together.

Strategies for Speaking to Diverse Audiences

Respecting Diversity Through Occasions for Public Speaking

In some situations, speakers may be tempted to say things that unintentionally demean listeners, such as by using inappropriate humor or falsely assuming that listeners share their values. These strategies will help you to avoid these pitfalls and to recognize audience diversity on the occasions when you speak.

1. Consider how some speaking situations may mix several of the situations discussed in this chapter. Pay attention to how the specific cultural situation in which you find yourself may modify the constraints and opportunities for your speech.
2. Avoid groupthink in group presentations. Listen carefully to others' ideas. But also keep in mind that different cultures may have varying expectations for when and how it is proper to talk. If a culture values age highly, for example, then a younger person may not be expected to speak as much as an older person.
3. Answer questions directly and with respect for the questioner. Use humor or deflection only if you can be sure that they will be taken in the right way.
4. In a ceremonial speech, invoke common values and experiences that unite audience members. Pay attention, though, to the polysemy of such an appeal; it can mean different things to different cultures or groups.
5. Avoid inappropriate or demeaning humor in a roast or after-dinner speech. When using humor, pay attention to previous speeches in the same situation, to get an idea of what type of humor is acceptable or expected.

The acceptance speech should also acknowledge the magnitude of the tasks ahead: winning office and carrying out its duties. It takes a careful combination of modesty and self-confidence to emphasize how difficult and important the position is and yet to pledge to perform capably if elected. Finally, the acceptance speech often concludes with a direct appeal for help from the audience. In accepting the Democratic presidential nomination in 1960, for example, John F. Kennedy asked listeners,"Give me your help, and your hand, and your voice, and your vote."

Acceptance speeches by presidential candidates in the United States have taken on new significance in recent years. Not since 1976 has there been any doubt about the names of the nominees by the time of the national conventions. Rather than focus on the formalities of accepting the nomination, therefore, this speech has become a means for the introduction of the candidate to a national audience and the launching of the general election campaign. For many people, the acceptance speeches are the first occasions when they pay attention to the political contest. Consequently, these speeches have dealt less with rallying the committed and more with swaying the undecided. They have become occasions for citizens to use the critical listening skills we explored in Chapter 4.

A slight variation on the acceptance speech occurs when there is no election campaign but the person nominated must still be approved by others. In 1993, when President Clinton nominated Judge Ruth Bader Ginsburg for a seat on the U.S. Supreme Court, her remarks revealed the typical features of an acceptance speech, as these brief excerpts indicate:

> Mr. President, I am grateful beyond measure for the confidence you have placed in me, and I will strive with all that I have to live up to your expectations in making this appointment. . . .
>
> The announcement the president just made is significant, I believe, because it contributes to the end of the days when women, at least half the talent pool in our society, appear in high places only as one-at-a-time performers. . . .
>
> I am indebted to so many for this extraordinary chance and challenge: to a revived women's movement in the 1970s that opened doors for people like me, to the civil rights movement of the 1960s from which the women's movement drew inspiration, to my teaching colleagues at Rutgers and Columbia and for thirteen years my D.C. Circuit colleagues who shaped and heightened my appreciation of the value of collegiality.

Justice Ginsburg expresses her appreciation for the nomination, notes the significance of the office, places her selection in a broader context, and acknowledges the help of those who have enabled her to reach this important milestone.

Inaugural Addresses. If the acceptance speech marks only the acceptance of candidacy rather than the assumption of office, the latter event is also often celebrated with a speech. Every four years, at the beginning of a term, the president of the United States delivers an **inaugural address**. Presidents, governors, mayors, or chairs of other organizations—whether colleges or universities, business or civic clubs, or professional organizations—may also be called upon to deliver an inaugural address. The inaugural may actually define the assumption of office, but sometimes, as with a university president, there is an interval of time between the official's taking over the office and delivering the inaugural address.

Watch the Video "Classic Speech: Franklin D. Roosevelt's First Inaugural Address (clip)" at **MyCommunicationLab**

inaugural address
A speech delivered when assuming an office to which one has been elected.

CHECKLIST 16.3

Speeches Combining Deliberative and Ceremonial Goals

1. Keynote speeches
2. Pep talks
3. After-dinner speeches
4. Commencement speeches
5. Speeches marking candidacy and election
   - ❐ Nominating speeches
   - ❐ Acceptance speeches
   - ❐ Inaugural addresses

An inaugural address includes several basic elements. First, the leader formally accepts the responsibilities of the office, stating that he or she understands the duties and will make every effort to fulfill them. Second, the new leader explicitly seeks to unify the audience. This is especially important if the campaign for office has been divisive; in effect, the new leader says that the campaign is over and reaches out for the help and support of everyone in the audience. After the bitter and close election of 1800, Thomas Jefferson introduced this aspect to the presidential inaugural address when he proclaimed:

> Let us then, fellow citizens, unite with one heart and one mind. Let us restore to social intercourse that harmony and affection without which liberty and even life itself are dreary things. . . . But every difference of opinion is not a difference of principle. We have called by different names brethren of the same principle. We are all Republicans, we are all Federalists.

President Jefferson's goal was to urge members of the two political parties of his day to overcome their differences and to unite for the common good. Most subsequent U.S. presidents have expressed similar sentiments in their inaugural address.

Third, the newly installed leader typically outlines the general goals to be pursued during his or her time in office. The inaugural address usually does not spell out specific proposals, but rather identifies general themes or goals. For example, in 2009, President Barack Obama combined a somber description of the conditions facing the United States with an expression of confidence that challenges would be met, and he sought to inspire among the American people the conviction and confidence that he said had been displayed by the nation's founders.

Finally, the inaugural address often puts the new leader's service into a larger context. He or she may speak of perpetuating the ideals of the organization or of fulfilling a dream held since childhood. Presidents of the United States have often concluded their inaugurals with a plea for divine assistance, which not only suggests humility but also places the presidency in the larger context of carrying out God's will.

Inaugural speeches in other contexts, though less lofty, are also significant. As you assume leadership of a campus organization, a brief speech thanking members for their support, stating your objectives, and appealing for help as you go forward will mark the occasion in an appropriate way.

What Have You Learned?

Objective 16.1: Explain how the nature of the speaking occasion and purpose influence the speech.

Any speaking occasion creates expectations that the speaker will want to observe or modify, but in any case will need to understand.

The purpose may be a combination of the following:

- Celebrating common bonds or values.
- Urging a course of action.
- Entertaining listeners.

Objective 16.2: Prepare a speech characterized by decorum, or "fittingness to the occasion."

Decorum, or fittingness to the occasion, influences a speaker's decisions about the following:

- The appropriate degree of formality
- The length of the speech
- The intensity of the speech
- The representativeness and types of supporting material
- How explicitly to identify with the audience.

A decorous speech is one that gives voice to the heretofore unexpressed sentiments of the audience.

Objective 16.3: Explain the nature of deliberative speaking and develop various kinds of deliberative speeches.

Speaking occasions can be classified as follows:

- Forensic, conducted in courts of law
- Deliberative, focusing on action
- Epideictic (ceremonial), emphasizing common bonds

Although forensic speaking is the work of professionally trained advocates, all public speakers engage in deliberative and ceremonial speaking.

Deliberative speaking aims to answer the question,"What shall we do?" It involves the following:

- Sharing of ideas, employing informative strategies
- Recommending a decision, employing persuasive strategies

Deliberative speaking takes place in a wide range of settings and includes the following:

- Community service and involvement
- Oral reports and presentations
- Speaking in small groups
- Public hearings and debates
- Responding to questions

Objective 16.4: Explain the nature of ceremonial speaking and develop various kinds of ceremonial speeches.

Ceremonial speaking is both argumentative and emotional in nature. It aims to do the following:

- Make people more aware of their common bonds
- Give a greater sense of presence to particular ideas, beliefs, or values

Strategies for ceremonial speaking include the following:

- Recalling a common past
- Invoking shared values
- Reinterpreting past events
- Paying tribute to symbolic heroes

Occasions for ceremonial speaking include the following:

- Speeches of greeting
- Speeches of tribute
- Commemorative celebrations
- Speeches marking awards

Objective 16.5: Develop types of speeches that combine deliberative and ceremonial elements.

Some occasions call for speeches that serve both deliberative and ceremonial functions, such as follows:

- Keynote speeches
- Pep talks
- After-dinner speeches
- Commencement speeches
- Speeches marking candidacy and election

Listen to the **Audio Chapter Summary** at **MyCommunicationLab**

Discussion Questions

1. Which types of special-occasion speeches discussed in this chapter have you heard? What were your expectations as an audience member? Did the speaker meet or neglect your expectations? Discuss your impressions with both deliberative and ceremonial speeches, including their appropriateness for the occasions at which they were presented.
2. In what ways might the strategic design of a speech differ for deliberative and ceremonial occasions? Identify potential differences in the speaker's arrangement of ideas, choice of supporting materials, and stylistic decisions.
3. When you discussed questions 1 and 2, how did the group dynamic of your class work? Did one person dominate the discussion? Did groupthink become a problem? Did anyone provide testimony to guide decision making? Was an individual who offered a claim asked to respond to questions? Were there any debates? Discuss and evaluate the public speaking that occurs in the group discussions of your class.
4. Several of the occasions described in this chapter were political in nature. You can learn a great deal about public speaking by watching politicians succeed or fail at the podium. What are some of the lessons you have learned from watching political speeches that might translate to other speaking situations? Although political examples are illustrative, what differences might make transferring their lessons difficult? Do you believe political examples will directly relate to your future public speaking experiences? Why or why not?

Activities

1. Attend a ceremony or event at which at least one speech will be given. In a short essay, critique a speech that you heard at that ceremony. Was the speech decorous? In what ways was it designed to fit the constraints of the occasion?
2. Observe a group discussion, taking care not to engage in that discussion. Write an essay describing what you learned from that experience. Considering the size of the group, the function of the meeting, and the particular dynamics of the group, comment on some of these speech goals:
   - Drawing up a group report
   - Speaking in small groups
   - Chairing a meeting
   - Responding to questions
3. Think about the expectations raised by the following real or imagined occasions, and prepare a decorous speech for one of them:
   a. A roast of your public speaking teacher
   b. An acceptance speech for an award that you hope to win someday
   c. A pep talk to your favorite sports team
   d. A eulogy for a friend, family member, or public figure
4. Find a video recording or transcript of Stephen Colbert's 2006 White House Correspondents' Dinner speech (discussed in this chapter). Discuss what you liked and disliked about the speech. Do you think that the speech was decorous? Think about the guidelines for the roast, and consider the people in attendance. Do you appreciate Colbert's approach to decorum, or do you think that the speech goes overboard?
5. Review transcripts or recordings of speeches and debates from the most recent political campaign. Identify where they follow the guidelines we have discussed for speeches marking candidacy and election, and also where they diverge. Try to find explanations for the differences.
6. Bring a two-liter bottle of soda and a package of plastic cups to class. Practice giving toasts to one another. Then discuss what distinguishes a good toast from a bad toast.

Key Terms

after-dinner speech **413**
ceremonial speaking **405**
chair **401**
commemorative celebration **409**
decorum **396**
deliberative speaking **397**
epideictic **405**
eulogy **407**
false dilemma **404**
forensic speaking **397**
groupthink **401**
inaugural address **417**
keynote speech **412**
loaded question **404**
motion **402**
multivocal **412**
nominating speech **414**
parliamentary procedure **402**
pep talk **413**
presence **405**
presentation speech **410**
resonance **405**
roast **409**
speech of acceptance **410**
symposium **401**
testimonial **407**
toast **408**

Study and **Review** the **Flashcards** at **MyCommunicationLab**

Notes

1 Two articles together capture this balance between constraint and creativity. Lloyd F. Bitzer, "The Rhetorical Situation," *Philosophy and Rhetoric* 1 (Winter 1968): 1–14, focuses on the need to respond to a rhetorical situation. Richard E. Vatz, "The Myth of the Rhetorical Situation," *Philosophy and Rhetoric* 6 (Summer 1973): 154–61, emphasizes that choices made by speakers actually shape the rhetorical situation.

2 Cicero emphasized the concept of decorum and made much of it. See Marcus Tullius Cicero, *Orator*, translated by H. M. Hubbel, Cambridge, MA: Harvard Univ. Press, 1939, 70–74.

3 For example, see Aristotle, *The Rhetoric*, translated by George Kennedy, New York: Oxford University Press, 1991, Book I, Chapter 3.

4 For more about speaking in small groups, see Gloria Galanes and Katherine Adams, *Effective Group Discussion: Theory and Practice*, 13th ed., New York: McGraw-Hill, 2009.

5 For more about parliamentary procedure, see Henry Martyn Robert, III, et al., *Robert's Rules of Order*, 11th ed., Philadelphia: DaCapo Press, 2011.

6 The way in which Reagan's eulogy was designed to respond to the occasion is discussed in more detail in Steven M. Mister, "Reagan's *Challenger* Tribute: Combining Generic Constraints and Situational Demands," *Central States Speech Journal* 37 (Fall 1986): 158–65.

7 For more about the use of humor in speeches, see Charles R. Gruner, "Advice to the Beginning Speaker on Using Humor—What the Research Tells Us," *Communication Education* 34 (April 1985): 142–47. For more information about how advanced public speakers utilize humor in motivating and connecting with their audience, see David Greatbatch and Timothy Clark, "Displaying Group Cohesiveness: Humour and Laughter in the Public Lectures of Management Gurus," *Human Relations* 56 (December 2003): 1515–44.

Appendix

Speeches for Analysis and Discussion

OUTLINE

The Internet and Intellectual Property

Charles Agbaje, Northwestern University

Immigration

Jaimie Sakumura, University of Kansas

Second Inaugural Address, 1865

Abraham Lincoln

Eulogy for the *Challenger* Astronauts, 1986

Ronald Reagan

Women's Rights Are Human Rights, 1995

Hillary Rodham Clinton

A More Perfect Union, 2008

Barack Obama

For Further Study

The first two speeches in this Appendix were delivered by students in Public Speaking classes probably similar to yours. Although both urge the audience to do specific things, they utilize a mix of informative and persuasive strategies as well as different approaches to arrangement, style, and use of evidence. They are good speeches but they are not perfect. As you study them, consider what you think is strong and what could be improved.

The other four are well-known speeches by public figures. They were selected because they were important when delivered and, in the opinion of most critics, have stood the test of time. Although you will not be likely to speak exactly like Abraham Lincoln, Ronald Reagan, Hillary Rodham Clinton, or Barack Obama, these speeches illustrate strategic choices about language, argument, structure, presentation, and audience analysis that are similar to choices you will need to make.

Several other speeches have been discussed in this book. Most of the public speeches (but not the student speeches) are easily available online. A particularly useful source for the texts of American speeches is www.americanrhetoric.com. At the end of this Appendix, you will find a listing of—and notes on—a few additional speeches that you can locate and use to study the concepts and techniques for effective public speaking.

The Internet and Intellectual Property

Charles Agbaje

Charles Agbaje delivered this speech in the fall of 2011, while he was a student at Northwestern University. The speech has several objectives: agenda setting, providing new information and perspective, strengthening or weakening commitment, and urging a specific action. Consider how these purposes call for a mix of informative and persuasive strategies. How well is this mix achieved? Also consider the strengths and weaknesses of this speech with respect to organization, style, technical terms, and the use of evidence. Was it well adapted to an audience of Public Speaking students? What if the audience had been, on average, 20 years older?

The Internet: quite possibly the greatest public forum in the history of mankind. It's the hub of free speech, interaction, and sharing. However, the industry of sharing is constantly under scrutiny and under fire from various corporations. Most recently, file sharing has come under fire from a recently proposed House bill called SOPA, the Stop Online Piracy Act. The purpose is reasonable, but I feel that the bill will ultimately do more harm than good.

Introduced on October 26, 2011, to combat online trafficking and copyright infringement on U.S. intellectual property, SOPA will effectively ban websites from advertising agents and payment facilities, such as PayPal, block websites from search engines, such as Google, or possibly even shut down websites entirely if they are found to be infringing on intellectual property. It will also make streaming copyrighted material into a felony.

The bill is proposed to promote prosperity, creativity, entrepreneurship, and innovation by combating the theft of intellectual property, which is the United States' greatest export. But in practice the way that the bill is phrased and worded is so vague and widespread that it gives powers that would effectively enact Internet censorship. Ultimately, I feel that the bill will infringe on free speech, job growth, and stifle the innovation necessary for the continued growth of the Internet. The bill must be stopped.

There is a clear divide between the parties that support and oppose the bill. Supporting the bill are trademark-based agencies such as Nike and copyright-based agencies such as the Motion Picture Association of America and the Recording Industry of American Artists. Opposing the bill are web-based properties such as Facebook, Mozilla, Google, and other Internet giants.

It speaks to a clear divide between the changing economic and business models of our day and age. On the one hand, we have these media and content producers who do deserve proper compensation for their work and for their contribution to society. On the other hand, we have these new innovative Web 2.0 properties that are continuously innovating and changing the way we live our lives day to day.

Because of this clear divide, there must be some sort of reconciliation. However, the policies of the bill, when enforced, will ultimately infringe upon the Internet, giving a great deal of power to corporations, in an effort to control the Internet in the same way that these corporations have controlled the advertising, television, and music industries throughout history.

As stated before, the bill is primarily targeted towards pirating efforts, such as the Pirate Bay, which I am sure many of you have heard of, if not used. It is the 89th most popular website worldwide. But because of the way the bill is phrased and the broad strokes that it paints, other websites such as YouTube, Wikipedia, and Dropbox could also come under fire for having users who share copyrighted content.

File-sharing, reposting of videos, and even covering pop songs would be addressed by the bill. Any copyright holder could potentially target even individual users for doing this, or the websites that they are hosted on for supporting them and not doing enough to combat the copyright infringement.

According to experts in the field, such as Lateef Mtima, the director of the Institute of Intellectual Property and Social Justice at Howard University, "perhaps the most dangerous aspect of the bill is that the conduct it would criminalize is so poorly defined. While on its face the bill seems to attempt to distinguish between commercial and non-commercial conduct, purportedly criminalizing the former and permitting the latter, in actuality the bill not only fails to accomplish this but, because of its lack of concrete definitions, it potentially criminalizes conduct that is currently permitted under the law." This is reminiscent of the basic file-sharing that is promoted on social media websites that we see each and every day.

Proponents of the bill say that it will ultimately protect jobs in the media industry, which is true. Michael O'Leary, a policy and external affairs officer at the Motion Picture Association of America, states that "the film industry alone supports 2 million American jobs and over 95,000 small businesses." And while those jobs are at risk due to pirating, the reform that this bill will enact over the Internet will ultimately do more harm than good by restricting Internet properties that are growing and flourishing.

While some of these jobs are admittedly being taken away, the Internet does create approximately 2.6 jobs for every one job that is lost in other sectors. The Internet is the fastest growing sector in the world right now and approximately

21% of GDP growth in the past five years can be attributed to it. Internet efficiency has stimulated $64 billion in the U.S. economy in 2009 alone.

Also, in recent studies by Booz & Company, funded by Google, approximately 80% of venture capitalists and other investors said that they would be less likely to invest in the environment proposed by SOPA in its current form. However, they would be 115% more likely to invest if SOPA was properly reformed and limited solely to pirating and not given these widespread powers. This is crucial because venture capitalists provide a large portion of the funding and jobs in these small and growing media industries, such as software, virus technology, electronics, computers, and telecommunications—all industries that are continuing to boom and continuing to change our lives and provide jobs.

Also, these industries are supporting small businesses and major corporations alike through social media marketing and other new and innovative ways that they can reach their audiences, advertising faster and further than they could do in any other form.

All that said, I am not advocating stopping the bill entirely because it does target piracy, which is incredibly important. Especially since I am planning on going into the media industry myself, and I know that there are a handful of film majors in the audience as well, the media industry is extremely time-consuming and expensive, so that these properties do need to be duly compensated. But at the expense of all these other factors? I feel as though there are better ways that this bill could be enforced. I believe that there are other bills that might be enacted to better address the issue.

For example, if the bill were to focus solely on pirating efforts and cracking down on pirating websites specifically, without encroaching onto other social media networks, that would be much better for it and for the social and economic environment. It would also be more effective if they were to enforce policies that really cracked down on people sneaking video cameras into movie theaters, for example, to repost the movies online later.

And while it doesn't call specifically for the iron fist of the Internet, the fact that the bill leaves such a potential open is something that we should all be aware of.

This is nothing new in our history. New technology has always come under fire from such major corporations, such as DVRs, CD players, and even VCRs back in their day, were all accused of copyright infringement. But after these companies were able to integrate these technologies instead of fighting back against them, they too were able to reap the benefits of them.

In sum, this bill is currently still working its way through the House and there are equivalent bills working their way through the Senate. We should all be very aware of these bills and we should do our parts to make sure that they are stopped before they fundamentally restructure the way the Internet is set up now.

There are several movements online that are trying to shut down these bills, such as AmericanCensorship.org, which hosted an American Censorship Day when several websites posted symbols to alert their followers and visitors that this issue was happening and that it was real and relevant. They also have a form right on their homepage that makes it very easy to get all the information that you need and contact your local statesman to make a difference.

That said, we should all be willing and able to go online to figure out the facts of this bill, because the Internet has become such an integral and daily part of our lives that if this goes into effect without us even knowing about it and without even having our voices heard, it would fundamentally change the way that we live our lives.

Jaimie Sakumura

Jaimie Sakumura presented this speech in class at the University of Kansas in 2006. She explores the issue of illegal immigration and argues that illegal immigrants should have the opportunity to become citizens. Consider what persuasive strategies Jaimie has used in this speech and how effective they are. Also examine whether the supporting material is adequate in amount and quality and whether the strategies of reasoning discussed in Chapter 8 are followed. Is the speech convincing? What changes, if any, would you suggest? How well is it adapted to a student audience? How might it be modified for a different audience?

Have you ever stopped to think about how lucky you are to be a citizen of the United States? Probably not very often, but there are millions of people in this world who would give anything to become one. The U.S. is a country built on immigration. Very few of us can say that our families have been here forever; most of us have immigration to the U.S. somewhere in our family tree. So should we really punish those people who are here now simply pursuing the same dreams that the people who founded our country pursued? As I mentioned in my first speech, the decisions made about immigration today will undoubtedly affect you at some point in your future, and it's important that we all understand the consequences of the decisions that could be made. I have studied both sides of the debate, and I understand the ramifications of each, and as a result of my extensive research, I have come to one conclusion. The treatment of illegal immigrants as felons is an impractical, inhumane way to deal with the problem, and it is actually distracting us from the bigger problem here. There are a few things that you should understand about this debate, and today I will discuss with you three of them. First of all, treating immigrants as felons is impractical and inhumane. Secondly, I'll talk about why we're being distracted from the bigger problem of our flawed immigration system as a whole. And lastly, I'll give you the best resolution in my opinion.

Let me begin by telling you why treating illegal immigrants as felons is an inhumane and impractical way to deal with this problem. Not providing illegal immigrants with the opportunity to obtain citizenship is, first of all, completely impractical. Sam Brownback, who is the Kansas Republican Senator, put it best in an April 6 article in the *Lawrence Journal-World* when he said, "The notion that we are going to go and round everybody up is ridiculous." According to the U.S. Census Bureau's American Community Survey, in 2004 there were about 10 million Mexican immigrants in the United States, and about 80 percent of them were here illegally. Now, since those numbers have dramatically increased since then, most sources estimate that there are about 11 million illegal immigrants in our country right now. Now, that's about 375 times the number of students at KU. Can you imagine trying to round up that many people and taking them back across the border? It would be close to impossible. Aside from the obvious impracticality of this method, it would have devastating effects on the immigrants themselves. Too often, we forget that when we talk about immigrants, even illegal ones, we're talking about people. These people have hopes, dreams, personal interests, and goals just like everybody else. Don't they deserve the opportunity to pursue those goals? It's easy to view immigrants as invaders and as burdens to our society. This image justifies the idea that they should be treated as criminals and deported back across the border. However, in Rachel Swarn's article entitled "Immigration Debate Framed by Family Ties," she explains the personal experience of New Mexican Republican Senator Pete Domenici. Mr. Domenici's mother was a kind, caring mother of four; she was a local PTA president, very active in the community. But she was also an illegal immigrant. In 1943, the authorities took her away from her family. Mr. Domenici, who was nine years old at the time, says that he remembers crying as he watched his mother disappear in a big black car. It's stories like these that are beginning to shed light on the previously unaddressed personal ramifications that uprooting immigrants could have.

Now, many of you are probably thinking: I don't discourage immigration altogether, I just discourage illegal immigration because that's what is causing the problem here. However, that is a common misconception. Our obsession with resolving the illegal immigration problem is actually taking our focus away from the real problem, which is our immigration policy as a whole. In his March 2006 article in the *National Review,* Ramesh Ponnuru, who is the senior editor of the *National Review* and author of *Party of Death,* points out that most of the concerns people have about illegal immigration are also true of legal immigration. For example, you might complain that illegal immigrants cost the federal and state governments billions of dollars every year. But legal immigrants cost the government money also. You might complain that illegal immigrants hurt low-income workers by driving wages down. But legal immigrants drive wages down, too. Or perhaps your biggest concern is that illegal immigrants present national security problems. But, with the way that our immigration system is working right now, legal immigrants are causing national security problems as well. Now, my intention here is not to say that immigration is a bad thing, at all. I just want to point out that it is our entire immigration system that is problematic, not just illegal immigration. Ponnuru also points out that we are focusing on illegal immigration in order to avoid facing the bigger problem of our immigration system as a whole. He explains that since illegal immigrants have broken the law, and therefore done something wrong, it is really easy to blame them for the failures in our immigration policy altogether.

So, what should be done about this situation? For my final point, I am going to tell you the best resolution to this problem. Clearly, immigration is one of the biggest debates facing our country today. In most Americans' opinions, this debate is bigger than abortion, bigger than gay marriage, bigger than the war in Iraq. So there are two major things that need to be done in order to resolve this debate. First of all, we need to treat illegal immigrants as people—not as felons. After all, the only crime they have committed is pursuing the American dream much like you and I are right now. Now, this approach involves putting them on some sort of path to citizenship. Janet Marguia, who is the president of the largest Hispanic civil rights organization in the United States, says in her April 24 interview with the *Lawrence Journal-World*: "We need guest-worker provisions and provisions that would allow for some path to permanent citizenship if we are going to deal with this issue in a comprehensible manner." She goes on to explain that many of these immigrants have been here for years—contributing to society, paying taxes, and in many cases, doing the hard labor that nobody else really wants to do. And most importantly, they're deeply rooted in their communities, and uprooting them at this point would be extremely unfair. Now, the second thing that needs to happen is that our immigration policy needs to be revised. Our immigration bureaucracy is bombarded with so many immigrants each year that it's becoming nearly impossible for them to regulate who is coming in and for what reasons. So, lowering the number of people allowed into the country every year would benefit not only the economy, but our national security as well.

So, now that you know a little bit more about the debate, I'd like to close by reminding you of the few things that you should keep in mind. Today I talked about why the decision not to give illegal immigrants the opportunity to gain citizenship is the wrong way to approach this problem. I've also told you how our emphasis on illegal immigration is actually distracting us from the underlying problem of our flawed immigration system as a whole. And I've talked about the best way to fix this situation. So the next time you hear about the immigration debate, I hope you remember that immigrants, even illegal ones, are people, not just statistics.

"Immigration" by Jaimie Sakumura. Reprinted by permission of the author.

Second Inaugural Address, 1865

Abraham Lincoln

By the time Lincoln took the presidential oath of office a second time, the outcome of the Civil War was certain. The disagreement was not about who would win the war but about the nature of the postwar Union. Lincoln needed to articulate how he planned to bring the nation back together, knowing that his approach would be highly controversial. To provide context for his reconstruction plan, he needed to explain or to account for the war. His Second Inaugural Address is devoted to this task. He both reaffirms that the war was about preservation of the Union and acknowledges that slavery was the underlying cause.

Lincoln's explanation fuses secular and sacred. He sees the war as divine punishment for human sins. By implication, changing attitudes about slavery was necessary to atone for sin, and only when that was done would "the scourge of war" pass away. It recalls values drawn from the past, puts forward the broad political principles of reconstruction, and acknowledges Executive limitations by placing the ultimate outcome in the hands of God.

Six weeks after delivering this speech, Abraham Lincoln lay dead, the first president to fall victim to assassination. In retrospect, the Second Inaugural Address takes on added significance as a kind of valedictory or farewell address, although it surely was not constructed with these purposes in mind.[1]

Fellow Countrymen: At this second appearing to take the oath of the Presidential office there is less occasion for an extended address than there was at the first. Then a statement somewhat in detail of a course to be pursued seemed fitting and proper. Now, at the expiration of four years, during which public declarations have been constantly called forth on every point and phase of the great contest which still absorbs the attention and engrosses the energies of the nation, little that is new could be presented. The progress of our arms, upon which all else chiefly depends, is as well known to the public as to myself, and it is, I trust, reasonably satisfactory and encouraging to all. With high hope for the future, no prediction in regard to it is ventured.

On the occasion corresponding to this four years ago all thoughts were anxiously directed to an impending civil war. All dreaded it, all sought to avert it. While the inaugural address was being delivered from this place, devoted altogether to *saving* the Union without war, insurgent agents were in the city seeking to *destroy* it without war—seeking to dissolve the Union and divide effects by negotiation. Both parties deprecated war, but one of them would *make* war rather than let the nation survive, and the other would *accept* war rather than let it perish, and the war came.

One-eighth of the whole population were colored slaves, not distributed generally over the Union, but localized in the southern part of it. These slaves constituted a peculiar and powerful interest. All knew that this interest was somehow the cause of the war. To strengthen, perpetuate, and extend this interest was the object for which the insurgents would rend the Union even by war, while the Government claimed no right to do more than to restrict the territorial enlargement of it. Neither party expected for the war the magnitude or the duration which it has already attained. Neither anticipated that the *cause* of the conflict might cease with or even before the conflict itself should cease. Each looked for an easier triumph, and a result less fundamental and astounding. Both read the same Bible and pray to the same God, and each invokes His aid against the other. It may seem strange that any men should dare to ask a just God's assistance in wringing their bread from the sweat of other men's faces, but let us judge not, that we be not judged. The prayers of both could not be answered. That of neither has been answered fully. The Almighty has His own purposes. "Woe unto the world because of offenses; for it must needs be that offenses come, but woe to that man by whom the offense cometh." If we shall suppose that American slavery is one of those offenses which, in the providence of God, must needs come, but which having continued through His appointed time, He now wills to remove, and that He gives to both North and South this terrible war as the woe due to those by whom the offense came, shall we discern therein any departure from those divine attributes which the believers in a living God always ascribe to Him? Fondly do we hope, fervently do we pray, that this mighty scourge of war may speedily pass away. Yet, if God wills that it continue until all the wealth piled by the bondsman's two hundred and fifty years of unrequited toil shall be sunk, and until every drop of blood drawn with the lash shall be paid by another drawn with the sword, as was said three thousand years ago, so still it must be said, "the judgments of the Lord are true and righteous altogether."

With malice toward none, with charity for all, with firmness in the right as God gives us to see the right, let us strive on to finish the work we are in, to bind up the nation's wounds, to care for him who shall have borne the battle and for his widow and his orphan, to do all which may achieve and cherish a just and lasting peace among ourselves and with all nations.

Eulogy for the *Challenger* Astronauts, 1986

Ronald Reagan

Giving meaning to tragic events is one key function of the eulogy. It honors the memory of the dead by finding a message for the living. Eulogies typically stress the virtues of the deceased to guide the beliefs and actions of listeners. Most eulogies are of interest to only a small number of people. When the tragedy is public, the eulogy takes on added significance.

Such a highly public tragedy occurred on the morning of January 28, 1986, when the space shuttle Challenger *exploded barely a minute after liftoff, killing all seven astronauts aboard. Schoolchildren and families across the country especially watched the launch because one of the astronauts was a teacher, Christa McAuliffe, the first civilian to travel in space. The explosion of the spacecraft was seen by millions of people on live television. These factors probably made the tragedy seem more immediate and "real" than the explosion of the* Columbia *as it reentered the earth's atmosphere in early 2003. Certainly for those old enough to remember, the* Columbia *disaster brought back to mind the tragic end of the* Challenger.

President Ronald Reagan had been scheduled to give a State of the Union address, but he postponed it and eulogized the Challenger *astronauts instead. Concerned that the tragedy might cause listeners to doubt the value of the space program, he chose instead to emphasize the pioneer virtues of the astronauts and to regard their death as an unfortunate but necessary price for progress. Did Reagan select an appropriate meaning to give to this tragedy? How did his choices in the speech work to accomplish his effect? Were better choices available? Was Reagan the most appropriate spokesperson on this occasion? Why or why not?*

Ladies and gentlemen, I'd planned to speak to you tonight to report on the state of the Union, but the events of earlier today have led me to change those plans. Today is a day of mourning and remembering. Nancy and I are pained to the core by the tragedy of the shuttle *Challenger*. We know we share this pain with all of the people of our country. This is truly a national loss.

Nineteen years ago, almost to the day, we lost three astronauts in a terrible accident on the ground. But we've never lost an astronaut in flight; we've never had a tragedy like this. And perhaps we've forgotten the courage it took for the crew of the shuttle. But they, the *Challenger* Seven, were aware of the dangers, but overcame them and did their jobs brilliantly. We mourn seven heroes: Michael Smith, Dick Scobee, Judith Resnik, Ronald McNair, Ellison Onizuka, Gregory Jarvis, and Christa McAuliffe. We mourn their loss as a nation together.

For the families of the seven, we cannot bear, as you do, the full impact of this tragedy. But we feel the loss, and we're thinking about you so very much. Your loved ones were daring and brave, and they had that special grace, that special spirit that says, "Give me a challenge, and I'll meet it with joy." They had a hunger to explore the universe and discover its truths. They wished to serve, and they did. They served all of us. We've grown used to wonders in this century. It's hard to dazzle us. But for twenty-five years the United States space program has been doing just that. We've grown used to the idea of space, and perhaps we forget that we've only just begun. We're still pioneers. They, the members of the *Challenger* crew, were pioneers.

And I want to say something to the schoolchildren of America who were watching the live coverage of the shuttle's take-off. I know it is hard to understand, but sometimes painful things like this happen. It's all part of the process of exploration and discovery. It's all part of taking a chance and expanding man's horizons. The future doesn't belong to the fainthearted; it belongs to the brave. The *Challenger* crew was pulling us into the future, and we'll continue to follow them.

I've always had great faith in and respect for our space program, and what happened today does nothing to diminish it. We don't hide our space program. We don't keep secrets and cover things up. We do it all up front and in public. That's the way freedom is, and we wouldn't change it for a minute. We'll continue our quest in space. There will be more shuttle flights and more shuttle crews and, yes, more volunteers, more civilians, more teachers in space. Nothing ends here; our hopes and our journeys continue. I want to add that I wish I could talk to every man and woman who works for NASA or who worked on this mission and tell them: "Your dedication and professionalism have moved and impressed us for decades. And we know of your anguish. We share it."

There's a coincidence today. On this day 390 years ago, the great explorer Sir Francis Drake died aboard ship off the coast of Panama. In his lifetime the great frontiers were the oceans, and an historian later said, "He lived by the sea, died on it, and was buried in it." Well, today we can say of the *Challenger* crew: Their dedication was, like Drake's, complete.

The crew of the space shuttle *Challenger* honored us by the manner in which they lived their lives. We will never forget them, nor the last time we saw them, this morning, as they prepared for their journey and waved goodbye and "slipped the surly bonds of earth" to "touch the face of God."

Women's Rights Are Human Rights, 1995

Hillary Rodham Clinton

Before being elected a U.S. Senator and before being named Secretary of State, Hillary Rodham Clinton was first lady of the United States from 1993 to 2001. In that role, she headed the U.S. delegation to the fourth United Nations Conference on Women, held in Beijing, China, in September of 1995. This is her opening speech to the conference.

We learned in Chapter 5 that speakers face special problems when their audience is heterogeneous, and that was certainly the case for Clinton. Not all who were attending the conference—and certainly not all who saw this speech or heard reports about it—shared her priorities or even her belief that it was urgent to protect and promote women's rights. Not all even shared Clinton's view of what those rights were. In this speech Clinton illustrates both of the strategies we studied for dealing with such a situation. First, she cumulates many specific examples, each of which will be meaningful to a particular segment of the audience. And second, she searches for a transcendent appeal by placing women's rights within the broader (and less controversial) category of human rights.

Clinton's speech also illustrates how persuasive definitions can be a strategic resource, a topic we examined in Chapter 12. Where in the speech do you find evidence of Clinton's putting this belief into practice?

Thank you very much, Gertrude Mongella, for your dedicated work that has brought us to this point, distinguished delegates, and guests. I would like to thank the Secretary General for inviting me to be part of the important United Nations Fourth World Conference on Women. This is truly a celebration, a celebration of the contributions women make in every aspect of life—in the home, on the job, in the community, as mothers, wives, sisters, daughters, learners, workers, citizens, and leaders.

It is also a coming together, much the way women come together every day in every country. We come together in fields and factories, in village markets and supermarkets, in living rooms and boardrooms. Whether it is while playing with our children in the park or washing clothes in a river or taking a break at the office water cooler, we come together and talk about our aspirations and concerns.

And time and again our talk turns to our children and our families. However different we may appear, there is far more that unites us than divides us. We share a common future. And we are here to find common ground so that we may help bring new dignity and respect to women and girls all over the world—and in so doing, bring new strength and stability to families as well.

By gathering in Beijing, we are focusing world attention on issues that matter most in our lives, the lives of women and their families—access to education, health care, jobs, and credit, the chance to enjoy basic legal and human rights and to participate fully in the political life of our countries.

There are some who question the reason for this conference. Let them listen to the voices of women in their homes, neighborhoods, and workplaces. There are some who wonder whether the lives of women and girls matter to economic and political progress around the globe. Let them look at the women gathered here and at Huairou—the homemakers and nurses, the teachers and lawyers, the policy makers and women who run their own businesses. It is conferences like this that compel governments and peoples everywhere to listen, look, and face the world's most pressing problems. Wasn't it, after all, after the women's conference in Nairobi ten years ago that the world focused for the first time on the crisis of domestic violence?

Earlier today, I participated in a World Health Organization forum. In that forum, we talked about ways that government officials, NGOs, and individual citizens are working to address the health problems of women and girls. Tomorrow, I will attend a gathering of the United Nations Development Fund for Women. There the discussion will focus on local—and highly successful—programs that give hardworking women access to credit so they can improve their own lives and the lives of their families.

What we are learning around the world is that if women are healthy and educated, their families will flourish. If women are free from violence, their families will flourish. If women have a chance to work and earn as full and equal partners in society, their families will flourish. And when families flourish, communities and nations do as well. That is why every woman, every man, every child, every family, and every nation on this planet does have a stake in the discussion that takes place here.

Over the past twenty-five years, I have worked persistently on issues relating to women, children, and families. Over the past two and a half years, I've had the opportunity to learn more about the challenges facing women in my own country and around the world.

I have met new mothers in Indonesia who come together regularly in their village to discuss nutrition, family planning, and baby care.

I have met working parents in Denmark who talk about the comfort they feel in knowing that their children can be cared for in safe and nurturing after-school centers.

I have met women in South Africa who helped lead the struggle to end apartheid and are now helping to build a new democracy,

I have met with the leading women of my own hemisphere who are working every day to promote literacy and better health care for children in their countries.

I have met women in India and Bangladesh who are taking out small loans to buy milk cows or rickshaws or thread in order to create a livelihood for themselves and their families.

I have met the doctors and nurses in Belarus and Ukraine who are trying to keep children alive in the aftermath of Chernobyl.

The great challenge of this conference is to give voice to women everywhere whose experiences go unnoticed, whose words go unheard.

Women comprise more than half the world's population, 70 percent of the world's poor, and two-thirds of those who are not taught to read and write. We are the primary caretakers for most of the world's children and elderly. Yet much of the work we do is not valued—not by economists, not by historians, not by popular culture, not by government leaders.

At this very moment, as we sit here, women around the world are giving birth, raising children, cooking meals, washing clothes, cleaning houses, planting crops, working on assembly lines, running companies, and running countries. Women also are dying from diseases that should have been prevented or treated. They are watching their children succumb to malnutrition caused by poverty and economic deprivation. They are being denied the right to go to school by their own fathers and brothers. They are being forced into prostitution, and they are being barred from the bank lending offices and banned from the ballot box.

Those of us who have the opportunity to be here have the responsibility to speak for those who could not. As an American, I want to speak for women in my own country—women who are raising children on the minimum wage, women who can't afford health care or child care, women whose lives are threatened by violence, including violence in their own homes. I want to speak up for mothers who are fighting for good schools, safe neighborhoods, clean air, and clean airwaves; for older women, some of them widows, who find that after raising their families, their skills and life experiences are not valued in the marketplace; for women who are working all night as nurses, hotel clerks, or fast-food chefs so that they can be at home during the day with their children; and for women everywhere who simply don't have time to do everything they are called upon to do each and every day.

Speaking to you today, I speak for them—just as each of us speaks for women around the world who are denied the chance to go to school or see a doctor or own property or have a say about the direction of their lives simply because they are women. The truth is that most women around the world work both inside and outside the home, usually by necessity.

We need to understand that there is no one formula for how women should lead our lives. That is why we must respect the choices that each woman makes for herself and her family. Every woman deserves the chance to realize her own God-given potential.

But we must recognize that women will never gain full dignity until their human rights are respected and protected. Our goals for this conference—to strengthen families and societies by empowering women to take greater control over their own destinies—cannot be fully achieved unless all governments, here and around the world, accept their responsibility to protect and promote internationally recognized human rights.

The international community has long acknowledged, and recently reaffirmed at Vienna, that both women and men are entitled to a range of protections and personal freedoms, from the right of personal security to the right to determine freely the number and spacing of the children they bear. No one, no one should be forced to remain silent for fear of religious or political persecution, arrest, abuse, or torture.

Tragically, women are most often the ones whose human rights are violated. Even now, in the late twentieth century, the rape of women continues to be used as an instrument of armed conflict. Women and children make up a large majority of the world's refugees, and when women are excluded from the political process, they become even more vulnerable to abuse.

I believe that now, on the eve of a new millennium, it is time to break the silence. It is time for us to say, here in Beijing and for the world to hear, that it is no longer acceptable to discuss women's rights as separate from human rights. These abuses have continued because, for too long, the history of women has been a history of silence. Even today there are those who are trying to silence our words. But the voices of this conference and of the women at Huairou must be heard loudly and clearly:

It is a violation of human rights when babies are denied food or drowned or suffocated or their spines broken simply because they are born girls.

It is a violation of human rights when women and girls are sold into the slavery of prostitution for human greed, and the kinds of reasons that are used to justify this practice should no longer be tolerated.

It is a violation of human rights when women are doused with gasoline, set on fire, and burned to death because their marriage dowries are deemed too small.

It is a violation of human rights when individual women are raped in their own communities and when thousands of women are subjected to rape as a tactic or prize of war.

It is a violation of human rights when a leading cause of death worldwide among women ages fourteen to forty-four is the violence they are subjected to in their own homes by their own relatives.

It is a violation of human rights when young girls are brutalized by the painful and degrading practice of genital mutilation.

It is a violation of human rights when women are denied the right to plan their own families—and that includes being forced to have abortions or being sterilized against their will.

If there is one message that echoes forth from this conference, let it be that human rights are women's rights and women's rights are human rights once and for all.

And among those rights are the right to speak freely and the right to be heard. Women must enjoy the rights to participate fully in the social and political lives of their countries if we want freedom and democracy to thrive and endure. It is indefensible that many women in nongovernmental organizations who wished to participate in this conference have not been able to attend or have been prohibited from fully taking part.

Let me be clear. Freedom means the right of people to assemble, organize, and debate openly. It means respecting the views of those who may disagree with the views of their governments. It means not taking citizens away from their loved ones and jailing them, mistreating them, or denying them their freedom or dignity because of the peaceful expression of their ideas and opinions.

In my country, we recently celebrated the seventy-fifth anniversary of women's suffrage. It took one hundred and fifty years after the signing of our Declaration of Independence for women to win the right to vote. It took seventy-two years of organized struggle before that happened, on the part of many courageous women and men.[2] It was one of America's most divisive philosophical wars. But it was a bloodless war. Suffrage was achieved without a shot being fired.

But we also have been reminded, in V-J Day observances last weekend, of the good that comes when men and women join together to combat the forces of tyranny and to build a better world. We have seen peace prevail in most places for a half century. We have avoided another world war. But we have not solved older, deeply rooted problems that continue to diminish the potential of half the world's population.

Now it is the time to act on behalf of women everywhere. If we take bold steps to better the lives of women, we will be taking bold steps to better the lives of children and families too. Families rely on mothers and wives for emotional support and care, families rely on women for labor in the home, and, increasingly, everywhere families rely on women for income needed to raise healthy children and care for other relatives. As long as discrimination and inequities remain so commonplace everywhere in the world—as long as girls and women are valued less, fed less, fed last, overworked, underpaid, not schooled, subjected to violence in and outside their homes—the potential of the human family to create a peaceful, prosperous world will not be realized.

Let, let this conference be our—and the world's—call to action. Let us heed that call so we can create a world in which every woman is treated with respect and dignity, every boy and girl is loved and cared for equally, and every family has the hope of a strong and stable future.

That is the work before you. That is the work before all of us who have a vision of the world we want to see for our children and our grandchildren. The time is now. We must move beyond rhetoric, we must move beyond recognition of problems, to working together to have the common efforts to build that common ground we hope to see.

God's blessings on you, your work, and all who will benefit from it. Godspeed, and thank you very much.

A More Perfect Union, 2008

Barack Obama

As a candidate for the U.S. Senate, Barack Obama catapulted to national fame as the result of a successful speech—the keynote address at the 2004 Democratic National Convention. He quickly developed a reputation for oratorical excellence based especially on his ability to transcend divisions of race, gender, and class through overarching appeals to basic common values.

This speech was delivered in the midst of an intense primary campaign for the Democratic presidential nomination in 2008. He came in for criticism when his pastor of many years, Reverend Jeremiah Wright, made remarks that were widely perceived as incendiary and unpatriotic. Obama spoke to this criticism in an address that not only focused on the immediate controversy but went beyond it to examine the complicated nature of race in American culture. The speech addressed a controversial subject head-on but tried to open a space for a more textured and rich national discussion of the topic. Which of the purposes for speeches discussed in Chapter 6 do you think Obama had in mind? How well was he able to achieve multiple purposes?[3]

"We the people, in order to form a more perfect union."

Two hundred and twenty-one years ago, in a hall that still stands across the street, a group of men gathered and, with these simple words, launched America's improbable experiment in democracy. Farmers and scholars, statesmen and patriots who had traveled across an ocean to escape tyranny and persecution finally made real their declaration of independence at a Philadelphia convention that lasted through the spring of 1787.

The document they produced was eventually signed but ultimately unfinished. It was stained by this nation's original sin of slavery, a question that divided the colonies and brought the convention to a stalemate until the founders chose to allow the slave trade to continue for at least twenty more years, and to leave any final resolution to future generations.

Of course, the answer to the slavery question was already embedded within our Constitution—a Constitution that had at its very core the ideal of equal citizenship under the law; a Constitution that promised its people liberty, and justice, and a union that could be and should be perfected over time.

And yet words on a parchment would not be enough to deliver slaves from bondage, or provide men and women of every color and creed their full rights and obligations as citizens of the United States. What would be needed were Americans in successive generations who were willing to do their part—through protests and struggle, on the streets and in the courts, through a civil war and civil disobedience and always at great risk—to narrow that gap between the promise of our ideals and the reality of their time.

This was one of the tasks we set forth at the beginning of this campaign—to continue the long march of those who came before us, a march for a more just, more equal, more free, more caring and more prosperous America. I chose to run for the presidency at this moment in history because I believe deeply that we cannot solve the challenges of our time unless we solve them together—unless we perfect our union by understanding that we may have different stories, but we hold common hopes; that we may not look the same and we may not have come from the same place, but we all want to move in the same direction—toward a better future for our children and our grandchildren.

This belief comes from my unyielding faith in the decency and generosity of the American people. But it also comes from my own American story.

I am the son of a black man from Kenya and a white woman from Kansas. I was raised with the help of a white grandfather who survived the Depression to serve in Patton's Army during World War II and a white grandmother who worked on a bomber assembly line at Fort Leavenworth while he was overseas. I've gone to some of the best schools in America and lived in one of the world's poorest nations. I am married to a black American who carries within her the blood of slaves and slaveowners—an inheritance we pass on to our two precious daughters. I have brothers, sisters, nieces, nephews, uncles and cousins, of every race and every hue, scattered across three continents, and for as long as I live, I will never forget that in no other country on Earth is my story even possible.

It's a story that hasn't made me the most conventional candidate. But it is a story that has seared into my genetic makeup the idea that this nation is more than the sum of its parts—that out of many, we are truly one.

Throughout the first year of this campaign, against all predictions to the contrary, we saw how hungry the American people were for this message of unity. Despite the temptation to view my candidacy through a purely racial lens, we won commanding victories in states with some of the whitest populations in the country. In South Carolina, where the Confederate flag still flies, we built a powerful coalition of African Americans and white Americans.

This is not to say that race has not been an issue in the campaign. At various stages in the campaign, some commentators have deemed me either "too black" or "not black enough." We saw racial tensions bubble to the surface during the week before the South Carolina primary. The press has scoured every exit poll for the latest evidence of racial polarization, not just in terms of white and black, but black and brown as well.

And yet, it has only been in the last couple of weeks that the discussion of race in this campaign has taken a particularly divisive turn.

On one end of the spectrum, we've heard the implication that my candidacy is somehow an exercise in affirmative action; that it's based solely on the desire of wide-eyed liberals to purchase racial reconciliation on the cheap. On the other end, we've heard my former pastor, Reverend Jeremiah Wright, use incendiary language to express views that have the potential not only to widen the racial divide, but views that denigrate both the greatness and the goodness of our nation; that rightly offend white and black alike.

I have already condemned, in unequivocal terms, the statements of Reverend Wright that have caused such controversy and in some cases pain. For some, nagging questions remain. Did I know him to be an occasionally fierce critic of American domestic and foreign policy? Of course. Did I ever hear him make remarks that could be considered controversial while I sat in the church? Yes. Did I strongly disagree with many of his political views? Absolutely—just as I'm sure many of you have heard remarks from your pastors, priests, or rabbis with which you strongly disagreed.

But the remarks that have caused this recent firestorm weren't simply controversial. They weren't simply a religious leader's effort to speak out against perceived injustice. Instead, they expressed a profoundly distorted view of this country—a view that sees white racism as endemic, and that elevates what is wrong with America above all that we know is right with America; a view that sees the conflicts in the Middle East as rooted primarily in the actions of stalwart allies like Israel, instead of emanating from the perverse and hateful ideologies of radical Islam.

As such, Reverend Wright's comments were not only wrong but divisive, divisive at a time when we need unity; racially charged at a time when we need to come together to solve a set of monumental problems—two wars, a terrorist threat, a falling economy, a chronic health care crisis, and potentially devastating climate change; problems that are neither black or white or Latino or Asian, but rather problems that confront us all.

Given my background, my politics, and my professed values and ideals, there will no doubt be those for whom my statements of condemnation are not enough. Why associate myself with Reverend Wright in the first place, they may ask? Why not join another church? And I confess that if all that I knew of Reverend Wright were the snippets of those sermons that have run in an endless loop on the television and YouTube, or if Trinity United Church of Christ conformed to the caricatures being peddled by some commentators, there is no doubt that I would react in much the same way.

But the truth is, that isn't all that I know of the man. The man I met more than 20 years ago is a man who helped introduce me to my Christian faith, a man who spoke to me about our obligations to love one another; to care for the sick and lift up the poor. He is a man who served his country as a U.S. Marine; who has studied and lectured at some of the finest universities and seminaries in the country, and who for over 30 years led a church that serves the community by doing God's work here on Earth—by housing the homeless, ministering to the needy, providing day care services and scholarships and prison ministries, and reaching out to those suffering from HIV/AIDS.

In my first book, *Dreams from My Father*, I described the experience of my first service at Trinity:

"People began to shout, to rise from their seats and clap and cry out, a forceful wind carrying the reverend's voice up into the rafters.... And in that single note—hope!—I heard something else; at the foot of that cross, inside the thousands of churches across the city, I imagined the stories of ordinary black people merging with the stories of David and Goliath, Moses and Pharaoh, the Christians in the lion's den, Ezekiel's field of dry bones. Those stories—of survival, and freedom, and hope—became our story, my story; the blood that had spilled was our blood, the tears our tears; until this black church, on this bright day, seemed once more a vessel carrying the story of a people into future generations and into a larger world. Our trials and triumphs became at once unique and universal, black and more than black; in chronicling our journey, the stories and songs gave us a means to reclaim memories that we didn't need to feel shame about ... memories that all people might study and cherish—and with which we could start to rebuild."

That has been my experience at Trinity. Like other predominantly black churches across the country, Trinity embodies the black community in its entirety—the doctor and the welfare mom, the model student and the former gang-banger. Like other black churches, Trinity's services are full of raucous laughter and sometimes bawdy humor. They are full of dancing, clapping, screaming, and shouting that may seem jarring to the untrained ear. The church contains in full the kindness and cruelty, the fierce intelligence and the shocking ignorance, the struggles and successes, the love, and yes, the bitterness and bias that make up the black experience in America.

And this helps explain, perhaps, my relationship with Reverend Wright. As imperfect as he may be, he has been like family to me. He strengthened my faith, officiated my wedding, and baptized my children. Not once in my conversations with him have I heard him talk about any ethnic group in derogatory terms, or treat whites with whom he interacted with anything but courtesy and respect. He contains within him the contradictions—the good and the bad—of the community that he has served diligently for so many years.

I can no more disown him than I can disown the black community. I can no more disown him than I can disown my white grandmother—a woman who helped raise me, a woman who sacrificed again and again for me, a woman who loves me as much as she loves anything in this world, but a woman who once confessed her fear of black men who passed her by on the street, and who on more than one occasion has uttered racial or ethnic stereotypes that made me cringe.

These people are a part of me. And they are a part of America, this country that I love.

Now some will see this as an attempt to justify or excuse comments that are simply inexcusable. I can assure you it is not. I suppose the politically safe thing to do would be to move on from this episode and just hope that it fades into the woodwork. We can dismiss Reverend Wright as a crank or a demagogue, just as some have dismissed Geraldine Ferraro, in the aftermath of her recent statements, as harboring some deep-seated racial bias.

But race is an issue that I believe this nation cannot afford to ignore right now. We would be making the same mistake that Reverend Wright made in his offending sermons about America—to simplify and stereotype and amplify the negative to the point that it distorts reality.

The fact is that the comments that have been made and the issues that have surfaced over the last few weeks reflect the complexities of race in this country that we've never really worked through—a part of our union that we have yet to perfect. And if we walk away now, if we simply retreat into our respective corners, we will never be able to come together and solve challenges like health care, or education, or the need to find good jobs for every American.

Understanding this reality requires a reminder of how we arrived at this point. As William Faulkner once wrote, "The past isn't dead and buried. In fact, it isn't even past." We do not need to recite here the history of racial injustice in this country. But we do need to remind ourselves that so many of the disparities that exist in the African American community today can be directly traced to inequalities passed on from an earlier generation that suffered under the brutal legacy of slavery and Jim Crow.

Segregated schools were, and are, inferior schools; we still haven't fixed them, 50 years after *Brown v. Board of Education*, and the inferior education they provided, then and now, helps explain the pervasive achievement gap between today's black and white students.

Legalized discrimination—where blacks were prevented, often through violence, from owning property, or loans were not granted to African American business owners, or black homeowners could not access FHA mortgages, or blacks were excluded from unions, or the police force, or fire departments—meant that black families could not amass any meaningful wealth to bequeath to future generations. That history helps explain the wealth and income gap between black and white, and the concentrated pockets of poverty that persists in so many of today's urban and rural communities.

A lack of economic opportunity among black men, and the shame and frustration that came from not being able to provide for one's family, contributed to the erosion of black families—a problem that welfare policies for many years may have worsened. And the lack of basic services in so many urban black neighborhoods—parks for kids to play in, police walking the beat, regular garbage pick-up and building code enforcement—all helped create a cycle of violence, blight and neglect that continue to haunt us.

This is the reality in which Reverend Wright and other African Americans of his generation grew up. They came of age in the late '50s and early '60s, a time when segregation was still the law of the land and opportunity was systematically constricted. What's remarkable is not how many failed in the face of discrimination, but rather how many men and women overcame the odds; how many were able to make a way out of no way for those like me who would come after them.

But for all those who scratched and clawed their way to get a piece of the American Dream, there were many who didn't make it—those who were ultimately defeated, in one way or another, by discrimination. That legacy of defeat was passed on to future generations—those young men and increasingly young women who we see standing on street corners or languishing in our prisons, without hope or prospects for the future. Even for those blacks who did make it, questions of race, and racism, continue to define their worldview in fundamental ways. For the men and women of Reverend Wright's generation, the memories of humiliation and doubt and fear have not gone away; nor has the anger and the bitterness of those years.

That anger may not get expressed in public, in front of white coworkers or white friends. But it does find voice in the barbershop or around the kitchen table. At times, that anger is exploited by politicians, to gin up votes along racial lines, or to make up for a politician's own failings.

And occasionally it finds voice in the church on Sunday morning, in the pulpit and in the pews. The fact that so many people are surprised to hear that anger in some of Reverend Wright's sermons simply reminds us of the old truism that the most segregated hour in American life occurs on Sunday morning.

That anger is not always productive; indeed, all too often it distracts attention from solving real problems; it keeps us from squarely facing our own complicity in our condition, and prevents the African American community from forging the alliances it needs to bring about real change. But the anger is real; it is powerful; and to simply wish it away, to condemn it without understanding its roots, only serves to widen the chasm of misunderstanding that exists between the races.

In fact, a similar anger exists within segments of the white community. Most working- and middle-class white Americans don't feel that they have been particularly privileged by their race. Their experience is the immigrant experience—as far as they're concerned, no one's handed them anything, they've built it from scratch. They've worked hard all their lives, many times only to see their jobs shipped overseas or their pension dumped after a lifetime of labor. They are anxious about their futures, and feel their dreams slipping away; in an era of stagnant wages and global competition, opportunity comes to be seen as a zero sum game, in which your dreams come at my expense. So when they are told to bus their children to a school across town; when they hear that an African American is getting an advantage in landing a good job or a spot in a good college because of an injustice that they themselves never committed; when they're told that their fears about crime in urban neighborhoods are somehow prejudiced, resentment builds over time.

Like the anger within the black community, these resentments aren't always expressed in polite company. But they have helped shape the political landscape for at least a generation. Anger over welfare and affirmative action helped forge the Reagan Coalition. Politicians routinely exploited fears of crime for their own electoral ends. Talk show hosts and conservative commentators built entire careers unmasking bogus claims of racism while dismissing legitimate discussions of racial injustice and inequality as mere political correctness or reverse racism.

Just as black anger often proved counterproductive, so have these white resentments distracted attention from the real culprits of the middle-class squeeze—a corporate culture rife with inside dealing, questionable accounting practices, and short-term greed; a Washington dominated by lobbyists and special interests; economic policies that favor the few over the many. And yet, to wish away the resentments of white Americans, to label them as misguided or even racist, without recognizing they are grounded in legitimate concerns—this too widens the racial divide, and blocks the path to understanding.

This is where we are right now. It's a racial stalemate we've been stuck in for years. Contrary to the claims of some of my critics, black and white, I have never been so naïve as to believe that we can get beyond our racial divisions in a single election cycle, or with a single candidacy—particularly a candidacy as imperfect as my own.

But I have asserted a firm conviction—a conviction rooted in my faith in God and my faith in the American people—that working together we can move beyond some of our old racial wounds, and that in fact we have no choice if we are to continue on the path of a more perfect union.

For the African American community, that path means embracing the burdens of our past without becoming victims of our past. It means continuing to insist on a full measure of justice in every aspect of American life. But it also means binding our particular grievances—for better health care, and better schools, and better jobs—to the larger aspirations of all Americans—the white woman struggling to break the glass ceiling, the white man whose been laid off, the immigrant trying to feed his family. And it means taking full responsibility for own lives—by demanding more from our fathers, and spending more time with our children, and reading to them, and teaching them that while they may face challenges and discrimination in their own lives, they must never succumb to despair or cynicism; they must always believe that they can write their own destiny.

Ironically, this quintessentially American—and yes, conservative—notion of self-help found frequent expression in Reverend Wright's sermons. But what my former pastor too often failed to understand is that embarking on a program of self-help also requires a belief that society can change.

The profound mistake of Reverend Wright's sermons is not that he spoke about racism in our society. It's that he spoke as if our society was static; as if no progress has been made; as if this country—a country that has made it possible for one of his own members to run for the highest office in the land and build a coalition of white and black; Latino and Asian, rich and poor, young and old—is still irrevocably bound to a tragic past. But what we know—what we have seen—is that America can change. That is the true genius of this nation. What we have already achieved gives us hope—the audacity to hope—for what we can and must achieve tomorrow.

In the white community, the path to a more perfect union means acknowledging that what ails the African American community does not just exist in the minds of black people; that the legacy of discrimination—and current incidents of discrimination, while less overt than in the past—are real and must be addressed. Not just with words, but with deeds—by investing in our schools and our communities; by enforcing our civil rights laws and ensuring fairness in our criminal justice system; by providing this generation with ladders of opportunity that were unavailable for previous generations. It requires all Americans to realize that your dreams do not have to come at the expense of my dreams; that investing in the health, welfare, and education of black and brown and white children will ultimately help all of America prosper.

In the end, then, what is called for is nothing more, and nothing less, than what all the world's great religions demand—that we do unto others as we would have them do unto us. Let us be our brother's keeper, Scripture tells us. Let us be our sister's keeper. Let us find that common stake we all have in one another, and let our politics reflect that spirit as well.

For we have a choice in this country. We can accept a politics that breeds division, and conflict, and cynicism. We can tackle race only as spectacle—as we did in the O.J. trial—or in the wake of tragedy, as we did in the aftermath of Katrina—or as fodder for the nightly news. We can play Reverend Wright's sermons on every channel, every day and talk about them from now until the election, and make the only question in this campaign whether or not the American people think that I somehow believe or sympathize with his most offensive words. We can pounce on some gaffe by a Hillary supporter as evidence that she's playing the race card, or we can speculate on whether white men will all flock to John McCain in the general election regardless of his policies.

We can do that.

But if we do, I can tell you that in the next election, we'll be talking about some other distraction. And then another one. And then another one. And nothing will change.

That is one option. Or, at this moment, in this election, we can come together and say, "Not this time." This time we want to talk about the crumbling schools that are stealing the future of black children and white children and Asian children and Hispanic children and Native American children. This time we want to reject the cynicism that tells us that these kids can't learn, that those kids who don't look like us are somebody else's problem. The children of America are not those kids, they are our kids, and we will not let them fall behind in a 21st-century economy. Not this time.

This time we want to talk about how the lines in the emergency room are filled with whites and blacks and Hispanics who do not have health care, who don't have the power on their own to overcome the special interests in Washington, but who can take them on if we do it together.

This time we want to talk about the shuttered mills that once provided a decent life for men and women of every race, and the homes for sale that once belonged to Americans from every religion, every region, every walk of life. This time we want to talk about the fact that the real problem is not that someone who doesn't look like you might take your job, it's that the corporation you work for will ship it overseas for nothing more than a profit.

This time we want to talk about the men and women of every color and creed who serve together, and fight together, and bleed together under the same proud flag. We want to talk about how to bring them home from a war that never should've been authorized and never should've been waged, and we want to talk about how we'll show our patriotism by caring for them, and their families, and giving them the benefits they have earned.

I would not be running for president if I didn't believe with all my heart that this is what the vast majority of Americans want for this country. This union may never be perfect, but generation after generation has shown that it can always be perfected. And today, whenever I find myself feeling doubtful or cynical about this possibility, what gives me the most hope is the next generation—the young people whose attitudes and beliefs and openness to change have already made history in this election.

There is one story in particularly that I'd like to leave you with today—a story I told when I had the great honor of speaking on Dr. King's birthday at his home church, Ebenezer Baptist, in Atlanta.

There is a young, twenty-three-year-old white woman named Ashley Baia who organized for our campaign in Florence, South Carolina. She had been working to organize a mostly African American community since the beginning of this campaign, and one day she was at a roundtable discussion where everyone went around telling their story and why they were there.

And Ashley said that when she was nine years old, her mother got cancer. And because she had to miss days of work, she was let go and lost her health care. They had to file for bankruptcy, and that's when Ashley decided that she had to do something to help her mom.

She knew that food was one of their most expensive costs, and so Ashley convinced her mother that what she really liked and really wanted to eat more than anything else was mustard and relish sandwiches. Because that was the cheapest way to eat.

She did this for a year until her mom got better, and she told everyone at the roundtable that the reason she joined our campaign was so that she could help the millions of other children in the country who want and need to help their parents too.

Now Ashley might have made a different choice. Perhaps somebody told her along the way that the source of her mother's problems were blacks who were on welfare and too lazy to work, or Hispanics who were coming into the country illegally. But she didn't. She sought out allies in her fight against injustice.

Anyway, Ashley finishes her story and then goes around the room and asks everyone else why they're supporting the campaign. They all have different stories and reasons. Many bring up a specific issue. And finally they come to this elderly black man who's been sitting there quietly the entire time. And Ashley asks him why he's there. And he does not bring up a specific issue. He does not say health care or the economy. He does not say education or the war. He does not say that he was there because of Barack Obama. He simply says to everyone in the room, "I am here because of Ashley."

"I'm here because of Ashley." By itself, that single moment of recognition between that young white girl and that old black man is not enough. It is not enough to give health care to the sick, or jobs to the jobless, or education to our children.

But it is where we start. It is where our union grows stronger. And as so many generations have come to realize over the course of the 221 years since a band of patriots signed that document in Philadelphia, that is where the perfection begins.

For Further Study

As mentioned at the beginning of this Appendix, you can find the texts of many additional speeches on the Internet. Depending on the speech, audio and video recordings may be available as well as the printed text.

One valuable list of speeches is Pearson's "Classic & Contemporary Speeches," which you can find online at MyCommunicationLab (mycommunicationlab.com; access code required). Here is a sampling of the more than 125 landmark speeches that you can access from there.

William Jennings Bryan, "The Cross of Gold," July 9, 1896

This keynote speech electrified the 1896 Democratic National Convention and made Bryan the nominee. It is a vigorous defense of agriculture against business and financial elites. Note especially Bryan's prophetic tone and the vividness of his imagery.

Barbara Bush, "Choices and Change," June 1, 1990

Delivered as the commencement address at Wellesley College, this speech extends the feminist concept of choice to include the choice of a traditional female role. Bush deploys a wry sense of humor and appeals to values and images that transcend conflict between traditional women and modern feminists. She also identifies well with her audience despite obvious differences in age.

George W. Bush, "The Warm Courage of National Unity," September 20, 2001

This speech was delivered to a joint session of Congress and the American people in the aftermath of the September 11, 2001, terrorist attacks. Bush characterizes the attacks as "war" yet distinguishes this from earlier wars and does not request sacrifice of the American people. The speech is organized as a series of answers to questions the people are said to be asking. The speech combines deliberative and epideictic elements, as discussed in Chapter 16.

Steve Jobs, Commencement Address at Stanford University, June 12, 2005

The inventor and entrepreneur discusses the relationship between his educational experiences and his phenomenal success. The speech illustrates a non-political commencement speech with a significant message in part about the role that chance and accident play in life's major decisions.

Martin Luther King, Jr., "I Have a Dream," August 28, 1963

Delivered at the 1963 March on Washington, this speech was selected by a national poll as the best speech given by an American during the twentieth century. King walked a tightrope between militancy and moderation, stressing the urgency of the situation but repudiating violence and avoiding attacks on whites. He grounded his ideals in "the American dream" and he merged political oratory with the preaching style of the Southern black church.

Abraham Lincoln, Gettysburg Address, November 19, 1863

This is probably the most famous speech in U.S. history. In fewer than 300 words, Lincoln captured the central meaning of the Civil War and used the dedication of a cemetery as the occasion to urge Americans to rededicate themselves to the task still remaining. Notice how little attention is given to the battle of Gettysburg itself, and how much is devoted to putting the battle within a larger category.

Richard Nixon, "The Great Silent Majority," November 3, 1969

President Nixon delivered this speech over national television to appeal for public support for his policies in Vietnam, which were being challenged by increasingly vocal protests. The speech illustrates how different segments of an audience can be targeted in the same address. Turning more fighting over to the South Vietnamese appealed to those who wanted to reduce the American role, while the claim that antiwar protests hurt the cause appealed to those motivated primarily by patriotism.

Barack Obama, "The Audacity of Hope," July 27, 2004

This is the speech that put Illinois State Senator Barack Obama on the national stage, propelling him to a U.S. Senate seat and four years later to the presidency.

The speech promotes John Kerry for president but it is most notable for its articulation of Obama's vision of national unity that overcomes partisan divisions. In a climate of political polarization, this message of common ground between "red" and "blue" states, supported with specific illustrations, was particularly welcome.

Franklin D. Roosevelt, First Inaugural Address, March 4, 1933

This speech was delivered in the depth of the Great Depression, and the new president's first task was to restore national confidence and hope. He promised action, called for national sacrifice, promised to seek whatever powers he would need, and asked for the help of God. Roosevelt had promised to take charge, and his inaugural address rallied the country around him at a time of great crisis.

Mary Church Terrell, "What It Means to Be Colored in the Capital of the United States," October 10, 1906

This speech was delivered to a predominantly white audience in the belief that ignorance was a major cause of racism. The speech makes vivid the reality of racial prejudice as it was experienced by African American women. It confronts listeners with the stark disparity between the ideals they profess and their actual practices.

Woodrow Wilson, War Message, April 2, 1917

After attempting to avoid American involvement in the First World War, Wilson delivered this speech to a joint session of Congress requesting a declaration of war. Significantly, war was not justified by traditional notions of national interest but by American idealism and principle. Wilson's line of reasoning would be repeated throughout the twentieth century as others argued for a unique American mission. The speech illustrates the nature of public discourse about U.S. foreign policy.

Notes

1 For a thorough analysis of this speech, see Ronald C. White, *Lincoln's Greatest Speech*, New York: Simon and Schuster, 2002.

2 Clinton is referring to the ratification of the Nineteenth Amendment to the U.S. Constitution in 1920, and to the 72 years that had passed since the 1848 convention in Seneca Falls, New York, had first called for extending women the right to vote.

3 Shortly after this speech was delivered, the distinguished historian Garry Wills wrote an essay comparing it to the speech that Abraham Lincoln delivered at Cooper Union in 1860. See Garry Wills, "Two Speeches on Race," *New York Review of Books,* May 1, 2008.

Photo Credits

Cover: © Geoffrey Kidd/Alamy, © CulturalEyes/W/Alamy; p. 2: © Golden Pixels LLC / Alamy; p. 5: © Reed Saxon/AP Wide World Photos; p. 14: © Ron Sachs/ CORBIS-NY; p. 18: © David R. Frazier Photolibrary, Inc./Alamy; p. 21: © Richard Graulich/Palm Beach Post/ZUMA Press/Newscom; p. 26: © Dwayne Newton/ PhotoEdit Inc.; p. 29: © Barbara Stitzer/PhotoEdit; p. 33: © Barbara Stitzer/ PhotoEdit; p. 37: Spencer Grant/PhotoEdit Inc.; p. 44: © Homer Sykes/Alamy; p. 56: © Jacob Silberberg/Reuters/Landov Media; p. 57: © Corbis Cusp/Alamy; p. 59: © Bob Daemmrich/PhotoEdit Inc.; p. 63: © Dave and Les Jacobs/Blend Images/SuperStock; p. 68: © Francesco Ridolfi/Fotolia; p. 73: © Visage/Alamy; p. 81: © Presselect/Alamy; p. 87: © Jeff Greenberg/PhotoEdit Inc.; p. 92: © Jim West/Alamy; p. 96: © Jeff Greenberg/Alamy Images; p. 98: © Visions of America, LLC/Alamy; p. 103: © Jordan Stead/ZUMA Press/Newscom; p. 106: Trevor Brown Jr./UPI/Newscom; p. 120: © Michael Newman/PhotoEdit; p. 132: © Stephen Chernin/Getty Images Inc.; p. 136: © Bob Daemmrich/PhotoEdit; p. 139: © Monika Graff/The Image Works; p. 146: © Ian Shaw/Alamy; p. 151: © Jeff Greenberg/ PhotoEdit; p. 160: © Blend Images/Alamy Images; p. 165: © Michael Newman/ PhotoEdit Inc.; p. 174: © Michael Newman/PhotoEdit Inc.; p. 178: © Mitch Wojnarowicz/Amsterdam Recorder, The Image Works; p. 182: © Dave & Les Jacobs/Thinkstock; p. 195: © Associated Press; p. 203: ©Syracuse Newspapers/ C. W. McKeen/The Image Works; p. 212: © blickwinkel/Alamy; p. 215: © Augusto Casasoli/A3/Contrasto/Redux Pictures; p. 218: © pressmaster/Fotolia; p. 221: © Jonathan Nourok/PhotoEdit Inc.; p. 236: © Jeff Greenberg/Alamy; p. 242: © Mike Groll/AP Wide World Photos; p. 250: © Michael Newman/PhotoEdit Inc.; p. 258: © John Moore/Getty Images Inc.; p. 262: © Images-USA/Alamy; p. 275: © Will Hart/PhotoEdit; p. 277: © Bob Daemmrich/PhotoEdit; p. 282: © DC Stock/Alamy; p. 285: © Danita Delimont/Alamy; p. 289: © Associated Press; p. 297: © Miami Herald/MCT, Landov Media; p. 312: © Richard Findler/ZUMA Press/Newscom; p. 315: © Everett Collection Inc./Alamy; p. 319: © Dmitry Vereshchagin; p. 324: © neiljohn/Alamy Images; p. 330: © Yahya Arhab/EPA/Newscom; p. 334: © AFP/ Getty Images; p. 345: © Harry Cabluck/AP Wide World Photos; p. 354: © Bernd Settnik/EPA/Newscom; p. 357: © Michael Newman/PhotoEdit Inc.; p. 364: © Tim E White/Alamy; p. 367: © Jeff Greenberg/PhotoEdit; p. 377: © ZUMA Press, Inc./ Alamy; p. 392: © Associated Press; p. 395: © ZUMA Press, Inc./Alamy; p. 404: © Associated Press; p. 406: © Corbis Bridge/Alamy; p. 413: © Associated Press.

Text Credits

p. 8: Courtesy Jeremy Johnson; p. 9: Courtesy Katie Jacobson; p. 20: Courtesy Mary O'Malley; p. 32: Courtesy of Teresa Madera; p. 32: Courtesy of Krupa Shah; p. 72: Based on How Are Your Listening Skills? A Quick Self-Rating Quiz," Taft College Learning Resource Center, http://www.taft.cc.ca.us/lrc/quizzes/listtest.htm, and Judi Brownell, *Listening: Attitudes, Principles, and Skills,* 5th ed., New York: Pearson, 2013, pp. 31–34; p. 86: Abraham Lincoln; p. 100: Barbara Jordan at the Democratic National Convention 1976; p. 102: An Inconvenient Truth, Al Gore; p. 104: Ronald Reagan; p. 131: 2005 Commencement speech by Steve Jobs, 2005; p. 131: Courtesy of Maria

Rogers; p. 132: Courtesy of Graig Hinners; p. 132: Hillary Clinton's 2008 concession speech; p. 133: Dorothy Hurst; p. 133: Courtesy of Rachel Samuels; p. 134: Courtesy of Sunny Lin; p. 149: Courtesy of Mitch Grissom; p. 151: Courtesy of Susan Anderson; p. 159: EBSCO Publishing; pp. 172–173: American Psychological Association (APA) and Modern Language Association (MLA); p. 183: Courtesy of Catherine Archer; p. 189: Courtesy of Sarah McAdams; p. 190: Senator Charles Robb, Congressional Record, 9/10/1996; p. 195: Courtesy of Roger Berkson; p. 197: Courtesy of Michael Leu; p. 198: Courtesy of Demetris Papademetriou; p. 199: Courtesy of Muhammad Gill; p. 201: Courtesy of Trisha Butcher; p. 206: Michael Dukakis; p. 226: Courtesy of Jennifer Aiello; p. 240: Courtesy of Michelle Ekanemesang; p. 231: Source: National Highway Traffic Safety Administration FARS data; p. 241: Courtesy of Rachel Venegas; p. 243: Mario Cuomo; p. 244: Elie Wiesel; p. 245: Courtesy of Stan Barkers; p. 246: Courtesy of Clayton Hottinger; p. 246: Courtesy of Andrea Richards; p. 251: Courtesy of Michelle Ekanemesang; p. 253: Courtesy of Todd McCullough; pp. 271–273: Courtesy of Christopher Chiyung; p. 293: Courtesy of Zana Kuljanian; p. 294: Courtesy of Jan Peterson; p. 297: Courtesy of Mark Nielsen; p. 300: Courtesy of Jennifer Frantz; p. 302: Courtesy of Beverly Watson; p. 303: Reprinted by permission of Monica Crane. All Rights Reserved; p. 315: Courtesy of Kimo Sanderson; p. 315: Courtesy of Krupa Shah; p. 319: Courtesy of Sonia Rubenstein; p. 322: Courtesy of Janet Wickstrom; p. 336: Courtesy of Michael Masdea; p. 337: Courtesy of Kevin Krebs; p. 349: Courtesy of Laura Davission; p. 352: Courtesy of Mitchell Johnson; p. 355: Courtesy of Margaret Orsingner; p. 370: Adapted from or data from Barry A. Kosmin, Egon Mayer, and Ariela Keysar, *American Religious Identification Survey* (ARIS, 2001). Institute for the Study of Secularism in Society and Culture, Trinity College, Hartford CT; p. 399: Courtesy of Laura Winston; p. 403: Courtesy of Janet Carpenter; p. 403: Courtesy of Richard Brinkley; p. 406: Courtesy of Jonathan Cherry; p. 407: President Ronald Reagan; p. 409: President Bill Clinton; p. 411: Elie Wiesel's 1986 Nobel Prize speech; p. 414: Kofi Annan, "Commencement Address at the Massachusetts Institute of Technology, 1997; p. 417: Ruth Bader Ginsburg's acceptance speech; p. 418: Thomas Jefferson; p. 424: Courtesy Charles Agbaje; p. 427: Reprinted by permission of Jaimie Sakumura. All Rights Reserved; p. 430: President Ronald Reagan, "Eulogy for the *Challenger* Astronauts, 1986; p. 432: Hillary Rodham Clinton, first lady of the United States; p. 436: President Barack Obama, "A More Perfect Union."

Index

D

E

F

G

H

I

J

K

L

M

N

T

U

V

W

Y

Z